John Muir (1838–1914) was born and raised in Dunbar, East Lothian. When his family emigrated to Wisconsin in 1849, young John was brought up to hard labour on his father's homestead. Yet he found time for reading and ingenious inventions which gave him an early reputation for brilliance.

After attending the University of Wisconsin, Muir pursued his mechanical skills until an industrial accident nearly blinded him. He set out on an epic walk from Indiana to the Gulf of Mexico, keeping a journal as he went, later published in 1916 as *A Thousand Mile Walk to the Gulf*. In 1868 he went to the Sierra Nevada mountains and spent five years in the Yosemite valley, which influenced the rest of his life. Living rough, Muir studied geology and the plant and animal life around him. His journals from this period, *My First Summer in the Sierra*, were published in 1911. In subsequent years he produced innumerable articles and lectures from the journals of regular summer trips to the mountains of California, Washington, Oregon, and Alaska. Marriage in 1880 took Muir out of the wilderness for a spell, until the need for its preservation involved him in a major campaign for the General Grant, Sequoia and Yosemite national parks, which were finally established in 1890. In the next ten years he overcame opposition from big business to the establishment of still more National Forest parks throughout the country and was a founder member of the Sierra Club which took up the cause of wilderness protection.

The Muir Woods National Monument was established in California in 1908, and John Muir has been honoured ever since as the 'father' of the modern environment movement.

John Muir

THE WILDERNESS JOURNEYS

The Story of
My Boyhood and Youth

A Thousand Mile Walk to the Gulf

My First Summer in the Sierra

Travels in Alaska

Stickeen

Introduced by Graham White

CANONGATE

CLASSICS

67

The Story of My Boyhood and Youth first published in 1913 in the United States by Houghton Mifflin Co. and as a Canongate Classic in 1987.

My First Summer in the Sierra first published in 1911 in the United States by Houghton Mifflin Co. and as a Canongate Classic in 1988.

A Thousand Mile Walk to the Gulf first published in 1916 in the United States by Houghton Mifflin Co.

Travels in Alaska first published in 1915 in the United States by Houghton Mifflin Co.

Stickeen first published in 1909 in the United States by Houghton Mifflin Co.

This edition published as a Canongate Classic in 1996 by Canongate Books Ltd, 14 High Street, Edinburgh EH1 1TE. Introduction © Graham White, 1996.

The publishers gratefully acknowledge general subsidy from the Scottish Arts Council towards the Canongate Classics series and a specific grant towards the publication of this volume.

Set in 10pt Plantin by Palimpsest Book Production Limited, Polmont, Stirlingshire. Printed and bound in Finland by WSOY.

Canongate Classics
Series Editor: Roderick Watson
Editorial Board: J.B. Pick and Cairns Craig

British Library Cataloguing in Publication Data
A catalogue record for this volume
is available on request from the
British Library.

ISBN 086241 586 1

Introduction

This omnibus edition restores to Scottish print *The Story of My Boyhood and Youth* and *My First Summer in the Sierra*, by John Muir, published for the first time as Canongate Classics in 1988. *A Thousand Mile Walk to the Gulf* and *Travels in Alaska* deal with the other great autobiographical journeys of Muir's life. The inclusion of *Stickeen* may at first seem odd, for it re-tells an incident included in *Travels in Alaska*; but told as a short story it reveals an aspect of Muir's concern for animals that is largely unknown in Britain, where it has rarely been available.

Together, these five books chart the epic journeys on which John Muir explored the geography and ecology of the American continent, from the snowy Alaskan glaciers to the alligators and orchids of the Florida swamps. They record the Odyssey of this great Scottish-American from humble origins in Victorian Scotland to his eventual enthronement as the elder statesman of Conservation: adviser to Presidents, lauded with honours by the universities, scientists and philosophers of his day.

In America John Muir is remembered as a climber, explorer, geologist, botanist and writer; but above all as the pioneer of conservation. In the 1870s, before 'mountaineering' existed as a sport in the USA, he made the first ascent of Mt Ritter (13,000 ft), the first ascent by the eastern route of Mt Whitney (14,500 ft), and early ascents of Mt Shasta (14,400 ft) and Mt Rainier (14,500 ft). He was first to ascend Cathedral Peak, a hazardous pinnacle in Yosemite National Park, and climbed many other peaks in the Sierra Nevada range. However, it was not the desire for fame, or bagging summits, which led him to risk his life in scaling these heights; he climbed in order to understand the geography of the unmapped areas he was exploring. But a deeper need also drew him to these remote summits, for here he found the beauty, cosmic mystery and spiritual insight which gave him his deepest fulfilment. Along the way he unwittingly pioneered 'clean climbing' for American mountaineers, for he normally climbed without crampons, ropes or pitons.

A self-taught geologist and glaciologist, he was the first to discover living glaciers in the High Sierra and to propose their role in sculpting entire mountain ranges. His theory, that slow-grinding glaciers had gouged out Yosemite Valley over vast epochs of time, was ridiculed by Josiah Whitney, the patriarch of Californian geology, who held to the 'catastrophist' doctrine, that giant earthquakes had dropped the valley floor. Whitney dismissed Muir's ideas with contempt: 'What does the sheep-herder know about geology?', but Louis Agassiz, the father of glaciology, later proved Muir correct. As a botanist and pioneer-ecologist Muir was consulted by the great scientists of his day, notably Asa Gray of Harvard and Joseph Hooker of Kew. He guided them on expeditions of discovery and they even named some of the plants he led them to in his honour! Ralph Waldo Emerson, the transcendental philosopher of New England, journeyed over 3,000 miles to visit Muir in the 'hang-nest', a wooden shack he had built in Yosemite. Emerson wrote that this self-reliant young Scot had the most original mind and powerful intellect of any man he had met in America; they became life-long friends.

But it is as the founder of the conservation movement, the first person to call clearly for the conservation and protection of wilderness and wildlife, that we remember John Muir. By the time of his death in 1914 he had become an almost mythic figure in the American pantheon, where today he ranks alongside Emerson, Thoreau, Lincoln and Kennedy as 'father of the national parks'. John Muir is truly revered, not as some intellectual fossil, enshrined in a marble hall of fame, but as a living spirit – an environmental *zeitgeist* – whose words and ideas reverberate through the conservation movement on both sides of the Atlantic with increasing resonance and relevance.

Americans have named over 200 sites in his honour,

including: Muir Glacier and Mount Muir in Alaska, Muir Woods and Muir Beach near San Francisco, and the John Muir Wilderness and John Muir Trail in the High Sierra. In 1964, Congress designated his Martinez home The John Muir National Historic Site, in recognition of his campaigns and the books in which he celebrated the natural heritage of the United States. This is just one of over 340 historic sites and parks, comprising over 80 million acres of wild land, cared for by the National Park Service, which Muir himself helped create. At Marquette County, Wisconsin, the John Muir Memorial Park is laid out near the Muir homestead at Fountain Lake. A granite slab among the wildflowers declares:

JOHN MUIR, Foster son of Wisconsin born in Scotland April 21, 1838
He came to America as a lad of eleven, spent his 'teen years in hard work clearing the farm across this lake, carving out a home in the wilderness. In the 'sunny woods, overlooking a flowery glacial meadow and a lake rimmed with water lilies', he found an environment that fanned the fire of his zeal and love for all nature, which, as a man, drove him to study, afoot, alone and unafraid, the forests, mountains and glaciers of the west to become the most rugged, fervent naturalist America has produced, and the Father of the National Parks of our country.

After Muir's death President Teddy Roosevelt wrote:

His was a dauntless soul. Not only are his books delightful, not only is he the author to whom all men turn when they think of the Sierras and Northern glaciers, and the giant trees of the California slope, but he was also – what few nature-lovers are – a man able to influence contemporary thought and action on the subjects to which he had devoted his life. He was a great factor in influencing the thought of California and the thought of the entire country so as to secure the preservation of those great natural

phenomena – wonderful canyons, giant trees, slopes
of flower-spangled hillsides . . . our generation owes
much to John Muir.

> President Theodore Roosevelt, January 6, 1915

Awareness of that historic debt remains undimmed in
the national consciousness. On April 21, 1988, the 150th
anniversary of Muir's birth it was resolved:

> . . . by the Senate and House of Representatives of
> the United States of America: that April 21, 1988,
> is designated as 'John Muir Day', and the President
> is authorized and requested to issue a proclamation
> calling upon the people of the United States to
> observe such day with appropriate ceremonies and
> activities.

Congress acknowledged Muir's role in conserving wilderness and in stressing an ecologically sound environment
as the basis of the quality of life for all people. The Rio
World Summit on the Environment in 1992 highlighted
the concept of 'sustainability' as the acid-test for survival in
the coming millennium; but John Muir was writing about
the sustainable use of the world's natural resources as long
ago as 1870.

These books record expeditions of courage, endurance
and extreme hardship; few would undertake them lightly,
even today, when rescue is only a mobile-phone away.
Muir traversed unmapped wildernesses, the country of
bears and mountain lions, with no prospect of help or of
rescue beyond total self-reliance. He went alone, equipped
only with hob-nailed boots, an old blanket, a hand-lens,
pencil and notebook. His food was a sack of brick-hard
bread, and 'a screw of tea' to add to the river water. He
never carried a gun to hunt game, or protect himself from
grizzlies, pumas and desperados.

The Story of My Boyhood and Youth (1913) was
written when Muir was over seventy, but he paints a
sparkling picture of his Dunbar days with clarity and
a wry humour. The opening paragraph is perhaps the

most famous evocation of a child's vision of nature ever written:

> When I was a boy in Scotland, I was fond of everything that was wild, and all my life I've been growing fonder and fonder of wild places and wild creatures. Fortunately, around my native town of Dunbar, by the stormy North Sea, there was no lack of wildness . . . with red blooded playmates, wild as myself, I loved to wander in the fields, to hear the birds sing, and along the seashore to gaze and wonder at the shells and seaweeds, eels and crabs in the pools among the rocks when the tide was low.

In this book Muir allows us to recapture a glimpse of the childhood Eden, from which most of us are barred as adults, to which somehow he always found the way home. He was born on April 21, 1838 in the fishing town of Dunbar, East Lothian, just 30 miles from Edinburgh; it was the year following Victoria's accession to the throne and two years after Darwin returned from his epic voyage on the *Beagle*. John was sent to school at three, and at seven entered Dunbar Grammar School, where English, Latin, French, Maths, and Geography were beaten into him along with the three Rs. Here he supped the salty broth of Scottish culture from Bannockburn and Flodden, to Burns and the Border Ballads. William Wallace and Robert the Bruce were his school-book heroes, and with school-mates he re-enacted the Wars of Independence daily. These fierce battles took place around Dunbar Castle, where Bruce and the Wallace had fought, first each other, and later the English. Muir was a passionate devotee of all things Scottish throughout his life, and even after 60 years in America, spoke and wrote in vernacular Scots.

In the 1840s, letters and newspapers from America filtered back to Dunbar. John Muir's imagination was sparked with fireside tales: of vast prairies and endless forests, inhabited by bears, wolves, mountain lions and wild, war-bonneted Indians; of maple trees dripping sweet sugar, and rocks studded with nuggets of yellow gold. A

country where ospreys and eagles perched on every branch,
and passenger pigeons darkened the sky from horizon to
horizon, in uncountable myriads. Emigration offered the
boundless possibilities of this young nation to millions of
poor Scots and Irish people.

In February 1849, encouraged by Scots already in
America, Daniel Muir set sail in search of religious
freedom, cheap land and a better life. At the age of
ten, John, with his sister Sarah and brother David, 'sailed
away from Glasgow, carefree as thistle seeds on the wings
of the winds, toward the glorious paradise over the sea.'
This entailed six weeks of winter voyage across the North
Atlantic, on a square-rigger packed with emigrants, some
fleeing the potato famine, others seeking land or gold.

The adults were wracked with anxiety, leaving their
homeland to face an uncertain future in a strange new
world. But Muir does not dwell on sea-sickness or the
stench of the steerage; he tells of his delight in the sailors'
songs, the thrill of setting canvas in a stiff breeze, of
dolphins playing in the green waters and of staring into
the eye of a great whale swimming alongside.

On arrival the family faced a lengthy journey by boat
up the Great Lakes and then by train and open wagon
to Kingston, Wisconsin, where Daniel Muir purchased a
section of virgin land.

Near the end of his life, Muir remembered his first
impression of Fountain Lake Farm:

This sudden splash into pure wildness – baptism in
Nature's warm heart – how utterly happy it made us!
Nature streaming into us, wooingly teaching her wonderful glowing lessons, so unlike the dismal grammar
ashes and cinders so long thrashed into us. Here,
without knowing it, we were still at school; every
wild lesson a love lesson, not whipped but charmed
into us. Oh, that glorious Wisconsin wilderness!

But it was dawn to dusk labour that dominated Muir's
first decade in Wisconsin, a period when he slaved as
unpaid 'ploughboy, well-digger and lumberjack' under

his father's despotism. Daniel Muir not only beat his sons frequently, but refused to call a doctor, or allow time from work, when John contracted mumps and even pneumonia. The boy survived; he escaped to the woods and the lake whenever he could, and immersed himself in books borrowed from neighbours. Self-taught from the age of ten, he showed signs of innate genius in his early teens, by the construction of a series of highly original machines. Clocks, barometers, thermometers, semi-automatic table saws, an 'early-rising machine' – all flowed from his hands, whittled from hickory or with metal scavenged from farm implements. It was the fame of these inventions which led him to university at Madison, Wisconsin, where for the first time he encountered minds like his own, and set his course for the future.

The second book, *A Thousand Mile Walk to the Gulf* (1916) was published after Muir's death by William Frederick Badé, his literary executor. Created from the journal written by Muir almost 50 years earlier, it recounts his epic walk to the Gulf of Mexico in the aftermath of the American Civil War. During the war years, Muir had avoided the slaughter by dodging the draft for over two years in Canada, where he earned his living in a woodwork factory. Later, his skills gained him the post of foreman-engineer at an Indianapolis carriage factory, where he automated production.

But a terrible accident had left Muir physically and mentally traumatised, marking a violent turning point in his life. While prising a metal staple from a drive-belt with the tang of a file, the tool slipped, his hand flew upward and the spike pierced his right eye. As the jelly of aqueous humour slid down his cheek, he ran to the window and realised he was blind; the agony increased when within hours, the other eye failed. Remarkably, after weeks lying bandaged in a darkened room, he recovered his sight; but this intimation of mortality caused him to flee industry forever and to follow his daemon to the wild places of America, determined as the Zen text exhorts, 'not to follow others, but to leave a trail that others might follow'.

It was on this journey to the Gulf that Muir first reflected on the anthropocentric view of nature and began to see that, far from being 'Lord of Creation', mankind was just one small part of the web of life; that all living creatures, plants and even rocks, existed for themselves in their own right, not merely for our utility. Before the word 'Ecology' was coined, Muir was already studying the 'inter-connectedness' of things. He saw humans as just one species in a world-community of beings – advocating 'deep ecology' a hundred years before modern thinkers came around to the same view. Central to his insight was the concept of 'flow', of the transference of energy, materials and life itself:

> One is constantly reminded of the infinite lavishness and fertility of Nature – inexhaustable abundance amid what seems enormous waste. And yet when we look into any of her operations that lie within reach of our minds, we learn that no particle of her material is wasted or worn out. It is eternally flowing from use to use, beauty to yet higher beauty; and we soon cease to lament waste and death, and rather rejoice and exult in the imperishable, unspendable wealth of the universe, and faithfully watch and wait the reappearance of everything that melts and fades and dies about us, feeling sure that its next appearance will be better and more beautiful than the last.

The third volume, *My First Summer in the Sierra* (1911), published by Badé from Muir's journals of forty years earlier, is perhaps Muir's best-loved book. It deals with the period following his arrival in California via the Panama Canal, after the thousand-mile walk. Landing in San Francisco in March 1868, he hiked across the central valley to find summer work as a shepherd in the Yosemite high country. For the next seven years, until February 1875, he was based more or less continuously in Yosemite, exploring the High Sierras, honing his skills in botany, geology and climbing. Self-taught as always, he would 'read from the great book of Nature', trusting only his own observations, verifying every fact and step along the way.

The *First Summer* has been called 'the journal of a soul on fire' and certainly Muir seems in a state of spiritual ecstasy and rapture as the glory of the Sierra peaks is revealed to him for the first time. A deeply spiritual person, though not in a conventional religious sense, he was steeped in scripture from his earliest days. In Dunbar, he had been forced to memorise the entire New Testament before the age of eleven, and claimed he had much of the Old Testament as well. But here, in the alpen-glow of the 'Range of Light', Muir forsook the narrow Scots Calvinism of his father for a new creed, whose prophets were Thoreau and Emerson, rather than Moses and Jeremiah. He remained a Christian but a profound nature-mysticism pervades all his writings from this period.

In the mountains he had what can only be described as a 'conversion experience' during which he saw a transcendent vision of Nature. Every rock, plant and animal in the landscape was transfigured into a divine manifestation, each one a golden thread in the infinite fabric of life, from which no fibre could be pulled without spoiling the whole tapestry. Muir sensed a divine presence behind all things, shining through them, imbuing them with infinite meaning and profound beauty. Even today this remains a truly cosmic vision:

> When we contemplate the whole globe as one great dewdrop, striped and dotted with continents and islands, flying through space with all the other stars, all singing and shining together as one, the whole universe appears as an infinite storm of beauty. This grand show is eternal. It is always sunrise somewhere, the dew is never all dried at once; a shower is forever falling; vapor ever rising. Eternal sunrise, eternal sunset, eternal dawn and gloaming on seas and continents and island, each in its turn, as the round earth rolls.

While others specialised in ever-narrower fields, gaining degrees and professorships, Muir allowed his jackdaw mind to roam free. Always seeking the inter-connections between things, rather than the limited perspective of just one field of study, he skipped from geology and geography to botany and zoology. The word 'Ecology' was coined in the late 1860s by Ernst Von Haeckel, but Muir was already ransacking the 'Earth household' and weaving his ecological synthesis, while the academics were still devising a label for his activities.

Travels in Alaska (1915) was also edited from Muir's journals by Badé and published post-humously. The book recounts just three of Muir's seven journeys to Alaska and is filled with adventures, discoveries and observations of plants, fish, animals, birds, rivers, mountains and, above all, glaciers. It includes his 'discovery' of Glacier Bay in the Klondyke territory, and his exploration of the islands, rivers and glaciers of the remote Wrangell area. Here he was inspired to name glaciers in honour of two Scots: Hugh Miller and Archibald Geikie, his geology mentors. The greatest glacier here is of course named Muir Glacier.

The book recounts the 500-mile canoe trip he made with the Stickeen indians, who made him an honorary chief and gave him the pet dog named 'Stickeen'. We witness encounters with the Sitka and Chilcat Indians, whose lodges he slept in, and with whom he navigated hundreds of miles of remote rivers and sea-passages in an open canoe. Later, as geological and botanical adviser to the Corwin and Harriman expeditions, he sailed over a thousand miles further north, to the Behring Straits and the coast of Siberia, and was present when Wrangell Land was annexed for the United States.

Stickeen is a much-loved story derived from a famous incident in which Muir almost lost his life in a desperate attempt to bridge a crevasse on an Alaskan glacier. He was a compulsive raconteur and this tale was told around the dinner table, to friends and family. He finally wrote it down for his daughters' amusement but it reveals an interesting side of Muir's nature-philosophy. In the 1890s scientific materialists claimed animals were only 'animated machines', devoid of soul, mind or intellect. Muir wrote that the little dog called Stickeen, who shared his perilous adventure on the glacier, had convinced him that even a dog had a mind and soul. Stickeen expanded Muir's vision of all living beings; it is a deeply affectionate tale, written as a kind of moral fable for Muir's daughters, but it remains relevant to today's debates.

During the 1870s Muir witnessed signs of environmental degradation in Yosemite and other areas which he had first encountered when pristine and undamaged. Everywhere he travelled he saw over-grazing of cattle and sheep, the clear-cutting of virgin forests, the devastation of mountains by hydraulic mining and valleys drowned for reservoirs. He knew that uncontrolled development would soon destroy the country's natural heritage, inexhaustible though it had once seemed. Encouraged by Robert Underwood Johnson, the influential editor of *Century* magazine, Muir began to write and lobby for the protection of wild places as national parks. But scientific arguments and inspirational writing would not guarantee protection; political struggle and legislation were the only way forward. In 1892 he played a key role in founding the Sierra Club to fight for conservation; as its first president he led the battle to enlarge the protected boundaries of Yosemite Valley, as America's second National Park.

Muir's success can be gauged from the fact that, during his lifetime, he influenced Presidents Roosevelt, Wilson and Taft in designating over 50 national parks, 200 national monuments and 140 million acres of National Forest. In the 1930s his example inspired David Brower, an unemployed student, to make first-ascents of over twenty peaks topping 13,000 ft in the High Sierra. Brower's experience of mountain beauty soon led him into the conservation movement and, following Muir's path, he became director of the Sierra Club in 1952. Seventeen years later he resigned and went on to found Friends of the Earth, which now has chapters in 53 countries. Muir's influence, working through people like David Brower, now extends across the globe.

But what of Scotland, the land of John Muir's birth, where he is still largely unknown among the mass of people? It is the most extensively de-forested country in Europe, with over 99 per cent of its trees long-gone and its natural heritage sadly impoverished as a result. There are signs that John Muir's spirit is at last coming home to inspire a new generation of conservationists. In 1976 the steady trickle of American pilgrims to Muir's birthplace in Dunbar inspired East Lothian District Council, under the prompting of Frank Tindall, the County Planning Officer, to designate John Muir Country Park – eight miles of wild sea-coast stretching from Belhaven Bay to Tyninghame and beyond.

In 1981 the Council opened the John Muir House Birthplace Museum at 128 High Street, Dunbar, which attracts visitors from all over the world. About the same time, the National Library of Scotland was given a complete microfilm edition of the John Muir Papers, containing copies of virtually every journal, book and letter that Muir ever wrote. This was gifted by the Holt Atherton Institute at the University of the Pacific in Stockton, where the original papers and much of John Muir's personal library are held. This historic archive is now available to scholars in Scotland and the United Kingdom for research into any aspect of Muir's writings.

In 1983 Muir's life inspired the creation of the John Muir Trust in Scotland, established to conserve wild land and protect it for future generations through purchase. To date the Trust has acquired four areas of wild land in Scotland: Li and Coire Dhorrcail in Knoydart (3,000 acres 1988), Torrin on the Isle of Skye (5,000 acres, 1991), Sandwood Bay, Sutherland (11,000 acres 1992), Strathaird and Bla Bheinn in the Skye Cuillin (15,000 acres 1994).

None of these areas is true 'wilderness' or 'wild' in the American sense; they all have crofting communities and people have farmed here for hundreds of years, possibly thousands. Whatever the label, these landscapes are among the most unspoiled in Britain and are sublimely beautiful. The John Muir Trust aims to demonstrate exemplary management of these areas, sharing responsibility with local communities for the sustainable use of the landscape, wildlife and natural resources. The Trust's Information and Education Committee also aims to foster a much wider knowledge of Muir's life and work, here in Britain.

In 1994 a group of local people founded Dunbar's John

Muir Association, with the support of the John Muir Trust. This new body aims to enhance knowledge of Muir and to reclaim him as a Scottish figure, for the educational and economic benefit of Scotland and Dunbar. It has submitted a bid to the Millennium Fund, for the creation of a John Muir Centre in Dunbar, as a beacon for environmental education and sustainability in Scotland. The Centre will function as an environmental gateway for visitors to Scotland, with stunning audio-visual facilities. It will allow children to experience distant wildernesses, anywhere on the planet, using advanced computer facilities, and will also enable schools to share environmental information and projects.

Every country needs heroes to fire the imagination with all that is excellent, and to provide inspiring role-models for children. Europe has no conservation hero to stand comparison with John Muir and it is timely that the John Muir Trust and Dunbar's John Muir Association are working to bring him home in time for the millennium. Muir's life and achievements represent a unique contribution to world conservation and it is vital that he should be brought back into the mainstream of Scottish culture and education.

John Muir never forgot his Dunbar roots and Scotland was always in his heart. His first decade in East Lothian was undoubtedly crucial. The foundations of his character: his dogged self-reliance, his hunger for knowledge, his endurance, his thirst for adventure and his profound love of nature, were laid down upon the sandstones and basalt of this rocky shore. Muir was not a systematiser; he wrote no textbooks and occupied no university chair. But it is arguable that the legacy of his books and successful battles on behalf of conservation, will ultimately have more enduring world-impact than any scientist or statesman of his day.

Late in life he wrote his 'Thoughts on the Birthday of Robert Burns':

It is glorious to know that one of the greatest men to appear in the last century was a Scotsman – Robert Burns – . . . this lesson of divine love and sympathy for humanity . . . which he sent forth white hot from his heart, has gone ringing and singing around the globe, stirring the heart of every nation and race. The men of science and natural history often lose sight of the essential oneness of all living beings in their seeking to classify them in kingdoms, orders, families, genera, species etc. . . . while the Poet and Seer never closes on the kinship of God's creatures and his heart ever beats in sympathy with the great and small as earth-born companions and fellow mortals dependent on Heaven's eternal laws.

Muir was a one-off, a unique personality who broke the mould: poet, philosopher and preacher as much as he was botanist or geologist. He is not amenable to simple analysis. The questions he asked about the survival of wild landscapes and wild creatures are as relevant today as when he first posed them. And his great vision of the whole of Nature as a divine manifestation, shining with beauty, brimming with purpose, filled with meaning, is one of the most potent rejoinders to the materialist and reductionist world-view that has ever been made. It is a vision that the world sorely needs as we approach the millennium, when mankind's search for spiritual truths, environmental values and practical strategies for sustainability has never been more urgent.

Graham White

The Story of My Boyhood and Youth

Contents

ONE

A Boyhood in Scotland

When I was a boy in Scotland I was fond of everything that was wild, and all my life I've been growing fonder and fonder of wild places and wild creatures. Fortunately around my native town of Dunbar, by the stormy North Sea, there was no lack of wildness, though most of the land lay in smooth cultivation. With red-blooded playmates, wild as myself, I loved to wander in the fields to hear the birds sing, and along the seashore to gaze and wonder at the shells and seaweeds, eels and crabs in the pools among the rocks when the tide was low; and best of all to watch the waves in awful storms thundering on the black headlands and craggy ruins of the old Dunbar Castle when the sea and the sky, the waves and the clouds, were mingled together as one. We never thought of playing truant, but after I was five or six years old I ran away to the seashore or the fields almost every Saturday, and every day in the school vacations except Sundays, though solemnly warned that I must play at home in the garden and back yard, lest I should learn to think bad thoughts and say bad words. All in vain. In spite of the sure sore punishments that followed like shadows, the natural inherited wildness in our blood ran true on its glorious course as invincible and unstoppable as stars.

My earliest recollections of the country were gained on short walks with my grandfather when I was perhaps not over three years old. On one of these walks grandfather took me to Lord Lauderdale's gardens, where I saw figs growing against a sunny wall and tasted some of them, and got as many apples to eat as I wished. On another memorable walk in a hayfield, when we sat down to rest on one of the haycocks I heard a sharp, prickly, stinging cry, and, jumping up eagerly, called grandfather's attention to it.

He said he heard only the wind, but I insisted on digging into the hay and turning it over until we discovered the source of the strange exciting sound – a mother field mouse with half a dozen naked young hanging to her teats. This to me was a wonderful discovery. No hunter could have been more excited on discovering a bear and her cubs in a wilderness den.

I was sent to school before I had completed my third year. The first schoolday was doubtless full of wonders, but I am not able to recall any of them. I remember the servant washing my face and getting soap in my eyes, and mother hanging a little green bag with my first book in it around my neck so I would not lose it, and its blowing back in the sea wind like a flag. But before I was sent to school my grandfather, as I was told, had taught me my letters from shop signs across the street. I can remember distinctly how proud I was when I had spelled my way through the little first book into the second, which seemed large and important, and so on to the third. Going from one book to another formed a grand triumphal advancement, the memories of which still stand out in clear relief.

The third book contained interesting stories as well as plain reading- and spelling-lessons. To me the best story of all was 'Llewellyn's Dog', the first animal that comes to mind after the needle-voiced field mouse. It so deeply interested and touched me and some of my classmates that we read it over and over with aching hearts, both in and out of school and shed bitter tears over the brave faithful dog, Gelert, slain by his own master, who imagined that he had devoured his son because he came to him all bloody when the boy was lost, though he had saved the child's life by killing a big wolf. We have to look far back to learn how great may be the capacity of a child's heart for sorrow and sympathy with animals as well as with human friends and neighbours. This auld-lang-syne story stands out in the throng of old schoolday memories as clearly as if I had myself been one of that Welsh hunting party – heard the bugles blowing, seen Gelert slain, joined in the search for the lost child, discovered it at last happy and smiling among the grass and bushes beside the dead, mangled wolf, and wept with Llewellyn over the sad fate of his noble, faithful dog friend.

Another favourite in this book was Southey's poem 'The Inchcape Bell', a story of a priest and a pirate. A good priest in order to warn seamen in dark stormy weather hung a big bell on the dangerous Inchcape Rock. The greater the storm and higher the waves, the louder rang the warning bell, until it was cut off and sunk by wicked Ralph the Rover. One fine day, as the story goes, when the bell was ringing gently, the pirate put out to the rock, saying, 'I'll sink that bell and plague the Abbot of Aberbrothok.' So he cut the rope, and down went the bell 'with a gurgling sound; the bubbles rose and burst around', etc. Then 'Ralph the Rover sailed away; he scoured the seas for many a day; and now, grown rich with plundered store, he steers his course for Scotland's shore.' Then came a terrible storm with cloud darkness and night darkness and high roaring waves. 'Now where we are,' cried the pirate, 'I cannot tell, but I wish I could hear the Inchcape bell.' And the story goes on to tell how the wretched rover 'tore his hair', and 'curst himself in his despair', when 'with a shivering shock' the stout ship struck on the Inchcape Rock, and went down with Ralph and his plunder beside the good priest's bell. The story appealed to our love of kind deeds and of wildness and fair play.

A lot of terrifying experiences connected with these first schooldays grew out of crimes committed by the keeper of a low lodging-house in Edinburgh, who allowed poor homeless wretches to sleep on benches or the floor for a penny or so a night, and, when kind Death came to their relief, sold the bodies for dissection to Dr Hare of the medical school. None of us children ever heard anything like the original story. The servant girls told us that 'Dandy Doctors', clad in long black cloaks and supplied with a store of sticking-plaster of wondrous adhesiveness, prowled at night about the country lanes and even the town streets, watching for children to choke and sell. The Dandy Doctor's business method, as the servants explained it, was with lightning quickness to clap a sticking-plaster on the face of a scholar, covering mouth and nose, preventing breathing or crying for help, then pop us under his long black cloak and carry us to Edinburgh to be sold and sliced into small pieces for folk to learn how we were made. We always mentioned the name 'Dandy Doctor' in a fearful whisper, and never dared venture out of doors after dark. In the short winter days it got dark before school closed, and in cloudy weather we sometimes had difficulty in finding our way home unless a servant with a lantern was sent for us; but during the Dandy Doctor period the school was closed earlier, for if detained until the usual hour the teacher could not get us to leave the schoolroom. We would rather stay all night supperless than dare the mysterious doctors supposed to be lying in wait for us. We had to go up a hill called the Davel Brae that lay between the schoolhouse and the main street. One evening just before dark, as we were running up the hill, one of the boys shouted, 'A Dandy Doctor! A Dandy Doctor!' and we all fled pellmell back into the schoolhouse to the astonishment of Mungo Siddons, the teacher. I can remember to this day the amused look on the good dominie's face as he stared and tried to guess what had got into us, until one of the older boys breathlessly explained that there was an awful big Dandy Doctor on the Brae and we couldna gang hame. Others corroborated the dreadful news. 'Yes! We saw him, plain as onything, with his lang black cloak to hide us in; and some of us thought we saw a sticken-plaister ready in his hand.' We were in such a state of fear and trembling that the teacher saw he wasn't going to get rid of us without going himself as leader. He went only a short distance, however, and turned us over to the care of the two biggest scholars, who led us to the top of the Brae and then left us to scurry home and dash into the door like pursued squirrels diving into their holes.

Just before school skaled (closed), we all arose and sang the fine hymn 'Lord, dismiss us with Thy blessing'. In the spring when the swallows were coming back from their winter homes we sang —

> Welcome, welcome, little stranger,
> Welcome from a foreign shore;
> Safe escaped from many a danger . . .

and while singing we all swayed in rhythm with the music. 'The Cuckoo', that always told his name in the spring of the year, was another favourite song, and when there was nothing in particular to call to mind any special bird or animal, the songs we sang were widely varied, such as

The whale, the whale is the beast for me,
Plunging along through the deep, deep sea.

But the best of all was 'Lord, dismiss us with Thy blessing', though at that time the most significant part I fear was the first three words.

With my school lessons father made me learn hymns and Bible verses. For learning 'Rock of Ages' he gave me a penny, and I thus became suddenly rich. Scotch boys are seldom spoiled with money. We thought more of a penny those economical days than the poorest American schoolboy thinks of a dollar. To decide what to do with that first penny was an extravagantly serious affair. I ran in great excitement up and down the street, examining the tempting goodies in the shop windows before venturing on so important an investment. My playmates also became excited when the wonderful news got abroad that Johnnie Muir had a penny, hoping to obtain a taste of the orange, apple, or candy it was likely to bring forth.

At this time infants were baptized and vaccinated a few days after birth. I remember very well a fight with the doctor when my brother David was vaccinated. This happened, I think, before I was sent to school. I couldn't imagine what the doctor, a tall, severe looking man in black, was doing to my brother, but as mother, who was holding him in her arms, offered no objection, I looked on quietly while he scratched the arm until I saw blood. Then, unable to trust even my mother, I managed to spring up high enough to grab and bite the doctor's arm, yelling that I wasna gan to let him hurt my bonnie brither, while to my utter astonishment mother and the doctor only laughed at me. So far from complete at times is sympathy between parents and children, and so much like wild beasts are baby boys, little fighting, biting, climbing pagans.

Father was proud of his garden and seemed always to be trying to make it as much like Eden as possible, and in a corner of it he gave each of us a little bit of ground for our very own in which we planted what we best liked, wondering how the hard dry seeds could change into soft leaves and flowers and find their way out to the light; and, to see how they were coming on, we used to dig up the larger ones, such as peas and beans, every day. My aunt had a corner assigned to her in our garden which she filled with lilies, and we all looked with the utmost respect and admiration at that precious lily-bed and wondered whether when we grew up we should ever be rich enough to own one anything like so grand. We imagined that each lily was worth an enormous sum of money and never dared to touch a single leaf or petal of them. We really stood in awe of them. Far, far was I then from the wild lily gardens of California that I was destined to see in their glory.

When I was a little boy at Mungo Siddons's school a flower-show was held in Dunbar, and I saw a number of the exhibitors carrying large handfuls of dahlias, the first I had ever seen. I thought them marvellous in size and beauty and, as in the case of my aunt's lilies, wondered if I should ever be rich enough to own some of them.

Although I never dared to touch my aunt's sacred lilies, I have good cause to remember stealing some common flowers from an apothecary, Peter Lawson, who also answered the purpose of a regular physician to most of the poor people of the town and adjacent country. He had a pony which was considered very wild and dangerous, and when he was called out of town he mounted this wonderful beast, which, after standing long in the stable, was frisky and boisterous, and often to our delight reared and jumped and danced about from side to side of the street before he could be persuaded to go ahead. We boys gazed in awful admiration and wondered how the druggist could be so brave and able as to get on and stay on that wild beast's back. This famous Peter loved flowers and had a fine garden surrounded by an iron fence, through the bars of which, when I thought no one saw me, I oftentimes snatched a flower and took to my heels. One day Peter discovered me in this mischief, dashed out into the street and caught me. I screamed that I wouldna steal any more if he would let me go. He didn't say anything but just dragged me along to the stable where he kept the wild pony, pushed me in right back of its heels, and shut the door. I was screaming, of course, but as soon as I was imprisoned the fear of being kicked quenched all noise. I hardly dared breathe. My only hope was in motionless silence. Imagine the agony I endured! I did not steal any more of his flowers. He was a good hard judge of boy nature.

I was in Peter's hands some time before this, when I was about two and a half years old. The servant girl bathed us small folk before putting us to bed. The smarting soapy scrubbings of the Saturday nights in preparation for the Sabbath were particularly severe, and we all dreaded them. My sister Sarah, the next older than me, wanted the long-legged stool I was sitting on awaiting my turn, so she just tipped me off. My chin struck on the edge of the bath-tub, and, as I was talking at the time, my tongue happened to be in the way of my teeth when they were closed by the blow, and a deep gash was cut on the side of it, which bled profusely. Mother came running at the noise I made, wrapped me up, put me in the servant girl's arms and told her to run with me through the garden and out by a back way to Peter Lawson to have something done to stop the bleeding. He simply pushed a wad of cotton into my mouth after soaking it in some brown astringent stuff, and told me to be sure to keep my mouth shut and all would soon be well. Mother put me to bed, calmed my fears, and told me to lie still and sleep like a gude bairn. But just as I was dropping off to sleep I swallowed the bulky wad of medicated cotton and with it, as I imagined, my tongue also. My screams over so great a loss brought mother, and when she anxiously took me in her arms and inquired what was the matter, I told her that I had swallowed my tongue. She only laughed at me, much to my astonishment, when I expected that she would bewail the awful loss her boy had sustained. My sisters, who were older than I, oftentimes said when I happened to be talking too much, 'It's a pity you hadn't swallowed at least half of that long tongue of yours when you were little.'

It appears natural for children to be fond of water, although the Scotch method of making every duty dismal contrived to make necessary bathing for health terrible to us. I well remember among the awful experiences of childhood being taken by the servant to the seashore when I was between two and three years old, stripped at the side of a deep pool in the rocks, plunged into it among crawling crawfish and slippery wriggling snake-like eels, and drawn up gasping and shrieking only to be plunged down again and again. As the time approached for this terrible bathing, I used to hide in the darkest corners of the house, and oftentimes a long search was required to find me. But after we were a few years older, we enjoyed bathing with other boys as we wandered along the shore, careful, however, not to get into a pool that had an invisible boy-devouring monster at the bottom of it. Such pools, miniature maelstroms, were called 'sookin-in-goats' and were well known to most of us. Nevertheless we never ventured into any pool on strange parts of the coast before we had thrust a stick into it. If the stick were not pulled out of our hands, we boldly entered and enjoyed plashing and ducking long ere we had learned to swim.

One of our best playgrounds was the famous old Dunbar Castle, to which King Edward fled after his defeat at Bannockburn. It was built more than a thousand years ago, and though we knew little of its history, we had heard many mysterious stories of the battles fought about its walls, and firmly believed that every bone we found in the ruins belonged to an ancient warrior. We tried to see who could climb highest on the crumbling peaks and crags, and took chances that no cautious mountaineer would try. That I did not fall and finish my rock-scrambling in those adventurous boyhood days seems now a reasonable wonder.

Among our best games were running, jumping, wrestling, and scrambling. I was so proud of my skill as a climber that when I first heard of hell from a servant girl who loved to tell its horrors and warn us that if we did anything wrong we would be cast into it, I always insisted that I could climb out of it. I imagined it was only a sooty pit with stone walls like those of the castle, and I felt sure there must be chinks and cracks in the masonry for fingers and toes. Anyhow the terrors of the horrible place seldom lasted long beyond the telling; for natural faith casts out fear.

Most of the Scotch children believe in ghosts, and some under peculiar conditions continue to believe in them all through life. Grave ghosts are deemed particularly dangerous, and many of the most credulous will go far out of their way to avoid passing through or near a graveyard in the dark. After being instructed by the servants in the nature, looks, and habits of the various black and white ghosts, boowuzzies, and witches we often speculated as to whether they could run fast, and tried to believe that we had a good chance to get away from most of them. To improve our speed and wind, we often took long runs into the country. Tam o'Shanter's mare outran a lot of witches – at least until she reached a place of safety beyond the keystone of the bridge – and we thought perhaps we also might be able to outrun them.

Our house formerly belonged to a physician, and a servant girl told us that the ghost of the dead doctor haunted one of the unoccupied rooms in the second story that was kept dark on account of a heavy window-tax. Our bedroom was adjacent to the ghost room, which had in it a lot of chemical apparatus – glass tubing, glass and brass retorts, test-tubes, flasks, etc – and we thought that those strange articles were still used by the old dead doctor in compounding physic. In the long summer days David and I were put to bed several hours before sunset. Mother tucked us in carefully, drew the curtains of the big old-fashioned bed, and told us to lie still and sleep like gude bairns; but we were usually out of bed, playing games of daring called 'scootchers', about as soon as our loving mother reached the foot of the stairs, for we couldn't lie still, however hard we might try. Going into the ghost room was regarded as a very great scootcher. After venturing in a few steps and rushing back in terror, I used to dare David to go as far without getting caught.

The roof of our house, as well as the crags and walls of the old castle, offered fine mountaineering exercise. Our bedroom was lighted by a dormer window. One night I opened it in search of good scootchers and hung myself out over the slates, holding on to the sill, while the wind was making a balloon of my nightgown. I then dared David to try the adventure, and he did. Then I went out again and hung by one hand, and David did the same. Then I hung by one finger, being careful not to slip, and he did that too. Then I stood on the sill and examined the edge of the left wall of the window, crept up the slates along its side by slight finger-holds, got astride of the roof, sat there a few minutes looking at the scenery over the garden wall while the wind was howling and threatening to blow me off, then managed to slip down, catch hold of the sill, and get safely back into the room. But before attempting this scootcher, recognizing its dangerous character, with commendable caution I warned David that in case I should happen to slip I would grip the rain-trough when I was going over the eaves and hang on, and that he must then run fast downstairs and tell father to get a ladder for me, and tell him to be quick because I would soon be tired hanging dangling in the wind by my hands. After my return from this capital scootcher, David, not to be outdone, crawled up to the top of the window-roof, and got bravely astride of it; but in trying to return he lost courage and began to greet (to cry), 'I canna get doon. Oh, I canna get doon.' I leaned out of the window and shouted encouragingly, 'Dinna greet, Davie, dinna greet, I'll help ye doon. If you greet, fayther will hear, and gie us baith an awfu' skelping.' Then, standing on the sill and holding on by one hand to the window-casing, I directed him to slip his feet down within reach, and, after securing a good hold, I jumped inside and dragged him in by his heels. This finished scootcher-scrambling for the night and frightened us into bed.

In the short winter days, when it was dark even at our early bedtime, we usually spent the hours before going to sleep playing voyages around the world under the bed-clothing. After mother had carefully covered us, bade us goodnight and gone downstairs, we set out on our travels. Burrowing like moles, we visited France, India, America, Australia, New Zealand, and all the places we had ever heard of; our travels never ending until we fell asleep. When mother came to take a last look at us, before she went to bed, to see that we were covered, we were oftentimes covered so well that she had difficulty in finding us, for we were hidden in all sorts of positions where sleep happened to overtake us, but in the morning we always found ourselves in good order, lying straight like gude bairns, as she said.

Some fifty years later, when I visited Scotland, I got one of my Dunbar schoolmates to introduce me to the owners of our old home, from whom I obtained permission to go upstairs to examine our bedroom window and judge what sort of adventure getting on its roof must have been, and with all my after experience in mountaineering, I found that what I had done in daring boyhood was now beyond my skill.

Boys are often at once cruel and merciful, thoughtlessly hard-hearted and tender-hearted, sympathetic, pitiful, and kind in ever changing contrasts. Love of neighbours, human or animal, grows up amid savage traits, coarse and fine. When father made out to get us securely locked up in the back yard to prevent our shore and field wanderings, we had to play away the comparatively dull time as best we could. One of our amusements was hunting cats without seriously hurting them. These sagacious animals knew, however, that, though not very dangerous, boys were not to be trusted. One time in particular I remember, when we began throwing stones at an experienced old Tom, not wishing to hurt him much, though he was a tempting mark. He soon saw what we were up to, fled to the stable, and climbed to the top of the hay manger. He was still within range, however, and we kept the stones flying faster and faster, but he just blinked and played possum without wincing either at our best shots or at the noise we made. I happened to strike him pretty hard with a good-sized pebble, but he still blinked and sat still as if without feeling. 'He must be mortally wounded,' I said, 'and now we must kill him to put him out of pain,' the savage in us rapidly growing with indulgence. All took heartily to this sort of cat mercy and began throwing the heaviest stones we could manage, but that old fellow knew what characters we were, and just as we imagined him mercifully dead he evidently thought the play was becoming too serious and that it was time to retreat; for suddenly with a wild whirr and gurr of energy he launched himself over our heads, rushed across the yard in a blur of speed, climbed to the roof of another building and over the garden wall, out of pain and bad company, with all his lives wideawake and in good working order.

After we had thus learned that Tom had at least nine lives, we tried to verify the common saying that no matter how far cats fell they always landed on their feet unhurt. We caught one in our back yard, not Tom but a smaller one of manageable size, and somehow got him smuggled up to the top story of the house. I don't know how in the world we managed to let go of him, for as soon as we opened the window and held him over the sill he knew his danger and made violent efforts to scratch and bite his way back into the room; but we determined to carry the thing through, and at last managed to drop him. I can remember to this day how the poor creature in danger of his life strained and balanced as he was falling and managed to alight on his feet. This was a cruel thing for even wild boys to do, and we never tried the experiment again, for we sincerely pitied the poor fellow when we saw him creeping slowly away, stunned and frightened, with a swollen black and blue chin.

Again – showing the natural savagery of boys – we delighted in dog-fights, and even in the horrid red work of slaughter-houses, often running long distances and climbing over walls and roofs to see a pig killed, as soon as we heard the desperately earnest squealing. And if the butcher was good-natured, we begged him to let us get a near view of the mysterious insides and to give us a bladder to blow up for a foot-ball.

But here is an illustration of the better side of boy nature. In our back yard there were three elm trees and in the one nearest the house a pair of robin-redbreasts had their nest. When the young were almost able to fly, a troop of the celebrated 'Scottish Grays' visited Dunbar, and three or four of the fine horses were lodged in our stable. When the soldiers were polishing their swords and helmets, they happened to notice the nest, and just as they were leaving, one of them climbed the tree and robbed it. With sore sympathy we watched the young birds as the hard-hearted robber pushed them one by one beneath his jacket – all but two that jumped out of the nest and tried to fly, but they were easily caught as they fluttered on the ground, and were hidden away with the rest. The distress of the bereaved parents, as they hovered and screamed over the frightened crying children they so long had loved and sheltered and fed, was pitiful to see; but the shining soldier rode grandly away on his big gray horse, caring only for the few pennies the young songbirds would bring and the beer they would buy, while we all, sisters and brothers, were crying and sobbing. I remember, as if it happened this day, how my heart fairly ached and choked me. Mother put us to bed and tried to comfort us, telling us that the little birds would be well fed and grow big, and soon learn to sing in pretty cages; but again and again we rehearsed the sad story of the poor bereaved birds and their frightened children, and could not be comforted. Father came into the room when we were half asleep and still sobbing, and I heard mother telling him that 'a' the bairns' hearts were broken over the robbing of the nest in the elm'.

After attaining the manly, belligerent age of five or six years, very few of my schooldays passed without a fist fight, and half a dozen was no uncommon number. When any classmate of our own age questioned our rank and standing as fighters, we always made haste to settle the matter at a quiet place on the Davel Brae. To be a 'gude fechter' was our highest ambition, our dearest aim in life in or out of school. To be a good scholar was a secondary consideration, though we tried hard to hold high places in our classes and gloried in being Dux.

We fairly revelled in the battle stories of glorious William Wallace and Robert the Bruce, with which every breath of Scotch air is saturated, and of course we were all going to be soldiers. On the Davel Brae battleground we often managed to bring on something like real war, greatly more exciting than personal combat. Choosing leaders, we divided into two armies. In winter damp snow furnished plenty of ammunition to make the thing serious, and in summer sand and grass sods. Cheering and shouting some battle-cry such as 'Bannockburn! Bannockburn! Scotland forever! The Last War in India!' we were led bravely on. For heavy battery work we stuffed our Scotch blue bonnets with snow and sand, sometimes mixed with gravel, and fired them at each other as cannon-balls.

Of course we always looked eagerly forward to vacation days and thought them slow in coming. Old Mungo Siddons gave us a lot of gooseberries or currants and wished us a happy time. Some sort of special closing-exercises – singing, recitations, etc – celebrated the great day, but I remember only the berries, freedom from school work, and opportunities for runaway rambles in the fields and along the wave-beaten seashore.

An exciting time came when at the age of seven or eight years I left the auld Davel Brae school for the grammar school. Of course I had a terrible lot of fighting to do, because a new scholar had to meet every one of his age who dared to challenge him, this being the common introduction to a new school. It was very strenuous for the first month or so, establishing my fighting rank, taking up new studies, especially Latin and French, getting acquainted with new classmates and the master and his rules. In the first few Latin and French lessons the new teacher, Mr Lyon, blandly smiled at our comical blunders, but pedagogical weather of the severest kind quickly set in, when for every mistake, everything short of perfection, the taws was promptly applied. We had to get three lessons every day in Latin, three in French, and as many in English, besides spelling, history, arithmetic, and geography. Word lessons in particular, the wouldst-couldst-shouldst-have-loved kind, were kept up, with much warlike thrashing, until I had committed the whole of the French, Latin, and English grammars to memory, and in connection with reading-lessons we were called on to recite parts of them with the rules over and over again, as if all the regular and irregular incomprehensible verb stuff was poetry. In addition to all this, father made me learn so many Bible verses every day that by the time I was eleven years of age I had about three fourths of the Old Testament and all of the New by heart and by sore flesh. I could recite the New Testament from the beginning of Matthew to the end of Revelation without a single stop. The dangers of cramming and of making scholars study at home instead of letting their little brains rest were never heard of in those days. We carried our school-books home in a strap every night and committed to memory our next day's lessons before we went to bed, and to do that we had to bend our attention as closely on our tasks as lawyers on great million-dollar cases. I can't conceive of anything that would now enable me to concentrate my attention more fully than when I was a mere stripling boy, and it was all done by whipping – thrashing in general. Old-fashioned Scotch teachers spent no time in seeking short roads to knowledge, or in trying any of the new-fangled psychological methods so much in vogue nowadays. There was nothing said about making the seats easy or the lessons easy. We were simply driven pointblank against our books like soldiers against the enemy, and sternly ordered, 'Up and at'em. Commit your lessons to memory!' If we failed in any part, however slight, we were whipped; for the grand, simple, all-sufficing Scotch discovery had been made that there was a close connection between the skin and the memory, and that irritating the skin excited the memory to any required degree.

Fighting was carried on still more vigorously in the high school than in the common school. Whenever any one was challenged, either the challenge was allowed or it was decided by a battle on the seashore, where with stubborn enthusiasm we battered each other as if we had not been sufficiently battered by the teacher. When we were so fortunate as to finish a fight without getting a black eye, we usually escaped a thrashing at home and another next morning at school, for other traces of the fray could be easily washed off at a well on the church brae, or concealed, or passed as results of playground accidents; but a black eye could never be explained away from downright fighting. A good double thrashing was the inevitable penalty, but all without avail; fighting went on without the slightest abatement, like natural storms; for no punishment less than death could quench the ancient inherited belligerence burning in our pagan blood. Nor could we be made to believe it was fair that father and teacher should thrash us so industriously for our good, while begrudging us the pleasure of thrashing each other for our good. All these various thrashings, however, were admirably influential in developing not only memory but fortitude as well. For if we did not endure our school punishments and fighting pains without flinching and making faces, we were mocked on the playground, and public opinion on a Scotch playground was a powerful agent in controlling behavior; therefore we at length managed to keep our features in smooth repose while enduring pain that would try anybody but an American Indian. Far from feeling that we were called on to endure too much pain, one of our playground games was thrashing each other with whips about two feet long made from the tough, wiry stems of a species of polygonum fastened together in a stiff, firm braid. One of us handing two of these whips to a companion to take his choice, we stood up close together and thrashed each other on the legs until one succumbed to the intolerable pain and thus lost the game. Nearly all of our playground games were strenuous – shin-battering shinny, wrestling, prisoners' base, and dogs and hares – all augmenting in no slight degree our lessons in fortitude. Moreover, we regarded our punishments and pains of every sort as training for war, since we were all going to be soldiers. Besides single combats we sometimes assembled on Saturdays to meet the scholars of another school, and very little was required for the growth of strained relations, and war. The immediate cause might be nothing more than a saucy stare. Perhaps the scholar stared at would insolently inquire, 'What are ye glowerin' at, Bob?' Bob would reply, 'I'll look where I hae a mind and hinder me if ye daur.' 'Weel, Bob,' the outraged stared-at scholar would reply, 'I'll soon let ye see whether I daur or no!' and give Bob a blow on the face. This opened the battle, and every good scholar belonging to either school was drawn into it. After both sides were sore and weary, a strong-lunged warrior would be heard above the din of battle shouting, 'I'll tell ye what we'll dae wi' ye. If ye'll let us alane we'll let ye alane!' and the school war ended as most wars between nations do; and some of them begin in much the same way.

Notwithstanding the great number of harshly enforced rules, not very good order was kept in school in my time. There were two schools within a few rods of each other, one for mathematics, navigation, etc., the other, called the grammar school, that I attended. The masters lived in a big freestone house within eight or ten yards of the schools, so that they could easily step out for anything they wanted or send one of the scholars. The moment our master disappeared, perhaps for a book or a drink, every scholar left his seat and his lessons, jumped on top of the benches and desks or crawled beneath them, tugging, rolling, wrestling, accomplishing in a minute a depth of disorder and din unbelievable save by a Scottish scholar. We even carried on war, class against class, in those wild, precious minutes. A watcher gave the alarm when the master opened his house-door to return, and it was a great feat to get into our places before he entered, adorned in awful majestic authority, shouting 'Silence!' and striking resounding blows with his cane on a desk or on some unfortunate scholar's back.

Forty-seven years after leaving this fighting school, I returned on a visit to Scotland, and a cousin in Dunbar introduced me to a minister who was acquainted with the history of the school, and obtained for me an invitation to dine with the new master. Of course I gladly accepted, for I wanted to see the old place of fun and pain, and the battleground on the sands. Mr Lyon, our able teacher and thrasher, I learned, had held his place as master of the school for twenty or thirty years after I left it, and had recently died in London, after preparing many young men for the English Universities. At the dinner-table, while I was recalling the amusements and fights of my old school-days, the minister remarked to the new master, 'Now, don't you wish that you had been teacher in those days, and gained the honor of walloping John Muir?' This pleasure so merrily suggested showed that the minister also had been a fighter in his youth. The old freestone school building was still perfectly sound, but the carved, ink-stained desks were almost whittled away.

The highest part of our playground back of the school commanded a view of the sea, and we loved to watch the passing ships and, judging by their rigging, make guesses as to the ports they had sailed from, those to which they were bound, what they were loaded with, their tonnage, etc. In stormy weather they were all smothered in clouds and spray, and showers of salt scud torn from the tops of the waves came flying over the playground wall. In those tremendous storms many a brave ship foundered or was tossed and smashed on the rocky shore. When a wreck occurred within a mile or two of the town, we often managed by running fast to reach it and pick up some of the spoils. In particular I remember visiting the battered fragments of an unfortunate brig or schooner that had been loaded with apples, and finding fine unpitiful sport in rushing into the spent waves and picking up the red-cheeked fruit from the frothy, seething foam.

All our school-books were extravagantly illustrated with drawings of every kind of sailing-vessel, and every boy owned some sort of craft whittled from a block of wood and trimmed with infinite pains – sloops, schooners, brigs, and full-rigged ships, with their sails and string ropes properly adjusted and named for us by some old sailor. These precious toy craft with lead keels we learned to sail on a pond near the town. With the sails set at the proper angle to the wind, they made fast straight voyages across the pond to boys on the other side, who readjusted the sails and started them back on the return voyages. Oftentimes fleets of half a dozen or more were started together in exciting races.

Our most exciting sport, however, was playing with gunpowder. We made guns out of gas-pipe, mounted them on sticks of any shape, clubbed our pennies together for powder, gleaned pieces of lead here and there and cut them into slugs, and, while one aimed, another applied a match to the touch-hole. With these awful weapons we wandered along the beach and fired at the gulls and solan-geese as they passed us. Fortunately we never hurt any of them that we knew of. We also dug holes in the ground, put in a handful or two of powder, tamped it well around a fuse made of a wheat-stalk, and, reaching cautiously forward, touched a match to the straw. This we called making earthquakes. Oftentimes we went home with singed hair and faces well peppered with powder-grains that could not be washed out. Then, of course, came a correspondingly severe punishment from both father and teacher.

Another favourite sport was climbing trees and scaling garden-walls. Boys eight or ten years of age could get over almost any wall by standing on each others' shoulders, thus making living ladders. To make walls secure against marauders, many of them were finished on top with broken bottles imbedded in lime, leaving the cutting edges sticking up; but with bunches of grass and weeds we could sit or stand in comfort on top of the jaggedest of them.

Like squirrels that begin to eat nuts before they are ripe, we began to eat apples about as soon as they were formed, causing, of course, desperate gastric disturbances to be cured by castor oil. Serious were the risks we ran in climbing and squeezing through hedges, and, of course, among the country folk we were far from welcome. Farmers passing us on the roads often shouted by way of greeting, 'Oh, you vagabonds! Back to the toon wi' ye. Gang back where ye belang. You're up to mischief, Ise warrant. I can see it. The gamekeeper'll catch ye, and maist like ye'll a' be hanged some day.'

Breakfast in those auld-lang-syne days was simple oatmeal porridge, usually with a little milk or treacle, served in wooden dishes called 'luggies', formed of staves hooped together like miniature tubs about four or five inches in diameter. One of the staves, the lug or ear, a few inches longer than the others, served as a handle, while the number of luggies ranged in a row on a dresser indicated the size of the family. We never dreamed of anything to come after the porridge, or of asking for more. Our portions were consumed in about a couple of minutes; then off to school. At noon we came racing home ravenously hungry. The midday meal, called dinner, was usually vegetable broth, a small piece of boiled mutton, and barley-meal scone. None of us liked the barley scone bread, therefore we got all we wanted of it, and in desperation had to eat it, for we were always hungry, about as hungry after as before meals. The evening meal was called 'tea' and was served on our return from school. It consisted, as far as we children were concerned, of half a slice of white bread without butter, barley scone, and warm water with a little milk and sugar in it, a beverage called 'content', which warmed but neither cheered nor inebriated. Immediately after tea we ran across the street with our books to Grandfather Gilrye, who took pleasure in seeing us and hearing us recite our next day's lessons. Then back home to supper, usually a boiled potato and piece of barley scone. Then family worship, and to bed.

Our amusements on Saturday afternoons and vacations depended mostly on getting away from home into the country, especially in the spring when the birds were calling loudest. Father sternly forbade David and me from playing truant in the fields with plundering wanderers like ourselves, fearing we might go on from bad to worse, get hurt in climbing over walls, caught by gamekeepers, or lost by falling over a cliff into the sea. 'Play as much as you like in the back yard and garden,' he said, 'and mind what you'll get when you forget and disobey.' Thus he warned us with an awfully stern countenance, looking very hard-hearted, while naturally his heart was far from hard, though he devoutly believed in eternal punishment for bad boys both here and hereafter. Nevertheless, like devout martyrs of wildness, we stole away to the seashore or the green, sunny fields with almost religious regularity, taking advantage of opportunities, when father was very busy, to join our companions, oftenest to hear the birds sing and hunt their nests, glorying in the number we had discovered and called our own. A sample of our nest chatter was something like this: Willie Chisholm would proudly exclaim, 'I ken (know) seventeen nests, and you, Johnnie, ken only fifteen.'

'But I wouldna gie my fifteen for your seventeen, for five of mine are larks and mavises. You ken only three o' the best singers.'

'Yes, Johnnie, but I ken six goldies and you ken only one. Maist of yours are only sparrows and linties and robin-redbreasts.'

Then perhaps Bob Richardson would loudly declare that he 'kenned mair nests than onybody, for he kenned twenty-three, with about fifty eggs in them and mair than fifty young birds – maybe a hundred. Some of them naething but raw gorblings but lots of them as big as their mithers and ready to flee. And aboot fifty craw's nests and three fox dens.'

'Oh, yes, Bob, but that's no fair, for naebody counts craw's nests and fox holes, and then you live in the country at Belle-haven where ye have the best chance.'

'Yes, but I ken a lot of bumbee's nests, baith the red-legged and the yellow-legged kind.'

'Oh, wha cares for bumbee's nests!'

'Weel, but here's something! Ma father let me gang to a fox hunt, and man, it was grand to see the hounds and the lang-legged horses lowpin the dykes and burns and hedges!'

The nests, I fear, with the beautiful eggs and young birds, were prized quite as highly as the songs of the glad parents, but no Scotch boy that I know of ever failed to listen with enthusiasm to the songs of the skylarks. Oftentimes on a broad meadow near Dunbar we stood for hours enjoying their marvellous singing and soaring. From the grass where the nest was hidden the male would suddenly rise, as straight as if shot up, to a height of perhaps thirty or forty feet, and, sustaining himself with rapid wing-beats, pour down the most delicious melody, sweet and clear and strong, overflowing all bounds, then suddenly he would soar higher again and again, ever higher and higher, soaring and singing until lost to sight even on perfectly clear days, and oftentimes in cloudy weather 'far in the downy cloud', as the poet says.

To test our eyes we often watched a lark until he seemed a faint speck in the sky and finally passed beyond the keenest-sighted of us all. 'I see him yet!' we would cry, 'I see him yet!' 'I see him yet!' 'I see him yet!' as he soared. And finally only one of us would be left to claim that he still saw him. At last he, too, would have to admit that the singer had soared beyond his sight, and still the music came pouring down to us in glorious profusion, from a height far above our vision, requiring marvellous power of wing and marvellous power of voice, for that rich, delicious, soft, and yet clear music was distinctly heard long after the bird was out of sight. Then, suddenly ceasing, the glorious singer would appear, falling like a bolt straight down to his nest, where his mate was sitting on the eggs.

It was far too common a practice among us to carry off a young lark just before it could fly, place it in a cage, and fondly, laboriously feed it. Sometimes we succeeded in keeping one alive for a year or two, and when awakened by the spring weather it was pitiful to see the quivering imprisoned soarer of the heavens rapidly beating its wings and singing as though it were flying and hovering in the air like its parents. To keep it in health we were taught that we must supply it with a sod of grass the size of the bottom of the cage, to make the poor bird feel as though it were at home on its native meadow – a meadow perhaps a foot or at most two feet square. Again and again it would try to hover over that miniature meadow from its minature sky just underneath the top of the cage. At last, conscience-stricken, we carried the beloved prisoner to the meadow west of Dunbar where it was born, and, blessing its sweet heart, bravely set it free, and our exceeding great reward was to see it fly and sing in the sky.

In the winter, when there was but little doing in the fields, we organized running-matches. A dozen or so of us would start out on races that were simply tests of endurance, running on and on along a public road over the breezy hills like hounds, without stopping or getting tired. The only serious trouble we ever felt in these long races was an occasional stitch in our sides. One of the boys started the story that sucking raw eggs was a sure cure for the stitches. We had hens in our back yard, and on the next Saturday we managed to swallow a couple of eggs apiece, a disgusting job, but we would do almost anything to mend our speed, and as soon as we could get away after taking the cure we set out on a ten or twenty mile run to prove its worth. We thought nothing of running right ahead ten or a dozen miles before turning back; for we knew nothing about taking time by the sun, and none of us had a watch in those days. Indeed, we never cared about time until it began to get dark. Then we thought of home and the thrashing that awaited us. Late or early, the thrashing was sure, unless father happened to be away. If he was expected to return soon, mother made haste to get us to bed before his arrival. We escaped the thrashing next morning, for father never felt like thrashing us in cold blood on the calm holy Sabbath. But no punishment, however sure and severe, was of any avail against the attraction of the fields and woods. It had other uses, developing memory, etc., but in keeping us at home it was of no use at all. Wildness was ever sounding in our ears, and Nature saw to it that besides school lessons and church lessons some of her own lessons should be learned, perhaps with a view to the time when we should be called to wander in wildness to our heart's content. Oh, the blessed enchantment of those Saturday runaways in the prime of the spring! How our young wondering eyes reveled in the sunny, breezy glory of the hills and the sky, every particle of us thrilling and tingling with the bees and glad birds and glad streams! Kings may be blessed; we were glorious, we were free – school cares and scoldings, heart thrashings and flesh thrashings alike, were forgotten in the fullness of Nature's glad wildness. These were my first excursions – the beginnings of lifelong wanderings.

TWO

A New World

Our grammar-school reader, called, I think, 'Maccoulough's Course of Reading', contained a few natural-history sketches that excited me very much and left a deep impression, especially a fine description of the fish hawk and the bald eagle by the Scotch ornithologist Wilson, who had the good fortune to wander for years in the American woods while the country was yet mostly wild. I read his description over and over again, till I got the vivid picture he drew by heart – the long-winged hawk circling over the heaving waves, every motion watched by the eagle perched on the top of a crag or dead tree; the fish hawk poising for a moment to take aim at a fish and plunging under the water; the eagle with kindling eye spreading his wings ready for instant flight in case the attack should prove successful; the hawk emerging with a struggling fish in his talons, and proud flight; the eagle launching himself in pursuit; the wonderful wing-work in the sky, the fish hawk, though encumbered with his prey, circling higher, higher, striving hard to keep above the robber eagle; the eagle at length soaring above him, compelling him with a cry of despair to drop his hard-won prey; then the eagle steadying himself for a moment to take aim, descending swift as a lightning-bolt, and seizing the falling fish before it reached the sea.

Not less exciting and memorable was Audubon's wonderful story of the passenger pigeon, a beautiful bird flying in vast flocks that darkened the sky like clouds, countless millions assembling to rest and sleep and rear their young in certain forests, miles in length and breadth, fifty or a hundred nests on a single tree; the overloaded branches bending low and often breaking; the farmers gathering from far and near, beating down countless thousands of the young and old birds from their nests and roosts with

long poles at night, and in the morning driving their bands
of hogs, some of them brought from farms a hundred miles
distant, to fatten on the dead and wounded covering the
ground.

In another of our reading-lessons some of the American
forests were described. The most interesting of the trees
to us boys was the sugar maple, and soon after we had
learned this sweet story we heard everybody talking about
the discovery of gold in the same wonder-filled country.

One night, when David and I were at grandfather's
fireside solemnly learning our lessons as usual, my father
came in with news, the most wonderful, most glorious, that
wild boys ever heard. 'Bairns,' he said, 'you needna learn
your lessons the nicht, for we're gan to America the morn!'
No more grammar, but boundless woods full of mysterious
good things; trees full of sugar, growing in ground full of
gold; hawks, eagles, pigeons, filling the sky; millions of
birds' nests, and no gamekeepers to stop us in all the wild,
happy land. We were utterly, blindly glorious. After father
left the room, grandfather gave David and me a gold coin
apiece for a keepsake, and looked very serious for he was
about to be deserted in his lonely old age. And when we
in fullness of young joy spoke of what we were going to do,
of the wonderful birds and their nests that we should find,
the sugar and gold, etc., and promised to send him a big
box full of that tree sugar packed in gold from the glorious
paradise over the sea, poor lonely grandfather, about to be
forsaken, looked with downcast eyes on the floor and said
in a low, trembling, troubled voice, 'Ah, poor laddies, poor
laddies, you'll find something else ower the sea forbye gold
and sugar, birds' nests and freedom fra lessons and schools.
You'll find plenty hard, hard work.' And so we did. But
nothing he could say could cloud our joy or abate the
fire of youthful, hopeful, fearless adventure. Nor could
we in the midst of such measureless excitement see or
feel the shadows and sorrows of his darkening old age. To
my schoolmates, met that night on the street, I shouted
the glorious news, 'I'm gan to Amaraka the morn!' None
could believe it. I said, 'Weel, just you see if I am at the
skule the morn!'

Next morning we went by rail to Glasgow and thence
joyfully sailed away from beloved Scotland, flying to our
fortunes on the wings of the winds, care-free as thistle
seeds. We could not then know what we were leaving,
what we were to encounter in the New World, nor what
our gains were likely to be. We were too young and full
of hope for fear or regret, but not too young to look
forward with eager enthusiasm to the wonderful schoolless
bookless American wilderness. Even the natural heart-pain
of parting from grandfather and grandmother Gilrye, who
loved us so well, and from mother and sisters and brother
was quickly quenched in young joy. Father took with
him only my sister Sarah (thirteen years of age), myself
(eleven), and brother David (nine), leaving my eldest
sister, Margaret, and the three youngest of the family,
Daniel, Mary, and Anna, with mother, to join us after a
farm had been found in the wilderness and a comfortable
house made to receive them.

In crossing the Atlantic before the days of steamships,
or even the American clippers, the voyages made in
old-fashioned sailing-vessels were very long. Ours was
six weeks and three days. But because we had no lessons
to get, that long voyage had not a dull moment for us
boys. Father and sister Sarah, with most of the old folk,
stayed below in rough weather, groaning in the miseries
of seasickness, many of the passengers wishing they had
never ventured in 'the auld rockin' creel', as they called
our bluff-bowed, wave-beating ship, and, when the weather
was moderately calm, singing songs in the evenings— 'The
Youthful Sailor Frank and Bold', 'Oh, why left I my hame,
why did I cross the deep', etc. But no matter how much
the old tub tossed about and battered the waves, we were
on deck every day, not in the least seasick, watching the
sailors at their rope-hauling and climbing work; joining in
their songs, learning the names of the ropes and sails and
helping them as far as they would let us; playing games
with other boys in calm weather when the deck was dry,
and in stormy weather rejoicing in sympathy with the big
curly-topped waves.

The captain occasionally called David and me into his

cabin and asked us about our schools, handed us books to read, and seemed surprised to find that Scotch boys could read and pronounce English with perfect accent and knew so much Latin and French. In Scotch schools only pure English was taught, although not a word of English was spoken out of school. All through life, however well educated, the Scotch spoke Scotch among their own folk, except at times when unduly excited on the only two subjects which Scotchmen get much excited, namely religion and politics. So long as the controversy went on with fairly level temper, only gude braid Scots was used, but if one became angry, as was likely to happen, then he immediately began speaking severely correct English, while his antagonist, drawing himself up, would say 'Weel, there's na use pursuing this subject ony further, for I see ye hae gotten to your English.'

As we neared the shore of the great new land, with what eager wonder we watched the whales and dolphins and porpoises and seabirds, and made the good-natured sailors teach us their names and tell us stories about them!

There were quite a large number of emigrants aboard, many of them newly married couples, and the advantages of the different parts of the New World they expected to settle in were often discussed. My father started with the intention of going to the backwoods of Upper Canada. Before the end of the voyage, however, he was persuaded that the States offered superior advantages, especially Wisconsin and Michigan, where the land was said to be as good as in Canada and far more easily brought under cultivation; for in Canada the woods were so close and heavy that a man might wear out his life in getting a few acres cleared of trees and stumps. So he changed his mind and concluded to go to one of the Western States.

On our wavering westward way a grain-dealer in Buffalo told father that most of the wheat he handled came from Wisconsin; and this influential information finally determined my father's choice. At Milwaukee a farmer who had come in from the country near Fort Winnebago with a load of wheat agreed to haul us and our formidable load of stuff to a little town called Kingston for thirty dollars.

On that hundred-mile journey, just after the spring thaw, the roads over the prairies were heavy and miry, causing no end of lamentation, for we often got stuck in the mud, and the poor farmer sadly declared that never, never again would he be tempted to try to haul such a cruel, heart-breaking, wagon-breaking, horse-killing load, no, not for a hundred dollars. In leaving Scotland, father, like many other home-seekers, burdened himself with far too much luggage, as if all America were still a wilderness in which little or nothing could be bought. One of his big iron-bound boxes must have weighed about four hundred pounds, for it contained an old-fashioned beam-scales with a complete set of cast-iron counterweights, two of them fifty-six pounds each, a twenty-eight, and so on down to a single pound. Also a lot of iron wedges, carpenter's tools, and so forth, and at Buffalo, as if on the very edge of the wilderness, he gladly added to his burden a big cast-iron stove with pots and pans, provisions enough for a long siege, and a scythe and cumbersome cradle for cutting wheat, all of which he succeeded in landing in the primeval Wisconsin woods.

A land-agent at Kingston gave father a note to a farmer by the name of Alexander Gray, who lived on the border of the settled part of the country, knew the section-lines, and would probably help him to find a good place for a farm. So father went away to spy out the land, and in the meantime left us children in Kingston in a rented room. It took us less than an hour to get acquainted with some of the boys in the village; we challenged them to wrestle, run races, climb trees, etc., and in a day or two we felt at home, carefree and happy, notwithstanding our family was so widely divided. When father returned he told us that he had found fine land for a farm in sunny open woods on the side of a lake, and that a team of three yoke of oxen with a big wagon was coming to haul us to Mr Gray's place.

We enjoyed the strange ten-mile ride through the woods very much, wondering how the great oxen could be so strong and wise and tame as to pull so heavy a load with no other harness than a chain and a crooked piece of wood on their necks, and how they could sway so obediently to right and left past roadside trees and stumps when the driver said *haw* and *gee*. At Mr Gray's house, father again left us for a few days to build a shanty on the quarter-section he had selected four or five miles to the westward. In the meanwhile we enjoyed our freedom as usual, wandering in the fields and meadows, looking at the trees and flowers, snakes and birds and squirrels. With the help of the nearest neighbours the little shanty was built in less than a day after the rough bur-oak logs for the walls and the white-oak boards for the floor and roof were got together.

To this charming hut, in the sunny woods, overlooking a flowery glacier meadow and a lake rimmed with white water-lilies, we were hauled by an ox-team across trackless carex swamps and low rolling hills sparsely dotted with round-headed oaks. Just as we arrived at the shanty, before we had time to look at it or the scenery about it, David and I jumped down in a hurry off the load of household goods, for we had discovered a blue jay's nest, and in a minute or so we were up the tree beside it, feasting our eyes on the beautiful green eggs and beautiful birds – our first memorable discovery. The handsome birds had not seen Scotch boys before and made a desperate screaming as if we were robbers like themselves; though we left the eggs untouched, feeling that we were already beginning to get rich, and wondering how many more nests we should find in the grand sunny woods. Then we ran along the brow of the hill that the shanty stood on, and down to the meadow, searching the trees and grass tufts and bushes, and soon discovered a bluebird's and a woodpecker's nest, and began an acquaintance with the frogs and snakes and turtles in the creeks and springs.

This sudden plash into pure wildness – baptism in Nature's warm heart – how utterly happy it made us! Nature streaming into us, wooingly teaching her wonderful glowing lessons, so unlike the dismal grammar ashes and cinders so long thrashed into us. Here without knowing it we still were at school; every wild lesson a love lesson, not whipped but charmed into us. Oh, that glorious Wisconsin wilderness! Everything new and pure in the very prime of the spring when Nature's pulses were beating highest and mysteriously keeping time with our own! Young hearts, young leaves, flowers, animals, the winds and the streams and the sparkling lake, all widely, gladly rejoicing together!

Next morning, when we climbed to the precious jay nest to take another admiring look at the eggs, we found it empty. Not a shell-fragment was left, and we wondered how in the world the birds were able to carry off their thin-shelled eggs either in their bills or in their feet without breaking them, and how they could be kept warm while a new nest was being built. Well, I am still asking these questions. When I was on the Harriman Expedition I asked Robert Ridgway, the eminent ornithologist, how these sudden flittings were accomplished, and he frankly confessed that he didn't know, but guessed that jays and many other birds carried their eggs in their mouths; and when I objected that a jay's mouth seemed too small to hold its eggs, he replied that birds' mouths were larger than the narrowness of their bills indicated. Then I asked him what he thought they did with the eggs while a new nest was being prepared. He didn't know; neither do I to this day. A specimen of the many puzzling problems presented to the naturalist.

We soon found many more nests belonging to birds that were not half so suspicious. The handsome and notorious blue jay plunders the nests of other birds and of course he could not trust us. Almost all the others – brown thrushes, bluebirds, song sparrows, kingbirds, hen-hawks, night-hawks, whip-poor-wills, woodpeckers, etc. – simply tried to avoid being seen, to draw or drive us away, or paid no attention to us.

We used to wonder how the woodpeckers could bore holes so perfectly round, true mathematical circles. We ourselves could not have done it even with gouges and chisels. We loved to watch them feeding their young, and wondered how they could glean food enough for so many clamorous, hungry, unsatisfiable babies, and how they managed to give each one its share; for after the young grew strong, one would get his head out of the door-hole and try to hold possession of it to meet the food-laden parents. How hard they worked to support their families, especially the red-headed and speckledy woodpeckers and flickers; digging, hammering on scaly bark and decaying trunks and branches from dawn to dark, coming and going at intervals of a few minutes all the livelong day!

We discovered a hen-hawk's nest on the top of a tall oak thirty or forty rods from the shanty and approached it cautiously. One of the pair always kept watch, soaring in wide circles high above the tree, and when we attempted to climb it, the big dangerous-looking bird came swooping down at us and drove us away.

We greatly admired the plucky kingbird. In Scotland our great ambition was to be good fighters, and we admired this quality in the handsome little chattering flycatcher that whips all the other birds. He was particularly angry when plundering jays and hawks came near his home, and took pains to thrash them not only away from the nest-tree but out of the neighbourhood. The nest was usually built on a bur oak near a meadow where insects were abundant, and where no undesirable visitor could approach without being discovered. When a hen-hawk hove in sight, the male immediately set off after him, and it was ridiculous to see that great, strong bird hurrying away as fast as his clumsy wings would carry him, as soon as he saw the little, waspish kingbird coming. But the kingbird easily overtook him, flew just a few feet above him, and with a lot of chattering, scolding notes kept diving and striking him on the back of the head until tired; then he alighted to rest on the hawk's broad shoulders, still scolding and chattering as he rode along, like an angry boy pouring out vials of wrath. Then, up and at him again with his sharp bill; and after he had thus driven and ridden his big enemy a mile or so from the nest, he went home to his mate, chuckling and bragging as if trying to tell her what a wonderful fellow he was.

This first spring, while some of the birds were still building their nests and very few young ones had yet tried to fly, father hired a Yankee to assist in clearing eight or ten acres of the best ground for a field. We found new wonders every day and often had to call on this Yankee to solve puzzling questions. We asked him one day if there was any bird in America that the kingbird couldn't whip. What about the sandhill crane? Could he whip that long-legged, long-billed fellow?

'A crane never goes near kingbirds' nests or notices so small a bird,' he said 'and therefore there could be no fighting between them.' So we hastily concluded that our hero could whip every bird in the country except perhaps the sandhill crane.

We never tired listening to the wonderful whip-poor-will. One came every night about dusk and sat on a log about twenty or thirty feet from our cabin door and began shouting 'Whip poor Will! Whip poor Will!' with loud emphatic earnestness. 'What's that? What's that?' we cried when this startling visitor first announced himself. 'What do you call it?'

'Why, it's telling you its name,' said the Yankee. 'Don't you hear it and what he wants you to do? He says his name is "Poor Will" and he wants you to whip him, and you may if you are able to catch him.' Poor Will seemed the most wonderful of all the strange creatures we had seen. What a wild, strong, bold voice he had, unlike any other we had ever heard on sea or land!

A near relative, the bull-bat, or nighthawk, seemed hardly less wonderful. Towards evening scattered flocks kept the sky lively as they circled around on their long wings a hundred feet or more above the ground, hunting moths and beetles, interrupting their rather slow but strong, regular wing-beats at short intervals with quick quivering strokes while uttering keen, squeaky cries something like *pfee, pfee*, and every now and then diving nearly to the ground with a loud ripping, bellowing sound, like bull-roaring, suggesting its name; then turning and gliding swiftly up again. These fine wild gray birds, about the size of a pigeon, lay their two eggs on bare ground without anything like a nest or even a concealing bush or grass-tuft. Nevertheless they are not easily seen, for they are coloured like the ground. While sitting on their eggs, they depend so much upon not being noticed that if you are walking rapidly ahead they allow you to step within an inch or two of them without flinching. But if they see by your looks that you have discovered them, they leave their eggs or young, and, like a good many other birds, pretend that they are sorely wounded, fluttering and rolling over on the ground and gasping as if dying, to draw you away. When pursued we were surprised to find that just when we were on the point of overtaking them they were always able to flutter a few yards further, until they had led us about a quarter of a mile from the nest; then, suddenly getting well, they quietly flew home by a roundabout way to their precious babies or eggs, o'er a' the ills of life victorious, bad boys among the worst. The Yankee took particular pleasure in encouraging us to pursue them.

Everything about us was so novel and wonderful that we could hardly believe our senses except when hungry or while father was thrashing us. When we first saw Fountain Lake Meadow, on a sultry evening, sprinkled with millions of lightning-bugs throbbing with light, the effect was so strange and beautiful that it seemed far too marvellous to be real. Looking from our shanty on the hill, I thought that the whole wonderful fairy show must be in my eyes; for only in fighting, when my eyes were struck, had I ever seen anything in the least like it. But when I asked my brother if he saw anything strange in the meadow he said, 'Yes, it's all covered with shaky fire-sparks.' Then I guessed that it might be something outside of us, and applied to our all-knowing Yankee to explain it. 'Oh, it's nothing but lightnin'-bugs,' he said, and kindly led us down the hill to the edge of the fiery meadow, caught a few of the wonderful bugs, dropped them into a cup, and carried them to the shanty, where we watched them throbbing and flashing out their mysterious light at regular intervals, as if each little passionate glow were caused by the beating of a heart. Once I saw a splendid display of glow-worm light in the foothills of the Himalayas, north of Calcutta, but glorious as it appeared in pure starry radiance, it was far less impressive than the extravagant abounding, quivering, dancing fire on our Wisconsin meadow.

Partridge drumming was another great marvel. When I

first heard the low, soft, solemn sound I thought it must be made by some strange disturbance in my head or stomach, but as all seemed serene within, I asked David whether he heard anything queer. 'Yes,' he said, 'I hear something saying *boomp, boomp, boomp,* and I'm wondering at it.' Then I was half satisfied that the source of the mysterious sound must be in something outside of us, coming perhaps from the ground or from some ghost or bogie or woodland fairy. Only after long watching and listening did we at last discover it in the wings of the plump brown bird.

The love-song of the common jack snipe seemed not a whit less mysterious than partridge drumming. It was usually heard on cloudy evenings, a strange, unearthly, winnowing, spiritlike sound, yet easily heard at a distance of a third of a mile. Our sharp eyes soon detected the bird while making it, as it circled high in the air over the meadow with wonderfully strong and rapid wing-beats, suddenly descending and rising, again and again, in deep, wide loops; the tones being very low and smooth at the beginning of the descent, rapidly increasing to a curious little whirling storm-roar at the bottom, and gradually fading lower and lower until the top was reached. It was long, however, before we identified this mysterious wing-singer as the little brown jack snipe that we knew so well and had so often watched as he silently probed the mud around the edges of our meadow stream and spring-holes, and made short zigzag flights over the grass uttering only little short, crisp quacks and chucks.

The love-songs of the frogs seemed hardly less wonderful than those of the birds, their musical notes varying from the sweet, tranquil, soothing peeping and purring of the hylas to the awfully deep low-bass blunt bellowing of the bullfrogs. Some of the smaller species have wonderfully clear, sharp voices and told us their good Bible names in musical tones about as plainly as the whip-poor-will. *Isaac, Isaac; Yacob, Yacob; Israel, Israel;* shouted in sharp, ringing, far-reaching tones, as if they had all been to school and severely drilled in elocution. In the still, warm evenings, big bunchy bullfrogs bellowed, *Drunk! Drunk! Drunk! fug o'rum! fug o'rum!* and early in the spring, countless thousands of the commonest species, up to the throat in cold water, sang in concert, making a mass of music, such as it was, loud enough to be heard at a distance of more than half a mile.

Far, far apart from this loud marsh music is that of the many species of hyla, a sort of soothing immortal melody filling the air like light.

We reveled in the glory of the sky scenery as well as that of the woods and meadows and rushy, lily-bordered lakes. The great thunderstorms in particular interested us, so unlike any seen in Scotland, exciting awful, wondering admiration. Gazing awe-stricken, we watched the upbuilding of the sublime cloud-mountains – glowing, sun-beaten pearl and alabaster cumuli, glorious in beauty and majesty and looking so firm and lasting that birds, we thought, might build their nests amid their downy bosses; the black-browed storm-clouds marching in awful grandeur across the landscape, trailing broad gray sheets of hail and rain like vast cataracts, and ever and anon flashing down vivid zigzag lightning followed by terrible crashing thunder. We saw several trees shattered, and one of them, a punky old oak, was set on fire, while we wondered why all the trees and everybody and everything did not share the same fate, for oftentimes the whole sky blazed. After sultry storm days, many of the nights were darkened by smooth black apparently structureless cloud-mantles which at short intervals were illumined with startling suddenness to a fiery glow by quick, quivering lightning-flashes, revealing the landscape in almost noonday brightness, to be instantly quenched in solid blackness.

But those first days and weeks of unmixed enjoyment and freedom, reveling in the wonderful wildness about us, were soon to be mingled with the hard work of making a farm. I was first put to burning brush in clearing land for the plough. Those magnificent brush fires with great white hearts and red flames, the first big, wild outdoor fires I had ever seen, were wonderful sights for young eyes. Again and again, when they were burning fiercest so that we could hardly approach near enough to throw on another branch, father put them to awfully practical use as warning lessons, comparing their heat with that of hell, and the branches with bad boys. 'Now, John,' he would say – 'now, John, just think what an awful thing it would be to be thrown into that fire – and then think of hellfire, that is so many times hotter. Into that fire all bad boys, with sinners of every sort who disobey God, will be cast as we are casting branches into this brush fire, and although suffering so much, their sufferings will never never end, because neither the fire nor the sinners can die.' But those terrible fire lessons quickly faded away in the blithe wilderness air; for no fire can be hotter than the heavenly fire of faith and hope that burns in every healthy boy's heart.

Soon after our arrival in the woods someone added a cat and puppy to the animals father had bought. The cat soon had kittens, and it was interesting to watch her feeding, protecting, and training them. After they were able to leave their nest and play, she went out hunting and brought in many kinds of birds and squirrels for them, mostly ground squirrels (spermophiles), called 'gophers' in Wisconsin. When she got within a dozen yards or so of the shanty, she announced her approach by a peculiar call, and the sleeping kittens immediately bounced up and ran to meet her, all racing for the first bite of they knew not what, and we too ran to see what she brought. She then lay down a few minutes to rest and enjoy the enjoyment of her feasting family, and again vanished in the grass and flowers, coming and going every half-hour or so. Sometimes she brought in birds that we had never seen before, and occasionally a flying squirrel, chipmunk, or big fox squirrel. We were just old enough, David and I, to regard all these creatures as wonders, the strange inhabitants of our new world.

The pup was a common cur, though very uncommon to us, a black and white short-haired mongrel that we named 'Watch'. We always gave him a pan of milk in the evening just before we knelt in family worship, while daylight still lingered in the shanty. And, instead of attending to the prayers, I too often studied the small wild creatures playing around us. Field mice scampered about the cabin as though it had been built for them alone, and their performances were very amusing. About dusk, on one of the calm, sultry nights so grateful to moths and beetles, when the puppy was lapping his milk, and we were on our knees, in through the door came a heavy broad-shouldered beetle about as big as a mouse, and after it had droned and boomed round the cabin two or three times, the pan of milk, showing white in the gloaming, caught its eyes, and, taking good aim, it alighted with a slanting, glinting plash in the middle of the pan like a duck alighting in a lake. Baby Watch, having never before seen anything like that beetle, started back, gazing in dumb astonishment and fear at the black sprawling monster trying to swim. Recovering somewhat from his fright, he began to bark at the creature, and ran round and round his milk-pan, wouf-woufing, gurring, growling, like an old dog barking at a wild-cat or a bear. The natural astonishment and curiosity of that boy dog getting his first entomological lesson in this wonderful world was so immoderately funny that I had great difficulty in keeping from laughing out loud.

Snapping turtles were common throughout the woods, and we were delighted to find that they would snap at a stick and hang on like bull-dogs; and we amused ourselves by introducing Watch to them, enjoying his curious behavior and theirs in getting acquainted with each other. One day we assisted one of the smallest of the turtles to get a good grip of poor Watch's ear. Then away he rushed, holding his head sidewise, yelping and terror-stricken, with the strange buglike reptile biting hard and clinging fast – a shameful amusement even for wild boys.

As a playmate Watch was too serious, though he learned more than any stranger would judge him capable of, was a bold, faithful watch-dog, and in his prime a grand fighter, able to whip all the other dogs in the neighbourhood. Comparing him with ourselves, we soon learned that although he could not read books he could read faces, was a good judge of character, always knew what was going on and what we were about to do, and liked to help us. We could run nearly as fast as he could, see about as far, and perhaps hear as well, but in sense of smell his nose was incomparably better than ours. One sharp winter morning when the ground was covered with snow, I noticed that when he was yawning and stretching himself after leaving his bed he suddenly caught the scent of something that excited him, went round the corner of the house, and looked intently to the westward across a tongue of land that we called West Bank, eagerly questioning the air with quivering nostrils, and bristling up as though he felt sure that there was something dangerous in that direction and had actually caught sight of it. Then he ran toward the Bank, and I followed him, curious to see what his nose had discovered. The top of the Bank commanded a view of the north end of our lake and meadow, and when we got there we saw an Indian hunter with a long spear, going from one muskrat cabin to another, approaching cautiously, careful to make no noise, and then suddenly thrusting his spear down through the house. If well aimed, the spear went through the poor beaver rat as it lay cuddled up in the snug nest it had made for itself in the fall with so much far-seeing care, and when the hunter felt the spear quivering, he dug down the mossy hut with his tomahawk and secured his prey – the flesh for food, and the skin to sell for a dime or so. This was a clear object lesson on dogs' keenness of scent. That Indian was more than half a mile away across a wooded ridge. Had the hunter been a white man, I suppose Watch would not have noticed him.

When he was about six or seven years old, he not only became cross, so that he would do only what he liked, but he fell on evil ways, and was accused by the neighbours who had settled around us of catching and devouring whole broods of chickens, some of them only a day or two out of the shell. We never imagined he would do anything so grossly undoglike. He never did at home. But several of the neighbours declared over and over again that they had caught him in the act, and insisted that he must be shot. At last, in spite of tearful protests, he was condemned and executed. Father examined the poor fellow's stomach in search of sure evidence, and discovered the heads of eight chickens that he had devoured at his last meal. So poor Watch was killed simply because his taste for chickens was too much like our own. Think of the millions of squabs that preaching, praying men and women kill and eat, with all sorts of other animals great and small, young and old, while eloquently discoursing on the coming of the blessed peaceful, bloodless millennium! Think of the passenger pigeons that fifty or sixty years ago filled the woods and sky over half the continent, now exterminated by beating down the young from the nests together with the brooding parents, before they could try their wonderful wings; by trapping them in nets, feeding them to hogs, etc. None of our fellow mortals is safe who eats what we eat, who in any way interferes with our pleasures, or who may be used for work or food, clothing or ornament, or mere cruel, sportish amusement. Fortunately many are too small to be seen, and therefore enjoy life beyond our reach. And in looking through God's great stone books made up of records reaching back millions and millions of years, it is a great comfort to learn that vast multitudes of creatures, great and small and infinite in number, lived and had a good time in God's love before man was created.

The old Scotch fashion of whipping for every act of disobedience or of simple, playful forgetfulness was still kept up in the wilderness, and of course many of those whippings fell upon me. Most of them were outrageously severe, and utterly barren of fun. But here is one that was nearly all fun.

Father was busy hauling lumber for the frame house that was to be got ready for the arrival of my mother, sisters, and brother, left behind in Scotland. One morning, when he was ready to start for another load, his ox-whip was not to be found. He asked me if I knew anything about it. I told him I didn't know where it was, but Scotch conscience compelled me to confess that when I was playing with it I had tied it to Watch's tail, and that he ran away, dragging it through the grass, and came back without it. 'It must have slipped off his tail,' I said, and so I didn't know where it was. This honest, straightforward little story made father so angry that he exclaimed with heavy, foreboding emphasis, 'The very deevil's in that boy!' David, who had been playing with me and was perhaps about as responsible for the loss of the whip as I was, said never a word, for he was always prudent enough to hold his tongue when the parental weather was stormy, and so escaped nearly all punishment. And, strange to say, this time I also escaped, all except a terrible scolding, though the thrashing weather seemed darker than ever. As if unwilling to let the sun see the shameful job, father took me into the cabin where the storm was to fall, and sent David to the woods for a switch. While he was out selecting the switch, father put in the spare time sketching my play-wickedness in awful colours, and of course referred again and again to the place prepared for bad boys. In the midst of this terrible word-storm, dreading most the impending thrashing, I whimpered that I was only playing because I couldn't help it; didn't know I was doing wrong; wouldn't do it again, and so forth. After this miserable dialogue was about exhausted, father became impatient at my brother for taking so long to find the switch; and so was I, for I wanted to have the thing over and done with. At last, in came David, a picture of open-hearted innocence, solemnly dragging a young bur-oak sapling, and handed the end of it to father, saying it was the best switch he could find. It was an awfully heavy one, about two and a half inches thick at the butt and ten feet long, almost big enough for a fence-pole. There wasn't room enough in the cabin to swing it, and the moment I saw it I burst out laughing in the midst of my fears. But father failed to see the fun and was very angry at David, heaved the bur-oak outside and passionately demanded his reason for fetching 'sic a muckle rail like that instead o' a switch? Do ye ca' that a switch? I have a gude mind to thrash you instead o' John.' David, with demure, downcast eyes, looked preternaturally righteous, but as usual prudently answered never a word.

It was a hard job in those days to bring up Scotch boys in the way they should go; and poor overworked father was determined to do it if enough of the right kind of switches could be found. But this time, as the sun was getting high, he hitched up old Tom and Jerry and made haste to the Kingston lumber-yard, leaving me unscathed and as innocently wicked as ever; for hardly had father got fairly out of sight among the oaks and hickories, ere all our troubles, hell-threatenings, and exhortations were forgotten in the fun we had lassoing a stubborn old sow and laboriously trying to teach her to go reasonably steady in rope harness. She was the first hog that father bought to stock the farm, and we boys regarded her as a very wonderful beast. In a few weeks she had a lot of pigs, and of all the queer, funny, animal children we had yet seen, none amused us more. They were so comic in size and shape, in their gait and gestures, their merry sham fights, and the false alarms they got up for the fun of scampering back to their mother and begging her in most persuasive little squeals to lie down and give them a drink.

After her darling short-snouted babies were about a month old, she took them out to the woods and gradually roamed farther and farther from the shanty in search of acorns and roots. One afternoon we heard a rifle-shot, a very noticeable thing, as we had no near neighbours, as yet. We thought it must have been fired by an Indian on the trail that followed the right bank of the Fox River between Portage and Packwaukee Lake and passed our shanty at a distance of about three quarters of a mile. Just a few minutes after that shot was heard, along came the poor mother rushing up to the shanty for protection, with her pigs, all out of breath and terror-stricken. One of them was missing, and we supposed of course that an Indian had shot it for food. Next day, I discovered a blood-puddle where the Indian trail crossed the outlet of our lake. One of father's hired men told us that the Indians thought nothing of levying this sort of blackmail whenever they were hungry. The solemn awe and fear in the eyes of that old mother and those little pigs I never can forget; it was as unmistakable and deadly a fear as I ever saw expressed by any human eye, and corroborates in no uncertain way the oneness of all of us.

THREE

Life on a Wisconsin Farm

Coming direct from school in Scotland while we were still hopefully ignorant and far from tame – notwithstanding the unnatural profusion of teaching and thrashing lavished upon us – getting acquainted with the animals about us was a never-failing source of wonder and delight. At first my father, like nearly all the backwoods settlers, bought a yoke of oxen to do the farm work, and as field after field was cleared, the number was gradually increased until we had five yoke. These wise, patient, plodding animals did all the ploughing, logging, hauling, and hard work of every sort for the first four or five years, and, never having seen oxen before, we looked at them with the same eager freshness of conception as we did at the wild animals. We worked with them, sympathized with them in their rest and toil and play, and thus learned to know them far better than we should had we been only trained scientific naturalists. We soon learned that each ox and cow and calf had individual character. Old white-faced Buck, one of the second yoke of oxen we owned, was a notably sagacious fellow. He seemed to reason sometimes almost like ourselves. In the fall we fed the cattle lots of pumpkins and had to split them open so that mouthfuls could be readily broken off. But Buck never waited for us to come to his help. The others, when they were hungry and impatient, tried to break through the hard rind with their teeth, but seldom with success if the pumpkin was full grown. Buck never wasted time in this mumbling, slavering way, but crushed them with his head. He went to the pile, picked out a good one, like a boy choosing an orange or apple, rolled it down on to the open ground, deliberately kneeled in front of it, placed his broad, flat brow on top of it, brought his weight hard down and crushed it, then quietly arose and went on with his meal in comfort. Some would call this 'instinct', as if so-called 'blind instinct' must necessarily make an ox stand on its head to break pumpkins when its teeth got sore, or when nobody came with an axe to split them. Another fine ox showed his skill when hungry by opening all the fences that stood in his way to the corn-fields.

The humanity we found in them came partly through the expression of their eyes when tired, their tones of voice when hungry and calling for food, their patient plodding and pulling in hot weather, their long-drawn-out sighing breath when exhausted and suffering like ourselves, and their enjoyment of rest with the same grateful looks as ours. We recognized their kinship also by their yawning like ourselves when sleepy and evidently enjoying the same peculiar pleasure at the roots of their jaws; by the way they stretched themselves in the morning after a good rest; by learning languages – Scotch, English, Irish, French, Dutch – a smattering of each as required in the faithful service they so willingly, wisely rendered; by their intelligent, alert curiosity, manifested in listening to strange sounds; their love of play; the attachments they made; and their mourning, long continued, when a companion was killed.

When we went to Portage, our nearest town, about ten or twelve miles from the farm, it would oftentimes be late before we got back, and in the summer-time, in sultry, rainy weather, the clouds were full of sheet lightning which every minute or two would suddenly illumine the landscape, revealing all its features, the hills and valleys, meadows and trees, about as fully and clearly as the noonday sunshine; then as suddenly the glorious light would be quenched, making the darkness seem denser than before. On such nights the cattle had to find the way home without any help from us, but they never got off the track, for they followed it by scent like dogs. Once, father, returning late from Portage or Kingston, compelled Tom and Jerry, our first oxen, to leave the dim track, imagining they must be going wrong. At last they stopped and refused to go farther. Then father unhitched them from the wagon, took hold of Tom's tail, and was thus led straight to the shanty. Next morning he set out to seek his wagon and found it on the brow of a steep hill above an impassable swamp. We learned less from the cows, because we did not enter so far into their lives, working with them, suffering heat and cold, hunger and thirst, and almost deadly weariness with them; but none with natural charity could fail to sympathize with them in their love for their calves, and to feel that it in no way differed from the divine mother-love of a woman in thoughtful, self-sacrificing care; for they would brave every danger, giving their lives for their offspring. Nor could we fail to sympathize with their awkward, blunt-nosed baby calves, with such beautiful, wondering eyes looking out on the world and slowly getting acquainted with things, all so strange to them, and awkwardly learning to use their legs, and play and fight.

Before leaving Scotland, father promised us a pony to ride when we got to America, and we saw to it that this promise was not forgotten. Only a week or two after our arrival in the woods he bought us a little Indian pony for thirteen dollars from a store-keeper in Kingston who had obtained him from a Winnebago or Menominee Indian in trade for goods. He was a stout handsome bay with long black mane and tail, and, though he was only two years old, the Indians had already taught him to carry all sorts of burdens, to stand without being tied, to go anywhere over all sorts of ground fast or slow, and to jump and swim and fear nothing – a truly wonderful creature, strangely different from shy, skittish, nervous, superstitious civilized beasts. We turned him loose, and, strange to say, he never ran away from us or refused to be caught, but behaved as if he had known Scotch boys all his life; probably because we were about as wild as young Indians.

One day when father happened to have a little leisure, he said, 'Noo, bairns, rin doon the meadow and get your powny and learn to ride him.' So we led him out to a smooth place near an Indian mound back of the shanty, where father directed us to begin. I mounted for the first memorable lesson, crossed the mound, and set out at a slow walk along the wagon-track made in hauling lumber; then father shouted, 'Whup him up, John, whup him up!

Make him gallop; gallopin' is easier and better than walkin' or trottin'.' Jack was willing, and away he sped at a good fast gallop. I managed to keep my balance fairly well by holding fast to the mane, but could not keep from bumping up and down, for I was plump and elastic and so was Jack; therefore about half of the time I was in the air.

After a quarter of a mile or so of this curious transportation, I cried, 'Whoa, Jack!' The wonderful creature seemed to understand Scotch, for he stopped so suddenly I flew over his head, but he stood perfectly still as if that flying method of dismounting were the regular way. Jumping on again, I bumped and bobbed back along the grassy, flowery track, over the Indian mound, cried, 'Whoa, Jack!', flew over his head, and alighted in father's arms as gracefully as if it were all intended for circus work.

After going over the course five or six times in the same free, picturesque style, I gave place to brother David, whose performances were much like my own. In a few weeks, however, or a month, we were taking adventurous rides more than a mile long out to a big meadow frequented by sandhill cranes, and returning safely with wonderful stories of the great long-legged birds we had seen, and how on the whole journey away and back we had fallen off only five or six times. Gradually we learned to gallop through the woods without roads of any sort, bareback and without rope or bridle, guiding only by leaning from side to side or by slight knee pressure. In this free way we used to amuse ourselves, riding at full speed across a big 'kettle' that was on our farm, without holding on by either mane or tail.

These so-called 'kettles' were formed by the melting of large detached blocks of ice that had been buried in moraine material thousands of years ago when the ice-sheet that covered all this region was receding. As the buried ice melted, of course the moraine material above and about it fell in, forming hopper-shaped hollows, while the grass growing on their sides and around them prevented the rain and wind from filling them up. The one we performed in was perhaps seventy or eighty feet wide and twenty or thirty feet deep; and without a saddle or hold of any kind it was not easy to keep from slipping over Jack's head in diving into it, or over his tail climbing out. This was fine sport on the long summer Sundays when we were able to steal away before meeting-time without being seen. We got very warm and red at it, and oftentimes poor Jack dripping with sweat like his riders, seemed to have been boiled in that kettle.

In Scotland we had often been admonished to be bold, and this advice we passed on to Jack, who had already got many a wild lesson from Indian boys. Once, when teaching him to jump muddy streams, I made him try the creek in our meadow at a place where it is about twelve feet wide. He jumped bravely enough, but came down with a grand splash hardly more than halfway over. The water was only about a foot in depth, but the black vegetable mud half afloat was unfathomable. I managed to wallow ashore, but poor Jack sank deeper and deeper until only his head was visible in the black abyss, and his Indian fortitude was desperately tried. His foundering so suddenly in the treacherous gulf recalled the story of the Abbot of Aberbrothok's bell, which went down with a gurgling sound while bubbles rose and burst around. I had to go to father for help. He tied a long hemp rope brought from Scotland around Jack's neck, and Tom and Jerry seemed to have all they could do to pull him out. After which I got a solemn scolding for asking the 'puir beast to jump intil sic a saft bottomless place'.

We moved into our frame house in the fall, when mother with the rest of the family arrived from Scotland, and, when the winter snow began to fly, our bur-oak shanty was made into a stable for Jack. Father told us that good meadow hay was all he required, but we fed him corn, lots of it, and he grew very frisky and fat. About the middle of winter his long hair was full of dust and, as we thought, required washing. So, without taking the frosty weather into account, we gave him a thorough soap and water scouring, and as we failed to get him rubbed dry, a row of icicles formed under his belly. Father happened to see him in this condition and angrily asked what we had been about. We said Jack was dirty and we had washed him to make him healthy. He told us we ought to be ashamed of ourselves, 'soaking the puir beast in cauld water at this time o' year'; that when we wanted to clean him we should have sense enough to use the brush and curry-comb.

In summer Dave or I had to ride after the cows every evening about sundown, and Jack got so accustomed to bringing in the drove that when we happened to be a few minutes late he used to go off alone at the regular time and bring them home at a gallop. It used to make father very angry to see Jack chasing the cows like a shepherd dog, running from one to the other and giving each a bite on the rump to keep them on the run, flying before him as if pursued by wolves. Father would declare at times that the wicked beast had the deevil in him and would be the death of the cattle. The corral and barn were just at the foot of a hill, and he made a great display of the drove on the home stretch as they walloped down that hill with their tails on end.

One evening when the pell-mell Wild West show was at its wildest, it made father so extravagantly mad that he ordered me to 'Shoot Jack!' I went to the house and brought the gun, suffering most horrible mental anguish, such as I suppose unhappy Abraham felt when commanded to slay Isaac. Jack's life was spared, however, though I can't tell what finally became of him. I wish I could. After father bought a span of work horses he was sold to a man who said he was going to ride him across the plains to California. We had him, I think, some five or six years. He was the stoutest, gentlest, bravest little horse I ever saw. He never seemed tired, could canter all day with a man about as heavy as himself on his back, and feared nothing. Once fifty or sixty pounds of beef that was tied on his back slid over his shoulders along his neck and weighed down his head to the ground, fairly anchoring him; but he stood patient and still for half an hour or so without making the slightest struggle to free himself, while I was away getting help to untie the pack-rope and set the load back in its place.

As I was the eldest boy I had the care of our first span of work horses. Their names were Nob and Nell. Nob was very intelligent, and even affectionate, and could learn almost anything. Nell was entirely different; balky and stubborn, though we managed to teach her a good many circus tricks; but she never seemed to like to play with us in anything like an affectionate way as Nob did. We turned them out one day into the pasture, and an Indian, hiding in the brush that had sprung up after the grass fires had been kept out, managed to catch Nob, tied a rope to her jaw for a bridle, rode her to Green Lake, about thirty or forty miles away, and tried to sell her for fifteen dollars. All our hearts were sore, as if one of the family had been lost. We hunted everywhere and could not at first imagine what had become of her. We discovered her track where the fence was broken down, and, following it for a few miles, made sure the track was Nob's; and a neighbour told us he had seen an Indian riding fast through the woods on a horse that looked like Nob. But we could find no farther trace of her until a month or two after she was lost, and we had given up hope of ever seeing her again. Then we learned that she had been taken from an Indian by a farmer at Green Lake because he saw that she had been shod and had worked in harness. So when the Indian tried to sell her the farmer said, 'You are a thief. That is a white man's horse. You stole her.'

'No,' said the Indian, 'I bought her from Prairie du Chien and she has always been mine.'

The man, pointing to her feet and the marks of the harness, said, 'You are lying. I will take that horse away from you and put her in my pasture, and if you come near it I will set the dogs on you.' Then he advertised her. One of our neighbours happened to see the advertisement and brought us the glad news, and great was our rejoicing when father brought her home. That Indian must have treated her with terrible cruelty, for when I was riding her through the pasture several years afterward, looking for another horse that we wanted to catch, as we approached the place where she had been captured she stood stock still gazing through the bushes, fearing the Indian might still be hiding there ready to spring; and she was so excited that she trembled, and her heartbeats were so loud that I could hear them distinctly as I sat on her back, *boomp, boomp, boomp*, like the drumming of a partridge. So vividly had she remembered her terrible experiences.

She was a great pet and favourite with the whole family, quickly learning playful tricks, came running when we called, seemed to know everything we said to her, and had the utmost confidence in our friendly kindness.

We used to cut and shock and husk the Indian corn in the fall, until a keen Yankee stopped overnight at our house and among other labor-saving notions convinced father that it was better to let it stand, and husk it at his leisure during the winter, then turn in the cattle to eat the leaves and trample down the stalks, so that they could be ploughed under in the spring. In this winter method each of us took two rows and husked into baskets, and emptied the corn on the ground in piles of fifteen to twenty basketfuls, then loaded it into the wagon to be hauled to the crib. This was cold, painful work, the temperature being oftentimes far below zero and the ground covered with dry, frosty snow, giving rise to miserable crops of chilblains and frosted fingers – a sad change from the merry Indian-summer husking, when the big yellow pumpkins covered the cleared fields: golden corn, golden pumpkins, gathered in the hazy golden weather. Sad change, indeed, but we occasionally got some fun out of the nipping, shivery work from hungry prairie chickens, and squirrels and mice that came about us.

The piles of corn were often left in the field several days, and while loading them into the wagon we usually found field mice in them – big, blunt-nosed, strong-scented fellows that we were taught to kill just because they nibbled a few grains of corn. I used to hold one while it was still warm, up to Nob's nose for the fun of seeing her make faces and snort at the smell of it; and I would say 'Here, Nob,' as if offering her a lump of sugar. One day I offered her an extra fine, fat, plump specimen, something like a little woodchuck, or muskrat, and to my astonishment, after smelling it curiously and doubtfully, as if wondering what the gift might be, and rubbing it back for forth in the palm of my hand with her upper lip, she deliberately took it into her mouth, crunched and munched and chewed it fine and swallowed it, bones, teeth, head, tail, everything.

Not a single hair of that mouse was wasted. When she was chewing it she nodded and grunted, as though critically tasting and relishing it.

My father was a steadfast enthusiast on religious matters, and, of course, attended almost every sort of church-meeting, especially revival meetings. They were occasionally held in summer, but mostly in winter when the sleighing was good and plenty of time available. One hot summer day father drove Nob to Portage and back, twenty-four miles over a sandy road. It was a hot, hard, sultry day's work, and she had evidently been over-driven in order to get home in time for one of these meetings. I shall never forget how tired and wilted she looked that evening when I unhitched her; how she drooped in her stall, too tired to eat or even to lie down. Next morning it was plain that her lungs were inflamed; all the dreadful symptoms were just the same as my own when I had pneumonia. Father sent for a Methodist minister, a very energetic, resourceful man, who was a blacksmith, farmer, butcher, and horse-doctor as well as minister; but all his gifts and skill were of no avail. Nob was doomed. We bathed her head and tried to get her to eat something, but she couldn't eat, and in about a couple of weeks we turned her loose to let her come around the house and see us in the weary suffering and loneliness of the shadow of death. She tried to follow us children, so long her friends and workmates and playmates. It was awfully touching. She had several hemorrhages, and in the forenoon of her last day, after she had had one of her dreadful spells of bleeding and gasping for breath, she came to me trembling, with beseeching, heartbreaking looks, and after I had bathed her head and tried to soothe and pet her, she lay down and gasped and died. All the family gathered about her, weeping, with aching hearts. Then dust to dust.

She was the most faithful, intelligent, playful, affectionate, human-like horse I ever knew, and she won all our hearts. Of the many advantages of farm life for boys one of the greatest is the gaining a real knowledge of animals as fellow-mortals, learning to respect them and love them, and even to win some of their love. Thus godlike sympathy grows and thrives and spreads far beyond the teachings of churches and schools, where too often the mean, blinding, loveless doctrine is taught that animals have neither mind nor soul, have no rights that we are bound to respect, and were made only for man, to be petted, spoiled, slaughtered, or enslaved.

At first we were afraid of snakes, but soon learned that most of them were harmless. The only venomous species seen on our farm were the rattlesnake and the copperhead, one of each. David saw the rattler, and we both saw the copperhead. One day, when my brother came in from his work, he reported that he had seen a snake that made a queer buzzy noise with its tail. This was the only rattlesnake seen on our farm, though we heard of them being common on limestone hills eight or ten miles distant. We discovered the copperhead when we were ploughing, and we saw and felt at the first long, fixed, half-charmed, admiring stare at him that he was an awfully dangerous fellow. Every fibre of his strong, lithe, quivering body, his burnished copper-coloured head, and above all his fierce, able eyes, seemed to be overflowing full of deadly power, and bade us beware. And yet it is only fair to say that this terrible, beautiful reptile showed no disposition to hurt us until we threw clods at him and tried to head him off from a log fence into which he was trying to escape. We were barefooted and of course afraid to let him get very near, while we vainly battered him with the loose sandy clods of the freshly ploughed field to hold him back until we could get a stick. Looking us in the eyes after a moment's pause, he probably saw we were afraid, and he came right straight at us, snapping and looking terrible, drove us out of his way, and won his fight.

Out on the open sandy hills there were a good many thick burly blow snakes, the kind that puff themselves up and hiss. Our Yankee declared that their breath was very poisonous and that we must not go near them. A handsome ringed species common in damp, shady places was, he told us, the most wonderful of all the snakes, for if chopped into pieces, however small, the fragments would wriggle themselves together again, and the restored snake would go on about its business as if nothing had happened. The commonest kinds were the striped slender species of the meadows and streams, good swimmers, that lived mostly on frogs.

Once I observed one of the larger ones, about two feet long, pursuing a frog in our meadow, and it was wonderful to see how fast the legless, footless, wingless, finless hunter could run. The frog, of course, knew its enemy and was making desperate efforts to escape to the water and hide in the marsh mud. He was a fine, sleek yellow muscular fellow and was springing over the tall grass in wide-arching jumps. The green-striped snake, gliding swiftly and steadily, was keeping the frog in sight and, had I not interfered, would probably have tired out the poor jumper. Then, perhaps, while digesting and enjoying his meal, the happy snake would himself be swallowed frog and all by a hawk. Again, to our astonishment, the small specimens were attacked by our hens. They pursued and pecked away at them until they killed and devoured them, oftentimes quarreling over the division of the spoil, though it was not easily divided.

We watched the habits of the swift-darting dragonflies, wild bees, butterflies, wasps, beetles, etc., and soon learned to discriminate between those that might be safely handled and the pinching or stinging species. But of all our wild neighbours the mosquitoes were the first with which we became very intimately acquainted.

The beautiful meadow lying warm in the spring sunshine, outspread between our lily-rimmed lake and the hill-slope that our shanty stood on, sent forth thirsty swarms of the little gray, speckledy, singing, stinging pests; and how tellingly they introduced themselves! Of little avail were the smudges that we made on muggy evenings to drive them away; and amid the many lessons which they insisted upon teaching us we wondered more and more at the extent of their knowledge, especially that in their tiny, flimsy bodies room could be found for such cunning palates. They would drink their fill from brown, smoky Indians, or from old white folk flavored with tobacco and whiskey, when no better could be had. But the surpassing fineness of their taste was best manifested by their enthusiastic appreciation of boys full of lively red blood, and of girls in full bloom fresh from cool Scotland or England. On these it was pleasant to witness their enjoyment as they feasted. Indians, we were told, believed that if they were brave fighters they would go after death to a happy country abounding in game, where there were no mosquitoes and no cowards. For cowards were driven away by themselves to a miserable country where there was no game fit to eat, and where the sky was always dark with huge gnats and mosquitoes as big as pigeons.

We were great admirers of the little black water-bugs. Their whole lives seemed to be play, skimming, swimming, swirling, and waltzing together in little groups on the edge of the lake and in the meadow springs, dancing to music we never could hear. The long-legged skaters, too, seemed wonderful fellows, shuffling about on top of the water, with air-bubbles like little bladders tangled under their hairy feet; and we often wished that we also might be shod in the same way to enable us to skate on the lake in summer as well as in icy winter. Not less wonderful were the boatmen, swimming on their backs, pulling themselves along with a pair of oar-like legs.

Great was the delight of brothers David and Daniel and myself when father gave us a few pine boards for a boat, and it was a memorable day when we got that boat built and launched into the lake. Never shall I forget our first sail over the gradually deepening water, the sunbeams pouring through it revealing the strange plants covering the bottom, and the fishes coming about us, staring and wondering as if the boat were a monstrous strange fish.

The water was so clear that it was almost invisible, and when we floated slowly out over the plants and fishes, we seemed to be miraculously sustained in the air while silently exploring a veritable fairyland.

We always had to work hard, but if we worked still harder we were occasionally allowed a little spell in the long summer evenings about sundown to fish, and on Sundays an hour or two to sail quietly without fishing-rod or gun when the lake was calm. Therefore we gradually learned something about its inhabitants – pickerel, sunfish, black bass, perch, shiners, pumpkin-seeds, ducks, loons, turtles, muskrats, etc. We saw the sunfishes making their nests in little openings in the rushes where the water was only a few feet deep, ploughing up and shoving away the soft gray mud with their noses, like pigs, forming round bowls five or six inches in depth and about two feet in diameter, in which their eggs were deposited. And with what beautiful, unweariable devotion they watched and hovered over them and chased away prowling spawn-eating enemies that ventured within a rod or two of the precious nest!

The pickerel is a savage fish endowed with marvellous strength and speed. It lies in wait for its prey on the bottom, perfectly motionless like a waterlogged stick, watching everything that moves, with fierce, hungry eyes. Oftentimes when we were fishing for some other kinds over the edge of the boat, a pickerel that we had not noticed would come like a bolt of lightning and seize the fish we had caught before we could get it into the boat. The very first pickerel that I ever caught jumped into the air to seize a small fish dangling on my line, and, missing its aim, fell plump into the boat as if it had dropped from the sky.

Some of our neighbours fished for pickerel through the ice in midwinter. They usually drove a wagon out on the lake, set a large number of lines baited with live minnows, hung a loop of the lines over a small bush planted at the side of each hole, and watched to see the loops pulled off when a fish had taken the bait. Large quantities of pickerel were often caught in this cruel way.

Our beautiful lake, named Fountain Lake by father, but Muir's Lake by the neighbours, is one of the many small glacier lakes that adorn the Wisconsin landscapes. It is fed by twenty or thirty meadow springs, is about half a mile long, half as wide, and surrounded by low finely-modeled hills dotted with oak and hickory, and meadows full of grasses and sedges and many beautiful orchids and ferns. First there is a zone of green, shining rushes, and just beyond the rushes a zone of white and orange water-lilies fifty or sixty feet wide forming a magnificent border. On bright days, when the lake was rippled by a breeze, the lilies and sun-spangles danced together in radiant beauty, and it became difficult to discriminate between them.

On Sundays, after or before chores and sermons and Bible-lessons, we drifted about on the lake for hours, especially in lily time, getting finest lessons and sermons from the water and flowers, ducks, fishes, and muskrats. In particular we took Christ's advice and devoutly 'considered the lilies' – how they grow up in beauty out of gray lime mud, and ride gloriously among the breezy sun-spangles. On our way home we gathered grand bouquets of them to be kept fresh all the week. No flower was hailed with greater wonder and admiration by the European settlers in general – Scotch, English, and Irish – than this white water-lily (*Nymphaea odorata*). It is a magnificent plant, queen of the inland waters, pure white, three or four inches in diameter, the most beautiful, sumptuous, and deliciously fragrant of all our Wisconsin flowers. No lily garden in civilization we had ever seen could compare with our lake garden.

The next most admirable flower in the estimation of settlers in this part of the new world was the pasque-flower or wind-flower (*Anemone patens* var. *Nuttalliana*). It is the very first to appear in the spring, covering the cold gray-black ground with cherry blossoms. Before the axe or plough had touched the 'oak openings' of Wisconsin, they were swept by running fires almost every autumn after the grass became dry. If from any cause, such as early snowstorms or late rains, they happened to escape the autumn fire besom, they were likely to be burned in the spring after the snow melted. But whether burned in the spring or fall, ashes and bits of charred twigs and grass stems made the whole country look dismal. Then, before a single grass-blade had sprouted, a hopeful multitude of large hairy, silky buds about as thick as one's thumb came to light, pushing up through the black and gray ashes and cinders, and before these buds were fairly free from the ground they opened wide and displayed purple blossoms about two inches in diameter, giving beauty for ashes in glorious abundance. Instead of remaining in the ground waiting for warm weather and companions, this admirable plant seemed to be in haste to rise and cheer the desolate landscape. Then at its leisure, after other plants had come to its help, it spread its leaves and grew up to a height of about two or three feet. The spreading leaves formed a whorl on the ground, and another about the middle of the stem as an involucre, and on the top of the stem the silky, hairy long-tailed seeds formed a head like a second flower. A little church was established among the earlier settlers and the meetings at first were held in our house. After working hard all the week it was difficult for boys to sit still through long sermons without falling asleep, especially in warm weather. In this drowsy trouble the charming anemone came to our help. A pocketful of the pungent seeds industriously nibbled while the discourses were at the dullest kept us awake and filled our minds with flowers.

The next great flower wonders on which we lavished admiration, not only for beauty of colour and size, but for their curious shapes, were the cypripediums, called 'lady's-slippers' or 'Indian moccasins'. They were so different from the familiar flowers of old Scotland. Several species grew in our meadow and on shady hillsides – yellow, rose-coloured, and some nearly white, an inch or more in diameter, and shaped exactly like Indian moccasins. They caught the eye of all the European settlers and made them gaze and wonder like children. And so did calopogon, pogonia, spiranthes, and many other fine plant people that lived in our meadow. The beautiful Turk's-turban (*Lilium superbum*) growing on stream-banks was rare in our neighbourhood, but the orange lily grew in abundance on dry ground beneath the bur-oaks and often brought Aunt Ray's lily-bed in Scotland to mind. The butterfly-weed, with its brilliant scarlet flowers, attracted flocks of butterflies and made fine masses of colour. With autumn came a glorious abundance and variety of asters, those beautiful plant stars, together with goldenrods, sunflowers, daisies, and liatris of different species, while around the shady margin of the meadow many ferns in beds and vaselike groups spread their beautiful fronds, especially the osmundas (*O.*

claytoniana, regalis, and *cinnamomea*) and the sensitive and ostrich ferns.

Early in summer we feasted on strawberries, that grew in rich beds beneath the meadow grasses and sedges as well as in the dry sunny woods. And in different bogs and marshes, and around their borders on our own farm and along the Fox River, we found dewberries and cranberries, and a glorious profusion of huckleberries, the fountain-heads of pies of wondrous taste and size, coloured in the heart like sunsets. Nor were we slow to discover the value of the hickory trees yielding both sugar and nuts. We carefully counted the different kinds on our farm, and every morning when we could steal a few minutes before breakfast after doing the chores, we visited the trees that had been wounded by the axe, to scrape off and enjoy the thick white delicious syrup that exuded from them, and gathered the nuts as they fell in the mellow Indian summer, making haste to get a fair share with the sapsuckers and squirrels. The hickory makes fine masses of colour in the fall, every leaf a flower, but it was the sweet sap and sweet nuts that first interested us. No harvest in the Wisconsin woods was ever gathered with more pleasure and care. Also, to our delight, we found plenty of hazelnuts, and in a few places abundance of wild apples. They were desperately sour, and we used to fill our pockets with them and dare each other to eat one without making a face – no easy feat.

One hot summer day father told us that we ought to learn to swim. This was one of the most interesting suggestions he had ever offered, but precious little time was allowed for trips to the lake, and he seldom tried to show us how. 'Go to the frogs,' he said, 'and they will give you all the lessons you need. Watch their arms and legs and see how smoothly they kick themselves along and dive and come up. When you want to dive, keep your arms by your side or over your head, and kick, and when you want to come up, let your legs drag and paddle with your hands.'

We found a little basin among the rushes at the south end of the lake, about waist-deep and a rod or two wide, shaped like a sunfish's nest. Here we kicked and plashed for many a lesson, faithfully trying to imitate frogs; but the smooth, comfortable sliding gait of our amphibious teachers seemed hopelessly hard to learn. When we tried to kick frog-fashion, down went our heads as if weighted with lead the moment our feet left the ground. One day it occurred to me to hold my breath as long as I could and let my head sink as far as it liked without paying any attention to it, and try to swim under the water instead of on the surface. This method was a great success, for at the very first trial I managed to cross the basin without touching bottom, and soon learned the use of my limbs. Then, of course, swimming with my head above water soon became so easy that it seemed perfectly natural. David tried the plan with the same success. Then we began to count the number of times that we could swim around the basin without stopping to rest, and after twenty or thirty rounds failed to tire us, we proudly thought that a little more practice would make us about as amphibious as frogs.

On the fourth of July of the swimming year one of the Lawson boys came to visit us, and we went down to the lake to spend the great warm day with the fishes and ducks and turtles. After gliding about on the smooth mirror water, telling stories and enjoying the company of the happy creatures about us, we rowed to our bathing-pool, and David and I went in for a swim, while our companion fished from the boat a little way out beyond the rushes. After a few turns in the pool, it occurred to me that it was now about time to try deep water. Swimming through the thick growth of rushes and lilies was somewhat dangerous, especially for a beginner, because one's arms and legs might be entangled among the long, limber stems; nevertheless I ventured and struck out boldly enough for the boat, where the water was twenty or thirty feet deep. When I reached the end of the little skiff I raised my right hand to take hold of it to surprise Lawson, whose back was toward me and who was not aware of my approach; but I failed to reach high enough, and, of course, the weight of my arm and the stroke against the overleaning stern of the boat shoved me down and I sank, struggling, frightened and confused. As soon as my feet touched the bottom, I slowly rose to the surface, but before I could get breath enough to call for help, sank back again and lost all control of myself. After sinking and rising I don't know how many times, some water got into my lungs and I began to drown. Then suddenly my mind seemed to clear. I remembered that I could swim under water, and, making a desperate struggle torward the shore, I reached a point where with my toes on the bottom I got my mouth above the surface, gasped for help, and was pulled into the boat.

This humiliating accident spoiled the day, and we all agreed to keep it a profound secret. My sister Sarah had heard my cry for help, and on our arrival at the house inquired what had happened. 'Were you drowning, John? I heard you cry you couldna get oot.' Lawson made haste to reply, 'Oh, no! He was juist haverin (making fun).'

I was very much ashamed of myself, and at night, after calmly reviewing the affair, concluded that there had been no reasonable cause for the accident, and that I ought to punish myself for so nearly losing my life from unmanly fear. Accordingly at the very first opportunity, I stole away to the lake by myself, got into my boat, and instead of going back to the old swimming-bowl for further practice, or to try to do sanely and well what I had so ignominiously failed to do in my first adventure, that is, to swim out through the rushes and lilies, I rowed directly out to the middle of the lake, stripped, stood up on the seat in the stern, and with grim deliberation took a header and dove straight down thirty or forty feet, turned easily, and, letting my feet drag, paddled straight to the surface with my hands as father had at first directed me to do. I then swam round the boat, glorying in my suddenly acquired confidence and victory over myself, climbed into it, and dived again, with the same triumphant success. I think I went down four or five times, and each time as I made the dive-spring shouted aloud, 'Take that!' feeling that I was getting most gloriously even with myself.

Never again from that day to this have I lost control of myself in water. If suddenly thrown overboard at sea in the dark, or even while asleep, I think I would immediately right myself in a way some would call 'instinct', rise among the waves, catch my breath, and try to plan what would better be done. Never was victory over self more complete. At a slow gait I think I could swim all day in smooth water moderate in temperature. When I was a student at Madison, I used to go on long swimming-journeys, called exploring expeditions, along the south shore of Lake Mendota, on Saturdays, sometimes alone, sometimes with another amphibious explorer by the name of Fuller.

My adventures in Fountain Lake call to mind the story of a boy who in climbing a tree to rob a crow's nest fell and broke his leg, but as soon as it healed compelled himself to climb to the top of the tree he had fallen from.

Like Scotch children in general we were taught grim self-denial, in season and out of season, to mortify the flesh, keep our bodies in subjection to Bible laws, and mercilessly punish ourselves for every fault imagined or committed. A little boy, while helping his sister to drive home the cows, happened to use a forbidden word. 'I'll have to tell fayther on ye,' said the horrified sister. 'I'll tell him that ye said a bad word.' 'Weel,' said the boy, by way of excuse, 'I couldna help the word comin' into me, and it's na waur to speak it oot than to let it rin through ye.'

A Scotch fiddler playing at a wedding drank so much whiskey that on the way home he fell by the roadside. In the morning he was ashamed and angry and determined to punish himself. Making haste to the house of a friend, a gamekeeper, he called him out, and requested the loan of a gun. The alarmed gamekeeper, not liking the fiddler's looks and voice, anxiously inquired what he was going to do with it. 'Surely,' said he, 'you're no gan to shoot yoursel.' 'No-o,' with characteristic candor replied the penitent fiddler, 'I dinna think that I'll just exactly kill mysel, but I'm gaun to tak a dander doon the burn (brook) wi' the gun and gie mysel a deevil o' a fleg (fright).'

One calm summer evening a red-headed woodpecker was drowned in our lake. The accident happened at the south end, opposite our memorable swimming-hole, a few rods from the place where I came so near being drowned years before. I had returned to the old home during a summer vacation of the State University, and, having made a beginning in botany, I was, of course, full of enthusiasm and ran eagerly to my beloved pogonia, calopogon, and cypripedium gardens, osmunda ferneries, and the lake lilies and pitcher-plants. A little before sundown the day-breeze died away, and the lake, reflecting the wooded hills like a mirror, was dimpled and dotted and streaked here and there where fishes and turtles were poking out their heads and muskrats were sculling themselves along with their flat tails making glittering tracks. After lingering a while, dreamily recalling the old, hard, half-happy days, and watching my favourite red-headed woodpeckers pursuing moths like regular flycatchers, I swam out through the rushes and up the middle of the lake to the north end and back, gliding slowly, looking about me, enjoying the scenery as I would in a saunter along the shore, and studying the habits of the animals as they were explained and recorded on the smooth glassy water.

On the way back, when I was within a hundred rods or so of the end of my voyage, I noticed a peculiar plashing disturbance that could not, I thought, be made by a jumping fish or any other inhabitant of the lake; for instead of low regular out-circling ripples such as are made by the popping up of a head, or like those raised by the quick splash of a leaping fish, or diving loon or muskrat, a continuous struggle was kept up for several minutes ere the outspreading, interfering ring-waves began to die away. Swimming hastily to the spot to try to discover what had happened, I found one of my woodpeckers floating motionless with outspread wings. All was over. Had I been a minute or two earlier, I might have saved him. He had glanced on the water I suppose in pursuit of a moth, was unable to rise from it, and died struggling, as I nearly did at this same spot. Like me he seemed to have lost his mind in blind confusion and fear. The water was warm, and had he kept still with his head a little above the surface, he would sooner or later have been wafted ashore. The best aimed flights of birds and man 'gang aft agley', but this was the first case I had witnessed of a bird losing its life by drowning.

Doubtless accidents to animals are far more common

than is generally known. I have seen quails killed by flying against our house when suddenly startled. Some birds get entangled in hairs of their own nests and die. Once I found a poor snipe in our meadow that was unable to fly on account of difficult egg-birth. Pitying the poor mother, I picked her up out of the grass and helped her as gently as I could, and as soon as the egg was born she flew gladly away. Oftentimes I have thought it strange that one could walk through the woods and mountains and plains for years without seeing a single blood-spot. Most wild animals get into the world and out of it without being noticed. Nevertheless we at last sadly learn that they are all subject to the vicissitudes of fortune like ourselves. Many birds lose their lives in storms. I remember a particularly severe Wisconsin winter, when the temperature was many degrees below zero and the snow was deep, preventing the quail, which feed on the ground, from getting anything like enough of food, as was pitifully shown by a flock I found on our farm frozen solid in a thicket of oak sprouts. They were in a circle about a foot wide, with their heads outward, packed close together for warmth. Yet all had died without a struggle, perhaps more from starvation than frost. Many small birds lose their lives in the storms of early spring, or even summer. One mild spring morning I picked up more than a score out of the grass and flowers, most of them darling singers that had perished in a sudden storm of sleety rain and hail.

In a hollow at the foot of an oak tree that I had chopped down one cold winter day, I found a poor ground squirrel frozen solid in its snug grassy nest, in the middle of a store of nearly a peck of wheat it had carefully gathered. I carried it home and gradually thawed and warmed it in the kitchen, hoping it would come to life like a pickerel I caught in our lake through a hole in the ice, which, after being frozen as hard as a bone and thawed at the fireside, squirmed itself out of the grasp of the cook when she began to scrape it, bounced off the table, and danced about on the floor, making wonderful springy jumps as if trying to find its way back home to the lake. But for the poor spermophile nothing I

could do in the way of revival was of any avail. Its
life had passed away without the slightest struggle, as
it lay asleep curled up like a ball, with its tail wrapped
about it.

FOUR

A Paradise of Birds

The Wisconsin oak openings were a summer paradise for song birds, and a fine place to get acquainted with them: for the trees stood wide apart, allowing one to see the happy homeseekers as they arrived in the spring, their mating, nest-building, the brooding and feeding of the young, and, after they were full-fledged and strong, to see all the families of the neighbourhood gathering and getting ready to leave in the fall. Excepting the geese and ducks and pigeons, nearly all our summer birds arrived singly or in small draggled flocks, but when frost and falling leaves brought their winter homes to mind they assembled in large flocks on dead or leafless trees by the side of a meadow or field, perhaps to get acquainted and talk the thing over. Some species held regular daily meetings for several weeks before finally setting forth on their long southern journeys. Strange to say, we never saw them start. Some morning we would find them gone. Doubtless they migrated in the night time. Comparatively few species remained all winter: the nuthatch, chickadee, owl, prairie chicken, quail, and a few stragglers from the main flocks of ducks, jays, hawks, and bluebirds. Only after the country was settled did either jays or bluebirds winter with us.

The brave, frost-defying chickadees and nuthatches stayed all the year wholly independent of farms and man's food and affairs.

With the first hints of spring came the brave little bluebirds, darling singers as blue as the best sky, and of course we all loved them. Their rich, crispy warbling is perfectly delightful, soothing and cheering, sweet and whisperingly low, Nature's fine love touches, every note going straight home into one's heart. And withal they are hardy and brave, fearless fighters in defense of home. When we boys approached their knot-hole nests, the bold little fellows kept scolding and diving at us and tried to strike us in the face, and oftentimes we were afraid they would prick our eyes. But the boldness of the little housekeepers only made us love them the more.

None of the bird people of Wisconsin welcomed us more heartily than the common robin. Far from showing alarm at the coming of settlers into their native woods, they reared their young around our gardens as if they liked us, and how heartily we admired the beauty and fine manners of these graceful birds and their loud cheery song of *Fear not, fear not, cheer up, cheer up*. It was easy to love them for they reminded us of the robin redbreast of Scotland. Like the bluebirds they dared every danger in defense of home, and we often wondered that birds so gentle could be so bold and that sweet-voiced singers could so fiercely fight and scold.

Of all the great singers that sweeten Wisconsin one of the best known and best loved is the brown thrush or thrasher, strong and able without being familiar, and easily seen and heard. Rosy purple evenings after thunder-showers are the favourite song-times, when the winds have died away and the steaming ground and the leaves and flowers fill the air with fragrance. Then the male makes haste to the topmost spray of an oak tree and sings loud and clear with delightful enthusiasm until sundown, mostly I suppose for his mate sitting on the precious eggs in a brush heap. And how faithful and watchful and daring he is! Woe to the snake or squirrel that ventured to go nigh the nest! We often saw him diving on them, pecking them about the head and driving them away as bravely as the kingbird drives away hawks. Their rich and varied strains make the air fairly quiver. We boys often tried to interpret the wild ringing melody and put it into words.

After the arrival of the thrushes came the bobolinks, gushing, gurgling, inexhaustible fountains of song, pouring forth floods of sweet notes over the broad Fox River meadows in wonderful variety and volume, crowded and mixed beyond description, as they hovered on quivering wings above their hidden nests in the grass. It seemed marvellous to us that birds so moderate in size could hold so much of this wonderful song stuff. Each one of them poured forth music enough for a whole flock, singing as if its whole body, feathers and all, were made up of music, flowing, glowing, bubbling melody interpenetrated here and there with small scintillating prickles and spicules. We never became so intimately acquainted with the bobolinks as with the thrushes, for they lived far out on the broad Fox River meadows, while the thrushes sang on the tree-tops around every home. The bobolinks were among the first of our great singers to leave us in the fall, going apparently direct to the rice-fields of the Southern States, where they grew fat and were slaughtered in countless numbers for food. Sad fate for singers so purely divine.

One of the gayest of the singers is the redwing blackbird. In the spring, when his scarlet epaulets shine brightest, and his little modest gray wife is sitting on the nest, built on rushes in a swamp, he sits on a nearby oak and devotedly sings almost all day. His rich simple strain is *baumpalee, baumpalee,* or *bobalee* as interpreted by some. In summer, after nesting cares are over, they assemble in flocks of hundreds and thousands to feast on Indian corn when it is in the milk. Scattering over a field, each selects an ear, strips the husk down far enough to lay bare an inch or two of the end of it, enjoys and exhilarating feast, and after all are full they rise simultaneously with a quick birr of wings like an old-fashioned church congregation fluttering to their feet when the minister after giving out the hymn says, 'Let the congregation arise and sing.' Alighting on nearby trees, they sing with a hearty vengeance, bursting out without any puttering prelude in gloriously glad concert, hundreds or thousands of exulting voices with sweet gurgling *baumpalees* mingled with chippy vibrant and exploding globules of musical notes, making a most enthusiastic, indescribable joy-song, a combination unlike anything to be heard elsewhere in the bird kingdom: something like bagpipes, flutes, violins, pianos, and human-like voices all bursting and bubbling at once. Then suddenly someone of the joyful congregation shouts *Chirr! Chirr!* and all stop as if shot.

The sweet-voiced meadowlark with its placid, simple song of *peery-eery-ódical* was another favourite, and we soon learned to admire the Baltimore oriole and its wonderful hanging nests, and the scarlet tanager glowing like fire amid the green leaves.

But no singer of them all got farther into our hearts than the little speckle-breasted song sparrow, one of the first to arrive and begin nest-building and singing. The richness, sweetness, and pathos of this small darling's song as he sat on a low bush often brought tears to our eyes.

The little cheery, modest chickadee midget, loved by every innocent boy and girl, man and woman, and by many not altogether innocent, was one of the first of the birds to attract our attention, drawing nearer and nearer to us as the winter advanced, bravely singing his faint silvery, lisping, tinkling notes ending with a bright *dee, dee, dee!* however frosty the weather.

The nuthatches, who also stayed all winter with us, were favourites with us boys. We loved to watch them as they traced the bark-furrows of the oaks and hickories head downward, deftly flicking off loose scales and splinters in search of insects, and braving the coldest weather as if their little sparks of life were as safely warm in winter as in summer, unquenchable by the severest frost. With the help of the chickadees they made a delightful stir in the solemn winter days, and when we were out chopping we never ceased to wonder how their slender naked toes could be kept warm when our own were so painfully frosted though clad in thick socks and boots. And we wondered and admired the more when we thought of the little midgets sleeping in knot-holes when the temperature was far below zero, sometimes thirty-five degrees below, and in the morning, after a minute breakfast of a few frozen insects and hoarfrost crystals, playing and chatting in cheery tones as if food, weather, and everything was according to their own warm hearts. Our Yankee told us that the name of this darling was Devil-downhead.

Their big neighbours the owls also made good winter music, singing out loud in wild, gallant strains bespeaking brave comfort, let the frost bite as it might. The solemn hooting of the species with the widest throat seemed to us the very wildest of all the winter sounds.

Prairie chickens came strolling in family flocks about the shanty, picking seeds and grasshoppers like domestic fowls, and they became still more abundant as wheat- and cornfields were multiplied, but also wilder, of course, when every shotgun in the country was aimed at them. The booming of the males during the mating-season was one of the loudest and strangest of the early spring sounds, being easily heard on calm mornings at a distance of a half or three fourths of a mile. As soon as the snow was off the ground, they assembled in flocks of a dozen or two on an open spot, usually on the side of a ploughed field, ruffled up their feathers, inflated the curious coloured sacks on the sides of their necks, and strutted about with queer gestures something like turkey gobblers, uttering strange loud, rounded, drumming calls – *boom! boom! boom!* interrupted by choking sounds. My brother Daniel caught one while she was sitting on her nest in our corn-field. The young are just like domestic chicks, run with the mother as soon as hatched, and stay with her until autumn, feeding on the ground, never taking wing unless disturbed. In winter, when full-grown, they assemble in large flocks, fly about sundown to selected roosting-places on tall trees, and to feeding-places in the morning – unhusked cornfields, if any are to be found in the neighbourhood, or thickets of dwarf birch and willows, the buds of which furnish a considerable part of their food when snow covers the ground.

The wild rice-marshes along the Fox River and around Pucaway Lake were the summer homes of millions of ducks, and in the Indian summer, when the rice was ripe, they grew very fat. The magnificent mallards in particular afforded our Yankee neighbours royal feasts almost without price, for often as many as a half-dozen were killed at a shot, but we seldom were allowed a single hour for hunting and so got very few. The autumn duck season was a glad time for the Indians also, for they feasted and grew fat not only on the ducks but on the wild rice, large quantities of which they gathered as they glided through the midst of the generous crop in canoes, bending down handfuls over the sides, and beating out the grain with small paddles.

The warmth of the deep spring fountains of the creek in our meadow kept it open all the year, and a few pairs of wood ducks, the most beautiful, we thought, of all the ducks, wintered in it. I well remember the first specimen I ever saw. Father shot it in the creek during a snowstorm, brought it into the house, and called us around him, saying, 'Come, bairns, and admire the work of God displayed in this bonnie bird. Naebody but God could paint feathers like these. Juist look at the colours, hoo they shine, and hoo fine they overlap and blend thegether like the colours o' the rainbow.' And we all agreed that never, never before had we seen so awfu' bonnie a bird. A pair nested every year in the hollow top of an oak stump about fifteen feet high that stood on the side of the meadow, and we used to wonder how they got the fluffy young ones down from the nest and across the meadow to the lake when they were only helpless, featherless midgets: whether the mother carried them to the water on her back or in her mouth. I never saw the thing done or found anybody who had until this summer, when Mr Holabird, a keen observer, told me that he once saw the mother carry them from the nest tree in her mouth, quickly coming and going to a nearby stream, and in a few minutes get them all together and proudly sail away.

Sometimes a flock of swans were seen passing over at a great height on their long journeys, and we admired their clear bugle notes, but they seldom visited any of the lakes in our neighbourhood, so seldom that when they did it was talked of for years. One was shot by a blacksmith on a millpond with a long-range Sharp's rifle, and many of the neighbours went far to see it.

The common gray goose, Canada honker, flying in regular harrow-shaped flocks, was one of the wildest and wariest of all the large birds that enlivened the spring and autumn. They seldom ventured to alight in our small lake, fearing, I suppose, that hunters might be concealed in the rushes, but on account of their fondness for the young leaves of winter wheat when they were a few inches high, they often alighted on our fields when passing on their way south, and occasionally even in our corn-fields when a snowstorm was blowing and they were hungry and wing-weary, with nearly an inch of snow on their backs. In such times of distress we used to pity them, even while trying to get a shot at them. They were exceedingly cautious and circumspect; usually flew several times round the adjacent thickets and fences to make sure that no enemy was near before settling down, and one always stood on guard, relieved from time to time, while the flock was feeding. Therefore there was no chance to creep up on them unobserved; you had to be well hidden before the flock arrived. It was the ambition of boys to be able to shoot these wary birds. I never got but two, both of them at one so-called lucky shot. When I ran to pick them up, one of them flew away, but as the poor fellow was sorely wounded he didn't fly far. When I caught him after a short chase, he uttered a piercing cry of terror and despair, which the leader of the flock heard at a distance of about a hundred rods. They had flown off in frightened disorder, of course, but had got into the regular harrow-shape order when the leader heard the cry, and I shall never forget how bravely he left his place at the head of the flock and hurried back screaming and struck at me in trying to save his companion. I dodged down and held my hands over my head, and thus escaped a blow of his elbows. Fortunately I had left my gun at the fence, and the life of this noble bird was spared after he had risked it in trying to save his wounded friend or neighbour or family relation. For so shy a bird boldly to attack a hunter showed wonderful sympathy and courage. This is one of my strangest hunting experiences. Never before had I regarded wild geese as dangerous, or capable of such noble self-sacrificing devotion.

The loud clear call of the handsome bob-whites was one of the pleasantest and most characteristic of our spring sounds, and we soon learned to imitate it so well that a bold cock often accepted our challenge and came flying to fight. The young run as soon as they are hatched and follow their parents until spring, roosting on the ground in a close bunch, heads out ready to scatter and fly. These fine birds were seldom seen when we first arrived in the wilderness, but when wheat-fields supplied abundance of food they multiplied very fast, although oftentimes sore pressed during hard winters when the snow reached a depth of two or three feet, covering their food, while the mercury fell to twenty or thirty degrees below zero. Occasionally, although shy on account of being persistently hunted, under pressure of extreme hunger in the very coldest weather when the snow was deepest they ventured into barnyards and even approached the doorsteps of houses, searching for any sort of scraps and crumbs, as if piteously begging for food. One of our neighbours saw a flock come creeping up through the snow, unable to fly, hardly able to walk, and while approaching the door several of them actually fell down and died; showing that birds, usually so vigorous and apparently independent of fortune, suffer and lose their lives in extreme weather like the rest of us, frozen to death like settlers caught in blizzards. None of our neighbours perished in storms, though many had feet, ears, and fingers frost-nipped or solidly frozen.

As soon as the lake ice melted, we heard the lonely cry of the loon, one of the wildest and most striking of all the wilderness sounds, a strange, sad, mournful, unearthly cry, half laughing, half wailing. Nevertheless the great northern diver, as our species is called, is a brave, hardy, beautiful bird, able to fly under water about as well as above it, and to spear and capture the swiftest fishes for food. Those that haunted our lake were so wary none was shot for years, though every boy hunter in the neighbourhood was ambitious to get one to prove his skill. On one of our bitter cold New Year holidays I was surprised to see a loon in the small open part of the lake at the mouth of the inlet that was kept from freezing by the warm spring water. I knew that it could not fly out of so small a place, for these heavy birds have to beat the water for half a mile or so before they can get fairly on the wing. Their narrow, finlike wings are very small as compared with the weight of the body and are evidently made for flying through water as well as through the air, and it is by means of their swift flight through the water and the swiftness of the blow they

strike with their long, spear-like bills that they are able
to capture the fishes on which they feed. I ran down the
meadow with the gun, got into my boat, and pursued that
poor winter-bound straggler. Of course he dived again and
again, but had to come up to breathe, and I at length got
a quick shot at his head and slightly wounded or stunned
him, caught him, and ran proudly back to the house with
my prize. I carried him in my arms; he didn't struggle to
get away or offer to strike me, and when I put him on the
floor in front of the kitchen stove, he just rested quietly on
his belly as noiseless and motionless as if he were a stuffed
specimen on a shelf, held his neck erect, gave no sign of
suffering from any wound, and though he was motionless,
his small black eyes seemed to be ever keenly watchful.
His formidable bill, very sharp, three or three and a half
inches long, and shaped like a pickaxe, was held perfectly
level. But the wonder was that he did not struggle or make
the slightest movement. We had a tortoise-shell cat, an old
Tom of great experience, who was so fond of lying under
the stove in frosty weather that it was difficult even to poke
him out with a broom; but when he saw and smelled that
strange big fishy, black and white, speckledy bird, the like
of which he had never before seen, he rushed wildly to
the farther corner of the kitchen, looked back cautiously
and suspiciously, and began to make a careful study of
the handsome but dangerous-looking stranger. Becoming more and more curious and interested, he at length
advanced a step or two for a nearer view and nearer smell;
and as the wonderful bird kept absolutely motionless, he
was encouraged to venture gradually nearer and nearer
until within perhaps five or six feet of its breast. Then
the wary loon, not liking Tom's looks in so near a view,
which perhaps recalled to his mind the plundering minks
and muskrats he had to fight when they approached his
nest, prepared to defend himself by slowly, almost imperceptibly drawing back his long pickaxe bill, and without
the slightest fuss or stir held it level and ready just over
his tail. With that dangerous bill drawn so far back out
of the way, Tom's confidence in the stranger's peaceful
intentions seemed almost complete, and, thus encouraged,

he at last ventured forward with wondering, questioning eyes and quivering nostrils until he was only eighteen or twenty inches from the loon's smooth white breast. When the beautiful bird, apparently as peaceful and inoffensive as a flower, saw that his hairy yellow enemy had arrived at the right distance, the loon, who evidently was fine judge of the reach of his spear, shot it forward quick as a lightning-flash, in marvellous contrast to the wonderful slowness of the preparatory poising, backward motion. The aim was true to a hair-breadth. Tom was struck right in the centre of his forehead, between the eyes. I thought his skull was cracked. Perhaps it was. The sudden astonishment of that outraged cat, the virtuous indignation and wrath, terror, and pain, are far beyond description. His eyes and screams and desperate retreat told all that. When the blow was received, he made a noise that I never heard a cat make before or since; an awfully deep, condensed, screechy, explosive *Wuck!* as he bounced straight up in the air like a bucking bronco; and when he alighted after his spring, he rushed madly across the room and made frantic efforts to climb up the hard-finished plaster wall. Not satisfied to get the width of the kitchen away from his mysterious enemy, for the first time that cold winter he tried to get out of the house, anyhow, anywhere out of that loon-infested room. When he finally ventured to look back and saw that the barbarous bird was still there, tranquil and motionless in front of the stove, he regained command of some of his shattered senses and carefully commenced to examine his wound. Backed against the wall in the farthest corner, and keeping his eye on the outrageous bird, he tenderly touched and washed the sore spot, wetting his paw with his tongue, pausing now and then as his courage increased to glare and stare and growl at his enemy with looks and tones wonderfully human, as if saying, 'You confounded fishy, unfair rascal! What did you do that for? What had I done to you? Faithless, legless, long-nosed wretch!' Intense experiences like the above bring out the humanity that is in all animals. One touch of nature, even a cat-and-loon touch, makes all the world kin.

It was a great memorable day when the first flock of

passenger pigeons came to our farm, calling to mind the
story we had read about them when we were at school
in Scotland. Of all God's feathered people that sailed
the Wisconsin sky, no other bird seemed to us so wonderful. The beautiful wanderers flew like the winds in
flocks of millions from climate to climate in accord with
the weather, finding their food – acorns, beechnuts, pine-
nuts, cranberries, strawberries, huckleberries, juniper berries, hackberries, buckwheat, rice, wheat, oats, corn – in
fields and forests thousands of miles apart. I have seen
flocks streaming south in the fall so large that they were
flowing over from horizon to horizon in an almost continuous stream all day long, at the rate of forty or fifty miles an
hour, like a mighty river in the sky, widening, contracting,
descending like falls and cataracts, and rising suddenly
here and there in huge ragged masses like high-plashing
spray. How wonderful the distances they flew in a day –
in a year – in a lifetime! They arrived in Wisconsin in the
spring just after the sun had cleared away the snow, and
alighted in the woods to feed on the fallen acorns that they
had missed the previous autumn. A comparatively small
flock swept thousands of acres perfectly clean of acorns
in a few minutes, by moving straight ahead with a broad
front. All got their share, for the rear constantly became the
van by flying over the flock and alighting in front, the entire
flock constantly changing from rear to front, revolving
something like a wheel with a low buzzing wing roar that
could be heard a long way off. In summer they feasted on
wheat and oats and were easily approached as they rested
on the trees along the sides of the field after a good full
meal, displaying beautiful iridescent colours as they moved
their necks backward and forward when we went very near
them. Every shotgun was aimed at them and everybody
feasted on pigeon pies, and not a few of the settlers feasted
also on the beauty of the wonderful birds. The breast of the
male is a fine rosy red, the lower part of the neck behind
and along the sides changing from the red of the breast to
gold, emerald green and rich crimson. The general colour of
the upper parts is grayish blue, the under parts white. The
extreme length of the bird is about seventeen inches; the

finely modeled slender tail about eight inches, and extent of wings twenty-four inches. The females are scarcely less beautiful. 'Oh, what bonnie, bonnie birds!' we exclaimed over the first that fell into our hands. 'Oh, what colours! Look at their breasts, bonnie as roses, and at their necks aglow wi' every colour juist like the wonderfu' wood ducks. Oh, the bonnie, bonnie creatures, they beat a'! Where did they a' come fra, and where are they a' gan? It's awfu' like a sin to kill them!' To this some smug, practical old sinner would remark, 'Aye, it's a peety, as ye say, to kill the bonnie things, but they were made to be killed, and sent for us to eat as the quails were sent to God's chosen people, the Israelites, when they were starving in the desert ayont the Red Sea. And I must confess that meat was never put up in neater, handsomer-painted packages.'

In the New England and Canada woods beechnuts were their best and most abundant food, farther north, cranberries and huckleberries. After everything was cleaned up in the north and winter was coming on, they went south for rice, corns, acorns, haws, wild grapes, crab-apples, sparkle-berries, etc. They seemed to require more than half of the continent for feeding-grounds, moving from one table to another, field to field, forest to forest, finding something ripe and wholesome all the year round. In going south in the fine Indian-summer weather they flew high and followed one another, though the head of the flock might be hundreds of miles in advance. But against head winds they took advantage of the inequalities of the ground, flying comparatively low. All followed the leader's ups and downs over hill and dale though far out of sight, never hesitating at any turn of the way, vertical or horizontal, that the leaders had taken, though the largest flocks stretched across several States, and belts of different kinds of weather.

There were no roosting- or breeding-places near our farm, and I never saw any of them until long after the great flocks were exterminated. I therefore quote, from Audubon's and Pokagon's vivid descriptions.

'Toward evening,' Audubon says, 'they depart for the roosting-place, which may be hundreds of miles distant.

One on the banks of Green River, Kentucky, was over three miles wide and forty long.

'My first view of it,' says the great naturalist, 'was about a fortnight after it had been chosen by the birds, and I arrived there nearly two hours before sunset. Few pigeons were then to be seen, but a great many persons with horses and wagons and armed with guns, long poles, sulphur pots, pine pitch torches, etc., had already established encampments on the borders. Two farmers had driven upwards of three hundred hogs a distance of more than a hundred miles to be fattened on slaughtered pigeons. Here and there the people employed in plucking and salting what had already been secured were sitting in the midst of piles of birds. Dung several inches thick covered the ground. Many trees two feet in diameter were broken off at no great distance from the ground, and the branches of many of the tallest and largest had given way, as if the forest had been swept by a tornado.

'Not a pigeon had arrived at sundown. Suddenly a general cry arose – "Here they come!" The noise they made, though still distant, reminded me of a hard gale at sea passing through the rigging of a close-reefed ship. Thousands were soon knocked down by the pole-men. The birds continued to pour in. The fires were lighted and a magnificent as well as terrifying sight presented itself. The pigeons pouring in alighted everywhere, one above another, until solid masses were formed on the branches all around. Here and there the perches gave way with a crash, and falling destroyed hundreds beneath, forcing down the dense groups with which every stick was loaded; a scene of uproar and conflict. I found it useless to speak or even to shout to those persons nearest me. Even the reports of the guns were seldom heard, and I was made aware of the firing only by seeing the shooters reloading. None dared venture within the line of devastation. The hogs had been penned up in due time, the picking up of the dead and wounded being left for the next morning's employment. The pigeons were constantly coming in and it was after midnight before I perceived a decrease in the number of those that arrived. The uproar continued all night, and anxious to know how far the sound reached I sent off a man who, returning two hours after, informed me that he had heard it distinctly three miles distant.

'Toward daylight the noise in some measure subsided; long before objects were distinguishable the pigeons began to move off in a direction quite different from that in which they had arrived the evening before, and at sunrise all that were able to fly had disappeared. The howling of the wolves now reached our ears, and the foxes, lynxes, cougars, bears, coons, opossums, and polecats were seen sneaking off, while eagles and hawks of different species, accompanied by a crowd of vultures, came to supplant them and enjoy a share of the spoil.

'Then the authors of all this devastation began their entry amongst the dead, the dying and mangled. The pigeons were picked up and piled in heaps until each had as many as they could possibly dispose of, when the hogs were let loose to feed on the remainder.

'The breeding-places are selected with reference to abundance of food, and countless myriads resort to them. At this period the note of the pigeon is coo coo coo, like that of the domestic species but much shorter. They caress by billing, and during incubation the male supplies the female with food. As the young grow, the tyrant of creation appears to disturb the peaceful scene, armed with axes to chop down the squab-laden trees, and the abomination of desolation and destruction produced far surpasses even that of the roosting places.'

Pokagon, an educated Indian writer, says: 'I saw one nesting-place in Wisconsin one hundred miles long and from three to ten miles wide. Every tree, some of them quite low and scrubby, had from one to fifty nests on each. Some of the nests overflow from the oaks to the hemlock and pine woods. When the pigeon hunters attack the breeding-places they sometimes cut the timber from thousands of acres. Millions are caught in nets with salt or grain for bait, and schooners, sometimes loaded down with the birds, are taken to New York where they are sold for a cent apiece.'

FIVE

Young Hunters

In the older eastern States it used to be considered great sport for an army of boys to assemble to hunt birds, squirrels, and every other unclaimed, unprotected live thing of shootable size. They dived into two squads, and, choosing leaders, scattered through the woods in different directions, and the party that killed the greatest number enjoyed a supper at the expense of the other. The whole neighbourhood seemed to enjoy the shameful sport especially the farmers afraid of their crops. With a great air of importance, laws were enacted to govern the gory business. For example, a gray squirrel must count four heads, a woodchuck six heads, common red squirrel two heads, black squirrel ten heads, a partridge five heads, the larger birds, such as whip-poor-wills and nighthawks two heads each, the wary crows three, and bob-whites three. But all the blessed company of mere songbirds, warblers, robins, thrushes, orioles, with nuthatches, chickadees, blue jays, woodpeckers, etc., counted only one head each. The heads of the birds were hastily wrung off and thrust into the game-bags to be counted, saving the bodies only of what were called game, the larger squirrels, bob-whites, partridges, etc. The blood-stained bags of the best slayers were soon bulging full. Then at a given hour all had to stop and repair to the town, empty their dripping sacks, count the heads, and go rejoicing to their dinner. Although, like other wild boys, I was fond of shooting, I never had anything to do with these abominable head-hunts. And now, the farmers having learned that birds are their friends, wholesale slaughter has been abolished.

We seldom saw deer, though their tracks were common. The Yankee explained that they traveled and fed mostly at night, and hid in tamarack swamps and brushy places in the daytime, and how the Indians knew all about them and could find them whenever they were hungry.

Indians belonging to the Menominee and Winnebago tribes occasionally visited us at our cabin to get a piece of bread or some matches, or to sharpen their knives on our grindstone, and we boys watched them closely to see that they didn't steal Jack. We wondered at their knowledge of animals when we saw them go direct to trees on our farm, chop holes in them with their tomahawks and take out coons, of the existence of which we had never noticed the slightest trace. In winter, after the first snow, we frequently saw three or four Indians hunting deer in company, running like hounds on the fresh, exciting tracks. The escape of the deer from these noiseless, tireless hunters was said to be well-nigh impossible; they were followed to the death.

Most of our neighbours brought some sort of gun from the old country, but seldom took time to hunt, even after the first hard work of fencing and clearing was over, except to shoot a duck or prairie chicken now and then that happened to come in their way. It was only the less industrious American settlers who left their work to go far a-hunting. Two or three of our most enterprising American neighbours went off every fall with their teams to the pine regions and cranberry marshes in the northern part of the State to hunt and gather berries. I well remember seeing their wagons loaded with game when they returned from a successful hunt. Their loads consisted usually of half a dozen deer or more, one or two black bears, and fifteen or twenty bushels of cranberries; all solidly frozen. Part of both the berries and meat was usually sold in Portage; the balance furnished their families with abundance of venison, bear grease, and pies.

Winter wheat is sown in the fall, and when it is a month or so old the deer, like the wild geese, are very fond of it, especially since other kinds of food are then becoming scarce. One of our neighbours across the Fox River killed a large number, some thirty or forty, on a small patch of wheat, simply by lying in wait for them every night. Our wheat-field was the first that was sown in the neighbourhood. The deer soon found it and came in every night to feast, but it was eight or nine years before we ever disturbed them. David then killed one deer, the only one killed by any of our family. He went out shortly after sundown at the time of full moon to one of our wheat-fields, carrying a double-barreled shotgun loaded with buck-shot. After lying in wait an hour or so, he saw a doe and her fawn jump the fence and come cautiously into the wheat. After they were within sixty or seventy yards of him, he was surprised when he tried to take aim that about half of the moon's disc was mysteriously darkened as if covered by the edge of a dense cloud. This proved to be an eclipse. Nevertheless, he fired at the mother, and she immediately ran off, jumped the fence, and took to the woods by the way she came. The fawn danced about bewildered, wondering what had become of its mother, but finally fled to the woods. David fired at the poor deserted thing as it ran past him but happily missed it. Hearing the shots, I joined David to learn his luck. He said he thought he must have wounded the mother, and when we were strolling about in the woods in search of her we saw three or four deer on their way to the wheat-field, led by a fine buck. They were walking rapidly, but cautiously halted at intervals of a few rods to listen and look ahead and scent the air. They failed to notice us, though by this time the moon was out of the eclipse shadow and we were standing only about fifty yards from them. I was carrying the gun. David had fired both barrels but when he was reloading one of them he happened to put the wad intended to cover the shot into the empty barrel, and so when we were climbing over the fence the buckshot had rolled out, and when I fired at the big buck I knew by the report that there was nothing but powder in the charge. The startled deer danced about in confusion for a few seconds, uncertain which way to run until they caught sight of us, when they bounded off through the woods. Next morning we found the poor mother lying about three hundred yards from the place where she was shot. She had run this distance and jumped a high fence after one of the buckshot had passed through her heart.

Excepting Sundays we boys had only two days of the year to ourselves, the 4th of July and the 1st of January. Sundays were less than half our own, on account of Bible lessons, Sunday-school lessons and church services; all the others were labor days, rain or shine, cold or warm. No wonder, then, that our two holidays were precious and that it was not easy to decide what to do with them. They were usually spent on the highest rocky hill in the neighbourhood, called the Observatory; in visiting our boy friends on adjacent farms to hunt, fish, wrestle, and play games; in reading some new favourite book we had managed to borrow or buy; or in making models of machines I had invented.

One of our July days was spent with two Scotch boys of our own age hunting redwing blackbirds then busy in the corn-fields. Our party had only one single-barreled shotgun, which, as the oldest and perhaps because I was thought to be the best shot, I had the honor of carrying. We marched through the corn without getting sight of a single redwing, but just as we reached the far side of the field, a redheaded woodpecker flew up, and the Lawson boys cried, 'Shoot him! Shoot him! he is just as bad as a blackbird. He eats corn!' This memorable woodpecker alighted in the top of a white oak tree about fifty feet high. I fired from a position almost immediately beneath him, and he fell straight down at my feet. When I picked him up and was admiring his plumage, he moved his legs slightly, and I said, 'Poor bird, he's no deed yet and we'll hae to kill him to put him oot o' pain,' – sincerely pitying him, after we had taken pleasure in shooting him. I had seen servant girls wringing chicken necks, so with desperate humanity I took the limp unfortunate by the head, swung him around three or four times thinking I was wringing his neck, and then threw him hard on the ground to quench the last possible spark of life and make quick death doubly sure. But to our astonishment the moment he struck the ground he gave a cry of alarm and flew right straight up like a rejoicing lark into the top of the same tree, and perhaps to the same branch he had fallen from, and began to adjust his ruffled feathers, nodding and chirping and looking down at us as if wondering what in the bird world we had been doing to him. This of course banished all thought of killing, as far as that revived woodpecker was concerned, no matter how many ears of corn he might spoil, and we all heartily congratulated him on his wonderful, triumphant resurrection from three kinds of death – shooting, neck-wringing, and destructive concussion. I suppose only one pellet had touched him, glancing on his head.

Another extraordinary shooting-affair happened one summer morning shortly after day-break. When I went to the stable to feed the horses I noticed a big white-breasted hawk on a tall oak in front of the chicken-house, evidently waiting for a chicken breakfast. I ran to the house for the gun, and when I fired he fell about halfway down the tree, caught a branch with his claws, hung back downward and fluttered a few seconds, then managed to stand erect. I fired again to put him out of pain, and to my surprise the second shot seemed to restore his strength instead of killing him, for he flew out of the tree and over the meadow with strong and regular wing-beats for thirty or forty rods apparently as well as ever, but died suddenly in the air and dropped like a stone.

We hunted muskrats whenever we had time to run down to the lake. They are brown bunchy animals about twenty-three inches long, the tail being about nine inches in length, black in colour and flattened vertically for sculling, and the hind feet are half-webbed. They look like little beavers, usually have from ten to a dozen young, are easily tamed and make interesting pets. We liked to watch them at their work and at their meals. In the spring when the snow vanishes and the lake ice begins to melt, the first open spot is always used as a feeding-place, where they dive from the edge of the ice and in a minute or less reappear with a mussel or a mouthful of pontederia or water-lily leaves, climb back on to the ice and sit up to nibble their food, handling it very much like squirrels or marmots. It is then that they are most easily shot, a solitary hunter oftentimes shooting thirty or forty in a single day. Their nests on the rushy margins of lakes and streams, far from being hidden like those of most birds, are conspicuously large, and conical in shape like Indian wigwams. They

are built of plants – rushes, sedges, mosses, etc. – and
ornamented around the base with mussel-shells. It was
always pleasant and interesting to see them in the fall
as soon as the nights began to be frosty, hard at work
cutting sedges on the edge of the meadow or swimming
out through the rushes, making long glittering ripples as
they sculled themselves along, diving where the water is
perhaps six or eight feet deep and reappearing in a minute
or so with large mouthfuls of the weedy tangled plants
gathered from the bottom, returning to their big wigwams,
climbing up and depositing their loads where most needed
to make them yet larger and firmer and warmer, foreseeing
the freezing weather just like ourselves when we banked up
our house to keep out the frost.

They lie snug and invisible all winter but do not hiber-
nate. Through a channel carefully kept open they swim
out under the ice for mussels, and the roots and stems
of water-lilies, etc., on which they feed just as they do
in summer. Sometimes the oldest and most enterprising
of them venture to orchards near the water in search of
fallen apples; very seldom, however, do they interfere with
anything belonging to their mortal enemy, man. Notwithstanding they are so well hidden and protected during the
winter, many of them are killed by Indian hunters, who
creep up softly and spear them through the thick walls of
their cabins. Indians are fond of their flesh, and so are
some of the wildest of the white trappers. They are easily
caught in steel traps, and after vainly trying to drag their
feet from the cruel crushing jaws, they sometimes in their
agony gnaw them off. Even after having gnawed off a leg
they are so guileless that they never seem to learn to know
and fear traps, for some are occasionally found that have
been caught twice and have gnawed off a second foot.
Many other animals suffering excruciating pain in these
cruel traps gnaw off their legs. Crabs and lobsters are so
fortunate as to be able to shed their limbs when caught or
merely frightened, apparently without suffering any pain,
simply by giving themselves a little shivery shake.

The muskrat is one of the most notable and widely distributed of American animals, and millions of the gentle,

industrious, beaver-like creatures are shot and trapped and speared every season for their skins, worth a dime or so – like shooting boys and girls for their garments.

Surely a better time must be drawing nigh when godlike human beings will become truly humane, and learn to put their animal fellow mortals in their hearts instead of on their backs or in their dinners. In the mean time we may just as well as not learn to live clean, innocent lives instead of slimy, bloody ones. All hale, red-blooded boys are savage, the best and boldest the savagest, fond of hunting and fishing. But when thoughtless childhood is past, the best rise the highest above all this bloody flesh and sport business, the wild foundational animal dying out day by day, as divine uplifting, transfiguring charity grows in.

Hares and rabbits were seldom seen when we first settled in the Wisconsin woods, but they multiplied rapidly after the animals that preyed upon them had been thinned out or exterminated, and food and shelter supplied in grain-fields and log fences and the thickets of young oaks that grew up in pastures after the annual grass fires were kept out. Catching hares in the winter-time, when they were hiddden in hollow fence-logs, was a favourite pastime with many of the boys whose fathers allowed them time to enjoy the sport. Occasionally a stout, lithe hare was carried out into an open snow-covered field, set free, and given a chance for its life in a race with a dog. When the snow was not too soft and deep, it usually made good its escape, for our dogs were only fat, short-legged mongrels. We sometimes discovered hares in standing hollow trees, crouching on decayed punky wood at the bottom, as far back as possible from the opening, but when alarmed they managed to climb to a considerable height if the hollow was not too wide, by bracing themselves against the sides.

Foxes, though not uncommon, we boys held steadily to work seldom saw, and as they found plenty of prairie chickens for themselves and families, they did not often come near the farmer's hen-roosts. Nevertheless the discovery of their dens was considered important. No matter how deep the den might be, it was thoroughly explored with pick and shovel by sport-loving settlers at a time when they judged the fox was likely to be at home, but I cannot remember any case in our neighbourhood where the fox was actually captured. In one of the dens a mile or two from our farm a lot of prairie chickens were found and some smaller birds.

Badger dens were far more common than fox dens. One of our fields was named Badger Hill from the number of badger holes in a hill at the end of it, but I cannot remember seeing a single one of the inhabitants.

On a stormy day in the middle of an unusually severe winter, a black bear, hungry, no doubt, and seeking something to eat, came strolling down through our neighbourhood from the northern pine woods. None had been seen here before, and it caused no little excitement and alarm, for the European settlers imagined that these poor, timid, bashful bears were as dangerous as man-eating lions and tigers, and that they would pursue any human being that came in their way. This species is common in the north part of the State, and few of our enterprising Yankee hunters who went to the pineries in the fall failed to shoot at least one of them.

We saw very little of the owlish, serious-looking coons, and no wonder, since they lie hidden nearly all day in hollow trees and we never had time to hunt them. We often heard their curious, quavering, whinnying cries on still evenings, but only once succeeded in tracing an unfortunate family through our corn-field to their den in a big oak and catching them all. One of our neighbours, Mr McRath, a Highland Scotchman, caught one and made a pet of it. It became very tame and had perfect confidence in the good intentions of its kind friend and master. He always addressed it in speaking to it as a 'little man'. When it came running to him and jumped on his lap or climbed up his trousers, he would say, while patting his head as if it were a dog or a child, 'Coonie, ma mannie, Coonie, ma mannie, hoo are ye the day? I think you're hungry,' – as the comical pet began to examine his pockets for nuts and bits of bread – 'Na, na, there's nathing in my pooch for ye the day, my wee mannie, but I'll get ye something.' He would then fetch something it liked – bread, nuts, a carrot, or perhaps a piece of fresh meat. Anything scattered for it on the floor it felt with its paw instead of looking at it, judging of its worth more by touch than sight.

The outlet of our Fountain Lake flowed past Mr McRath's door, and the coon was very fond of swimming in it and searching for frogs and mussels. It seemed perfectly satisfied to stay about the house without being confined, occupied a comfortable bed in a section of a hollow tree, and never wandered far. How long it lived after the death of its kind master I don't know.

I suppose that almost any wild animal may be made a pet, simply by sympathizing with it and entering as much as possible into its life. In Alaska I saw one of the common gray mountain marmots kept as a pet in an Indian family. When its master entered the house it always seemed glad, almost like a dog, and when cold or tired it snuggled up in a fold of his blanket with the utmost confidence.

We have all heard of ferocious animals, lions and tigers, etc., that were fed and spoken to only by their masters, becoming perfectly tame; and, as is well known, the faithful dog that follows man and serves him, and looks up to him and loves him as if he were a god, is a descendant of the blood-thirsty wolf or jackal. Even frogs and toads and fishes may be tamed, provided they have the uniform sympathy of one person, with whom they become intimately acquainted without the distracting and varying attentions of strangers. And surely all God's people, however serious and savage, great or small, like to play. Whales and elephants, dancing, humming gnats, and invisibly small mischievous microbes – all are warm with divine radium and must have lots of fun in them.

As far as I know, all wild creatures keep themselves clean. Birds, it seems to me, take more pains to bathe and dress themselves than any other animals. Even ducks, though living so much in water, dip and scatter cleansing showers over their backs, and shake and preen their feathers as carefully as land-birds. Watching small singers taking their morning baths is very interesting, particularly when the weather is cold. Alighting in a shallow pool, they oftentimes show a sort of dread of dipping into it, like children hesitating about taking a plunge, as if they felt the same kind of shock, and this makes it easy for us to sympathize with the little feathered people.

Occasionally I have seen from my study-window red-headed linnets bathing in dew when water elsewhere was scarce. A large Monterey cypress with broad branches and innumerable leaves on which the dew lodges in still nights made favourite bathing-places. Alighting gently, as if afraid to waste the dew, they would pause and fidget as they do before beginning to plash in pools, then dip and scatter the drops in showers and get as thorough a bath as they would in a pool. I have also seen the same kind of baths taken by birds on the boughs of silver firs on the edge of a glacier meadow, but nowhere have I seen the dew-drops so abundant as on the Monterey cypress; and the picture made by the quivering wings and irised dew was memorably beautiful. Children, too, make fine pictures plashing and crowing in their little tubs. How widely different from wallowing pigs, bathing with great show of comfort and rubbing themselves dry against rough-barked trees!

Some of our own species seem fairly to dread the touch of water. When the necessity of absolute cleanliness by means of frequent baths was being preached by a friend who had been reading Combe's Physiology, in which he had learned something of the wonders of the skin with its millions of pores that had to be kept open for health, one of our neighbours remarked, 'Oh! that's unnatural. It's well enough to wash in a tub maybe once or twice a year, but not to be paddling in the water all the time like a frog in a spring-hole.' Another neighbour, who prided himself on his knowledge of big words, said with great solemnity, 'I never can believe that man is amphibious!'

Natives of tropic islands pass a large part of their lives in water, and seem as much at home in the sea as on the land: swim and dive, pursue fishes, play in the waves like surfducks and seals, and explore the coral gardens and groves and seaweed meadows as if truly amphibious. Even the natives of the far north bathe at times. I once saw a lot of Eskimo boys ducking and plashing right merrily in the Arctic Ocean.

It seemed very wonderful to us that the wild animals could keep themselves warm and strong in winter when the temperature was far below zero. Feeble-looking rabbits scud away over the snow, lithe and elastic, as if glorying in the frosty, sparkling weather and sure of their dinners. I have seen gray squirrels dragging ears of corn about as heavy as themselves out of our field through loose snow and up a tree, balancing them on limbs and eating in comfort with their dry, electric tails spread airily over their backs. Once I saw a fine hardy fellow go into a knot-hole. Thrusting in my hand I caught him and pulled him out. As soon as he guessed what I was up to, he took the end of my thumb in his mouth and sunk his teeth right through it, but I gripped him hard by the neck, carried him home, and shut him up in a box that contained about half a bushel of hazel- and hickory-nuts, hoping that he would not be too frightened and discouraged to eat while thus imprisoned after the rough handling he had suffered. I soon learned, however, that sympathy in this direction was wasted, for no sooner did I pop him in than he fell to with right hearty appetite, gnawing and munching the nuts as if he had gathered them himself and was very hungry that day. Therefore, after allowing time enough for a good square meal, I made haste to get him out of the nut-box and shut him up in a spare bedroom, in which father had hung a lot of selected ears of Indian corn for seed. They were hung up by the husks on cords stretched across from side to side of the room. The squirrel managed to jump from the top of one of the bed-posts to the corn, cut off an ear, and let it drop to the floor. He then jumped down, got a good grip of the heavy ear, carried it to the top of one of the slippery, polished bed-posts, seated himself comfortably, and, holding it well balanced, deliberately pried out one kernel at a time with his long chisel teeth, ate the soft, sweet germ, and dropped the hard part of the kernel. In this masterly way, working at high speed, he demolished several ears a day, and with a good warm bed in a box made himself at home and grew fat. Then naturally, I suppose, free romping in the snow and tree-tops with companions came to mind. Anyhow he began to look for a way of escape. Of course he first tried the window, but found that his teeth made no impression on the glass. Next he tried the sash and gnawed the wood off level with the glass; then father happened to come upstairs and discovered the mischief that was being done to his seed corn and window and immediately ordered him out of the house.

The flying squirrel was one of the most interesting of the little animals we found in the woods, a beautiful brown creature, with fine eyes and smooth, soft fur like that of a mole or field mouse. He is about half as long as the gray squirrel, but his wide-spread tail and the folds of skin along his sides that form the wings make him look broad and flat, something like a kite. In the evenings our cat often brought them to her kittens at the shanty, and later we saw them fly during the day from the trees we were chopping. They jumped and glided off smoothly and apparently without effort, like birds, as soon as they heard and felt the breaking shock of the strained fibres at the stump, when the trees they were in began to totter and groan. They can fly, or rather glide, twenty or thirty yards from the top of a tree twenty or thirty feet high to the foot of another, gliding upward as they reach the trunk, or if the distance is too great they alight comfortably on the ground and make haste to the nearest tree, and climb just like the wingless squirrels.

Every boy and girl loves the little fairy, airy striped chipmunk, half squirrel, half spermophile. He is about the size of a field mouse, and often made us think of linnets and song sparrows as he frisked about gathering nuts and berries. He likes almost all kinds of grain, berries, and nuts – hazel-nuts, hickory-nuts, strawberries, huckle-berries, wheat, oats, corn – he is fond of them all and thrives on them. Most of the hazel bushes on our farm grew along the fences as if they had been planted for the chipmunks alone, for the rail fences were their favourite highways. We never wearied watching them, especially when the hazel-nuts were ripe and the little fellows were sitting on the rails nibbling and handling them like tree-squirrels. We used to notice too that, although they are very neat animals, their lips and fingers were dyed red like our own when the strawberries and huckleberries were ripe. We could always tell when the wheat and oats were in the milk by seeing the chipmunks feeding on the ears. They kept nibbling at the wheat until it was harvested and then gleaned in the stubble, keeping up a careful watch for their enemies – dogs, hawks, and shrikes. They are as widely distributed over the continent as the squirrels, various species inhabiting different regions on the mountains and lowlands, but all the different kinds have the same general characteristics of light, airy cheerfulness and good nature.

Before the arrival of farmers in the Wisconsin woods the small ground squirrels, called 'gophers', lived chiefly on the seeds of wild grasses and weeds, but after the country was cleared and ploughed no feasting animal fell to more heartily on the farmer's wheat and corn. Increasing rapidly in numbers and knowledge, they became very destructive, especially in the spring when the corn was planted, for they learned to trace the rows and dig up and eat the three or four seeds in each hill about as fast as the poor farmers could cover them. And unless great pains were taken to diminish the numbers of the cunning little robbers, the fields had to be planted two or three times over, and even then large gaps in the rows would be found. The loss of the grain they consumed after it was ripe, together with the winter stores laid up in their burrows, amounted to little as compared with the loss of the seed on which the whole crop depended.

One evening about sundown, when my father sent me out with the shotgun to hunt them in a stubble field, I learned something curious and interesting in connection with these mischievous gophers, though just then they were doing no harm. As I strolled through the stubble watching for a chance for a shot, a shrike flew past me and alighted on an open spot at the mouth of a burrow about thirty yards ahead of me. Curious to see what he was up to, I stood still to watch him. He looked down the gopher hole in a listening attitude, then looked back at me to see if I was coming, looked down again and listened, and looked back at me. I stood perfectly still, and he kept twitching his tail, seeming uneasy and doubtful about venturing to do the savage job that I soon learned he had in his mind. Finally, encouraged by my keeping so still, to my astonishment he suddenly vanished in the gopher hole.

A bird going down a deep narrow hole in the ground like a ferret or a weasel seemed very strange, and I thought it would be a fine thing to run forward, clap my hand over the hole, and have the fun of imprisoning him and seeing what he would do when he tried to get out. So I ran forward but stopped when I got within a dozen or fifteen yards of the hole, thinking it might perhaps be more interesting to wait and see what would naturally happen without my interference. While I stood there looking and listening, I heard a great disturbance going on in the burrow, a mixed lot of keen squeaking, shrieking, distressful cries, telling that down in the dark something terrible was being done. Then suddenly out popped a half-grown gopher, four and a half or five inches long, and, without stopping a single moment to choose a way of escape, ran screaming through the stubble straight away from its home, quickly followed by another and another, until some half-dozen were driven out, all of them crying and running in different directions as if at this dreadful time home, sweet home, was the most dangerous and least desirable of any place in the wide world. Then out came the shrike, flew above the runaway gopher children, and, diving on them, killed them one after another with blows at the back of the skull. He then seized one of them, dragged it to the top of a small clod so as to be able to get a start, and laboriously made out to fly with it about ten or fifteen yards, when he alighted to rest. Then he dragged it to the top of another clod and flew with it about the same distance, repeating this hard work over and over again until he managed to get one of the gophers on to the top of a log fence. How much he ate of his hard-won prey, or what he did with the others, I can't tell, for by this time the sun was down and I had to hurry home to my chores.

SIX

The Ploughboy

At first, wheat, corn, and potatoes were the principal crops we raised; wheat especially. But in four or five years the soil was so exhausted that only five or six bushels an acre, even in the better fields, was obtained, although when first ploughed twenty and twenty-five bushels was about the ordinary yield. More attention was then paid to corn, but without fertilizers the corn-crop also became very meagre. At last it was discovered that English clover would grow on even the exhausted fields, and that when ploughed under and planted with corn, or even wheat, wonderful crops were raised. This caused a complete change in farming methods; the farmers raised fertilizing clover, planted corn, and fed the crop to cattle and hogs.

But no crop raised in our wilderness was so surprisingly rich and sweet and purely generous to us boys and, indeed, to everybody as the watermelons and muskmelons. We planted a large patch on a sunny hill-slope the very first spring, and it seemed miraculous that a few handfuls of little flat seeds should in a few months send up a hundred wagonloads of crisp, sumptuous, red-hearted and yellow-hearted fruits covering all the hill. We soon learned to know when they were in their prime, and when over-ripe and mealy. Also that if a second crop was taken from the same ground without fertilizing it, the melons would be small and what we called soapy; that is, soft and smooth, utterly uncrisp, and without a trace of the lively freshness and sweetness of those raised on virgin soil. Coming in from the farm work at noon, the half-dozen or so of melons we had placed in our cold spring were a glorious luxury that only weary barefooted farm boys can ever know.

Spring was not very trying as to temperature, and refreshing rains fell at short intervals. The work of ploughing commenced as soon as the frost was out of the ground. Corn- and potato-planting and the sowing of spring wheat was comparatively light work, while the nesting birds sang cheerily, grass and flowers covered the marshes and meadows and all the wild, uncleared parts of the farm, and the trees put forth their new leaves, those of the oaks forming beautiful purple masses as if every leaf were a petal; and with all this we enjoyed the mild soothing winds, the humming of innumerable small insects and hylas, and the freshness and fragrance of everything. Then, too, came the wonderful passenger pigeons streaming from the south, and flocks of geese and cranes, filling all the sky with whistling wings.

The summer work, on the contrary, was deadly heavy, especially harvesting and corn-hoeing. All the ground had to be hoed over for the first few years, before father bought cultivators or small weed-covering ploughs, and we were not allowed a moment's rest. The hoes had to be kept working up and down as steadily as if they were moved by machinery. Ploughing for winter wheat was comparatively easy, when we walked barefooted in the furrows, while the fine autumn tints kindled in the woods, and the hillsides were covered with golden pumpkins.

In summer the chores were grinding scythes, feeding the animals, chopping stove-wood, and carrying water up the hill from the spring on the edge of the meadow, etc. Then breakfast, and to the harvest or hay-field. I was foolishly ambitious to be first in mowing and cradling, and by the time I was sixteen led all the hired men. An hour was allowed at noon for dinner and more chores. We stayed in the field until dark, then supper, and still more chores, family worship, and to bed; making altogether a hard, sweaty day of about sixteen or seventeen hours. Think of that, ye blessed eight-hour-day laborers!

In winter father came to the foot of the stairs and called us at six o'clock to feed the horses and cattle, grind axes, bring in wood, and do any other chores required, then breakfast, and out to work in the mealy, frosty snow by daybreak, chopping, fencing, etc. So in general our winter work was about as restless and trying as that of the long-day summer. No matter what the weather, there was always something to do. During heavy rains or snow-storms we worked in the barn, shelling corn, fanning wheat, thrashing with the flail, making axe-handles or ox-yokes, mending things, or sprouting and sorting potatoes in the cellar.

No pains were taken to diminish or in any way soften the natural hardships of this pioneer farm life; nor did any of the Europeans seem to know how to find reasonable ease and comfort if they would. The very best oak and hickory fuel was embarrassingly abundant and cost nothing but cutting and common sense; but instead of hauling great heart-cheering loads of it for wide, open, all-welcoming, climate-changing, beauty-making, Godlike ingle-fires, it was hauled with weary heart-breaking industry into fences and waste places to get it out of the way of the plough, and out of the way of doing good. The only fire for the whole house was the kitchen stove, with a fire-box about eighteen inches long and eight inches wide and deep – scant space for three or four small sticks, around which in hard zero weather all the family of ten persons shivered, and beneath which in the morning we found our socks and coarse, soggy boots frozen solid. We were not allowed to start even this despicable little fire in its black box to thaw them. No, we had to squeeze our throbbing, aching, chilblained feet into them, causing greater pain than tooth-ache, and hurry out to chores. Fortunately the miserable chilblain pain began to abate as soon as the temperature of our feet approached the freezing-point, enabling us in spite of hard work and hard frost to enjoy the winter beauty – the wonderful radiance of the snow when it was starry with crystals, and the dawns and the sunsets and white noons, and the cheery, enlivening company of the brave chickadees and nuthatches.

The winter stars far surpassed those of our stormy Scotland in brightness, and we gazed and gazed as though we had never seen stars before. Oftentimes the heavens were made still more glorious by auroras, the long lance rays, called 'Merry Dancers' in Scotland, streaming with startling tremulous motion to the zenith. Usually the electric auroral light is white or pale yellow, but in the third or fourth of our Wisconsin winters there was a magnificently coloured aurora that was seen and admired over nearly all the continent. The whole sky was draped in graceful purple and crimson folds glorious beyond description. Father called us out into the yard in front of the house where we had a wide view, crying, 'Come! Come, mother! Come, bairns! and see the glory of God. All the sky is clad in a robe of red light. Look straight up to the crown where the folds are gathered. Hush and wonder and adore, for surely this is the clothing of the Lord Himself, and perhaps He will even now appear looking down from his high heaven.' This celestial show was far more glorious than anything we had ever yet beheld, and throughout that wonderful winter hardly anything else was spoken of.

We even enjoyed the snowstorms; the thronging crystals, like daisies, coming down separate and distinct, were very different from the tufted flakes we enjoyed so much in Scotland, when we ran into the midst of the slow-falling feathery throng shouting with enthusiasm, 'Jennie's plucking her doos! Jennie's plucking her doos (doves)!'

Nature has many ways of thinning and pruning and trimming her forests – lightning-stikes, heavy snow, and stormwinds to shatter and blow down whole trees here and there or break off branches as required. The results of these methods I have observed in different forests, but only once have I seen pruning by rain. The rain froze on the trees as it fell and grew so thick and heavy that many of them lost a third or more of their branches. The view of the woods after the storm had passed and the sun shone forth was something never to be forgotten. Every twig and branch and rugged trunk was encased in pure crystal ice, and each oak and hickory and willow became a fairy crystal palace. Such dazzling brilliance, such effects of white light and irised light glowing and flashing I had never seen before, nor have I since. This sudden change of the leafless woods to glowing silver was, like the great aurora, spoken of for years, and is one of the most beautiful of the many pictures that enriches my life. And besides the great shows there were thousands of others even in the coldest weather manifesting the utmost fineness and tenderness of beauty and affording noble compensation for hardship and pain.

One of the most striking of the winter sounds was the loud roaring and rumbling of the ice on our lake, from its shrinking and expanding with the changes of the weather. The fishermen who were catching pickerel said that they had no luck when this roaring was going on above the fish. I remember how frightened we boys were when on one of our New Year holidays we were taking a walk on the ice and heard for the first time the sudden rumbling roar beneath our feet and running on ahead of us, creaking and whooping as if all the ice eighteen or twenty inches thick was breaking.

In the neighbourhood of our Wisconsin farm there were extensive swamps consisting in great part of a thick sod of very tough carex roots covering thin, watery lakes of mud. They originated in glacier lakes that were gradually overgrown. This sod was so tough that oxen with loaded wagons could be driven over it without cutting down through it, although it was afloat. The carpenters who came to build our frame house, noticing how the sedges sunk beneath their feet, said that if they should break through, they would probably be well on their way to California before touching bottom. On the contrary, all these lake-basins are shallow as compared with their width. When we went into the Wisconsin woods there was not a single wheel-track or cattle-track. The only man-made road was an Indian trail along the Fox River between Portage and Packwauckee Lake. Of course the deer, foxes, badgers, coons, skunks, and even the squirrels had well-beaten tracks from their dens and hiding-places in thickets, hollow trees, and the ground, but they did not reach far, and but little noise was made by the soft-footed travelers in passing over them, only a slight rustling and swishing among fallen leaves and grass.

Corduroying the swamps formed the principal part of road-making among the early settlers for many a day. At these annual road-making gatherings opportunity was offered for discussion of the news, politics, religion, war, the state of the crops, comparative advantages of the new country over the old, and so forth, but the principal opportunities, recurring every week, were the hours after

Sunday church services. I remember hearing long talks on the wonderful beauty of the Indian corn; the wonderful melons, so wondrous fine for 'sloken a body on hot days'; their contempt for tomatoes, so fine to look at with their sunny colours and so disappointing in taste; the miserable cucumbers the 'Yankee bodies' ate, though tasteless as rushes; the character of the Yankees, etc. Then there were long discussions about the Russian war, news of which was eagerly gleaned from Greeley's 'New York Tribune'; the great battles of the Alma, the charges at Balaklava and Inkerman; the siege of Sebastopol; the military genius of Todleben; the character of Nicholas; the character of the Russian soldier, his stubborn bravery, who for the first time in history withstood the British bayonet charges; the probable outcome of the terrible war; the fate of Turkey, and so forth.

Very few of our old-country neighbours gave much heed to what are called spirit-rappings. On the contrary, they were regarded as a sort of sleight-of-hand humbug. Some of these spirits seem to be stout able-bodied fellows, judging by the weights they lift and the heavy furniture they bang about. But they do no good work that I know of; never saw wood, grind corn, cook, feed the hungry, or go to the help of poor anxious mothers at the bedsides of their sick children. I noticed when I was a boy that it was not the strongest characters who followed so-called mediums. When a rapping-storm was at its height in Wisconsin, one of our neighbours, an old Scotchman, remarked, 'They puir silly medium-bodies may gang to the deil wi' their rappin' speerits, for they dae nae gude, and I think the deil's their fayther.'

Although in the spring of 1849 there was no other settler within a radius of four miles of our Fountain Lake farm, in three or four years almost every quarter-section of government land was taken up, mostly by enthusiastic home-seekers from Great Britain, with only here and there Yankee families from adjacent states, who had come drifting indefinitely westward in covered wagons, seeking their fortunes like winged seeds; all alike striking root and gripping the glacial drift soil as naturally as oak and hickory trees; happy and hopeful, establishing homes and making wider and wider fields in the hospitable wilderness. The axe and plough were kept very busy; cattle, horses, sheep, and pigs multiplied; barns and corn-cribs were filled up, and man and beast were well fed; a schoolhouse was built, which was used also for a church; and in a very short time the new country began to look like an old one.

Comparatively few of the first settlers suffered from serious accidents. One of our neighbours had a finger shot off, and on a bitter, frosty night had to be taken to a surgeon in Portage, in a sled drawn by slow, plodding oxen, to have the shattered stump dressed. Another fell from his wagon and was killed by the wheel passing over his body. An acre of ground was reserved and fenced for graves, and soon consumption came to fill it. One of the saddest instances was that of a Scotch family from Edinburgh, consisting of a father, son, and daughter, who settled on eighty acres of land within half a mile of our place. The daughter died of consumption the third year after their arrival, the son one or two years later, and at last the father followed his two children. Thus sadly ended bright hopes and dreams of a happy home in rich and free America.

Another neighbour, I remember, after a lingering illness died of the same disease in mid-winter, and his funeral was attended by the neighbours in sleighs during a driving snow-storm when the thermometer was fifteen or twenty degrees below zero. The great white plague carried off another of our near neighbours, a fine Scotchman, the father of eight promising boys, when he was only about forty-five years of age. Most of those who suffered from this disease seemed hopeful and cheerful up to a very short time before their death, but Mr Reid, I remember, on one of his last visits to our house, said with brave resignation, 'I know that never more in this world can I be well, but I must just submit. I must just submit.'

One of the saddest deaths from other causes than consumption was that of a poor feeble-minded man whose brother, a sturdy, devout, severe puritan, was a very hard taskmaster. Poor half-witted Charlie was kept steadily at work – although he was not able to do much, for his body was about as feeble as his mind. He never could be taught the right use of an axe, and when he was set to chopping down trees for firewood he feebly hacked and chipped round and round them, sometimes spending several days in nibbling down a tree that a beaver might have gnawed down in half the time. Occasionally when he had an extra large tree to chop, he would go home and report that the tree was too tough and strong for him and that he could never make it fall. Then his brother, calling him a useless creature, would fell it with a few well-directed strokes, and leave Charlie to nibble away at it for weeks trying to make it into stove-wood.

His guardian brother, delighting in hard work and able for anything, was as remarkable for strength of body and mind as poor Charlie for childishness. All the neighbours pitied Charlie, especially the women, who never missed an opportunity to give him kind words, cookies, and pie; above all, they bestowed natural sympathy on the poor imbecile as if he were an unfortunate motherless child. In particular, his nearest neighbours, Scotch Highlanders, warmly welcomed him to their home and never wearied in doing everything that tender sympathy could suggest. To those friends he ran gladly at every opportunity. But after years of suffering from overwork and illness his feeble health failed, and he told his Scotch friends one day that he was not able to work any more or do anything that his brother wanted him to do, that he was tired of life, and that he had come to thank them for their kindness and to bid them good-bye, for he was going to drown himself in Muir's lake. 'Oh, Charlie! Charlie!' they cried, 'you mustn't talk that way. Cheer up! You will soon be stronger. We all love you. Cheer up! Cheer up! And always come here whenever you need anything.'

'Oh, no! my friends,' he pathetically replied, 'I know you love me, but I can't cheer up any more. My heart's gone, and I want to die.'

Next day, when Mr Anderson, a carpenter whose house was on the west shore of our lake, was going to a spring he saw a man wade out through the rushes and lily-pads and throw himself forward into deep water. This was poor

Charlie. Fortunately, Mr Anderson had a skiff close by, and as the distance was not great he reached the broken-hearted imbecile in time to save his life, and after trying to cheer him took him home to his brother. But even this terrible proof of despair failed to soften his brother. He seemed to regard the attempt at suicide simply as a crime calculated to bring harm to religion. Though snatched from the lake to his bed, poor Charlie lived only a few days longer. A physician who was called when his health first became seriously impaired reported that he was suffering from Bright's disease. After all was over, the stoical brother walked over to the neighbour who had saved Charlie from drowning, and, after talking on ordinary affairs, crops, the weather, etc., said in a careless tone, 'I have a little job of carpenter work for you, Mr Anderson.' 'What is it, Mr – ?' 'I want you to make a coffin.' 'A coffin!' said the startled carpenter. 'Who is dead?' 'Charlie,' he coolly replied. All the neighbours were in tears over the poor child man's fate. But, strange to say, the brother who had faithfully cared for him controlled and concealed all his natural affection as incompatible with sound faith.

The mixed lot of settlers around us offered a favorable field for observation of the different kinds of people of our own race. We were swift to note the way they behaved, the differences in their religion and morals, and in their ways of drawing a living from the same kind of soil under the same general conditions; how they protected themselves from the weather; how they were influenced by new doctrines and old ones seen in new lights in preaching, lecturing, debating, bringing up their children, etc., and how they regarded the Indians, those first settlers and owners of the ground that was being made into farms.

I well remember my father's discussing with a Scotch neighbour, a Mr George Mair, the Indian question as to the rightful ownership of the soil. Mr Mair remarked one day that it was pitiful to see how the unfortunate Indians, children of Nature, living on the natural products of the soil, hunting, fishing, and even cultivating small corn-fields on the most fertile spots, were now being robbed of their lands and pushed ruthlessly back into narrower and narrower limits by alien races who were cutting off their means of livelihood. Father replied that surely it could never have been the intention of God to allow Indians to rove and hunt over so fertile a country and hold it forever in unproductive wildness, while Scotch and Irish and English farmers could put it to so much better use. Where an Indian required thousands of acres for his family, these acres in the hands of industrious, God-fearing farmers would support ten or a hundred times more people in a far worthier manner, while at the same time helping to spread the gospel.

Mr Mair urged that such farming as our first immigrants were practising was in many ways rude and full of the mistakes of ignorance, yet, rude as it was, and ill-tilled as were most of our Wisconsin farms by unskillful, inexperienced settlers who had been merchants and mechanics and servants in the old countries, how should we like to have specially trained and educated farmers drive us out of our homes and farms, such as they were, making use of the same argument, that God could never have intended such ignorant, unprofitable, devastating farmers as we were to occupy land upon which scientific farmers could raise five or ten times as much on each acre as we did? And I well remember thinking that Mr Mair had the better side of the argument. It then seemed to me that, whatever the final outcome might be, it was at this stage of the fight only an example of the rule of might with but little or no thought for the right or welfare of the other fellow if he were the weaker; that 'they should take who had the power, and they should keep who can', as Wordsworth makes the marauding Scottish Highlanders say.

Many of our old neighbours toiled and sweated and grubbed themselves into their graves years before their natural dying days, in getting a living on a quarter-section of land and vaguely trying to get rich, while bread and raiment might have been serenely won on less than a fourth of this land, and time gained to get better acquainted with God.

I was put to the plough at the age of twelve, when my head reached but little above the handles, and for many years I had to do the greater part of the ploughing. It was hard work for so small a boy; nevertheless, as good ploughing was exacted from me as if I were a man, and very soon I had become a good ploughman, or rather ploughboy. None could draw a straighter furrow. For the first few years the work was particularly hard on account of the tree-stumps that had to be dodged. Later the stumps were all dug and chopped out to make way for the McCormick reaper, and because I proved to be the best chopper and stump-digger I had nearly all of it to myself. It was dull, hard work leaning over on my knees all day, chopping out those tough oak and hickory stumps, deep down below the crowns of the big roots. Some, though fortunately not many, were two feet or more in diameter.

And as I was the eldest boy, the greater part of all the other hard work of the farm quite naturally fell on me. I had to split rails for long lines of zigzag fences. The trees that were tall enough and straight enough to afford one or two logs ten feet long were used for rails, the others, too knotty or cross-grained, were disposed of in log and cord-wood fences. Making rails was hard work and required no little skill. I used to cut and split a hundred a day from our short, knotty oak timber, swinging the axe and heavy mallet, often with sore hands, from early morning to night. Father was not successful as a rail-splitter. After trying the work with me a day or two, he in despair left it all to me. I rather liked it, for I was proud of my skill, and tried to believe that I was as tough as the timber I mauled, though this and other heavy jobs stopped my growth and earned for me the title 'Runt of the family'.

In those early days, long before the great labor-saving machines came to our help, almost everything connected with wheat-raising abounded in trying work – cradling in the long, sweaty dog-days, raking and binding, stacking, thrashing – and it often seemed to me that our fierce, overindustrious way of getting the grain from the ground was too closely connected with grave-digging. The staff of life, naturally beautiful, oftentimes suggested the grave-digger's spade. Men and boys, and in those days even women and girls, were cut down while cutting the wheat. The fat folk grew lean and the lean leaner, while the rosy cheeks brought from Scotland and other cool countries across the sea faded to yellow like the wheat. We were all made slaves through the vice of over-industry. The same was in great part true in making hay to keep the cattle and horses through the long winters. We were called in the morning at four o'clock and seldom got to bed before nine, making a broiling, seething day seventeen hours long loaded with heavy work, while I was only a small stunted boy; and a few years later my brothers David and Daniel and my older sisters had to endure about as much as I did. In the harvest dog-days and dog-nights and dog-mornings, when we arose from our clammy beds, our cotton shirts clung to our backs as wet with sweat as the bathing-suits of swimmers, and remained so all the long, sweltering days. In mowing and cradling, the most exhausting of all the farm work, I made matters worse by foolish ambition in keeping ahead of the hired men. Never a warning word was spoken of the dangers of overwork. On the contrary, even when sick we were held to our tasks as long as we could stand. Once in harvest-time I had the mumps and was unable to swallow any food except milk, but this was not allowed to make any difference, while I staggered with weakness and sometimes fell headlong among the sheaves. Only once was I allowed to leave the harvest-field – when I was stricken down with pneumonia. I lay gasping for weeks, but the Scotch are hard to kill and I pulled through. No physician was called, for father was an enthusiast, and always said and believed that God and hard work were by far the best doctors.

None of our neighbours were so excessively industrious as father; though nearly all of the Scotch, English, and Irish worked too hard, trying to make good homes and to lay up money enough for comfortable independence. Excepting small garden-patches, few of them had owned land in the old country. Here their craving land-hunger was satisfied, and they were naturally proud of their farms and tried to keep them as neat and clean and well-tilled as gardens. To accomplish this without the means for hiring help was impossible. Flowers were planted about the neatly kept log or frame houses; barnyards, granaries, etc., were kept in about as neat order as the homes, and the fences and corn-rows were rigidly straight. But every uncut weed distressed them; so also did every ungathered ear of grain, and all that was lost by birds and gophers; and this overcarefulness bred endless work and worry.

As for money, for many a year there was precious little of it in the country for anybody. Eggs sold at six cents a dozen in trade, and five-cent calico was exchanged at twenty-five cents a yard. Wheat brought fifty cents a bushel in trade. To get cash for it before the Portage Railway was built, it had to be hauled to Milwaukee, a hundred miles away. On the other hand, food was abundant – eggs, chickens, pigs, cattle, wheat, corn, potatoes, garden vegetables of the best, and wonderful melons as luxuries. No other wild country I have ever known extended a kinder welcome to poor immigrants. On the arrival in the spring, a log house could be built, a few acres ploughed, the virgin sod planted with corn, potatoes, etc., and enough raised to keep a family comfortably the very first year; and wild hay for cows and oxen grew in abundance on the numerous meadows. The American settlers were wisely content with smaller fields and less of everything, kept indoors during excessively hot or cold weather, rested when tired, went off fishing and hunting at the most favorable times and seasons of the day and year, gathered nuts and berries, and in general tranquilly accepted all the good things the fertile wilderness offered.

After eight years of this dreary work of clearing the Fountain Lake farm, fencing it and getting it in perfect order, building a frame house and the necessary out-buildings for the cattle and horses – after all this had been victoriously accomplished, and we had made out to escape with life – father bought a half-section of wild land about four or five miles to the eastward and began all over again to clear and fence and break up other fields for a new farm, doubling all the stunting, heartbreaking chopping, grubbing, stump-digging, rail-splitting, fence-building, barn-building, house-building, and so forth.

By this time I had learned to run the breaking plough. Most of these ploughs were very large, turning furrows from eighteen inches to two feet wide, and were drawn by four or five yoke of oxen. They were used only for the first ploughing, in breaking up the wild sod woven into a tough mass, chiefly by the cordlike roots of perennial grasses, reinforced by the tap-roots of oak and hickory bushes, called 'grubs', some of which were more than a century old and four or five inches in diameter. In the hardest ploughing on the most difficult ground, the grubs were said to be as thick as the hair on a dog's back. If in good trim, the plough cut through and turned over these grubs as if the century-old wood were soft like the flesh of carrots and turnips; but if not in good trim the grubs promptly tossed the plough out of the ground. A stout Highland Scot, our neighbour, whose plough was in bad order and who did not know how to trim it, was vainly trying to keep it in the ground by main strength, while his son, who was driving and merrily whipping up the cattle, would cry encouragingly, 'Haud her in, fayther! Haud her in!'

'But hoo i' the deil can I haud her in when she'll no *stop* in?' his perspiring father would reply, gasping for breath between each word. On the contrary, with the share and coulter sharp and nicely adjusted, the plough, instead of shying at every grub and jumping out, ran straight ahead without need of steering or holding, and gripped the ground so firmly that it could hardly be thrown out at the end of the furrow.

Our breaker turned a furrow two feet wide, and on our best land, where the sod was toughest, held so firm a grip that at the end of the field my brother, who was driving the oxen, had to come to my assistance in throwing it over on its side to be drawn around the end of the landing; and it was all I could do to set it up again. But I learned to keep that plough in such trim that after I got started on a new furrow I used to ride on the crossbar between the handles with my feet resting comfortably on the beam, without having to steady or steer it in any way on the whole length of the field, unless we had to go round a stump, for it sawed through the biggest grubs without flinching.

The growth of these grubs was interesting to me. When an acorn of hickory-nut had sent up its first season's sprout, a few inches long, it was burned off in the autumn grass fires; but the root continued to hold on to life, formed a callus over the wound and sent up one or more shoots the next spring. Next autumn these new shoots were burned off, but the root and calloused head, about level with the surface of the ground, continued to grow and send up more new shoots; and so on, almost every year until very old, probably far more than a century, while the tops, which would naturally have become tall broad-headed trees, were only mere sprouts seldom more than two years old. Thus the ground was kept open like a prairie, with only five or six trees to the acre, which had escaped the fire by having the good fortune to grow on a bare spot at the door of a fox or badger den, or between straggling grass-tufts wide apart on the poorest sandy soil.

The uniformly rich soil of the Illinois and Wisconsin prairies produced so close and tall a growth of grasses for fires that no tree could live on it. Had there been no fires, these fine prairies, so marked a feature of the country, would have been covered by the heaviest forests. As soon as the oak openings in our neighbourhood were settled, and the farmers had prevented running grass-fires, the grubs grew up into trees and formed tall thickets so dense that it was difficult to walk through them and every trace of the sunny 'openings' vanished.

We called our second farm Hickory Hill, from its many fine hickory trees and the long gentle slope leading up to it. Compared with Fountain Lake farm it lay high and dry. The land was better, but it had no living water, no spring or stream or meadow or lake. A well ninety feet deep had to be dug, all except the first ten feet or so in fine-grained sandstone. When the sandstone was struck, my father, on the advice of a man who had worked in mines, tried to blast the rock; but from lack of skill the blasting went on very slowly, and father decided to have me do all the work with mason's chisels, a long, hard job, with a good deal of danger in it. I had to sit cramped in a space about three feet in diameter, and wearily chip, chip, with heavy hammer and chisels from early morning until dark, day after day, for weeks and months. In the morning, father and David lowered me in a wooden bucket by a windlass, hauled up what chips were left from the night before, then went away to the farm work and left me until noon, when they hoisted me out for dinner. After dinner I was promptly lowered again, the forenoon's accumulation of chips hoisted out of the way, and I was left until night.

One morning, after the dreary bore was about eighty feet deep, my life was all but lost in deadly choke-damp – carbonic acid gas that had settled at the bottom during the night. Instead of clearing away the chips as usual when I was lowered to the bottom, I swayed back and forth and began to sink under the poison. Father, alarmed that I did not make any noise, shouted, 'What's keeping you so still?' to which he got no reply. Just as I was settling down against the side of the wall, I happened to catch a glimpse of a branch of a bur-oak tree which leaned out over the mouth of the shaft. This suddenly awakened me, and to father's excited shouting I feebly murmured, 'Take me out.' But when he began to hoist he found I was not in the bucket and in wild alarm shouted, 'Get in! Get in the bucket and hold on! Hold on!' Somehow I managed to get into the bucket, and that is all I remembered until I was dragged out, violently gasping for breath.

One of our near neighbours, a stone mason and miner by the name of William Duncan, came to see me, and after hearing the particulars of the accident he solemnly said, 'Weel, Johnnie, it's God's mercy that you're alive. Many a companion of mine have I seen dead with choke-damp, but none that I ever saw or heard of was so near to death in it as you were and escaped without help.' Mr Duncan taught father to throw water down the shaft to absorb the gas, and also to drop a bundle of brush or hay attached to a light rope, dropping it again and again to carry down pure air and stir up the poison. When, after a day or two, I had recovered from the shock, father lowered me again to my work, after taking the precaution to test the air with a candle and stir it up well with a brush-and-hay bundle. The weary hammer-and-chisel-chipping went on as before, only more slowly, until ninety feet down, when at last I struck a fine, hearty gush of water. Constant dropping wears away stone. So does constant chipping, while at the same time wearing away the chipper. Father never spent an hour in that well. He trusted me to sink it straight and plumb, and I did, and built a fine covered top over it, and swung two iron-bound buckets in it from which we all drank for many a day.

The honey-bee arrived in America long before we boys did, but several years passed ere we noticed any on our farm. The introduction of the honey-bee into flowery America formed a grand epoch in bee history. This sweet humming creature, companion and friend of the flowers, is now distributed over the greater part of the continent, filling countless hollows in rocks and trees with honey as well as the millions of hives prepared for them by honey-farmers, who keep and tend their flocks of sweet winged cattle, as shepherds keep sheep – a charming employment, 'like directing sunbeams', as Thoreau says. The Indians call the honey-bee the white man's fly; and though they had long been acquainted with several species of bumblebees that yielded more or less honey, how gladly surprised they must have been when they discovered that, in the hollow trees where before they had found only coons or squirrels, they found swarms of brown flies with fifty or even a hundred pounds of honey sealed up in beautiful cells. With their keen hunting senses they of course were not slow to learn the habits of the little brown immigrants and the best methods of tracing them to their sweet homes, however well hidden. During the first few years none were seen on our farm, though we sometimes heard father's hired men talking about 'lining bees'. None of us boys ever found a bee tree, or tried to find any until about ten years after our arrival in the woods. On the Hickory Hill farm there is a ridge of moraine material, rather dry, but flowery with goldenrods and asters of many species, upon which we saw bees feeding in the late autumn just when their hives were fullest of honey, and it occurred to me one day after I was of age and my own master that I must try to find a bee tree. I made a little box about six inches long and four inches deep and wide; bought half a pound of honey, went to the goldenrod hill, swept a bee into the box and closed it. The lid had a pane of glass in it so I could see when the bee had sucked its fill and was ready to go home. At first it groped around trying to get out, but, smelling the honey, it seemed to forget everything else, and while it was feasting I carried the box and a small sharp-pointed stake to an open spot, where I could see about me, fixed the stake in the ground, and placed the box on the flat top of it. When I thought that the little feaster must be about full, I opened the box, but it was in no hurry to fly. It slowly crawled up to the edge of the box, lingered a minute or two cleaning its legs that had become sticky with honey, and when it took wing, instead of making what is called a bee-line for home, it buzzed around the box and minutely examined it as if trying to fix a clear picture of it in its mind so as to be able to recognize it when it returned for another load, then circled around at a little distance as if looking for something to locate it by. I was the nearest object, and the thoughtful worker buzzed in front of my face and took a good stare at me, and then flew up on to the top of an oak on the side of the open spot in the centre of which the honey-box was. Keeping a keen watch, after a minute or two of rest or wing-cleaning, I saw it fly in wide circles round the tops of the trees nearest the honey-box, and, after apparently satisfying itself, make a bee-line for the hive. Looking endwise on the line of flight, I saw that what is called a bee-line is not an absolutely straight line, but a line in general straight made of many slight, wavering, lateral curves. After taking as true a bearing as I could, I waited and watched. In a few minutes, probably ten, I was surprised to see that bee arrive at the end of the outleaning limb of the oak mentioned above, as though that was the first point it had fixed in its memory to be depended on in retracing the way back to the honey-box. From the tree-top it came straight to my head, thence straight to the box, entered without the least hesitation, filled up and started off after the same preparatory dressing and taking of bearings as before. Then I took particular pains to lay down the exact course so I would be able to trace it to the hive. Before doing so, however, I made an experiment to test the worth of the impression I had that the little insect found the way back to the box by fixing telling points in its mind. While it was away, I picked up the honey-box and set it on the stake a few rods from the position it had thus far occupied, and stood there watching. In a few minutes I saw the bee arrive at its guide-mark, the overleaning branch on the tree-top, and thence came bouncing down right to the spaces in the air which had been occupied by my head and the honey-box, and when the cunning little honey-gleaner found nothing there but empty air it whirled round and round as if confused and lost; and although I was standing with the open honey-box within fifty or sixty feet of the former feasting-spot, it could not, or at least did not, find it.

Now that I had learned the general direction of the hive, I pushed on in search of it. I had gone perhaps a quarter of a mile when I caught another bee, which, after getting loaded, went through the same performance of circling round and round the honey-box, buzzing in front of me and staring me in the face to be able to recognize me; but as if the adjacent trees and bushes were sufficiently well known, it simply looked around at them and bolted off without much dressing, indicating, I thought, that the distance to the hive was not great. I followed on and very soon discovered it in the bottom log of a corn-field fence, but some lucky fellow had discovered it before me and robbed it. The robbers had chopped a large hole in the log, taken out most of the honey, and left the poor bees late in the fall, when winter was approaching, to make haste to gather all the honey they could from the latest flowers to avoid starvation in the winter.

SEVEN

Knowledge and Inventions

I learned arithmetic in Scotland without understanding any of it, though I had the rules by heart. But when I was about fifteen or sixteen years of age, I began to grow hungry for real knowledge, and persuaded father, who was willing enough to have me study provided my farm work was kept up, to buy me a higher arithmetic. Beginning at the beginning, in one summer I easily finished it without assistance, in the short intervals between the end of dinner and the afternoon start for the harvest- and hay-fields, accomplishing more without a teacher in a few scraps of time than in years in school before my mind was ready for such work. Then in succession I took up algebra, geometry, and trigonometry and made some little progress in each, and reviewed grammar. I was fond of reading, but father had brought only a few religious books from Scotland. Fortunately, several of our neighbours had brought a dozen or two of all sorts of books, which I borrowed and read, keeping all of them except the religious ones carefully hidden from father's eye. Among these were Scott's novels, which, like all other novels, were strictly forbidden, but devoured with glorious pleasure in secret. Father was easily persuaded to buy Josephus's *War of the Jews*, and D'Aubigné's *History of the Reformation*, and I tried hard to get him to buy Plutarch's *Lives*, which, as I told him, everybody, even religious people, praised as a grand good book; but he would have nothing to do with the old pagan until the graham bread and anti-flesh doctrines came suddenly into our backwoods neighbourhood, making a stir something like phrenology and spirit-rappings, which were as mysterious in their attacks as influenza. He then thought it possible that Plutarch might be turned to account on the food question by revealing what those old Greeks and Romans ate to make them strong; and so at last we gained our glorious Plutarch. Dick's *Christian Philosopher*, which I borrowed from a neighbour, I thought I might venture to read in the open, trusting that the word 'Christian' would be proof against its cautious condemnation. But father balked at the word 'Philosopher', and quoted from the Bible a verse which spoke of 'Philosophy falsely so-called'. I then ventured to speak in defense of the book, arguing that we could not do without at least a little of the most useful kinds of philosophy.

'Yes, we can,' he said with enthusiasm, 'The Bible is the only book human beings can possibly require throughout all the journey from earth to heaven.'

'But how,' I contended, 'can we find the way to heaven without the Bible, and how after we grow old can we read the Bible without a little helpful science? Just think, father, you cannot read your Bible without spectacles, and millions of others are in the same fix; and spectacles cannot be made without some knowledge of the science of optics.'

'Oh!' he replied, perceiving the drift of the argument, 'there will always be plenty of wordly people to make spectacles.'

To this I stubbornly replied with a quotation from the Bible with reference to the time coming when 'all shall know the Lord from the least even to the greatest', and then who will make the spectacles? But he still objected to my reading that book, called me a contumacious quibbler too fond of disputation, and ordered me to return it to the accommodating owner. I managed, however, to read it later.

On the food question father insisted that those who argued for a vegetable diet were in the right, because our teeth showed plainly that they were made with reference to fruit and grain and not for flesh like those of dogs and wolves and tigers. He therefore promptly adopted a vegetable diet and requested mother to make the bread from graham flour instead of bolted flour. Mother put both kinds on the table, and meat also, to let all the family take their choice, and while father was insisting on the foolishness of eating flesh, I came to her help by calling father's attention to the passage in the Bible which told the story of Elijah the prophet who, when he was pursued by enemies who wanted to take his life, was hidden by the Lord by the brook Cherith, and fed by ravens; and surely the Lord knew what was good to eat, whether bread or meat. And on what, I asked, did the Lord feed Elijah? On vegetables or graham bread? No, he directed the ravens to feed his prophet on flesh. The Bible being the sole rule, father at once acknowledged that he was mistaken. The Lord would never have sent flesh to Elijah by the ravens if graham bread were better.

I remember as a great and sudden discovery that the poetry of the Bible, Shakespeare, and Milton was a source of inspiring, exhilarating, uplifting pleasure; and I became anxious to know all the poets, and saved up small sums to buy as many of their books as possible. Within three or four years I was the proud possessor of parts of Shakespeare's, Milton's, Cowper's, Henry Kirke White's, Campbell's, and Akenside's works, and quite a number of others seldom read nowadays. I think it was in my fifteenth year that I began to relish good literature with enthusiasm, and smack my lips over favourite lines, but there was desperately little time for reading, even in the winter evenings – only a few stolen minutes now and then. Father's strict rule was, straight to bed immediately after family worship, which in winter was usually over by eight o'clock. I was in the habit of lingering in the kitchen with a book and candle after the rest of the family had retired, and considered myself fortunate if I got five minutes' reading before father noticed the light and ordered me to bed; an order that of course I immediately obeyed. But night after night I tried to steal minutes in the same lingering way, and how keenly precious those minutes were, few nowadays can know. Father failed perhaps two or three times in a whole winter to notice my light for nearly ten minutes, magnificent golden blocks of time, long to be remembered like holidays or geological periods. One evening when I was reading Church history father was particularly irritable, and called out with hope-killing emphasis, '*John, go to bed*! Must I give you a separate order every night to get you to go to bed? Now, I will have no irregularity in the family; you *must* go when the rest go, and without my having to tell you.' Then, as an afterthought, as if judging that his words and tone of voice were too severe for so pardonable an offense as reading a religious book he unwarily added, 'If you *will* read, get up in the morning and read. You may get up in the morning as early as you like.'

That night I went to bed wishing with all my heart and soul that somebody or something might call me out of sleep to avail myself of this wonderful indulgence; and next morning to my joyful surprise I awoke before father called me. A boy sleeps soundly after working all day in the snowy woods, but that frosty morning I sprang out of bed as if called by a trumpet blast, rushed downstairs, scarce feeling my chilblains, enormously eager to see how much time I had won; and when I held up my candle to a little clock that stood on a bracket in the kitchen I found that it was only one o'clock. I had gained five hours, almost half a day! 'Five hours to myself!' I said, 'five huge, solid hours!' I can hardly think of any other event in my life, any discovery I ever made that gave birth to joy so transportingly glorious as the possession of these five frosty hours.

In the glad, tumultuous excitement of so much suddenly acquired time-wealth, I hardly knew what to do with it. I first thought of going on with my reading, but the zero weather would make a fire necessary, and it occurred to me that father might object to the cost of fire-wood that took time to chop. Therefore, I prudently decided to go down to the cellar, and begin work on a model of a self-setting sawmill I had invented. Next morning I managed to get up at the same gloriously early hour, and though the temperature of the cellar was a little below the freezing point, and my light was only a tallow candle the mill work went joyfully on. There were a few tools in a corner of the cellar – a vise, files, a hammer, chisels, etc., that father had brought from Scotland, but no saw excepting a coarse crooked one that was unfit for sawing dry hickory or oak. So I made a fine-tooth saw suitable for my work out of a strip of steel that had formed part of an old-fashioned corset, that cut the hardest wood smoothly. I also made my own bradawls, punches, and a pair of compasses, out of wire and old files.

My workshop was immediately under father's bed, and the filing and tapping in making cogwheels, journals, cams, etc., must, no doubt, have annoyed him, but with the permission he had granted in his mind, and doubtless hoping that I would soon tire of getting up at one o'clock, he impatiently waited about two weeks before saying a word. I did not vary more than five minutes from one o'clock all winter, nor did I feel any bad effects whatever, nor did I think at all about the subject as to whether so little sleep might be in any way injurious; it was a grand triumph of will-power over cold and common comfort and work-weariness in abruptly cutting down my ten hours' allowance of sleep to five. I simply felt that I was rich beyond anything I could have dreamed of or hoped for. I was far more than happy. Like Tam o'Shanter I was glorious, 'O'er a' the ills o' life victorious'.

Father, as was customary in Scotland, gave thanks and asked a blessing before meals, not merely as a matter of form and decent Christian manners, for he regarded food as a gift derived directly from the hands of the Father in heaven. Therefore every meal to him was a sacrament requiring conduct and attitude of mind not unlike that befitting the Lord's Supper. No idle word was allowed to be spoken at our table, much less any laughing or fun or story-telling. When we were at the breakfast-table, about two weeks after the great golden time-discovery, father cleared his throat preliminary, as we all knew, to saying something considered important. I feared that it was to be on the subject of my early rising, and dreaded the withdrawal of the permission he had granted on account of the noise I made, but still hoping that, as he had given his word that I might get up as early as I wished, he would as a Scotchman stand to it, even though it was given in an unguarded moment and taken in a sense unreasonably far-reaching. The solemn sacramental silence was broken by the dreaded question:

'John, what time is it when you get up in the morning?'

'About one o'clock,' I replied in a low, meek, guilty tone of voice.

'And what kind of a time is that, getting up in the middle of the night and disturbing the whole family?'

I simply reminded him of the permission he had freely granted me to get up as early as I wished.

'I *know* it,' he said, in an almost agonized tone of voice, 'I *know* I gave you that miserable permission, but I never imagined that you would get up in the middle of the night.'

To this I cautiously made no reply, but continued to listen for the heavenly one-o'clock call, and it never failed.

After completing my self-setting sawmill I dammed one of the streams in the meadow and put the mill in operation. This invention was speedily followed by a lot of others – water-wheels, curious doorlocks and latches, themometers, hygrometers, pyrometers, clocks, a barometer, an automatic contrivance for feeding the horses at any required hour, a lamp-lighter and fire-lighter, an early-or-late-rising machine, and so forth.

After the sawmill was proved and discharged from my mind, I happened to think it would be a fine thing to make a timekeeper which would tell the day of the week and the day of the month, as well as strike like a common clock and point out the hours; also to have an attachment whereby it could be connected with a bedstead to set me on my feet at any hour in the morning; also to start fires, light lamps, etc. I had learned the time laws of the pendulum from a book, but with this exception I knew nothing of timekeepers, for I had never seen the inside of any sort of clock or watch. After long brooding, the novel clock was at length completed in my mind, and was tried and found to be durable and to work well and look well before I had begun to build it in wood. I carried small parts of it in my pocket to whittle at when I was out at work on the farm, using every spare or stolen moment within reach without father's knowing anything about it. In the middle of summer, when harvesting was in progress, the novel time-machine was nearly completed. It was hidden upstairs in a spare bedroom where some tools were kept. I did the making and mending on the farm, but one day at noon, when I happened to be away, father went upstairs for a hammer or something and discovered the mysterious machine back of the bedstead. My sister Margaret saw him on his knees examining it, and at the first opportunity whispered in my ear, 'John, fayther saw that thing you're making upstairs.' None of the family knew what I was doing but they knew very well that all such work was frowned on by father, and kindly warned me of any danger that threatened my plans. The fine invention seemed doomed to destruction before its time-ticking commenced, though I thought it handsome, had so long carried it in my mind, and like the nest of Burns's wee mousie it had cost me mony a weary whittling nibble. When we were at dinner several days after the sad discovery, father began to clear his throat to speak, and I feared the doom of martyrdom was about to be pronounced on my grand clock.

'John,' he inquired, 'what is that thing you are making upstairs?'

I replied in desperation that I didn't know what to call it.

'What! You mean to say you don't know what you are trying to do?'

'Oh, yes,' I said, 'I know very well what I am doing.'

'What, then, is the thing for?'

'It's for a lot of things,' I replied, 'but getting people up early in the morning is one of the main things it is intended for; therefore it might perhaps be called an early-rising machine.'

After getting up so extravagantly early all the last memorable winter, to make a machine for getting up perhaps still earlier seemed so ridiculous that he very nearly laughed. But after controlling himself and getting command of a sufficiently solemn face and voice he said severely, 'Do you not think it is very wrong to waste your time on such nonsense?'

'No,' I said meekly, 'I don't thing I'm doing any wrong.'

'Well,' he replied, 'I assure you I do; and if you were only half as zealous in the study of religion as you are in contriving and whittling these useless, nonsensical things, it would be infinitely better for you. I want you to be like Paul, who said that he desired to know nothing among men but Christ and Him crucified.'

To this I made no reply, gloomily believing my fine machine was to be burned, but still taking what comfort I could in realizing that anyhow I had enjoyed inventing and making it.

After a few days, finding that nothing more was to be said, and that father after all had not had the heart to destroy it, all necessity for secrecy being ended, I finished it in the half-hours that we had at noon and set it in the parlor between two chairs, hung moraine boulders that had come from the direction of Lake Superior on it for weights, and set it running. We were then hauling grain into the barn. Father at this period devoted himself entirely to the Bible and did no farm work whatever. The clock had a good loud tick, and when he heard it strike, one of my sisters told me that he left his study, went to the parlor, got down on his knees and carefully examined the machinery, which was all in plain sight, not being enclosed in a case. This he did repeatedly, and evidently seemed a little proud of my ability to invent and whittle such a thing, though careful to give no encouragement for anything more of the kind in future.

But somehow it seemed impossible to stop. Inventing and whittling faster than ever, I made another hickory clock, shaped like a scythe to symbolize the scythe of Father Time. The pendulum is a bunch of arrows symbolizing the flight of time. It hangs on a leafless mossy oak snag showing the effect of time, and on the snath is written, 'All flesh is grass.' This, especially the inscription, rather pleased father, and, of course, mother and all my sisters and brothers admired it. Like the first it indicates the days of the week and month, starts fires and beds at any given hour and minute, and, though made more than fifty years ago, is still a good timekeeper.

My mind still running on clocks, I invented a big one like a town clock with four dials, with the time-figures so large they could be read by all our immediate neighbours as well as ourselves when at work in the fields, and on the side next the house the days of the week and month were indicated. It was to be placed on the peak of the barn roof. But just as it was all but finished, father stopped me, saying that it would bring too many people around the barn. I then asked permission to put it on the top of a black-oak tree near the house. Studying the larger main branches, I thought I could secure a sufficiently rigid foundation for it, while the trimmed sprays and leaves would conceal the angles of the cabin required to shelter the works from the weather, and the two-second pendulum, fourteen feet long, could be snugly encased on the side of the trunk. Nothing about the grand, useful timekeeper, I argued, would disfigure the tree, for it would look something like a big hawk's nest. 'But that,' he objected, 'would draw still bigger bothersome trampling crowds about the place, for who ever heard of anything so queer as a big clock on the top of a tree?' So I had to lay aside its big wheels and cams and rest content with the pleasure of inventing it, and looking at it in my mind and listening to the deep solemn throbbing of its long two-second pendulum with its two old axes back to back for the bob.

One of my inventions was a large thermometer made of an iron rod, about three feet long and five eighths of an inch in diameter, that had formed part of a wagon-box. The expansion and contraction of this rod was multiplied by a series of levers made of strips of hoop iron. The pressure of the rod against the levers was kept constant by a small counterweight, so that the slightest change in the length of the rod was instantly shown on a dial about three feet wide multiplied about thirty-two thousand times. The zero-point was gained by packing the rod in wet snow. The scale was so large that the big black hand on the white-painted dial could be seen distinctly and the temperature read while we were ploughing in the field below the house. The extremes of heat and cold caused the hand to make several revolutions. The number of these revolutions was indicated on a small dial marked on the larger one. This thermometer was fastened on the side of the house, and was so sensitive that when anyone approached it within four or five feet the heat radiated from the observer's body caused the hand of the dial to move so fast that the motion was plainly visible, and when he stepped back, the hand moved slowly back to its normal position. It was regarded as a great wonder by the neighbours and even by my own all-Bible father.

Boys are fond of the books of travelers, and I remember that one day, after I had been reading Mungo Park's travels in Africa, mother said, 'Weel, John, maybe you will travel like Park and Humboldt some day.' Father overheard her and cried out in solemn deprecation, 'Oh, Anne! dinna put sic notions in the laddie's heed.' But at this time there was precious little need of such prayers. My brothers left the farm when they came of age, but I stayed a year longer, loath to leave home. Mother hoped I might be a minister some day; my sisters that I would be a great inventor. I often thought I should like to be a physician, but I saw no way of making money and getting the necessary education, excepting as an inventor. So, as a beginning, I decided to try to get into a big shop or factory and live a while among machines. But I was naturally extremely shy and had been taught to have a poor opinion of myself, as of no account, though all our neighbours encouragingly called me a genius, sure to rise in the world. When I was talking over plans one day with a friendly neighbour, he said, 'Now, John, if you wish to get into a machine-shop, just take some of your inventions to the State Fair, and you may be sure that as soon as they are seen they will open the door of any shop in the country for you. You will be welcomed everywhere.' And when I doubtingly asked if people would care to look at things made of wood, he said, 'Made of wood! Made of wood! What does it matter what they're made of when they are so out-and-out original. There's nothing else like them in the world. That is what will attract attention, and besides they're mighty handsome things anyway to come from the backwoods.' So I was encouraged to leave home and go at his direction to the State Fair when it was being held in Madison.

EIGHT

The World and the University

When I told father that I was about to leave home, and inquired whether, if I should happen to be in need of money, he would send me a little, he said, 'No; depend entirely on yourself.' Good advice, I suppose, but surely needlessly severe for a bashful, home-loving boy who had worked so hard. I had the gold sovereign that my grandfather had given me when I left Scotland, and a few dollars, perhaps ten, that I had made by raising a few bushels of grain on a little patch of sandy abandoned ground. So when I left home to try the world I had only about fifteen dollars in my pocket.

Strange to say, father carefully taught us to consider ourselves very poor worms of the dust, conceived in sin, etc., and devoutly believed that quenching every spark of pride and self-confidence was a sacred duty, without realizing that in so doing he might at the same time be quenching everything else. Praise he considered most venomous, and tried to assure me that when I was fairly out in the wicked world making my own way I would soon learn that although I might have thought him a hard taskmaster at times, strangers were far harder. On the contrary, I found no lack of kindness and sympathy. All the baggage I carried was a package made up of the two clocks and a small thermometer made of a piece of old washboard, all three tied together, with no covering or case of any sort, the whole looking like one very complicated machine.

The aching parting from mother and my sisters was, of course, hard to bear. Father let David drive me down to Pardeeville, a place I had never before seen, though it was only nine miles south of the Hickory Hill home. When we arrived at the village tavern, it seemed deserted.

Not a single person was in sight. I set my clock baggage on the rickety platform. David said good-bye and started for home, leaving me alone in the world. The grinding noise made by the wagon in turning short brought out the landlord, and the first thing that caught his eye was my strange bundle. Then he looked at me and said, 'Hello, young man, what's this?'

'Machines,' I said, 'for keeping time and getting up in the morning, and so forth.'

'Well! Well! That's a mighty queer get-up. You must be a Down-East Yankee. Where did you get the pattern for such a thing?'

'In my head,' I said.

Some one down the street happened to notice the landlord looking intently at something and came to see what it was. Three or four people in that little village formed an attractive crowd, and in fifteen or twenty minutes the greater part of the population of Pardeeville stood gazing in a circle around my strange hickory belongings. I kept outside of the circle to avoid being seen, and had the advantage of hearing the remarks without being embarrassed. Almost every one as he came up would say, 'What's that? What's it for? Who made it?' The landlord would answer them all alike, 'Why, a young man that lives out in the country somewhere made it, and he says it's a thing for keeping time, getting up in the morning, and something that I didn't understand. I don't know what he meant.' 'Oh, no!' one of the crowd would say, 'that can't be. It's for something else – something mysterious. Mark my words, you'll see all about it in the newspapers some of these days.' A curious little fellow came running up the street, joined the crowd, stood on tiptoe to get sight of the wonder, quickly made up his mind, and shouted in crisp, confident, cock-crowing style, 'I know what that contraption's for. It's a machine for taking the bones out of fish.'

This was in the time of the great popular phrenology craze, when the fences and barns along the roads through-out the country were plastered with big skull-bump post-ers, headed, 'Know Thyself', and advising everybody to attend schoolhouse lectures to have their heads explained and be told what they were good for and whom they ought to marry. My mechanical bundle seemed to bring a good deal of this phrenology to mind, for many of the onlookers would say, 'I wish I could see that boy's head – he must have a tremendous bump of invention.' Others complimented me by saying, 'I wish I had that fellow's head. I'd rather have it than the best farm in the State.'

I stayed overnight at this little tavern, waiting for a train. In the morning I went to the station, and set my bundle on the platform. Along came the thundering train, a glorious sight, the first train I had ever waited for. When the conductor saw my queer baggage, he cried, 'Hello! What have we here?'

'Inventions for keeping time, early rising, and so forth. May I take them into the car with me?'

'You can take them where you like,' he replied, 'but you had better give them to the baggage-master. If you take them into the car they will draw a crowd and might get broken.'

So I gave them to the baggage-master and made haste to ask the conductor whether I might ride on the engine. He good-naturedly said, 'Yes, it's the right place for you. Run ahead, and tell the engineer what I say.' But the engineer bluntly refused to let me on, saying, 'It don't matter what the conductor told you. *I* say you can't ride on my engine.'

By this time the conductor, standing ready to start his train, was watching to see what luck I had, and when he saw me returning came ahead to meet me.

'The engineer won't let me on,' I reported.

'Won't he?' said the kind conductor. 'Oh! I guess he will. You come down with me.' And so he actually took the time and patience to walk the length of that long train to get me on to the engine.

'Charlie,' said he, addressing the engineer, 'don't you ever take a passenger?'

'Very seldom,' he replied.

'Anyhow, I wish you would take this young man on. He has the strangest machines in the baggage-car I ever saw in my life. I believe he could make a locomotive. He wants to see the engine running. Let him on.' Then in a low whisper he told me to jump on, which I did gladly, the engineer offering neither encouragement nor objection.

As soon as the train was started, the engineer asked what the 'strange thing' the conductor spoke of really was.

'Only inventions for keeping time, getting folk up in the morning, and so forth,' I hastily replied, and before he could ask any more questions I asked permission to go outside of the cab to see the machinery. This he kindly granted, adding, 'Be careful not to fall off, and when you hear me whistling for a station you come back, because if it is reported against me to the superintendent that I allow boys to run all over my engine I might lose my job.'

Assuring him that I would come back promptly, I went out and walked along the foot-board on the side of the boiler, watching the magnificent machine rushing through the landscapes as if glorying in its strength like a living creature. While seated on the cow-catcher platform, I seemed to be fairly flying, and the wonderful display of power and motion was enchanting. This was the first time I had ever been on a train, much less a locomotive, since I had left Scotland. When I got to Madison, I thanked the kind conductor and engineer for my glorious ride, inquired the way to the Fair, shouldered my inventions, and walked to the Fair Ground.

When I applied for an admission ticket at a window by the gate I told the agent that I had something to exhibit.

'What is it?' he inquired.

'Well, here it is. Look at it.'

When he craned his neck through the window and got a glimpse of my bundle, he cried excitedly, 'Oh! *you* don't need a ticket – come right in.'

When I inquired of the agent where such things as mine should be exhibited, he said, 'You see that building up on the hill with a big flag on it? That's the Fine Arts Hall, and it's just the place for your wonderful invention.'

So I went up to the Fine Arts Hall and looked in, wondering if they would allow wooden things in so fine a place.

I was met at the door by a dignified gentleman, who

greeted me kindly and said, 'Young man, what have we got here?'

'Two clocks and a thermometer,' I replied.

'Did you make these? They look wonderfully beautiful and novel and must, I think, prove the most interesting feature of the fair.'

'Where shall I place them?' I inquired.

'Just look around, young man, and choose the place you like best, whether it is occupied or not. You can have your pick of all the building, and a carpenter to make the necessary shelving and assist you every way possible!'

So I quickly had a shelf made large enough for all of them, went out on the hill and picked up some glacial boulders of the right size for weights, and in fifteen or twenty minutes the clocks were running. They seemed to attract more attention than anything else in the hall. I got lots of praise from the crowd and the newspaper-reporters. The local press reports were copied into the Eastern papers. It was considered wonderful that a boy on a farm had been able to invent and make such things, and almost every spectator foretold good fortune. But I had been so lectured by my father above all things to avoid praise that I was afraid to read those kind newspaper notices, and never clipped out or preserved any of them, just glanced at them and turned away my eyes from beholding vanity. They gave me a prize of ten or fifteen dollars and a diploma for wonderful things not down in the list of exhibits.

Many years later, after I had written articles and books, I received a letter from the gentleman who had charge of the Fine Arts Hall. He proved to be the Professor of English Literature in the University of Wisconsin at this Fair time, and long afterward he sent me clippings of reports of his lectures. He had a lecture on me, discussing style, etc., and telling how well he remembered my arrival at the Hall in my shirt-sleeves with those mechanical wonders on my shoulder, and so forth, and so forth. These inventions, though of little importance, opened all doors for me and made marks that have lasted many years, simply, I suppose, because they were original and promising.

I was looking around in the mean time to find out where

I should go to seek my fortune. An inventor at the Fair, by the name of Wiard, was exhibiting an iceboat he had invented to run on the upper Mississippi from Prairie du Chien to St Paul during the winter months, explaining how useful it would be thus to make a highway of the river while it was closed to ordinary navigation by ice. After he saw my inventions he offered me a place in his foundry and machine-shop in Prairie du Chien and promised to assist me all he could. So I made up my mind to accept his offer and rode with him to Prairie du Chien in his iceboat, which was mounted on a flat car. I soon found, however, that he was seldom at home and that I was not likely to learn much at his small shop. I found a place where I could work for my board and devote my spare hours to mechanical drawing, geometry, and physics, making but little headway, however, although the Pelton family, for whom I worked, were very kind. I made up my mind after a few months' stay in Prairie du Chien to return to Madison, hoping that in some way I might be able to gain an education.

At Madison I raised a few dollars by making and selling a few of those bedsteads that set the sleepers on their feet in the morning – inserting in the footboard the works of an ordinary clock that could be bought for a dollar. I also made a few dollars addressing circulars in an insurance office, while at the same time I was paying my board by taking care of a pair of horses and going errands. This is of no great interest except that I was thus winning my bread while hoping that something would turn up that might enable me to make money enough to enter the State University. This was my ambition, and it never wavered no matter what I was doing. No University, it seemed to me, could be more admirably situated, and as I sauntered about it, charmed with its fine lawns and trees and beautiful lakes, and saw the students going and coming with their books, and occasionally practising with a theodolite in measuring distances, I thought that if I could only join them it would be the greatest joy of life. I was desperately hungry and thirsty for knowledge and willing to endure anything to get it.

One day I chanced to meet a student who had noticed my inventions at the Fair and now recognized me. And when I said, 'You are fortunate fellows to be allowed to study in this beautiful place. I wish I could join you.' 'Well, why don't you?' he asked. 'I haven't money enough,' I said. 'Oh, as to money,' he reassuringly explained, 'very little is required. I presume you're able to enter the Freshman class, and you can board yourself as quite a number of us do at a cost of about a dollar a week. The baker and milkman come every day. You can live on bread and milk.' Well, I thought, maybe I have money enough for at least one beginning term. Anyhow I couldn't help trying.

With fear and trembling, overladen with ignorance, I called on Professor Stirling, the Dean of the Faculty, who was then Acting President, presented my case, and told him how far I had got on with my studies at home, and that I hadn't been to school since leaving Scotland at the age of eleven years, excepting one short term of a couple of months at a district school, because I could not be spared from the farm work. After hearing my story, the kind professor welcomed me to the glorious University – next, it seemed to me, to the Kingdom of Heaven. After a few weeks in the preparatory department I entered the Freshman class. In Latin I found that one of the books in use I had already studied in Scotland. So, after an interruption of a dozen years, I began my Latin over again where I had left off; and, strange to say, most of it came back to me, especially the grammar which I had committed to memory at the Dunbar Grammar School.

During the four years that I was in the University, I earned enough in the harvest-fields during the long summer vacations to carry me through the balance of each year, working very hard, cutting with a cradle four acres of wheat a day, and helping to put it in the shock. But, having to buy books and paying, I think, thirty-two dollars a year for instruction, and occasionally buying acids and retorts, glass tubing, bell-glasses, flasks, etc., I had to cut down expenses for board now and then to half a dollar a week.

One winter I taught school ten miles south of Madison, earning much-needed money at the rate of twenty dollars a month, 'boarding round', and keeping up my University work by studying at night. As I was not then well enough off to own a watch, I used one of my hickory clocks, not only for keeping time, but for starting the school fire in the cold mornings, and regulating class-times. I carried it out on my shoulder to the old log schoolhouse, and set it to work on a little shelf nailed to one of the knotty, bulging logs. The winter was very cold, and I had to go to the schoolhouse and start the fire about eight o'clock to warm it before the arrival of the scholars. This was a rather trying job, and one that my clock might easily be made to do. Therefore, after supper one evening I told the head of the family with whom I was boarding that if he would give me a candle I would go back to the schoolhouse and make arrangements for lighting the fire at eight o'clock, without my having to be present until time to open the school at nine. He said, 'Oh! young man, you have some curious things in the school-room, but I don't think you can do that.' I said, 'Oh, yes! It's easy,' and in hardly more than an hour the simple job was completed. I had only to place a teaspoonful of powdered chlorate of potash and sugar on the stove-hearth near a few shavings and kindling, and at the required time make the clock, through a simple arrangement, touch the inflammable mixture with a drop of sulphuric acid. Every evening after school was dismissed, I shoveled out what was left of the fire into the snow, put in a little kindling, filled up the big box stove with heavy oak wood, placed the lighting arrangement on the hearth, and set the clock to drop the acid at the hour of eight; all this requiring only a few minutes.

The first morning after I had made this simple arrangement I invited the doubting farmer to watch the old squat schoolhouse from a window that overlooked it, to see if a good smoke did not rise from the stovepipe. Sure enough, on the minute, he saw a tall column curling gracefully up through the frosty air, but instead of congratulating me on my success he solemnly shook his head and said in a hollow, lugubrious voice, 'Young man, you will be setting fire to the schoolhouse.' All winter long that faithful clock fire never failed, and by the time I got to the schoolhouse the stove was usually red-hot.

At the beginning of the long summer vacations I returned to the Hickory Hill farm to earn the means in the harvest-fields to continue my University course, walking all the way to save railroad fares. And although I cradled four acres of wheat a day, I made the long, hard, sweaty day's work still longer and harder by keeping up my study of plants. At the noon hour I collected a large handful, put them in water to keep them fresh, and after supper got to work on them and sat up till after midnight, analyzing and classifying, thus leaving only four hours for sleep; and by the end of the first year, after taking up botany, I knew the principal flowering plants of the region.

I received my first lesson in botany from a student by the name of Griswold, who is now County Judge of the County of Waukesha, Wisconsin. In the University he was often laughed at on account of his anxiety to instruct others, and his frequently saying with fine emphasis, 'Imparting instruction is my greatest enjoyment.' One memorable day in June, when I was standing on the stone steps of the north dormitory, Mr Griswold joined me and at once began to teach. He reached up, plucked a flower from an overspreading branch of a locust tree, and, handing it to me, said, 'Muir, do you know what family this tree belongs to?'

'No,' I said, 'I don't know anything about botany.'

'Well, no matter,' said he, 'what is it like?'

'It's like a pea flower,' I replied.

'That's right. You're right,' he said, 'it belongs to the Pea Family.'

'But how can that be,' I objected, 'when the pea is a weak, clinging, straggling herb, and the locust a big, thorny hardwood tree?'

'Yes, that is true,' he replied, 'as to the difference in size, but it is also true that in all their essential characters they are alike, and therefore they must belong to one and the same family. Just look at the peculiar form of the locust flower; you see that the upper petal, called the banner, is broad and erect, and so is the upper petal of the pea flower;

the two lower petals, called the wings, are outspread and wingshaped; so are those of the pea; and the two petals below the wings are united on their edges, curve upward, and form what is called the keel, and so you see are the corresponding petals of the pea flower. And now look at the stamens and pistils. You see that nine of the ten stamens have their filaments united into a sheath around the pistil, but the tenth stamen has its filament free. These are very marked characters, are they not? And, strange to say, you will find them the same in the tree and in the vine. Now look at the ovules or seeds of the locust, and you will see that they are arranged in a pod or legume like those of the pea. And look at the leaves. You see the leaf of the locust is made up of several leaflets, and so also is the leaf of the pea. Now taste the locust leaf.'

I did so and found that it tasted like the leaf of the pea. Nature has used the same seasoning for both, though one is a straggling vine, the other a big tree.

'Now, surely you cannot imagine that all these similar characters are mere coincidences. Do they not rather go to show that the Creator in making the pea vine and locust tree had the same idea in mind, and that plants are not classified arbitrarily? Man has nothing to do with their classification. Nature has attended to all that, giving essential unity with boundless variety, so that the botanist has only to examine plants to learn the harmony of their relations.'

This fine lesson charmed me and sent me flying to the woods and meadows in wild enthusiasm. Like everybody else I was always fond of flowers, attracted by their external beauty and purity. Now my eyes were opened to their inner beauty, all alike revealing glorious traces of the thoughts of God, and leading on and on into the infinite cosmos. I wandered away at every opportunity, making long excursions round the lakes, gathering specimens and keeping them fresh in a bucket in my room to study at night after my regular class tasks were learned; for my eyes never closed on the plant glory I had seen.

Nevertheless, I still indulged my love of mechanical inventions. I invented a desk in which the books I had to study were arranged in order at the beginning of each term. I also made a bed which set me on my feet every morning at the hour determined on, and in dark winter mornings just as the bed set me on the floor it lighted a lamp. Then, after the minutes allowed for dressing had elapsed, a click was heard and the first book to be studied was pushed up from a rack below the top of the desk, thrown open, and allowed to remain there the number of minutes required. Then the machinery closed the book and allowed it to drop back into its stall, then moved the rack forward and threw up the next in order, and so on, all the day being divided according to the times of recitation, and time required and allotted to each study. Besides this, I thought it would be a fine thing in the summer-time when the sun rose early, to dispense with the clock-controlled bed machinery, and make use of sunbeams instead. This I did simply by taking a lens out of my small spy-glass, fixing it on a frame on the sill of my bedroom window, and pointing it to the sunrise; the sunbeams focused on a thread, burned it through, allowing the bed machinery to put me on my feet. When I wished to arise at any given time after sunrise, I had only to turn the pivoted frame that held the lens the requisite number of degrees or minutes. Thus I took Emerson's advice and hitched my dumping-wagon bed to a star.

I also invented a machine to make visible the growth of plants and the action of the sunlight, a very delicate contrivance, enclosed in glass. Besides this I invented a barometer and a lot of novel scientific apparatus. My room was regarded as a sort of show place by the professors, who oftentimes brought visitors to it on Saturdays and holidays. And when, some eighteen years after I had left the University, I was sauntering over the campus in time of vacation, and spoke to a man who seemed to be taking some charge of the grounds, he informed me that he was the janitor; and when I inquired what had become of Pat, the janitor in my time, and a favourite with the students, he replied that Pat was still alive and well, but now too old to do much work. And when I pointed to the dormitory room that I long ago occupied, he said, 'Oh! then I know who you are,' and mentioned my name. 'How comes it that you know my name?' I inquired. He explained that 'Pat always pointed out that room to newcomers and told long stories about the wonders that used to be in it.' So long had the memory of my little inventions survived.

Although I was four years at the University, I did not take the regular course of studies, but instead picked out what I thought would be most useful to me, particularly chemistry, which opened a new world, and mathematics and physics, a little Greek and Latin, botany and geology. I was far from satisfied with what I had learned, and should have stayed longer. Anyhow I wandered away on a glorious botanical and geological excursion, which has lasted nearly fifty years and is not yet completed, always happy and free, poor and rich, without thought of a diploma or of making a name, urged on and on through endless, inspiring, Godful beauty.

From the top of a hill on the north side of Lake Mendota I gained a last wistful, lingering view of the beautiful University grounds and buildings where I had spent so many hungry and happy and hopeful days. There with streaming eyes I bade my blessed Alma Mater farewell. But I was only leaving one University for another, the Wisconsin University for the University of the Wilderness.

A Thousand Mile Walk
to the Gulf

Contents

ONE

Kentucky Forests and Caves

I had long been looking from the wild woods and gardens of the Northern States to those of the warm South, and at last, all drawbacks overcome, I set forth (from Indianapolis) on the first day of September, 1867, joyful and free, on a thousand-mile walk to the Gulf of Mexico. (The trip to Jeffersonville, on the banks of the Ohio, was made by rail.) Crossing the Ohio at Louisville (2 September), I steered through the big city by compass without speaking a word to any one. Beyond the city I found a road running southward, and after passing a scatterment of suburban cabins and cottages I reached the green woods and spread out my pocket map to rough-hew a plan for my journey.

My plan was simply to push on in a general southward direction by the wildest, leafiest, and least trodden way I could find, promising the greatest extent of virgin forest. Folding my map, I shouldered my little bag and plant press and strode away among the old Kentucky oaks, rejoicing in splendid visions of pines and palms and tropic flowers in glorious array, not, however, without a few cold shadows of loneliness, although the great oaks seemed to spread their arms in welcome.

I have seen oaks of many species in many kinds of exposure and soil, but those of Kentucky excel in grandeur all I had ever before beheld. They are broad and dense and bright green. In the leafy bowers and caves of their long branches dwell magnificent avenues of shade, and every tree seems to be blessed with a double portion of strong exulting life. Walked twenty miles, mostly on river bottom, and found shelter in a rickety tavern.

3 September. Escaped from the dust and squalor of my garret bedroom to the glorious forest. All the streams that I tasted hereabouts are salty and so are the wells. Salt

River was nearly dry. Much of my way this forenoon was over naked limestone. After passing the level ground that extended twenty-five or thirty miles from the river I came to a region of rolling hills called Kentucky Knobs – hills of denudation, covered with trees to the top. Some of them have a few pines. For a few hours I followed the farmers' paths, but soon wandered away from roads and encountered many a tribe of twisted vines difficult to pass.

Emerging about noon from a grove of giant sunflowers, I found myself on the brink of a tumbling rocky stream (Rolling Fork). I did not expect to find bridges on my wild ways, and at once started to ford, when a negro woman on the opposite bank earnestly called on me to wait until she could tell the 'men folks' to bring me a horse – that the river was too deep and rapid to wade and that I would 'sartain be drowned' if I attempted to cross. I replied that my bag and plants would ballast me; that the water did not appear to be deep, and that if I were carried away, I was a good swimmer and would soon dry in the sunshine. But the cautious old soul replied that no one ever waded that river and set off for a horse, saying that it was no trouble at all.

In a few minutes the ferry horse came gingerly down the bank through vines and weeds. His long stilt legs proved him a natural wader. He was white and the little sable negro boy that rode him looked like a bug on his back. After many a tottering halt the outward voyage was safely made, and I mounted behind little Nig. He was a queer specimen, puffy and jet as an India rubber doll and his hair was matted in sections like the wool of a merino sheep. The old horse, overladen with his black and white burden, rocked and stumbled on his stilt legs with fair promises of a fall. But all ducking signs failed and we arrived in safety among the weeds and vines of the rugged bank. A salt bath would have done us no harm. I could swim and little Afric looked as if he might float like a bladder.

I called at the homestead where my ferryman informed me I would find 'tollable' water. But, like all the water of this section that I have tasted, it was intolerable with salt. Everything about this old Kentucky home bespoke plenty, unpolished and unmeasured. The house was built in true Southern style, airy, large, and with a transverse central hall that looks like a railway tunnel, and heavy rough outside chimneys. The negro quarters and other buildings are enough in number for a village, altogether an interesting representative of a genuine old Kentucky home, embosomed in orchards, corn fields and green wooded hills.

Passed gangs of woodmen engaged in felling and hewing the grand oaks for market. Fruit very abundant. Magnificent flowing hill scenery all afternoon. Walked southeast from Elizabethtown till wearied and lay down in the bushes by guess.

4 September. The sun was gilding the hilltops when I was awakened by the alarm notes of birds whose dwelling in a hazel thicket I had disturbed. They flitted excitedly close to my head, as if scolding or asking angry questions, while several beautiful plants, strangers to me, were looking me full in the face. The first botanical discovery in bed! This was one of the most delightful camp grounds, though groped for in the dark, and I lingered about it enjoying its trees and soft lights and music.

Walked ten miles of forest. Met a strange oak with willow-looking leaves. Entered a sandy stretch of black oak called 'Barrens,' many of which were sixty or seventy feet in height, and are said to have grown since the fires were kept off, forty years ago. The farmers hereabouts are tall, stout, happy fellows, fond of guns and horses. Enjoyed friendly chats with them. Arrived at dark in a village that seemed to be drawing its last breath. Was guided to the 'tavern' by a negro who was extremely accommodating. 'No trouble at all,' he said.

5 September. No bird or flower or friendly tree above me this morning; only squalid garret rubbish and dust. Escaped to the woods. Came to the region of caves. At the mouth of the first I discovered, I was surprised to find ferns which belonged to the coolest nooks of Wisconsin and northward, but soon observed that each cave rim has a zone of climate peculiar to itself, and it is always cool. This cave had an opening about ten feet in diameter, and twenty-five feet perpendicular depth. A strong cold wind issued from it and I could hear the sounds of running water. A long pole was set against its walls as if intended for a ladder, but in some places it was slippery and smooth as a mast and would test the climbing powers of a monkey. The walls and rim of this natural reservoir were finely carved and flowered. Bushes leaned over it with shading leaves, and beautiful ferns and mosses were in rows and sheets on its slopes and shelves. Lingered here a long happy while, pressing specimens and printing this beauty into memory.

Arrived about noon at Munfordville; was soon discovered and examined by Mr Munford himself, a pioneer and father of the village. He is a surveyor – has held all country offices, and every seeker of roads and lands applies to him for information. He regards all the villagers as his children, and all strangers who enter Munfordville as his own visitors. Of course he inquired my business, destination, et cetera, and invited me to his house.

After refreshing me with 'parrs' he complacently covered the table with bits of rocks, plants, et cetera, things new and old which he had gathered in his surveying walks and supposed to be full of scientific interest. He informed me that all scientific men applied to him for information, and as I was a botanist, he either possessed, or ought to possess, the knowledge I was seeking, and so I received long lessons concerning roots and herbs for every mortal ill. Thanking my benefactor for his kindness, I escaped to the fields and followed a railroad along the base of a grand hill ridge. As evening came on all the dwellings I found seemed to repel me, and I could not muster courage enough to ask entertainment at any of them. Took refuge in a log schoolhouse that stood on a hillside beneath stately oaks and slept on the softest looking of the benches.

6 September. Started at the earliest bird song in hopes of seeing the great Mammoth Cave before evening. Overtook an old negro driving an ox team. Rode with him a few miles and had some interesting chat concerning war, wild fruits of the woods, et cetera. 'Right heah,' said he, 'is where the Rebs was a-tearin' up the track, and they all a sudden thought they seed the Yankees a-comin', obah dem big hills dar, and Lo'd, how dey run.' I asked him if he would like a renewal of these sad war times, when his flexible face suddenly calmed, and he said with intense earnestness, 'Oh, Lo'd, want no mo wa, Lo'd no.' Many of these Kentucky negroes are shrewd and intelligent, and when warmed upon a subject that interests them, are eloquent in no mean degree.

Arrived at Horse Cave, about ten miles from the great cave. The entrance is by a long easy slope of several hundred yards. It seems like a noble gateway to the birthplace of springs and fountains and the dark treasuries of the mineral kingdom. This cave is in a village (of the same name) which it supplies with an abundance of cold water, and cold air that issues from its fern clad lips. In hot weather crowds of people sit about it in the shade of the trees that guard it. This magnificent fan is capable of cooling everybody in the town at once.

Those who live near lofty mountains may climb to cool weather in a day or two, but the overheated Kentuckians can find a patch of cool climate in almost every glen in the State. The villager who accompanied me said that Horse Cave had never been fully explored, but that it was several miles in length at least. He told me that he had never been at Mammoth Cave – that it was not worth going ten miles to see, as it was nothing but a hole in the ground, and I found that his was no rare case. He was one of the useful, practical men – too wise to waste precious time with weeds, caves, fossils, or anything else that he could not eat.

Arrived at the great Mammoth Cave. I was surprised to find it in so complete naturalness. A large hotel with fine walks and gardens is near it. But fortunately the cave has been unimproved, and were it not for the narrow trail that leads down the glen to its door, one would not know that it had been visited. There are house-rooms and halls whose entrances give but slight hint of their grandeur. And so also this magnificent hall in the mineral kingdom of Kentucky has a door comparatively small and unpromising. One might pass within a few yards of it without noticing it. A strong cool breeze issues constantly from it, creating a northern climate for the ferns that adorn its rocky front.

I never before saw Nature's grandeur in so abrupt contrast with paltry artificial gardens. The fashionable hotel grounds are in exact parlour taste, with many a beautiful plant cultivated to deformity, and arranged in strict geometrical beds, the whole pretty affair a laborious failure side by side with Divine beauty. The trees around the mouth of the cave are smooth and tall and bent forward at the bottom, then straight upwards. Only a butternut seems, by its angular knotty branches, to sympathize with and belong to the cave, with a fine growth of *Cystopteris* and *Hypnum*.

Started for Glasgow Junction. Got belated in the hill woods. Inquired my way at a farmhouse and was invited to stay overnight in a rare, hearty, hospitable manner. Engaged in familiar running talk on politics, war times, and theology. The old Kentuckian seemed to take a liking to me and advised me to stay in these hills until next spring, assuring me that I would find much to interest me in and about the Great Cave; also, that he was one of the school officials and was sure that I could obtain their school for the winter term. I sincerely thanked him for his kind plans, but pursued my own.

7 September. Left the hospitable Kentuckians with their sincere good wishes and bore away southwards again through the deep green woods. In noble forests all day. Saw mistletoe for the first time. Part of the day I travelled with a Kentuckian from near Burkesville. He spoke to all the negroes he met with familiar kindly greetings, addressing them always as 'Uncles' and 'Aunts'. All travellers one meets on these roads, white and black, male and female, travel on horseback. Glasgow is one of the few Southern towns that shows ordinary American life. At night with a well-to-do farmer.

8 September. Deep, green, bossy sea of waving, flowing hilltops. Corn and cotton and tobacco fields scattered here and there. I had imagined that a cotton field in flower was something magnificent. But cotton is a coarse, rough, straggling, unhappy looking plant, not half as good-looking as a field of Irish potatoes.

Met a great many negroes going to meeting, dressed in

their Sunday best. Fat, happy looking, and contented. The scenery on approaching the Cumberland River becomes still grander. Burkesville, in beautiful location, is embosomed in a glorious array of verdant flowing hills. The Cumberland must be a happy stream. I think I could enjoy travelling with it in the midst of such beauty all my life. This evening I could find none willing to take me in, and so lay down on a hillside and fell asleep muttering praises to the happy abounding beauty of Kentucky.

9 September. Another day in the most favoured province of bird and flower. Many rapid streams, flowing in beautiful flower-bordered canyons embosomed in dense woods. Am seated on a grand hill-slope that leans back against the sky like a picture. Amid the wide waves of green wood there are spots of autumnal yellow and the atmosphere, too, has the dawnings of autumn in colours and sounds. The soft light of morning falls upon ripening forests of oak and elm, walnut and hickory, and all Nature is thoughtful and calm. Kentucky is the greenest, leafiest State I have yet seen. The sea of soft temperate plant-green is deepest here.

Comparing volumes of vegetable verdure in different countries to a wedge, the thick end would be in the forests of Kentucky, the other in the lichens and mosses of the North. This verdure wedge would not be perfect in its lines. From Kentucky it would maintain its thickness long and well in passing the level forests of Indiana and Canada. From the maples and pines of Canada it would slope rapidly to the bleak Arctic hills with dwarf birches and alders; thence it would thin out in a long edge among hardy lichens and liverworts and mosses to the dwelling-places of everlasting frost. Far the grandest of all Kentucky plants are her noble oaks. They are the master existences of her exuberant forests. Here is the Eden, the paradise of oaks. Passed the Kentucky line towards evening and obtained food and shelter from a thrifty Tennessee farmer, after he had made use of all the ordinary anti-hospitable arguments of cautious comfortable families.

10 September. Escaped from a heap of uncordial kindness to the generous bosom of the woods. After a few miles of level ground in luxuriant tangles of brooding vines,

I began the ascent of the Cumberland Mountains, the first real mountains that my foot ever touched or eyes beheld. The ascent was by a nearly regular zigzag slope, mostly covered up like a tunnel by overarching oaks. But there were a few openings where the glorious forest road of Kentucky was grandly seen, stretching over hill and valley, adjusted to every slope and curve by the hands of Nature – the most sublime and comprehensive picture that ever entered my eyes. Reached the summit in six or seven hours – a strangely long period of up-grade work to one accustomed only to the hillocky levels of Wisconsin and adjacent States.

TWO

Crossing the Cumberland Mountains

I had climbed but a short distance when I was overtaken by a young man on horseback, who soon showed that he intended to rob me if he should find the job worth while. After he had inquired where I came from, and where I was going, he offered to carry my bag. I told him that it was so light that I did not feel it at all a burden; but he insisted and coaxed until I allowed him to carry it. As soon as he had gained possession I noticed that he gradually increased his speed, evidently trying to get far enough ahead of me to examine the contents without being observed. But I was too good a walker and runner for him to get far. At a turn of the road, after trotting his horse for about half an hour, and when he thought he was out of sight, I caught him rummaging my poor bag. Finding there only a comb, brush, towel, soap, a change of underclothing, a copy of Burns's poems, Milton's Paradise Lost, and a small New Testament, he waited for me, handed back my bag, and returned down the hill, saying that he had forgotten something.

I found splendid growths of shining-leaved *Ericaceæ* (heathworts) for which the Alleghany Mountains are noted. Also ferns of which *Osmunda cinnamomea* (Cinnamon Fern) is the largest and perhaps the most abundant. *Osmunda regalis* (Flowering Fern) is also common here, but not large. In Wood's and Gray's Botany *Osmunda cinnamomea* is said to be a much larger fern than *Osmunda Claytoniana*. This I found to be true in Tennessee and southward, but in Indiana, part of Illinois, and Wisconsin the opposite is true. Found here the beautiful, sensitive *Schrankia*, or sensitive brier. It is a long, prickly, leguminous vine, with dense heads of small, yellow fragrant flowers.

Vines growing on roadsides receive many a tormenting blow, simply because they give evidence of feeling. Sensitive people are served in the same way. But the roadside vine soon becomes less sensitive, like people getting used to teasing – Nature, in this instance, making for the comfort of flower creatures the same benevolent arrangement as for man. Thus I found that the *Schrankia* vines growing along footpaths leading to a backwoods schoolhouse were much less sensitive than those in the adjacent unfrequented woods, having learned to pay but slight attention to the tingling strokes they get from teasing scholars.

It is startling to see the pairs of pinnate leaves rising quickly out of the grass and folding themselves close in regular succession from the root to the end of the prostrate stems, ten to twenty feet in length. How little we know as yet of the life of plants – their hopes and fears, pains and enjoyments!

Travelled a few miles with an old Tennessee farmer who was much excited on account of the news he had just heard. 'Three kingdoms, England, Ireland, and Russia, have declared war agin the United States. Oh, it's terrible, terrible,' said he. 'This big war comin' so quick after our own big fight. Well, it can't be helped, and all I have to say is, Amerricay forever, but I'd a heap rather they didn't fight.'

'But are you sure the news is true?' I inquired. 'Oh, yes, quite sure,' he replied, 'for me and some of my neighbours were down at the store last night, and Jim Smith can read, and he found out all about it in a newspaper.'

Passed the poor, rickety, thrice-dead village of Jamestown, an incredibly dreary place. Toward the top of the Cumberland grade, about two hours before sundown I came to a log house, and as I had been warned that all the broad plateau of the range for forty or fifty miles was desolate, I began thus early to seek a lodging for the night. Knocking at the door, a motherly old lady replied to my request for supper and bed and breakfast, that I was welcome to the best she had, provided that I had the necessary change to pay my bill. When I told her that unfortunately I had nothing smaller than a five-dollar greenback, she said, 'Well, I'm sorry, but cannot afford to keep you. Not long ago ten soldiers came across from North Carolina, and in the morning they offered a greenback that I couldn't change, and so I got nothing for keeping them, which I was ill able to afford.'

'Very well,' I said, 'I'm glad you spoke of this before-hand, for I would rather go hungry than impose on your hospitality.'

As I turned to leave, after bidding her goodbye, she, evidently pitying me for my tired looks, called me back and asked me if I would like a drink of milk. This I gladly accepted, thinking that perhaps I might not be successful in getting any other nourishment for a day or two. Then I inquired whether there were any more houses on the road, nearer than North Carolina, forty or fifty miles away. 'Yes,' she said, 'it's only two miles to the next house, but beyond that there are no houses that I know of except empty ones whose owners have been killed or driven away during the war.'

Arriving at the last house, my knock at the door was answered by a bright, good-natured, good-looking little woman, who in reply to my request for a night's lodging and food, said, 'Oh, I guess so. I think you can stay. Come in and I'll call my husband.' 'But I must first warn you,' I said, 'that I have nothing smaller to offer you than a five-dollar bill for my entertainment. I don't want you to think that I am trying to impose on your hospitality.'

She then called her husband, a blacksmith, who was at work at his forge. He came out, hammer in hand, bare-breasted, sweaty, begrimed, and covered with shaggy black hair. In reply to his wife's statement, that this young man wished to stop over night, he quickly replied, 'That's all right; tell him to go into the house.' He was turning to go back to his shop, when his wife added, 'But he says he hasn't any change to pay. He has nothing smaller than a five-dollar bill.' Hesitating only a moment, he turned on his heel and said, 'Tell him to go into the house. A man that comes right out like that beforehand is welcome to eat my bread.'

When he came in after his hard day's work and sat down

to dinner, he solemnly asked a blessing on the frugal meal, consisting solely of corn bread and bacon. Then, looking across the table at me, he said, 'Young man, what are you doing down here?' I replied that I was looking at plants. 'Plants? What kind of plants?' I said, 'Oh, all kinds; grass, weeds, flowers, trees, mosses, ferns – almost everything that grows is interesting to me.'

'Well, young man,' he queried, 'you mean to say that you are not employed by the Government on some private business?' 'No,' I said, 'I am not employed by any one except just myself. I love all kinds of plants, and I came down here to these Southern States to get acquainted with as many of them as possible.'

'You look like a strong-minded man,' he replied, 'and surely you are able to do something better than wander over the country and look at weeds and blossoms. These are hard times, and real work is required of every man that is able. Picking up blossoms doesn't seem to be a man's work at all in any kind of times.'

To this I replied, 'You are a believer in the Bible, are you not?' 'Oh, yes.' 'Well, you know Solomon was a strong-minded man, and he is generally believed to have been the very wisest man the world ever saw, and yet he considered it was worth while to study plants; not only to go and pick them up as I am doing, but to study them; and you know we are told that he wrote a book about plants, not only of the great cedars of Lebanon, but of little bits of things growing in the cracks of the walls.

'Therefore, you see that Solomon differed very much more from you than from me in this matter. I'll warrant you he had many a long ramble in the mountains of Judea, and had he been a Yankee he would likely have visited every weed in the land. And again, do you not remember that Christ told his disciples to "consider the lilies how they grow," and compared their beauty with Solomon in all his glory? Now, whose advice am I to take, yours or Christ's? Christ says, "Consider the lilies." You say, "Don't consider them. It isn't worthwhile for any strong-minded man."'

This evidently satisfied him, and he acknowledged that

he had never thought of blossoms in that way before. He repeated again and again that I must be a very strong-minded man, and admitted that no doubt I was fully justified in picking up blossoms. He then told me that although the war was over, walking across the Cumberland Mountains still was far from safe on account of small bands of guerrillas who were in hiding along the roads, and earnestly entreated me to turn back and not to think of walking so far as the Gulf of Mexico until the country became quiet and orderly once more.

I replied that I had no fear, that I had but very little to lose, and that nobody was likely to think it worth while to rob me; that, anyhow, I always had good luck. In the morning he repeated the warning and entreated me to turn back, which never for a moment interfered with my resolution to pursue my glorious walk.

11 September. Long stretch of level sandstone plateau, lightly furrowed and dimpled with shallow groove-like valleys and hills. The trees are mostly oaks, planted wide apart like those in the Wisconsin woods. A good many pine trees here and there, forty to eighty feet high, and most of the ground is covered with showy flowers. Polygalas (milkworts), solidagoes (goldenrods), and asters were especially abundant. I came to a cool clear brook every half mile or so, the banks planted with *Osmunda regalis*, *Osmunda cinnamomea*, and handsome sedges. The few larger streams were fringed with laurels and azaleas. Large areas beneath the trees are covered with formidable green briers and brambles, armed with hooked claws, and almost impenetrable. Houses are far apart and uninhabited, orchards and fences in ruins – sad marks of war.

About noon my road became dim and at last vanished among desolate fields. Lost and hungry, I knew my direction but could not keep it on account of the briers. My path was indeed strewn with flowers, but as thorny, also, as mortal as ever trod. In trying to force a way through these cat-plants one is not simply clawed and pricked through all one's clothing, but caught and held fast. The toothed arching branches come down over you and above you like cruel living arms, and the more you struggle the more desperately you are entangled, and your wounds deepened and multiplied. The South has plant fly-catchers. It also has plant man-catchers.

After a great deal of defensive fighting and struggling I escaped to a road and a house, but failed to find food or shelter. Towards sundown, as I was walking rapidly along a straight stretch in the road, I suddenly came in sight of ten mounted men riding abreast. They undoubtedly had seen me before I discovered them, for they had stopped their horses and were evidently watching me. I saw at once that it was useless to attempt to avoid them, for the ground thereabout was quite open. I knew that there was nothing for it but to face them fearlessly, without showing the slightest suspicion of foul play. Therefore, without halting even for a moment, I advanced rapidly with long strides as though I intended to walk through the midst of them. When I got within a rod or so I looked up in their faces and smilingly bade them 'Howdy.' Stopping never an instant, I turned to one side and walked around them to get on the road again, and kept on without venturing to look back or to betray the slightest fear of being robbed.

After I had gone about one hundred or one hundred and fifty yards, I ventured a quick glance back, without stopping, and saw in this flash of an eye that all the ten had turned their horses towards me and were evidently talking about me; supposedly, with reference to what my object was, where I was going, and whether it would be worth while to rob me. They all were mounted on rather scrawny horses, and all wore long hair hanging down on their shoulders. Evidently they belonged to the most irreclaimable of the guerrilla bands who, long accustomed to plunder, deplored the coming of peace. I was not followed, however, probably because the plants projecting from my plant press made them believe that I was a poor herb doctor, a common occupation in these mountain regions.

About dark I discovered, a little off the road, another house, inhabited by negroes, where I succeeded in obtaining a much needed meal of string beans, buttermilk, and corn bread. At the table I was seated in a bottomless chair, and as I became sore and heavy, I sank deeper and deeper, pressing my knees against my breast, and my mouth settled to the level of my plate. But wild hunger cares for none of these things, and my curiously compressed position prevented the too free indulgence of boisterous appetite. Of course, I was compelled to sleep with the trees in the one great bedroom of the open night.

12 September. Awoke drenched with mountain mist, which made a grand show, as it moved away before the hot sun. Passed Montgomery, a shabby village at the head of the east slope of the Cumberland Mountains. Obtained breakfast in a clean house and began the descent of the mountains. Obtained fine views of a wide, open country, and distant flanking ridges and spurs. Crossed a wide cool stream (Emory River), a branch of the Clinch River. There is nothing more eloquent in Nature than a mountain stream, and this is the first I ever saw. Its banks are luxuriantly peopled with rare and lovely flowers and overarching trees, making one of Nature's coolest and most hospitable places. Every tree, every flower, every ripple and eddy of this lovely stream seemed solemnly to feel the presence of the great Creator. Lingered in this sanctuary a long time thanking the Lord with all my heart for his goodness in allowing me to enter and enjoy it.

Discovered two ferns, *Dicksonia* and a small matted polypod on trees, common farther South. Also a species of magnolia with very large leaves and scarlet conical fruit. Near this stream I spent some joyous time in a grand rock-dwelling full of mosses, birds, and flowers. Most heavenly place I ever entered. The long narrow valleys of the mountainside, all well watered and nobly adorned with oaks, magnolias, laurels, azaleas, asters, ferns, Hypnum mosses, Madotheca (Scale-mosses), etc. Also towering clumps of beautiful hemlocks. The hemlock, judging from the common species of Canada, I regarded as the least noble of the conifers. But those of the eastern valleys of the Cumberland Mountains are as perfect in form and regal in port as the pines themselves. The latter abundant. Obtained fine glimpses from open places as I descended to the great valley between these mountains and the Unaka Mountains on the state line. Forded the Clinch, a beautiful clear stream, that knows many of the dearest mountain retreats that ever heard the music of running water. Reached Kingston before dark. Sent back my plant collections by express to my brother in Wisconsin.

13 September. Walked all day across small parallel valleys that flute the surface of the one wide valley. These flutings appear to have been formed by lateral pressure, are fertile, and contain some fine forms, though the seal of war is on all things. The roads never seem to proceed with any fixed purpose, but wander as if lost. In seeking the way to Philadelphia (in Loudon County, Tennessee), I was told by a buxom Tennessee 'gal' that over the hills was much the nearer way, that she always went that way, and that surely I could travel it.

I started over the flint-ridges, but soon reached a set of enchanted little valleys among which, no matter how or in what direction I travelled, I could not get a foot nearer to Philadelphia. At last, consulting my map and compass, I neglected all directions and finally reached the house of a negro driver, with whom I put up for the night. Received a good deal of knowledge which may be of use should I ever be a negro teamster.

14 September. Philadelphia is a very filthy village in a beautiful situation. More or less of pine. Black oak most abundant. *Polypodium hexagonopterum* and *Aspidium acrostichoides* (Christmas Fern) most abundant of ferns and most generally distributed. *Osmunda claytoniana* rare, not in fruit, small. *Dicksonia* abundant, after leaving the Cumberland Mountains. *Asplenium ebeneum* (Ebony Spleenwort) quite common in Tennessee and many parts of Kentucky. *Cystopteris* (Bladder Fern), and *Asplenium filix-foemina* not common through the same range. *Pteris aquilina* (Common Brake) abundant, but small.

Walked through many a leafy valley, shady grove, and cool brooklet. Reached Madisonville, a brisk village. Came in full view of the Unaka Mountains, a magnificent sight. Stayed over night with a pleasant young farmer.

15 September. Most glorious billowy mountain scenery. Made many a halt at open places to take breath and to admire. The road, in many places cut into the rock, goes winding about the knobs and gorges. Dense growth of asters, liatris, and grapevines.

Reached a house before night, and asked leave to stop. 'Well, you're welcome to stop,' said the mountaineer, 'if you think you can live till morning on what I have to live on all the time.' Found the old gentleman very communicative. Was favoured with long 'bar' stories, deer hunts, etc., and in the morning was pressed to stay a day or two.

16 September. 'I will take you,' said he, 'to the highest ridge in the country, where you can see both ways. You will have a view of all the world on one side of the mountains and all creation on the other. Besides, you, who are travelling for curiosity and wonder, ought to see our gold mines. I agreed to stay and went to the mines. Gold is found in small quantities throughout the Alleghanies, and many farmers work at mining a few weeks or months every year when their time is not more valuable for other pursuits. In this neighbourhood miners are earning from half a dollar to two dollars a day. There are several large quartz mills not far from here. Common labour is worth ten dollars a month.

17 September. Spent the day in botanizing, blacksmithing, and examining a grist mill. Grist mills, in the less settled parts of Tennessee and North Carolina, are remarkably simple affairs. A small stone, that a man might carry under his arm, is fastened to the vertical shaft of a little home-made, boyish-looking, back-action water-wheel, which, with a hopper and a box to receive the meal, is the whole affair. The walls of the mill are of undressed poles cut from seedling trees and there is no floor, as lumber is dear. No dam is built. The water is conveyed along some hillside until sufficient fall is obtained, a thing easily done in the mountains.

On Sundays you may see wild, unshorn, uncombed men coming out of the woods, each with a bag of corn on his back. From a peck to a bushel is a common grist. They go to the mill along verdant footpaths, winding up and down over hill and valley, and crossing many a rhododendron glen. The flowers and shining leaves brush against their shoulders and knees, occasionally knocking off their coon-skin caps. The first arrived throws his corn into the hopper, turns on the water, and goes to the house. After chatting and smoking he returns to see if his grist is done. Should the stones run empty for an hour or two, it does no harm.

This is a fair average in equipment and capacity of a score of mills that I saw in Tennessee. This one was built by John Vohn, who claimed that he could make it grind twenty bushels a day. But since it fell into other hands it can be made to grind only ten per day. All the machines of Kentucky and Tennessee are far behind the age. There is scarce a trace of that restless spirit of speculation and invention so characteristic of the North. But one way of doing things obtains here, as if laws had been passed making attempts at improvement a crime. Spinning and weaving are done in every one of these mountain cabins wherever the least pretensions are made to thrift and economy. The practice of these ancient arts they deem marks of advancement rather than of backwardness. 'There's a place back heah,' said my worthy entertainer, 'whar there's a mill-house, an' a store-house, an' a still-house, an' a spring-house, an' a blacksmith shop – all in the same yard! Cows too, an' heaps of big gals a-milkin' them.'

This is the most primitive country I have seen, primitive in everything. The remotest hidden parts of Wisconsin are far in advance of the mountain regions of Tennessee and North Carolina. But my host speaks of the 'old-fashioned unenlightened times,' like a philosopher in the best light of civilization. 'I believe in Providence,' said he. 'Our fathers came into these valleys, got the richest of them, and skimmed off the cream of the soil. The worn-out ground won't yield no roastin' ears now. But the Lord foresaw this state of affairs, and prepared something else for us. And what is it? Why, He meant us to bust open these copper mines and gold mines, so that we may have money to buy the corn that we cannot raise.' A most profound observation.

18 September. Up the mountain on the state line. The scenery is far grander than any I ever before beheld. The view extends from the Cumberland Mountains on the north far into Georgia and North Carolina to the south, an area of about five thousand square miles. Such an ocean of wooded, waving, swelling mountain beauty and grandeur is not to be described. Countless forest-clad hills, side by side in rows and groups, seemed to be enjoying the rich sunshine and remaining motionless only because they were so eagerly absorbing it. All were united by curves and slopes of inimitable softness and beauty. Oh, these forest gardens of our Father! What perfection, what divinity, in their architecture! What simplicity and mysterious complexity of detail! Who shall read the teaching of these sylvan pages, the glad brotherhood of rills that sing in the valleys, and all the happy creatures that dwell in them under the tender keeping of a Father's care?

19 September. Received another solemn warning of dangers on my way through the mountains. Was told by my worthy entertainer of a wondrous gap in the mountains which he advised me to see. 'It is called Track Gap,' said he, 'from the great number of tracks in the rocks – bird tracks, bear tracks, hoss tracks, men tracks, all in the solid rock as if it had been mud.' Bidding farewell to my worthy mountaineer and all his comfortable wonders, I pursued my way to the South.

As I was leaving, he repeated the warnings of danger ahead, saying that there were a good many people living like wild beasts on whatever they could steal, and that murders were sometimes committed for four or five dollars, and even less. While stopping with him I noticed that a man came regularly after dark to the house for his supper. He was armed with a gun, a pistol, and a long knife. My host told me that this man was at feud with one of his neighbours, and that they were prepared to shoot one another at sight. That neither of them could do any regular work or sleep in the same place two nights in succession. That they visited houses only for food, and as soon as the one that I saw had got his supper he went out and slept in the woods, without of course making a fire. His enemy did the same.

My entertainer told me that he was trying to make peace between these two men, because they both were good men, and if they would agree to stop their quarrel, they could then both go to work. Most of the food in this house was coffee without sugar, corn bread, and sometimes bacon. But the coffee was the greatest luxury which these people knew. The only way of obtaining it was by selling skins, or, in particular, 'sang,' that is ginseng, which found a market in far-off China.

My path all today led me along the leafy banks of the Hiwassee, a most impressive mountain river. Its channel is very rough, as it crosses the edges of upturned rock strata, some·of them standing at right angles, or glancing off obliquely to right and left. Thus a multitude of short, resounding cataracts are produced, and the river is restrained from the headlong speed due to its volume and the inclination of its bed.

All the larger streams of uncultivated countries are mysteriously charming and beautiful, whether flowing in mountains or through swamps and plains. Their channels are interestingly sculptured, far more so than the grandest architectural works of man. The finest of the forests are usually found along their banks, and in the multitude of falls and rapids the wilderness finds a voice. Such a river is the Hiwassee, with its surface broken to a thousand sparkling gems, and its forest walls vine-draped and flowery as Eden. And how fine the song it sings!

In Murphy (North Carolina) I was hailed by the sheriff who could not determine by my colours and rigging to what country or craft I belonged. Since the war, every other stranger in these lonely parts is supposed to be a criminal, and all are objects of curiosity or apprehensive concern. After a few minutes' conversation with this chief man of Murphy I was pronounced harmless, and invited to his house, where for the first time since leaving home I found a house decked with flowers and vines, clean within and without, and stamped with the comforts of culture and refinement in all its arrangements. Striking contrast to the uncouth transitionist establishments from the wigwams of savages to the clumsy but clean log castle of the thrifty pioneer.

20 September. All day among the groves and gorges of Murphy with Mr Beale. Was shown the site of Camp Butler where General Scott had his headquarters when he removed the Cherokee Indians to a new home in the West. Found a number of rare and strange plants on the rocky banks of the River Hiwassee. In the afternoon, from the summit of a commanding ridge, I obtained a magnificent view of blue, softly curved mountain scenery. Among the trees I saw *Ilex* (Holly) for the first time. Mr Beale informed me that the paleness of most of the women in his neighbourhood, and the mountains in general hereabouts, was caused chiefly by smoking and by what is called 'dipping'. I had never even heard of dipping. The term simply describes the application of snuff to the gum by means of a small swab.

21 September. Most luxuriant forest. Many brooks running across the road. Blairsville (Georgia), which I passed in the forenoon, seems a shapeless and insignificant village, but grandly encircled with banded hills. At night I was cordially received by a farmer whose wife, though smart and neat in her appearance, was an inveterate smoker.

22 September. Hills becoming small, sparsely covered with soil. They are called 'knob land' and are cultivated, or scratched, with a kind of one-tooth cultivator. Every rain robs them of their fertility, while the bottoms are of course correspondingly enriched. About noon I reached the last mountain summit on my way to the sea. It is called the Blue Ridge and before it lies a prospect very different from any I had passed, namely, a vast uniform expanse of dark pine woods, extending to the sea; an impressive view at any time and under any circumstances, but particularly so to one emerging from the mountains.

Travelled in the wake of three poor but merry mountaineers – an old woman, a young woman, and a young man – who sat, leaned, and lay in the box of a shackly wagon that seemed to be held together by spiritualism, and was kept in agitation by a very large and a very small mule. In going down hill the looseness of the harness and the joints of the wagon allowed the mules to back nearly out of sight beneath the box, and the three who occupied it were slid against the front boards in a heap over the mules' ears. Before they could unravel their limbs from this unmannerly and impolite disorder, a new ridge in the road frequently tilted them with a swish and a bump against the back boards in a mixing that was still more grotesque.

I expected to see man, women, and mules mingled in piebald ruin at the bottom of some rocky hollow, but they seemed to have full confidence in the back board and front board of the wagon-box. So they continued to slide comfortably up and down, from end to end, in slippery obedience to the law of gravitation, as the grades demanded. Where the jolting was moderate, they engaged in conversation on love, marriage, and camp-meeting, according to the custom of the country. The old lady, through all the vicissitudes of the transportation, held a bouquet of French marigolds.

The hillsides hereabouts were bearing a fine harvest of asters. Reached Mount Yonah in the evening. Had a long conversation with an old Methodist slaveholder and mine owner. Was hospitably refreshed with a drink of fine cider.

THREE

Through the River Country of Georgia

23 September. Am now fairly out of the mountains. Thus far the climate has not changed in any marked degree, the decrease in latitude being balanced by the increase in altitude. These mountains are highways on which northern plants may extend their colonies southward. The plants of the North and of the South have many minor places of meeting along the way I have travelled; but it is here on the southern slope of the Alleghanies that the greatest number of hardy, enterprising representatives of the two climates are assembled.

Passed the comfortable, finely shaded little town of Gainesville. The Chattahoochee River is richly embanked with massive, bossy, dark green water oaks, and wreathed with a dense growth of muscadine grapevines, whose ornate foliage, so well adapted to bank embroidery, was enriched with other interweaving species of vines and brightly coloured flowers. This is the first truly southern stream I have met.

At night I reached the home of a young man with whom I had worked in Indiana, Mr Prater. He was down here on a visit to his father and mother. This was a plain back-woods family, living out of sight among knobby timbered hillocks not far from the river. The evening was passed in mixed conversation on southern and northern generalities.

24 September. Spent this day with Mr Prater sailing on the Chattahoochee, feasting on grapes that had dropped from the overhanging vines. This remarkable species of wild grape has a stout stem, sometimes five or six inches in diameter, smooth bark and hard wood, quite unlike any other wild or cultivated grapevine that I have seen. The grapes are very large, some of them nearly an inch in diameter, globular and fine flavoured. Usually there are but three or four berries in a cluster, and when mature they drop off instead of decaying on the vine. Those which fall into the river are often found in large quantities in the eddies along the bank, where they are collected by men in boats and sometimes made into wine. I think another name for this grape is the Scuppernong, though called 'muscadine' here.

Besides sailing on the river, we had a long walk among the plant bowers and tangles of the Chattahoochee bottom lands.

25 September. Bade good-bye to this friendly family. Mr Prater accompanied me a short distance from the house and warned me over and over again to be on the outlook for rattlesnakes. They are now leaving the damp lowlands, he told me, so that the danger is much greater because they are on their travels. Thus warned, I set out for Savannah, but got lost in the vine-fenced hills and hollows of the river bottom. Was unable to find the ford to which I had been directed by Mr Prater.

I then determined to push on southward regardless of roads and fords. After repeated failures I succeeded in finding a place on the river bank where I could force my way into the stream through the vine tangles. I succeeded in crossing the river by wading and swimming, careless of wetting, knowing that I would soon dry in the hot sunshine.

Out near the middle of the river I found great difficulty in resisting the rapid current. Though I braced myself with a stout stick, I was at length carried away in spite of all my efforts. But I succeeded in swimming to the shallows on the farther side, luckily caught hold of a rock, and after a rest swam and waded ashore. Dragging myself up the steep bank by the overhanging vines, I spread out myself, my paper money, and my plants to dry.

Debated with myself whether to proceed down the river valley until I could buy a boat, or lumber to make one, for a sail instead of a march through Georgia. I was intoxicated with the beauty of these glorious river banks, which I fancied might increase in grandeur as I approached the sea. But I finally concluded that such a pleasure sail would be less profitable than a walk, and so sauntered on southward as soon as I was dry. Rattlesnakes abundant. Lodged at a farmhouse. Found a few tropical plants in the garden.

Cotton is the principal crop hereabouts, and picking is now going on merrily. Only the lower bolls are now ripe. Those higher on the plants are green and unopened. Higher still, there are buds and flowers, some of which, if the plants be thrifty and the season favourable, will continue to produce ripe bolls until January.

The negroes are easy-going and merry, making a great deal of noise and doing little work. One energetic white man, working with a will, would easily pick as much cotton as half a dozen Sambos and Sallies. The forest here is almost entirely made up of dim-green, knotty, sparsely planted pines. The soil is mostly white, fine-grained sand.

26 September. Reached Athens in the afternoon, a remarkably beautiful and aristocratic town, containing many classic and magnificent mansions of wealthy planters, who formerly owned large negro-stocked plantations in the best cotton and sugar regions farther south. Unmistakable marks of culture and refinement, as well as wealth, were everywhere apparent. This is the most beautiful town I have seen on the journey, so far, and the only one in the South that I would like to revisit.

The negroes here have been well trained and are extremely polite. When they come in sight of a white man on the road, off go their hats, even at a distance of forty or fifty yards, and they walk bare-headed until he is out of sight.

27 September. Long zigzag walk amid the old plantations, a few of which are still cultivated in the old way by the same negroes that worked them before the war, and who still occupy their former 'quarters'. They are now paid seven to ten dollars a month.

The weather is very hot on these sandy, lightly shaded, lowland levels. When very thirsty I discovered a beautiful spring in a sandstone basin overhung with shady bushes and vines, where I enjoyed to the utmost the blessing of pure cold water. Discovered here a fine southern fern, some new grasses, etc. Fancied that I might have been directed here by Providence, while fainting with thirst. It is not often hereabouts that the joys of cool water, cool shade, and rare plants are so delightfully combined.

Witnessed the most gorgeous sunset I ever enjoyed in this bright world of light. The sunny South is indeed sunny. Was directed by a very civil negro to lodgings for the night. Daily bread hereabouts means sweet potatoes and rusty bacon.

28 September. The water oak is abundant on stream banks and in damp hollows. Grasses are becoming tall and cane-like and do not cover the ground with their leaves as at the North. Strange plants are crowding about me now. Scarce a familiar face appears among all the flowers of the day's walk.

29 September. Today I met a magnificent grass, ten or twelve feet in stature, with a superb panicle of glossy purple flowers. Its leaves, too, are of princely mould and dimensions. Its home is in sunny meadows and along the wet borders of slow streams and swamps. It seems to be fully aware of its high rank, and waves with the grace and solemn majesty of a mountain pine. I wish I could place one of these regal plants among the grass settlements of our Western prairies. Surely every panicle would wave and bow in joyous allegiance and acknowledge their king.

30 September. Between Thomson and Augusta I found many new and beautiful grasses, tall gerardias, liatris, club mosses, etc. Here, too, is the northern limit of the remarkable long-leafed pine, a tree from sixty to seventy feet in height, from twenty to thirty inches in diameter, with leaves ten to fifteen inches long, in dense radiant masses at the ends of the naked branches. The wood is strong, hard, and very resinous. It makes excellent ship spars, bridge timbers and flooring. Much of it is shipped to the West India Islands, New York, and Galveston.

The seedlings, five or six years old, are very striking objects to one from the North, consisting as they do, of the straight, leafless stem, surmounted by a crown of deep green leaves, arching and spreading like a palm. Children fancy that they resemble brooms, and use them as such in their picnic playhouses. *Pinus palustris* is most abundant in Georgia and Florida.

The sandy soil here is sparingly seamed with rolled quartz pebbles and clay. Denudation, going on slowly, allows the thorough removal of these clay seams, leaving only the sand. Notwithstanding the sandiness of the soil, much of the surface of the country is covered with standing water, which is easily accounted for by the presence of the above-mentioned impermeable seams.

Travelled today more than forty miles without dinner or supper. No family would receive me, so I had to push on to Augusta. Went hungry to bed and awoke with a sore stomach – sore, I suppose, from its walls rubbing on each other without anything to grind. A negro kindly directed me to the best hotel, called, I think, the Planter's. Got a good bed for a dollar.

1 October. Found a cheap breakfast in a market-place; then set off along the Savannah River to Savannah. Splendid grasses and rich, dense, vine-clad forests. Muscadine grapes in cart-loads. Asters and solidagoes becoming scarce. Carices (sedges) quite rare. Leguminous plants abundant. A species of passion flower is common, reaching back into Tennessee. It is here called 'apricot vine,' has a superb flower, and the most delicious fruit I have ever eaten.

The pomegranate is cultivated here. The fruit is about the size of an orange, has a thick, tough skin, and when opened resembles a many-chambered box full of translucent purple candies.

Toward evening I came to the country of one of the most striking of southern plants, the so-called 'Long Moss' or Spanish Moss (Tillandsia), though it is a flowering plant and belongs to the same family as the pineapple (Bromelworts). The trees hereabouts have all their branches draped with it, producing a remarkable effect.

Here, too, I found an impenetrable cypress swamp. This remarkable tree, called cypress, is a taxodium, grows large and high, and is remarkable for its flat crown. The whole forest seems almost level on the top, as if each tree had grown up against a ceiling, or had been rolled while growing. This taxodium is the only level-topped tree that I have seen. The branches, though spreading, are careful not to pass each other, and stop suddenly on reaching the general level, as if they had grown up against a ceiling.

The groves and thickets of smaller trees are full of blooming evergreen vines. These vines are not arranged in separate groups, or in delicate wreaths, but in bossy walls and heavy, mound-like heaps and banks. Am made to feel that I am now in a strange land. I know hardly any of the plants, but few of the birds, and I am unable to see the country for the solemn, dark, mysterious cypress woods which cover everything.

The winds are full of strange sounds, making one feel far from the people and plants and fruitful fields of home. Night is coming on and I am filled with indescribable loneliness. Felt feverish; bathed in a black, silent stream; nervously watchful for alligators. Obtained lodging in a planter's house among cotton fields. Although the family seemed to be pretty well-off, the only light in the house was bits of pitch-pine wood burned in the fireplace.

2 October. In the low bottom forest of the Savannah River. Very busy with new specimens. Most exquisitely planned wrecks of *Agrostis scabra* (Rough Hair Grass). Pines in glorious array with open, welcoming, approachable plants.

Met a young African with whom I had a long talk. Was amused with his eloquent narrative of coon hunting, alligators, and many superstitions. He showed me a place where a railroad train had run off the track, and assured me that the ghosts of the killed may be seen every dark night.

Had a long walk after sundown. At last was received at the house of Dr Perkins. Saw Cape Jasmine (*Gardenia florida*) in the garden. Heard long recitals of war happenings, discussion of the slave question, and Northern politics; a thoroughly characteristic Southern family, refined in manners and kind, but immovably prejudiced on everything connected with slavery.

The family table was unlike any I ever saw before. It

was circular, and the central part of it revolved. When any one wished to be helped, he placed his plate on the revolving part, which was whirled around to the host, and then whirled back with its new load. Thus every plate was revolved into place, without the assistance of any of the family.

3 October. In 'pine barrens' most of the day. Low, level, sandy tracts; the pines wide apart; the sunny spaces between full of beautiful abounding grasses, liatris, long, wand-like solidago, saw palmettos, etc., covering the ground in garden style. Here I sauntered in delightful freedom, meeting none of the cat-clawed vines, or shrubs, of the alluvial bottoms. Dwarf live-oaks common.

Toward evening I arrived at the home of Mr Cameron, a wealthy planter, who had large bands of slaves at work in his cotton fields. They still call him 'Massa.' He tells me that labour costs him less now than it did before the emancipation of the negroes. When I arrived I found him busily engaged in scouring the rust off some cotton-gin saws which had been lying for months at the bottom of his mill-pond to prevent Sherman's 'bummers' from destroying them. The most valuable parts of the grist-mill and cotton-press were hidden in the same way. 'If Bill Sherman,' he said, 'should come down now without his army, he would never go back.'

When I asked him if he could give me food and lodging for the night he said, 'No, no, we have no accommodation for travellers.' I said, 'But I am travelling as a botanist and either have to find lodgings when night overtakes me or lie outdoors, which I often have had to do in my long walk from Indiana. But you see that the country here is very swampy; if you will at least sell me a piece of bread, and give me a drink at your well, I shall have to look around for a dry spot to lie down on.'

Then, asking me a few questions, and narrowly examining me, he said, 'Well, it is barely possible that we may find a place for you, and if you will come to the house I will ask my wife.' Evidently he was cautious to get his wife's opinion of the kind of creature I was before committing himself to hospitality. He halted me at the door and called out his wife, a fine-looking woman, who also questioned me narrowly as to my object in coming so far down through the South, so soon after the war. She said to her husband that she thought they could, perhaps, give me a place to sleep.

After supper, as we sat by the fire talking on my favourite subject of botany, I described the country I had passed through, its botanical character, etc. Then, evidently, all doubt as to my being a decent man vanished, and they both said that they wouldn't for anything have turned me away; but I must excuse their caution, for perhaps fewer than one in a hundred, who passed through this unfrequented part of the country, were to be relied upon. 'Only a short time ago we entertained a man who was well spoken and well dressed, and he vanished some time during the night with some valuable silverware.'

Mr Cameron told me that when I arrived he tried me for a Mason, and finding that I was not a Mason he wondered still more that I would venture into the country without being able to gain the assistance of brother Masons in these troublous times.

'Young man,' he said, after hearing my talks on botany, 'I see that your hobby is botany. My hobby is e-lec-tricity. I believe that the time is coming, though we may not live to see it, when that mysterious power or force, used now only for telegraphy, will eventually supply the power for running railroad trains and steamships, for lighting, and, in a word, electricity will do all the work of the world.'

Many times since then I have thought of the wonderfully correct vision of this Georgia planter, so far in advance of almost everybody else in the world. Already nearly all that he foresaw has been accomplished, and the use of electricity is being extended more and more every year.

4 October. New plants constantly appearing. All day in dense, wet, dark mysterious forest of flat-topped taxodiums.

5 October. Saw the stately banana for the first time, growing luxuriantly in the wayside gardens. At night with a very pleasant, intelligent Savannah family, but as usual was admitted only after I had undergone a severe course of questioning.

6 October. Immense swamps, still more completely fenced and darkened, that are never ruffled with winds or scorched with drought. Many of them seem to be thoroughly aquatic.

7 October. Impenetrable taxodium swamp, seemingly boundless. The silvery skeins of tillandsia becoming longer and more abundant. Passed the night with a very pleasant family of Georgians, after the usual questions and cross questions.

8 October. Found the first woody *compositæ*, a most notable discovery. Took them to be such at a considerable distance. Almost all trees and shrubs are evergreens here with thick polished leaves. *Magnolia grandiflora* becoming common. A magnificent tree in fruit and foliage as well as in flower. Near Savannah I found waste places covered with a dense growth of woody leguminous plants, eight or ten feet high, with pinnate leaves and suspended rattling pods.

Reached Savannah, but find no word from home, and the money that I had ordered to be sent by express from Portage (Wisconsin) by my brother has not yet arrived. Feel dreadfully lonesome and poor. Went to the meanest looking lodging-house that I could find, on account of its cheapness.

FOUR

Camping Among the Tombs

9 October. After going again to the express office and post office, and wandering about the streets, I found a road which led me to the Bonaventure graveyard. If that burying-ground across the Sea of Galilee, mentioned in Scripture, was half as beautiful as Bonaventure, I do not wonder that a man should dwell among the tombs. It is only three or four miles from Savannah, and is reached by a smooth white shell road.

There is but little to be seen on the way in land, water, or sky, that would lead one to hope for the glories of Bonaventure. The ragged desolate fields, on both sides of the road, are overrun with coarse rank weeds, and show scarce a trace of cultivation. But soon all is changed. Rickety log huts, broken fences, and the last patch of weedy rice-stubble are left behind. You come to beds of purple liatris and living wild-wood trees. You hear the song of birds, cross a small stream, and are with Nature in the grand old forest graveyard, so beautiful that almost any sensible person would choose to dwell here with the dead rather than with the lazy, disorderly living.

Part of the grounds was cultivated and planted with live-oak, about a hundred years ago, by a wealthy gentleman who had his country residence here. But much the greater part is undisturbed. Even those spots which are disordered by art, Nature is ever at work to reclaim, and to make them look as if the foot of man had never known them. Only a small plot of ground is occupied with graves and the old mansion is in ruins.

The most conspicuous glory of Bonaventure is its noble avenue of live-oaks. They are the most magnificent planted trees I have ever seen, about fifty feet high and perhaps three or four feet in diameter, with broad spreading leafy heads. The main branches reach out horizontally until they come together over the driveway, embowering it throughout its entire length, while each branch is adorned like a garden with ferns, flowers, grasses, and dwarf palmettos.

But of all the plants of these curious tree-gardens the most striking and characteristic is the so-called Long Moss (*Tillandsia usneoides*). It drapes all the branches from top to bottom, hanging in long silvery-grey skeins, reaching a length of not less than eight or ten feet, and when slowly waving in the wind they produce a solemn funeral effect singularly impressive.

There are also thousands of smaller trees and clustered bushes, covered almost from sight in the glorious brightness of their own light. The place is half surrounded by the salt marshes and islands of the river, their reeds and sedges making a delightful fringe. Many bald eagles roost among the trees along the side of the marsh. Their screams are heard every morning, joined with the noise of crows and the songs of countless warblers, hidden deep in their dwellings of leafy bowers. Large flocks of butterflies, all kinds of happy insects, seem to be in a perfect fever of joy and sportive gladness. The whole place seems like a centre of life. The dead do not reign there alone.

Bonaventure to me is one of the most impressive assemblages of animal and plant creatures I ever met. I was fresh from the Western prairies, the garden-like openings of Wisconsin, the beech and maple and oak woods of Indiana and Kentucky, the dark mysterious Savannah cypress forests; but never since I was allowed to walk the woods have I found so impressive a company of trees as the tillandsia-draped oaks of Bonaventure.

I gazed awe-stricken as one new-arrived from another world. Bonaventure is called a graveyard, a town of the dead, but the few graves are powerless in such a depth of life. The rippling of living waters, the song of birds, the joyous confidence of flowers, the calm, undisturbable grandeur of the oaks, mark this place of graves as one of the Lord's most favoured abodes of life and light.

On no subject are our ideas more warped and pitiable than on death. Instead of the sympathy, the friendly union, of life and death so apparent in Nature, we are taught that death is an accident, a deplorable punishment for the oldest sin, the arch-enemy of life, etc. Town children, especially, are steeped in this death orthodoxy, for the natural beauties of death are seldom seen or taught in towns.

Of death among our own species, to say nothing of the thousand styles and modes of murder, our best memories, even among happy deaths, yield groans and tears, mingled with morbid exultation; burial companies, black in cloth and countenance; and, last of all, a black box burial in an ill-omened place, haunted by imaginary glooms and ghosts of every degree. Thus death becomes fearful, and the most notable and incredible thing heard around a death-bed is, 'I fear not to die.'

But let children walk with Nature, let them see the beautiful blendings and communions of death and life, their joyous inseparable unity, as taught in woods and meadows, plains and mountains and streams of our blessed star, and they will learn that death is stingless indeed, and as beautiful as life, and that the grave has no victory, for it never fights. All is divine harmony.

Most of the few graves of Bonaventure are planted with flowers. There is generally a magnolia at the head, near the strictly erect marble, a rose-bush or two at the foot, and some violets and showy exotics along the sides or on the tops. All is enclosed by a black iron railing, composed of rigid bars that might have been spears or bludgeons from a battlefield in Pandemonium.

It is interesting to observe how assiduously Nature seeks to remedy these laboured art blunders. She corrodes the iron and marble, and gradually levels the hill which is always heaped up, as if a sufficiently heavy quantity of clods could not be laid on the dead. Arching grasses come one by one; seeds come flying on downy wings, silent as fate, to give life's dearest beauty for the ashes of art; and strong evergreen arms laden with ferns and tillandsia drapery are spread over all – Life at work everywhere, obliterating all memory of the confusion of man.

In Georgia many graves are covered with a common shingle roof, supported on four posts as the cover of a well, as if rain and sunshine were not regarded as blessings. Perhaps, in this hot and insalubrious climate, moisture and sunheat are considered necessary evils to which they do not wish to expose their dead.

The money package that I was expecting did not arrive until the following week. After stopping the first night at the cheap, disreputable-looking hotel, I had only about a dollar and a half left in my purse, and so was compelled to camp out to make it last in buying only bread. I went out of the noisy town to seek a sleeping-place that was not marshy. After gaining the outskirts of the town toward the sea, I found some low sand dunes, yellow with flowering solidagoes.

I wandered wearily from dune to dune sinking ankle-deep in the sand, searching for a place to sleep beneath the tall flowers, free from insects and snakes, and above all from my fellow man. But idle negroes were prowling about everywhere, and I was afraid. The wind had strange sounds, waving the heavy panicles over my head, and I feared sickness from malaria so prevalent here, when I suddenly thought of the graveyard.

'There,' thought I, 'is an ideal place for a penniless wanderer. There no superstitious prowling mischief maker dares venture for fear of haunting ghosts, while for me there will be God's rest and peace. And then, if I am to be exposed to unhealthy vapours, I shall have capital compensation in seeing those grand oaks in the moonlight, with all the impressive and nameless influences of this lonely beautiful place.'

By this time it was near sunset, and I hastened across the common to the road and set off for Bonaventure, delighted with my choice, and almost glad to find that necessity had furnished me with so good an excuse for doing what I knew my mother would censure; for she made me promise I would not lie out of doors if I could possibly avoid it. The sun was set ere I was past the negroes' huts and rice fields, and I arrived near the graves in the silent hour of the gloaming.

I was very thirsty after walking so long in the muggy heat, a distance of three or four miles from the city, to get to this graveyard. A dull, sluggish, coffee-coloured stream flows under the road just outside the graveyard garden park, from which I managed to get a drink after breaking a way down to the water through a dense fringe of bushes, daring the snakes and alligators in the dark. Thus refreshed I entered the weird and beautiful abode of the dead.

All the avenue where I walked was in shadow, but an exposed tombstone frequently shone out in startling whiteness on either hand, and thickets of sparkleberry bushes gleamed like heaps of crystal. Not a breath of air moved the grey moss, and the great black arms of the trees met overhead and covered the avenue. But the canopy was fissured by many a netted seam and leafy-edged opening, through which the moonlight sifted in auroral rays, broidering the blackness in silvery light. Though tired, I sauntered a while enchanted, then lay down under one of the great oaks. I found a little mound that served for a pillow, placed my plant press and bag beside me and rested fairly well, though somewhat disturbed by large prickly-footed beetles creeping across my hands and face, and by a lot of hungry stinging mosquitoes.

When I awoke, the sun was up and all Nature was rejoicing. Some birds had discovered me as an intruder, and were making a great ado in interesting language and gestures. I heard the screaming of the bald eagles, and of some strange waders in the rushes. I heard the hum of Savannah with the long jarring hallows of negroes far away. On rising I found that my head had been resting on a grave, and though my sleep had not been quite so sound as that of the person below, I arose refreshed, and looking about me, the morning sunbeams pouring through the oaks and gardens dripping with dew, the beauty displayed was so glorious and exhilarating that hunger and care seemed only a dream.

Eating a breakfast cracker or two and watching for a few hours the beautiful light, birds, squirrels, and insects, I returned to Savannah, to find that my money package had not yet arrived. I then decided to go early to the graveyard and make a nest with a roof to keep off the dew, as there was no way of finding out how long I might have to stay.

I chose a hidden spot in a dense thicket of sparkleberry bushes, near the right bank of the Savannah River, where the bald eagles and a multitude of singing birds roosted. It was so well hidden that I had to carefully fix its compass bearing in my mind from a mark I made on the side of the main avenue, that I might be able to find it at bedtime.

I used four of the bushes as corner posts for my little hut, which was about four or five feet long by about three or four in width, tied little branches across from forks in the bushes to support a roof of rushes, and spread a thick mattress of Long Moss over the floor for a bed. My whole establishment was on so small a scale that I could have taken up, not only my bed, but my whole house, and walked. There I lay that night, eating a few crackers.

Next day I returned to the town and was disappointed as usual in obtaining money. So after spending the day looking at the plants in the gardens of the fine residences and town squares, I returned to my graveyard home. That I might not be observed and suspected of hiding, as if I had committed a crime, I always went home after dark, and one night, as I lay down in my moss nest, I felt some cold-blooded creature in it; whether a snake or simply a frog or toad I do not know, but instinctively, instead of drawing back my hand, I grasped the poor creature and threw it over the tops of the bushes. That was the only significant disturbance or fright that I got.

In the morning everything seemed divine. Only squirrels, sunbeams, and birds came about me. I was awakened every morning by these little singers after they discovered my nest. Instead of serenely singing their morning songs they at first came within two or three feet of the hut, and, looking in at me through the leaves, chattered and scolded in half-angry, half-wondering tones. The crowd constantly increased, attracted by the disturbance. Thus I began to get acquainted with my bird neighbours in this blessed wilderness, and after they learned that I meant them no ill they scolded less and sang more.

After five days of this graveyard life I saw that even with living on three or four cents a day my last twenty-five cents would soon be spent, and after trying again and again unsuccessfully to find some employment began to think that I must strike farther out into the country, but still within reach of town, until I came to some grain or rice field that had not yet been harvested, trusting that I could live indefinitely on toasted or raw corn, or rice.

By this time I was becoming faint, and in making the journey to the town was alarmed to find myself growing staggery and giddy. The ground ahead seemed to be rising up in front of me, and the little streams in the ditches on the sides of the road seemed to be flowing up hill. Then I realized that I was becoming dangerously hungry and became more than ever anxious to receive that money package.

To my delight this fifth or sixth morning, when I inquired if the money package had come, the clerk replied that it had, but that he could not deliver it without my being identified. I said, 'Well, here! read my brother's letter,' handing it to him. 'It states the amount in the package, where it came from, the day it was put into the office at Portage City, and I should think that would be enough.' He said, 'No, that is not enough. How do I know that this letter is yours? You may have stolen it. How do I know that you are John Muir?'

I said, 'Well, don't you see that this letter indicates that I am a botanist? For in it my brother says, 'I hope you are having a good time and finding many new plants.'' Now, you say that I might have stolen this letter from John Muir, and in that way have become aware of there being a money package to arrive from Portage for him. But the letter proves that John Muir must be a botanist, and though, as you say, his letter might have been stolen, it would hardly be likely that the robber would be able to steal John Muir's knowledge of botany. Now I suppose, of course, that you have been to school and know something of botany. Examine me and see if I know anything about it.'

At this he laughed good-naturedly, evidently feeling the force of my argument, and, perhaps, pitying me on account of looking pale and hungry, he turned and rapped at the door of a private office – probably the Manager's –

called him out and said, 'Mr So and So, here is a man who has inquired every day for the last week or so for a money package from Portage, Wisconsin. He is a stranger in the city with no one to identify him. He states correctly the amount and the name of the sender. He has shown me a letter which indicates that Mr Muir is a botanist, and that although a travelling companion may have stolen Mr Muir's letter, he could not have stolen his botany, and requests us to examine him.'

The head official smiled, took a good stare into my face, waved his hand, and said, 'Let him have it.' Gladly I pocketed my money, and had not gone along the street more than a few rods before I met a very large negro woman with a tray of gingerbread, in which I immediately invested some of my new wealth, and walked rejoicingly, munching along the street, making no attempt to conceal the pleasure I had in eating. Then, still hunting for more food, I found a sort of eating-place in a market and had a large regular meal on top of the gingerbread! Thus my 'marching through Georgia' terminated handsomely in a jubilee of bread.

FIVE

Through Florida Swamps and Forests

Of the people of the States that I have now passed, I best liked the Georgians. They have charming manners, and their dwellings are mostly larger and better than those of adjacent States. However costly or ornamental their homes or their manners, they do not, like those of the New Englander, appear as the fruits of intense and painful sacrifice and training, but are entirely divested of artificial weights and measures, and seem to pervade and twine about their characters as spontaneous growths with the durability and charm of living nature.

In particular, Georgians, even the commonest, have a most charmingly cordial way of saying to strangers, as they proceed on their journey, 'I wish you well, sir.' The negroes of Georgia, too, are extremely mannerly and polite, and appear always to be delighted to find opportunity for obliging anybody.

Athens contains many beautiful residences. I never before saw so much about a home that was so evidently done for beauty only, although this is by no means a universal characteristic of Georgian homes. Nearly all well-to-do farmers' families in Georgia and Tennessee spin and weave their own cloth. This work is almost all done by the mothers and daughters and consumes much of their time.

The traces of war are not only apparent on the broken fields, burnt fences, mills and woods ruthlessly slaughtered, but also on the countenances of the people. A few years after a forest has been burned another generation of bright and happy trees arises, in purest, freshest vigour; only the old trees, wholly or half dead, bear marks of the calamity. So with the people of this war-field. Happy, unscarred, and unclouded youth is growing up around the aged, half-consumed, and fallen parents, who bear in sad measure the ineffaceable marks of the farthest-reaching and most infernal of all civilized calamities.

Since the commencement of my floral pilgrimage I have seen much that is not only new, but altogether unallied, unacquainted with the plants of my former life. I have seen magnolias, tupelo, live-oak, Kentucky oak, tillandsia, long-leafed pine, palmetto, schrankia, and whole forests of strange trees and vine-tied thickets of blooming shrubs; whole meadowfuls of magnificent bamboo and lakefuls of lilies, all new to me; yet I still press eagerly on to Florida as the special home of the tropical plants I am looking for, and I feel sure I shall not be disappointed.

The same day on which the money arrived I took passage on the steamship Sylvan Shore for Fernandina, Florida. The daylight part of this sail along the coast of Florida was full of novelty, and by association awakened memories of my Scottish days at Dunbar on the Firth of Forth.

On board I had civilized conversation with a Southern planter on topics that are found floating in the mind of every white man down here who has a single thought. I also met a brother Scotchman, who was especially interesting and had some ideas outside of Southern politics. Altogether my half-day and night on board the steamer were pleasant, and carried me past a very sickly, entangled, overflowed, and unwalkable piece of forest.

It is pretty well known that a short geological time ago the ocean covered the sandy level margin, extending from the foot of the Alleghanies to the present coast-line, and in receding left many basins for lakes and swamps. The land is still encroaching on the sea, and it does so not evenly, in a regular line, but in fringing lagoons and inlets and dotlike coral islands.

It is on the coast strip of isles and peninsulas that sea-island cotton is grown. Some of these small islands are afloat, anchored only by the roots of mangroves and rushes. For a few hours our steamer sailed in the open sea, exposed to its waves, but most of the time she threaded her way among the lagoons, the home of alligators and countless ducks and waders.

15 October. Today, at last, I reached Florida, the so-called 'Land of Flowers,' that I had so long waited for, wondering if after all my longings and prayers would be in vain, and I should die without a glimpse of the flowery Canaan. But here it is, at the distance of a few yards! – a flat, watery, reedy coast, with clumps of mangrove and forests of moss-dressed, strange trees appearing low in the distance. The steamer finds her way among the reedy islands like a duck, and I step on a rickety wharf. A few steps more take me to a rickety town, Fernandina. I discover a baker, buy some bread, and without asking a single question, make for the shady, gloomy groves.

In visiting Florida in dreams, of either day or night, I always came suddenly on a close forest of trees, every one in flower, and bent down and entangled to network by luxuriant, bright-blooming vines, and over all a flood of bright sunlight. But such was not the gate by which I entered the promised land. Salt marshes, belonging more to the sea than to the land; with groves here and there, green and unflowered, sunk to the shoulders in sedges and rushes; with trees farther back, ill defined in their boundary, and instead of rising in hilly waves and swellings, stretching inland in low water-like levels.

We were all discharged by the captain of the steamer without breakfast, and, after meeting and examining the new plants that crowded about me, I threw down my press and little bag beneath a thicket, where there was a dry spot on some broken heaps of grass and roots, something like a deserted muskrat house, and applied myself to my bread breakfast. Everything in earth and sky had an impression of strangeness; not a mark of friendly recognition, not a breath, not a spirit whisper of sympathy came from anything about me, and of course I was lonely. I lay on my elbow eating my bread, gazing, and listening to the profound strangeness.

While thus engaged I was startled from these gatherings of melancholy by a rustling sound in the rushes behind me. Had my mind been in health, and my body not starved, I should only have turned calmly to the noise. But in this half-starved, unfriended condition I could have no healthy thought, and I at once believed that the sound came from an alligator. I fancied I could feel the stroke of his long notched tail, and could see his big jaws and rows of teeth, closing with a springy snap on me, as I had seen in pictures.

Well, I don't know the exact measure of my fright either in time or pain, but when I did come to a knowledge of the truth, my man-eating alligator became a tall white crane, handsome as a minister from spirit land – 'only that.' I was ashamed and tried to excuse myself on account of Bonaventure anxiety and hunger.

Florida is so watery and vine-tied that pathless wanderings are not easily possible in any direction. I started to cross the State by a gap hewn for the locomotive, walking sometimes between the rails, stepping from tie to tie, or walking on the strip of sand at the sides, gazing into the mysterious forest, Nature's own. It is impossible to write the dimmest picture of plant grandeur so redundant, unfathomable.

Short was the measure of my walk to-day. A new, canelike grass, or big lily, or gorgeous flower belonging to tree or vine, would catch my attention, and I would throw down my bag and press and splash through the coffee-brown water for specimens. Frequently I sank deeper and deeper until compelled to turn back and make the attempt in another and still another place. Oftentimes I was tangled in a labyrinth of armed vines like a fly in a spider-web. At all times, whether wading or climbing a tree for specimens of fruit, I was overwhelmed with the vastness and unapproachableness of the great guarded sea of sunny plants.

Magnolia grandiflora I had seen in Georgia; but its home, its better land, is here. Its large dark-green leaves, glossy bright above and rusty brown beneath, gleam and mirror the sunbeams most gloriously among countless flowerheaps of the climbing, smothering vines. It is bright also in fruit and more tropical in form and expression than the orange. It speaks itself a prince among its fellows.

Occasionally, I came to a little strip of open sand, planted with pine (*Pinus palustris* or *Cubensis*). Even these spots were mostly wet, though lighted with free sunshine, and adorned with purple liatris, and orange-coloured *Osmunda cinnamomea*. But the grandest discovery of this great wild day was the palmetto.

I was meeting so many strange plants that I was much excited, making many stops to get specimens. But I could not force my way far through the swampy forest, although so tempting and full of promise. Regardless of water snakes or insects, I endeavoured repeatedly to force a way through the tough vine-tangles, but seldom succeeded in getting farther than a few hundred yards.

It was while feeling sad to think that I was only walking on the edge of the vast wood, that I caught sight of the first palmetto in a grassy place, standing almost alone. A few magnolias were near it, and bald cypresses, but it was not shaded by them. They tell us that plants are perishable, soulless creatures, that only man is immortal, etc.; but this, I think, is something that we know very nearly nothing about. Anyhow, this palm was indescribably impressive and told me grander things than I ever got from human priest.

This vegetable has a plain grey shaft, round as a broom-handle, and a crown of varnished channelled leaves. It is a plainer plant than the humblest of Wisconsin oaks; but, whether rocking and rustling in the wind or poised thoughtful and calm in the sunshine, it has a power of expression not excelled by any plant high or low that I have met in my whole walk thus far.

This, my first specimen, was not very tall, only about twenty-five feet high, with fifteen or twenty leaves, arching equally and evenly all around. Each leaf was about ten feet in length, the blade four feet, the stalk six. The leaves are channelled like half-open clams and are highly polished, so that they reflect the sunlight like glass. The undeveloped leaves on the top stand erect, closely folded, all together forming an oval crown over which the tropic light is poured and reflected from its slanting mirrors in sparks and splinters and long-rayed stars.

I am now in the hot gardens of the sun, where the palm meets the pine, longed and prayed for and often visited in dreams, and, though lonely tonight amid this multitude of strangers, strange plants, strange winds blowing gently, whispering, cooing, in a language I never learned, and strange birds also, everything solid or spiritual full of influences that I never before felt, yet I thank the Lord with all my heart for his goodness in granting me admission to this magnificent realm.

16 *October.* Last evening when I was in the trackless woods, the great mysterious night becoming more mysterious in the thickening darkness, I gave up hope of finding food or a house bed, and searched only for a dry spot on which to sleep safely hidden from wild, runaway negroes. I walked rapidly for hours in the wet, level woods, but not a foot of dry ground could I find. Hollow-voiced owls were calling without intermission. All manner of night sounds came from strange insects and beasts, one by one, or crowded together. All had a home but I. Jacob on the dry plains of Padanaram, with a stone pillow, must have been comparatively happy.

When I came to an open place where pines grew, it was about ten o'clock, and I thought that now at last I would find dry ground. But even the sandy barren was wet, and I had to grope in the dark a long time, feeling the ground with my hands when my feet ceased to plash, before I at last discovered a little hillock dry enough to lie down on. I ate a piece of bread that I fortunately had in my bag, drank some of the brown water about my precious hillock, and lay down. The noisiest of the unseen witnesses around me were the owls, who pronounced their gloomy speeches with profound emphasis, but did not prevent the coming of sleep to heal weariness.

In the morning I was cold and wet with dew, and I set out breakfastless. Flowers and beauty I had in abundance, but no bread. A serious matter is this bread which perishes, and, could it be dispensed with, I doubt if civilization would ever see me again. I walked briskly, watching for a house, as well as the grand assemblies of novel plants.

Near the middle of the forenoon I came to a shanty where a party of loggers were getting out long pines for ship spars. They were the wildest of all the white savages I have met. The long-haired ex-guerrillas of the mountains of Tennessee and North Carolina are uncivilized fellows; but for downright barbarism these Florida loggers excel. Nevertheless, they gave me a portion of their yellow pork and hominy without either apparent hospitality or a grudge, and I was glad to escape to the forest again.

A few hours later I dined with three men and three dogs. I was viciously attacked by the latter, who undertook to undress me with their teeth. I was nearly dragged down backward, but escaped unbitten. Liver pie, mixed with sweet potatoes and fat duff, was set before me, and after I had finished a moderate portion, one of the men, turning to his companion, remarked: 'Wall, I guess that man quit eatin' 'cause he had nothin' more to eat. I'll get him more potato.'

Arrived at a place on the margin of a stagnant pool where an alligator had been rolling and sunning himself. 'See,' said a man who lived here, 'see, what a track that is! He must have been a mighty big fellow. Alligators wallow like hogs and like to lie in the sun. I'd like a shot at that fellow.' Here followed a long recital of bloody combats with the scaly enemy, in many of which he had, of course, taken an important part. Alligators are said to be extremely fond of negroes and dogs, and naturally the dogs and negroes are afraid of them.

Another man that I met today pointed to a shallow, grassy pond before his door. 'There,' said he, 'I once had a tough fight with an alligator. He caught my dog. I heard him howling, and as he was one of my best hunters I tried hard to save him. The water was only about knee-deep and I ran up to the alligator. It was only a small one about four feet long, and was having trouble in its efforts to drown the dog in the shallow water. I scared him and made him let go his hold, but before the poor crippled dog could reach the shore, he was caught again, and when I went at the alligator with a knife, it seized my arm. If it had been a little stronger it might have eaten me instead of my dog.'

I never in all my travels saw more than one, though they are said to be abundant in most of the swamps, and frequently attain a length of nine or ten feet. It is reported, also, that they are very savage, oftentimes attacking men in boats. These independent inhabitants of the sluggish waters of this low coast cannot be called the friends of man, though I heard of one big fellow that was caught young and was partially civilized and made to work in harness.

Many good people believe that alligators were created by the Devil, thus accounting for their all-consuming appetite and ugliness. But doubtless these creatures are happy and fill the place assigned them by the great Creator of us all. Fierce and cruel they appear to us, but beautiful in the eyes of God. They, also, are his children, for He hears their cries, cares for them tenderly, and provides their daily bread.

The antipathies existing in the Lord's great animal family must be wisely planned, like balanced repulsion and attraction in the mineral kingdom. How narrow we selfish, conceited creatures are in our sympathies! how blind to the rights of all the rest of creation! With what dismal irreverence we speak of our fellow mortals! Though alligators, snakes, etc., naturally repel us, they are not mysterious evils. They dwell happily in these flowery wilds, are part of God's family, unfallen, undepraved, and cared for with the same species of tenderness and love as is bestowed on angels in heaven or saints on earth.

I think that most of the antipathies which haunt and terrify us are morbid productions of ignorance and weakness. I have better thoughts of those alligators now that I have seen them at home. Honourable representatives of the great saurians of an older creation, may you long enjoy your lilies and rushes, and be blessed now and then with a mouthful of terror-stricken man by way of dainty!

Found a beautiful lycopodium today, and many grasses in the dry sunlit places called 'barrens,' 'hummocks,' 'savannas,' etc. Ferns also are abundant. What a flood of heat and light is daily poured out on these beautiful openings and intertangled woods! 'The land of the sunny South,' we say, but no part of our diversified country is more shaded and covered from sunshine. Many a sunny sheet of plain and prairie break the continuity of the forests of the North and West, and the forests themselves are mostly lighted also, pierced with direct ray lances, or (the sunlight) passing to the earth and the lowly plants in filtered softness through translucent leaves. But in the dense Florida forests sunlight cannot enter. It falls on the evergreen roof and rebounds in long silvery lances and flashy spray. In many places there is not light sufficient to feed a single green leaf on these dark forest floors. All that the eye can reach is just a maze of tree stems and crooked leafless vine strings. All the flowers, all the verdure, all the glory is up in the light.

The streams of Florida are still young, and in many places are untraceable. I expected to find these streams a little discoloured from the vegetable matter that I knew they must contain, and I was sure that in so flat a country I should not find any considerable falls or long rapids. The streams of upper Georgia are almost unapproachable in some places on account of luxuriant bordering vines, but the banks are nevertheless high and well defined. Florida streams are not yet possessed of banks and braes and definite channels. Their waters in deep places are black as ink, perfectly opaque, and glossy on the surface as if varnished. It often is difficult to ascertain which way they are flowing or creeping, so slowly and so widely do they circulate through the tree-tangles and swamps of the woods. The flowers here are strangers to me, but not more so than the rivers and lakes. Most streams appear to travel through a country with thoughts and plans for something beyond. But those of Florida are at home, do not appear to be travelling at all, and seem to know nothing of the sea.

17 October. Found a small, silvery-leafed magnolia, a bush ten feet high. Passed through a good many miles of open level pine barrens, as bounteously lighted as the 'openings' of Wisconsin. The pines are rather small, are planted sparsely and pretty evenly on these sandy flats not long risen from the sea. Scarcely a specimen of any other tree is to be found associated with the pine. But there are some thickets of the little saw palmettos and a magnificent assemblage of tall grasses, their splendid panicles waving grandly in the warm wind, and making low tuneful changes in the glistening light that is flashed from their bent stems.

Not a pine, not a palm, in all this garden excels these stately grass plants in beauty of wind-waving gestures. Here are panicles that are one mass of refined purple; others that have flowers as yellow as ripe oranges, and stems polished and shining like steel wire. Some of the species are grouped in groves and thickets like trees, while others may be seen waving without any companions in sight. Some of them have wide-branching panicles like Kentucky oaks, others with a few tassels of spikelets drooping from a tall, leafless stem. But all of them are beautiful beyond the reach of language. I rejoice that God has 'so clothed the grass of the field.' How strangely we are blinded to beauty and colour, form and motion, by comparative size! For example, we measure grasses by our own stature and by the height and bulkiness of trees. But what is the size of the greatest man, or the tallest tree that ever overtopped a grass! Compared with other things in God's creation the difference is nothing. We all are only microscopic animalcula.

18 October. Am walking on land that is almost dry. The dead levels are interrupted here and there by sandy waves a few feet in height. It is said that not a point in all Florida is more than three hundred feet above sea-level – a country where but little grading is required for roads, but much bridging, and boring of many tunnels through forests.

Before reaching this open ground, in a lonely, swampy place in the woods, I met a large, muscular, brawny young negro, who eyed me with glaring, wistful curiosity. I was very thirsty at the time, and inquired of the man if there were any houses or springs near by where I could get a drink. 'Oh yes,' he replied, still eagerly searching me with his wild eyes. Then he inquired where I came from, where I was going, and what brought me to such a wild country, where I was liable to be robbed, and perhaps killed.

'Oh, I am not afraid of any one robbing me,' I said, 'for I don't carry anything worth stealing.' 'Yes,' said he, 'but you can't travel without money.' I started to walk on, but he blocked my way. Then I noticed that he was trembling, and it flashed upon me all at once that he was thinking of knocking me down in order to rob me. After glaring at my pockets as if searching for weapons, he stammered in a quavering voice, 'Do you carry shooting-irons?' His motives, which I ought to have noted sooner, now were apparent to me. Though I had no pistol, I instinctively threw my hand back to my pistol pocket and, with my eyes fixed on his, I marched up close to him and said, 'I allow people to find out if I am armed or not.' Then he quailed, stepped aside, and allowed me to pass, for fear of being shot. This was evidently a narrow escape.

A few miles farther on I came to a cottonfield, to patches of sugar cane carefully fenced, and some respectable-looking houses with gardens. These little fenced fields look as if they were intended to be for plants what cages are for birds. Discovered a large, treelike cactus in a dooryard; a small species was abundant on the sand-hillocks. Reached Gainesville late in the night.

When within three or four miles of the town I noticed a light off in the pine woods. As I was very thirsty, I thought I would venture toward it with the hope of obtaining water. In creeping cautiously and noiselessly through the grass to discover whether or no it was a camp of robber negroes, I came suddenly in full view of the best-lighted and most primitive of all the domestic establishments I have yet seen in town or grove. There was, first of all, a big, glowing log fire, illuminating the overleaning bushes and trees, bringing out leaf and spray with more than noonday distinctness, and making still darker the surrounding wood. In the centre of this globe of light sat two negroes. I could see their ivory gleaming from the great lips, and their smooth cheeks flashing off light as if made of glass. Seen anywhere but in the South, the glossy pair would have been taken for twin devils, but here it was only a negro and his wife at their supper.

I ventured forward to the radiant presence of the black pair, and, after being stared at with that desperate fixedness which is said to subdue the lion, I was handed water in a gourd from somewhere out of the darkness. I was standing for a moment beside the big fire, looking at the unsurpassable simplicity of the establishment, and asking questions about the road to Gainesville, when my attention was called to a black lump of something lying in the ashes of the fire. It seemed to be made of rubber; but ere I had time for much speculation, the woman bent wooingly over the black object and said with motherly kindness, 'Come, honey, eat yo' hominy.'

At the sound of 'hominy' the rubber gave strong manifestations of vitality and proved to be a burly little negro boy, rising from the earth naked as to the earth he came. Had he emerged from the black muck of a marsh, we might easily have believed that the Lord had manufactured him like Adam direct from the earth.

Surely, thought I, as I started for Gainesville, surely I am now coming to the tropics, where the inhabitants wear nothing but their own skins. This fashion is sufficiently simple, – 'no troublesome disguises,' as Milton calls clothing – but it certainly is not quite in harmony with Nature. Birds make nests and nearly all beasts make some kind of bed for their young; but these negroes allow their younglings to lie nestless and naked in the dirt.

Gainesville is rather attractive – an oasis in the desert, compared with other villages. It gets its life from the few plantations located about it on dry ground that rises islandlike a few feet above the swamps. Obtained food and lodging at a sort of tavern.

19 October. Dry land nearly all day. Encountered limestone, flint, coral, shells, etc. Passed several thrifty cotton plantations with comfortable residences, contrasting sharply with the squalid hovels of my first days in Florida. Found a single specimen of a handsome little plant, which at once, in some mysterious way, brought to mind a young friend in Indiana. How wonderfully our thoughts and impressions are stored! There is that in the glance of a flower which may at times control the greatest of creation's braggart lords.

The magnolia is much more abundant here. It forms groves and almost exclusively forests the edge of ponds and the banks of streams. The easy, dignified simplicity of this noble tree, its plain leaf endowed with superb richness of colour and form, its open branches festooned with graceful vines and tillandsia, its showy crimson fruit, and its magnificent fragrant white flowers make *Magnolia grandiflora* the most lovable of Florida trees.

Discovered a great many beautiful polygonums, petalostemons, and yellow leguminous vines. Passed over fine sunny areas of the long-leafed and Cuban pines, which were everywhere accompanied by fine grasses and solidagoes. Wild orange groves are said to be rather common here, but I have seen only limes growing wild in the woods.

Came to a hut about noon, and, being weary and hungry, asked if I could have dinner. After serious consultation I was told to wait, that dinner would soon be ready. I saw only the man and his wife. If they had children, they may have been hidden in the weeds on account of nakedness. Both were suffering from malarial fever, and were very dirty. But they did not appear to have any realizing sense of discomfort from either the one or the other of these misfortunes. The dirt which encircled the countenances of these people did not, like the common dirt of the North, stick on the skin in bold union like plaster or paint, but appeared to stand out a little on contact like a hazy, misty, half-aerial mud envelope, the most diseased and incurable dirt that I ever saw, evidently desperately chronic and hereditary.

It seems impossible that children from such parents could ever be clean. Dirt and disease are dreadful enough when separate, but combined are inconceivably horrible. The neat cottage with a fragrant circumference of thyme and honeysuckle is almost unknown here. I have seen dirt on garments regularly stratified, the various strata no doubt indicating different periods of life. Some of them, perhaps, were annual layers, furnishing, like those of trees, a means of determining the age. Man and other civilized animals are the only creatures that ever become dirty.

Slept in the barrens at the side of a log. Suffered from cold and was drenched with dew. What a comfort a companion would be in the dark loneliness of such nights! Did not dare to make a fire for fear of discovery by robber negroes, who, I was warned, would kill a man for a dollar or two. Had a long walk after nightfall, hoping to discover a house. Became very thirsty and often was compelled to drink from slimy pools groped for in the grass, with the fear of alligators before my eyes.

20 October. Swamp very dense during this day's journey. Almost one continuous sheet of water covered with aquatic trees and vines. No stream that I crossed today appeared to have the least idea where it was going. Saw an alligator plash into the sedgy brown water by the roadside from an old log.

Arrived at night at the house of Captain Simmons, one of the very few scholarly, intelligent men that I have met in Florida. He had been an officer in the Confederate army in the war and was, of course, prejudiced against the North, but polite and kind to me, nevertheless. Our conversation, as we sat by the light of the fire, was on the one great question, slavery and its concomitants. I managed, however, to switch off to something more congenial occasionally – the birds of the neighbourhood, the animals, the climate, and what spring, summer, and winter are like in these parts.

About the climate, I could not get much information, as he had always lived in the South and, of course, saw nothing extraordinary in weather to which he had always been accustomed. But in speaking of animals, he at once became enthusiastic and told many stories of hairbreadth escapes, in the woods about his house, from bears, hungry alligators, wounded deer, etc. 'and now,' said he, forgetting in his kindness that I was from the hated North, 'you must stay with me a few days. Deer are abundant. I will lend you a rifle and we'll go hunting. I hunt whenever I wish venison, and I can get it about as easily from the woods nearby as a shepherd can get mutton out of his flock. And perhaps we will see a bear, for they are far from scarce here, and there are some big grey wolves, too.'

I expressed a wish to see some large alligators. 'Oh, well,' said he, 'I can take you where you will see plenty of those fellows, but they are not much to look at. I once got a good look at an alligator that was lying at the bottom of still, transparent water, and I think that his eyes were the most impressively cold and cruel of any animal I have seen. Many alligators go out to sea among the keys. These sea alligators are the largest and most ferocious, and sometimes attack people by trying to strike them with their tails when they are out fishing in boats.

'Another thing I wish you to see,' he continued, 'is a palmetto grove on a rich hummock a few miles from here. The grove is about seven miles in length by three in breadth. The ground is covered with long grass, uninterrupted with bushes or other trees. It is the finest grove of palmettos I have ever seen and I have oftentimes thought that it would make a fine subject for an artist.'

I concluded to stop – more to see this wonderful palmetto hummock than to hunt. Besides, I was weary and the prospect of getting a little rest was a tempting consideration after so many restless nights and long, hard walks by day.

21 October. Having outlived the sanguinary hunters' tales of my loquacious host, and breakfasted sumptuously on fresh venison and 'caller' fish from the sea, I set out for the grand palm grove. I had seen these dazzling sun-children in every day of my walk through Florida, but they were usually standing solitary, or in groups of three or four; but today I was to see them by the mile. The captain led me a short distance through his corn field and showed me a trail which would conduct me to the palmy hummock. He pointed out the general direction, which I noted upon my compass.

'Now,' said he, 'at the other side of my farthest field you will come to a jungle of cat-briers, but will be able to pass them if you manage to keep the trail. You will find that the way is not by any means well marked, for in passing through a broad swamp, the trail makes a good many abrupt turns to avoid deep water, fallen trees, or impenetrable thickets. You will have to wade a good deal, and in passing the water-covered places you will have to watch for the point where the trail comes out on the opposite side.'

I made my way through the briers, which in strength and ferocity equalled those of Tennessee, followed the path through all of its dim waverings, waded the many opposing pools, and, emerging suddenly from the leafy darkness of the swamp forest, at last stood free and unshaded on the border of the sundrenched palm garden. It was a level area of grasses and sedges, smooth as a prairie, well starred with flowers, and bounded like a clearing by a wall of vine-laden trees.

The palms had full possession and appeared to enjoy their sunny home. There was no jostling, no apparent effort to outgrow each other. Abundance of sunlight was there for every crown, and plenty to fall between. I walked enchanted in their midst. What a landscape! Only palms as far as the eye could reach! Smooth pillars rising from the grass, each capped with a sphere of leaves, shining in the sun as bright as a star. The silence and calm were as deep as ever I found in the dark, solemn pine woods of Canada, and that contentment which is an attribute of the best of God's plant people was as impressively felt in this alligator wilderness as in the homes of the happy, healthy people of the North.

The admirable Linnaeus calls palms 'the princes of the vegetable world.' I know that there is grandeur and nobility in their character, and that there are palms nobler far than these. But in rank they appear to me to stand below both the oak and the pine. The motions of the palms, their gestures, are not very graceful. They appear to best advantage when perfectly motionless in the noontide calm and intensity of light. But they rustle and rock in the evening wind. I have seen grasses waving with far more dignity. And when our northern pines are waving and bowing in signs of worship with the winter storm-winds, where is the prince of palms that could have the conscience to demand their homage!

Members of this palm congregation were of all sizes with respect to their stems; but their glorious crowns were all alike. In development there is only the terminal bud to consider. The young palm of this species emerges from the ground in full strength, one cluster of leaves arched every way, making a sphere about ten or twelve feet in diameter. The outside lower leaves gradually become yellow, wither, and break off, the petiole snapping squarely across, a few inches from the stem. New leaves develop with wonderful rapidity. They stand erect at first, but gradually arch outward as they expand their blades and lengthen their petioles.

New leaves arise constantly from the centre of the grand bud, while old ones break away from the outside. The splendid crowns are thus kept about the same size, perhaps a little larger than in youth while they are yet on the ground. As the development of the central axis goes on, the crown is gradually raised on a stem of about six to twelve inches in diameter. This stem is of equal thickness at the top and at the bottom and when young is roughened with the broken petioles. But these petiole-stumps fall off and disappear as they become old, and the trunk becomes smooth as if turned in a lathe.

After some hours in this charming forest I started on the return journey before night, on account of the difficulties of the swamp and the brier patch. On leaving the palmettos and entering the vine-tangled, half-submerged forest I sought long and carefully, but in vain, for the trail, for I had drifted about too incautiously in search of plants. But, recollecting the direction that I had followed in the morning, I took a compass bearing and started to penetrate the swamp in a direct line.

Of course I had a sore weary time, pushing through the tanglement of falling, standing, and half-fallen trees and bushes, to say nothing of knotted vines as remarkable for their efficient army of interlocking and lancing prickers as for their length and the number of their blossoms. But these were not my greatest obstacles, nor yet the pools and lagoons full of dead leaves and alligators. It was the army of cat-briers that I most dreaded. I knew that I would have to find the narrow slit of a lane before dark or spend the night with mosquitoes and alligators, without food or fire. The entire distance was not great, but a traveller in open woods can form no idea of the crooked and strange difficulties of pathless locomotion in these thorny, watery Southern tangles, especially in pitch darkness. I struggled hard and kept my course, leaving the general direction only when drawn aside by a plant of extraordinary promise, that I wanted for a specimen, or when I had to make the half-circuit of a pile of trees, or of a deep lagoon or pond.

In wading I never attempted to keep my clothes dry, because the water was too deep, and the necessary care would consume too much time. Had the water that I was forced to wade been transparent it would have lost much of its difficulty. But as it was, I constantly expected to plant my feet on an alligator, and therefore proceeded with strained caution. The opacity of the water caused uneasiness also on account of my inability to determine its depth. In many places I was compelled to turn back, after wading forty or fifty yards, and to try again a score of times before I succeeded in getting across a single lagoon.

At length, after miles of wading and wallowing, I arrived at the grand cat-brier encampment which guarded the whole forest in solid phalanx, unmeasured miles up and down across my way. Alas! the trail by which I had crossed in the morning was not to be found, and night was near. In vain I scrambled back and forth in search of an opening. There was not even a strip of dry ground on which to rest. Everywhere the long briers arched over to the vines and bushes of the watery swamp, leaving no standing-ground between them. I began to think of building some sort of a scaffold in a tree to rest on through the night, but concluded to make one more desperate effort to find the narrow track.

After calm, concentrated recollection of my course, I made a long exploration toward the left down the brier line, and after scrambling a mile or so, perspiring and bleeding, I discovered the blessed trail and escaped to dry land and the light. Reached the captain at sundown. Dined on milk and johnny-cake and fresh venison. Was congratulated on my singular good fortune and woodcraft, and soon after supper was sleeping the deep sleep of the weary and the safe.

22 October. This morning I was easily prevailed upon by the captain and an ex-judge, who was rusticating here, to join in a deer hunt. Had a delightful ramble in the long grass and flowery barrens. Started one deer but did not draw a single shot. The captain, the judge, and myself stood at different stations where the deer was expected to pass, while a brother of the captain entered the woods to arouse the game from cover. The one deer that he started took a different direction from any which this particular old buck had ever been known to take in times past, and in so doing was cordially cursed as being the 'd – dest deer that ever ran unshot.' To me it appeared as 'd – dest' work to slaughter God's cattle for sport. 'They were made for us,' say these self-approving preachers; 'for our food, our recreation, or other uses not yet discovered.' As truthfully we might say on behalf of a bear, when he deals successfully with an unfortunate hunter, 'Men and other bipeds were made for bears, and thanks be to God for claws and teeth so long.'

Let a Christian hunter go to the Lord's woods and kill his well-kept beasts, or wild Indians, and it is well, but let an enterprising specimen of these proper, predestined victims go to houses and fields and kill the most worthless person of the vertical godlike killers – oh! that is horribly unorthodox, and on the part of the Indians atrocious murder! Well, I have precious little sympathy for the selfish propriety of civilized man, and if a war of races should occur between the wild beasts and Lord Man, I would be tempted to sympathize with the bears.

SIX

Cedar Keys

23 October. Today I reached the sea. While I was yet many miles back in the palmy woods, I caught the scent of the salt sea breeze which, although I had so many years lived far from sea breezes, suddenly conjured up Dunbar, its rocky coast, winds and waves; and my whole childhood, that seemed to have utterly vanished in the New World, was now restored amid the Florida woods by that one breath from the sea. Forgotten were the palms and magnolias and the thousand flowers that enclosed me. I could see only dulse and tangle, long-winged gulls, the Bass Rock in the Firth of Forth, and the old castle, schools, churches, and long country rambles in search of birds' nests. I do not wonder that the weary camels coming from the scorching African deserts should be able to scent the Nile.

How imperishable are all the impressions that ever vibrate one's life! We cannot forget anything. Memories may escape the action of will, may sleep a long time, but when stirred by the right influence, though that influence be light as a shadow, they flash into full stature and life with everything in place. For nineteen years my vision was bounded by forests, but today emerging from a multitude of tropical plants, I beheld the Gulf of Mexico stretching away unbounded, except by the sky. What dreams and speculative matter for thought arose as I stood on the strand, gazing out on the burnished, treeless plain!

But now at the seaside I was in difficulty. I had reached a point that I could not ford, and Cedar Keys had an empty harbour. Would I proceed down the peninsula to Tampa and Key West, where I would be sure to find a vessel for Cuba, or would I wait here, like Crusoe, and pray for a ship. Full of these thoughts, I stepped into a little store which had a considerable trade in quinine and alligator and rattlesnake skins, and inquired about shipping, means of travel, etc.

The proprietor informed me that one of several sawmills near the village was running, and that a schooner chartered to carry a load of lumber to Galveston, Texas, was expected at the mills for a load. This mill was situated on a tongue of land a few miles along the coast from Cedar Keys, and I determined to see Mr Hodgson, the owner, to find out particulars about the expected schooner, the time she would take to load, whether I would be likely to obtain passage on her, etc.

Found Mr Hodgson at his mill. Stated my case, and was kindly furnished the desired information. I determined to wait the two weeks likely to elapse before she sailed, and go on her to the flowery plains of Texas, from any of whose ports, I fancied, I could easily find passage to the West Indies. I agreed to work for Mr Hodgson in the mill until I sailed, as I had but little money. He invited me to his spacious house, which occupied a shell hillock and commanded a fine view of the Gulf and many gems of palmy islets, called 'keys,' that fringe the shore like huge bouquets – not too big, however, for the spacious waters. Mr Hodgson's family welcomed me with that open, unconstrained cordiality which is characteristic of the better class of Southern people.

At the sawmill a new cover had been put on the main driving pulley, which, made of rough plank, had to be turned off and smoothed. He asked me if I was able to do this job and I told him that I could. Fixing a rest and making a tool out of an old file, I directed the engineer to start the engine and run slow. After turning down the pulley and getting it true, I put a keen edge on a common carpenter's plane, quickly finished the job, and was assigned a bunk in one of the employee's lodging-houses.

The next day I felt a strange dullness and headache while I was botanizing along the coast. Thinking that a bath in the salt water might refresh me, I plunged in and swam a little distance, but this seemed only to make me feel worse. I felt anxious for something sour, and walked back to the village to buy lemons.

Thus and here my long walk was interrupted. I thought that a few days' sail would land me among the famous flower-beds of Texas. But the expected ship came and went while I was helpless with fever. The very day after reaching the sea I began to be weighed down by inexorable leaden numbness, which I resisted and tried to shake off for three days, by bathing in the Gulf, by dragging myself about among the palms, plants, and strange shells of the shore, and by doing a little mill work. I did not fear any serious illness, for I never was sick before, and was unwilling to pay attention to my feelings.

But yet heavier and more remorselessly pressed the growing fever, rapidly gaining on my strength. On the third day after my arrival I could not take any nourishment, but craved acid. Cedar Keys was only a mile or two distant, and I managed to walk there to buy lemons. On returning, about the middle of the afternoon, the fever broke on me like a storm, and before I had staggered halfway to the mill I fell down unconscious on the narrow trail among dwarf palmettos.

When I awoke from the hot fever sleep, the stars were shining, and I was at a loss to know which end of the trail to take, but fortunately, as it afterwards proved, I guessed right. Subsequently, as I fell again and again after walking only a hundred yards or so, I was careful to lie with my head in the direction in which I thought the mill was. I rose, staggered, and fell, I know not how many times, in delirious bewilderment, gasping and throbbing with only moments of consciousness. Thus passed the hours till after midnight, when I reached the mill lodging-house.

The watchman on his rounds found me lying on a heap of sawdust at the foot of the stairs. I asked him to assist me up the steps to bed, but he thought my difficulty was only intoxication and refused to help me. The mill hands, especially on Saturday nights, often returned from the village drunk. This was the cause of the watchman's refusal. Feeling that I must get to bed, I made out to reach it on hands and knees, tumbled in after a desperate struggle, and immediately became oblivious to everything.

I awoke at a strange hour on a strange day to hear Mr

Hodgson ask a watcher beside me whether I had yet spoken, and when he replied that I had not, he said: 'Well, you must keep on pouring in quinine. That's all we can do.' How long I lay unconscious I never found out, but it must have been many days. Some time or other I was moved on a horse from the mill quarters to Mr Hodgson's house, where I was nursed about three months with unfailing kindness, and to the skill and care of Mr and Mrs Hodgson I doubtless owe my life. Through quinine and calomel – in sorry abundance – with other milder medicines, my malarial fever became typhoid. I had night sweats, and my legs became like posts of the temper and consistency of clay on account of dropsy. So on until January, a weary time.

As soon as I was able to get out of bed, I crept away to the edge of the wood, and sat day after day beneath a moss-draped live-oak, watching birds feeding on the shore when the tide was out. Later, as I gathered some strength, I sailed in a little skiff from one key to another. Nearly all the shrubs and trees here are evergreen, and a few of the smaller plants are in flower all winter. The principal trees on this Cedar Key are the juniper, long-leafed pine, and live-oak. All of the latter, living and dead, are heavily draped with tillandsia, like those of Bonaventure. The leaf is oval, about two inches long, three fourths of an inch wide, glossy and dark green above, pale beneath. The trunk is usually much divided, and is extremely unwedgeable. The specimen on the opposite page [of the original journal] is growing in the dooryard of Mr Hodgson's house. It is a grand old king, whose crown gleamed in the bright sky long ere the Spanish shipbuilders felled a single tree of this noble species.

The live-oaks of these keys divide empire with the long-leafed pine and palmetto, but in many places on the mainland there are large tracts exclusively occupied by them. Like the Bonaventure oaks they have the upper side of their main spreading branches thickly planted with ferns, grasses, small saw palmettos, etc. There is also a dwarf oak here, which forms dense thickets. The oaks of this key are not, like those of the Wisconsin openings, growing on grassy slopes, but stand, sunk to the shoulders, in flowering magnolias, heathworts, etc.

During my long sojourn here as a convalescent I used to lie on my back for whole days beneath the ample arms of these great trees, listening to the winds and the birds. There is an extensive shallow on the coast, close by, which the receding tide exposes daily. This is the feeding-ground of thousands of waders of all sizes, plumage, and language, and they make a lively picture and noise when they gather at the great family board to eat their daily bread, so bountifully provided for them.

Their leisure in time of high tide they spend in various ways and places. Some go in large flocks to reedy margins about the islands and wade and stand about quarrelling or making sport, occasionally finding a stray mouthful to eat. Some stand on the mangroves of the solitary shore, now and then plunging into the water after a fish. Some go long journeys inland, up creeks and inlets. A few lonely old herons of solemn look and wing retire to favourite oaks. It was my delight to watch those old white sages of immaculate feather as they stood erect drowsing away the dull hours between tides, curtained by long skeins of tillandsia. White-bearded hermits gazing dreamily from dark caves could not appear more solemn or more becomingly shrouded from the rest of their fellow beings.

One of the characteristic plants of these keys is the Spanish bayonet, a species of yucca, about eight or ten feet in height, and with a trunk three or four inches in diameter when full grown. It belongs to the lily family and develops palmlike from terminal buds. The stout leaves are very rigid, sharp-pointed and bayonet-like. By one of these leaves a man might be as seriously stabbed as by an army bayonet, and woe to the luckless wanderer who dares to urge his way through these armed gardens after dark. Vegetable cats of many species will rob him of his clothes and claw his flesh, while dwarf palmettos will saw his bones, and the bayonets will glide to his joints and marrow without the smallest consideration for Lord Man.

The climate of these precious islets is simply warm summer and warmer summer, corresponding in time with winter and summer in the North. The weather goes smoothly over the points of union betwixt the twin summers. Few of the storms are very loud or variable. The average temperature during the day, in December, was about sixty-five degrees in the shade, but on one day a little damp snow fell.

Cedar Key is two and one half or three miles in diameter and its highest point is forty-four feet above mean tidewater. It is surrounded by scores of other keys, many of them looking like a clump of palms, arranged like a tasteful bouquet, and placed in the sea to be kept fresh. Others have quite a sprinkling of oaks and junipers, beautifully united with vines. Still others consist of shells, with a few grasses and mangroves, circled with a rim of rushes. Those which have sedgy margins furnish a favourite retreat for countless waders and divers, especially for pelicans that frequently whiten the shore like a ring of foam.

It is delightful to observe the assembling of these feathered people from the woods and reedy isles; herons white as wave-tops, or blue as the sky, winnowing the warm air on wide quiet wing; pelicans coming with baskets to fill, and the multitude of smaller sailors of the air, swift as swallows, gracefully taking their places at Nature's family table for their daily bread. Happy birds!

The mockingbird is graceful in form and a fine singer, plainly dressed, rather familiar in habits, frequently coming like robins to doorsills for crumbs – a noble fellow, beloved by everybody. Wild geese are abundant in winter, associated with brant, some species of which I have never seen in the North. Also great flocks of robins, mourning doves, bluebirds, and the delightful brown thrashers. A large number of the smaller birds are fine singers. Crows, too, are here, some of them cawing with a foreign accent. The common bob-white quail I observed as far south as middle Georgia.

Lime Key is a fair specimen of the Florida Keys on this part of the coast. The cactus, *Opuntia*, sketched on another page, [of the original journal] is from the above-named key, and is abundant there. The fruit, an inch in length, is gathered, and made into a sauce, of which some people are fond. This species forms thorny, impenetrable thickets. One joint that I measured was fifteen inches long.

The mainland of Florida is less salubrious than the islands, but no portion of this coast, nor of the flat border which sweeps from Maryland to Texas, is quite free from malaria. All the inhabitants of this region, whether black or white, are liable to be prostrated by the ever-present fever and ague, to say nothing of the plagues of cholera and yellow fever that come and go suddenly like storms, prostrating the population and cutting gaps in it like hurricanes in woods.

The world, we are told, was made especially for man – a presumption not supported by all the facts. A numerous class of men are painfully astonished whenever they find anything, living or dead, in all God's universe, which they cannot eat or render in some way what they call useful to themselves. They have precise dogmatic insight of the intentions of the Creator, and it is hardly possible to be guilty of irreverence in speaking of *their* God any more than of heathen idols. He is regarded as a civilized, law-abiding gentleman in favour either of a republican form of government or of a limited monarchy; believes in the literature and language of England; is a warm supporter of the English constitution and Sunday schools and missionary societies; and is as purely a manufactured article as any puppet of a halfpenny theatre.

With such views of the Creator it is, of course, not surprising that erroneous views should be entertained of the creation. To such properly trimmed people, the sheep, for example, is an easy problem – food and clothing 'for us,' eating grass and daisies white by divine appointment for this predestined purpose, on perceiving the demand for wool that would be occasioned by the eating of the apple in the Garden of Eden.

In the same pleasant plan, whales are storehouses of oil for us, to help out the stars in lighting our dark ways until the discovery of the Pennsylvania oil wells. Among plants, hemp, to say nothing of the cereals, is a case of evident destination for ships' rigging, wrapping packages, and hanging the wicked. Cotton is another plain case of clothing. Iron was made for hammers and ploughs, and lead for bullets; all intended for us. And so of other small handfuls of insignificant things.

But if we should ask these profound expositors of God's intentions, How about those man-eating animals – lions, tigers, alligators – which smack their lips over raw man? Or about those myriads of noxious insects that destroy labour and drink his blood? Doubtless man was intended for food and drink for all these? Oh, no! Not at all! These are unresolvable difficulties connected with Eden's apple and the Devil. Why does water drown its lord? Why do so many minerals poison him? Why are so many plants and fishes deadly enemies? Why is the lord of creation subjected to the same laws of life as his subjects? Oh, all these things are satanic, or in some way connected with the first garden.

Now, it never seems to occur to these far-seeing teachers that Nature's object in making animals and plants might possibly be first of all the happiness of each one of them, not the creation of all for the happiness of one. Why should man value himself as more than a small part of the one great unit of creation? And what creature of all that the Lord has taken the pains to make is not essential to the completeness of that unit – the cosmos? The universe would be incomplete without man; but it would also be incomplete without the smallest transmicroscopic creature that dwells beyond our conceitful eyes and knowledge.

From the dust of the earth, from the common elementary fund, the Creator has made *Homo sapiens*. From the same material he has made every other creature, however noxious and insignificant to us. They are earth-born companions and our fellow mortals. The fearfully good, the orthodox, of this laborious patchwork of modern civilization cry 'Heresy' on every one whose sympathies reach a single hair's breadth beyond the boundary epidermis of our own species. Not content with taking all of earth, they also claim the celestial country as the only ones who possess the kind of souls for which that imponderable empire was planned.

This star, our own good earth, made many a successful

journey around the heavens ere man was made, and whole kingdoms of creatures enjoyed existence and returned to dust ere man appeared to claim them. After human beings have also played their part in Creation's plan, they too may disappear without any general burning or extraordinary commotion whatever.

Plants are credited with but dim and uncertain sensation, and minerals with positively none at all. But why may not even a mineral arrangement of matter be endowed with sensation of a kind that we in our blind exclusive perfection can have no manner of communication with?

But I have wandered from my object. I stated above that man claimed the earth was made for him, and I was going to say that venomous beasts, thorny plants, and deadly diseases of certain parts of the earth prove that the whole world was not made for him. When an animal from a tropical climate is taken to high latitudes, it may perish of cold, and we say that such an animal was never intended for so severe a climate. But when man betakes himself to sickly parts of the tropics and perishes, he cannot see that he was never intended for such deadly climates. No, he will rather accuse the first mother of the cause of the difficulty, though she may never have seen a fever district; or will consider it a providential chastisement for some self-invented form of sin.

Furthermore, all uneatable and uncivilizable animals, and all plants which carry prickles, are deplorable evils which, according to closet researches of clergy, require the cleansing chemistry of universal planetary combustion. But more than aught else mankind requires burning, as being in great part wicked, and if that transmundane furnace can be so applied and regulated as to smelt and purify us into conformity with the rest of the terrestrial creation, then the tophetisation of the erratic genus Homo were a consummation devoutly to be prayed for. But, glad to leave these ecclesiastical fires and blunders, I joyfully return to the immortal truth and immortal beauty of Nature.

SEVEN

A Sojourn in Cuba

One day in January I climbed to the housetop to get a
view of another of the fine sunsets of this land of flowers.
The landscape was a strip of clear Gulf water, a strip of
sylvan coast, a tranquil company of shell and coral keys,
and a gloriously coloured sky without a threatening cloud.
All the winds were hushed and the calm of the heavens
was as profound as that of the palmy islands and their
encircling waters. As I gazed from one to another of
the palm-crowned keys, enclosed by the sunset-coloured
dome, my eyes chanced to rest upon the fluttering sails of
a Yankee schooner that was threading the tortuous channel
in the coral reef leading to the harbour of Cedar Keys.
'There,' thought I, 'perhaps I may sail in that pretty white
moth.' She proved to be the schooner Island Belle.

One day soon after her arrival I went over the key to the
harbour, for I was now strong enough to walk. Some of
her crew were ashore after water. I waited until their casks
were filled, and went with them to the vessel in their boat.
Ascertained that she was ready to sail with her cargo of
lumber for Cuba. I engaged passage on her for twenty-five
dollars, and asked her sharpvisaged captain when he would
sail. 'Just as soon,' said he, 'as we get a north wind. We
have had northers enough when we did not want them,
and now we have this dying breath from the south.'

Hurrying back to the house, I gathered my plants,
took leave of my kind friends, and went aboard, and
soon, as if to calm the captain's complaints, Boreas came
foaming loud and strong. The little craft was quickly
trimmed and snugged, her inviting sails spread open,
and away she dashed to her ocean home like an exulting
war-horse to the battle. Islet after islet speedily grew
dim and sank beneath the horizon. Deeper became the

blue of the water, and in a few hours all of Florida vanished.

This excursion on the sea, the first one after twenty years in the woods, was of course exceedingly interesting, and I was full of hope, glad to be once more on my journey to the South. Boreas increased in power and the Island Belle appeared to glory in her speed and managed her full-spread wings as gracefully as a sea-bird. In less than a day our norther increased in strength to the storm point. Deeper and wider became the valleys, and yet higher the hills of the round plain of water. The flying jib and gaff topsails were lowered and mainsails close-reefed, and our deck was white with broken wave-tops.

'You had better go below,' said the captain. 'The Gulf Stream, opposed by this wind, is raising a heavy sea and you will be sick. No landsman can stand this long.' I replied that I hoped the storm would be as violent as his ship could bear, that I enjoyed the scenery of such a sea so much that it was impossible to be sick, that I had long waited in the woods for just such a storm, and that, now that the precious thing had come, I would remain on deck and enjoy it. 'Well,' said he, 'if you can stand this, you are the first landsman I ever saw that could.'

I remained on deck, holding on by a rope to keep from being washed overboard, and watched the behaviour of the Belle as she dared nobly on; but my attention was mostly directed among the glorious fields of foam-topped waves. The wind had a mysterious voice and carried nothing now of the songs of birds or of the rustling of palms and fragrant vines. Its burden was gathered from a stormy expanse of crested waves and briny tangles. I could see no striving in those magnificent wave-motions, no raging; all the storm was apparently inspired with nature's beauty and harmony. Every wave was obedient and harmonious as the smoothest ripple of a forest lake, and after dark all the water was phosphorescent like silver fire, a glorious sight.

Our luminous storm was all too short for me. Cuba's rock-waves loomed above the white waters early in the morning. The sailors, accustomed to detect the faintest land line, pointed out well-known guiding harbour-marks back of the Morro Castle long before I could see them through the flying spray. We sailed landward for several hours, the misty shore becoming gradually more earthlike. A flock of white-plumaged ships was departing from the Havana harbour, or, like us, seeking to enter it. No sooner had our little schooner flapped her sails in the lee of the Castle than she was boarded by a swarm of daintily dressed officials who were good-naturedly and good-gesturedly making all sorts of inquiries, while our busy captain, paying little attention to them, was giving orders to his crew.

The neck of the harbour is narrow and it is seldom posible to sail in to appointed anchorage without the aid of a steam tug. Our captain wished to save his money, but after much profitless tacking was compelled to take the proffered aid of steam, when we soon reached our quiet mid-harbour quarters and dropped anchor among ships of every size from every sea.

I was still four or five hundred yards from land and could determine no plant in sight excepting the long arched leaf banners of the banana and the palm, which made a brave show on the Morro Hill. When we were approaching the land, I observed that in some places it was distinctly yellow, and I wondered while we were yet some miles distant whether the colour belonged to the ground or to sheets of flowers. From our harbour home I could now see that the colour was plant-gold. On one side of the habour was a city of these yellow plants; on the other, a city of yellow stucco houses, narrowly and confusedly congregated.

'Do you want to go ashore?' said the captain to me. 'Yes,' I replied, 'but I wish to go to the plant side of the harbour.' 'Oh well,' he said, 'come with me now. There are some fine squares and gardens in the city, full of all sorts of trees and flowers. Enjoy these today, and some other day we will all go over the Morro Hill with you and gather shells. All kinds of shells are over there; but these yellow slopes that you see are covered only with weeds.'

We jumped into the boat and a couple of sailors pulled us

to the thronged, noisy wharf. It was Sunday afternoon,[1] the noisiest day of a Havana week. Cathedral bells and prayers in the forenoon, theatres and bull-fight bells and bellowings in the afternoon! Lowly whispered prayers to the saints and the Virgin, followed by shouts of praise or reproach to bulls and matadors! I made free with fine oranges and bananas and many other fruits. Pineapple I had never seen before. Wandered about the narrow streets, stunned with the babel of strange sounds and sights; went gazing, also, among the gorgeously flowered garden squares, and then waited among some boxed merchandise until our captain, detained by business, arrived. Was glad to escape to our little schooner Belle again, weary and heavy laden with excitement and tempting fruits.

As night came on, a thousand lights starred the great town. I was now in one of my happy dreamlands, the fairest of West India islands. But how, I wondered, shall I be able to escape from this great city of confusion? How shall I reach nature in this delectable land? Consulting my map, I longed to climb the central mountain range of the island and trace it through all its forests and valleys and over its summit peaks, a distance of seven or eight hundred miles. But alas! though out of Florida swamps, fever was yet weighing me down, and a mile of city walking was quite exhausting. The weather too was oppressively warm and sultry.

16 January. During the few days since our arrival the sun usually has risen unclouded, pouring down pure gold, rich and dense, for one or two hours. Then islandlike masses of white-edged cumuli suddenly appeared, grew to storm size, and in a few minutes discharged rain in tepid plashing bucketfuls, accompanied with high wind. This was followed by a short space of calm, half-cloudy sky, delightfully fragrant with flowers, and again the air would become hot, thick, and sultry.

This weather, as may readily be perceived, was severe to one so weak and feverish, and after a dozen trials of strength over the Morro Hill and along the coast northward

[1] Doubtless 12 January 1868.

for shells and flowers, I was sadly compelled to see that no enthusiasm could enable me to walk to the interior. So I was obliged to limit my researches to within ten or twelve miles of Havana. Captain Parsons offered his ship as my headquarters, and my weakness prevented me from spending a single night ashore.

The daily programme for nearly all the month that I spent here was about as follows: After breakfast a sailor rowed me ashore on the north side of the harbour. A few minutes' walk took me past the Morro Castle and out of sight of the town on a broad cactus common, about as solitary and untrodden as the tangles of Florida. Here I zigzagged and gathered prizes among unnumbered plants and shells along the shore, stopping to press the plant specimens and to rest in the shade of vine-heaps and bushes until sundown. The happy hours stole away until I had to return to the schooner. Either I was seen by the sailors who usually came for me, or I hired a boat to take me back. Arrived, I reached up my press and a big handful of flowers, and with a little help climbed up the side of my floating home.

Refreshed with supper and rest, I recounted my adventures in the vine tangles, cactus thickets, sunflower swamps, and along the shore among the breakers. My flower specimens, also, and pocketfuls of shells and corals had to be reviewed. Next followed a cool, dreamy hour on deck amid the lights of the town and the various vessels coming and departing.

Many strange sounds were heard: the vociferous, unsmotherable bells, the heavy thundering of cannon from the Castle, and the shouts of the sentinels in measured time. Combined they made the most incessant sharp-angled mass of noise that I ever was doomed to hear. Nine or ten o'clock found me in a small bunk with the harbour wavelets tinkling outside close to my ear. The hours of sleep were filled with dreams of heavy heat, or fruitless efforts for the disentanglement of vines, or of running from curling breakers back to the Morro, etc. Thus my days and nights went on.

Occasionally I was persuaded by the captain to go ashore

in the evening on his side of the harbour, accompanied perhaps by two or three other captains. After landing and telling the sailors when to call for us, we hired a carriage and drove to the upper end of the city, to a fine public square adorned with shady walks and magnificent plants. A brass band in imposing uniform played the characteristic lance-noted martial airs of the Spanish. Evening is the fashionable hour for aristocratic drives about the streets and squares, the only time that is delightfully cool. I never saw elsewhere people so neatly and becomingly dressed. The proud best-family Cubans may fairly be called beautiful, are under- rather than over-sized, with features exquisitely moulded, and set off with silks and broadcloth in excellent taste. Strange that their amusements should be so coarse. Bull-fighting, brain-splitting bell-ringing, and the most piercing artificial music appeal to their taste.

The rank and wealth of Havana nobility, when out driving, seems to be indicated by the distance of their horses from the body of the carriage. The higher the rank, the longer the shafts of the carriage, and the clumsier and more ponderous are the wheels, which are not unlike those of a cannon-cart. A few of these carriages have shafts twenty-five feet in length, and the brilliant-liveried negro driver on the lead horse, twenty or thirty feet in advance of the horse in the shafts, is beyond calling distance of his master.

Havana abounds in public squares, which in all my random strolls throughout the big town I found to be well watered, well cared for, well planted, and full of exceedingly showy and interesting plants, rare even amid the exhaustless luxuriance of Cuba. These squares also contained fine marble statuary and were furnished with seats in the shadiest places. Many of the walks were paved instead of gravelled.

The streets of Havana are crooked, labyrinthic, and exceedingly narrow. The sidewalks are only about a foot wide. A traveller experiences delightful relief when, heated and wearied by raids through the breadth of the dingy yellow town, dodging a way through crowds of men and mules lumbering carts and carriages, he at length finds shelter in the spacious, dustless, cool, flowery squares; still more when, emerging from all the din and darkness of these lanelike streets, he suddenly finds himself out in the middle of the harbour, inhaling full-drawn breaths of the sea breezes.

The interior of the better houses which came under my observation struck me with the profusion of dumpy, ill-proportioned pillars at the entrances and in the halls, and with the spacious open-fielded appearance of their enclosed square house-gardens or courts. Cubans in general appear to me superfinely polished, polite, and agreeable in society, but in their treatment of animals they are cruel. I saw more downright brutal cruelty to mules and horses during the few weeks I stayed there than in my whole life elsewhere. Live chickens and hogs are tied in bunches by the legs and carried to market thus, slung on a mule. In their general treatment of all sorts of animals they seem to have no thought for them beyond cold-blooded, selfish interest.

In tropical regions it is easy to build towns, but it is difficult to subdue their armed and united plant inhabitants, and to clear fields and make them blossom with breadstuff. The plant people of temperate regions, feeble, unarmed, unallied, disappear under the trampling feet of flocks, herds, and man, leaving their homes to enslavable plants which follow the will of man and furnish him with food. But the armed and united plants of the tropics hold their rightful kingdom plantfully, nor, since the first appearance of Lord Man, have they ever suffered defeat.

A large number of Cuba's wild plants circle closely about Havana. In five minutes' walk from the wharf I could reach the undisturbed settlements of Nature. The field of the greater portion of my rambling researches was a strip of rocky common, silent and unfrequented by anybody save an occasional beggar at Nature's door asking for a few roots and seeds. This natural strip extended ten miles along the coast northward, with but few large-sized trees and bushes, but rich in magnificent vines, cacti-composites, leguminous plants, grasses, etc. The wild flowers of this seaside field are a happy band, closely joined in splendid array. The trees shine with blossoms and with light reflected from the leaves. The individuality of the vines is lost in trackless, interlacing, twisting, overheaping union.

Our American 'South' is rich in flowery vines. In some districts almost every tree is crowned with them, aiding each other in grace and beauty. Indiana, Kentucky, and Tennessee have the grapevine in predominant numbers and development. Farther south dwell the greenbriers and countless leguminous vines. A vine common among the Florida islets, perhaps belonging to the dogbane family, overruns live-oaks and palmettos, with frequently more than a hundred stems twisted into one cable. Yet in no section of the South are there such complicated and such gorgeously flowered vine-tangles as flourish in armed safety in the hot and humid wild gardens of Cuba.

The longest and the shortest vine that I found in Cuba were both leguminous. I have said that the harbour side of the Morro Hill is clothed with tall yellow-flowered composites through which it is difficult to pass. But there are smooth, velvety, lawnlike patches in these *Compositae* forests. Coming suddenly upon one of these open places, I stopped to admire its greenness and smoothness, when I observed a sprinkling of large papilionaceous blossoms among the short green grass. The long composites that bordered this little lawn were entwined and almost smothered with vines which bore similar corollas in tropic abundance.

I at once decided that these sprinkled flowers had been blown off the encompassing tangles and had been kept fresh by dew and by spray from the sea. But, on stooping to pick one of them up, I was surprised to find that it was attached to Mother Earth by a short, prostrate, slender hair of a vine stem, bearing, besides the one large blossom, a pair or two of linear leaves. The flower weighed more than stem, root, and leaves combined. Thus, in a land of creeping and twining giants, we find also this charming, diminutive simplicity – the vine reduced to its lowest terms.

The longest vine, prostrate and untwined like its little neighbour, covers patches of several hundred square yards with its countless branches and close growth of upright, trifoliate, smooth green leaves. The flowers are as plain and un-showy in size and colour as those of the sweet peas of gardens. The seeds are large and satiny. The whole plant is noble in its motions and features, covering the ground with a depth of unconfused leafage which I have never seen equalled by any other plant. The extent of leaf-surface is greater, I think, than that of a large Kentucky oak. It grows, as far as my observation has reached, only upon shores, in a soil composed of broken shells and corals, and extends exactly to the water-line of the highest-reaching waves. The same plant is abundant in Florida.

The cacti form an important part of the plant population of my ramble ground. They are various as the vines, consisting now of a diminutive joint or two hid in the weeds, now rising into bushy trees, wide-topped, with trunks a foot in diameter, and with glossy, dark-green joints that reflect light like the silex-varnished palms. They are planted for fences, together with the Spanish bayonet and agave.

In one of my first walks I was laboriously scrambling among some low rocks gathering ferns and vines, when I was startled by finding my face close to a great snake, whose body was disposed carelessly like a castaway rope among the weeds and stones. After escaping and coming to my senses, I discovered that the snake was a member of the vegetable kingdom, capable of no dangerous amount of locomotion, but possessed of many a fang, and prostrate as though under the curse of Eden, 'Upon thy belly shalt thou go and dust shalt thou eat.'

One day, after luxuriating in the riches of my Morro pasture, and pressing many new specimens, I went down to the bank of brilliant wave-washed shells to rest awhile in their beauty, and to watch the breakers that a powerful norther was heaving in splendid rank along the coral boundary. I gathered pocketfuls of shells, mostly small but fine in colour and form, and bits of rosy coral. Then I amused myself by noting the varying colours of the waves and the different forms of their curved and blossoming crests. While thus alone and free it was interesting to learn the richly varied songs, or what we mortals call the roar, of expiring breakers. I compared their variation with the different distances to which the broken wave-water reached landward in its farthest-flung foam-wreaths, and endeavoured to form some idea of the one great song sounding forever all around the white-blooming shores of the world.

Rising from my shell seat, I watched a wave leaping from the deep and coming far up the bevelled strand to bloom and die in a mass of white. Then I followed the spent waters in their return to the blue deep, wading in their spangled, decaying fragments until chased back up the bank by the coming of another wave. While thus playing half studiously, I discovered in the rough, beaten deathbed of the wave a little plant with closed flowers. It was crouching in a hollow of the brown wave-washed rock, and one by one the chanting, dying waves rolled over it. The tips of its delicate pink petals peered above the clasping green calyx. 'Surely,' said I, as I stooped over it for a moment, before the oncoming of another wave, 'surely you cannot be living here! You must have been blown from some warm bank, and rolled into this little hollow crack like a dead shell.' But, running back after every retiring wave, I found that its roots were wedged into a shallow wrinkle of the coral rock, and that this wave-beaten chink was indeed its dwelling-place.

I had oftentimes admired the adaptation displayed in the structure of the stately dulse and other seaweeds, but never thought to find a highbred flowering plant dwelling amid waves in the stormy, roaring domain of the sea. This little plant has smooth globular leaves, fleshy and translucent like beads, but green like those of other land plants. The flower is about five eighths of an inch in diameter, rose-purple, opening in calm weather, when deserted by the waves. In general appearance it is like a small portulaca. The strand, as far as I walked it, was luxuriantly fringed with woody *Compositæ*, two or three feet in height, their tops purple and golden with a profusion of flowers. Among these I discovered a small bush whose yellow flowers were ideal; all the parts were present regularly alternate and in fives, and all separate, a plain harmony.

When a page is written over but once it may be easily

read; but if it be written over and over with characters of every size and style, it soon becomes unreadable, although not a single confused meaningless mark or thought may concur among all the written characters to mar its perfection. Our limited powers are similarly perplexed and overtaxed in reading the inexhaustible pages of nature, for they are written over and over uncountable times, written in characters of every size and colour, sentences composed of sentences, every part of a character a sentence. There is not a fragment in nature, for every relative fragment of one thing is a full harmonious unit in itself. All together form the one grand palimpsest of the world.

One of the most common plants of my pasture was the agave. It is sometimes used for fencing. One day, in looking back from the top of the Morro Hill, as I was returning to the Island Belle, I chanced to observe two poplar-like trees about twenty-five feet in height. They were growing in a dense patch of cactus and vine-knotted sunflowers. I was anxious to see anything so homelike as a poplar, and so made haste towards the two strange trees, making a way through the cactus and sunflower jungle that protected them. I was surprised to find that what I took to be poplars were agaves in flower, the first I had seen. They were almost out of flower, and fast becoming wilted at the approach of death. Bulbs were scattered about, and a good many still remained on the branches, which gave it a fruited appearance.

The stem of the agave seems enormous in size when one considers that it is the growth of a few weeks. This plant is said to make a mighty effort to flower and mature its seeds and then to die of exhaustion. Now there is not, so far as I have seen, a mighty effort or the need of one, in wild Nature. She accomplishes her ends without unquiet effort, and perhaps there is nothing more mighty in the development of the flower-stem of the agave than in the development of a grass panicle.

Havana has a fine botanical garden. I spent pleasant hours in its magnificent flowery arbours and around its shady fountains. There is a palm avenue which is considered wonderfully stately and beautiful, fifty palms in two straight lines, each rigidly perpendicular. The smooth round shafts, slightly thicker in the middle, appear to be productions of the lathe, rather than vegetable stems. The fifty arched crowns, inimitably balanced, blaze in the sunshine like heaps of stars that have fallen from the skies. The stems were about sixty or seventy feet in height, the crowns about fifteen feet in diameter.

Along a stream-bank were tall, waving bamboos, leafy as willows, and infinitely graceful in wind gestures. There was one species of palm, with immense bipinnate leaves and leaflets fringed, jagged, and one-sided, like those of *Adiantum*. Hundreds of the most gorgeous-flowered plants, some of them large trees, belonging to the *Leguminosæ*. Compared with what I have before seen in artificial flower-gardens, this is past comparison the grandest. It is a perfect metropolis of the brightest and most exuberant of garden plants, watered by handsome fountains, while gravelled and finely bordered walks slant and curve in all directions, and in all kinds of fanciful playground styles, more like the fairy gardens of the Arabian Nights than any ordinary manmade pleasure-ground.

In Havana I saw the strongest and ugliest negroes that I have met in my whole walk. The stevedores of the Havana wharf are muscled in true giant style, enabling them to tumble and toss ponderous casks and boxes of sugar weighing hundreds of pounds as if they were empty. I heard our own brawny sailors, after watching them at work a few minutes, express unbounded admiration of their strength, and wish that their hard outbulging muscles were for sale. The countenances of some of the negro orange-selling dames express a devout good-natured ugliness that I never could have conceived any arrangement of flesh and blood to be capable of. Besides oranges they sold pineapples, bananas, and lottery tickets.

EIGHT

By a Crooked Route to California

After passing a month in this magnificent island, and finding that my health was not improving, I made up my mind to push on to South America while my stock of strength, such as it was, lasted. But fortunately I could not find passage for any South American port. I had long wished to visit the Orinoco basin and in particular the basin of the Amazon. My plan was to get ashore anywhere on the north end of the continent, push on southward through the wilderness around the headwaters of the Orinoco, until I reached a tributary of the Amazon, and float down on a raft or skiff the whole length of the great river to its mouth. It seems strange that such a trip should ever have entered the dreams of any person, however enthusiastic and full of youthful daring, particularly under the disadvantages of poor health, of funds less than a hundred dollars, and of the insalubrity of the Amazon Valley.

Fortunately, as I said, after visiting all the shipping agencies, I could not find a vessel of any sort bound for South America, and so made up a plan to go north, to the longed-for cold weather of New York, and thence to the forests and mountains of California. There, I thought, I shall find health and new plants and mountains, and after a year spent in that interesting country I can carry out my Amazon plans.

It seemed hard to leave Cuba thus unseen and unwalked, but illness forbade my stay and I had to comfort myself with the hope of returning to its waiting treasures in full health. In the mean time I prepared for immediate departure. When I was resting in one of the Havana gardens, I noticed in a New York paper an advertisement for cheap fares to California. I consulted Captain Parsons concerning a passage to New York, where I could find a ship for California. At this time none of the California ships touched at Cuba.

'Well,' said he, pointing toward the middle of the harbour, 'there is a trim little schooner loaded with oranges for New York, and these little fruiters are fast sailers. You had better see her captain about a passage, for she must be about ready to sail.' So I jumped into the dinghy and a sailor rowed me over to the fruiter. Going aboard, I inquired for the captain, who soon appeared on deck and readily agreed to carry me to New York for twenty-five dollars. Inquiring when he would sail, 'Tomorrow morning at daylight,' he replied, 'if this norther slacks a little; but my papers are made out, and you will have to see the American consul to get permission to leave on my ship.'

I immediately went to the city, but was unable to find the consul, whereupon I determined to sail for New York without any formal leave. Early next morning, after leaving the Island Belle and bidding Captain Parsons goodbye, I was rowed to the fruiter and got aboard. Notwithstanding the north wind was still as boisterous as ever, our Dutch captain was resolved to face it, confident in the strength of his all-oak little schooner.

Vessels leaving the harbour are stopped at the Morro Castle to have their clearance papers examined; in particular, to see that no runaway slaves were being carried away. The officials came alongside our little ship, but did not come aboard. They were satisfied by a glance at the consul's clearance paper, and with the declaration of the captain, when asked whether he had any negroes, that he had 'not a d – d one.' 'All right, then,' shouted the officials, 'farewell! A pleasant voyage to you!' As my name was not on the ship's papers, I stayed below, out of sight, until I felt the heaving of the waves and knew that we were fairly out on the open sea. The Castle towers, the hills, the palms, and the wave-white strand, all faded in the distance, and our mimic sea-bird was at home in the open stormy gulf, curtsying to every wave and facing bravely to the wind.

Two thousand years ago our Saviour told Nicodemus that he did not know where the winds came from, nor where they were going. And now in this Golden Age, though we Gentiles know the birthplace of many a wind and also 'whither it is going,' yet we know about as little of winds in general as those Palestinian Jews, and our ignorance, despite the powers of science, can never be much less profound than it is at present.

The substance of the winds is too thin for human eyes, their written language is too difficult for human minds, and their spoken language mostly too faint for the ears. A mechanism is said to have been invented whereby the human organs of speech are made to write their own utterances. But without any extra mechanical contrivance, every speaker also writes as he speaks. All things in the creation of God register their own acts. The poet was mistaken when he said, 'From the wing no scar the sky sustains.' His eyes were simply too dim to see the scar. In sailing past Cuba I could see a fringe of foam along the coast, but could hear no sound of waves, simply because my ears could not hear wave-dashing at that distance. Yet every bit of spray was sounding in my ears.

The subject brings to mind a few recollections of the winds I heard in my late journey. In my walk from Indiana to the Gulf, earth and sky, plants and people, and all things changeable were constantly changing. Even in Kentucky nature and art have many a characteristic shibboleth. The people differ in language and in customs. Their architecture is generically different from that of their immediate neighbours in the north, not only in planters' mansions, but in barns and granaries and the cabins of the poor. But thousands of familiar flower faces looked from every hill and valley. I noted no difference in the sky, and the winds spoke the same things. I did not feel myself in a strange land.

In Tennessee my eyes rested upon the first mountain scenery I ever beheld. I was rising higher than ever before; strange trees were beginning to appear; alpine flowers and shrubs were meeting me at every step. But these Cumberland Mountains were timbered with oak, and were not unlike Wisconsin hills piled upon each other, and the strange plants were like those that were not strange. The sky was changed only a little, and the winds not by a single detectable note. Therefore, neither was Tennessee a strange land.

But soon came changes thick and fast. After passing the mountainous corner of North Carolina and a little way into Georgia, I beheld from one of the last ridge-summits of the Alleghanies that vast, smooth, sandy slope that reaches from the mountains to the sea. It is wooded with dark, branchy pines which were all strangers to me. Here the grasses, which are an earth-covering at the north, grow wide apart in tall clumps and tufts like saplings. My known flower companions were leaving me now, not one by one as in Kentucky and Tennessee, but in whole tribes and genera, and companies of shining strangers came trooping upon me in countless ranks. The sky, too, was changed, and I could detect strange sounds in the winds. Now I began to feel myself 'a stranger in a strange land.'

But in Florida came the greatest changes of all, for here grows the palmetto, and here blow the winds so strangely toned by them. These palms and these winds severed the last strands of the cord that united me with home. Now I was a stranger, indeed. I was delighted, astonished, confounded, and gazed in wonderment blank and overwhelming as if I had fallen upon another star. But in all of this long, complex series of changes, one of the greatest, and the last of all, was the change I found in the tone and language of the winds. They no longer came with the old home music gathered from open prairies and waving fields of oak, but they passed over many a strange string. The leaves of magnolia, smooth like polished steel, the immense inverted forests of tillandsia banks, and the princely crowns of palms – upon these the winds made strange music, and at the coming-on of night had overwhelming power to present the distance from friends and home, and the completeness of my isolation from all things familiar.

Elsewhere I have already noted that when I was a day's journey from the Gulf, a wind blew upon me from the sea – the first sea breeze that had touched me in twenty years. I was plodding along with my satchel and plants, leaning wearily forward, a little sore from approaching fever, when suddenly I felt the salt air, and before I had time to think, a whole flood of long-dormant associations rolled in upon me. The Firth of Forth, the Bass Rock, Dunbar Castle, and the winds and rocks and hills came upon the wings of that wind, and stood in as clear and sudden light as a landscape flashed upon the view by a blaze of lightning in a dark night.

I like to cling to a small chip of a ship like ours when the sea is rough, and long, comet-tailed streamers are blowing from the curled top of every wave. A big vessel responds awkwardly with mixed gestures to several waves at once, lumbering along like a loose floating island. But our little schooner, buoyant as a gull, glides up one side and down the other of each wave hill in delightful rhythm. As we advanced the scenery increased in grandeur and beauty. The waves heaved higher and grew wider, with corresponding motion. It was delightful to ride over this unsullied country of ever-changing water, and when looking upward from the shallow vales, or abroad over the round expanse from the tops of the wave hills, I almost forgot at times that the glassy, treeless country was forbidden to walkers. How delightful it would be to ramble over it on foot, enjoying the transparent crystal ground, and the music of its rising and falling hillocks, unmarred by the ropes and spars of a ship; to study the plants of these waving plains and their stream-currents; to sleep in wild weather in a bed of phosphorescent wave-foam, or briny scented seaweeds; to see the fishes by night in pathways of phosphorescent light; to walk the glassy plain in calm, with birds and flocks of glittering flying fishes here and there, or by night with every star pictured in its bosom!

But even of the land only a small portion is free to man, and if he, among other journeys on forbidden paths, ventures among the ice lands and hot lands, or up in the air in balloon bubbles, or on the ocean in ships, or down into it a little way in smothering diving-bells – in all such small adventures man is admonished and often punished in ways which clearly show him that he is in places for which, to use an approved phrase, he was never designed. However, in view of the rapid advancement of our time, no one can tell how far our star may finally be subdued to man's will. At all events I enjoyed this drifting locomotion to some extent.

The tar-scented community of a ship is a study in itself – a despotism on the small territory of a few drifting planks pinned together. But as our crew consisted only of four sailors, a mate, and the captain, there were no signs of despotism. We all dined at one table, enjoying our fine store of salt mackerel and plum duff, with endless abundance of oranges. Not only was the hold of our little ship filled with loose, unboxed oranges, but the deck also was filled up level with the rails, and we had to walk over the top of the golden fruit on boards.

Flocks of flying fishes often flew acros the ship, one or two occasionally falling among the oranges. These the sailors were glad to capture to sell in New York as curiosities, or to give away to friends. But the captain had a large Newfoundland dog who got the largest share of these unfortunate fishes. He used to jump from a dozing sleep as soon as he heard the fluttering of their wings, then pounce and feast leisurely on them before the sailors could reach the spot where they fell.

In passing through the Straits of Florida the winds died away and the sea was smoothed to unruffled calm. The water here is very transparent and of delightfully pure pale-blue colour, as different from ordinary dull-coloured water as town smoke from mountain air. I could see the bottom as distinctly as one sees the ground when riding over it. It seemed strange that our ship should be upborne in such an ethereal liquid as this, and that we did not run aground where the bottom seemed so near.

One morning, while among the Bahama dots of islands, we had calm sky and calm sea. The sun had risen in cloudless glory, when I observed a large flock of flying fish, a short distance from us, closely pursued by a dolphin. These fish-swallows rose in pretty good order, skimmed swiftly ahead for fifty or a hundred yards in a low arc, then dipped below the surface. Dripping and sparkling, they rose again in a few seconds and glanced back into the lucid brine with wonderful speed, but without apparent terror.

At length the dolphin, gaining on the flock, dashed into the midst of them, and now all order was at an end. They rose in scattering disorder, in all directions, like a flock of birds charged by a hawk. The pursuing dolphin also leaped into the air, showing his splendid colours and wonderful speed. After the first scattering flight all steady pursuit was useless, and the dolphin had but to pounce about in the broken mob of its weary prey until satisfied with his meal.

We are apt to look out on the great ocean and regard it as but a half-blank part of our globe – a sort of desert, 'a waste of water.' But, land animals though we be, land is about as unknown to us as the sea, for the turbid glances we gain of the ocean in general through commercial eyes are comparatively worthless. Now that science is making comprehensive surveys of the life of the sea, and the forms of its basins, and similar surveys are being made into the land deserts, hot and cold, we may at length discover that the sea is as full of life as the land. None can tell how far man's knowledge may yet reach.

After passing the Straits and sailing up the coast, when about opposite the south end of the Carolina coast, we had stiff head winds all the way to New York and our able little vessel was drenched all day long. Of course our load of oranges suffered, and since they were boarded over level with the rail, we had difficulty in walking and had many chances of being washed overboard. The flying fishes of Cape Hatteras appeared to take pleasure in shooting across from wave-top to wave-top. They avoided the ship during the day, but frequently fell among the oranges at night. The sailors caught many, but our big Newfoundland dog jumped for them faster than the sailors, and so almost monopolised the game.

When dark night fell on the stormy sea, the breaking waves of phosphorescent light were a glorious sight. On such nights I stood on the bowsprit holding on by a rope for hours in order to enjoy this phenomenon. How wonderful this light is! Developed in the sea by myriads of organised beings, it gloriously illuminates the pathways of the fishes, and every breaking wave, and in some places glows over large areas like sheet lightning. We sailed through large fields of seaweed, of which I procured specimens. I thoroughly enjoyed life in this novel little tar-and-oakum home, and, as the end of our voyage drew nigh, I was sorry at the thought of leaving it.

We were now, on the twelfth day, approaching New York, the big ship metropolis. We were in sight of the coast all day. The leafless trees and the snow appeared wonderfully strange. It was now about the end of February and snow covered the ground nearly to the water's edge. Arriving, as we did, in this rough winter weather from the intense heat and general tropical luxuriance of Cuba, the leafless, snow-white woods of New York struck us with all the novelty and impressiveness of a new world. A frosty blast was sweeping seaward from Sandy Hook. The sailors explored their wardrobes for their long-cast-off woollens, and pulled the ropes and managed the sails while muffled in clothing to the rotundity of Eskimos. For myself, long burdened with fever, the frosty wind, as it sifted through my loosened bones, was more delicious and grateful than ever was a spring-scented breeze.

We now had plenty of company; fleets of vessels were on the wing from all countries. Our taut little racer outwinded without exception all who, like her, were going to the port. Toward evening we were grinding and wedging our way through the ice-field of the river delta, which we passed with difficulty. Arrived in port at nine o'clock. The ship was deposited, like a cart at market, in a proper slip, and next morning we and our load of oranges, one third rotten, were landed. Thus all the purposes of our voyage were accomplished.

On our arrival the captain, knowing something of the lightness of my purse, told me that I could continue to occupy my bed on the ship until I sailed for California, getting my meals at a near-by restaurant. 'This is the way we are all doing,' he said. Consulting the newspapers, I found that the first ship, the Nebraska, sailed for Aspinwall in about ten days, and that the steerage passage to San Francisco by way of the Isthmus was only forty dollars.

In the meantime I wandered about the city without

knowing a single person in it. My walks extended but little beyond the sight of my little schooner home. I saw the name Central Park on some of the street-cars and thought I would like to visit it, but, fearing that I might not be able to find my way back, I dared not make the adventure. I felt completely lost in the vast throngs of people, the noise of the streets, and the immense size of the buildings. Often I thought I would like to explore the city if, like a lot of wild hills and valleys, it was clear of inhabitants.

The day before the sailing of the Panama ship I bought a pocket map of California and allowed myself to be persuaded to buy a dozen large maps, mounted on rollers, with a map of the world on one side and the United States on the other. In vain I said I had no use for them. 'But surely you want to make money in California, don't you? Everything out there is very dear. We'll sell you a dozen of these fine maps for two dollars each and you can easily sell them in California for ten dollars apiece.' I foolishly allowed myself to be persuaded. The maps made a very large, awkward bundle, but fortunately it was the only baggage I had except my little plant press and a small bag. I laid them in my berth in the steerage, for they were too large to be stolen and concealed.

There was a savage contrast between life in the steerage and my fine home on the little ship fruiter. Never before had I seen such a barbarous mob, especially at meals. Arrived at Aspinwall – Colon, we had half a day to ramble about before starting across the Isthmus. Never shall I forget the glorious flora, especially for the first fifteen or twenty miles along the Chagres River. The riotous exuberance of great forest trees, glowing in purple, red, and yellow flowers, far surpassed anything I had ever seen, especially of flowering trees, either in Florida or Cuba. I gazed from the car-platform enchanted. I fairly cried for joy and hoped that sometime I should be able to return and enjoy and study this most glorious of forests to my heart's content. We reached San Fransisco about the first of April, and I remained there only one day, before starting for Yosemite Valley.

I followed the Diablo foothills along the San José Valley to Gilroy, thence over the Diablo Mountains to the valley of the San Joaquin by the Pacheco Pass, thence down the valley opposite the mouth of the Merced River, thence across the San Joaquin, and up into the Sierra Nevada to the mammoth trees of Mariposa, and the glorious Yosemite, and thence down the Merced to this place. The goodness of the weather as I journeyed toward Pacheco was beyond all praise and description – fragrant, mellow, and bright. The sky was perfectly delicious, sweet enough for the breath of angels; every draught of it gave a separate and distinct piece of pleasure. I do not believe that Adam and Eve ever tasted better in their balmiest nook.

The last of the Coast Range foothills were in near view all the way to Gilroy. Their union with the valley is by curves and slopes of inimitable beauty. They were robed with the greenest grass and richest light I ever beheld, and were coloured and shaded with myriads of flowers of every hue, chiefly of purple and golden yellow. Hundreds of crystal rills joined song with the larks, filling all the valley with music like a sea, making it Eden from end to end.

The scenery, too, and all of nature in the Pass is fairly enchanting. Strange and beautiful mountain ferns are there, low in the dark canyons and high upon the rocky sunlit peaks; banks of blooming shrubs, and sprinklings and gatherings of garment flowers, precious and pure as ever enjoyed the sweets of a mountain home. And oh! what streams are there! beaming, glancing, each with music of its own, singing as they go, in shadow and light, onward upon their lovely, changing pathways to the sea. And hills rise over hills, and mountains over mountains, heaving, waving, swelling, in most glorious, overpowering, unreadable majesty.

When at last, stricken and faint like a crushed insect, you hope to escape from all the terrible grandeur of these mountain powers, other fountains, other oceans break forth before you; for there, in clear view, over heaps and rows of foothills, is laid a grand, smooth, outspread plain, watered by a river, and another range of peaky, snow-capped mountains a hundred miles in the distance. That plain is the valley of the San Joaquin, and those mountains are the great Sierra Nevada. The valley of the San Joaquin is the floweriest piece of world I ever walked, one vast, level, even flower-bed, a sheet of flowers, a smooth sea, ruffled a little in the middle by the tree fringing of the river and of smaller cross-streams here and there, from the mountains.

Florida is indeed a 'land of flowers,' but for every flower creature that dwells in its most delightsome places more than a hundred are living here. Here, here is Florida! Here they are not sprinkled apart with grass between as on our prairies, but grasses are sprinkled among the flowers; not as in Cuba, flowers piled upon flowers, heaped and gathered into deep, glowing masses, but side by side, flower to flower, petal to petal, touching but not entwined, branches weaving past and past each other, yet free and separate – one smooth garment, mosses next the ground, grasses above, petalled flowers between.

Before studying the flowers of this valley and their sky, and all of the furniture and sounds and adornments of their home, one can scarce believe that their vast assemblies are permanent; but rather that, actuated by some plant purpose, they had convened from every plain and mountain and meadow of their kingdom, and that the different colouring of patches, acres, and miles marks the bounds of the various tribes and family encampments.

NINE

Twenty Hill Hollow

Were we to cross-cut the Sierra Nevada into blocks a dozen miles or so in thickness, each section would contain a Yosemite Valley and a river, together with a bright array of lakes and meadows, rocks and forests. The grandeur and inexhaustible beauty of each block would be so vast and over-satisfying that to choose among them would be like selecting slices of bread cut from the same loaf. One bread-slice might have burnt spots, answering to craters; another would be more browned; another, more crusted or raggedly cut; but all essentially the same. In no greater degree would the Sierra slices differ in general character. Nevertheless, we all would choose the Merced slice, because, being easier of access, it has been nibbled and tasted, and pronounced very good; and because of the concentrated form of its Yosemite, caused by certain conditions of baking, yeasting, and glacier-frosting of this portion of the great Sierra loaf. In like manner, we readily perceive that the great central plain is one batch of bread – one golden cake – and we are loath to leave these magnificent loaves for crumbs, however good.

After our smoky sky has been washed in the rains of winter, the whole complex row of Sierras appears from the plain as a simple wall, slightly bevelled, and coloured in horizontal bands laid one above another, as if entirely composed of partially straightened rainbows. So, also, the plain seen from the mountains has the same simplicity of smooth surface, coloured purple, and yellow, like a patchwork of irised clouds. But when we descend to this smooth-furred sheet, we discover complexity in its physical conditions equal to that of the mountains, though less strongly marked. In particular, that portion of the plain lying between the Merced and the Tuolumne, within ten miles of the slaty foothills, is most elaborately carved into valleys, hollows, and smooth undulations, and among them is laid the Merced Yosemite of the plain – Twenty Hill Hollow.

This delightful Hollow is less than a mile in length, and of just sufficient width to form a well-proportioned oval. It is situated about midway between the two rivers, and five miles from the Sierra foothills. Its banks are formed of twenty hemispherical hills; hence its name. They surround and enclose it on all sides, leaving only one narrow opening toward the southwest for the escape of its waters. The bottom of the Hollow is about two hundred feet below the level of the surrounding plain, and the tops of its hills are slightly below the general level. Here is no towering dome, no Tissiack, to mark its place; and one may ramble close upon its rim before he is made aware of its existence. Its twenty hills are as wonderfully regular in size and position as in form. They are like big marbles half buried in the ground, each poised and settled daintily into its place at a regular distance from its fellows, making a charming fairy-land of hills, with small, grassy valleys between, each valley having a tiny stream of its own, which leaps and sparkles out into the open hollow, uniting to form Hollow Creek.

Like all others in the immediate neighbourhood, these twenty hills are composed of stratified lavas mixed with mountain drift in varying proportions. Some strata are almost wholly made up of volcanic matter – lava and cinders – thoroughly ground and mixed by the waters that deposited them; others are largely composed of slate and quartz boulders of all degrees of coarseness, forming conglomerates. A few clear, open sections occur, exposing an elaborate history of seas, and glaciers, and volcanic floods – chapters of cinders and ashes that picture dark days when these bright snowy mountains were clouded in smoke and rivered and laked with living fire. A fearful age, say mortals, when these Sierras flowed lava to the sea. What horizons of flame! What atmospheres of ashes and smoke!

The conglomerates and lavas of this region are readily

denuded by water. In the time when their parent sea was removed to form this golden plain, their regular surface, in great part covered with shallow lakes, showed little variation from motionless level until torrents of rain and floods from the mountains gradually sculptured the simple page to the present diversity of bank and brae, creating, in the section between the Merced and the Tuolumne, Twenty Hill Hollow, Lily Hollow, and the lovely valleys of Cascade and Castle Creeks, with many others nameless and unknown, seen only by hunters and shepherds, sunk in the wide bosom of the plain, like undiscovered gold. Twenty Hill Hollow is a fine illustration of a valley created by erosion of water. Here are no Washington columns, no angular El Capitans. The hollow canyons, cut in soft lavas, are not so deep as to require a single earthquake at the hands of science, much less a baker's dozen of those convenient tools demanded for the making of mountain Yosemites, and our moderate arithmetical standards are not outraged by a single magnitude of this simple, comprehensible hollow.

The present rate of denudation of this portion of the plain seems to be about one tenth of an inch per year. This approximation is based upon observations made upon stream-banks and perennial plants. Rains and winds remove mountains without disturbing their plant or animal inhabitants. Hovering petrels, the fishes and floating plants of ocean, sink and rise in beautiful rhythm with its waves; and, in like manner, the birds and plants of the plain sink and rise with these waves of land, the only difference being that the fluctuations are more rapid in the one case than in the other.

In March and April the bottom of the Hollow and every one of its hills are smoothly covered and plushed with yellow and purple flowers, the yellow predominating. They are mostly social *Compositæ*, with a few claytonias, gilias, eschscholtzias, white and yellow violets, blue and yellow lilies, dodecatheons, and eriogonums set in a half-floating maze of purple grasses. There is but one vine in the Hollow – the *Megarrhiza* (*Echinocystis* T. & D.) or 'Big Root.' The only bush within a mile of it, about four feet in height, forms so remarkable an object upon the universal smoothness that my dog barks furiously around it, at a cautious distance, as if it were a bear. Some of the hills have rock ribs that are brightly coloured with red and yellow lichens, and in moist nooks there are luxuriant mosses – *Bartramia, Dicranum, Funaria*, and several *Hypnums*. In cool, sunless coves the mosses are companioned with ferns – a *Cystopteris* and the little gold-dusted rock fern, *Gymnogramma triangularis*.

The Hollow is not rich in birds. The meadowlark homes there, and the little burrowing owl, the killdeer, and a species of sparrow. Occasionally a few ducks pay a visit to its waters, a few tall herons – the blue and the white – may at times be seen stalking along the creek; and the sparrow hawk and grey eagle come to hunt. The lark, who does nearly all the singing for the Hollow, is not identical in species with the meadowlark of the East, though closely resembling it; richer flowers and skies have inspired him with a better song than was ever known to the Atlantic lark.

I have noted three distinct lark-songs here. The words of the first, which I committed to memory at one of their special meetings, spelled as sung are, 'Wee-ro spee-ro wee-o weer-ly wee-it.' On the 20th of January, 1869, they sang 'Queed-lix boodle,' repeating it with great regularity, for hours together, to music sweet as the sky that gave it. On the 22nd of the same month, they sang 'Chee chool chee-dildy choodildy.' An inspiration is this song of the blessed lark, and universally absorbable by human souls. It seems to be the only bird-song of these hills that has been created with any direct reference to us. Music is one of the attributes of matter, into whatever forms it may be organized. Drops and sprays of air are specialized, and made to plash and churn in the bosom of a lark, as infinitesimal portions of air plash and sing about the angles and hollows of sand-grains, as perfectly composed and predestined as the rejoicing anthems of worlds; but our senses are not fine enough to catch the tones. Fancy the waving, pulsing melody of the vast flower-congregations of the Hollow flowing from myriad voices of tuned petal and pistil, and heaps of sculptured pollen. Scarce one note is for us; nevertheless, God be thanked for this blessed instrument hid beneath the feathers of a lark.

The eagle does not dwell in the Hollow; he only floats there to hunt the long-eared hare. One day I saw a fine specimen alight upon a hillside. I was at first puzzled to know what power could fetch the sky-king down into the grass with the larks. Watching him attentively, I soon discovered the cause of his earthiness. He was hungry and stood watching a long-eared hare, which stood erect at the door of his burrow, staring his winged fellow mortal full in the face. They were about ten feet apart. Should the eagle attempt to snatch the hare, he would instantly disappear in the ground. Should long-ears, tired of inaction, venture to skim the hill to some neighbouring burrow, the eagle would swoop above him and strike him dead with a blow of his pinions, bear him to some favourite rock table, satisfy his hunger, wipe off all marks of grossness, and go again to the sky.

Since antelopes have been driven away, the hare is the swiftest animal of the Hollow. When chased by a dog he will not seek a burrow, as when the eagle wings in sight, but skims wavily from hill to hill across connecting curves, swift and effortless as a bird-shadow. One that I measured was twelve inches in height at the shoulders. His body was eighteen inches, from nose-tip to tail. His great ears measured six and a half inches in length and two in width. His ears – which, notwithstanding their great size, he wears gracefully and becomingly, have procured for him the homely nickname, by which he is commonly known, of 'Jackass rabbit.' Hares are very abundant over all the plain and up in the sunny, lightly wooded foothills, but their range does not extend into the close pine forests.

Coyotes, or California wolves, are occasionally seen gliding about the Hollow, but they are not numerous, vast numbers having been slain by the traps and poisons of sheep-raisers. The coyote is about the size of a small shepherd-dog, beautiful and graceful in motion, with erect ears, and a bushy tail, like a fox. Inasmuch as he is fond of mutton, he is cordially detested by 'sheep-men' and nearly all cultured people.

The ground-squirrel is the most common animal of the Hollow. In several hills there is a soft stratum in which they have tunnelled their homes. It is interesting to observe these rodent towns in time of alarm. Their one circular street resounds with sharp, lancing outcries of 'Seekit, seek, seek, seekit!' Near neighbours, peeping cautiously half out of doors, engage in low, purring chat. Others, bolt upright on the doorsill or on the rock above, shout excitedly as if calling attention to the motions and aspects of the enemy. Like the wolf, this little animal is accursed, because of his relish for grain. What a pity that Nature should have made so many small mouths palated like our own!

All the seasons of the Hollow are warm and bright, and flowers bloom through the whole year. But the grand commencement of the annual genesis of plant and insect life is governed by the setting-in of the rains, in December or January. The air, hot and opaque, is then washed and cooled. Plant seeds, which for six months have lain on the ground dry as if garnered in a farmer's bin, at once unfold their treasured life. Flies hum their delicate tunes. Butterflies come from their coffins, like cotyledons from their husks. The network of dry water-courses, spread over valleys and hollows, suddenly gushes with bright waters, sparkling and pouring from pool to pool, like dusty mummies risen from the dead and set living and laughing with colour and blood. The weather grows in beauty, like a flower. Its roots in the ground develop day-clusters a week or two in size, divided by and shaded in foliage of clouds; or round hours of ripe sunshine wave and spray in sky-shadows, like racemes of berries half hidden in leaves.

These months of so-called rainy season are not filled with rain. Nowhere else in North America, perhaps in the world, are Januarys so balmed and glowed with vital sunlight. Referring to my notes of 1868 and 1869, I find that the first heavy general rain of the season fell on the 18th of December. January yielded to the Hollow, during the day, only twenty hours of rain, which was divided among six rainy days. February had only three days on which rain fell, amounting to eighteen and one-half hours in all. March had five rainy days. April had three, yielding seven hours of rain. May also had three wet days, yielding nine hours of rain, and completed the so-called 'rainy season' for that year, which is probably about an average one. It must be remembered that this rain record has nothing to do with what fell in the night.

The ordinary rainstorm of this region has little of that outward pomp and sublimity of structure so characteristic of the storms of the Mississippi Valley. Nevertheless, we have experienced rainstorms out on these treeless plains, in nights of solid darkness, as impressively sublime as the noblest storms of the mountains. The wind, which in settled weather blows from the northwest, veers to the southeast; the sky curdles gradually and evenly to a grainless, seamless, homogeneous cloud; and then comes the rain, pouring steadily and often driven aslant by strong winds. In 1869, more than three fourths of the winter rains came from the southeast. One magnificent storm from the northwest occurred on the 21st of March; an immense, round-browed cloud came sailing over the flowery hills in most imposing majesty, bestowing water as from a sea. The passionate rain-gush lasted only about one minute, but was nevertheless the most magnificent cataract of the sky mountains that I ever beheld. A portion of calm sky toward the Sierras was brushed with thin, white cloud-tissue, upon which the rain-torrent showed to a great height – a cloud waterfall, which, like those of Yosemite, was neither spray, rain, nor solid water. In the same year the cloudiness of January, omitting rainy days, averaged 0.32; February, 0.13; March, 0.20; April, 0.10; May, 0.08. The greater portion of this cloudiness was gathered into a few days, leaving the others blocks of solid, universal sunshine in every chink and pore.

At the end of January, four plants were in flower: a small white cress, growing in large patches, a low-set, umbelled plant, with yellow flowers; an eriogonum, with flowers in leafless spangles; and a small boragewort. Five or six mosses had adjusted their hoods, and were in the prime of life. In February, squirrels, hares, and flowers were in springtime joy. Bright plant-constellations shone everywhere about the Hollow. Ants were getting ready for work, rubbing and sunning their limbs upon the husk-piles around their doors; fat, pollen-dusted, 'burly, dozing humble-bees' were rumbling among the flowers; and spiders were busy mending up old webs, or weaving new ones. Flowers were born every day, and came gushing from the ground like gaily dressed children from a church. The bright air became daily more songful with fly-wings, and sweeter with breath of plants.

In March, plant-life is more than doubled. The little pioneer cress, by this time, goes to seed, wearing daintily embroidered silicles. Several claytonias appear; also, a large white leptosiphon(?), and two nemophilas. A small plantago becomes tall enough to wave and show silky ripples of shade. Towards the end of this month or the beginning of April, plant-life is at its greatest height. Few have any just conception of its amazing richness. Count the flowers of any portion of these twenty hills, or of the bottom of the Hollow, among the streams: you will find that there are from one to ten thousand upon every square yard, counting the heads of *Compositae* as single flowers. Yellow *Compositae* from by far the greater portion of this goldy-way. Well may the sun feed them with his richest light, for these shining sunlets are his very children – rays of his ray, beams of his beam! One would fancy that these California days receive more gold from the ground than they give to it. The earth has indeed become a sky; and the two cloudless skies, raying toward each other flower-beams and sunbeams, are fused and congolded into one glowing heaven. By the end of April most of the Hollow plants have ripened their seeds and died; but, undecayed, still assist the landscape with colour from persistent involucres and corolla-like heads of chaffy scales.

In May, only a few deep-set lilies and eriogonums are left alive. June, July, August, and September are the season of plant rest, followed, in October, by a most extraordinary outgush of plant-life, at the very driest time of the whole year. A small, unobtrusive plant, *Hemizonia virgata*, from six inches to three feet in height, with pale, glandular leaves, suddenly bursts into bloom, in patches miles in extent, like a resurrection of the gold of April. I have counted upward of three thousand heads upon one plant. Both leaves and pedicles are so small as to be nearly invisible among so vast a number of daisy golden-heads that seem to keep their places unsupported, like stars in the sky. The heads are about five eighths of an inch in diameter; rays and disk-flowers, yellow; stamens, purple. The rays have a rich, furred appearance, like the petals of garden pansies. The prevailing summer wind makes all the heads turn to the southeast. The waxy secretion of its leaves and involucres has suggested its grim name of 'tarweed', by which it is generally known. In our estimation, it is the most delightful member of the whole Composite Family of the plain. It remains in flower until November, uniting with an eriogonum that continues the floral chain across December to the spring plants of January. Thus, although nearly all of the year's plant-life is crowded into February, March, and April, the flower circle around the Twenty Hill Hollow is never broken.

The Hollow may easily be visited by tourists *en route* for Yosemite, as it is distant only about six miles from Snelling's. It is at all seasons interesting to the naturalist; but it has little that would interest the majority of tourists earlier than January or later than April. If you wish to see how much of light, life, and joy can be got into a January, go to this blessed Hollow. If you wish to see a plant-resurrection – myriads of bright flowers crowding from the ground, like souls to a judgment – go to Twenty Hills in February. If you are travelling for health, play truant to doctors and friends, fill your pocket with biscuits, and hide in the hills of the Hollow, lave in its waters, tan in its golds, bask in its flower-shine, and your baptisms will make you a new creature indeed. Or, choked in the sediments of society, so tired of the world, here will your hard doubts disappear, your carnal incrustations melt off, and your soul breathe deep and free in God's shoreless atmosphere of beauty and love.

Never shall I forget my baptism in this font. It happened in January, a resurrection day for many a plant and for me.

I suddenly found myself on one of its hills; the Hollow overflowed with light, as a fountain, and only small, sunless nooks were kept for mosseries and ferneries. Hollow Creek spangled and mazed like a river. The ground steamed with fragrance. Light, of unspeakable richness, was brooding the flowers. Truly, said I, is California the Golden State – in metallic gold, in sun gold, and in plant gold. The sunshine for a whole summer seemed condensed into the chambers of that one glowing day. Every trace of dimness had been washed from the sky; the mountains were dusted and wiped clean with clouds – Pacheco Peak and Mount Diablo, and the waved blue wall between; the grand Sierra stood along the plain, coloured in four horizontal bands: – the lowest, rose purple; the next higher, dark purple; the next, blue; and, above all, the white rows of summits pointing to the heavens.

It may be asked, What have mountains fifty or a hundred miles away to do with Twenty Hill Hollow? To lovers of the wild, these mountains are not a hundred miles away. Their spiritual power and the goodness of the sky make them near, as a circle of friends. They rise as a portion of the hilled walls of the Hollow. You cannot feel yourself out of doors; plain, sky, and mountains ray beauty which you feel. You bathe in these spirit-beams, turning round and round, as if warming at a camp-fire. Presently you lose consciousness of your own separate existence: you blend with the landscape, and become part and parcel of nature.

My First Summer
in the Sierra

Contents

ONE

Through the Foothills with a Flock of Sheep

In the great Central Valley of California there are only two seasons – spring and summer. The spring begins with the first rain-storm, which usually falls in November. In a few months the wonderful flowery vegetation is in full bloom and by the end of May it is dead and dry and crisp, as if every plant had been roasted in an oven.

Then the lolling, panting flocks and herds are driven to the high, cool, green pastures of the Sierra. I was longing for the mountains about this time, but money was scarce and I couldn't see how a bread supply was to be kept up. While I was anxiously brooding on the bread problem, so troublesome to wanderers, and trying to believe that I might learn to live like the wild animals, gleaning nourishment here and there from seeds and berries, sauntering and climbing in joyful independence of money or baggage, Mr Delaney, a sheep-owner, for whom I had worked a few weeks, called on me and offered to engage me to go with his shepherd and flock to the headwaters of the Merced and Tuolumne rivers – the very region I had most in mind. I was in the mood to accept work of any kind that would take me into the mountains whose treasures I had tasted last summer in the Yosemite region. The flock, he explained, would be moved gradually higher through the successive forest belts as the snow melted, stopping for a few weeks at the best places we came to. These I thought would be good centres of observation from which I might be able to make many telling excursions within a radius of eight or ten miles of the camps to learn something of the plants, animals and rocks; for he assured me that I should be left perfectly free to follow my studies. I judged, however, that I was in no way the right man for the place, and freely explained my shortcomings, confessing that I was wholly unacquainted with the topography of the upper mountains, the streams that would have to be crossed, and the wild sheep-eating animals; in short that, what with bears, coyotes, rivers, canyons and thorny, bewildering chaparral, I feared that half or more of his flock would be lost. Fortunately these shortcomings seemed insignificant to Mr Delaney. The main thing he said, was to have a man about the camp whom he could trust to see that the shepherd did his duty, and he assured me that the difficulties that seemed so formidable at a distance would vanish as we went on; encouraging me further by saying that the shepherd would do all the herding, that I could study plants and rocks and scenery as much as I liked, and that he would himself accompany us to the first main camp and make occasional visits to our higher ones to replenish our store of provisions and see how we prospered. Therefore I concluded to go, though still fearing, when I saw the silly sheep bouncing one by one through the narrow gate of the home corral to be counted, that of the two thousand and fifty many would never return.

I was fortunate in getting a fine St Bernard dog for a companion. His master, a hunter with whom I was slightly acquainted, came to me as soon as he heard that I was going to spend the summer in the Sierra and begged me to take his favourite dog, Carlo, with me, for he feared that if he were compelled to stay all summer on the plains the fierce heat might be the death of him. 'I think I can trust you to be kind to him,' he said, 'and I am sure he will be good to you. He knows all about the mountain animals, will guard the camp, assist in managing the sheep and in every way be found able and faithful.' Carlo knew we were talking about him, watched our faces and listened so attentively that I fancied he understood us. Calling him by name, I asked him if he was willing to go with me. He looked me in the face with eyes expressing wonderful intelligence, then turned to his master, and after permission was given by a wave of the hand toward me and a farewell patting caress, he quietly followed me as if he perfectly understood all that had been said and had known me always.

*   *   *

June 3, 1869. This morning provisions, camp-kettles, blankets, plant press etc., were packed on two horses, the flock headed for the tawny foothills, and away we sauntered in a cloud of dust: Mr Delaney, bony and tall, with sharply hacked profile like Don Quixote, leading the packhorses, Billy the proud shepherd, a Chinaman and a Digger Indian to assist in driving for the first few days in the brushy foothills, and myself with notebook tied to my belt.

The home ranch from which we set out is on the south side of the Tuolumne River near French Bar, where the foothills of metamorphic gold-bearing slates dip below the stratified deposits of the Central Valley. We had not gone more than a mile before some of the old leaders of the flock showed by the eager, inquiring way they ran and looked ahead that they were thinking of the high pastures they had enjoyed last summer. Soon the whole flock seemed to be hopefully excited, the mothers calling their lambs, the lambs replying in tones wonderfully human, their fondly quavering calls interrupted now and then by hastily snatched mouthfuls of withered grass. Amid all this seeming babel of baas as they streamed over the hills every mother and child recognised each other's voice. In case a tired lamb, half asleep in the smothering dust, should fail to answer, its mother would come running back through the flock toward the spot whence its last response was heard, and refused to be comforted until she found it, the one of a thousand, though to our eyes and ears all seemed alike.

The flock travelled at the rate of about a mile an hour, outspread in the form of an irregular triangle, about a hundred yards wide at the base and a hundred and fifty yards long, with a crooked, ever changing point made up of the strongest foragers, called the 'leaders,' which, with the most active of those scattered along the ragged sides of the 'main body,' hastily explored nooks in the rocks and bushes for grass and leaves; the lambs and feeble old mothers dawdling in the rear were called the 'tail end.'

About noon the heat was hard to bear; the poor sheep panted pitifully and tried to stop in the shade of every tree they came to, while we gazed with eager longing through the dim burning glare toward the snowy mountains and streams, though not one was in sight. The landscape is only wavering foothills roughened here and there with bushes and trees and outcropping masses of slate. The trees, mostly the blue oak (*Quercus Douglasii*), are about thirty to forty feet high with pale blue-green leaves and white bark, sparsely planted on the thinnest soil or in crevices of rocks beyond the reach of grass fires. The slates in many places rise abruptly through the tawny grass in sharp lichen-covered slabs like tombstones in deserted burying grounds. With the exception of the oak and four or five species of manzanita and ceanothus, the vegetation of the foothills is mostly the same as that of the plains. I saw this region in the early spring, when it was a charming landscape garden full of birds and bees and flowers. Now the scorching weather makes everything dreary. The ground is full of cracks, lizards glide about on the rocks and ants in amazing numbers, whose tiny sparks of life only burn the brighter with the heat, fairly quiver with unquenchable energy as they run in long lines to fight and gather food. How it comes that they do not dry to a crisp in a few seconds exposure to such sun-fire is marvellous. A few rattlesnakes lie coiled in out of the way places, but are seldom seen. Magpies and crows, usually so noisy, are silent now, standing in mixed flocks on the ground beneath the best shade trees, with bills wide open and wings drooped, too breathless to speak; the quails also are trying to keep in the shade about the few tepid alkaline waterholes; cottontail rabbits are running from shade to shade among the ceanothus brush and occasionally the long-eared hare is seen cantering gracefully across the wider openings.

After a short noon rest in a grove, the poor dust-choked flock was again driven ahead over the brushy hills, but the dim roadway we had been following faded away just where it was most needed, compelling us to stop to look about us and get our bearings. The Chinaman seemed to think we were lost, and chattered in pidgin English concerning the abundance of 'litty stick' (chaparral), while the Indian silently scanned the billowy ridges and gulches for openings. Pushing through the thorny jungle, we at length discovered a road trending toward Coulterville, which we followed until an hour before sunset, when we reached a dry ranch and camped for the night.

Camping in the foothills with a flock of sheep is simple and easy but far from pleasant. The sheep were allowed to pick what they could find in the neighbourhood until after sunset, watched by the shepherd, while the others gathered wood, made a fire, cooked, unpacked and fed the horses, etc. About dusk the weary sheep were gathered on the highest open spot near camp where they willingly bunched close together and after each mother had found her lamb and suckled it, all lay down and required no attention until morning.

Supper was announced by the call, 'Grub!' Each with a tin plate helped himself direct from the pots and pans while chatting about such camp studies as sheep-feed, mines, coyotes, bears, or adventures during the memorable gold days of pay dirt. The Indian kept in the background, saying never a word, as if he belonged to another species. The meal finished, the dogs were fed, the smokers smoked by the fire, and under the influences of fullness and tobacco the calm that settled on their faces seemed almost divine, something like the mellow meditative glow portrayed on the countenances of saints. Then suddenly, as if awakening from a dream, each with a sigh or a grunt knocked the ashes out of his pipe, yawned, gazed at the fire a few moments, said, 'Well, I believe I'll turn in,' and straightway vanished beneath his blankets. The fire smouldered and flickered an hour or two longer; the stars shone brighter; coons, coyotes and owls stirred the silence here and there, while crickets and hylas made a cheerful, continuous music, so fitting and full that it seemed a part of the very body of the night. The only discordance came from a snoring sleeper and the coughing sheep with dust in their throats. In the starlight the flock looked like a big grey blanket.

June 4. The camp was astir at daybreak; coffee, bacon and beans formed the breakfast, followed by quick dish-washing and packing. A general bleating began about sunrise. As soon as a mother ewe arose, her lamb came bounding and bunting for its breakfast and after the thousand youngsters had been suckled the flock began to nibble and spread. The restless wethers with ravenous appetites were the first to move but dared not go far from the main body. Billy and the Indian and the Chinaman kept them headed along the weary road, and allowed them to pick up what little they could find on a breadth of about a quarter of a mile. But as several flocks had already gone ahead of us, scarce a leaf, green or dry, was left; therefore the starving flock had to be hurried on over the bare, hot hills to the nearest of the green pastures, about twenty or thirty miles from here.

The pack-animals were led by Don Quixote, a heavy rifle over his shoulder intended for bears and wolves. This day has been as hot and dusty as the first, leading over gently sloping brown hills with mostly the same vegetation, excepting the strange looking Sabine pine (*Pinus Sabiniana*), which here forms small groves or is scattered among the blue oaks. The trunk divides at a height of fifteen or twenty feet into two or more stems, outleaning or nearly upright with many straggling branches and long grey needles, casting but little shade. In general appearance this tree looks more like a palm than a pine. The cones are about six or seven inches long, about five in diameter, very heavy, and last long after they fall so that the ground beneath the trees is covered with them. They make fine resiny, light giving campfires, next to ears of Indian corn the most beautiful fuel I've ever seen. The nuts, the Don tells me, are gathered in large quantities by the Digger Indians for food. They are about as large and hard-shelled as hazelnuts – food and fire fit for the gods from the same fruit.

June 5. This morning a few hours after setting out with the crawling sheep cloud, we gained the summit of the first well-defined bench on the mountain flank at Pino Blanco. The Sabine pines interest me greatly. They are so airy and strangely palm-like I was eager to sketch them and was in a fever of excitement without accomplishing much. I managed to halt long enough however to make a tolerably fair sketch of Pino Blanco peak from the southwest side, where there is a small field and vineyard irrigated by a stream that makes a pretty fall on its way down a gorge by the roadside.

After gaining the open summit of this first bench, feeling the natural exhilaration due to the slight elevation of a thousand feet or so and the hopes excited concerning the outlook to be obtained, a magnificent section of the Merced Valley at what is called Horseshoe Bend came full in sight – a glorious wilderness that seemed to be calling with a thousand songful voices. Bold, down-sweeping slopes, feathered with pines and clumps of manzanita with sunny, open spaces between them, make up most of the foreground; the middle and background present fold beyond fold of finely modelled hills and ridges rising into mountain-like masses in the distance, all covered with a shaggy growth of chaparral, mostly adenostoma, planted so marvellously close and even that it looks like soft, rich plush without a single tree or bare spot. As far as the eye can reach it extends, a heaving, swelling sea of green as regular and continuous as that produced by the heaths of Scotland. The sculpture of the landscape is as striking in its main lines as in its lavish richness of detail; a grand congregation of massive heights with the river shining between, each carved into smooth, graceful folds without leaving a single rocky angle exposed, as if the delicate fluting and ridging fashioned out of metamorphic slates had been carefully sandpapered. The whole landscape showed design, like man's noblest sculptures. How wonderful the power of its beauty! Gazing awestricken, I might have left everything for it. Glad, endless work would then be mine tracing the forces that have brought forth its features, its rocks and plants and animals and glorious weather. Beauty beyond thought everywhere, beneath, above, made and being made forever. I gazed and gazed and longed and admired until the dusty sheep and packs were far out of sight, made hurried notes and a sketch, though there was no need of either, for the colours and lines and expression of this divine landscape countenance are so burned into mind and heart they surely can never grow dim.

The evening of this charmed day is cool, calm, cloudless
and full of a kind of lightning I have never seen before –
white glowing cloud shaped masses down among the trees
and bushes, like quick throbbing fire-flies in the Wisconsin
meadows rather than the so called 'wild fire.' The spreading
hairs of the horses' tails and sparks from our blankets show
how highly charged the air is.

June 6. We are now on what may be called the second
bench or plateau of the range, after making many small
ups and downs over belts of hill waves, with of course,
corresponding changes in the vegetation. In open spots
many of the lowland compositae are still to be found
and some of the Mariposa tulips and other conspicuous
members of the lily family; but the characteristic blue
oak of the foothills is left below and its place is taken
by a fine large species (*Quercus Californica*) with deeply
lobed deciduous leaves, picturesquely divided trunk, and
broad, massy, finely lobed and modelled head. Here also
at a height of about twenty five hundred feet we come to
the edge of the great coniferous forest, made up mostly
of yellow pine with just a few sugar pines. We are now in
the mountains and they are in us, kindling enthusiasm,
making every nerve quiver, filling every pore and cell of
us. Our flesh and bone tabernacle seems transparent as
glass to the beauty about us, as if truly an inseparable part
of it, thrilling with the air and trees, streams and rocks,
in the waves of the sun, – a part of all nature, neither
old nor young, sick nor well, but immortal. Just now I
can hardly conceive of any bodily condition dependent
on food or breath any more than the ground or the sky.
How glorious a conversion, so complete and wholesome
it is, scarce memory enough of old bondage days left as a
standpoint to view it from! In this newness of life we seem
to have been so always.

Through a meadow opening in the pine woods I see
snowy peaks about the headwaters of the Merced above
Yosemite. How near they seem and how clear their outlines
on the blue air, or rather *in* the blue air; for they seem to
be saturated with it. How consuming strong the invitation
they extend! Shall I be allowed to go to them? Night and

day I'll pray that I may, but it seems too good to be true. Some one worthy will go, able for the Godful work, yet as far as I can I must drift about these love monument mountains, glad to be a servant of servants in so holy a wilderness.

Found a lovely lily (*Calochortus albus*) in a shady adenostoma thicket near Coulterville, in company with *Adiantum Chilense*. It is white with a faint purplish tinge inside at the base of the petals, a most impressive plant, pure as a snow crystal, one of the plant saints that all must love and be made so much the purer by it every time it is seen. It puts the roughest mountaineer on his good behaviour. With this plant the whole world would seem rich though none other existed. It is not easy to keep on with the camp cloud while such plant people are standing preaching by the wayside.

During the afternoon we passed a fine meadow bounded by stately pines, mostly the arrowy yellow pine, with here and there a noble sugar pine, its feathery arms outspread above the spires of its companion species in marked contrast; a glorious tree, its cones fifteen to twenty inches long, swinging like tassels at the ends of the branches with superb ornamental effect. Saw some logs of this species at the Greeley Mill. They are round and regular as if turned in a lathe, excepting the butt cuts, which have a few buttressing projections. The fragrance of the sugary sap is delicious and scents the mill and lumber yard. How beautiful the ground beneath this pine thickly strewn with slender needles and grand cones and the piles of cone scales, seed-wings and shells around the instep of each tree where the squirrels have been feasting! They get the seeds by cutting off the scales at the base in regular order, following their spiral arrangement, and the two seeds at the base of each scale, a hundred or two in a cone, must make a good meal. The yellow pine cones and those of most other species and genera are held upside down on the ground by the Douglas squirrel and turned around gradually until stripped, while he sits usually with his back to a tree, probably for safety. Strange to say, he never seems to get himself smeared with gum, not even his paws or whiskers – and how cleanly and beautiful in colour the cone-litter kitchen-middens he makes.

We are now approaching the region of clouds and cool streams. Magnificent white cumuli appeared about noon above the Yosemite region, – floating fountains refreshing the glorious wilderness, – sky mountains in whose pearly hills and dales the streams take their rise, – blessing with cooling shadows and rain. No rock landscape is more varied in sculpture, none more delicately modelled than these landscapes of the sky; domes and peaks rising, swelling, white as finest marble and firmly outlined, a most impressive manifestation of world building. Every rain cloud, however fleeting, leaves its mark, not only on trees and flowers whose pulses are quickened and on the replenished streams and lakes, but also on the rocks are its marks engraved whether we can see them or not.

I have been examining the curious and influential shrub *Adenostoma fasciculata*, first noticed about Horseshoe Bend. It is very abundant on the lower slopes of the second plateau near Coulterville, forming a dense, almost impenetrable growth that looks dark in the distance. It belongs to the rose family, is about six or eight feet high, has small white flowers in racemes eight to twelve inches long, round needle-like leaves, and reddish bark that becomes shreddy when old. It grows on sunbeaten slopes and like the grass is often swept away by running fires, but is quickly renewed from the roots. Any trees that may have established themselves in its midst are at length killed by these fires and this no doubt is the secret of the unbroken character of its broad belts. A few manzanitas, which also rise again from the root after consuming fires, make out to dwell with it, also a few bush compositae – baccharis and linosyris and some liliaceous plants, mostly calochortus and brodiaea, with deepset bulbs safe from fire. A multitude of birds and 'wee, sleekit, cow'rin', tim'rous beasties' find good homes in its deepest thickets, and the open bays and lanes that fringe the margins of its main belts offer shelter and food to the deer when winter storms drive them down from their high mountain pastures. A most admirable plant! It is now in bloom, and I like to wear its pretty fragrant racemes in my buttonhole.

Azalea occidentalis, another charming shrub, grows beside cool streams hereabouts and much higher in the Yosemite region. We found it this evening in bloom a few miles above Greeley's Mill, where we are camped for the night. It is closely related to the rhododendrons, is very showy and fragrant, and everybody must like it not only for itself but for the shady alders and willows, ferny meadows, and living water associated with it.

Another conifer was met today – incense cedar (*Libocedrus decurrens*), a large tree with warm yellow green foliage in flat plumes like those of arborvitae, bark cinnamon-coloured, and as the boles of the old trees are without limbs they make striking pillars in the woods where the sun chances to shine on them – a worthy companion of the kingly sugar and yellow pines. I feel strangely attracted to this tree. The brown close-grained wood, as well as the small scale-like leaves, is fragrant, and the flat overlapping plumes make fine beds, and must shed the rain well. It would be delightful to be stormbound beneath one of these noble, hospitable, inviting old trees, its broad sheltering arms bent down like a tent, incense rising from the fire made from its dry fallen branches, and a hearty wind chanting overhead. But the weather is calm tonight, and our camp is only a sheep camp. We are near the north fork of the Merced. The night wind is telling the wonders of the upper mountains, their snow fountains and gardens, forests and groves; even their topography is in its tones. And the stars, the everlasting sky lilies, how bright they are now that we have climbed above the lowland dust! The horizon is bounded and adorned by a spiry wall of pines, every tree harmoniously related to every other; definite symbols, divine hieroglyphics written with sunbeams. Would I could understand them! The stream flowing past the camp through ferns and lilies and alders makes sweet music to the ear, but the pines marshalled around the edge of the sky make a yet sweeter music to the eye. Divine beauty all. Here I could stay tethered forever with just bread and water, nor would I be lonely; loved friends and neighbours, as love for everything increased, would seem all the nearer however many the miles and mountains between us.

June 7. The sheep were sick last night, and many of them are still far from well, hardly able to leave camp, coughing, groaning, looking wretched and pitiful, all from eating the leaves of the blessed azalea. So at least say the shepherd and the Don. Having had but little grass since they left the plains, they are starving, and so eat anything green they can get. 'Sheep men' call azalea 'sheep-poison,' and wonder what the Creator was thinking about when he made it – so desperately does sheep business blind and degrade, though supposed to have a refining influence in the good old days we read of. The California sheep-owner is in haste to get rich, and often does, now that pasturage costs nothing, while the climate is so favourable that no winter food supply, shelter pens, or barns are required. Therefore large flocks may be kept at slight expense and large profits realised, the money invested doubling, it is claimed, every other year. This quickly acquired wealth usually creates desire for more. Then indeed the wool is drawn close down over the poor fellow's eyes, dimming or shutting out almost everything worth seeing.

As for the shepherd, his case is still worse, especially in winter when he lives alone in a cabin. For, though stimulated at times by hopes of one day owning a flock and getting rich like his boss, he at the same time is likely to be degraded by the life he leads, and seldom reaches the dignity or advantage – or disadvantage – of ownership. The degradation in his case has for cause one not far to seek. He is solitary most of the year, and solitude to most people seems hard to bear. He seldom has much good mental work or recreation in the way of books. Coming into his dingy hovel cabin at night, stupidly weary, he finds nothing to balance and level his life with the universe. No, after his dull drag all day after the sheep, he must get his supper; he is likely to slight this task and try to satisfy his hunger with whatever comes handy. Perhaps no bread is baked; then he just makes a few grimy flapjacks in his unwashed frying-pan, boils a handful of tea, and perhaps fries a few strips of rusty bacon. Usually there are dried peaches or apples in the cabin, but he hates to be bothered with the cooking of them, just swallows the bacon and flapjacks, and depends on the genial stupefaction of tobacco for the rest. Then to bed, often without removing the clothing worn during the day. Of course his health suffers, reacting on his mind; and seeing nobody for weeks or months, he finally becomes semi insane or wholly so.

The shepherd in Scotland seldom thinks of being anything but a shepherd. He has probably descended from a race of shepherds and inherited a love and aptitude for the business almost as marked as that of his collie. He has but a small flock to look after, sees his family and neighbours, has time for reading in fine weather and often carries books to the fields with which he may converse with kings. The oriental shepherd, we read, called his sheep by name; they knew his voice and followed him. The flocks must have been small and easily managed, allowing piping on the hills and ample leisure for reading and thinking. But whatever the blessings of sheep culture in other times and countries, the California shepherd, as far as I've seen or heard, is never quite sane for any considerable time. Of all Nature's voices baa is about all he hears. Even the howls and ki-yis of coyotes might be blessings if well heard, but he hears them only through a blur of mutton and wool, and they do him no good.

The sick sheep are getting well and the shepherd is discoursing on the various poisons lurking in these high pastures – azalea, kalmia, alkali. After crossing the north fork of the Merced we turned to the left toward Pilot Peak and made a considerable ascent on a rocky, brush-covered ridge to Brown's Flat, where for the first time since leaving the plains the flock is enjoying plenty of green grass. Mr Delaney intends to seek a permanent camp somewhere in the neighbourhood, to last several weeks.

Before noon we passed Bower Cave, a delightful marble palace, not dark and dripping but filled with sunshine, which pours into it through its wide-open mouth facing the south. It has a fine, deep, clear little lake with mossy banks embowered with broad-leaved maples, all under ground, wholly unlike anything I have seen in the cave line even in Kentucky, where a large part of the State is honeycombed with caves. This curious specimen of subterranean scenery is located on a belt of marble that is said to extend from the north end of the range to the extreme south. Many other caves occur on the belt, but none like this as far as I have learned, combining as it does sunny outdoor brightness and vegetation with the crystalline beauty of the underworld. It is claimed by a Frenchman, who has fenced and locked it, placed a boat on the lakelet and seats on the mossy bank under the maple trees, and charges a dollar admission fee. Being on one of the ways to the Yosemite Valley, a good many tourists visit it during the travel months of summer, regarding it as an interesting addition to their Yosemite wonders.

Poison oak or poison ivy (*Rhus diversiloba*), both as a bush and a scrambler up trees and rocks, is common throughout the foothill region up to a height of at least three thousand feet above the sea. It is somewhat trouble-some to most travellers, inflaming the skin and eyes, but blends harmoniously with its companion plants, and many a charming flower leans confidingly upon it for protection and shade. I have oftentimes found the curious twining lily (*Stropholirion Californicum*) climbing its branches, showing no fear but rather congenial companionship. Sheep eat it without apparent ill effects; so do horses to some extent, though not fond of it, and to many persons it is harmless. Like most other things not apparently useful to man, it has few friends, and the blind question, 'Why was it made?' goes on and on with never a guess that first of all it might have been made for itself.

Brown's Flat is a shallow fertile valley on the top of the divide between the north fork of the Merced and Bull Creek, commanding magnificent views in every direction. Here the adventurous pioneer David Brown made his headquarters for many years, dividing his time between gold-hunting and bear-hunting. Where could lonely hunter find a better solitude? Game in the woods, gold in the rocks, health and exhilaration in the air, while the colours and cloud furniture of the sky are ever inspiring through all sorts of weather. Though sternly practical, like most pioneers, old David seems to have been uncommonly fond of scenery. Mr Delaney, who knew him well, tells me that he dearly loved to climb to the summit of a commanding ridge to gaze abroad over the forest to the snow-clad peaks and sources of the rivers, and over the foreground valleys and gulches to note where miners were at work or claims were abandoned, judging by smoke from cabins and camp-fires, the sounds of axes, etc.; and when a rifle-shot was heard, to guess who was the hunter, whether Indian or some poacher on his wide domain. His dog Sandy accompanied him everywhere, and well the little hairy mountaineer knew and loved his master and his master's aims. In deer-hunting he had but little to do, trotting behind his master as he slowly made his way through the wood, careful not to step heavily on dry twigs, scanning open spots in the chaparral, where the game loves to feed in the early morning and towards sunset; peering cautiously over ridges as new outlooks were reached, and along the meadowy borders of streams. But when bears were hunted, little Sandy became more important, and it was as a bear hunter that Brown became famous. His hunting method, as described by Mr Delaney, who had passed many a night with him in his lonely cabin and learned his stories, was simply to go slowly and silently through the best bear pastures, with his dog and rifle and a few pounds of flour, until he found a fresh track and then follow it to the death, paying no heed to the time required. Wherever the bear went he followed, led by little Sandy, who had a keen nose and never lost the track, however rocky the ground. When high open points were reached, the likeliest places were carefully scanned. The time of year enabled the hunter to determine approximately where the bear would be found – in the spring and early summer on open spots about the banks of streams and springy places eating grass and clover and lupines, or in dry meadows feasting on strawberries; toward the end of summer, on dry ridges, feasting on manzanita berries, sitting on his haunches, pulling down the laden branches with his paws and pressing them together so as to get good compact mouthfuls however much mixed with twigs and leaves; in the Indian summer, beneath the pines, chewing the cones cut off by the squirrels, or occasionally climbing a tree to gnaw and break off the fruitful branches. In late autumn, when acorns are ripe, Bruin's favourite feeding grounds are groves of the California oak in park-like canyon flats. Always the cunning hunter knew where to look, and seldom came upon Bruin unawares. When the hot scent showed the dangerous game was nigh, a long halt was made, and the intricacies of the topography and vegetation leisurely scanned to catch a glimpse of the shaggy wanderer, or to at least determine where he was most likely to be.

'Whenever,' said the hunter, 'I saw a bear before it saw me I had no trouble in killing it. I just studied the lay of the land and got to leeward of it no matter how far around I had to go, and then worked up to within a few hundred yards or so, at the foot of a tree that I could easily climb, but too small for the bear to climb. Then I looked well to the condition of my rifle, took off my boots so as to climb well if necessary, and waited until the bear turned its side in clear view when I could make a sure or at least a good shot. In case it showed fight I climbed out of reach. But bears are slow and awkward with their eyes, and being to leeward of them they could not scent me, and I often got in a second shot before they noticed the smoke. Usually, however, they run when wounded and hide in the brush. I let them run a good safe time before I ventured to follow them and Sandy was pretty sure to find them dead. If not, he barked and drew their attention and occasionally rushed in for a distracting bite, so that I was able to get to a safe distance for a final shot. Oh, yes, bear hunting is safe enough when followed in a safe way, though like every other business it has its accidents, and little doggie and I have had some close calls. Bears like to keep out of the way of men as a general thing, but if an old, lean, hungry mother with cubs met a man on her own ground she would, in my opinion, try to catch and eat him. This would be only fair play anyhow, for we eat them, but nobody hereabout has been used for bear grub that I know of.'

Brown had left his mountain home ere we arrived, but

a considerable number of Digger Indians still linger in their cedar bark huts on the edge of the flat. They were attracted in the first place by the white hunter whom they had learned to respect, and to whom they looked for guidance and protection against their enemies the Pah Utes, who sometimes made raids across from the east side of the range to plunder the stores of the comparatively feeble Diggers and steal their wives.

TWO

In Camp on the North Fork of the Merced

June 8. The sheep, now grassy and good-natured, slowly nibbled their way down into the valley of the north fork of the Merced at the foot of Pilot Peak Ridge to the place selected by the Don for our first central camp, a picturesque hopper-shaped hollow formed by converging hill slopes at a bend of the river. Here racks for dishes and provisions were made in the shade of the riverbank trees, and beds of fern fronds, cedar plumes, and various flowers, each to the taste of its owner, and a corral back on the open flat for the wool.

June 9. How deep our sleep last night in the mountain's heart, beneath the trees and stars, hushed by solemn-sounding waterfalls and many small soothing voices in sweet accord whispering peace! And our first pure mountain day, warm, calm, cloudless, – how immeasurable it seems, how serenely wild! I can scarcely remember its beginning. Along the river, over the hills, in the ground, in the sky, spring work is going on with joyful enthusiasm, new life, new beauty, unfolding, unrolling in glorious exuberant extravagance, – new birds in their nests, new winged creatures in the air, and new leaves, new flowers, spreading, shining, rejoicing everywhere.

The trees about the camp stand close, giving ample shade for ferns and lilies, while back from the bank most of the sunshine reaches the ground, calling up the grasses and flowers in glorious array, tall bromus waving like bam-boos, starry compositae, monardella, Mariposa tulips, lupines, gilias, violets, glad children of light. Soon every fern frond will be unrolled, great beds of common pteris and woodwardia along the river, wreaths and rosettes of pellaea and cheilanthes on sunny rocks. Some of the woodwardia fronds are already six feet high.

A handsome little shrub, *Chamoebatia foliolosa*, belonging to the rose family, spreads a yellow-green mantle beneath the sugar pines for miles without a break, not mixed or roughened with other plants. Only here and there a Washington lily may be seen nodding above its even surface, or a bunch or two of tall bromus as if for ornament. This fine carpet shrub begins to appear at, say, twenty five hundred or three thousand feet above sea level, is about knee high or less, has brown branches, and the largest stems are only about half an inch in diameter. The leaves, light yellow-green, thrice pinnate and finely cut, give them a rich ferny appearance, and they are dotted with minute glands that secrete wax with a peculiar pleasant odour that blends finely with the spicy fragrance of the pines. The flowers are white, five eighths of an inch in diameter and look like those of the strawberry. Am delighted with this little bush. It is the only true carpet shrub of this part of the Sierra. The manzanita, rhamnus, and most of the species of ceanothus make shaggy rugs and border fringes rather than carpets or mantles.

The sheep do not take kindly to their new pastures, perhaps from being too closely hemmed in by the hills. They are never fully at rest. Last night they were frightened, probably by bears or coyotes prowling and planning for a share of the grand mass of mutton.

June 10. Very warm. We get water for the camp from a rock basin at the foot of a picturesque cascading reach of the river where it is well stirred and made lively without being beaten into dusty foam. The rock here is black metamorphic slate, worn into smooth knobs in the stream channels, contrasting with the fine grey and white cascading water as it glides and glances and falls in lace-like sheets and braided overfolding currents. Tufts of sedge growing on the rock knobs that rise above the surface produce a charming effect, the long elastic leaves arching over in every direction, the tips of the longest drooping into the current, which dividing against the projecting rocks makes still finer lines, uniting with the sedges to see how beautiful the happy stream can be made. Nor is this all, for the giant saxifrage also is growing on some of the knob rock islets, firmly anchored and displaying their broad, round, umbrella-like leaves in showy groups by themselves, or above the sedge tufts. The flowers of this species (*Saxifraga peltata*) are purple, and form tall glandular racemes that are in bloom before the appearance of the leaves. The fleshy root stocks grip the rock in cracks and hollows, and thus enable the plant to hold on against occasional floods, – a marked species employed by Nature to make yet more beautiful the most interesting portions of these cool clear streams. Near camp the trees arch over from bank to bank, making a leafy tunnel full of soft subdued light, through which the young river sings and shines like a happy living creature.

Heard a few peals of thunder from the upper Sierra and saw firm white bossy cumuli rising back of the pines. This was about noon.

June 11. On one of the eastern branches of the river discovered some charming cascades with a pool at the foot of each of them. White dashing water, a few bushes and tufts of carex on ledges leaning over with fine effect, and large orange lilies assembled in superb groups on fertile soil beds beside the pools.

There are no large meadows or grassy plains near camp to supply lasting pasture for our thousands of busy nibblers. The main dependence is ceanothus brush on the hills and tufted grass patches here and there, with lupines and pea vines among the flowers on sunny open spaces. Large areas have already been stripped bare, or nearly so, compelling the poor hungry wool bundles to scatter far and wide, keeping the shepherds and dogs at the top of their speed to hold them within bounds. Mr Delaney has gone back to the plains, taking the Indian and Chinaman with him, leaving instruction to keep the flock here or hereabouts until his return, which he promised would not be long delayed.

How fine the weather is! Nothing more celestial can I conceive. How gently the winds blow! Scarce can these tranquil air currents be called winds. They seem the very breath of Nature, whispering peace to every living thing. Down in the camp dell there is no swaying of treetops; most of the time not a leaf moves. I don't remember having seen a single lily swinging on its stalk, though they are so tall the least breeze would rock them. What grand bells these lilies have! Some of them big enough for children's bonnets. I have been sketching them, and would fain draw every leaf of their wide shining whorls and every curved and spotted petal. More beautiful, better kept gardens cannot be imagined. The species is *Lilium pardalinum*, five to six feet high, leaf whorls a foot wide, flowers about six inches wide, bright orange, purple spotted in the throat, segments revolute – a majestic plant.

June 12. A slight sprinkle of rain – large drops far apart, falling with hearty pat and plash on leaves and stones and into the mouths of the flowers. Cumuli rising to the eastward. How beautiful their pearly bosses! How well they harmonise with the upswelling rocks beneath them. Mountains of the sky, solid-looking, finely sculptured, their richly varied topography wonderfully defined. Never before have I seen clouds so substantial looking in form and texture. Nearly every day toward noon they rise with visible swelling motion as if new worlds were being created. And how fondly they brood and hover over the gardens and forests with their cooling shadows and showers, keeping every petal and leaf in glad health and heart. One may fancy the clouds themselves are plants, springing up in the sky-fields at the call of the sun, growing in beauty until they reach their prime, scattering rain and hail like berries and seeds, then wilting and dying.

The mountain live oak, common here and a thousand feet or so higher, is like the live oak of Florida, not only in general appearance, foliage, bark, and wide-branching habit, but in its tough, knotty, unwedgeable wood. Standing alone with plenty of elbow room, the largest trees are about seven to eight feet in diameter near the ground, sixty feet high and as wide or wider across the head. The leaves are small and undivided, mostly without teeth or wavy edging, though on young shoots some are sharply serrated, both kinds being found on the same tree. The cups of the medium-sized acorns are shallow, thick walled and covered with a golden dust of minute hairs. Some of the trees have hardly any main trunk, dividing near the ground into large wide-spreading limbs, and these, dividing again and again, terminate in long, drooping, cord-like branchlets, many of which reach nearly to the ground, while a dense canopy of short, shining, leafy branchlets forms a round head which looks something like a cumulus cloud when the sunshine is pouring over it.

A marked plant is the bush poppy (*Dendromecon rigidum*), found on the hot hillsides near camp, the only woody member of the order I have yet met in all my walks. Its flowers are bright orange yellow, an inch to two inches wide, fruit pods three or four inches long, slender and curving, – height of bushes about four feet, made up of many slim, straight branches, radiating from the root, – a companion of the manzanita and other sun loving chaparral shrubs.

June 13 . Another glorious Sierra day in which one seems to be dissolved and absorbed and sent pulsing onward we know not where. Life seems neither long nor short, and we take no more heed to save time or make haste than do the trees and stars. This is true freedom, a good practical sort of immortality. Yonder rises another white skyland. How sharply the yellow pine spires and the palm-like crowns of the sugar pines are outlined on its smooth white domes. And hark! the grand thunder billows booming, rolling from ridge to ridge, followed by the faithful shower.

A good many herbaceous plants come thus far up the mountains from the plains and are now in flower, two months later than their lowland relatives. Saw a few columbines today. Most of the ferns are in their prime, – rock ferns on the sunny hillsides, cheilanthes, pellaea, gymno-gramme; woodwardia, aspidium, woodsia along the stream banks, and the common *Pteris aquilina* on sandy flats. This last, however common, is here making shows of strong, exuberant, abounding beauty to set the botanist wild with admiration. I measured some scarce full grown that are more than seven feet high. Though the commonest and most widely distributed of all the ferns, I might almost say that I never saw it before. The broad-shouldered fronds held high on smooth stout stalks growing close together, overleaning and overlapping, make a complete ceiling, beneath which one may walk erect over several acres without being seen, as if beneath a roof. And how soft and lovely the light streaming through this living ceiling, revealing the arching branching ribs and veins of the fronds as the framework of countless panes of pale green and yellow plant glass nicely fitted together – a fairyland created out of the commonest fern-stuff.

The smaller animals wander about as if in a tropical forest. I saw the entire flock of sheep vanish at one side of a patch and reappear a hundred yards farther on at the other, their progress betrayed only by the jerking and trembling of the fronds; and strange to say very few of the stout woody stalks were broken. I sat a long time beneath the tallest fronds and never enjoyed anything in the way of a bower of wild leaves more strangely impressive. Only spread a fern frond over a man's head and worldly cares are cast out, and freedom and beauty and peace come in. The waving of a pine tree on the top of a mountain, – a magic wand in Nature's hand, – every devout mountaineer knows its power; but the marvellous beauty value of what the Scotch call 'a breckan in a still dell,' what poet has sung this? It would seem impossible that any one, however incrusted with care, could escape the Godful influence of these sacred fern forests. Yet this very day I saw a shepherd pass through one of the finest of them without betraying more feeling than his sheep. 'What do you think of these grand ferns?' I asked. 'Oh, they're only d – d big brakes,' he replied.

Lizards of every temper, style, and colour dwell here, seemingly as happy and companionable as the birds and squirrels. Lowly, gentle fellow mortals, enjoying God's sunshine, and doing the best they can in getting a living, I like to watch them at their work and play. They bear acquaintance well, and one likes them the better the longer one looks into their beautiful, innocent eyes. They are easily tamed and one soon learns to love them, as they dart about on the hot rocks, swift as dragonflies. The eye can hardly follow them; but they never make long sustained runs, usually only about ten or twelve feet, then a sudden stop and as sudden a start again; going all their journeys by quick, jerking impulses. These many stops I find are necessary as rests, for they are short-winded and when pursued steadily are soon out of breath, pant pitifully and are easily caught. Their bodies are more than half tail, but these tails are well managed, never heavily dragged nor curved up as if hard to carry; on the contrary, they seem to follow the body lightly of their own will. Some are coloured like the sky, bright as bluebirds, others grey like the lichened rocks on which they hunt and bask. Even the horned toad of the plains is a mild, harmless creature and so are the snake-like species which glide in curves with true snake motion, while their small, undeveloped limbs drag as useless appendages. One specimen fourteen inches long which I observed closely made no use whatever of its tender, sprouting limbs, but glided with all the soft, sly ease and grace of a snake. Here comes a little, grey, dusty fellow who seems to know and trust me, running about my feet and looking up cunningly into my face. Carlo is watching, makes a quick pounce on him, for the fun of the thing I suppose; but Liz has shot away from his paws like an arrow, and is safe in the recesses of a clump of chaparral. Gentle saurians, dragons, descendants of an ancient and mighty race, Heaven bless you all and make your virtues known! for few of us know as yet that scales may cover fellow creatures as gentle and lovable as feathers, or hair, or cloth.

Mastodons and elephants used to live here no great geological time ago, as shown by their bones, often discovered by miners in washing gold-gravel. And bears of at least two species are here now, besides the California lion or panther, and wild cats, wolves, foxes, snakes, scorpions, wasps, tarantulas; but one is almost tempted at times to regard a small savage black ant as the master existence of this vast mountain world. These fearless, restless, wandering imps, though only about a quarter of an inch long, are fonder of fighting and biting than any beast I know. They attack every living thing around their homes, often without cause as far as I can see. Their bodies are mostly jaws curved like ice hooks, and to get work for these weapons seems to be their chief aim and pleasure. Most of their colonies are established in living oaks somewhat decayed or hollowed, in which they can conveniently build their cells. These are chosen probably because of their strength as opposed to the attacks of animals and storms. They work both day and night, creep into dark caves, climb the highest trees, wander and hunt through cool ravines as well as on hot, unshaded ridges, and extend their highways and byways over everything but water and sky. From the foothills to a mile above the level of the sea nothing can stir without their knowledge; and alarms are spread in an incredibly short time, without any howl or cry that we can hear. I can't understand the need of their ferocious courage; there seems to be no common sense in it. Sometimes, no doubt, they fight in defence of their homes but they fight anywhere and always wherever they can find anything to bite. As soon as a vulnerable spot is discovered on man or beast, they stand on their heads and sink their jaws, and though torn limb from limb, they will yet hold on and die biting deeper. When I contemplate this fierce creature so widely distributed and strongly intrenched, I see that much remains to be done ere the world is brought under the rule of universal peace and love.

On my way to camp a few minutes ago, I passed a dead pine nearly ten feet in diameter. It has been enveloped in fire from top to bottom so that now it looks like a grand black pillar set up as a monument. In this noble shaft a colony of large jet black ants have established themselves, laboriously cutting tunnels and cells through the wood, whether sound or decayed. The entire trunk seems to have been honey-combed, judging by the size of the talus of gnawed chips like sawdust piled up around its base. They are more intelligent looking than their small, belligerent, strong-scented brethren and have better manners, though quick to fight when required. Their towns are carved in fallen trunks as well as in those left standing, but never in sound, living trees or in the ground. When you happen to sit down to rest or take notes near a colony, some wandering hunter is sure to find you and come cautiously forward to discover the nature of the intruder and what ought to be done. If you are not too near the town and keep perfectly still he may run across your feet a few times, over your legs and hands and face, up your trousers, as if taking your measure and getting comprehensive views, then go in peace without raising an alarm. If, however, a tempting spot is offered or some suspicious movement excites him, a bite follows, and such a bite! I fancy that a bear or wolf bite is not to be compared with it. A quick electric flame of pain flashes along the outraged nerves, and you discover for the first time how great is the capacity for sensation you are possessed of. A shriek, a grab for the animal, and a bewildered stare follow this bite of bites as one comes back to consciousness from sudden eclipse. Fortunately, if careful, one need not be bitten oftener than once or twice in a lifetime. This wonderful electric species is about three fourths of an inch long. Bears are fond of them, and tear and gnaw their home logs to pieces, and roughly devour the eggs, larvae, parent ants, and the rotten or sound wood of the cells, all in one spicy acid hash. The Digger Indians also are fond of the larvae and even of the perfect ants, so I have been told by old mountaineers. They bite off and reject the head and eat the tickly acid body with keen relish. Thus are the poor biters bitten, like every other biter, big or little, in the world's great family.

There is also a fine, active, intelligent looking red species, intermediate in size between the above. They dwell in the ground and build large piles of seed husks, leaves, straw, etc., over their nests. Their food seems to be mostly insects and plant leaves, seeds and sap. How many mouths Nature has to fill, how many neighbours we have, how little we know about them and how seldom we get in each other's way! Then to think of the infinite numbers of smaller fellow mortals, invisibly small, compared with which the smallest ants are as mastodons.

June 14. The pool basins below the falls and cascades hereabouts, formed by the heavy down-plunging currents, are kept nicely clean and clear of detritus. The heavier parts of the material swept over the falls are heaped up a short distance in front of the basins in the form of a dam, thus tending, together with erosion, to increase their size. Sudden changes, however, are effected during the spring floods, when the snow is melting and the upper tributaries are roaring loud from 'bank to brae.' Then boulders that have fallen into the channels and which the ordinary summer and winter currents were unable to move, are suddenly swept forward as by a mighty besom, hurled over the falls into these pools and piled up in a new dam together with part of the old one, while some of the smaller boulders are carried farther down stream and variously lodged according to size and shape, all seeking rest where the force of the current is less than the resistance they are able to offer. But the greatest changes made in these relations of fall, pool, and dam are caused, not by the ordinary spring floods, but by extraordinary ones that occur at irregular intervals. The testimony of trees growing on flood boulder deposits shows that a century or more has passed since the last master flood came to awaken everything movable to go swirling and dancing on wonderful journeys. These floods may occur during the summer, when heavy thunder showers, called 'cloud bursts,' fall on wide, steeply inclined stream basins furrowed by converging channels which suddenly gather the waters together into the main trunk in booming torrents of enormous transporting power, though short lived.

One of these ancient flood boulders stands firm in the middle of the stream channel, just below the lower edge of the pool dam at the foot of the fall nearest our camp. It is a nearly cubical mass of granite about eight feet high, plushed with mosses over the top and down the sides to ordinary high-water mark. When I climbed on top of it today and lay down to rest, it seemed the most romantic spot I had yet found – the one big stone with its mossy level top and smooth sides standing square and firm and solitary, like an altar, the fall in front of it bathing it lightly with the finest of the spray, just enough to keep its moss cover fresh; the clear green pool beneath, with its foam-bells and its half circle of lilies leaning forward like a band of admirers, and flowering dogwood and alder trees leaning over all in sun sifted arches. How soothingly, restfully cool it is beneath that leafy, translucent ceiling, and how delightful the water music – the deep bass tones of the fall, the clashing, ringing spray, and infinite variety of small low tones of the current gliding past the side of the boulder island, and glinting against a thousand smaller stones down the ferny channel! All this shut in; every one of these influences acting at short range as if in a quiet room. The place seemed holy, where one might hope to see God.

After dark, when the camp was at rest, I groped my way back to the altar boulder and passed the night on it, – above the water, beneath the leaves and stars, – everything still more impressive than by day, the fall seen dimly white, singing Nature's old love song with solemn enthusiasm, while the stars peering through the leaf roof seemed to join in the white water's song. Precious night, precious day to abide in me forever. Thanks be to God for this immortal gift.

June 15. Another reviving morning. Down the long mountain slopes the sunbeams pour, gilding the awakening pines, cheering every needle, filling every living thing with joy. Robins are singing in the alder and maple groves, the same old song that has cheered and sweetened countless seasons over almost all of our blessed continent. In this mountain hollow they seem as much at home as in farmers' orchards. Bullock's oriole and the Louisiana tanager are here also, with many warblers and other little mountain troubadours, most of them now busy about their nests.

Discovered another magnificent specimen of the goldcup oak six feet in diameter, a Douglas spruce seven feet and a twining lily (*Stropholirion*), with stem eight feet long, and sixty rose-coloured flowers.

Sugar pine cones are cylindrical, slightly tapered at the end and rounded at the base. Found one today nearly twenty four inches long and six in diameter, the scales being open. Another specimen nineteen inches long; the average length of full grown cones on trees favourably situated is nearly eighteen inches. On the lower edge of the belt at a height of about twenty five hundred feet above the sea they are smaller, say a foot to fifteen inches long, and at a height of seven thousand feet or more near the upper limits of its growth in the Yosemite region they are about the same size. This noble tree is an inexhaustible study and source of pleasure. I never weary of gazing at its grand tassel cones, its perfectly round bole one hundred feet or more without a limb, the fine purplish colour of its bark, and its magnificent outsweeping, down-curving feathery arms forming a crown always bold and striking and exhilarating. In habit and general port it looks somewhat like a palm, but no palm that I have yet seen displays such majesty of form and behaviour either when poised silent and thoughtful in sunshine, or wide awake waving in storm winds with every needle quivering. When young it is very straight and regular in form like most other conifers; but at the age of fifty to one hundred years it begins to acquire individuality, so that no two are alike in their prime or old age. Every tree calls for special admiration. I have been making many sketches and regret that I cannot draw every needle. It is said to reach a height of three hundred feet, though the tallest I have measured falls short of this stature sixty feet or more. The diameter of the largest near the ground is about ten feet, though I've heard of some twelve feet thick or even fifteen. The diameter is held to a great height, the taper being almost imperceptibly gradual. Its companion, the yellow pine, is almost as large. The long silvery foliage of the younger specimens forms magnificent cylindrical brushes on the top shoots and the ends of the upturned branches, and when the wind sways the needles all one way at a certain angle every tree becomes a tower of white quivering sun-fire. Well may this shining species be called the silver pine. The needles are sometimes more than a foot long, almost as long as those of the long-leaf pine of Florida. But though in size the yellow pine almost equals the sugar pine, and in rugged enduring strength seems to surpass it, it is far less marked in general habit and expression, with its regular conventional spire and its comparatively small cones clustered stiffly among the needles. Were there no sugar pine, then would this be the king of the world's eighty or ninety species, the brightest of the bright, waving, worshipping multitude. Were they mere mechanical sculptures, what noble objects they would still be! How much more throbbing, thrilling, overflowing, full

of life in every fibre and cell, grand glowing silver rods –
the very gods of the plant kingdom, living their sublime
century lives in sight of Heaven, watched and loved and
admired from generation to generation! And how many
other radiant resiny sun trees are here and higher up,
– libocedrus, Douglas spruce, silver fir, sequoia. How
rich our inheritance in these blessed mountains, the tree
pastures into which our eyes are turned!

Now comes sundown. The west is all a glory of colour
transfiguring everything. Far up the Pilot Peak Ridge
the radiant host of trees stand hushed and thoughtful,
receiving the Sun's goodnight, as solemn and impressive
a leave-taking as if sun and trees were to meet no more.
The daylight fades, the colour spell is broken, and the
forest breathes free in the night breeze beneath the stars.

June 16. One of the Indians from Brown's Flat got right
into the middle of the camp this morning, unobserved.
I was seated on a stone, looking over my notes and
sketches and happening to look up, was startled to see
him standing grim and silent within a few steps of me,
as motionless and weather-stained as an old tree-stump
that had stood there for centuries. All Indians seem to
have learned this wonderful way of walking unseen, –
making themselves invisible like certain spiders I have
been observing here, which, in case of alarm, caused for
example by a bird alighting on the bush their webs are
spread upon, immediately bounce themselves up and down
on their elastic threads so rapidly that only a blur is visible.
The wild Indian power of escaping observation, even where
there is little or no cover to hide in, was probably slowly
acquired in hard hunting and fighting lessons while trying
to approach game, take enemies by surprise, or get safely
away when compelled to retreat. And this experience
transmitted through many generations seems at length to
have become what is vaguely called instinct.

How smooth and changeless seems the surface of the
mountains about us! Scarce a track is to be found beyond
the range of the sheep except on small open spots on the
sides of the streams, or where the forest carpets are thin
or wanting. On the smoothest of these open strips and

patches deer tracks may be seen, and the great suggestive footprints of bears, which, with those of the many small animals, are scarce enough to answer as a kind of light ornamental stitching or embroidery. Along the main ridges and larger branches of the river Indian trails may be traced, but they are not nearly as distinct as one would expect to find them. How many centuries Indians have roamed these woods nobody knows, probably a great many, extending far beyond the time that Columbus touched our shores, and it seems strange that heavier marks have not been made. Indians walk softly and hurt the landscape hardly more than the birds and squirrels, and their brush and bark huts last hardly longer than those of wood rats, while their more enduring monuments, excepting those wrought on the forests by the fires they made to improve their hunting grounds, vanish in a few centuries.

How different are most of those of the white man, especially on the lower gold region – roads blasted in the solid rock, wild streams dammed and tamed and turned out of their channels and led along the sides of canyons and valleys to work in mines like slaves. Crossing from ridge to ridge, high in the air, on long straddling trestles as if flowing on stilts, or down and up across valleys and hills imprisoned in iron pipes to strike and wash away hills and miles of the skin of the mountain's face, riddling, stripping every gold gully and flat. These are the white man's marks made in a few feverish years, to say nothing of mills, fields, villages, scattered hundreds of miles along the flank of the range. Long will it be ere these marks are effaced, though Nature is doing what she can, replanting, gardening, sweeping away old dams and flumes, levelling gravel and boulder piles, patiently trying to heal every raw scar. The main gold storm is over. Calm enough are the grey old miners scratching a bare living in waste diggings here and there. Thundering underground blasting is still going on to feed the pounding quartz mills, but their influence on the landscape is light as compared with that of the pick and shovel storms waged a few years ago. Fortunately for Sierra scenery the gold-bearing slates are mostly restricted to the foothills. The region about our camp is still wild, and higher lies the snow about as trackless as the sky.

Only a few hills and domes of cloudland were built yesterday and none at all today. The light is peculiarly white and thin, though pleasantly warm. The serenity of this mountain weather in the spring, just when Nature's pulses are beating highest, is one of its greatest charms. There is only a moderate breeze from the summits of the range at night, and a slight breathing from the sea and the lowland hills and plains during the day, or stillness so complete no leaf stirs. The trees hereabouts have but little wind history to tell.

Sheep, like people, are ungovernable when hungry. Excepting my guarded lily gardens, almost every leaf that these hoofed locusts can reach within a radius of a mile or two from camp has been devoured. Even the bushes are stripped bare and in spite of dogs and shepherds the sheep scatter to all points of the compass and vanish in dust. I fear some are lost, for one of the sixteen black ones is missing.

June 17. Counted the wool bundles this morning as they bounced through the narrow corral gate. About three hundred are missing, and as the shepherd could not go to seek them, I had to go. I tied a crust of bread to my belt, and with Carlo set out for the upper slopes of the Pilot Peak Ridge and had a good day, notwithstanding the care of seeking the silly runaways. I went out for wool, and did not come back shorn. A peculiar light circled around the horizon, white and thin like that often seen over the auroral corona, blending into the blue of the upper sky. The only clouds were a few faint flossy pencillings like combed silk. I pushed direct to the boundary of the usual range of the flock, and around it until I found the outgoing trail of the wanderers. It led far up the ridge into an open place surrounded by a hedge-like growth of ceanothus chaparral. Carlo knew what I was about, and eagerly followed the scent until we came up to them, huddled in a timid, silent bunch. They had evidently been here all night and all the forenoon, afraid to go out to feed. Having escaped restraint, they were, like some people we know of, afraid of their freedom, did not know what to do with it, and seemed glad to get back into the old familiar bondage.

June 18. Another inspiring morning, nothing better in any world can be conceived. No description of Heaven that I have ever heard or read of seems half so fine. At noon the clouds occupied about five per cent of the sky, white filmy touches drawn delicately on the azure.

The high ridges and hilltops beyond the woolly locusts are now gay with monardella, clarkia, coreopsis, and tall tufted grasses, some of them tall enough to wave like pines. The lupines, of which there are many ill-defined species, are now mostly out of flower, and many of the compositae are beginning to fade, their radiant corollas vanishing in fluffy pappus like stars in mist.

We had another visitor from Brown's Flat today, an old Indian woman with a basket on her back. Like our first caller from the village, she got fairly into camp and was standing in plain view when discovered. How long she had been quietly looking on, I cannot say. Even the dogs failed to notice her stealthy approach. She was on her way, I suppose, to some wild garden, probably for lupine and starchy saxifrage leaves and rootstocks. Her dress was calico rags, far from clean. In every way she seemed sadly unlike Nature's neat well-dressed animals, though living like them on the bounty of the wilderness. Strange that mankind alone is dirty. Had she been clad in fur, or cloth woven of grass or shreddy bark, like the juniper and libocedrus mats, she might then have seemed a rightful part of the wilderness; like a good wolf at least, or bear. But from no point of view that I have found are such debased fellow beings a whit more natural than the glaring tailored tourists we saw that frightened the birds and squirrels.

June 19. Pure sunshine all day. How beautiful a rock is made by leaf shadows! Those of the live oak are particularly clear and distinct, and beyond all art in grace and delicacy, now still as if painted on stone, now gliding softly as if afraid of noise, now dancing, waltzing in swift, merry swirls, or jumping on and off sunny rocks in quick dashes like wave embroidery on seashore cliffs. How true and substantial is this shadow beauty, and with what sublime extravagance is beauty thus multiplied! The big orange lilies are now arrayed in all their glory of leaf and flower. Noble plants, in perfect health, Nature's darlings.

June 20. Some of the silly sheep got caught fast in a tangle of chaparral this morning, like flies in a spider's web and had to be helped out. Carlo found them and tried to drive them from the trap by the easiest way. How far above sheep are intelligent dogs! No friend and helper can be more affectionate and constant than Carlo. The noble St Bernard is an honour to his race.

The air is distinctly fragrant with balsam and resin and mint, – every breath of it a gift we may well thank God for. Who could ever guess that so rough a wilderness should yet be so fine, so full of good things. One seems to be in a majestic domed pavilion in which a grand play is being acted with scenery and music and incense, – all the furniture and action so interesting we are in no danger of being called on to endure one dull moment. God himself seems to be always doing his best here, working like a man in a glow of enthusiasm.

June 21. Sauntered along the riverbank to my lily gardens. The perfection of beauty in these lilies of the wilderness is a never ending source of admiration and wonder. Their rhizomes are set in black mould accumulated in hollows of the metamorphic slates beside the pools, where they are well watered without being subjected to flood action. Every leaf in the level whorls around the tall polished stalks is as finely finished as the petals, and the light and heat required are measured for them and tempered in passing through the branches of overleaning trees. However strong the winds from the noon rain-storms, they are securely sheltered. Beautiful hypnum carpets bordered with ferns are spread beneath them, violets too, and a few daisies. Everything around them sweet and fresh like themselves.

Cloudland today is only a solitary white mountain; but it is so enriched with sunshine and shade, the tones of colour on its big domed head and bossy outbulging ridges, and in the hollows and ravines between them, are ineffably fine.

June 22. Unusually cloudy. Besides the periodical shower-bearing cumuli there is a thin, diffused, fog-like cloud overhead. About seventy five per cent in all.

June 23. Oh, these vast, calm, measureless mountain days, inciting at once to work and rest! Days in whose light everything seems equally divine, opening a thousand windows to show us God. Nevermore, however weary, should one faint by the way who gains the blessings of one mountain day; whatever his fate, long life, short life, stormy or calm, he is rich forever.

June 24. Our regular allowance of clouds and thunder. Shepherd Billy is in a peck of trouble about the sheep; he declares that they are possessed with more of the evil one than any other flock from the beginning of the invention of mutton and wool to the last batch of it. No matter how many are missing, he will not, he says, go a step to seek them, because, as he reasons, while getting back one wanderer he would probably lose ten. Therefore runaway hunting must be Carlo's and mine. Billy's little dog Jack is also giving trouble by leaving camp every night to visit his neighbours up the mountain at Brown's Flat. He is a common-looking cur of no particular breed, but tremendously enterprising in love and war. He has cut all the ropes and leather straps he has been tied with, until his master in desperation, after climbing the brushy mountain again and again to drag him back, fastened him with a pole attached to his collar under his chin at one end, and to a stout sapling at the other. But the pole gave good leverage, and by constant twisting during the night, the fastening at the sapling end was chaffed off, and he set out on his usual journey, dragging the pole through the brush, and reached the Indian settlement in safety. His master followed, and making no allowance, gave him a beating, and swore in bad terms that next evening he would 'fix that infatuated pup' by anchoring him unmercifully to the heavy cast iron lid of our Dutch oven, weighing about as much as the dog. It was linked directly to his collar close up under the chin, so that the poor fellow seemed unable to stir. He stood quite discouraged until after dark, unable to look about him, or even to lie down unless he stretched himself out with his front feet across the lid, and his head close down between his paws. Before morning, however, Jack was heard far up the height howling Excelsior, cast iron anchor to the contrary notwithstanding. He must have walked, or rather climbed, erect on his hind legs, clasping the heavy lid like a shield against his breast, a formidable ironclad condition in which to meet his rivals. Next night, dog, pot lid and all, were tied up in an old bean sack, and thus at last angry Billy gained the victory. Just before leaving home, Jack was bitten in the lower jaw by a rattlesnake, and for a week or so his head and neck were swollen to more than double the normal size; nevertheless he ran about as brisk and lively as ever, and is now completely recovered. The only treatment he got was fresh milk – a gallon or two at a time forcibly poured down his sore, poisoned throat.

June 25. Though only a sheep camp, this grand mountain hollow is home, sweet home, every day growing sweeter, and I shall be sorry to leave it. The lily gardens are safe as yet from the trampling flock. Poor, dusty, raggedy, famishing creatures, I heartily pity them. Many a mile they must go every day to gather their fifteen or twenty tons of chaparral and grass.

June 26. Nuttall's flowering dogwood makes a fine show when in bloom. The whole tree is then snowy white. The involucres are six to eight inches wide. Along the streams it is a good-sized tree thirty to fifty feet high, with a broad head when not crowded by companions. Its showy involucres attract a crowd of moths, butterflies, and other winged people about it for their own, and I suppose, the tree's advantage. It likes plenty of cool water, and is a great drinker like the alder, willow and cottonwood, and flourishes best on stream banks, though it often wanders far from streams in damp shady glens beneath the pines, where it is much smaller. When the leaves ripen in the fall, they become more beautiful than the flowers, displaying charming tones of red, purple and lavender. Another species grows in abundance as a chaparral shrub on the shady sides of the hills, probably *Cornus sessilis*. The leaves are eaten by the sheep. – Heard a few lightning strokes in the distance, with rumbling, mumbling reverberations.

June 27. The beaked hazel (*Corylus rostrata*, var. *Californica*) is common on cool slopes up toward the summit of the Pilot Peak Ridge. There is something peculiarly attractive in the hazel, like the oaks and heaths of the cool countries of our forefathers, and through them our love for these plants has, I suppose, been transmitted. This species is four or five feet high, leaves soft and hairy, grateful to the touch, and the delicious nuts are eagerly gathered by Indians and squirrels. The sky as usual adorned with white noon clouds.

June 28. Warm, mellow summer. The glowing sunbeams make every nerve tingle. The new needles of the pines and firs are nearly full grown and shine gloriously. Lizards are glinting about on the hot rocks; some that live near the camp are more than half tame. They seem attentive to every movement on our part, as if curious to simply look on without suspicion of harm, turning their heads to look back, and making a variety of pretty gestures. Gentle, guileless creatures with beautiful eyes, I shall be sorry to leave them when we leave camp.

June 29. I have been making the acquaintance of a very interesting little bird that flits about the falls and rapids of the main branches of the river. It is not a water bird in structure, though it gets its living in the water, and never leaves the streams. It is not web-footed, yet it dives fearlessly into deep swirling rapids, evidently to feed at the bottom, using its wings to swim with under water just as ducks and loons do. Sometimes it wades about in shallow places, thrusting its head under from time to time in a jerking, nodding, frisky way that is sure to attract attention. It is about the size of a robin, has short crisp wings serviceable for flying either in water or air, and a tail of moderate size slanted upward, giving it, with its nodding, bobbing manners, a wrennish look. Its colour is plain bluish ash, with a tinge of brown on the head and shoulders. It flies from fall to fall, rapid to rapid, with a solid whirr of wing beats like those of a quail, follows the windings of the stream, and usually alights on some rock jutting up out of the current, or on some stranded snag, or rarely on the dry limb of an overhanging tree, perching

like regular tree birds when it suits its convenience. It has
the oddest, daintiest mincing manners imaginable; and
the little fellow can sing too, a sweet, thrushy, fluty song,
rather low, not the least boisterous, and much less keen and
accentuated than from its vigorous briskness one would be
led to look for. What a romantic life this little bird leads
on the most beautiful portions of the streams, in a genial
climate with shade and cool water and spray to temper the
summer heat. No wonder it is a fine singer, considering
the stream songs it hears day and night. Every breath the
little poet draws is part of a song, for all the air about the
rapids and falls is beaten into music, and its first lessons
must begin before it is born by the thrilling and quivering
of the eggs in unison with the tones of the falls. I have not
yet found its nest, but it must be near the streams, for it
never leaves them.

June 30. Half cloudy, half sunny, clouds lustrous white.
The tall pines crowded along the top of the Pilot Peak
Ridge look like six-inch miniatures exquisitely outlined
on the satiny sky. Average cloudiness for the day about
twenty five per cent. No rain. And so this memorable
month ends, a stream of beauty unmeasured, no more to
be sectioned off by almanac arithmetic than sun radiance
or the currents of seas and rivers – a peaceful, joyful stream
of beauty. Every morning, arising from the death of sleep,
the happy plants and all our fellow animal creatures great
and small, and even the rocks, seemed to be shouting,
'Awake, awake, rejoice, rejoice, come love us and join
in our song. Come! Come!' Looking back through the
stillness and romantic enchanting beauty and peace of the
camp grove, this June seems the greatest of all the months
of my life, the most truly, divinely free, boundless like
eternity, immortal. Everything in it seems equally divine
– one smooth, pure, wild glow of Heaven's love, never to
be blotted or blurred by anything past or to come.

July 1. Summer is ripe. Flocks of seeds are already
out of their cups and pods seeking their predestined
places. Some will strike root and grow up beside their
parents, others flying on the wings of the wind far from
them, among strangers. Most of the young birds are full

feathered and out of their nests, though still looked after by both father and mother, protected and fed and to some extent educated. How beautiful the home life of birds! No wonder we all love them.

I like to watch the squirrels. There are two species here, the large California grey and the Douglas. The latter is the brightest of all the squirrels I have ever seen, a hot spark of life, making every tree tingle with his prickly toes, a condensed nugget of fresh mountain vigour and valour, as free from disease as a sunbeam. One cannot think of such an animal ever being weary or sick. He seems to think the mountains belong to him and at first tried to drive away the whole flock of sheep as well as the shepherd and dogs. How he scolds and what faces he makes, all eyes, teeth and whiskers! If not so comically small, he would indeed be a dreadful fellow. I should like to know more about his bringing up, his life in the home knot-hole, as well as in the treetops, throughout all seasons. Strange that I have not yet found a nest full of young ones. The Douglas is nearly allied to the red squirrel of the Atlantic slope, and may have been distributed to this side of the continent by way of the great unbroken forests of the north.

The California grey is one of the most beautiful, and next to the Douglas, the most interesting of our hairy neighbours. Compared with the Douglas he is twice as large, but far less lively and influential as a worker in the woods and he manages to make his way through leaves and branches with less stir than his small brother. I have never heard him bark at anything except our dogs. When in search of food he glides silently from branch to branch, examining last year's cones to see whether some few seeds may not be left between the scales, or gleans fallen ones among the leaves on the ground, since none of the present season's crop is yet available. His tail floats now behind him, now above him, level or gracefully curled like a wisp of cirrus cloud, every hair in its place, clean and shining and radiant as thistledown in spite of rough, gummy work. His whole body seems about as unsubstantial as his tail. The little Douglas is fiery, peppery, full of brag and fight and show, with movements so quick and keen they almost sting the onlooker, and the harlequin gyrating show he makes of himself turns one giddy to see. The grey is shy, and oftentimes stealthy in his movements, as if half expecting an enemy in every tree and bush and back of every log, wishing only to be let alone apparently, and manifesting no desire to be seen or admired or feared. The Indians hunt this species for food, a good cause for caution, not to mention other enemies – hawks, snakes, wild cats. In woods where food is abundant they wear paths through sheltering thickets and over prostrate trees to some favourite pool where in hot and dry weather they drink at nearly the same hour every day. These pools are said to be narrowly watched, especially by the boys, who lie in ambush with bow and arrow and kill without noise. But, in spite of enemies, squirrels are happy fellows, forest favourites, types of tireless life. Of all Nature's wild beasts they seem to me the wildest. May we come to know each other better.

The chaparral-covered hill slope to the south of the camp, besides furnishing nesting places for countless merry birds, is the home and hiding place of the curious wood rat (*Neotoma*), a handsome, interesting animal, always attracting attention wherever seen. It is more like a squirrel than a rat, is much larger, has delicate, thick, soft fur of a bluish slate colour, white on the belly; ears large, thin and translucent; eyes soft, full and liquid; claws slender, sharp as needles; and as his limbs are strong, he can climb about as well as a squirrel. No rat or squirrel has so innocent a look, is so easily approached or expresses such confidence in one's good intentions. He seems too fine for the thorny thickets he inhabits and his hut also is as unlike himself as may be, though softly furnished inside. No other animal inhabitant of these mountains builds houses so large and striking in appearance. The traveller coming suddenly upon a group of them for the first time will not be likely to forget them. They are built of all kinds of sticks, old rotten pieces picked up anywhere, and green prickly twigs bitten from the nearest bushes, the whole mixed with miscellaneous odds and ends of everything movable, such as bits of cloddy earth, stones, bones and deerhorn, piled up in a conical mass as if it were got ready for burning. Some of these curious cabins are six feet high and as wide at the base, and a dozen or more of them are occasionally grouped together, less perhaps for the sake of society than for advantages of food and shelter. Coming through the dense shaggy thickets of some lonely hillside, the solitary explorer happening into one of these strange villages is startled at the sight, and may fancy himself in an Indian settlement, and begin to wonder what kind of reception he is likely to get. But no savage face will he see, perhaps not a single inhabitant, or at most two or three seated on top of their wigwams, looking at the stranger with the mildest of wild eyes and allowing a near approach. In the centre of the rough spiky hut a soft nest is made of the inner fibres of bark chewed to tow, and lined with feathers and the down of various seeds, such as willow and milkweed. The delicate creature in its prickly, thick-walled home suggests a tender flower in a thorny involucre. Some of the nests are built in trees thirty or forty feet from the ground and even in garrets, as if seeking the company and protection of man, like swallows and linnets, though accustomed to the wildest solitude. Among housekeepers Neotoma has the reputation of a thief, because he carries away everything transportable to his queer hut, – knives, forks, combs, nails, tin cups and spectacles, – merely however to strengthen his fortifications, I guess. His food at home, as far as I have learned, is nearly the same as that of the squirrels – nuts, berries, seeds and sometimes the bark and tender shoots of the various species of ceanothus.

July 2. Warm, sunny day, thrilling plant and animals and rocks alike, making sap and blood flow fast and making every particle of the crystal mountains throb and swirl and dance in glad accord like stardust. No dullness anywhere visible or thinkable. No stagnation, no death. Everything kept in joyful rhythmic motion in the pulses of Nature's big heart.

Pearl cumuli over the higher mountains – clouds, not with a silver lining, but all silver. The brightest, crispest, rockiest looking clouds, most varied in features and keenest in outline I ever saw at any time of year in any country.

The daily building and unbuilding of these snowy cloud ranges – the highest Sierra – is a prime marvel to me and I gaze at the stupendous white domes, miles high, with ever fresh admiration. But in the midst of these sky and mountain affairs a change of diet is pulling us down. We have been out of bread a few days, and begin to miss it more than seems reasonable, for we have plenty of meat and sugar and tea. Strange we should feel food-poor in so rich a wilderness. The Indians put us to shame, so do the squirrels, – starchy roots and seeds and bark in abundance, yet the failure of the meal sack disturbs our bodily balance, and threatens our best enjoyments.

July 3. Warm. Breeze just enough to sift through the woods and waft fragrance from their thousand fountains. The pine and fir cones are growing well, resin and balsam dripping from every tree, and seeds are ripening fast, promising a fine harvest. The squirrels will have bread. They eat all kinds of nuts long before they are ripe and yet never seem to suffer in stomach.

THREE

A Bread Famine

July 4. The air beyond the flock range, full of the essences of the woods, is growing sweeter and more fragrant from day to day, like ripening fruit.

Mr Delaney is expected to arrive soon from the lowlands with a new stock of provisions and as the flock is to be moved to fresh pastures we shall all be well fed. In the meantime our stock of beans as well as flour has failed – everything but mutton, sugar and tea. The shepherd is somewhat demoralised and seems to care but little what becomes of his flock. He says that since the boss has failed to feed him he is not rightly bound to feed the sheep and swears that no decent white man can climb these steep mountains on mutton alone. 'It's not fittin' grub for a white man really white. For dogs and coyotes and Indians it's different. Good grub, good sheep. That's what I say.' Such was Billy's Fourth of July oration.

July 5. The clouds of noon on the high Sierra seem yet more marvellously, indescribably beautiful from day to day as one becomes more wakeful to see them. The smoke of the gunpowder burned yesterday on the lowlands and the eloquence of the orators has probably settled or been blown away by this time. Here every day is a holiday, a jubilee ever sounding with serene enthusiasm, without wear or waste or cloying weariness. Everything rejoicing. Not a single cell or crystal unvisited or forgotten.

July 6. Mr Delaney has not arrived, and the bread famine is sore. We must eat mutton a while longer, though it seems hard to get accustomed to it. I have heard of Texas pioneers living without bread or anything made from the cereals for months without suffering, using the breast meat of wild turkeys for bread. Of this kind they had plenty in the good old days when life, though considered less safe, was fussed over the less. The trappers and fur traders of early days in the Rocky Mountain regions lived on bison and beaver meat for months. Salmon eaters too, there are among both Indians and whites who seem to suffer little or not at all from the want of bread. Just at this moment mutton seems the least desirable of food, though of good quality. We pick out the leanest bits, and down they go against heavy disgust, causing nausea and an effort to reject the offensive stuff. Tea makes matters worse, if possible. The stomach begins to assert itself as an independent creature with a will of its own. We should boil lupine leaves, clover, starchy petioles and saxifrage rootstocks like the Indians. We try to ignore our gastric troubles, rise and gaze about us, turn our eyes to the mountains and climb doggedly up through brush and rocks into the heart of the scenery. A stifled calm comes on, and the day's duties and even enjoyments are languidly got through with. We chew a few leaves of ceanothus by way of luncheon and smell or chew the spicy monardella for the dull headache and stomach ache that now lightens, now comes muffling down upon us and into us like fog. At night more mutton, flesh to flesh, down with it, not too much and there are the stars shining through the cedar plumes and branches above our beds.

July 7. Rather weak and sickish this morning and all about a piece of bread. Can scarce command attention to my best studies, as if one couldn't take a few days' saunter in the Godful woods without maintaining a base on a wheatfield and grist mill. Like caged parrots we want a cracker, any of the hundred kinds, – the remainder biscuit of a voyage around the world would answer well enough, nor would the wholesomeness of saleratus biscuit be questioned. Bread without flesh is a good diet, as on many botanical excursions I have proved. Tea also may easily be ignored. Just bread and water and delightful toil is all I need, – not unreasonably much, yet one ought to be trained and tempered to enjoy life in these brave wilds in full independence of any particular kind of nourishment. That this may be accomplished is manifest, as far as bodily welfare is concerned, in the lives of people of other climes. The Eskimo, for example, gets a living far north of the wheat line, from oily seals and whales. Meat, berries, bitter weeds and blubber, or only the last, for months at a time; and yet these people all around the frozen shores of our continent are said to be hearty, jolly, stout and brave. We hear, too, of fish eaters, carnivorous as spiders, yet well enough as far as stomachs are concerned, while we are so ridiculously helpless, making wry faces over our fare, looking sheepish in digestive distress amid rumbling, grumbling sounds that might well pass for smothered baas. We have a large supply of sugar, and this evening it occurred to me that these belligerent stomachs might possibly, like complaining children, be coaxed with candy. Accordingly the frying pan was cleansed and a lot of sugar cooked in it to a sort of wax, but this stuff only made matters worse.

Man seems to be the only animal whose food soils him, making necessary much washing and shield-like bibs and napkins. Moles living in the earth and eating slimy worms are yet as clean as seals or fishes, whose lives are one perpetual wash. And, as we have seen, the squirrels in these resiny woods keep themselves clean in some mysterious way; not a hair is sticky, though they handle the gummy cones, and glide about apparently without care. The birds, too, are clean, though they seem to make a good deal of fuss washing and cleaning their feathers. Certain flies and ants I see are in a fix, entangled and sealed up in the sugar wax we threw away, like some of their ancestors in amber. Our stomachs, like tired muscles, are sore with long squirming. Once I was very hungry in the Bonaventure graveyard near Savannah, Georgia, having fasted for several days; then the empty stomach seemed to chafe in much the same way as now and a somewhat similar tenderness and aching was produced, hard to bear, though the pain was not acute. We dream of bread, a sure sign we need it. Like the Indians, we ought to know how to get the starch out of fern and saxifrage stalks, lily bulbs, pine bark, etc. Our education has been sadly neglected for many generations. Wild rice would be good. I noticed a leersia in wet meadow edges, but the seeds are small. Acorns are not ripe, nor pine nuts, nor filberts. The inner bark of pine or spruce might be

tried. Drank tea until half intoxicated. Man seems to crave
a stimulant when anything extraordinary is going on and
this is the only one I use. Billy chews great quantities of
tobacco, which I suppose helps to stupefy and moderate
his misery. We look and listen for the Don every hour. How
beautiful upon the mountains his big feet would be!

In the warm, hospitable Sierra, shepherds and mountain
men in general, as far as I have seen, are easily satisfied as
to food supplies and bedding. Most of them are heartily
content to 'rough it,' ignoring Nature's fineness as bothersome or unmanly. The shepherd's bed is often only the
bare ground and a pair of blankets, with a stone, a piece
of wood or a pack-saddle for a pillow. In choosing the spot,
he shows less care than the dogs, for they usually deliberate
before making up their minds in so important an affair,
going from place to place, scraping away loose sticks and
pebbles and trying for comfort by making many changes,
while the shepherd casts himself down anywhere, seemingly
the least skilled of all rest seekers. His food too, even when
he has all he wants, is usually far from delicate, either in
kind or cooking. Beans, bread of any sort, bacon, mutton,
dried peaches and sometimes potatoes and onions, make
up his bill of fare, the two latter articles being regarded as
luxuries on account of their weight as compared with the
nourishment they contain; a half sack or so of each may
be put into the pack in setting out from the home ranch
and in a few days they are done. Beans are the main
standby, portable, wholesome and capable of going far,
besides being easily cooked, although curiously enough a
great deal of mystery is supposed to lie about the bean
pot. No two cooks quite agree on the methods of making
beans do their best, and after petting and coaxing and
nursing the savoury mess, – well oiled and mellowed with
bacon boiled into the heart of it, – the proud cook will ask,
after dishing out a quart or two for trial, 'Well, how do
you like *my* beans?' as if by no possibility could they be
like any other beans cooked in the same way, but must
needs possess some special virtue of which he alone is
master. Molasses, sugar, or pepper may be used to give
desired flavours; or the first water may be poured off and

a spoonful or two of ashes or soda added to dissolve or soften the skins more fully, according to various tastes and notions. But, like casks of wine, no two potfuls are exactly alike to every palate. Some are supposed to be spoiled by the moon, by some unlucky day, by the beans having been grown on soil not suitable; or the whole year may be to blame as not favourable for beans.

Coffee too, has its marvels in the camp kitchen but not so many and not so inscrutable as those that beset the bean pot. A low complacent grunt follows a mouthful drawn in with a gurgle and the remark cast forth aimlessly, 'That's good coffee.' Then another gurgling sip and repetition of the judgment, '*Yes sir*, that *is* good coffee.' As to tea, there are but two kinds, weak and strong, the stronger the better. The only remark heard is, 'That tea's weak,' otherwise it is good enough and not worth mentioning. If it has been boiled an hour or two or smoked on a pitchy fire, no matter, – who cares for a little tannin or creosote? they make the black beverage all the stronger and more attractive to tobacco tanned palates.

Sheep-camp bread, like most California camp bread, is baked in Dutch ovens, some of it in the form of yeast powder biscuit, an unwholesome sticky compound leading straight to dyspepsia. The greater part, however, is fermented with sour dough, a handful from each batch being saved and put away in the mouth of the flour sack to inoculate the next. The oven is simply a cast iron pot, about five inches deep and from twelve to eighteen inches wide. After the batch has been mixed and kneaded in a tin pan, the oven is slightly heated and rubbed with a piece of tallow or pork rind. The dough is then placed in it, pressed out against the sides, and left to rise. When ready for baking a shovelful of coals is spread out by the side of the fire and the oven set upon them, while another shovelful is placed on top of the lid, which is raised from time to time to see that the requisite amount of heat is being kept up. With care good bread may be made in this way, though it is liable to be burned or to be sour, or raised too much, and the weight of the oven is a serious objection.

At last Don Delaney comes doon the lang glen, – hunger vanishes, we turn our eyes to the mountains, and tomorrow we go climbing toward cloudland.

Never while anything is left of me shall this first camp be forgotten. It has fairly grown into me, not merely as memory pictures, but as part and parcel of mind and body alike. The deep hopper-like hollow, with its majestic trees through which all the wonderful nights the stars poured their beauty. The flowery wildness of the high steep slope toward Brown's Flat, and its bloom-fragrance descending at the close of the still days. The embowered river-reaches with their multitude of voices making melody, the stately flow and rush and glad exulting onsweeping currents caressing the dipping sedge-leaves and bushes and mossy stones, swirling in pools, dividing against little flowery islands, breaking grey and white here and there, ever rejoicing, yet with deep solemn undertones recalling the ocean, – the brave little bird ever beside them, singing with sweet human tones among the waltzing foam-bells, and like a blessed evangel explaining God's love. And the Pilot Peak Ridge, its long withdrawing slopes gracefully modelled and braided, reaching from climate to climate, feathered with trees that are the kings of their race, their ranks nobly marshalled to view, spire above spire, crown above crown, waving their long, leafy arms, tossing their cones like ringing bells, – blessed sun-fed mountaineers rejoicing in their strength, every tree tuneful, a harp for the winds and the sun. The hazel and buckthorn pastures of the deer, the sun-beaten brows purple and yellow with mint and golden-rods, carpeted with chamoebatia, humming with bees. And the dawns and sunrises and sundowns of these mountain days, – the rose light creeping higher among the stars, changing to daffodil yellow, the level beams bursting forth, streaming across the ridges, touching pine after pine, awakening and warming all the mighty host to do gladly their shining day's work. The great sun-gold noons, the alabaster cloud mountains, the landscape beaming with consciousness like the face of a god. The sunsets, when the trees stood hushed awaiting their goodnight blessings. Divine, enduring, unwastable wealth.

FOUR

To the High Mountains

July 8. Now away we go toward the topmost mountains. Many still, small voices, as well as the noon thunder, are calling, 'Come higher.' Farewell, blessed dell, woods, gardens, streams, birds, squirrels, lizards and a thousand others. Farewell. Farewell.

Up through the woods the hoofed locusts streamed beneath a cloud of brown dust. Scarcely were they driven a hundred yards from the old corral ere they seemed to know that at last they were going to new pastures, and rushed wildly ahead, crowding through gaps in the brush, jumping, tumbling like exulting, hurrahing flood waters escaping through a broken dam. A man on each flank kept shouting advice to the leaders, who in their famishing condition were behaving like Gadarene swine; two other drivers were busy with stragglers, helping them out of brush tangles; the Indian, calm, alert, silently watched for wanderers likely to be overlooked; the two dogs ran here and there, at a loss to know what was best to be done, while the Don, soon far in the rear, was trying to keep in sight of his troublesome wealth.

As soon as the boundary of the old eaten out range was passed the hungry horde suddenly became calm, like a mountain stream in a meadow. Thenceforward they were allowed to eat their way as slowly as they wished, care being taken only to keep them headed toward the summit of the Merced and Tuolumne divide. Soon the two thousand flattened paunches were bulged out with sweetpea vines and grass and the gaunt, desperate creatures, more like wolves than sheep, became bland and governable, while the howling drivers changed to gentle shepherds, and sauntered in peace.

Toward sundown we reached Hazel Green, a charming

spot on the summit of the dividing ridge between the basins of the Merced and Tuolumne, where there is a small brook flowing through hazel and dogwood thickets beneath magnificent silver firs and pines. Here we are camped for the night, our big fire, heaped high with rosiny logs and branches, is blazing like a sunrise, gladly giving back the light slowly sifted from the sunbeams of centuries of summers; and in the glow of that old sunlight how impressively surrounding objects are brought forward in relief against the outer darkness! Grasses, larkspurs, columbines, lilies, hazel bushes, and the great trees form a circle around the fire like thoughtful spectators, gazing and listening with human-like enthusiasm. The night breeze is cool, for all day we have been climbing into the upper sky, the home of the cloud mountains we so long have admired. How sweet and keen the air! Every breath a blessing. Here the sugar pine reaches its fullest development in size and beauty and number of individuals, filling every swell and hollow and down-plunging ravine almost to the exclusion of other species. A few yellow pines are still to be found as companions, and in the coolest places silver firs; but noble as these are, the sugar pine is king, and spreads long protecting arms above them while they rock and wave in sign of recognition.

We have now reached a height of six thousand feet. In the forenoon we passed along a flat part of the dividing ridge that is planted with manzanita (*Arctostaphylos*), some specimens the largest I have seen. I measured one, the bole of which is four feet in diameter and only eighteen inches high from the ground, where it dissolves into many widespreading branches forming a broad round head about ten or twelve feet high, covered with clusters of small narrow-throated pink bells. The leaves are pale green, glandular, and set on edge by a twist of the petiole. The branches seem naked; for the chocolate-coloured bark is very smooth and thin, and is shed off in flakes that curl when dry. The wood is red, close-grained, hard, and heavy. I wonder how old these curious tree bushes are, probably as old as the great pines. Indians and bears and birds and fat grubs feast on the berries, which look like small apples, often rosy on one side, green on the other. The Indians are said to make a kind of beer or cider out of them. There are many species. This one, *Arctostaphylos pungens*, is common hereabouts. No need have they to fear the wind, so low they are and steadfastly rooted. Even the fires that sweep the woods seldom destroy them utterly, for they rise again from the root and some of the dry ridges they grow on are seldom touched by fire. I must try to know them better.

I miss my river songs tonight. Here Hazel Creek at its topmost springs has a voice like a bird. The wind tones in the great trees overhead are strangely impressive, all the more because not a leaf stirs below them. But it grows late and I must to bed. The camp is silent; everybody asleep. It seems extravagant to spend hours so precious in sleep. 'He giveth his beloved sleep.' Pity the poor beloved needs it, weak, weary, forspent; oh, the pity of it, to sleep in the midst of eternal, beautiful motion instead of gazing forever, like the stars.

July 9. Exhilarated with the mountain air, I feel like shouting this morning with excess of wild animal joy. The Indian lay down away from the fire last night without blankets, having nothing on, by way of clothing, but a pair of blue overalls and a calico shirt wet with sweat. The night air is chilly at this elevation, and we gave him some horse blankets, but he didn't seem to care for them. A fine thing to be independent of clothing where it is so hard to carry. When food is scarce, he can live on whatever comes in his way, – a few berries, roots, bird eggs, grasshoppers, black ants, fat wasp or bumblebee larvae, without feeling that he is doing anything worth mention, so I have been told.

Our course today was along the broad top of the main ridge to a hollow beyond Crane Flat. It is scarce at all rocky, and is covered with the noblest pines and spruces I have yet seen. Sugar pines from six to eight feet in diameter are not uncommon, with a height of two hundred feet or even more. The silver firs (*Abies concolour* and *A. magnifica*) are exceedingly beautiful, especially the *magnifica*, which becomes more abundant the higher we go. It is of great size, one of the most notable in every way of the gaint conifers of the Sierra. I saw specimens that measured seven

feet in diameter and over two hundred feet in height, while
the average size for what might be called full grown mature
trees can hardly be less than one hundred and eighty or two
hundred feet high and five or six feet in diameter; and with
these noble dimensions there is a symmetry and perfection
of finish not to be seen in any other tree, hereabout at
least. The branches are whorled in fives mostly, and
stand out from the tall, straight, exquisitely tapered bole
in level collars, each branch regularly pinnated like the
fronds of ferns, and densely clad with leaves all around
the branchlets, thus giving them a singularly rich and
sumptuous appearance. The extreme top of the tree is
a thick blunt shoot pointing straight to the zenith like
an admonishing finger. The cones stand erect like casks
on the upper branches. They are about six inches long,
three in diameter, blunt, velvety, and cylindrical in form,
and very rich and precious looking. The seeds are about
three quarters of an inch long, dark reddish brown with
brilliant iridescent purple wings, and when ripe, the cone
falls to pieces, and the seeds thus set free at a height of one
hundred and fifty or two hundred feet have a good send
off and may fly considerable distances in a good breeze;
and it is when a good breeze is blowing that most of them
are shaken free to fly.

The other species, *Abies concolour*, attains nearly as great
a height and thickness as the *magnifica*, but the branches
do not form such regular whorls, nor are they so exactly
pinnated or richly leaf-clad. Instead of growing all around
the branchlets, the leaves are mostly arranged in two flat
horizontal rows. The cones and seeds are like those of the
magnifica in form but less than half as large. The bark of
the *magnifica* is reddish purple and closely furrowed, that
of the *concolour* grey and widely furrowed. A noble pair.

At Crane Flat we climbed a thousand feet or more in a
distance of about two miles, the forest growing more dense
and the silvery *magnifica* fir forming a still greater portion
of the whole. Crane Flat is a meadow with a wide sandy
border lying on the top of the divide. It is often visited by
blue cranes to rest and feed on their long journeys, hence
the name. It is about half a mile long, draining into the

Merced, sedgy in the middle with a margin bright with lilies, columbines, larkspurs, lupines, castilleia then an outer zone of dry, gently sloping ground starred with a multitude of small flowers, – eunanus, mimulus, gilia, with rosettes of spraguea and tufts of several species of eriogonum and the brilliant zauschneria. The noble forest wall about it is made up of the two silver firs and the yellow and sugar pines, which here seem to reach their highest pitch of beauty and grandeur; for the elevation, six thousand feet or a little more, is not too great for the sugar and yellow pines or too low for the *magnifica* fir, while the *concolour* seems to find this elevation the best possible. About a mile from the north end of the flat there is a grove of *Sequoia gigantea*, the king of all the conifers. Furthermore, the Douglas spruce (*Pseudotsuga Douglasii*) and *Libocedrus decurrens*, and a few two-leaved pines, occur here and there, forming a small part of the forest. Three pines, two silver firs, one Douglas spruce, one sequoia, – all of them, except the two-leaved pine, colossal trees, – are found here together, an assemblage of conifers unrivalled on the globe.

We passed a number of charming garden-like meadows lying on top of the divide or hanging like ribbons down its sides, imbedded in the glorious forest. Some are taken up chiefly with the tall white-flowered *Veratrum Californicum*, with boat-shaped leaves about a foot long, eight or ten inches wide and veined like those of cypripedium, – a robust, hearty, liliaceous plant, fond of water and determined to be seen. Columbine and larkspur grow on the dryer edges of the meadows, with a tall handsome lupine standing waist-deep in long grasses and sedges. Castilleias, too, of several species make a bright show with beds of violets at their feet. But the glory of these forest meadows is a lily (*L. parvum*). The tallest are from seven to eight feet high with magnificent racemes of ten to twenty or more small orange-coloured flowers; they stand out free in open ground, with just enough grass and other companion plants about them to fringe their feet, and show them off to best advantage. This is a grand addition to my lily acquaintances, – a true mountaineer, reaching prime vigour and beauty at a height of seven thousand feet or thereabouts. It varies, I find, very much in size even in the same meadow, not only with the soil, but with age. I saw a specimen that had only one flower, and another within a stone's throw had twenty five. And to think that the sheep should be allowed in these lily meadows! after how many centuries of Nature's care planting and watering them, tucking the bulbs in snugly below winter frost, shading the tender shoots with clouds drawn above them like curtains, pouring refreshing rain, making them perfect in beauty, and keeping them safe by a thousand miracles; yet, strange to say, allowing the trampling of devastating sheep. One might reasonably look for a wall of fire to fence such gardens. So extravagant is nature with her choicest treasures, spending plant beauty as she spends sunshine, pouring it forth into land and sea, garden and desert. And so the beauty of lilies falls on angels and men, bears and squirrels, wolves and sheep, birds and bees, but as far as I have seen, man alone, and the animals he tames, destroy these gardens. Awkward, lumbering bears, the Don tells me, love to wallow in them in hot weather, and deer with their sharp feet cross them again and again, sauntering and feeding, yet never a lily have I seen spoiled by them. Rather, like gardeners, they seem to cultivate them, pressing and dibbling as required. Anyhow not a leaf or petal seems misplaced.

The trees round about them seem as perfect in beauty and form as the lilies, their boughs whorled like lily leaves in exact order. This evening, as usual, the glow of our campfire is working enchantment on everything within reach of its rays. Lying beneath the firs, it is glorious to see them dipping their spires in the starry sky, the sky like one vast lily meadow in bloom! How can I close my eyes on so precious a night?

July 10. A Douglas squirrel, peppery, pungent autocrat of the woods, is barking overhead this morning and the small forest birds, so seldom seen when one travels noisily, are out on sunny branches along the edge of the meadow getting warm, taking a sun bath and dew bath – a fine sight. How charming the sprightly confident looks and ways of these little feathered people of the trees! They seem sure of dainty, wholesome breakfasts, and where are so many breakfasts to come from? How helpless should we find ourselves should we try to set a table for them of such buds, seeds, insects, etc., as would keep them in the pure wild health they enjoy! Not a headache or any other ache amongst them, I guess. As for the irrepressible Douglas squirrels, one never thinks of their breakfasts or the possibility of hunger, sickness or death; rather they seem like stars above chance or change, even though we may see them at times busy gathering burrs, working hard for a living.

On through the forest ever higher we go, a cloud of dust dimming the way, thousands of feet, trampling leaves and flowers, but in this mighty wilderness they seem but a feeble band, and a thousand gardens will escape their blighting touch. They cannot hurt the trees, though some of the seedlings suffer, and should the woolly locusts be greatly multiplied, as on account of dollar value they are likely to be, then the forests too, may in time be destroyed. Only the sky will then be safe, though hid from view by dust and smoke, incense of a bad sacrifice. Poor, helpless, hungry sheep, in great part misbegotten, without good right to be, semi-manufactured, made less by God than man, born out of time and place, yet their voices are strangely human and call out one's pity.

Our way is still along the Merced and Tuolumne divide, the streams on our right going to swell the songful Yosemite River, those on our left to the songful Tuolumne, slipping through sunny carex and lily meadows and breaking into song down a thousand ravines almost as soon as they are born. A more tuneful set of streams surely nowhere exists, or more sparkling crystal pure, now gliding with tinkling whisper, now with merry dimpling rush, in and out through sunshine and shade, shimmering in pools, uniting their currents, bouncing, dancing from form to form over cliffs and inclines, ever more beautiful the farther they go until they pour into the main glacial rivers.

All day I have been gazing in growing admiration at the noble groups of the magnificent silver fir which more and more is taking the ground to itself. The woods above Crane Flat still continue comparatively open, letting in the sunshine on the brown needle-strewn ground. Not only are the individual trees admirable in symmetry and superb in foliage and port, but half a dozen or more, often form temple groves in which the trees are so nicely graded in size and position as to seem one. Here indeed, is the tree-lover's paradise. The dullest eye in the world must surely be quickened by such trees as these.

Fortunately the sheep need little attention, as they are driven slowly and allowed to nip and nibble as they like. Since leaving Hazel Green we have been following the Yosemite trail; visitors to the famous valley coming by way of Coulterville and Chinese Camp pass this way – the two trails uniting at Crane Flat – and enter the valley on the north side. Another trail enters on the south side by way of Mariposa. The tourists we saw were in parties of from three or four to fifteen or twenty, mounted on mules or small mustang ponies. A strange show they made, winding single file through the solemn woods in gaudy attire, scaring the wild creatures, and one might fancy that even the great pines would be disturbed and groan aghast. But what may we say of ourselves and the flock?

We are now camped at Tamarack Flat, within four or five miles of the lower end of Yosemite. Here is another fine meadow embosomed in the woods, with a deep, clear stream gliding through it, its banks rounded and bevelled with a thatch of dipping sedges. The flat is named after the two leaved pine (*Pinus contorta*, var. *Murrayana*), common here, especially around the cool margin of the meadow. On rocky ground it is a rough, thickset tree, about forty to sixty feet high and one to three feet in diameter, bark thin and gummy, branches rather naked, tassels, leaves and cones small. But in damp, rich soil it grows close and slender, and reaches a height at times of nearly a hundred feet. Specimens only six inches in diameter at the ground are often fifty or sixty feet in height, as slender and sharp in outline as arrows, like the true tamarack (larch) of the Eastern States; hence the name, though it is a pine.

July 11. The Don has gone ahead on one of the pack

animals to spy out the land to the north of Yosemite in search of the best point for a central camp. Much higher than this we cannot now go, for the upper pastures, said to be better than any hereabouts, are still buried in heavy winter snow. Glad I am that camp is to be fixed in the Yosemite region, for many a glorious ramble I'll have along the top of the walls, and then what landscapes I shall find with their new mountains and canyons, forests and gardens, lakes and streams and falls.

We are now about seven thousand feet above the sea and the nights are so cool we have to pile coats and extra clothing on top of our blankets. Tamarack Creek is icy cold, delicious, exhilarating champagne water. It is flowing bank full in the meadow with silent speed, but only a few hundred yards below our camp the ground is bare grey granite strewn with boulders, large spaces being without a single tree or only a small one here and there anchored in narrow seams and cracks. The boulders, many of them very large, are not in piles or scattered like rubbish among loose crumbling debris as if weathered out of the solid as boulders of disintegration; they mostly occur singly, and are lying on a clean pavement on which the sunshine falls in a glare that contrasts with the shimmer of light and shade we have been accustomed to in the leafy woods. And strange to say, these boulders lying so still and deserted, with no moving force near them, no boulder carrier anywhere in sight, were nevertheless brought from a distance, as difference in colour and composition shows, quarried and carried and laid down here each in its place; nor have they stirred, most of them, through calm and storm since first they arrived. They look lonely here, strangers in a strange land, – huge blocks, angular mountain chips, the largest twenty or thirty feet in diameter, the chips that Nature has made in modelling her landscapes, fashioning the forms of her mountains and valleys. And with what tool were they quarried and carried? On the pavement we find its marks. The most resisting unweathered portion of the surface is scored and striated in a rigidly parallel way, indicating that the region has been overswept by a glacier from the north-eastward, grinding down the general mass of the mountains, scoring and polishing, producing a strange, raw, wiped appearance, and dropping whatever boulders it chanced to be carrying at the time it was melted at the close of the Glacial Period. A fine discovery this. As for the forests we have been passing through, they are probably growing on deposits of soil most of which has been laid down by this same ice agent in the form of moraines of different sorts, now in great part disintegrated and outspread by post-glacial weathering.

Out of the grassy meadow and down over this ice-planed granite runs the glad young Tamarack Creek, rejoicing, exulting, chanting, dancing in white, glowing, irised falls and cascades on its way to the Merced Canyon, a few miles below Yosemite, falling more than three thousand feet in a distance of about two miles.

All the Merced streams are wonderful singers, and Yosemite is the centre where the main tributaries meet. From a point about half a mile from our camp we can see into the lower end of the famous valley, with its wonderful cliffs and groves, a grand page of mountain manuscript that I would gladly give my life to be able to read. How vast it seems, how short human life when we happen to think of it, and how little we may learn, however hard we try! Yet why bewail our poor inevitable ignorance? Some of the external beauty is always in sight, enough to keep every fibre of us tingling, and this we are able to gloriously enjoy though the methods of its creation may lie beyond our ken. Sing on, brave Tamarack Creek, fresh from your snowy fountains, plash and swirl and dance to your fate in the sea; bathing, cheering every living thing along your way.

Have greatly enjoyed all this huge day, sauntering and seeing, steeping in the mountain influences, sketching, noting, pressing flowers, drinking ozone and Tamarack water. Found the white fragrant Washington lily, the finest of all the Sierra lilies. Its bulbs are buried in shaggy chaparral tangles, I suppose for safety from pawing bears; and its magnificent panicles sway and rock over the top of the rough snow-pressed bushes, while big, bold, blunt-nosed bees drone and mumble in its polleny bells. A lovely flower, worth going hungry and footsore endless miles to see. The whole world seems richer now that I have found this plant in so noble a landscape.

A log house serves to mark a claim to the Tamarack meadow, which may become valuable as a station in case travel to Yosemite should greatly increase. Belated parties occasionally stop here. A white man with an Indian woman is holding possession of the place.

Sauntered up the meadow about sundown, out of sight of camp and sheep and all human mark, into the deep peace of the solemn old woods, everything glowing with Heaven's unquenchable enthusiasm.

July 12. The Don has returned, and again we go on pilgrimage. 'Looking over the Yosemite Creek country,' he said, 'from the tops of the hills you see nothing but rocks and patches of trees; but when you go down into the rocky desert you find no end of small grassy banks and meadows, and so the country is not half so lean as it looks. There we'll go and stay until the snow is melted from the upper country.'

I was glad to hear that the high snow made a stay in the Yosemite region necessary, for I am anxious to see as much of it as possible. What fine times I shall have sketching, studying plants and rocks, and scrambling about the brink of the great valley alone, out of sight and sound of camp!

We saw another party of Yosemite tourists today. Somehow most of these travellers seem to care but little for the glorious objects about them, though enough to spend time and money and endure long rides to see the famous valley. And when they are fairly within the mighty walls of the temple and hear the psalms of the falls, they will forget themselves and become devout. Blessed indeed, should be every pilgrim in these holy mountains!

We moved slowly eastward along the Mono Trail, and early in the afternoon unpacked and camped on the bank of Cascade Creek. The Mono Trail crosses the range by the Bloody Canyon Pass to gold mines near the north end of Mono Lake. These mines were reported to be rich when first discovered, and a grand rush took place, making a trail necessary. A few small bridges were built over streams where fording was not practicable on account of the softness of the bottom, sections of fallen trees cut out and lanes made through thickets wide enough to allow the passage of bulky packs; but over the greater part of the way scarce a stone or shovelful of earth has been moved.

The woods we passed through are composed almost wholly of *Abies magnifica*, the companion species, *concolor*, being mostly left behind on account of altitude, while the increasing elevation seems grateful to the charming *magnifica*. No words can do anything like justice to this noble tree. At one place many had fallen during some heavy wind storm, owing to the loose sandy character of the soil, which offered no secure anchorage. The soil is mostly decomposed and disintegrated moraine material.

The sheep are lying down on a bare rocky spot such as they like, chewing the cud in grassy peace. Cooking is going on, appetites growing keener every day. No lowlander can appreciate the mountain appetite, and the facility with which heavy food called 'grub' is disposed of. Eating, walking, resting, seem alike delightful, and one feels inclined to shout lustily on rising in the morning like a crowing cock. Sleep and digestion as clear as the air. Fine spicy plush boughs for bedding we shall have tonight, and a glorious lullaby from this cascading creek. Never was stream more fittingly named, for as far as I have traced it above and below our camp it is one continuous bouncing, dancing, white bloom of cascades. And at the very last unwearied it finishes its wild course in a grand leap of three hundred feet or more to the bottom of the main Yosemite canyon near the fall of Tamarack Creek, a few miles below the foot of the valley. These falls almost rival some of the far famed Yosemite falls. Never shall I forget these glad cascade songs, the low booming, the roaring, the keen, silvery clashing of the cool water rushing exulting from form to form beneath irised spray; or in the deep still night seen white in the darkness, and its multitude of voices sounding still more impressively sublime. Here I find the little water ouzel as much at home as any linnet in a leafy grove, seeming to take the greater delight the more boisterous the stream.

The dizzy precipices, the swift dashing energy displayed, and the thunder tones of the sheer falls are awe-inspiring, but there is nothing awful about this little bird. Its song is sweet and low, and all its gestures, as it flits about amid the loud uproar, bespeak strength and peace and joy. Contemplating these darlings of Nature coming forth from spray sprinkled nests on the brink of savage streams, Samson's riddle comes to mind, 'Out of the strong cometh forth sweetness.' A yet finer bloom is this little bird than the foam bells in eddying pools. Gentle bird, a precious message you bring me. We may miss the meaning of the torrent, but thy sweet voice, only love is in it.

July 13. Our course all day has been eastward over the rim of Yosemite Creek basin and down about halfway to the bottom, where we have encamped on a sheet of glacier-polished granite, a firm foundation for beds. Saw the tracks of a very large bear on the trail, and the don talked of bears in general. I said I should like to see the maker of these immense tracks as he marched along, and follow him for days, without disturbing him, to learn something of the life of this master beast of the wilderness. Lambs, the Don told me, born in the lowland, that never saw or heard a bear, snort and run in terror when they catch the scent, showing how fully they have inherited a knowledge of their enemy. Hogs, mules, horses and cattle are afraid of bears, and are seized with ungovernable terror when they approach, particularly hogs and mules. Hogs are frequently driven to pastures in the foothills of the Coast Range and Sierra where acorns are abundant and are herded in droves of hundreds like sheep. When a bear comes to the range they promptly leave it, emigrating in a body, usually in the night time, the keepers being powerless to prevent; they thus show more sense than sheep, that simply scatter in the rocks and brush and await their fate. Mules flee like the wind with or without riders when they see a bear, and, if picketed, sometimes break their necks in trying to break their ropes, though I have not heard of bears killing mules or horses. Of hogs they are said to be particularly fond, bolting small ones, bones and all, without choice of parts. In particular, Mr Delaney assured me that all kinds of bears in the Sierra are very shy, and that hunters found far greater difficulty in getting within gunshot of them than of deer or indeed any other animal in the Sierra and if I was anxious to see much of them I should have to wait and watch with endless Indian patience and pay no attention to anything else.

Night is coming on, the grey rock waves are growing dim in the twilight. How raw and young this region appears! Had the ice sheet that swept over it vanished but yesterday, its traces on the more resisting portions about our camp could hardly be more distinct than they now are. The horses and sheep and all of us, indeed, slipped on the smoothest places.

July 14. How deathlike is sleep in this mountain air, and quick the awakening into newness of life! A calm dawn, yellow and purple, then floods of sun-gold, making everything tingle and glow.

In an hour or two we came to Yosemite Creek, the stream that makes the greatest of all the Yosemite falls. It is about forty feet wide at the Mono Trail crossing, and now about four feet in average depth, flowing about three miles an hour. The distance to the verge of the Yosemite wall, where it makes its tremendous plunge, is only about two miles from here. Calm, beautiful, and nearly silent, it glides with stately gestures, a dense growth of the slender two-leaved pine along its banks, and a fringe of willow, purple spirea, sedges, daisies, lilies and columbines. Some of the sedges and willow boughs dip into the current, and just outside of the close ranks of trees there is a sunny flat of washed gravelly sand which seems to have been deposited by some ancient flood. It is covered with millions of erethrea, eriogonum, and oxytheca, with more flowers than leaves, forming an even growth, slightly dimpled and ruffled here and there by rosettes of *Spraguea umbellata*. Back of this flowery strip there is a wavy upsloping plain of solid granite, so smoothly ice-polished in many places that it glistens in the sun like glass. In shallow hollows there are patches of trees, mostly the rough form of the two-leaved pine, rather scrawny looking where there is little or no soil. Also a few junipers (*Juniperus occidentalis*), short and stout, with bright cinnamon-coloured bark and grey foliage, standing alone mostly, on the sun-beaten pavement, safe from fire, clinging by slight joints, – a sturdy storm-enduring mountaineer of a tree, living on sunshine and snow, maintaining tough health on this diet for perhaps more than a thousand years.

Up towards the head of the basin I see groups of domes rising above the wavelike ridges, and some picturesque castellated masses, and dark strips and patches of silver fir, indicating deposits of fertile soil. Would that I could command the time to study them! What rich excursions one could make in this well-defined basin! Its glacial inscriptions and sculptures, how marvellous they seem, how noble the studies they offer! I tremble with excitement in the dawn of these glorious mountain sublimities, but I can only gaze and wonder, and, like a child, gather here and there a lily, half hoping I may be able to study and learn in years to come.

The drivers and dogs had a lively, laborious time getting the sheep across the creek, the second large stream thus far that they have been compelled to cross without a bridge; the first being the north fork of the Merced near Bower Cave. Men and dogs, shouting and barking, drove the timid, water-fearing creatures in a close crowd against the bank, but not one of the flock would launch away. While thus jammed, the Don and the shepherd rushed through the frightened crowd to stampede those in front, but this would only cause a break backward, and away they would scamper through the stream bank trees and scatter over the rocky pavement. Then with the aid of the dogs the runaways would again be gathered and made to face the stream, and again the compacted mass would break away, amid wild shouting and barking that might well have disturbed the stream itself and marred the music of its falls, to which visitors no doubt from all quarters of the globe were listening. 'Hold them there! Now hold them there!' shouted the Don; 'the front ranks will soon tire of the pressure, and be glad to take to the water, then all will jump in and cross in a hurry.' But they did nothing of the kind; they only avoided the pressure by breaking back in scores and hundreds, leaving the beauty of the banks sadly trampled.

If only one could be got to cross over, all would make haste to follow; but that one could not be found. A lamb was caught, carried across, and tied to a bush on the opposite bank, where it cried piteously for its mother. But though greatly concerned, the mother only called it back. That play on maternal affection failed, and we began to fear that we should be forced to make a long roundabout drive and cross the widespread tributaries of the creek in succession. This would require several days, but it had its advantages, for I was eager to see the sources of so famous a stream. Don Quixote, however, determined that they must ford just here, and immediately began a sort of siege by cutting down slender pines on the bank and building a corral barely large enough to hold the flock when well pressed together. And as the stream would form one side of the corral he believed that they could easily be forced into the water.

In a few hours the enclosure was completed, and the silly animals were driven in and rammed hard against the brink of the ford. Then the Don, forcing a way through the compacted mass, pitched a few of the terrified unfortunates into the stream by main strength; but instead of crossing over, they swam about close to the bank, making desperate attempts to get back into the flock. Then a dozen or more were shoved off, and the Don, tall like a crane and a good natural wader, jumped in after them, seized a struggling wether, and dragged it to the opposite shore. But no sooner did he let it go than it jumped into the stream and swam back to its frightened companions in the corral, thus manifesting sheep nature as unchangeable as gravitation. Pan with his pipes would have had no better luck, I fear. We were now pretty well baffled. The silly creatures would suffer any sort of death rather than cross that stream. Calling a council, the dripping Don declared that starvation was now the only likely scheme to try, and that we might as well camp here in comfort and let the besieged flock grow hungry and cool and come to their senses, if they had any. In a few minutes after being thus let alone, an adventurer in the foremost rank plunged in and swam bravely to the farther shore. Then suddenly all rushed in pell-mell together, trampling one another under water, while we vainly tried to hold them back. The Don jumped into the thickest of the gasping, gurgling, drowning mass, and shoved them right and left as if each sheep was a piece of floating timber. The current also served to drift them apart; a long bent column was soon formed and in a few minutes all were over and began baaing and feeding as if nothing out of the common had happened. That none were drowned seems wonderful. I fully expected that hundreds would gain the romantic fate of being swept into Yosemite over the highest waterfall in the world.

As the day was far spent we camped a little way back from the ford and let the dripping flock scatter and feed until sundown. The wool is dry now, and calm, cud-chewing peace has fallen on all the comfortable band, leaving no trace of the watery battle. I have seen fish driven out of the water with less ado than was made in driving these animals into it. Sheep brain must surely be poor stuff. Compare today's exhibition with the performances of deer swimming quietly across broad and rapid rivers, and from island to island in seas and lakes; or with dogs, or even with the squirrels that, as the story goes, cross the Mississippi River on selected chips, with tails for sails comfortably trimmed to the breeze. A sheep can hardly be called an animal; an entire flock is required to make one foolish individual.

FIVE

The Yosemite

July 15. Followed the Mono Trail up the eastern rim of the basin nearly to its summit, then turned off southward to a small shallow valley that extends to the edge of the Yosemite, which we reached about noon, and encamped. After luncheon I made haste to high ground, and from the top of the ridge on the west side of Indian Canyon gained the noblest view of the summit peaks I have ever yet enjoyed. Nearly all the upper basin of the Merced was displayed, with its sublime domes and canyons, dark upsweeping forests, and glorious array of white peaks deep in the sky, every feature glowing, radiating beauty that pours into our flesh and bones like heat rays from fire. Sunshine over all; no breath of wind to stir the brooding calm. Never before had I seen so glorious a landscape, so boundless an affluence of sublime mountain beauty. The most extravagant description I might give of this view to any one who has not seen similar landscapes with his own eyes would not so much as hint its grandeur and the spiritual glow that covered it. I shouted and gesticulated in a wild burst of ecstasy, much to the astonishment of St Bernard Carlo, who came running up to me, manifesting in his intelligent eyes a puzzled concern that was very ludicrous, which had the effect of bringing me to my senses. A brown bear, too, it would seem, had been a spectator of the show I had made of myself, for I had gone but a few yards when I started one from a thicket of brush. He evidently considered me dangerous, for he ran away very fast, tumbling over the tops of the tangled manzanita bushes in his haste. Carlo drew back, with his ears depressed as if afraid, and kept looking me in the face, as if expecting me to pursue and shoot, for he had seen many a bear battle in his day.

Following the ridge, which made a gradual descent to the south, I came at length to the brow of that massive cliff that stands between Indian Canyon and Yosemite Falls, and here the far-famed valley came suddenly into view throughout almost its whole extent. The noble walls – sculptured into endless variety of domes and gables, spires and battlements and plain mural precipices – all atremble with the thunder tones of the falling water. The level bottom seemed to be dressed like a garden – sunny meadows here and there, and groves of pine and oak; the river of Mercy sweeping in majesty through the midst of them and flashing back the sunbeams. The great Tissiack, or Half-Dome, rising at the upper end of the valley to a height of nearly a mile, is nobly proportioned and lifelike, the most impressive of all the rocks, holding the eye in devout admiration, calling it back again and again from falls or meadows, or even the mountains beyond, – marvellous cliffs, marvellous in sheer dizzy depth and sculpture, types of endurance. Thousands of years have they stood in the sky exposed to rain, snow, frost, earthquake and avalanche, yet they still wear the bloom of youth.

I rambled along the valley rim to the westward; most of it is rounded off on the very brink, so that it is not easy to find places where one may look clear down the face of the wall to the bottom. When such places were found and I had cautiously set my feet and drawn my body erect, I could not help fearing a little that the rock might split off and let me down, and what a down! – more than three thousand feet. Still my limbs did not tremble, nor did I feel the least uncertainty as to the reliance to be placed on them. My only fear was that a flake of the granite, which in some places showed joints more or less open and running parallel with the face of the cliff, might give way. After withdrawing from such places, excited with the view I had got, I would say to myself, 'Now don't go out on the verge again.' But in the face of Yosemite scenery cautious remonstrance is vain; under its spell one's body seems to go where it likes with a will over which we seem to have scarce any control.

After a mile or so of this memorable cliff work I

approached Yosemite Creek, admiring its easy, graceful, confident gestures as it comes bravely forward in its narrow channel, singing the last of its mountain songs on its way to its fate – a few rods more over the shining granite, then down half a mile in showy foam to another world, to be lost in the Merced, where climate, vegetation, inhabitants, all are different. Emerging from its last gorge, it glides in wide lace-like rapids down a smooth incline into a pool where it seems to rest and compose its grey, agitated waters before taking the grand plunge, then slowly slipping over the lip of the pool basin, it descends another glossy slope with rapidly accelerated speed to the brink of the tremendous cliff, and with sublime, fateful confidence springs out free in the air.

I took off my shoes and stockings and worked my way cautiously down alongside the rushing flood, keeping my feet and hands pressed firmly on the polished rock. The booming, roaring water, rushing past close to my head, was very exciting. I had expected that the sloping apron would terminate with the perpendicular wall of the valley, and that from the foot of it, where it is less steeply inclined, I should be able to lean far enough out to see the forms and behaviour of the fall all the way down to the bottom. But I found that there was yet another small brow over which I could not see, and which appeared to be too steep for mortal feet. Scanning it keenly, I discovered a narrow shelf about three inches wide on the very brink, just wide enough for a rest for one's heels. But there seemed to be no way of reaching it over so steep a brow. At length, after careful scrutiny of the surface, I found an irregular edge of a flake of the rock some distance back from the margin of the torrent. If I was to get down to the brink at all that rough edge, which might offer slight finger holds, was the only way. But the slope beside it looked dangerously smooth and steep, and the swift roaring flood beneath, overhead, and beside me was very nerve trying. I therefore concluded not to venture farther, but did nevertheless. Tufts of artemisia were growing in clefts of the rock near by, and I filled my mouth with the bitter leaves, hoping they might help to prevent giddiness. Then, with a caution not known in ordinary circumstances, I crept down safely to the little ledge, got my heels well planted on it, then shuffled in a horizontal direction twenty or thirty feet until close to the outplunging current, which, by the time it had descended thus far, was already white. Here I obtained a perfectly free view down into the heart of the snowy, chanting throng of comet-like streamers, into which the body of the fall soon separates.

While perched on that narrow niche I was not distinctly conscious of danger. The tremendous grandeur of the fall in form and sound and motion, acting at close range, smothered the sense of fear, and in such places one's body takes keen care for safety on its own account. How long I remained down there, or how I returned, I can hardly tell. Anyhow I had a glorious time, and got back to camp about dark, enjoying triumphant exhilaration soon followed by dull weariness. Hereafter I'll try to keep from such extravagant, nerve straining places. Yet such a day is well worth venturing for. My first view of the High Sierra, first view looking down into Yosemite, the death song of Yosemite Creek, and its flight over the vast cliff, each one of these is of itself enough for a great lifelong landscape fortune – a most memorable day of days – enjoyment enough to kill if that were possible.

July 16. My enjoyments yesterday afternoon, especially at the head of the fall, were too great for good sleep. Kept starting up last night in a nervous tremor, half awake, fancying that the foundation of the mountain we were camped on had given way and was falling into Yosemite Valley. In vain I roused myself to make a new beginning for sound sleep. The nerve strain had been too great, and again and again I dreamed I was rushing through the air above a glorious avalanche of water and rocks. One time, springing to my feet, I said, 'This time it is real – all must die, and where could mountaineer find a more glorious death!'

Left camp soon after sunrise for an all day ramble eastward. Crossed the head of Indian Basin, forested with *Abies magnifica*, underbrush mostly *Ceanothus cordulatus* and manzanita, a mixture not easily trampled over or penetrated, for the ceanothus is thorny and grows in dense snow-pressed masses, and the manzanita has exceedingly crooked, stubborn branches. From the head of the canyon continued on past North Dome into the basin of Dome or Porcupine Creek. Here are many fine meadows embedded in the woods, gay with *Lilium parvum* and its companions; the elevation, about eight thousand feet, seems to be best suited for it – saw specimens that were a foot or two higher than my head. Had more magnificent views of the upper mountains, and of the great South Dome, said to be the grandest rock in the world. Well it may be, since it is of such noble dimensions and sculpture. A wonderfully impressive monument, its lines exquisite in fineness, and though sublime in size, is finished like the finest work of art, and seems to be alive.

July 17. A new camp was made today in a magnificent silver fir grove at the head of a small stream that flows into Yosemite by way of Indian Canyon. Here we intend to stay several weeks, – a fine location from which to make excursions about the great valley and its fountains. Glorious days I'll have sketching, pressing plants, studying the wonderful topography and the wild animals, our happy fellow mortals and neighbours. But the vast mountains in the distance, shall I ever know them, shall I be allowed to enter into their midst and dwell with them?

We were pelted about noon by a short, heavy rain-storm, sublime thunder reverberating among the mountains and canyons, – some strokes near, crashing, ringing in the tense crisp air with startling keenness, while the distant peaks loomed gloriously through the cloud fringes and sheets of rain. Now the storm is past, and the fresh washed air is full of the essences of the flower gardens and groves. Winter storms in Yosemite must be glorious. May I see them!

Have got my bed made in our new camp, – plushy, sumptuous, and deliciously fragrant, most of it *magnifica* fir plumes, of course, with a variety of sweet flowers in the pillow. Hope to sleep tonight without tottering nerve dreams. Watched a deer eating ceanothus leaves and twigs.

July 18. Slept pretty well; the valley walls did not seem to fall, though I still fancied myself at the brink, alongside the white, plunging flood, especially when half asleep. Strange the danger of that adventure should be more troublesome now that I am in the bosom of the peaceful woods, a mile or more from the fall, than it was while I was on the brink of it.

Bears seem to be common here, judging by their tracks. About noon we had another rain-storm with keen startling thunder, the metallic, ringing, clashing, clanging notes gradually fading into low bass rolling and muttering in the distance. For a few minutes the rain came in a grand torrent like a waterfall, then hail; some of the hailstones an inch in diameter, hard, icy, and irregular in form, like those oftentimes seen in Wisconsin. Carlo watched them with intelligent astonishment as they came pelting and thrashing through the quivering branches of the trees. The cloud scenery sublime. Afternoon calm, sunful, and clear, with delicious freshness and fragrance from the firs and flowers and steaming ground.

July 19. Watching the daybreak and sunrise. The pale rose and purple sky changing softly to daffodil yellow and white, sunbeams pouring through the passes between the peaks and over the Yosemite domes, making their edges burn; the silver firs in the middle ground catching the glow on their spiry tops, and our camp grove fills and thrills with the glorious light. Everything awakening alert and joyful; the birds begin to stir and innumerable insect people. Deer quietly withdraw into leafy hiding places in the chaparral; the dew vanishes, flowers spread their petals, every pulse beats high, every life cell rejoices, the very rocks seem to thrill with life. The whole landscape glows like a human face in a glory of enthusiasm, and the blue sky, pale around the horizon, bends peacefully down over all like one vast flower.

About noon, as usual, big bossy cumuli began to grow above the forest, and the rainstorm pouring from them is the most imposing I have yet seen. The silvery zigzag lightning lances are longer than usual and the thunder gloriously impressive, keen, crashing, intensely concentrated, speaking with such tremendous energy it would seem that an entire mountain is being shattered at every stroke, but probably only a few trees are being shattered, many of which I have seen on my walks hereabouts strewing the ground. At last the clear ringing strokes are succeeded by deep low tones that grow gradually fainter as they roll afar into the recesses of the echoing mountains, where they seem to be welcomed home. Then another and another peal, or rather crashing, splintering stroke, follows in quick succession, perchance splitting some giant pine or fir from top to bottom into long rails and slivers, and scattering them to all points of the compass. Now comes the rain, with corresponding extravagant grandeur, covering the ground high and low with a sheet of flowing water, a transparent film fitted like a skin upon the rugged anatomy of the landscape, making the rocks glitter and glow, gathering in the ravines, flooding the streams, and making them shout and boom in reply to the thunder.

How interesting to trace the history of a single raindrop! It is not long, geologically speaking, as we have seen, since the first raindrops fell on the newborn leafless Sierra landscapes. How different the lot of these falling now! Happy the showers that fall on so fair a wilderness, – scarce a single drop can fail to find a beautiful spot, – on the tops of the peaks, on the shining glacier pavements, on the great smooth domes, on forests and gardens and brushy moraines, plashing, glinting, pattering, laving. Some go to the high snowy fountains to swell their well-saved stores; some into the lakes, washing the mountain windows, patting their smooth glassy levels, making dimples and bubbles and spray; some into the waterfalls and cascades, as if eager to join in their dance and song and beat their foam yet finer; good luck and good work for the happy mountain raindrops, each one of them a high waterfall in itself, descending from the cliffs and hollows of the clouds to the cliffs and hollows of the rocks, out of the sky-thunder into the thunder of the falling rivers. Some, falling on meadows and bogs, creep silently out of sight to the grass roots, hiding softly as in a nest, slipping, oozing hither, thither, seeking and finding their appointed work. Some, descending through the spires of the woods, sift spray through the shining needles, whispering peace and good cheer to each one of them. Some drops with happy aim glint on the sides of crystals, – quartz, hornblende, garnet, zircon, tourmaline, feldspar, – patter on grains of gold and heavy way-worn nuggets; some, with blunt plap-plap and low bass drumming, fall on the broad leaves of veratrum, saxifrage, cypripedium. Some happy drops fall straight into the cups of flowers, kissing the lips of lilies. How far they have to go, how many cups to fill, great and small, cells too small to be seen, cups holding half a drop as well as lake basins between the hills, each replenished with equal care, every drop in all the blessed throng a silvery newborn star with lake and river, garden and grove, valley and mountain, all that the landscape holds reflected in its crystal depths, God's messenger, angel of love sent on its way with majesty and pomp and display of power that make man's greatest shows ridiculous.

Now the storm is over, the sky is clear, the last rolling thunder-wave is spent on the peaks, and where are the raindrops now – what has become of all the shining throng? In winged vapour rising some are already hastening back to the sky, some have gone into the plants, creeping through invisible doors into the round rooms of cells, some are locked in crystals of ice, some in rock crystals, some in porous moraines to keep their small springs flowing, some have gone journeying on in the rivers to join the larger raindrop of the ocean. From form to form, beauty to beauty, ever changing, never resting, all are speeding on with love's enthusiasm, singing with the stars the eternal song of creation.

July 20. Fine calm morning; air tense and clear; not the slightest breeze astir; everything shining, the rocks with wet crystals, the plants with dew, each receiving its portion of irised dewdrops and sunshine like living creatures getting their breakfast, their dew manna coming down from the starry sky like swarms of smaller stars. How wondrous fine are the particles in showers of dew, thousands required for a single drop, growing in the dark as silently as the grass! What pains are taken to keep this wilderness in health, – showers of snow, showers of rain, showers of dew, floods of light, floods of invisible vapour, clouds, winds, all sorts of weather, interaction of plant on plant and animal on animal, beyond thought! How fine Nature's methods! How deeply with beauty is beauty overlaid! the ground covered with crystals, the crystals with mosses and lichens and low-spreading grasses and flowers, these with larger plants leaf over leaf with ever changing colour and form, the broad palms of the firs outspread over these, the azure dome over all like a bell-flower, and star above star.

Yonder stands the South Dome, its crown high above our camp, though its base is four thousand feet below us; a most noble rock, it seems full of thought, clothed with living light, no sense of dead stone about it, all spiritualised, neither heavy looking nor light, steadfast in serene strength like a god.

Our shepherd is a queer character and hard to place in this wilderness. His bed is a hollow made in red dry rot punky dust beside a log which forms a portion of the south wall of the corral. Here he lies with his wonderful everlasting clothing on, wrapped in a red blanket, breathing not only the dust of the decayed wood but also that of the corral, as if determined to take ammoniacal snuff all night after chewing tobacco all day. Following the sheep he carries a heavy six-shooter swung from his belt on one side and his luncheon on the other. The ancient cloth in which the meat, fresh from the frying pan, is tied serves as a filter through which the clear fat and gravy juices drip down on his right hip and leg in clustering stalactites. This oleaginous formation is soon broken up however, and diffused and rubbed evenly into his scanty apparel, by sitting down, rolling over, crossing his legs while resting on logs, making shirt and trousers watertight and shiny. His trousers, in particular, have become so adhesive with the mixed fat and resin that pine needles, thin flakes and fibres of bark, hair, mica scales and minute grains of quartz, hornblende, etc., feathers, seed wings, moth and butterfly wings, legs and antennae of innumerable insects, or even whole insects such as the small beetles, moths and mosquitoes, with flower petals, pollen dust and indeed bits of all plants, animals, and minerals of the region adhere to them and are safely embedded, so that though far from being a naturalist he collects fragmentary specimens of everything and becomes richer than he knows. His specimens are kept passably fresh too, by the purity of the air and the resiny bituminous beds into which they are pressed. Man is a microcosm, at least our shepherd is, or rather his trousers. These precious overalls are never taken off, and nobody knows how old they are, though one may guess by their thickness and concentric structure. Instead of wearing thin they wear thick, and in their stratification have no small geological significance.

Besides herding the sheep, Billy is the butcher, while I have agreed to wash the few iron and tin utensils and make the bread. Then, these small duties done, by the time the sun is fairly above the mountain tops I am beyond the flock, free to rove and revel in the wilderness all the big immortal days.

Sketching on the North Dome. It commands views of nearly all the valley besides a few of the high mountains. I would fain draw everything in sight – rock, tree, and leaf. But little can I do beyond mere outlines, – marks with meanings like words, readable only to myself, – yet I sharpen my pencils and work on as if others might possibly be benefited. Whether these picture-sheets are to vanish like fallen leaves or go to friends like letters, matters not much; for little can they tell to those who have not themselves seen similar wildness, and like a language have learned it. No pain here, no dull empty hours, no fear of the past, no fear of the future. These blessed mountains are so compactly filled with God's beauty, no petty personal hope or experience has room to be. Drinking this champagne water is pure pleasure, so is breathing the living air, and every movement of limbs is pleasure, while the whole body seems to feel beauty when exposed to it as it feels the campfire or sunshine, entering not by the eyes alone, but equally through all one's flesh like radiant heat, making a passionate ecstatic pleasure glow not explainable. One's body then seems homogeneous throughout, sound as a crystal.

Perched like a fly on this Yosemite dome, I gaze and sketch and bask, oftentimes settling down into dumb admiration without definite hope of ever learning much, yet with the longing, unresting effort that lies at the door of hope, humbly prostrate before the vast display of God's power, and eager to offer self-denial and renunciation with eternal toil to learn any lesson in the divine manuscript.

It is easier to feel than to realise, or in any way explain, Yosemite grandeur. The magnitudes of the rocks and trees and streams are so delicately harmonised they are mostly hidden. Sheer precipices three thousand feet high are fringed with tall trees growing close like grass on the brow of a lowland hill, and extending along the feet of these precipices a ribbon of meadow a mile wide and seven or eight long, that seems like a strip a farmer might mow in less than a day. Waterfalls, five hundred to one or two thousand feet high, are so subordinated to the mighty cliffs over which they pour that they seem like wisps of smoke, gentle as floating clouds, though their voices fill the valley and make the rocks tremble. The mountains too, along the eastern sky, and the domes in front of them, and the succession of smooth rounded waves between, swelling higher, higher, with dark woods in their hollows, serene in massive exuberant bulk and beauty, tend yet more to hide the grandeur of the Yosemite temple and make it appear as a subdued subordinate feature of the vast harmonious landscape. Thus every attempt to appreciate any one feature is beaten down by the overwhelming influence of all the others. And, as if this were not enough, lo! in the sky arises another mountain range with topography as rugged and substantial-looking as the one beneath it – snowy peaks and domes and shadowy Yosemite valley – another version of the snowy Sierra, a new creation heralded by a thunderstorm. How fiercely, devoutly wild is Nature in the midst of her beauty-loving tenderness! – painting lilies, watering them, caressing them with gentle hand, going from flower to flower like a gardener while building rock mountains and cloud mountains full of lightning and rain. Gladly we run for shelter beneath an overhanging cliff and examine the reassuring ferns and mosses, gentle love tokens growing in cracks and chinks. Daisies too, and ivesias, confiding wild children of light, too small to fear. To these one's heart goes home, and the voices of the storm become gentle. Now the sun breaks forth and fragrant steam arises. The birds are out singing on the edges of the groves. The west is flaming in gold and purple, ready for the ceremony of the sunset, and back I go to camp with my notes and pictures, the best of them printed in my mind as dreams. A fruitful day, without measured beginning or ending. A terrestrial eternity. A gift of good God.

Wrote to my mother and a few friends, mountain hints to each. They seem as near as if within voice-reach or touch. The deeper the solitude the less the sense of loneliness, and the nearer our friends. Now bread and tea, fir bed and goodnight to Carlo, a look at the sky lilies, and death sleep until the dawn of another Sierra tomorrow.

July 21. Sketching on the Dome – no rain; clouds at noon about quarter filled the sky, casting shadows with fine effect on the white mountains at the heads of the streams, and a soothing cover over the gardens during the warm hours.

Saw a common house fly and a grasshopper and a brown bear. The fly and grasshopper paid me a merry visit on the top of the Dome, and I paid a visit to the bear in the middle of a small garden meadow between the Dome and the camp where he was standing alert among the flowers as if willing to be seen to advantage. I had not gone more than half a mile from camp this morning, when Carlo, who was trotting on a few yards ahead of me, came to a sudden, cautious standstill. Down went tail and ears, and forward went his knowing nose, while he seemed to be saying, 'Ha, what's this? A bear, I guess.' Then a cautious advance of a few steps, setting his feet down softly like a hunting cat, and questioning the air as to the scent he had caught until all doubt vanished. Then he came back to me, looked me in the face, and with his speaking eyes reported a bear near by; then led on softly, careful, like an experienced hunter, not to make the slightest noise, and frequently looking back as if whispering, 'Yes, it's a bear; come and I'll show you.' Presently we came to where the sunbeams were streaming through between the purple shafts of the firs, which showed that we were nearing an open spot, and here Carlo came behind me, evidently sure that the bear was very near. So I crept to a low ridge of moraine boulders on the edge of a narrow garden meadow, and in this meadow I felt pretty sure the bear must be. I was anxious to get a good look at the sturdy mountaineer without alarming him; so drawing myself up noiselessly back of one of the largest of the trees I peered past its bulging buttresses, exposing only a part of my head, and there stood neighbour Bruin within a stone's throw, his hips covered by tall grass and flowers, and his front feet on the trunk of a fir that had fallen out into the meadow, which raised his head so high that he seemed to be standing erect. He had not yet seen me, but was looking and listening attentively, showing that in some way he was aware of our approach. I watched his gestures and tried to make the most of my opportunity to learn what I could about him, fearing he would catch sight of me and run away. For I had been told that this sort of bear, the cinnamon, always ran from his bad brother man, never showing fight unless wounded or in defence of young. He made a telling picture standing alert in the sunny forest garden. How well he played his part, harmonising in bulk and colour and shaggy hair with the trunks of the trees and lush vegetation, as natural a feature as any other in the landscape. After examination at leisure, noting the sharp muzzle thrust inquiringly forward, the long shaggy hair on his broad chest, the stiff, erect ears nearly buried in hair, and the slow, heavy way he moved his head, I thought I should like to see his gait in running, so I made a sudden rush at him, shouting and swinging my hat to frighten him, expecting to see him make haste to get away. But to my dismay he did not run or show any sign of running. On the contrary, he stood his ground ready to fight and defend himself, lowered his head, thrust it forward, and looked sharply and fiercely at me. Then I suddenly began to fear that upon me would fall the work of running; but I was afraid to run, and therefore, like the bear, held my ground. We stood staring at each other in solemn silence within a dozen yards or thereabouts, while I fervently hoped that the power of the human eye over wild beasts would prove as great as it is said to be. How long our awfully strenuous interview lasted, I don't know; but at length in the slow fullness of time he pulled his huge paws down off the log, and with magnificent deliberation turned and walked leisurely up the meadow, stopping frequently to look back over his shoulder to see whether I was pursuing him, then moving on again, evidently neither fearing me very much nor trusting me. He was probably about five hundred pounds in weight, a broad, rusty bundle of ungovernable wildness, a happy fellow whose lines have fallen in pleasant places. The flowery glade in which I saw him so well, framed like a picture, is one of the best of all I have yet discovered, a conservatory of Nature's precious plant people. Tall lilies were swinging their bells over that bear's back, with geraniums, larkspurs, columbines, and daisies brushing against his sides. A place for angels, one would say, instead of bears.

In the great canyons Bruin reigns supreme. Happy fellow, whom no famine can reach while one of his thousand kinds of food is spared him. His bread is sure at all seasons, ranged on the mountain shelves like stores in a pantry. From one to the other, up or down he climbs, tasting and enjoying each in turn in different climates, as if he had journeyed thousands of miles to other countries north or south to enjoy their varied productions. I should like to know my hairy brothers better – though after this particular Yosemite bear, my very neighbour, had sauntered out of sight this morning, I reluctantly went back to camp for the Don's rifle to shoot him, if necessary, in defence of the flock. Fortunately I couldn't find him, and after tracking him a mile or two towards Mount Hoffman I bade him Godspeed and gladly returned to my work on the Yosemite Dome.

The house fly also seemed at home and buzzed about me as I sat sketching, and enjoying my bear interview now it was over. I wonder what draws house flies so far up the mountains, heavy gross feeders as they are, sensitive to cold, and fond of domestic ease. How have they been distributed from continent to continent, across seas and deserts and mountain chains, usually so influential in determining boundaries of species both of plants and animals. Beetles and butterflies are sometimes restricted to small areas. Each mountain in a range, and even the different zones of a mountain, may have its own peculiar species. But the house fly seems to be everywhere. I wonder if any island in mid-ocean is flyless. The bluebottle is abundant in these Yosemite woods, ever ready with his marvellous store of eggs to make all dead flesh fly. Bumblebees are here, and are well fed on boundless stores of nectar and pollen. The honeybee, though abundant in the foothills, has not yet got so high. It is only a few years since the first swarm was brought to California.

A queer fellow and a jolly fellow is the grasshopper. Up the mountains he comes on excursions, how high I don't know, but at least as far and high as Yosemite tourists. I was much interested with the hearty enjoyment of the one that danced and sang for me on the Dome this afternoon. He seemed brimful of glad, hilarious energy, manifested by springing into the air to a height of twenty or thirty feet, then diving and springing up again and making a sharp musical rattle just as the lowest point in the descent was reached. Up and down a dozen times or so he danced and sang, then alighted to rest, then up and at it again. The curves he described in the air in diving and rattling resembled those made by cords hanging loosely and attached at the same height at the ends, the loops nearly covering each other. Braver, heartier, keener, carefree enjoyment of life I have never seen or heard in any creature, great or small. The life of this comic redlegs, the mountain's merriest child, seems to be made up of pure, condensed gaiety. The Douglas squirrel is the only living creature that I can compare him with in exuberant, rollicking, irrepressible jollity. Wonderful that these sublime mountains are so loudly cheered and brightened by a creature so queer. Nature in him seems to be snapping her fingers in the face of all earthly dejection and melancholy with a boyish hip hip hurrah. How the sound is made I do not understand. When he was on the ground he made not the slightest noise, nor when he was simply flying from place to place, but only when diving in curves, the motion seeming to be required for the sound; for the more vigorous the diving the more energetic the corresponding outbursts of jolly rattling. I tried to observe him closely while he was resting in the intervals of his performances; but he would not allow a near approach, always getting his jumping legs ready to spring for immediate flight, and keeping his eyes on me. A fine sermon the little fellow danced for me on the Dome, a likely place to look for sermons in stones, but not for grass-hopper sermons. A large and imposing pulpit for so small a preacher. No danger of weakness in the knees of the world while Nature can spring such a rattle at this. Even the bear did not express for me the mountain's wild health and strength and happiness so tellingly as did this comical little hopper. No cloud of care in his day, no winter of discontent in sight. To him every day is a holiday; and when at length his sun sets, I fancy he will cuddle down on the forest floor and die like the leaves and flowers, and like them leave no unsightly remains calling for burial.

Sundown, and I must to camp. Goodnight, friends three, – brown bear, rugged boulder of energy in groves and gardens fair as Eden; restless, fussy fly with gauzy wings stirring the air around all the world; and grasshopper, crisp, electric spark of joy enlivening the massy sublimity of the mountains like the laugh of a child. Thank you, thank you all three for your quickening company. Heaven guide every wing and leg. Goodnight friends three, goodnight.

July 22. A fine specimen of the black-tailed deer went bounding past camp this morning. A buck with wide spread of antlers, showing admirable vigour and grace. Wonderful the beauty, strength, and graceful movements of animals in wildernesses, cared for by Nature only, when our experience with domestic animals would lead us to fear that all the so-called neglected wild beasts would degenerate. Yet the upshot of Nature's method of breeding and teaching seems to lead to excellence of every sort. Deer, like all wild animals, are as clean as plants. The beauties of their gestures and attitudes, alert or in repose, surprise yet more than their bounding exuberant strength. Every movement and posture is graceful, the very poetry of manners and motion. Mother Nature is too often spoken of as in reality no mother at all. Yet how wisely, sternly, tenderly she loves and looks after her children in all sorts of weather and wildernesses. The more I see of deer the more I admire them as mountaineers. They make their way into the heart of the roughest solitudes with smooth reserve of strength, through dense belts of brush and forest encumbered with fallen trees and boulder piles, across canyons, roaring streams, and snowfields, ever showing forth beauty and courage. Over nearly all the continent the deer find homes. In the Florida savannas and hummocks, in the Canada woods, in the far north, roaming over mossy tundras, swimming lakes and rivers and arms of the sea from island to island washed with waves, or climbing rocky mountains, everywhere healthy and able, adding beauty to every landscape, – a truly admirable creature and great credit to Nature.

Have been sketching a silver fir that stands on a granite ridge a few hundred yards to the eastward of camp – a fine tree with a particular snowstorm story to tell. It is about one hundred feet high, growing on bare rock, thrusting its roots into a weathered joint less than an inch wide, and bulging out to form a base to bear its weight. The storm came from the north while it was young and broke it down nearly to the ground, as is shown by the old, dead, weatherbeaten top leaning out from the living trunk built up from a new shoot below the break. The annual rings of the trunk that have overgrown the dead sapling tell the year of the storm. Wonderful that a side branch forming a portion of one of the level collars that encircle the trunk of this species (*Abies magnifica*) should bend upward, grow erect, and take the place of the lost axis to form a new tree.

Many others, pines as well as firs, bear testimony to the crushing severity of this particular storm. Trees, some of them fifty to seventy five feet high, were bent to the ground and buried like grass, whole groves vanishing as if the forest had been cleared away, leaving not a branch or needle visible until the spring thaw. Then the more elastic undamaged saplings rose again, aided by the wind, some reaching a nearly erect attitude, others remaining more or less bent, while those with broken backs endeavoured to specialise a side branch below the break and make a leader of it to form a new axis of development. It is as if a man, whose back was broken or nearly so and who was compelled to go bent, should find a branch backbone sprouting straight up from below the break and should gradually develop new arms and shoulders and head, while the old damaged portion of his body died.

Grand white cloud mountains and domes created about noon as usual, ridges and ranges of endless variety, as if Nature dearly loved this sort of work, doing it again and again nearly every day with infinite industry, and producing beauty that never palls. A few zigzags of lightning, five minutes shower, then a gradual wilting and clearing.

July 23. Another midday cloudland, displaying power and beauty that one never wearies in beholding, but hopelessly unsketchable and untellable. What can poor mortals say about clouds? While a description of their huge glowing domes and ridges, shadowy gulfs and canyons, and feather-edged ravines is being tried, they vanish, leaving no visible ruins. Nevertheless, these fleeting sky mountains are as substantial and significant as the more lasting upheavals of granite beneath them. Both alike are built up and die, and in God's calendar difference of duration is nothing. We can only dream about them in wondering, worshipping admiration, happier than we dare tell even to friends who see farthest in sympathy, glad to know that not a crystal or vapour particle of them, hard or soft, is lost; that they sink and vanish only to rise again and again in higher and higher beauty. As to our own work, duty, influence, etc., concerning which so much fussy pother is made, it will not fail of its due effect, though, like a lichen on a stone, we keep silent.

July 24. Clouds at noon occupying about half the sky gave half an hour of heavy rain to wash one of the cleanest landscapes in the world. How well it is washed! The sea is hardly less dusty than the ice-burnished pavements and ridges, domes and canyons, and summit peaks plashed with snow like waves with foam. How fresh the woods are and calm after the last films of clouds have been wiped from the sky! A few minutes ago every tree was excited, bowing to the roaring storm, waving, swirling, tossing their branches in glorious enthusiasm like worship. But though to the outer ear these trees are now silent, their songs never cease. Every hidden cell is throbbing with music and life, every fibre thrilling like harp strings, while incense is ever flowing from the balsam bells and leaves. No wonder the hills and groves were God's first temples, and the more they are cut down and hewn into cathedrals and churches, the farther off and dimmer seems the Lord himself. The same may be said of stone temples. Yonder, to the eastward of our camp grove, stands one of Nature's cathedrals, hewn from the living rock, almost conventional in form, about two thousand feet high, nobly adorned with spires and pinnacles, thrilling under floods of sunshine as if alive like a grove-temple, and well named 'Cathedral Peak.' Even Shepherd Billy turns at times to this wonderful mountain building, though apparently deaf to all stone sermons. Snow that refused to melt in fire would hardly be more wonderful than unchanging dullness in the rays of God's beauty. I have been trying to get him to walk to the brink of Yosemite for a view, offering to watch the sheep for a day, while he should enjoy what tourists come from all over the world to see. But though within a mile of the famous valley, he will not go to it even out of mere curiosity. 'What,' says he, 'is Yosemite but a canyon – a lot of rocks – a hole in the ground – a place dangerous about falling into – a d – d good place to keep away from.' 'But think of the waterfalls, Billy – just think of that, and the sound it makes. You can hear it now like the roar of the sea.' Thus I pressed Yosemite upon him like a missionary offering the gospel, but he would have none of it. 'I should be afraid to look over so high a wall,' he said. 'It would make my head swim. There is nothing worth seeing anywhere, only rocks, and I see plenty of them here. Tourists that spend their money to see rocks and falls are fools, that's all. You can't humbug me. I've been in this country too long for that.' Such souls, I suppose, are asleep, or smothered and befogged beneath mean pleasures and cares.

July 25. Another cloudland. Some clouds have an overripe decaying look, watery and bedraggled and drawn out into wind-torn shreds and patches, giving the sky a littered appearance; not so these Sierra summer midday clouds. All are beautiful with smooth definite outlines and curves like those of glacier-polished domes. They begin to grow about eleven o'clock, and seem so wonderfully near and clear from this high camp one is tempted to try to climb them and trace the streams that pour like cataracts from their shadowy fountains. The rain to which they give birth is often very heavy, a sort of waterfall as imposing as if pouring from rock mountains. Never in all my travels have I found anything more truly novel and interesting than these midday mountains of the sky, their fine tones of colour, majestic visible growth, and ever-changing scenery and general effects, though mostly as well let alone as far as description goes. I oftentimes think of Shelley's cloud poem, 'I sift the snow on the mountains below.'

SIX

Mount Hoffman and Lake Tenaya

July 26. Ramble to the summit of Mount Hoffman, eleven thousand feet high, the highest point in life's journey my feet have yet touched. And what glorious landscapes are about me, new plants, new animals, new crystals, and multitudes of new mountains far higher than Hoffman, towering in glorious array along the axis of the range, serene, majestic, snow-laden, sun-drenched, vast domes and ridges shining below them, forests, lakes, and meadows in the hollows, the pure blue bell-flower sky brooding them all, – a glory day of admission into a new realm of wonders as if Nature had wooingly whispered, 'Come higher.' What questions I asked, and how little I know of all the vast show, and how eagerly, tremulously hopeful of some day knowing more, learning the meaning of these divine symbols crowded together on this wondrous page.

Mount Hoffman is the highest part of a ridge or spur about fourteen miles from the axis of the main range, perhaps a remnant brought into relief and isolated by unequal denudation. The southern slopes shed their waters into Yosemite Valley by Tenaya and Dome Creeks, the northern in part into the Tuolumne River, but mostly into the Merced by Yosemite Creek. The rock is mostly granite, with some small piles and crests rising here and there in picturesque pillared and castellated remnants of red metamorphic slates. Both the granite and slates are divided by joints, making them separable into blocks like the stones of artificial masonry, suggesting the Scripture 'He hath builded the mountains.' Great banks of snow and ice are piled in hollows on the cool precipitous north side forming the highest perennial sources of Yosemite Creek. The southern slopes are much more gradual and accessible. Narrow slot-like gorges extend across the summit at

right angles, which look like lanes, formed evidently by
the erosion of less resisting beds. They are usually called
'devil's slides,' though they lie far above the region usually
haunted by the devil; for though we read that he once
climbed an exceeding high mountain, he cannot be much
of a mountaineer, for his tracks are seldom seen above the
timber line.

The broad grey summit is barren and desolate-looking
in general views, wasted by ages of gnawing storms; but
looking at the surface in detail, one finds it covered by
thousands and millions of charming plants with leaves
and flowers so small they form no mass of colour visible at a distance of a few hundred yards. Beds of azure
daisies smile confidingly in moist hollows, and along the
banks of small rills, with several species of eriogonum,
silky-leaved ivesia, pentstemon, orthocarpus, and patches
of *Primula suffruticosa*, a beautiful shrubby species. Here
also I found bryanthus, a charming heathwort covered
with purple flowers and dark green foliage like heather,
and three trees new to me – a hemlock and two pines. The
hemlock (*Tsuga Mertensiana*) is the most beautiful conifer
I have ever seen; the branches and also the main axis droop
in a singularly graceful way, and the dense foliage covers
the delicate, sensitive, swaying branchlets all around. It is
now in full bloom, and the flowers, together with thousands of last season's cones still clinging to the drooping
sprays, display wonderful wealth of colour, brown and
purple and blue. Gladly I climbed the first tree I found to
revel in the midst of it. How the touch of the flowers makes
one's flesh tingle! The pistillate are dark, rich purple, and
almost translucent, the staminate blue, – a vivid, pure tone
of blue like the mountain sky, – the most uncommonly
beautiful of all the Sierra tree flowers I have seen. How
wonderful that, with all its delicate feminine grace and
beauty of form and dress and behaviour, this lovely tree
up here, exposed to the wildest blasts, has already endured
the storms of centuries of winters!

The two pines also are brave storm-enduring trees, the
mountain pine (*Pinus monticola*) and the dwarf pine (*Pinus
albicaulis*). The mountain pine is closely related to the

sugar pine, though the cones are only about four to six inches long. The largest trees are from five to six feet in diameter at four feet above the ground, the bark rich brown. Only a few storm-beaten adventurers approach the summit of the mountain. The dwarf or white-bark pine is the species that forms the timber line, where it is so completely dwarfed that one may walk over the top of a bed of it as over snow-pressed chaparral.

How boundless the day seems as we revel in these stormbeaten sky gardens amid so vast a congregation of onlooking mountains! Strange and admirable it is that the more savage and chilly and storm-chafed the mountains, the finer the glow on their faces and the finer the plants they bear. The myriads of flowers tingeing the mountain top do not seem to have grown out of the dry, rough gravel of disintegration, but rather they appear as visitors, a cloud of witnesses to Nature's love in what we in our timid ignorance and unbelief call howling desert. The surface of the ground, so dull and forbidding at first sight, besides being rich in plants, shines and sparkles with crystals: mica, hornblende, feldspar, quartz, tourmaline. The radiance in some places is so great as to be fairly dazzling, keen lance rays of every colour flashing, sparkling in glorious abundance, joining the plants in their fine, brave beauty work – every crystal, every flower a window opening into heaven, a mirror reflecting the Creator.

From garden to garden, ridge to ridge, I drifted enchanted, now on my knees gazing into the face of a daisy, now climbing again and again among the purple and azure flowers of the hemlocks, now down into the treasuries of the snow, or gazing afar over domes and peaks, lakes and woods, and the billowy glaciated fields of the upper Tuolumne, and trying to sketch them. In the midst of such beauty, pierced with its rays, one's body is all one tingling palate. Who wouldn't be a mountaineer! Up here all the world's prizes seem nothing.

The largest of the many glacier lakes in sight, and the one with the finest shore scenery, is Tenaya, about a mile long, with an imposing mountain dipping its feet into it on the south side, Cathedral Peak a few miles above its head, many smooth swelling rock-waves and domes on the north, and in the distance southward a multitude of snowy peaks, the fountain-heads of rivers. Lake Hoffman lies shimmering beneath my feet, mountain pines around its shining rim. To the northward the picturesque basin of Yosemite Creek glitters with lakelets and pools; but the eye is soon drawn away from these bright mirror wells, however attractive, to revel in the glorious congregation of peaks on the axis of the range in their robes of snow and light.

Carlo caught an unfortunate woodchuck when it was running from a grassy spot to its boulder pile home – one of the hardiest of the mountain animals. I tried hard to save him, but in vain. After telling Carlo that he must be careful not to kill anything, I caught sight, for the first time, of the curious pika, or little chief hare, that cuts large quantities of lupines and other plants and lays them out to dry in the sun for hay, which it stores in underground barns to last through the long, snowy winter. Coming upon these plants freshly cut and lying in handfuls here and there on the rocks has a startling effect of busy life on the lonely mountain top. These little haymakers, endowed with brain stuff something like our own, – God up here looking after them, – what lessons they teach, how they widen our sympathy!

An eagle soaring above a sheer cliff, where I suppose its nest is, makes another striking show of life, and helps to bring to mind the other people of the so-called solitude – deer in the forest caring for their young; the strong, well-clad, well-fed bears; the lively throng of squirrels; the blessed birds, great and small, stirring and sweetening the groves; and the clouds of happy insects filling the sky with joyous hum as part and parcel of the down-pouring sunshine. All these come to mind, as well as the plant people, and the glad streams singing their way to the sea. But most impressive of all is the vast glowing countenance of the wilderness in awful, infinite repose.

Toward sunset, enjoyed a fine run to camp, down the long south slopes, across ridges and ravines, gardens and avalanche gaps, through the firs and chaparral, enjoying wild excitement and excess of strength, and so ends a day that will never end.

July 27. Up and away to Lake Tenaya, – another big day, enough for a lifetime. The rocks, the air, everything speaking with audible voice or silent; joyful, wonderful, enchanting, banishing weariness and sense of time. No longing for anything now or hereafter as we go home into the mountain's heart. The level sunbeams are touching the fir tops, every leaf shining with dew. Am holding an easterly course, the deep canyon of Tenaya Creek on the right hand, Mount Hoffman on the left, and the lake straight ahead about ten miles distant, the summit of Mount Hoffman about three thousand feet above me, Tenaya Creek four thousand feet below and separated from the shallow, irregular valley, along which most of the way lies, by smooth domes and wave-ridges. Many mossy emerald bogs, meadows and gardens in rocky hollows to wade and saunter through – and what fine plants they give me, what joyful streams I have to cross, and how many views are displayed of the Hoffman and Cathedral Peak masonry, and what a wondrous breadth of shining granite pavement to walk over for the first time about the shores of the lake! On I sauntered in freedom complete; body without weight as far as I was aware; now wading through starry parnassia bogs, now through gardens shoulder deep in larkspur and lilies, grasses and rushes, shaking off showers of dew; crossing piles of crystalline moraine boulders, bright mirror pavements, and cool, cheery streams going to Yosemite; crossing bryanthus carpets and the scoured pathways of avalanches, and thickets of snow-pressed ceanothus; then down a broad, majestic stairway into the ice-sculptured lake basin.

The snow on the high mountains is melting fast, and the streams are singing bank-full, swaying softly through the level meadows and bogs, quivering with sun-spangles, swirling in potholes, resting in deep pools, leaping, shouting in wild, exulting energy over rough boulder dams, joyful, beautiful in all their forms. No Sierra landscape that I have seen holds anything truly dead or dull, or any trace of what in manufactories is called rubbish or waste;

everything is perfectly clean and pure and full of divine lessons. This quick, inevitable interest attaching to everything seems marvellous until the hand of God becomes visible; then it seems reasonable that what interests Him may well interest us. When we try to pick out anything by itself, we find it hitched to everything else in the universe. One fancies a heart like our own must be beating in every crystal and cell, and we feel like stopping to speak to the plants and animals as friendly fellow mountaineers. Nature as a poet, an enthusiastic workingman, becomes more and more visible the farther and higher we go; for the mountains are fountains – beginning places, however related to sources beyond mortal ken.

I found three kinds of meadows: (1) Those contained in basins not yet filled with earth enough to make a dry surface. They are planted with several species of carex, and have their margins diversified with robust flowering plants such as veratrum, larkspur and lupine, etc. (2) Those contained in the same sort of basins, once lakes like the first, but so situated in relation to the streams that flow through them and beds of transportable sand, gravel, etc., that they are now high and dry and well drained. This dry condition and corresponding difference in their vegetation may be caused by no superiority of position, or power of transporting filling material in the streams that belong to them, but simply by the basin being shallow and therefore sooner filled. They are planted with grasses, mostly fine, silky, and rather short-leaved, *Calamagrostis* and *Agrostis* being the principal genera. They form delightfully smooth, level sods in which one finds two or three species of gentian and as many of purple and yellow orthocarpus, violet, vaccinium, kalmia, bryanthus, and lonicera. (3) Meadows hanging on ridge and mountain slopes, not in basins at all, but made and held in place by masses of boulders and fallen trees, which, forming dams one above another in close succession on small, outspread, channelless streams, have collected soil enough for the growth of grasses, carices and many flowering plants, and being kept well watered, without being subject to currents sufficiently strong to carry them away, a hanging or sloping meadow is the result. Their surfaces are seldom so smooth as the others, being roughened more or less by the projecting tops of the dam rocks or logs; but at a little distance this roughness is not noticed and the effect is very striking – bright green, fluent, down-sweeping flowery ribbons on grey slopes. The broad shallow streams these meadows belong to are mostly derived from banks of snow and because the soil is well drained in some places, while in others the dam rocks are packed close and caulked with bits of wood and leaves, making boggy patches; the vegetation, of course, is correspondingly varied. I saw patches of willow, bryanthus, and a fine show of lilies on some of them, not forming a margin, but scattered about among the carex and grass. Most of these meadows are now in their prime. How wonderful must be the temper of the elastic leaves of grasses and sedges to make curves so perfect and fine. Tempered a little harder, they would stand erect, stiff and bristly, like strips of metal; a little softer, and every leaf would lie flat. And what fine painting and tinting there is on the glumes and pales, stamens and feathery pistils. Butterflies coloured like the flowers waver above them in wonderful profusion, and many other beautiful winged people, numbered and known and loved only by the Lord, are waltzing together high overhead, seemingly in pure play and hilarious enjoyment of their little sparks of life. How wonderful they are! How do they get a living, and endure the weather? How are their little bodies, with muscles, nerves, organs, kept warm and jolly in such admirable exuberant health? Regarded only as mechanical inventions, how wonderful they are! Compared with these, Godlike man's greatest machines are as nothing.

Most of the sandy gardens on moraines are in prime beauty like the meadows, though some on the north sides of rocks and beneath groves of sapling pines have not yet bloomed. On sunny sheets of crystal soil along the slopes of the Hoffman Mountains, I saw extensive patches of ivesia and purple gilia with scarce a green leaf, making fine clouds of colour. Ribes bushes, vaccinium and kalmia, now in flower, make beautiful rugs and borders along the banks of the streams. Shaggy beds of dwarf oak (*Quercus chrysolepis*, var. *vaccinifolia*) over which one may walk are common on rocky moraines, yet this is the same species as the large live oak seen near Brown's Flat. The most beautiful of the shrubs is the purple-flowered bryanthus, here making glorious carpets at an elevation of nine thousand feet.

The principal tree for the first mile or two from camp is the magnificent silver fir, which reaches perfection here both in size and form of individual trees, and in the mode of grouping in groves with open spaces between. So trim and tasteful are these silvery, spiry groves one would fancy they must have been placed in position by some master landscape gardener, their regularity seeming almost conventional. But Nature is the only gardener able to do work so fine. A few noble specimens two hundred feet high occupy central positions in the groups with younger trees around them; and outside of these another circle of yet smaller ones, the whole arranged like tastefully symmetrical bouquets, every tree fitting nicely the place assigned to it as if made especially for it; small roses and eriogonums are usually found blooming on the open spaces about the groves, forming charming pleasure grounds. Higher, the firs gradually become smaller and less perfect, many showing double summits, indicating storm stress. Still, where good moraine soil is found, even on the rim of the lake basin, specimens one hundred and fifty feet in height and five feet in diameter occur nearly nine thousand feet above the sea. The saplings I find, are mostly bent with the crushing weight of the winter snow, which at this elevation must be at least eight or ten feet deep, judging by marks on the trees; and this depth of compacted snow is heavy enough to bend and bury young trees twenty or thirty feet in height and hold them down for four or five months. Some are broken; the others spring up when the snow melts and at length attain a size that enables them to withstand the snow pressure. Yet even in trees five feet thick the traces of this early discipline are still plainly to be seen in their curved insteps, and frequently in old dried saplings protruding from the trunk, partially overgrown by the new axis developed from a branch below the break. Yet through all this stress the forest is maintained in marvellous beauty.

Beyond the silver firs I find the two-leaved pine (*Pinus contorta*, var. *Murrayana*) forms the bulk of the forest up to an elevation of ten thousand feet or more – the highest timber-belt of the Sierra. I saw a specimen nearly five feet in diameter growing on deep, well watered soil at an elevation of about nine thousand feet. The form of this species varies very much with position, exposure and soil, etc. On stream banks, where it is closely planted, it is very slender; some specimens seventy five feet high do not exceed five inches in diameter at the ground, but the ordinary form, as far as I have seen, is well proportioned. The average diameter when full grown at this elevation is about twelve or fourteen inches, height forty or fifty feet, the straggling branches bent up at the end, the bark thin and bedraggled with amber-coloured resin. The pistillate flowers form little crimson rosettes a fourth of an inch in diameter on the ends of the branchlets, mostly hidden in the leaf tassels; the staminate are about three eighths of an inch in diameter, sulphur-yellow, in showy clusters, giving a remarkably rich effect – a brave, hardy mountaineer pine, growing cheerily on rough beds of avalanche boulders and joints of rock pavements, as well as in fertile hollows, standing up to the waist in snow every winter for centuries, facing a thousand storms and blooming every year in colours as bright as those worn by the sun-drenched trees of the tropics.

A still hardier mountaineer is the Sierra juniper (*Juniperus occidentalis*), growing mostly on domes and ridges and glacier pavements. A thickset, sturdy, picturesque highlander, seemingly content to live for more than a score of centuries on sunshine and snow; a truly wonderful fellow, dogged endurance expressed in every feature, lasting about as long as the granite he stands on. Some are nearly as broad as high. I saw one on the shore of the lake nearly ten feet in diameter, and many six to eight feet. The bark, cinnamon-coloured, flakes off in long ribbon-like strips with a satiny lustre. Surely the most enduring of all tree mountaineers, it never seems to die a natural death, or even to fall after it has been killed. If protected from accidents, it would perhaps be immortal. I saw some that had withstood

an avalanche from snowy Mount Hoffman cheerily putting
out new branches, as if repeating, like Grip, 'Never say
die.' Some were simply standing on the pavement where
no fissure more than half an inch wide offered a hold for
its roots. The common height for these rock dwellers is from
ten to twenty feet; most of the old ones have broken tops,
and are mere stumps, with a few tufted branches, forming
picturesque brown pillars on bare pavements, with plenty
of elbow room and a clear view in every direction. On good
moraine soil it reaches a height of from forty to sixty feet,
with dense grey foliage. The rings of the trunk are very thin,
eighty to an inch of diameter in some specimens I examined.
Those ten feet in diameter must be very old – thousands of
years. Wish I could live, like these junipers, on sunshine and
snow, and stand beside them on the shore of Lake Tenaya
for a thousand years. How much I should see, and how
delightful it would be! Everything in the mountains would
find me and come to me, and everything from the heavens
like light.

The lake was named for one of the chiefs of the Yosemite
tribe. Old Tenaya is said to have been a good Indian to
his tribe. When a company of soldiers followed his band
into Yosemite to punish them for cattle stealing and other
crimes, they fled to this lake by a trail that leads out of the
upper end of the valley, early in the spring, while the snow
was still deep; but being pursued, they lost heart and sur-
rendered. A fine monument the old man has in this bright
lake, and likely to last a long time, though lakes die as well
as Indians, being gradually filled with detritus carried in
by the feeding streams, and to some extent also by snow
avalanches and rain and wind. A considerable portion of
the Tenaya basin is already changed into a forested flat and
meadow at the upper end, where the main tributary enters
from Cathedral Peak. Two other tributaries come from
the Hoffman Range. The outlet flows westward through
Tenaya Canyon to join the Merced River in Yosemite.
Scarce a handful of loose soil is to be seen on the north
shore. All is bare, shining granite, suggesting the Indian
name of the lake, Pywiack, meaning shining rock. The
basin seems to have been slowly excavated by the ancient

glaciers, a marvellous work requiring countless thousands of years. On the south side an imposing mountain rises from the water's edge to a height of three thousand feet or more, feathered with hemlock and pine; and huge shining domes on the east, over the tops of which the grinding, wasting, moulding glacier must have swept as the wind does today.

July 28. No cloud mountains, only curly currus wisps scarce perceptible, and the want of thunder to strike the noon hour seems strange, as if the Sierra clock had stopped. Have been studying the *magnifica* fir – measured one near two hundred and forty feet high, the tallest I have yet seen. This species is the most symmetrical of all conifers, but though gigantic in size it seldom lives more than four or five hundred years. Most of the trees die from the attacks of a fungus at the age of two or three centuries. This dry-rot fungus perhaps enters the trunk by way of the stumps of limbs broken off by the snow that loads the broad palmate branches. The younger specimens are marvels of symmetry, straight and erect as a plumb line, their branches in regular level whorls of five mostly, each branch as exact in its divisions as a fern frond, and thickly covered by the leaves, making a rich plush over all the tree, excepting only the trunk and a small portion of the main limbs. The leaves turn upward, especially on the branchlets, and are stiff and sharp, pointed on all the upper portion of the tree. They remain on the tree about eight or ten years, and as the growth is rapid it is not rare to find the leaves still in place on the upper part of the axis where it is three to four inches in diameter, wide apart of course, and their spiral arrangement beautifully displayed. The leaf scars are conspicuous for twenty years or more, but there is a good deal of variation in different trees as to the thickness and sharpness of the leaves.

After the excursion to Mount Hoffman I had seen a complete cross section of the Sierra forest, and I find that *Abies magnifica* is the most symmetrical tree of all the noble coniferous company. The cones are grand affairs, superb in form, size, and colour, cylindrical, stand erect on the upper branches like casks, and are from five to eight inches in length by three or four in diameter, greenish grey, and covered with fine down which has a silvery lustre in the sunshine, and their brilliance is augmented by beads of transparent balsam which seems to have been poured over each cone, bringing to mind the old ceremonies of anointing with oil. If possible, the inside of the cone is more beautiful than the outside; the scales, bracts, and seed wings are tinted with the loveliest rosy purple with a bright lustrous iridescence; the seeds, three fourths of an inch long, are dark brown. When the cones are ripe the scales and bracts fall off, setting the seeds free to fly to their predestined places, while the dead spike-like axes are left on the branches for many years to mark the positions of the vanished cones, excepting those cut off when green by the Douglas squirrel. How he gets his teeth under the broad bases of the sessile cones, I don't know. Climbing these trees on a sunny day to visit the growing cones and to gaze over the tops of the forest is one of my best enjoyments.

July 29. Bright, cool, exhilarating. Clouds about five per cent. Another glorious day of rambling, sketching, and universal enjoyment.

July 30. Clouds, twenty per cent, but the regular shower did not reach us, though thunder was heard a few miles off striking the noon hour. Ants, flies and mosquitoes seem to enjoy this fine climate. A few house flies have discovered our camp. The Sierra mosquitoes are courageous and of good size, some of them measuring nearly an inch from tip of sting to tip of folded wings. Though less abundant than in most wildernesses, they occasionally make quite a hum and stir, and pay but little attention to time or place. They sting anywhere, any time of day, wherever they can find anything worth while, until they are themselves stung by frost. The large, jet-black ants are only ticklish and troublesome when one is lying down under the trees. Noticed a borer drilling a silver fir. Ovipositor about an inch and a half in length, polished and straight like a needle. When not in use, it is folded back in a sheath, which extends straight behind like the legs of a crane in flying. This drilling, I suppose, is to save nest building, and the after care of feeding the young. Who would guess that in the brain of a fly so much knowledge could find lodgment? How do they know that their eggs will hatch in such holes, or, after they hatch, that the soft, helpless grubs will find the right sort of nourishment in silver fir sap? This domestic arrangement calls to mind the curious family of gallflies. Each species seems to know what kind of plant will respond to the irritation or stimulus of the puncture it makes and the eggs it lays, in forming a growth that not only answers for a nest and home but also provides food for the young. Probably these gallflies make mistakes at times like anybody else; but when they do, there is simply a failure of that particular brood, while enough to perpetuate the species do find the proper plants and nourishment. Many mistakes of this kind might be made without being discovered by us. Once a pair of wrens made the mistake of building a nest in the sleeve of a workman's coat, which was called for at sundown, much to the consternation and discomfiture of the birds. Still the marvel remains that any of the children of such small people as gnats and mosquitoes should escape their own and their parents' mistakes, as well as the vicissitudes of the weather and hosts of enemies, and come forth in full vigour and perfection to enjoy the sunny world. When we think of the small creatures that are visible, we are led to think of many that are smaller still and lead us on and on into infinite mystery.

July 31. Another glorious day, the air as delicious to the lungs as nectar to the tongue; indeed the body seems one palate, and tingles equally throughout. Cloudiness about five per cent, but our ordinary shower has not yet reached us, though I hear thunder in the distance.

The cheery little chipmunk, so common about Brown's Flat, is common here also, and perhaps other species. In their light, airy habits they recall the familiar species of the Eastern States, which we admired in the oak openings of Wisconsin as they skimmed along the zigzag rail fences. These Sierra chipmunks are more arboreal and squirrel-like. I first noticed them on the lower edge of the coniferous belt, where the Sabine and yellow pines meet, – exceedingly interesting little fellows, full of odd, funny ways, and without being true squirrels, have most of their accomplishments without their aggressive quarrelsomeness. I never weary watching them as they frisk about in the bushes gathering seeds and berries, like song sparrows poising daintily on slender twigs, and making even less stir than most birds of the same size. Few of the Sierra animals interest me more; they are so able, gentle, confiding, and beautiful, they take one's heart, and get themselves adopted as darlings. Though weighing hardly more than field mice, they are laborious collectors of seeds, nuts, and cones, and are therefore well fed, but never in the least swollen with fat or lazily full. On the contrary, of their frisky, birdlike liveliness there is no end. They have a great variety of notes corresponding with their movements, some sweet and liquid, like water dripping with tinkling sounds into pools. They seem dearly to love teasing a dog, coming frequently almost within reach, then frisking away with lively chipping, like sparrows, beating time to their music with their tails, which at each chip describe half circles from side to side. Not even the Douglas squirrel is surer-footed or more fearless. I have seen them running about on sheer precipices of the Yosemite walls seemingly holding on with as little effort as flies, and as unconscious of danger, where, if the slightest slip were made, they would have fallen two or three thousand feet. How fine it would be could we mountaineers climb these tremendous cliffs with the same sure grip! The venture I made the other day for a view of the Yosemite Fall and which tried my nerves so sorely, this little Tamias would have made for an ear of grass.

The woodchuck (*Arctomys monax*) of the bleak mountain tops is a very different sort of mountaineer – the most bovine of rodents, a heavy eater, fat, aldermanic in bulk and fairly bloated, in his high pastures, like a cow in a clover field. One woodchuck would outweigh a hundred chipmunks and yet he is by no means a dull animal. In the midst of what we regard as storm-beaten desolation he pipes and whistles right cheerily, and enjoys long life in his skyland homes. His burrow is made in disintegrated rocks or beneath large boulders. Coming out of his den in the cold hoarfrost mornings, he takes a sun-bath on some favourite flat-topped rock, then goes to breakfast in garden hollows, eats grass and flowers until comfortably swollen, then goes a-visiting to fight and play. How long a woodchuck lives in this bracing air I don't know, but some of them are rusty and grey like lichen-covered boulders.

August 1. A grand cloudland and five minute shower, refreshing the blessed wilderness, already so fragrant and fresh, steeping the black meadow mould and dead leaves like tea.

The waycup, or flicker, so familiar to every boy in the old Middle West States, is one of the most common of the woodpeckers hereabouts, and makes one feel at home. I can see no difference in plumage or habits from the Eastern species, though the climate here is so different, – a fine, brave, confiding, beautiful bird. The robin too, is here, with all his familiar notes and gestures, tripping daintily on open garden spots and high meadows. Over all America he seems to be at home, moving from the plains to the mountains and from north to south, back and forth, up and down, with the march of the seasons and food supply. How admirable the constitution and temper of this brave singer, keeping in cheery health over so vast and varied a range! Oftentimes, as I wander through these solemn woods, awe-stricken and silent, I hear the reassuring voice of this fellow wanderer ringing out, sweet and clear, 'Fear not! fear not!'

The mountain quail (*Oreortyx ricta*) I often meet in my walks – a small brown partridge with a very long, slender, ornamental crest worn jauntily like a feather in a boy's cap, giving it a very marked appearance. This species is considerably larger than the valley quail, so common on the hot foothills. They seldom alight in trees, but love to wander in flocks of from five or six to twenty through the ceanothus and manzanita thickets and over open, dry meadows and rocks of the ridges where the forest is less dense or wanting, uttering a low clucking sound to enable them to keep together. When disturbed they rise with a strong birr of wingbeats, and scatter as if exploded to a distance of a quarter of a mile or so. After the danger is past they call one another together with a loud piping note – Nature's beautiful mountain chickens. I have not yet found their nests. The young of this season are already hatched and away – new broods of happy wanderers half as large as their parents. I wonder how they live through the long winters, when the ground is snow-covered ten feet deep. They must go down towards the lower edge of the forest, like the deer, though I have not heard of them there.

The blue, or dusky, grouse is also common here. They like the deepest and closest fir woods, and when disturbed, burst from the branches of the trees with a strong, loud whirr of wingbeats, and vanish in a wavering, silent slide, without moving a feather – a stout, beautiful bird about the size of the prairie chicken of the old west, spending most of the time in the trees, excepting the breeding season, when it keeps to the ground. The young are now able to fly. When scattered by man or dog, they keep still until the danger is supposed to be passed, then the mother calls them together. The chicks can hear the call a distance of several hundred yards, though it is not loud. Should the young be unable to fly, the mother feigns desperate lameness or death to draw one away, throwing herself at one's feet within two or three yards, rolling over on her back, kicking and gasping, so as to deceive man or beast. They are said to stay all the year in the woods hereabouts, taking shelter in dense tufted branches of fir and yellow pine during snowstorms, and feeding on the young buds of these trees. Their legs are feathered down to their toes, and I have never heard of their suffering in any sort of weather. Able to live on pine and fir buds, they are forever independent in the matter of food, which troubles so many of us and controls our movements. Gladly, if I could, I would live forever on pine buds, however full of turpentine and pitch, for the sake of this grand independence. Just to think of our sufferings last month merely for grist-mill flour. Man seems to have more difficulty in gaining food than any other of the Lord's creatures. For many in towns it is a consuming, lifelong struggle; for others, the danger of coming to want is so great, the deadly habit of endless hoarding for the future is formed, which smothers all real life, and is continued long after every reasonable need has been over-supplied.

On Mount Hoffman I saw a curious dove-coloured bird that seemed half woodpecker, half magpie, or crow. It screams something like a crow, but flies like a woodpecker, and has a long, straight bill, with which I saw it opening the cones of the mountain and white-barked pines. It seems to keep to the heights, though no doubt it comes down for shelter during winter, if not for food. So far as food is concerned, these bird-mountaineers, I guess, can glean nuts enough, even in winter, from the different kinds of conifers; for always there are a few that have been unable to fly out of the cones and remain for hungry winter gleaners.

SEVEN

A Strange Experience

August 2. Clouds and showers, about the same as yesterday. Sketching all day on the North Dome until four or five
o'clock in the afternoon, when, as I was busily employed
thinking only of the glorious Yosemite landscape, trying
to draw every tree and every line and feature of the rocks,
I was suddenly and without warning, possessed with the
notion that my friend, Professor J D Butler, of the State
University of Wisconsin, was below me in the valley, and
I jumped up full of the idea of meeting him, with almost as
much startling excitement as if he had suddenly touched
me to make me look up. Leaving my work without the
slightest deliberation, I ran down the western slope of the
Dome and along the brink of the valley wall, looking for a
way to the bottom, until I came to a side canyon which,
judging by its apparently continuous growth of trees and
bushes, I thought might afford a practical way into the
valley, and immediately began to make the descent, late
as it was, as if drawn irresistibly. But after a little, common
sense stopped me and explained that it would be long
after dark ere I could possibly reach the hotel, that the
visitors would be asleep, that nobody would know me,
that I had no money in my pockets, and moreover was
without a coat. I therefore compelled myself to stop, and
finally succeeded in reasoning myself out of the notion of
seeking my friend in the dark, whose presence I only felt in
a strange, telepathic way. I succeeded in dragging myself
back through the woods to camp, never for a moment
wavering however, in my determination to go down to
him next morning. This I think is the most unexplainable
notion that ever struck me. Had some one whispered in
my ear while I sat on the Dome, where I had spent so
many days, that Professor Butler was in the valley, I could

not have been more surprised and startled. When I was leaving the university, he said, 'Now, John, I want to hold you in sight and watch your career. Promise to write me at least once a year.' I received a letter from him in July, at our first camp in the Hollow, written in May, in which he said that he might possibly visit California some time this summer, and therefore hoped to meet me. But inasmuch as he named no meeting place, and gave no directions as to the course he would probably follow, and as I should be in the wilderness all summer, I had not the slightest hope of seeing him, and all thought of the matter had vanished from my mind until this afternoon, when he seemed to be wafted bodily almost against my face. Well, tomorrow I shall see; for, reasonable or unreasonable, I feel I must go.

August 3. Had a wonderful day. Found Professor Butler as the compass needle finds the pole. So last evening's telepathy, transcendental revelation, or whatever else it may be called, was true; for strange to say, he had just entered the valley by way of the Coulterville Trail and was coming up the valley past El Capitan when his presence struck me. Had he then looked toward the North Dome with a good glass when it first came in sight, he might have seen me jump up from my work and run toward him. This seems the one well-defined marvel of my life of the kind called supernatural; for, absorbed in glad Nature, spirit rappings, second sight, ghost stories, etc., have never interested me since boyhood, seeming comparatively useless and infinitely less wonderful than Nature's open, harmonious, songful, sunny, everyday beauty.

This morning, when I thought of having to appear among tourists at a hotel, I was troubled because I had no suitable clothes and at best am desperately bashful and shy. I was determined to go however, to see my old friend after two years among strangers; got on a clean pair of overalls, a cashmere shirt, and a sort of jacket, – the best my camp wardrobe afforded, – tied my notebook on my belt, and strode away on my strange journey, followed by Carlo. I made my way through the gap discovered last evening, which proved to be Indian Canyon. There was no trail in it, and the rocks and brush were so rough that Carlo frequently called me back to help him down precipitous places. Emerging from the canyon shadows, I found a man making hay on one of the meadows and asked him whether Professor Butler was in the valley. 'I don't know,' he replied; 'but you can easily find out at the hotel. There are but few visitors in the valley just now. A small party came in yesterday afternoon, and I heard some one called Professor Butler, or Butterfield, or some name like that.'

In front of the gloomy hotel I found a tourist party adjusting their fishing tackle. They all stared at me in silent wonderment, as if I had been seen dropping down through the trees from the clouds, mostly, I suppose, on account of my strange garb. Inquiring for the office, I was told it was locked, and that the landlord was away, but I might find the landlady, Mrs Hutchings, in the parlour. I entered in a sad state of embarrassment, and after I had waited in the big, empty room and knocked at several doors the landlady at length appeared, and in reply to my question said she rather thought Professor Butler *was* in the valley, but to make sure, she would bring the register from the office. Among the names of the last arrivals I soon discovered the Professor's familiar handwriting, at the sight of which bashfulness vanished; and having learned that his party had gone up the valley, – probably to the Vernal and Nevada Falls, – I pushed on in glad pursuit, my heart now sure of its prey. In less than an hour I reached the head of the Nevada Canyon at the Vernal Fall, and just outside of the spray discovered a distinguished-looking gentleman, who, like everybody else I have seen today, regarded me curiously as I approached. When I made bold to inquire if he knew where Professor Butler was, he seemed yet more curious to know what could possibly have happened that required a messenger for the Professor, and instead of answering my question he asked with military sharpness, 'Who wants him?' 'I want him,' I replied with equal sharpness. 'Why? Do *you* know him?' 'Yes,' I said. 'Do *you* know him?' Astonished that any one in the mountains could possibly know Professor Butler and find him as soon as he had reached the valley, he came down to meet the strange mountaineer on equal terms, and courteously replied, 'Yes, I know Professor Butler very well. I am General Alvord, and we were fellow students in Rutland, Vermont, long ago, when we were both young.' 'But where is he now?' I persisted, cutting short his story. 'He has gone beyond the falls with a companion, to try to climb that big rock, the top of which you see from here.' His guide now volunteered the information that it was the Liberty Cap Professor Butler and his companion had gone to climb, and that if I waited at the head of the fall I should be sure to find them on their way down. I therefore climbed the ladders alongside the Vernal Fall, and was pushing forward, determined to go to the top of Liberty Cap rock in my hurry, rather than wait, if I should not meet my friend sooner. So heart-hungry at times may one be to see a friend in the flesh, however happily full and carefree one's life may be. I had gone but a short distance however, above the brow of the Vernal Fall when I caught sight of him in the brush and rocks, half erect, groping his way, his sleeves rolled up, vest open, hat in his hand, evidently very hot and tired. When he saw me coming he sat down on a boulder to wipe the perspiration from his brow and neck, and taking me for one of the valley guides, he inquired the way to the fall ladders. I pointed out the path marked with little piles of stones, on seeing which he called his companion, saying that the way was found; but he did not yet recognize me. Then I stood directly in front of him, looked him in the face, and held out my hand. He thought I was offering to assist him in rising. 'Never mind,' he said. Then I said, 'Professor Butler, don't you know me?' 'I think not,' he replied; but catching my eye, sudden recognition followed, and astonishment that I should have found him just when he was lost in the brush and did not know that I was within hundreds of miles of him. 'John Muir, John Muir, where have you come from?' Then I told him the story of my feeling his presence when he entered the valley last evening, when he was four or five miles distant, as I sat sketching on the North Dome. This, of course, only made him wonder the more. Below the foot of the Vernal Fall the guide was waiting with his saddle-horse, and I walked along the trail, chatting all the way back to the hotel, talking of school days, friends in Madison, of the students, how each had prospered, ever and anon gazing at the stupendous rocks about us, now growing indistinct in the gloaming, and again quoting from the poets – a rare ramble.

It was late ere we reached the hotel, and General Alvord was waiting the Professor's arrival for dinner. When I was introduced he seemed yet more astonished than the Professor at my descent from cloudland and going straight to my friend without knowing in any ordinary way that he was even in California. They had come on direct from the East, had not yet visited any of their friends in the state, and considered themselves undiscoverable. As we sat at dinner, the General leaned back in his chair, and looking down the table, thus introduced me to the dozen guests or so, including the staring fisherman mentioned above: 'This man, you know, came down out of these huge, trackless mountains, you know, to find his friend Professor Butler here, the very day he arrived; and how did he know he was here? He just felt him, he says. This is the queerest case of Scotch farsightedness I ever heard of,' etc., etc. While my friend quoted Shakespeare: 'More things in heaven and earth, Horatio, than are dreamt of in your philosophy,' 'As the sun, ere he has risen, sometimes paints his image in the firmament, e'en so the shadows of events precede the events, and in today already walks tomorrow.'

Had a long conversation, after dinner, over Madison days. The Professor wants me to promise to go with him, sometime, on a camping trip in the Hawaiian Islands, while I tried to get him to go back with me to camp in the high Sierra. But he says, 'Not now.' He must not leave the General; and I was surprised to learn they are to leave the valley tomorrow or next day. I'm glad I'm not great enough to be missed in the busy world.

August 4. It seemed strange to sleep in a paltry hotel chamber after the spacious magnificence and luxury of the starry sky and silver fir grove. Bade farewell to my friend and the General. The old soldier was very kind, and an interesting talker. He told me long stories of the Florida Seminole war, in which he took part, and invited me to visit him in Omaha. Calling Carlo, I scrambled home through the Indian Canyon gate, rejoicing, pitying the poor Professor and General, bound by clocks, almanacs, orders and duties, and compelled to dwell with lowland care and dust and din, where Nature is covered and her voice smothered, while the poor, insignificant wanderer enjoys the freedom and glory of God's wilderness.

Apart from the human interest of my visit today, I greatly enjoyed Yosemite, which I had visited only once before, having spent eight days last spring in rambling amid its rocks and waters. Wherever we go in the mountains, or indeed in any of God's wild fields, we find more than we seek. Descending four thousand feet in a few hours, we enter a new world – climate, plants, sounds, inhabitants, and scenery all new or changed. Near camp the goldcup oak forms sheets of chaparral, on top of which we may make our beds. Going down the Indian Canyon we observe this little bush changing by regular gradations to a large bush, to a small tree, and then larger, until on the rocky taluses near the bottom of the valley we find it developed into a broad, wide-spreading, gnarled, picturesque tree from four to eight feet in diameter, and forty or fifty feet high. Innumerable are the forms of water displayed. Every gliding reach, cascade, and fall has characters of its own. Had a good view of the Vernal and Nevada, two of the main falls of the valley, less than a mile apart, and offering striking differences in voice, form and colour. The Vernal, four hundred feet high and about seventy five or eighty feet wide, drops smoothly over a round-lipped precipice and forms a superb apron of embroidery, green and white, slightly folded and fluted, maintaining this form nearly to the bottom, where it is suddenly veiled in quick-flying billows of spray and mist, in which the afternoon sunbeams play with ravishing beauty of rainbow colours. The Nevada is white from its first appearance as it leaps out into the freedom of the air. At the head it presents a twisted appearance, by an overfolding of the current from striking on the side of its channel just before the first free outbounding leap is made. About two thirds of the way down, the hurrying throng of comet-shaped masses glance on an inclined part of the face of the precipice and are beaten into yet whiter foam, greatly expanded, and sent bounding outward, making an indescribably glorious show, especially when the afternoon sunshine is pouring into it. In this fall – one of the most wonderful in the world – the water does not seem to be under the dominion of ordinary laws, but rather as if it were a living creature, full of the strength of the mountains and their huge, wild joy.

From beneath heavy throbbing blasts of spray the broken river is seen emerging in ragged boulder-chafed strips. These are speedily gathered into a roaring torrent, showing that the young river is still gloriously alive. On it goes, shouting, roaring, exulting in its strength, passes through a gorge with sublime display of energy, then suddenly expands on a gently inclined pavement, down which it rushes in thin sheets and folds of lacework into a quiet pool, – 'Emerald Pool,' as it is called, – a stopping place, a period separating two grand sentences. Resting here long enough to part with its foam-bells and grey mixtures of air, it glides quietly to the verge of the Vernal precipice in a broad sheet and makes its new display in the Vernal Fall; then more rapids and rock tossings down the canyon, shaded by live oak, Douglas spruce, fir, maple, and dogwood. It receives the Illilouette tributary, and makes a long sweep out into the level, sun-filled valley to join the other streams which, like itself, have danced and sung their way down from snowy heights to form the main Merced – the river of Mercy. But of this there is no end, and life, when one thinks of it, is so short. Never mind, one day in the midst of these divine glories is well worth living and toiling and starving for.

Before parting with Professor Butler he gave me a book, and I gave him one of my pencil sketches for his little son Henry, who is a favourite of mine. He used to make many visits to my room when I was a student. Never shall I forget his patriotic speeches for the Union, mounted on a tall stool, when he was only six years old.

It seems strange that visitors to Yosemite should be so little influenced by its novel grandeur, as if their eyes were bandaged and their ears stopped. Most of those I saw yesterday were looking down as if wholly unconscious of anything going on about them, while the sublime rocks were trembling with the tones of the mighty chanting congregation of waters gathered from all the mountains round about, making music that might draw angels out of heaven. Yet respectable-looking, even wise-looking people were fixing bits of worms on bent pieces of wire to catch trout. Sport they called it. Should churchgoers try to pass the time fishing in baptismal fonts while dull sermons were being preached, the so-called sport might not be so bad; but to play in the Yosemite temple, seeking pleasure in the pain of fishes struggling for their lives, while God himself is preaching his sublimest water and stone sermons!

Now I'm back at the campfire, and cannot help thinking about my recognition of my friend's presence in the valley while he was four or five miles away, and while I had no means of knowing that he was not thousands of miles away. It seems supernatural, but only because it is not understood. Anyhow, it seems silly to make so much of it, while the natural and common is more truly marvellous and mysterious than the so-called supernatural. Indeed most of the miracles we hear of are infinitely less wonderful than the commonest of natural phenomena, when fairly seen. Perhaps the invisible rays that struck me while I sat at work on the Dome are something like those which attract and repel people at first sight, concerning which so much nonsense has been written. The worst apparent effect of these mysterious odd things is blindness to all that is divinely common. Hawthorne, I fancy, could weave one of his weird romances out of this little telepathic episode, the one strange marvel of my life, probably replacing my good old Professor by an attractive woman.

August 5. We were awakened this morning before day-break by the furious barking of Carlo and Jack and the sound of stampeding sheep. Billy fled from his punk bed to the fire, and refused to stir into the darkness to try to gather the scattered flock, or ascertain the nature of the disturbance. It was a bear attack, as we afterward learned, and I suppose little was gained by attempting to do anything before daylight. Nevertheless, being anxious to know what was up, Carlo and I groped our way through the woods, guided by the rustling sound made by fragments of the flock, not fearing the bear, for I knew that the runaways would go from their enemy as far as possible and Carlo's nose was also to be depended upon. About half a mile east of the corral we overtook twenty or thirty of the flock and succeeded in driving them back; then turning to the westward, we traced another band of fugitives and got them back to the flock. After daybreak I discovered the remains of a sheep carcass, still warm, showing that Bruin must have been enjoying his early mutton breakfast while I was seeking the runaways. He had eaten about half of it. Six dead sheep lay in the corral, evidently smothered by the crowding and piling up of the flock against the side of the corral wall when the bear entered. Making a wide circuit of the camp, Carlo and I discovered a third band of fugitives and drove them back to camp. We also discovered another dead sheep half eaten, showing there had been two of the shaggy freebooters at this early breakfast. They were easily traced. They had each caught a sheep, jumped over the corral fence with them, carrying them as a cat carries a mouse, laid them at the foot of fir trees a hundred yards or so back from the corral, and eaten their fill. After breakfast I set out to seek more of the lost, and found seventy five at a considerable distance from camp. In the afternoon I succeeded, with Carlo's help, in getting them back to the flock. I don't know whether all are together again or not. I shall make a big fire this evening and keep watch.

When I asked Billy why he made his bed against the corral in rotten wood, when so many better places offered, he replied that he 'wished to be as near the sheep as possible in case bears should attack them.' Now that the bears have come, he has moved his bed to the far side of the camp, and seems afraid that he may be mistaken for a sheep.

This has been mostly a sheep day, and of course studies have been interrupted. Nevertheless, the walk through the gloom of the woods before the dawn was worth while, and I have learned something about these noble bears. Their tracks are very telling, and so are their breakfasts. Scarce a trace of clouds today, and of course our ordinary midday thunder is wanting.

August 6. Enjoyed the grand illumination of the camp grove, last night, from the fire we made to frighten the bears – compensation for loss of sleep and sheep. The noble pillars of verdure, vividly aglow, seemed to shoot into the sky like the flames that lighted them. Nevertheless, one of the bears paid us another visit, as if more attracted than repelled by the fire, climbed into the corral, killed a sheep and made off with it without being seen, while still another was lost by trampling and suffocation against the side of the corral. Now that our mutton has been tasted, I suppose it will be difficult to put a stop to the ravages of these freebooters.

The Don arrived today from the lowlands with provisions and a letter. On learning the losses he had sustained, he determined to move the flock at once to the Upper Tuolumne region, saying that the bears would be sure to visit the camp every night as long as we stayed, and that no fire or noise we might make would avail to frighten them. No clouds save a few thin, lustrous touches on the eastern horizon. Thunder heard in the distance.

EIGHT

The Mono Trail

August 7. Early this morning bade goodbye to the bears and blessed silver fir camp, and moved slowly eastward along the Mono Trail. At sundown camped for the night on one of the many small flowery meadows so greatly enjoyed on my excursion to Lake Tenaya. The dusty, noisy flock seems outrageously foreign and out of place in these nature gardens, more so than bears among sheep. The harm they do goes to the heart, but glorious hope lifts above all the dust and din and bids me look forward to a good time coming, when money enough will be earned to enable me to go walking where I like in pure wildness, with what I can carry on my back, and when the bread sack is empty, run down to the nearest point on the breadline for more. Nor will these run-downs be blanks, for, whether up or down, every step and jump on these blessed mountains is full of fine lessons.

August 8. Camp at the west end of Lake Tenaya. Arriving early, I took a walk on the glacier-polished pavements along the north shore, and climbed the magnificent mountain rock at the east end of the lake, now shining in the late afternoon light. Almost every yard of its surface shows the scoring and polishing action of a great glacier that enveloped it and swept heavily over its summit, though it is about two thousand feet high above the lake and ten thousand above sea level. This majestic, ancient ice-flood came from the eastward, as the scoring and crushing of the surface shows. Even below the waters of the lake the rock in some places is still grooved and polished; the lapping of the waves and their disintegrating action have not as yet obliterated even the superficial marks of glaciation. In climbing the steepest polished places I had to take off shoes and stockings. A fine region this for study of glacial action in mountain-making. I found many charming plants: arctic daisies, phlox, white spiraea, bryanthus, and rock ferns, – pellaea, cheilanthes, allosorus, – fringing weathered seams all the way up to the summit; and sturdy junipers, grand old grey and brown monuments, stood bravely erect on fissured spots here and there, telling storm and avalanche stories of hundreds of winters. The view of the lake from the top is, I think, the best of all. There is another rock, more striking in form than this, standing isolated at the head of the lake, but it is not more than half as high. It is a knob or knot of burnished granite, perhaps about a thousand feet high, apparently as flawless and strong in structure as a wave-worn pebble, and probably owes its existence to the superior resistance it offered to the action of the overflowing ice-flood.

Made sketch of the lake, and sauntered back to camp, my iron-shod shoes clanking on the pavements disturbing the chipmunks and birds. After dark went out to the shore, – not a breath of air astir, the lake a perfect mirror reflecting the sky and mountains with their stars and trees and wonderful sculpture, all their grandeur refined and doubled, – a marvellously impressive picture, that seemed to belong more to heaven than earth.

August 9. I went ahead of the flock, and crossed over the divide between the Merced and Tuolumne Basins. The gap between the east end of the Hoffman spur and the mass of mountain rocks about Cathedral Peak, though roughened by ridges and waving folds, seems to be one of the channels of a broad ancient glacier that came from the mountains on the summit of the range. In crossing this divide the ice-river made an ascent of about five hundred feet from the Tuolumne meadows. This entire region must have been overswept by ice.

From the top of the divide, and also from the big Tuolumne Meadows, the wonderful mountain called Cathedral Peak is in sight. From every point of view it shows marked individuality. It is a majestic temple of one stone, hewn from the living rock, and adorned with spires and pinnacles in regular cathedral style. The dwarf pines on the roof look like mosses. I hope some time to climb to it to say my prayers and hear the stone sermons.

The big Tuolumne Meadows are flowery lawns, lying along the south fork of the Tuolumne River at a height of about eighty five hundred to nine thousand feet above the sea, partially separated by forests and bars of glaciated granite. Here the mountains seem to have been cleared away or set back, so that wide open views may be had in every direction. The upper end of the series lies at the base of Mount Lyell, the lower below the east end of the Hoffman Range, so the length must be about ten or twelve miles. They vary in width from a quarter of a mile to perhaps three quarters, and a good many branch meadows put out along the banks of the tributary streams. This is the most spacious and delightful high pleasure ground I have yet seen. The air is keen and bracing, yet warm during the day; and though lying high in the sky, the surrounding mountains are so much higher, one feels protected as if in a grand hall. Mounts Dana and Gibbs, massive red mountains, perhaps thirteen thousand feet high or more, bound the view on the east, the Cathedral and Unicorn Peaks, with many nameless peaks, on the south, the Hoffman Range on the west, and a number of peaks unnamed, as far as I know, on the north. One of these last is much like the Cathedral. The grass of the meadows is mostly fine and silky, with exceedingly slender leaves, making a close sod, above which the panicles of minute purple flowers seem to float in airy, misty lightness, while the sod is enriched with at least three species of gentian and as many or more of orthocarpus, potentilla, ivesia, solidago, pentstemon, with their gay colours, – purple, blue, yellow, and red, – all of which I may know better ere long. A central camp will probably be made in this region, from which I hope to make long excursions into the surrounding mountains.

On the return trip I met the flock about three miles east of Lake Tenaya. Here we camped for the night near a small lake lying on top of the divide in a clump of the two-leaved pine. We are now about nine thousand feet above the sea. Small lakes abound in all sorts of situations, – on ridges, along mountain sides, and in piles of moraine boulders, most of them mere pools. Only in those canyons of the larger streams at the foot of declivities, where the down thrust of the glaciers was heaviest, do we find lakes of considerable size and depth. How grateful a task it would be to trace them all and study them! How pure their waters are, clear as crystal in polished stone basins! None of them, so far as I have seen, have fishes, I suppose on account of falls making them inaccessible. Yet one would think their eggs might get into these lakes by some chance or other; on ducks' feet, for example, or in their mouths, or in their crops, as some plant seeds are distributed. Nature has so many ways of doing such things. How did the frogs, found in all the bogs and pools and lakes, however high, manage to get up these mountains? Surely not by jumping. Such excursions through miles of dry brush and boulders would be very hard on frogs. Perhaps their stringy gelatinous spawn is occasionally entangled or glued on the feet of water birds. Anyhow, they are here and in hearty health and voice. I like their cheery tronk and crink. They take the place of song-birds at a pinch.

August 10. Another of those charming exhilarating days that make the blood dance and excite nerve currents that render one unweariable and well nigh immortal. Had another view of the broad ice-ploughed divide, and gazed again and again at the Sierra temple and the great red mountains east of the meadows.

We are camped near the Soda Springs on the north side of the river. A hard time we had getting the sheep across. They were driven into a horseshoe bend and fairly crowded off the bank. They seemed willing to suffer death rather than risk getting wet, though they swim well enough when they have to. Why sheep should be so unreasonably afraid of water, I don't know, but they do fear it as soon as they are born and perhaps before. I once saw a lamb only a few hours old approach a shallow stream about two feet wide and an inch deep, after it had walked only about a hundred yards on its life journey. All the flock to which it belonged had crossed this inch-deep stream, and as the mother and her lamb were the last to cross, I had a good opportunity to observe them. As soon as the flock was out of the way, the anxious mother crossed over and called the youngster. It walked cautiously to the brink, gazed at the water, bleated piteously, and refused to venture. The patient mother went back to it again and again to encourage it, but long without avail. Like the pilgrim on Jordan's stormy bank it feared to launch away. At length, gathering its trembling inexperienced legs for the mightly effort, throwing up its head as if it knew all about drowning, and was anxious to keep its nose above water, it made the tremendous leap, and landed in the middle of the inch-deep stream. It seemed astonished to find that, instead of sinking over head and ears, only its toes were wet, gazed at the shining water a few seconds, and then sprang to the shore safe and dry through the dreadful adventure. All kinds of wild sheep are mountain animals, and their descendants' dread of water is not easily accounted for.

August 11 . Fine shining weather, with a ten minutes noon thunderstorm and rain. Rambling all day getting acquainted with the region north of the river. Found a small lake and many charming glacier meadows embosomed in an extensive forest of the two-leaved pine. The forest is growing on broad, almost continuous deposits of moraine material, is remarkably even in its growth, and the trees are much closer together than in any of the fir or pine woods farther down the range. The evenness of the growth would seem to indicate that the trees are all of the same age or nearly so. This regularity has probably been in great part the result of fire. I saw several large patches and strips of dead bleached spars, the ground beneath them covered with a young even growth. Fire can run in these woods, not only because the thin bark of the trees is dripping with resin, but because the growth is close, and the comparatively rich soil produces good crops of tall broad-leaved grasses on which fire can travel, even when the weather is calm. Besides these fire-killed patches there are a good many fallen uprooted trees here and there, some with the bark and needles still on, as if they had lately been blown down in some thunderstorm blast. Saw a large black-tailed deer, a buck with antlers like the upturned roots of a fallen pine.

After a long ramble through the dense encumbered woods I emerged upon a smooth meadow full of sunshine like a lake of light, about a mile and a half long, a quarter to half a mile wide, and bounded by tall arrowy pines. The sod, like that of all the glacier meadows hereabouts, is made of silky agrostis and calamagrostis chiefly; their panicles of purple flowers and purple stems, exceedingly light and airy, seem to float above the green plush of leaves like a thin misty cloud, while the sod is brightened by several species of gentian, potentilla, ivesia, orthocarpus, and their corresponding bees and butterflies. All the glacier meadows are beautiful, but few are so perfect as this one. Compared with it the most carefully levelled, licked, snipped artificial lawns of pleasure grounds are coarse things. I should like to live here always. It is so calm and withdrawn while open to the universe in full communion with everything good. To the north of this glorious meadow I discovered the camp of some Indian hunters. Their fire was still burning, but they had not yet returned from the chase.

From meadow to meadow, every one beautiful beyond telling, and from lake to lake through groves and belts of arrowy trees, I held my way northward toward Mount Conness, finding telling beauty everywhere, while the encompassing mountains were calling 'Come.' Hope I may climb them all.

August 12 . The sky scenery has changed but little so far with the change in elevation. Clouds about five per cent. Glorious pearly cumuli tinted with purple of ineffable fineness of tone. Moved camp to the side of the glacier meadow mentioned above. To let sheep trample so divinely fine a place seems barbarous. Fortunately they prefer the succulent broad-leaved triticum and other woodland grasses to the silky species of the meadows, and therefore seldom bite them or set foot on them.

The shepherd and the Don cannot agree about methods of herding. Billy sets his dog Jack on the sheep far too often, so the Don thinks; and after some dispute today, in which the shepherd loudly claimed the right to dog the sheep as often as he pleased, he started for the plains. Now I suppose the care of the sheep will fall on me, though Mr Delaney promises to do the herding himself for a while, then return to the lowlands and bring another shepherd, so as to leave me free to rove as I like.

Had another rich ramble. Pushed northward beyond the forests to the head of the general basin, where traces of glacial action are strikingly clear and interesting. The recesses among the peaks look like quarries, so raw and fresh are the moraine chips and boulders that strew the ground in Nature's glacial workshops.

Soon after my return to camp we received a visit from an Indian, probably one of the hunters whose camp I had discovered. He came from Mono, he said, with others of his tribe, to hunt deer. One that he had killed a short distance from here he was carrying on his back, its legs tied together in an ornamental bunch on his forehead. Throwing down his burden, he gazed stolidly for a few minutes in silent Indian fashion, then cut off eight or ten pounds of venison for us, and begged a 'lill' (little) of everything he saw or could think of – flour, bread, sugar, tobacco, whiskey and needles, etc. We gave a fair price for the meat in flour and sugar and added a few needles. A strangely dirty and irregular life these dark-eyed, dark-haired, half happy savages lead in this clean wilderness, – starvation and abundance, death-like calm, indolence, and admirable, indefatigable action succeeding each other in stormy rhythm like winter and summer. Two things they have that civilised toilers might well envy them – pure air and pure water. These go far to cover and cure the grossness of their lives. Their food is mostly good berries, pine nuts, clover, lily bulbs, wild sheep, antelope, deer, grouse, sage hens, and the larvae of ants, wasps, bees, and other insects.

August 13. Day all sunshine, dawn and evening purple, noon gold, no clouds, air motionless. Mr Delaney arrived with two shepherds, one of them an Indian. On his way up from the plains he left some provisions at the Portuguese camp on Porcupine Creek near our old Yosemite camp, and I set out this morning with one of the pack animals to fetch them. Arrived at the Porcupine camp at noon, and might have returned to the Tuolumne late in the evening, but concluded to stay overnight with the Portuguese shepherds at their pressing invitation. They had sad stories to tell of losses from the Yosemite bears, and were so discouraged they seemed on the point of leaving the mountains; for the bears came every night and helped themselves to one or several of the flock in spite of all their efforts to keep them off.

I spent the afternoon in a grand ramble along the Yosemite walls. From the highest of the rocks called the Three Brothers, I enjoyed a magnificent view comprehending all the upper half of the floor of the valley and nearly all the rocks of the walls on both sides and at the head, with snowy peaks in the background. Saw also the Vernal and Nevada Falls, a truly glorious picture, – rocky strength and permanence combined with beauty of plants frail and fine and evanescent; water descending in thunder, and the same water gliding through meadows and groves in gentlest beauty. This standpoint is about eight thousand feet above the sea, or four thousand feet above the floor of the valley, and every tree, though looking small and feathery, stands in admirable clearness, and the shadows they cast are as distinct in outline as if seen at a distance of a few yards. They appeared even more so. No words will ever describe the exquisite beauty and charm of this mountain park – Nature's landscape garden at once tenderly beautiful and sublime. No wonder it draws nature-lovers from all over the world.

Glacial action even on this lofty summit is plainly displayed. Not only has all the lovely valley now smiling in sunshine been filled to the brim with ice, but it has been deeply overflowed.

I visited our old Yosemite camp ground on the head of Indian Creek, and found it fairly patted and smoothed down with bear tracks. The bears had eaten all the sheep that were smothered in the corral, and some of the grand animals must have died, for Mr Delaney, before leaving camp, put a large quantity of poison in the carcasses. All sheep men carry strychnine to kill coyotes, bears, and panthers, though neither coyotes nor panthers are at all numerous in the upper mountains. The little dog-like wolves are far more numerous in the foothill region and on the plains, where they find a better supply of food, – saw only one panther track above eight thousand feet.

On my return after sunset to the Portuguese camp I found the shepherds greatly excited over the behaviour of the bears that have learned to like mutton. 'They are getting worse and worse,' they lamented. Not willing to wait decently until after dark for their suppers, they come and kill and eat their fill in broad daylight. The evening before my arrival, when the two shepherds were leisurely driving the flock toward camp half an hour before sunset, a hungry bear came out of the chaparral within a few yards of them and shuffled deliberately toward the flock. 'Portuguese Joe,' who always carried a gun loaded with buckshot, fired excitedly, threw down his gun, fled to the nearest suitable tree, and climbed to a safe height without waiting to see the effect of his shot. His companion also ran, but said that he saw the bear rise on its hind legs and throw out its arms as if feeling for somebody, and then go into the brush as if wounded.

At another of their camps in this neighbourhood, a bear with two cubs attacked the flock before sunset, just as they were approaching the corral. Joe promptly climbed a tree out of danger, while Antone, rebuking his companion for cowardice in abandoning his charge, said that he was not going to let bears 'eat up his sheeps' in daylight, and rushed towards the bears, shouting and setting his dog on them. The frightened cubs climbed a tree, but the mother ran to meet the shepherd and seemed anxious to fight. Antone stood astonished for a moment, eyeing the oncoming bear, then turned and fled, closely pursued. Unable to reach a suitable tree for climbing, he ran to the camp and scrambled up to the roof of the little cabin; the bear followed, but did not climb to the roof, – only stood glaring up at him for a few minutes, threatening him and holding him in mortal terror, then went to her cubs, called them down, went to the flock, caught a sheep for supper, and vanished in the brush. As soon as the bear left the cabin, the trembling Antone begged Joe to show him a good safe tree, up which he climbed like a sailor climbing a mast, and remained as long as he could hold on, the tree being almost branchless. After these disastrous experiences the two shepherds chopped and gathered large piles of dry wood and made a ring of fire around the corral every night, while one with a gun kept watch from a comfortable stage built on a neighbouring pine that commanded a view of the corral. This evening the show made by the circle of fire was very fine, bringing out the surrounding trees in most impressive relief, and making the thousands of sheep eyes glow like a glorious bed of diamonds.

August 14. Up to the time I went to bed last night all was quiet, though we expected the shaggy freebooters every minute. They did not come till near midnight, when a pair walked boldly to the corral between two of the great fires, climbed in, killed two sheep and smothered ten, while the frightened watcher in the tree did not fire a single shot, saying that he was afraid he might kill some of the sheep, for the bears got into the corral before he got a good clear view of them. I told the shepherds they should at once move the flock to another camp. 'Oh, no use, no use,' they lamented; 'where we go, the bears go too. See my poor dead sheeps – soon all dead. No use try another camp. We go down to the plains.' And as I afterwards learned, they were driven out of the mountains a month before the usual time. Were bears much more numerous and destructive, the sheep would be kept away altogether.

It seems strange that bears, so fond of all sorts of flesh, running the risks of guns and fires and poison, should never attack men except in defence of their young. How easily and safely a bear could pick us up as we lie asleep! Only wolves and tigers seem to have learned to hunt man for food, and perhaps sharks and crocodiles. Mosquitoes and other insects would, I suppose, devour a helpless man in some parts of the world, and so might lions, leopards, wolves, hyenas, and panthers at times if pressed by hunger, – but under ordinary circumstances perhaps, only the tiger among land animals may be said to be a man-eater, – unless we add man himself.

Clouds as usual about five per cent. Another glorious Sierra day, warm, crisp, fragrant, and clear. Many of the flowering plants have gone to seed, but many others are unfolding their petals every day, and the firs and pines are more fragrant than ever. Their seeds are nearly ripe, and will soon be flying in the merriest flocks that ever spread a wing.

On the way back to our Tuolumne camp, I enjoyed the scenery if possible more than when it first came to view. Every feature already seems familiar as if I had lived here always. I never weary gazing at the wonderful Cathedral. It has more individual character than any other rock or mountain I ever saw, excepting perhaps the Yosemite South Dome. The forests, too, seem kindly familiar, and the lakes and meadows and glad singing streams. I should like to dwell with them forever. Here with bread and water I should be content. Even if not allowed to roam and climb, tethered to a stake or tree in some meadow or grove, even then I should be content forever. Bathed in such beauty, watching the expressions ever varying on the faces of the mountains, watching the stars, which here have a glory that the lowlander never dreams of, watching the circling seasons, listening to the songs of the waters and winds and birds, would be endless pleasure. And what glorious cloudlands I should see, storms and calms, – a new heaven and a new earth every day, aye and new inhabitants. And how many visitors I should have. I feel sure I should not have one dull moment. And why should this appear extravagant? It is only common sense, a sign of health, genuine, natural, all awake health. One would be at an endless Godful play, and what speeches and music and acting and scenery and lights! – sun, moon, stars, auroras. Creation just beginning, the morning stars 'still singing together and all the sons of God shouting for joy.'

NINE

Bloody Canyon and Mono Lake

August 21. Have just returned from a fine wild excursion across the range to Mono Lake, by way of the Mono or Bloody Canyon Pass. Mr Delaney has been good to me all summer, lending a helping, sympathising hand at every opportunity, as if my wild notions and rambles and studies were his own. He is one of those remarkable California men who have been overflowed and denuded and remodelled by the excitements of the gold fields, like the Sierra landscapes by grinding ice, bringing the harder bosses and ridges of character into relief, – a tall, lean, big-boned, big-hearted Irishman, educated for a priest in Maynooth College, – lots of good in him, shining out now and then in this mountain light. Recognising my love of wild places, he told me one evening that I ought to go through Bloody Canyon, for he was sure I should find it wild enough. He had not been there himself, he said, but had heard many of his mining friends speak of it as the wildest of all the Sierra passes. Of course I was glad to go. It lies just to the east of our camp and swoops down from the summit of the range to the edge of the Mono Desert, making a descent of about four thousand feet in a distance of about four miles. It was known and travelled as a pass by wild animals and the Indians long before its discovery by white men in the gold year of 1858, as is shown by old trails which come together at the head of it. The name may have been suggested by the red colour of the metamorphic slates in which the canyon abounds, or by the bloodstains on the rocks from the unfortunate animals that were compelled to slide and shuffle over the sharp-angled boulders.

Early in the morning I tied my notebook and some bread to my belt, and strode away full of eager hope, feeling that I was going to have a glorious revel. The glacier meadows that lay along my way served to soothe my morning speed, for the sod was full of blue gentians and daisies, kalmia and dwarf vaccinium, calling for recognition as old friends, and I had to stop many times to examine the shining rocks over which the ancient glacier had passed with tremendous pressure, polishing them so well that they reflected the sunlight like glass in some places, while fine striae, seen clearly through a lens, indicated the direction in which the ice had flowed. On some of the sloping polished pavements abrupt steps occur, showing that occasionally large masses of the rock had given way before the glacial pressure, as well as small particles; moraines, too, some scattered, others regular like long curving embankments and dams, occur here and there, giving the general surface of the region a young, new-made appearance. I watched the gradual dwarfing of the pines as I ascended, and the corresponding dwarfing of nearly all the rest of the vegetation. On the slopes of Mammoth Mountain, to the south of the pass, I saw many gaps in the woods reaching from the upper edge of the timber-line down to the level meadows, where avalanches of snow had descended, sweeping away every tree in their paths as well as the soil they were growing in, leaving the bedrock bare. The trees are nearly all uprooted, but a few that had been extremely well anchored in clefts of the rock were broken off near the ground. It seems strange at first sight that trees that had been allowed to grow for a century or more undisturbed should in their old age be thus swished away at a stroke. Such avalanches can only occur under rare conditions of weather and snowfall. No doubt on some positions of the mountain slopes the inclination and smoothness of the surface is such that avalanches must occur every winter, or even after every heavy snowstorm, and of course no trees or even bushes can grow in their channels. I noticed a few clean-swept slopes of this kind. The uprooted trees that had grown in the pathway of what might be called 'century avalanches' were piled in windrows, and tucked snugly against the wall-trees of the gaps, heads downward, excepting a few that were carried out into the open ground of the meadows, where the heads of the avalanches had stopped. Young pines, mostly the two-leaved and the white-barked, are already springing up in these cleared gaps. It would be interesting to ascertain the age of these saplings, for thus we should gain a fair approximation to the year that the great avalanches occurred. Perhaps most or all of them occurred the same winter. How glad I should be if free to pursue such studies!

Near the summit at the head of the pass I found a species of dwarf willow lying perfectly flat on the ground, making a nice, soft, silky grey carpet, not a single stem or branch more than three inches high; but the catkins, which are now nearly ripe, stand erect and make a close, nearly regular grey growth, being larger than all the rest of the plants. Some of these interesting dwarfs have only one catkin – willow bushes reduced to their lowest terms. I found patches of dwarf vaccinium also forming smooth carpets, closely pressed to the ground or against the sides of stones, and covered with round pink flowers in lavish abundance as if they had fallen from the sky like hail. A little higher, almost at the very head of the pass, I found the blue arctic daisy and purple-flowered bryanthus, the mountain's own darlings, gentle mountaineers face to face with the sky, kept safe and warm by a thousand miracles, seeming always the finer and purer the wilder and stormier their homes. The trees, tough and resiny, seem unable to go a step farther; but up and up, far above the tree line, these tender plants climb, cheerily spreading their grey and pink carpets right up to the very edges of the snow banks in deep hollows and shadows. Here, too, is the familiar robin, tripping on the flowery lawns, bravely singing the same cheery song I first heard when a boy in Wisconsin newly arrived from old Scotland. In this fine company sauntering enchanted, taking no heed of time, I at length entered the gate of the pass, and the huge rocks began to close around me in all their mysterious impressiveness. Just then I was startled by a lot of queer, hairy, muffled creatures coming shuffling, shambling, wallowing towards me as if they had no bones in their bodies. Had I discovered them while they were yet a good way off, I should have tried to avoid them. What a picture they made contrasted with the others I had just been admiring. When I came up to them, I found that they were only a band of Indians from Mono on their way to Yosemite for a load of acorns. They were wrapped in blankets made of the skins of sage-rabbits. The dirt on some of the faces seemed almost old enough and thick enough to have a geological significance; some were strangely blurred and divided into sections by seams and wrinkles that looked like cleavage joints, and had a worn abraded look as if they had lain exposed to the weather for ages. I tried to pass them without stopping, but they wouldn't let me; forming a dismal circle about me, I was closely besieged while they begged whiskey or tobacco, and it was hard to convince them that I hadn't any. How glad I was to get away from the grey grim crowd and see them vanish down the trail! Yet it seems sad to feel such desperate repulsion from one's fellow beings, however degraded. To prefer the society of squirrels and woodchucks to that of our own species must surely be unnatural. So with a fresh breeze and a hill or mountain between us I must wish them Godspeed and try to pray and sing with Burns, 'It's coming yet, for a' that, that man to man, the warld o'er, shall brothers be for a' that.'

How the day passed I hardly know. By the map I have come only about ten or twelve miles, though the sun is already low in the west, showing how long I must have lingered, observing, sketching, taking notes among the glaciated rocks and moraines and Alpine flower beds.

At sundown the sombre crags and peaks were inspired with the ineffable beauty of the alpenglow, and a solemn, awful stillness hushed everything in the landscape. Then I crept into a hollow by the side of a small lake near the head of the canyon, smoothed a sheltered spot, and gathered a few pine tassels for a bed. After the short twilight began to fade I kindled a sunny fire, made a tin cupful of tea, and lay down to watch the stars. Soon the night-wind began to flow from the snowy peaks overhead, at first only a gentle breathing, then gaining strength, in less than an hour rumbled in massive volume something like a boisterous stream in a boulder-choked channel, roaring and moaning down the canyon as if the work it had to do was tremendously important and fateful; and mingled with these storm tones were those of the waterfalls on the north side of the canyon, now sounding distinctly, now smothered by the heavier cataracts of air, making a glorious psalm of savage wildness. My fire squirmed and struggled as if ill at ease, for though in a sheltered nook, detached masses of icy wind often fell like icebergs on top of it, scattering sparks and coals, so that I had to keep well back to avoid being burned. But the big resiny roots and knots of the dwarf pine could neither be beaten out nor blown away, and the flames, now rushing up in long lances, now flattened and twisted on the rocky ground, roared as if trying to tell the storm stories of the trees they belonged to, as the light given out was telling the story of the sunshine they had gathered in centuries of summers.

The stars shone clear in the strip of sky between the huge dark cliffs; and as I lay recalling the lessons of the day, suddenly the full moon looked down over the canyon wall, her face apparently filled with eager concern, which had a startling effect, as if she had left her place in the sky and had come down to gaze on me alone, like a person entering one's bedroom. It was hard to realise that she was in her place in the sky, and was looking abroad on half the globe, land and sea, mountains, plains, lakes, rivers, oceans, ships, cities with their myriads of inhabitants sleeping and waking, sick and well. No, she seemed to be just on the rim of Bloody Canyon and looking only at me. This was indeed getting near to Nature. I remember watching the harvest moon rising above the oak trees in Wisconsin apparently as big as a cartwheel and not farther than half a mile distant. With these exceptions I might say I never before had seen the moon, and this night she seemed so full of life and so near, the effect was marvellously impressive and made me forget the Indians, the great black rocks above me, and the wild uproar of the winds and waters making their way down the huge jagged gorge. Of course I slept but little and gladly welcomed the dawn over the Mono Desert. By the time I had made a cupful of tea the sunbeams were pouring through the canyon, and I set forth, gazing eagerly at the tremendous walls of red slates savagely hacked and scarred and apparently ready to fall in avalanches great enough to choke the pass and fill up the chain of lakelets. But soon its beauties came to view, and I bounded lightly from rock to rock, admiring the polished bosses shining in the slant sunshine with glorious effect in the general roughness of moraines and avalanche taluses, even toward the head of the canyon near the highest fountains of the ice. Here, too, are most of the lowly plant people seen yesterday on the other side of the divide now opening their beautiful eyes. None could fail to glory in Nature's tender care for them in so wild a place. The little ouzel is flitting from rock to rock along the rapid swirling Canyon Creek, diving for breakfast in icy pools, and merrily singing as if the huge rugged avalanche-swept gorge was the most delightful of all its mountain homes. Besides a high fall on the north wall of the canyon, apparently coming direct from the sky, there are many narrow cascades, bright silvery ribbons zig-zagging down the red cliffs, tracing the diagonal cleavage joints of the metamorphic slates, now contracted and out of sight, now leaping from ledge to ledge in filmy sheets through which the sunbeams sift. And on the main Canyon Creek, to which all these are tributary, is a series of small falls, cascades, and rapids extending all the way down to the foot of the canyon, interrupted only by the lakes in which the tossed and beaten waters rest. One of the finest of the cascades is outspread on the face of a precipice, its waters separated into ribbon-like strips, and woven into a diamond-like pattern by tracing the cleavage joints of the rock, while tufts of bryanthus, grass, sedge, saxifrage form beautiful fringes. Who could imagine beauty so fine in so savage a place? Gardens are blooming in all sorts of nooks and hollows, – at the head alpine eriogonums, erigerons, saxifrages, gentians, cowania, bush primula; in the middle region larkspur, columbine, orthocarpus, castilleia, hare-bell, epilobium, violets, mints, yarrow; near the foot sun-flowers, lilies, brier rose, iris, lonicera, clematis.

One of the smallest of the cascades, which I name the Bower Cascade, is in the lower region of the pass, where the vegetation is snowy and luxuriant. Wild rose and dogwood form dense masses overarching the stream, and out of this bower the creek, grown strong with many indashing tributaries, leaps forth into the light, and descends in a fluted curve thick-sown with crisp flashing spray. At the foot of the canyon there is a lake formed in part at least by the damming of the stream by a terminal moraine. The three other lakes in the canyon are in basins eroded from the solid rock, where the pressure of the glacier was greatest, and the most resisting portions of the basin rims are beautifully, tellingly polished. Below Moraine Lake at the foot of the canyon there are several old lake basins lying between the large lateral moraines which extend out into the desert. These basins are now completely filled up by the material carried in by the streams, and changed to dry sandy flats covered mostly by grass and artemisia and sun-loving flowers. All these lower lake basins were evidently formed by terminal moraine dams deposited where the receding glacier had lingered during short periods of less waste, or greater snowfall, or both.

Looking up the canyon from the warm sunny edge of the Mono plain my morning ramble seems a dream, so great is the change in the vegetation and climate. The lilies on the bank of Moraine Lake are higher than my head, and the sunshine is hot enough for palms. Yet the snow round the arctic gardens at the summit of the pass is plainly visible, only about four miles away, and between lie specimen zones of all the principal climates of the globe. In little more than an hour one may swoop down from winter to summer, from an Arctic to a torrid region, through as great changes of climate as one would encounter in travelling from Labrador to Florida.

The Indians I had met near the head of the canyon had camped at the foot of it the night before they made the ascent, and I found their fire still smoking on the side of a small tributary stream near Moraine Lake; and on the edge of what is called the Mono Desert, four or five miles from the lake, I came to a patch of elymus, or wild rye, growing in magnificent waving clumps six or eight feet high, bearing heads six to eight inches long. The crop was ripe, and Indian women were gathering the grain in baskets by bending down large handfuls, beating out the seed, and fanning it in the wind. The grains are about five eighths of an inch long, dark-coloured and sweet. I fancy the bread made from it must be as good as wheat bread. A fine squirrelish employment this wild grain gathering seems, and the women were evidently enjoying it, laughing and chattering and looking almost natural, though most Indians I have seen are not a whit more natural in their lives that we civilised whites. Perhaps if I knew them better I should like them better. The worst thing about them is their uncleanliness. Nothing truly wild is unclean. Down on the shore of Mono Lake I saw a number of their flimsy huts on the banks of streams that dash swiftly into that dead sea, – mere brush tents where they lie and eat at their ease. Some of the men were feasting on buffalo berries, lying beneath the tall bushes now red with fruit. The berries are rather insipid, but they must needs be wholesome, since for days and weeks the Indians, it is said, eat nothing else. In the season they in like manner depend chiefly on the fat larvae of a fly that breeds in the saltwater of the lake, or on the big fat corrugated caterpillars of a species of silkworm that feeds on the leaves of the yellow pine. Occasionally a grand rabbit-drive is organised and hundreds are slain with clubs on the lake shore, chased and frightened into a dense crowd by dogs, boys, girls, men and women, and rings of sage brush fire, when of course they are quickly killed. The skins are made into blankets. In the autumn the more enterprising of the hunters bring in a good many deer, and rarely a wild sheep from the high peaks. Antelopes used to be abundant on the desert at the base of the interior mountain ranges. Sage hens, grouse, and squirrels help to vary their wild diet of worms; pine nuts also from the small interesting *Pinus monophylla*, and good bread and good mush are made from acorns and wild rye. Strange to say, they seem to like the lake larvae best of all. Long windrows are washed up on the shore, which they gather and dry like grain for winter use. It is said that wars, on account of encroachments on each other's worm grounds, are of common occurrence among the various tribes and families. Each claims a certain marked portion of the shore.

The pine nuts are delicious – large quantities are gathered every autumn. The tribes of the west flank of the range trade acorns for worms and pine nuts. The squaws carry immense loads on their backs across the rough passes and down the range, making journeys of about forty or fifty miles each way.

The desert around the lake is surprisingly flowery. In many places among the sage bushes I saw mentzelia, abronia, aster, bigelovia, and gilia, all of which seemed to enjoy the hot sunshine. The abronia, in particular, is a delicate, fragrant, and most charming plant.

Opposite the mouth of the canyon a range of volcanic cones extends southward from the lake, rising abruptly out of the desert like a chain of mountains. The largest of the cones are about twenty five hundred feet high above the lake level, have well-formed craters, and all of them are evidently comparatively recent additions to the landscape. At a distance of a few miles they look like heaps of loose ashes that have never been blest by either rain or snow, but, for a' that and a' that, yellow pines are climbing their grey slopes, trying to clothe them and give beauty for ashes. A country of wonderful contrasts. Hot deserts bounded by snow laden mountains, – cinders and ashes scattered on glacier polished pavements – frost and fire working together in the making of beauty. In the lake are several volcanic islands, which show that the waters were once mingled with fire.

Glad to get back to the green side of the mountains, though I have greatly enjoyed the grey east side and hope to see more of it. Reading these grand mountain manuscripts displayed through every vicissitude of heat and cold, calm and storm, upheaving volcanoes and down-grinding glaciers, we see that everything in Nature called destruction must be creation – a change from beauty to beauty.

Our glacier meadow camp north of the Soda Springs seems more beautiful every day. The grass covers all the ground though the leaves are thread-like in fineness, and in walking on the sod it seems like a plush carpet of marvellous richness and softness, and the purple panicles brushing against one's feet are not felt. This is a typical glacier meadow, occupying the basin of a vanished lake, very definitely bounded by walls of the arrowy two-leaved pines drawn up in a handsome orderly array like soldiers on parade. There are many other meadows of the same kind hereabouts embedded in the woods. The main big meadows along the river are the same in general and extend with but little interruption for ten or twelve miles, but none I have seen are so finely finished and perfect as this one. It is richer in flowering plants than the prairies of Wisconsin and Illinois were when in all their wild glory. The showy flowers are mostly three species of gentian, a purple and yellow orthocarpus, a golden-rod or two, a small blue pentstemon almost like a gentian, potentilla, ivesia, pedicularis, white violet, kalmia, and bryanthus. There are no coarse weedy plants. Through this flowery lawn flows a stream silently gliding, swirling, slipping as if careful not to make the slightest noise. It is only about three feet wide in most places, widening here and there into pools six or eight feet in diameter with no apparent current, the banks bossily rounded by the down-curving mossy sod, grass panicles over-leaning like miniature pine trees, and rugs of bryanthus spreading here and there over sunken boulders. At the foot of the meadow the stream, rich with the juices of the plants it has refreshed, sings merrily down over shelving rock ledges on its way to the Tuolumne River. The sublime, massive Mount Dana and its companions, green, red, and white, loom impressively above the pines along the eastern horizon; a range or spur of grey rugged granite crags and mountains on the north; the curiously crested and battlemented Mount Hoffman on the west; and the Cathedral Range on the south with its grand Cathedral Peak, Cathedral Spires, Unicorn Peak, and several others, grey and pointed or massively rounded.

TEN

The Tuolumne Camp

August 22. Clouds none, cool west wind, slight hoarfrost on the meadows. Carlo is missing; have been seeking him all day. In the thick woods between camp and the river, among tall grass and fallen pines, I discovered a baby fawn. At first it seemed inclined to come to me; but when I tried to catch it, and got within a rod or two, it turned and walked softly away, choosing its steps like a cautious, stealthy, hunting cat. Then, as if suddenly called or alarmed, it began to buck and run like a grown deer, jumping high above the fallen trunks, and was soon out of sight. Possibly its mother may have called it, but I did not hear her. I don't think fawns ever leave the home thicket or follow their mothers until they are called or frightened. I am distressed about Carlo. There are several other camps and dogs not many miles from here, and I still hope to find him. He never left me before. Panthers are very rare here, and I don't think any of these cats would dare touch him. He knows bears too well to be caught by them, and as for Indians, they don't want him.

August 23. Cool, bright day, hinting Indian summer. Mr Delaney has gone to the Smith Ranch, on the Tuolumne below Hetch-Hetchy Valley, thirty five or forty miles from here, so I'll be alone for a week or more, – not really alone, for Carlo has come back. He was at a camp a few miles to the northwestward. He looked sheepish and ashamed when I asked him where he had been and why he had gone away without leave. He is now trying to get me to caress him and show signs of forgiveness. A wondrous wise dog. A great load is off my mind. I could not have left the mountains without him. He seems very glad to get back to me.

Rose and crimson sunset, and soon after the stars appeared the moon rose in most impressive majesty over the top of Mount Dana. I sauntered up the meadow in the white light. The jet-black tree shadows were so wonderfully distinct and substantial looking, I often stepped high in crossing them, taking them for black charred logs.

August 24. Another charming day, warm and calm soon after sunrise, clouds only about one per cent, – faint, silky cirrus wisps, scarcely visible. Slight frost, Indian summerish, the mountains growing softer in outline and dreamy looking, their rough angles melted off, apparently. Sky at evening with fine, dark, subdued purple, almost like the evening purple of the San Joaquin plains in settled weather. The moon is now gazing over the summit of Dana. Glorious exhilarating air. I wonder if in all the world there is another mountain range of equal height blessed with weather so fine, and so openly kind and hospitable and approachable.

August 25. Cool as usual in the morning, quickly changing to the ordinary serene generous warmth and brightness. Toward evening the west wind was cool and sent us to the campfire. Of all Nature's flowery carpeted mountain halls none can be finer than this glacier meadow. Bees and butterflies seem as abundant as ever. The birds are still here, showing no sign of leaving for winter quarters though the frost must bring them to mind. For my part I should like to stay here all winter or all my life or even all eternity.

August 26. Frost this morning; all the meadow grass and some of the pine needles sparkling with irised crystals, – flowers of light. Large picturesque clouds, craggy like rocks, are piled on Mount Dana, reddish in colour like the mountain itself; the sky for a few degrees around the horizon is pale purple, into which the pines dip their spires with fine effect. Spent the day as usual looking about me, watching the changing lights, the ripening autumn colours of the grass, seeds, late-blooming gentians, asters, golden-rods; parting the meadow grass here and there and looking down into the underworld of mosses and liverworts; watching the busy ants and beetles and other small people at work and play like squirrels and bears in a forest; studying the formation of lakes and meadows, moraines, mountain sculpture; making small beginnings in these directions, charmed by the serene beauty of everything.

The day has been extra cloudy, though bright on the whole, for the clouds were brighter than common. Clouds about fifteen per cent, which in Switzerland would be considered extra clear. Probably more free sunshine falls on this majestic range than on any other in the world I've ever seen or heard of. It has the brightest weather, brightest glacier-polished rocks, the greatest abundance of irised spray from its glorious waterfalls, the brightest forests of silver firs and silver pines, more starshine, moonshine, and perhaps more crystalshine than any other mountain chain, and its countless mirror lakes, having more light poured into them, glow and spangle most. And how glorious the shining after the short summer showers and after frosty nights when the morning sunbeams are pouring through the crystals on the grass and pine needles, and how ineffably spiritually fine is the morning glow on the mountain tops and the alpenglow of evening. Well may the Sierra be named, not the Snowy Range, but the Range of Light.

August 27. Clouds only five per cent, – mostly white and pink cumuli over the Hoffman spur towards evening, – frosty morning. Crystals grow in marvellous beauty and perfection of form these still nights, every one built as carefully as the grandest holiest temple, as if planned to endure forever.

Contemplating the lace-like fabric of streams outspread over the mountains, we are reminded that everything is flowing – going somewhere, animals and so-called lifeless rocks as well as water. Thus the snow flows fast or slow in grand beauty-making glaciers and avalanches; the air in majestic floods carrying minerals, plant leaves, seeds, spores, with streams of music and fragrance; water streams carrying rocks both in solution and in the form of mud particles, sand, pebbles, and boulders. Rocks flow from volcanoes like water from springs, and animals flock together and flow in currents modified by stepping, leaping, gliding, flying and swimming, etc. While the stars go streaming through space pulsed on and on forever like blood globules in Nature's warm heart.

August 28. The dawn a glorious song of colour. Sky absolutely cloudless. A fine crop of hoarfrost. Warm after ten o'clock. The gentians don't mind the first frost though their petals seem so delicate; they close every night as if going to sleep, and awake fresh as ever in the morning sun glory. The grass is a shade browner since last week, but there are no nipped wilted plants of any sort as far as I have seen. Butterflies and the grand host of smaller flies are benumbed every night, but they hover and dance in the sunbeams over the meadows before noon with no apparent lack of playful, joyful life. Soon they must all fall like petals in an orchard, dry and wrinkled, not a wing of all the mighty host left to tingle the air. Nevertheless new myriads will arise in the spring, rejoicing, exulting, as if laughing cold death to scorn.

August 29. Clouds about five per cent, slight frost. Bland serene Indian summer weather. Have been gazing all day at the mountains, watching the changing lights. More and more plainly are they clothed with light as a garment, white tinged with pale purple, palest during the midday hours, richest in the morning and evening. Everything seems consciously peaceful, thoughtful, faithfully waiting God's will.

August 30. This day just like yesterday. A few clouds motionless and apparently with no work to do beyond looking beautiful. Frost enough for crystal building, – glorious fields of ice diamonds destined to last but a night. How lavish is Nature building, pulling down, creating, destroying, chasing every material particle from form to form, ever changing, ever beautiful.

Mr Delaney arrived this morning. Felt not a trace of loneliness while he was gone. On the contrary, I never enjoyed grander company. The whole wilderness seems to be alive and familiar, full of humanity. The very stones seem talkative, sympathetic, brotherly. No wonder when we consider that we all have the same Father and Mother.

August 31. Clouds five per cent. Silky cirrus wisps and fringes so fine they almost escape notice. Frost enough for another crop of crystals on the meadows but none on the forests. The gentians, goldenrods and asters don't seem to feel it; neither petals nor leaves are touched though they seem so tender. Every day opens and closes like a flower, noiseless, effortless. Divine peace glows on all the majestic landscape like the silent enthusiastic joy that sometimes transfigures a noble human face.

September 1. Clouds five per cent – motionless, of no particular colour – ornaments with no hint of rain or snow in them. Day all calm – another grand throb of Nature's heart, ripening late flowers and seeds for next summer, full of life and the thoughts and plans of life to come, and full of ripe and ready death beautiful as life, telling divine wisdom and goodness and immortality. Have been up Mount Dana, making haste to see as much as I can now that the time of departure is drawing nigh. The views from the summit reach far and wide, eastward over the Mono Lake and Desert; mountains beyond mountains looking strangely barren and grey and bare like heaps of ashes dumped from the sky. The lake, eight or ten miles in diameter, shines like a burnished disc of silver, no trees about its grey, ashy, cindery shores. Looking westward, the glorious forests are seen sweeping over countless ridges and hills, girdling domes and subordinate mountains, fringing in long curving lines the dividing ridges, and filling every hollow where the glaciers have spread soil beds however rocky or smooth. Looking northward and southward along the axis of the range, you see the glorious array of high mountains, crags and peaks and snow, the fountain-heads of rivers that are flowing west to the sea through the famous Golden Gate, and east to hot salt lakes and deserts to evaporate and hurry back into the sky. Innumerable lakes are shining like eyes beneath heavy rock brows, bare or tree fringed, or embedded in black forests. Meadow openings in the woods seem as numerous as the lakes or perhaps more so. Far up the moraine-covered slopes and among crumbling rocks I found many delicate hardy plants, some of them still in flower. The best gains of this trip were the lessons of unity and interrelation of all the features of the landscape revealed in general views. The lakes and meadows are located just where the ancient glaciers bore heaviest at the foot of the steepest parts of their channels, and of course their longest diameters are approximately parallel with each other and with the belts of forests growing in long curving lines on the lateral and medial moraines, and in broad outspreading fields on the terminal beds deposited toward the end of the ice period when the glaciers were receding. The domes, ridges, and spurs also show the influence of glacial action in their forms, which approximately seem to be the forms of greatest strength with reference to the stress of oversweeping, past-sweeping, down-grinding ice-streams; survivals of the most resisting masses, or those most favourably situated. How interesting everything is! Every rock, mountain, stream, plant, lake, lawn, forest, garden, bird, beast, insect seems to call and invite us to come and learn something of its history and relationship. But shall the poor ignorant scholar be allowed to try the lessons they offer? It seems too great and good to be true. Soon I'll be going to the lowlands. The bread camp must soon be removed. If I had a few sacks of flour, an axe, and some matches, I would build a cabin of pine logs, pile up plenty of firewood about it and stay all winter to see the grand fertile snowstorms, watch the birds and animals that winter thus high, how they live, how the forests look snow-laden or buried, and how the avalanches look and sound on their way down the mountains. But now I'll have to go, for there is nothing to spare in the way of provisions. I'll surely be back, however, surely I'll be back. No other place has ever so overwhelmingly attracted me as this hospitable, Godful wilderness.

September 2. A grand, red, rosy, crimson day, – a perfect glory of a day. What it means I don't know. It is the first marked change from tranquil sunshine with purple mornings and evenings and still, white noons. There is nothing like a storm, however. The average cloudiness only about eight per cent, and there is no sighing in the woods to betoken a big weather change. The sky was red in the morning and evening, the colour not diffused like the ordinary purple glow, but loaded upon separate well-defined clouds that remained motionless, as if anchored around the jagged mountain-fenced horizon. A deep red cap, bluffy around its sides, lingered a long time on Mount

Dana and Mount Gibbs, drooping so low as to hide most of their bases, but leaving Dana's round summit free, which seemed to float separate and alone over the big crimson cloud. Mammoth Mountain, to the south of Gibbs and Bloody Canyon, striped and spotted with snow banks and clumps of dwarf pine, was also favoured with a glorious crimson cap, in the making of which there was no trace of economy – a huge bossy pile coloured with a perfect passion of crimson that seemed important enough to be sent off to burn among the stars in majestic independence. One is constantly reminded of the infinite lavishness and fertility of Nature – inexhaustible abundance amid what seems enormous wastage. And yet when we look into any of her operations that lie within reach of our minds, we learn that no particle of her material is wasted or worn out. It is eternally flowing from use to use, beauty to yet higher beauty; and we soon cease to lament waste and death, and rather rejoice and exult in the imperishable, unspendable wealth of the universe, and faithfully watch and wait the reappearance of everything that melts and fades and dies about us, feeling sure that its next appearance will be better and more beautiful than the last.

I watched the growth of these red lands of the sky as eagerly as if new mountain ranges were being built. Soon the group of snowy peaks in whose recesses lie the highest fountains of the Tuolumne, Merced, and North Fork of the San Joaquin were decorated with majestic coloured clouds like those already described, but more complicated, to correspond with the grand fountain-heads of the rivers they overshadowed. The Sierra Cathedral, to the south of camp, was overshadowed like Sinai. Never before noticed so fine a union of rock and cloud in form and colour and substance, drawing earth and sky together as one; and so human is it, every feature and tint of colour goes to one's heart, and we shout, exulting in wild enthusiasm as if all the divine show were our own. More and more, in a place like this, we feel ourselves part of wild Nature, kin to everything. Spent most of the day high up on the north rim of the valley, commanding views of the clouds in all their red glory spreading their wonderful light over all the basin, while the rocks and trees and small Alpine plants at my feet seemed hushed and thoughtful, as if they also were conscious spectators of the glorious new cloud world.

Here and there, as I plodded farther and higher, I came to small garden patches and ferneries just where one would naturally decide that no plant-creature could possibly live. But, as in the region about the head of Mono Pass and the top of Dana, it was in the wildest, highest places that the most beautiful and tender and enthusiastic plant-people were found. Again and again, as I lingered over these charming plants, I said, How came you here? How do you live through the winter? Our roots, they explained, reach far down the joints of the summer-warmed rocks, and beneath our fine snow mantle killing frosts cannot reach us, while we sleep away the dark half of the year dreaming of spring.

Ever since I was allowed entrance into these mountains I have been looking for cassiope, said to be the most beautiful and best loved of the heathworts, but, strange to say, I have not yet found it. On my high mountain walks I keep muttering, 'Cassiope, cassiope.' This name, as Calvinists say, is driven in upon me, notwithstanding the glorious host of plants that come about me uncalled as soon as I show myself. Cassiope seems the highest name of all the small mountain-heath people, and as if conscious of her worth, keeps out of my way. I must find her soon, if at all this year.

September 4. All the vast sky dome is clear, filled only with mellow Indian summer light. The pine and hemlock and fir cones are nearly ripe and are falling fast from morning to night, cut off and gathered by the busy squirrels. Almost all the plants have matured their seeds, their summer work done; and the summer crop of birds and deer will soon be able to follow their parents to the foothills and plains at the approach of winter, when the snow begins to fly.

September 5. No clouds. Weather cool, calm, bright as if no great thing was yet ready to be done. Have been sketching the North Tuolumne Church. The sunset gloriously coloured.

September 6. Still another perfectly cloudless day, purple evening and morning, all the middle hours one mass of pure serene sunshine. Soon after sunrise the air grew warm, and there was no wind. One naturally halted to see what Nature intended to do. There is a suggestion of real Indian summer in the hushed brooding, faintly hazy weather. The yellow atmosphere, though thin, is still plainly of the same general character as that of eastern Indian summer. The peculiar mellowness is perhaps in part caused by myriads of ripe spores adrift in the sky.

Mr Delaney now keeps up a solemn talk about the need of getting away from these high mountains, telling sad stories of flocks that perished in storms that broke suddenly into the midst of fine innocent weather like this we are now enjoying. 'In no case,' said he, 'will I venture to stay so high and far back in the mountains as we now are later than the middle of this month, no matter how warm and sunny it may be.' He would move the flock slowly at first, a few miles a day until the Yosemite Creek basin was reached and crossed, then while lingering in the heavy pine woods should the weather threaten he could hurry down to the foothills, where the snow never falls deep enough to smother a sheep. Of course I am anxious to see as much of the wilderness as possible in the few days left me, and I say again, – May the good time come when I can stay as long as I like with plenty of bread, far and free from trampling flocks, though I may well be thankful for this generous foodful inspiring summer. Anyhow we never know where we must go nor what guides we are to get, – men, storms, guardian angels, or sheep. Perhaps almost everybody in the least natural is guarded more than he is ever aware of. All the wilderness seems to be full of tricks and plans to drive and draw us up into God's Light.

Have been busy planning, and baking bread for at least one more good wild excursion among the high peaks, and surely none however hopefully aiming at fortune or fame, ever felt so gloriously happily excited by the outlook.

September 7. Left camp at daybreak and made direct for Cathedral Peak, intending to strike eastward and southward from that point among the peaks and ridges at the heads of the Tuolumne, Merced, and San Joaquin Rivers. Down through the pine woods I made my way, across the Tuolumne River and meadows, and up the heavily timbered slope forming the south boundary of the upper Tuolumne basin, along the east side of Cathedral Peak, and up to its topmost spire, which I reached at noon, having loitered by the way to study the fine trees – two-leaved pine, mountain pine, albicaulis pine, silver fir, and the most charming, most graceful of all the evergreens, the mountain hemlock. High, cool, late flowering meadows also detained me, and lakelets and avalanche tracks and huge quarries of moraine rocks above the forests.

All the way up from the Big Meadows to the base of the Cathedral the ground is covered with moraine material, the left lateral moraine of the great glacier that must have completely filled this upper Tuolumne basin. Higher there are several small terminal moraines of residual glaciers shoved forward at right angles against the grand simple lateral of the main Tuolumne Glacier. A fine place to study mountain sculpture and soil making. The view from the Cathedral Spires is very fine and telling in every direction. Innumerable peaks, ridges, domes, meadows, lakes, and woods; the forests extending in long curving lines and broad fields wherever the glaciers have left soil for them to grow on, while the sides of the highest mountains show a straggling dwarf growth clinging to rifts in the rocks apparently independent of soil. The dark heath-like growth on the Cathedral roof I found to be dwarf snow-pressed albicaulis pine, about three or four feet high, but very old looking. Many of them are bearing cones, and the noisy Clarke crow is eating the seeds, using his long bill like a woodpecker in digging them out of the cones. A good many flowers are still in bloom about the base of the peak, and even on the roof among the little pines, especially a woody yellow-flowered eriogonum and a hand-some aster. The body of the Cathedral is nearly square, and the roof slopes are wonderfully regular and symmetrical, the ridge trending northeast and southwest. This direction has apparently been determined by structure joints in the granite. The gable on the northeast end is magnificent in size and simplicity, and at its base there is a big snow bank protected by the shadow of the building. The front is adorned with many pinnacles and a tall spire of curious workmanship. Here too the joints in the rock are seen to have played an important part in determining their forms and size and general arrangement. The Cathedral is said to be about eleven thousand feet above the sea, but the height of the building itself above the level of the ridge it stands on is about fifteen hundred feet. A mile or so to the westward there is a handsome lake, and the glacier-polished granite about it is shining so brightly it is not easy in some places to trace the line between the rock and water, both shining alike. Of this lake with its silvery basin and bits of meadow and groves I have a fine view from the spires; also of Lake Tenaya, Cloud's Rest and the South Dome of Yosemite, Mount Starr King, Mount Hoffman, the Merced peaks, and the vast multitude of snowy fountain peaks extending far north and south along the axis of the range. No feature, however, of all the noble landscape as seen from here seems more wonderful than the Cathedral itself, a temple display-ing Nature's best masonry and sermons in stones. How often I have gazed at it from the tops of hills and ridges, and through openings in the forests on my many short excursions, devoutly wondering, admiring, longing! This I may say is the first time I have been at church in California, led here at last, every door graciously opened for the poor lonely worshipper. In our best times everything turns into religion, all the world seems a church and the mountains altars. And lo, here at last in front of the Cathedral is blessed cassiope, ringing her thousands of sweet-toned bells, the sweetest church music I ever enjoyed. Listening, admiring, until late in the afternoon I compelled myself to hasten away eastward back of rough, sharp, spiry, splintery peaks, all of them granite like the Cathedral, sparkling with crystals – feldspar, quartz, hornblende, mica, tourmaline. Had a rather difficult walk and creep across an immense snow and ice cliff which gradually increased in steepness as I advanced until it was almost impassable. Slipped on a dangerous place, but managed to stop by digging my heels into the thawing surface just on the brink of a yawning ice gulf. Camped beside a little pool and a group of crinkled dwarf pines; and as I sit by the fire trying to write notes the shallow pool seems fathomless with the infinite starry heavens in it, while the onlooking rocks and trees, tiny shrubs and daisies and sedges, brought forward in the fireglow, seem full of thought as if about to speak aloud and tell all their wild stories. A marvellously impressive meeting in which every one has something worthwhile to tell. And beyond the firebeams out in the solemn darkness, how impressive is the music of a choir of rills singing their way down from the snow to the river! And when we call to mind that thousands of these rejoicing rills are assembled in each one of the main streams, we wonder the less that our Sierra rivers are songful all the way to the sea.

About sundown saw a flock of dun greyish sparrows going to roost in crevices of a crag above the big snowfield. Charming little mountaineers! Found a species of sedge in flower within eight or ten feet of a snowbank. Judging by the looks of the ground, it can hardly have been out in the sunshine much longer than a week, and it is likely to be buried again in fresh snow in a month or so, thus making a winter about ten months long, while spring, summer, and autumn are crowded and hurried into two months. How delightful it is to be alone here! How wild everything is – wild as the sky and as pure! Never shall I forget this big, divine day – the Cathedral and its thousands of cassiope bells, and the landscapes around them, and this camp in the grey crags above the woods, with its stars and streams and snow.

September 8. Day of climbing, scrambling, sliding on the peaks around the highest source of the Tuolumne and Merced. Climbed three of the most commanding of the mountains, whose names I don't know; crossed streams and huge beds of ice and snow more than I could keep count of. Neither could I keep count of the lakes scattered on tablelands and in the cirques of the peaks, and in chains in the canyons, linked together by the streams – a tremendously wild grey wilderness of hacked, shattered crags, ridges, and peaks, a few clouds drifting over and through the midst of them as if looking for work. In general views all the immense round landscape seems raw and lifeless as a quarry, yet the most charming flowers were found rejoicing in countless nooks and garden-like patches everywhere. I must have done three or four days' climbing work in this one. Limbs perfectly tireless until near sundown, when I descended into the main upper Tuolumne valley at the foot of Mount Lyell, the camp still eight or ten miles distant. Going up through the pine woods past the Soda Springs Dome in the dark, where there is much fallen timber, and when all the excitement of seeing things was wanting, I was tired. Arrived at the main camp at nine o'clock, and soon was sleeping sound as death.

ELEVEN

Back to the Lowlands

September 9. Weariness rested away and I feel eager and ready for another excursion a month or two long in the same wonderful wilderness. Now, however, I must turn toward the lowlands, praying and hoping Heaven will shove me back again.

The most telling thing learned in these mountain excursions is the influence of cleavage joints on the features sculptured from the general mass of the range. Evidently the denudation has been enormous, while the inevitable outcome is subtle balanced beauty. Comprehended in general views, the features of the wildest landscape seem to be as harmoniously related as the features of a human face. Indeed, they look human and radiate spiritual beauty, divine thought, however covered and concealed by rock and snow.

Mr Delaney has hardly had time to ask me how I enjoyed my trip, though he has facilitated and encouraged my plans all summer, and declares I'll be famous some day, a kind guess that seems strange and incredible to a wandering wilderness-lover with never a thought or dream of fame while humbly trying to trace and learn and enjoy Nature's lessons.

The camp stuff is now packed on the horses, and the flock is headed for the home ranch. Away we go, down through the pines, leaving the lovely lawn where we have camped so long. I wonder if I'll ever see it again. The sod is so tough and close it is scarcely at all injured by the sheep. Fortunately they are not fond of silky glacier meadow grass. The day is perfectly clear, not a cloud or the faintest hint of a cloud is visible, and there is no wind. I wonder if in all the world, at a height of nine thousand feet, weather so steadily, faithfully calm and bright and hospitable may anywhere else be found. We are going away fearing destructive storms, though it is difficult to conceive weather changes so great.

Though the water is now low in the river, the usual difficulty occurred in getting the flock across it. Every sheep seemed to be invincibly determined to die any sort of dry death rather than wet its feet. Carlo has learned the sheep business as perfectly as the best shepherd, and it is interesting to watch his intelligent efforts to push or frighten the silly creatures into the water. They had to be fairly crowded and shoved over the bank; and when at last one crossed because it could not push its way back, the whole flock suddenly plunged in headlong together, as if the river was the only desirable part of the world. Aside from mere money profit one would rather herd wolves than sheep. As soon as they clambered up the opposite bank, they began baaing and feeding as if nothing unusual had happened. We crossed the meadows and drove slowly up the south rim of the valley through the same woods I had passed on my way to Cathedral Peak, and camped for the night by the side of a small pond on top of the big lateral moraine.

September 10. In the morning at daybreak not one of the two thousand sheep was in sight. Examining the tracks, we discovered that they had been scattered, perhaps by a bear. In a few hours all were found and gathered into one flock again. Had fine view of a deer. How graceful and perfect in every way it seemed as compared with the silly, dusty, tousled sheep! From the high ground hereabouts had another grand view to the northward – a heaving, swelling sea of domes and round-backed ridges fringed with pines, and bounded by innumerable sharp-pointed peaks, grey and barren-looking, though so full of beautiful life. Another day of the calm, cloudless kind, purple in the morning and evening. The evening glow has been very marked for the last two or three weeks. Perhaps the 'zodiacal light.'

September 11. Cloudless. Slight frost. Calm. Fairly started downhill, and now are camped at the west end meadows of Lake Tenaya – a charming place. Lake smooth as glass, mirroring its miles of glacier-polished pavements and bold mountain walls. Find aster still in flower. Here is about the upper limit of the dwarf form of the goldcup oak, – eight thousand feet above sea level, – reaching about two thousand feet higher than the California black oak (*Quercus Californica*). Lovely evening, the lake reflections after dark marvellously impressive.

September 12 . Cloudless day, all pure sungold. Among the magnificent silver firs once more, within two miles of the brink of Yosemite, at the famous Portuguese bear camp. Chaparral of goldcup oak, manzanita, and ceanothus abundant hereabouts, wanting about the Tuolumne meadows, although the elevation is but little higher there. The two-leaved pine, though far more abundant about the Tuolumne meadow region, reaches its greatest size on stream sides hereabouts and around meadows that are rather boggy. All the best dry ground is taken by the magnificent silver fir, which here reaches its greatest size and forms a well-defined belt. A glorious tree. Have fine bed of its boughs tonight.

September 13 . Camp this evening at Yosemite Creek, close to the stream, on a little sand flat near our old camp ground. The vegetation is already brown and yellow and dry; the creek almost dry also. The slender form of the two-leaved pine on its banks is, I think, the handsomest I have anywhere seen. It might easily pass at first sight for a distinct species, though surely only a variety (*Murrayana*), due to crowded and rapid growth on good soil. The yellow pine is as variable, or perhaps more so. The form here and a thousand feet higher, on crumbling rocks, is broad branching, with closely furrowed, reddish bark, large cones, and long leaves. It is one of the hardiest of pines, and has wonderful vitality. The tassels of long, stout needles shining silvery in the sun, when the wind is blowing them all in the same direction, is one of the most splendid spectacles these glorious Sierra forests have to show. This variety of *Pinus ponderosa* is regarded as a distinct species, *Pinus Jeffreyi*, by some botanists. The basin of this famous Yosemite stream is extremely rocky, – seems fairly to be paved with domes like a street with big cobblestones. I wonder if I shall ever be allowed to explore it. It draws me so strongly, I would make any sacrifice to try to read its lessons. I thank God for this glimpse of it. The charms of these mountains are beyond all common reason, unexplainable and mysterious as life itself.

September 14. Nearly all day in magnificent fir forest, the top branches laden with superb erect grey cones shining with beads of pure balsam. The squirrels are cutting them off at a great rate. Bump, bump, I hear them falling, soon to be gathered and stored for winter bread. Those that chance to be left by the industrious harvesters drop the scales and bracts when fully ripe, and it is fine to see the purple-winged seeds flying in swirling, merry looking flocks seeking their fortunes. The bole and dead limbs of nearly every tree in the main forest belt are ornamented by conspicuous tufts and strips of a yellow lichen.

Camped for the night at Cascade Creek, near the Mono Trail crossing. Manzanita berries now ripe. Cloudiness today about ten per cent. The sunset very rich, flaming purple and crimson showing gloriously through the aisles of the woods.

September 15. The weather pure gold, cloudiness about five per cent, white cirrus flecks and pencillings around the horizon. Move two or three miles and camp at Tamarack Flat. Wandering in the woods here back of the pines which bound the meadows, I found very noble specimens of the magnificent silver fir, the tallest about two hundred and forty feet high and five feet in diameter four feet from the ground.

September 16. Crawled slowly four or five miles today through the glorious forest to Crane Flat, where we are camped for the night. The forests we so admired in summer seem still more beautiful and sublime in this mellow autumn light. Lovely starry night, the tall, spiring treetops relieved in jet black against the sky. I linger by the fire, loath to go to bed.

September 17. Left camp early. Ran over the Tuolomne divide and down a few miles to a grove of sequoias that I had heard of, directed by the Don. They occupy an area of perhaps less than a hundred acres. Some of the trees are noble, colossal old giants, surrounded by magnificent sugar pines and Douglas spruces. The perfect specimens not burned or broken are singularly regular and symmetrical, though not at all conventional, showing infinite variety in general unity and harmony; the noble shafts with rich purplish brown fluted bark, free of limbs for one hundred and fifty feet or so, ornamented here and there with leafy rosettes; main branches of the oldest trees very large, crooked and rugged, zigzagging stiffly outward seemingly lawless, yet unexpectedly stooping just at the right distance from the trunk and dissolving in dense bossy masses of branchlets, thus making a regular though greatly varied outline, – a cylinder of leafy, outbulging spray masses, terminating in a noble dome, that may be recognised while yet far off upheaved against the sky above the dark bed of pines and firs and spruces, the king of all conifers, not only in size but in sublime majesty of behaviour and port. I found a black, charred stump about thirty feet in diameter and eighty or ninety feet high – a venerable, impressive old monument of a tree that in its prime may have been the monarch of the grove; seedlings and saplings growing up here and there, thrifty and hopeful, giving no hint of the dying out of the species. Not any unfavourable change of climate, but only fire, threatens the existence of these noblest of God's trees. Sorry I was not able to get a count of the old monument's annual rings.

Camp this evening at Hazel Green, on the broad back of the dividing ridge near our old camp ground when we were on the way up the mountains in the spring. This ridge has the finest sugar pine groves and finest manzanita and ceanothus thickets I have yet found on all this wonderful summer journey.

September 18. Made a long descent on the south side of the divide to Brown's Flat, the grand forests now left above us, though the sugar pine still flourishes fairly well, and with the yellow pine, libocedrus, and Douglas spruce, makes forests that would be considered most wonderful in any other part of the world.

The Indians here, with great concern, pointed to an old

garden patch on the flat and told us to keep away from it. Perhaps some of their tribe are buried here.

September 19. Camped this evening at Smith's Mill, on the first broad mountain bench or plateau reached in ascending the range, where pines grow large enough for good lumber. Here wheat, apples, peaches and grapes grow, and we were treated to wine and apples. The wine I didn't like, but Mr Delaney and the Indian driver and the shepherd seemed to think the stuff divine. Compared to sparkling Sierra water fresh from the heavens, it seemed a dull, muddy, stupid drink. But the apples, best of fruits, how delicious they were – fit for gods or men.

On the way down from Brown's Flat we stopped at Bower Cave, and I spent an hour in it – one of the most novel and interesting of all Nature's underground mansions. Plenty of sunlight pours into it through the leaves of the four maple trees growing in its mouth, illuminating its clear, calm pool and marble chambers, – a charming place, ravishingly beautiful, but the accessible parts of the walls sadly disfigured with names of vandals.

September 20. The weather still golden and calm, but hot. We are now in the foothills, and all the conifers are left behind except the grey Sabine pine. Camped at the Dutch Boy's Ranch, where there are extensive barley fields now showing nothing save dusty stubble.

September 21. A terribly hot, dusty, sunburned day, and as nothing was to be gained by loitering where the flock could find nothing to eat save thorny twigs and chaparral, we made a long drive, and before sundown reached the home ranch on the yellow San Joaquin plain.

September 22. The sheep were let out of the corral one by one, this morning, and counted, and strange to say, after all their adventurous wanderings in bewildering rocks and brush and streams, scattered by bears, poisoned by azalea, kalmia, alkali, all are accounted for. Of the two thousand and fifty that left the corral in the spring lean and weak, two thousand and twenty-five have returned fat and strong. The losses are: ten killed by bears, one by a rattle-snake, one that had to be killed after it had broken its leg on a boulder slope, and one that ran away in blind terror on being accidentally separated from the flock, – thirteen all told. Of the other twelve doomed never to return, three were sold to ranchmen and nine were made camp mutton.

Here ends my forever memorable first High Sierra excursion. I have crossed the Range of Light, surely the brightest and best of all the Lord has built; and rejoicing in its glory, I gladly, gratefully, hopefully pray I may see it again.

Travels in Alaska

Contents

Puget Sound and British Columbia

After eleven years of study and exploration in the Sierra Nevada of California and the mountain-ranges of the Great Basin, studying in particular their glaciers, forests, and wild life, above all their ancient glaciers and the influence they exerted in sculpturing the rocks over which they passed with tremendous pressure, making new landscapes, scenery, and beauty which so mysteriously influence every human being, and to some extent all life, I was anxious to gain some knowledge of the regions to the northward, about Puget Sound and Alaska. With this grand object in view I left San Francisco in May, 1879, on the steamer Dakota, without any definite plan, as with the exception of a few of the Oregon peaks and their forests all the wild north was new to me.

To the mountaineer a sea voyage is a grand, inspiring, restful change. For forests and plains with their flowers and fruits we have new scenery, new life of every sort; water hills and dales in eternal visible motion for rock waves, types of permanence.

It was curious to note how suddenly the eager countenances of the passengers were darkened as soon as the good ship passed through the Golden Gate and began to heave on the waves of the open ocean. The crowded deck was speedily deserted on account of seasickness. It seemed strange that nearly every one afflicted should be more or less ashamed.

Next morning a strong wind was blowing, and the sea was grey and white, with long breaking waves, across which the Dakota was racing half-buried in spray. Very few passengers were on deck to enjoy the wild scenery. Every wave seemed to be making enthusiastic, eager haste to the shore, with long, irised tresses streaming from its

tops, some of its outer fringes borne away in scud to refresh
the wind, all the rolling, pitching, flying water exulting in
the beauty of rainbow light. Gulls and albatrosses, strong,
glad life in the midst of the stormy beauty, skimmed
the waves against the wind, seemingly without effort,
oftentimes flying nearly a mile without a single wing-beat,
gracefully swaying from side to side and tracing the curves
of the briny water hills with the finest precision, now and
then just grazing the highest.

And yonder, glistening amid the irised spray, is a still
more striking revelation of warm life in the so-called
howling waste – a half-dozen whales, their broad backs
like glaciated bosses of granite heaving aloft in near view,
spouting lustily, drawing a long breath, and plunging down
home in colossal health and comfort. A merry school
of porpoises, a square mile of them, suddenly appear,
tossing themselves into the air in abounding strength and
hilarity, adding foam to the waves and making all the
wilderness wilder. One cannot but feel sympathy with
and be proud of these brave neighbours, fellow citizens
in the commonwealth of the world, making a living like
the rest of us. Our good ship also seemed like a thing
of life, its great iron heart beating on through calm and
storm, a truly noble spectacle. But think of the hearts of
these whales, beating warm against the sea, day and night,
through dark and light, on and on for centuries; how the
red blood must rush and gurgle in and out, bucketfuls,
barrelfuls at a beat!

The cloud colours of one of the four sunsets enjoyed on
the voyage were remarkably pure and rich in tone. There
was a well-defined range of cumuli a few degrees above
the horizon, and a massive, dark-grey rain-cloud above it,
from which depended long, bent fringes overlapping the
lower cumuli and partially veiling them; and from time
to time sunbeams poured through narrow openings and
painted the exposed bosses and fringes in ripe yellow tones,
which, with the reflections on the water, made magnificent
pictures. The scenery of the ocean, however sublime in vast
expanse, seems far less beautiful to us dry-shod animals
than that of the land seen only in comparatively small

patches; but when we contemplate the whole globe as one great dewdrop, striped and dotted with continents and islands, flying through space with other stars all singing and shining together as one, the whole universe appears as an infinite storm of beauty.

The California coast-hills and cliffs look bare and uninviting as seen from the ship, the magnificent forests keeping well back out of sight beyond the reach of the sea winds; those of Oregon and Washington are in some places clad with conifers nearly down to the shore; even the little detached islets, so marked a feature to the northward, are mostly tree-crowned. Up through the Straits of Juan de Fuca the forests, sheltered from the ocean gales and favoured with abundant rains, flourish in marvellous luxuriance on the glacier-sculptured mountains of the Olympic Range.

We arrived in Esquimault Harbour, three miles from Victoria, on the evening of the fourth day, and drove to the town through a magnificent forest of Douglas spruce – with an undergrowth in open spots of oak, madrone, hazel, dogwood, alder, spiraea, willow, and wild rose – and around many an upswelling *moutonné* rock, freshly glaciated and furred with yellow mosses and lichens.

Victoria, the capital of British Columbia, was in 1879 a small old-fashioned English town on the south end of Vancouver Island. It was said to contain about six thousand inhabitants. The government buildings and some of the business blocks were noticeable, but the attention of the traveller was more worthily attracted to the neat cottage homes found here, embowered in the freshest and floweriest climbing roses and honeysuckles conceivable. Californians may well be proud of their home roses loading sunny verandas, climbing to the tops of the roofs and falling over the gables in white and red cascades. But here, with so much bland fog and dew and gentle laving rain, a still finer development of some of the commonest garden plants is reached. English honeysuckle seems to have found here a most congenial home. Still more beautiful were the wild roses, blooming in wonderful luxuriance along the woodland paths, with corollas two and three inches wide.

This rose and three species of spiraea fairly filled the air with fragrance after showers; and how brightly then did the red dogwood berries shine amid the green leaves beneath trees two hundred and fifty feet high.

Strange to say, all of this exuberant forest and flower vegetation was growing upon fresh moraine material scarcely at all moved or in any way modified by post-glacial agents. In the town gardens and orchards, peaches and apples fell upon glacier-polished rocks, and the streets were graded in moraine gravel; and I observed scratched and grooved rock bosses as unweathered and telling as those of the High Sierra of California eight thousand feet or more above sea-level. The Victoria Harbour is plainly glacial in origin, eroded from the solid; and the rock islets that rise here and there in it are unchanged to any appreciable extent by all the waves that have broken over them since first they came to light toward the close of the glacial period. The shores also of the harbour are strikingly grooved and scratched and in every way as glacial in all their characteristics as those of new-born glacial lakes. That the domain of the sea is being slowly extended over the land by incessant wave-action is well known; but in this freshly glaciated region the shores have been so short a time exposed to wave-action that they are scarcely at all wasted. The extension of the sea affected by its own action in post-glacial times is probably less than the millionth part of that affected by glacial action during the last glacier period. The direction of the flow of the ice-sheet to which all the main features of this wonderful region are due was in general southward.

From this quiet little English town I made many short excursions – up the coast to Nanaimo, to Burrard Inlet, now the terminus of the Canadian Pacific Railroad, to Puget Sound, up Frazer River to New Westminster and Yale at the head of navigation, charmed everywhere with the wild, new-born scenery. The most interesting of these and the most difficult to leave was the Puget Sound region, famous the world over for the wonderful forests of gigantic trees about its shores. It is an arm and many-fingered hand of the sea, reaching southward from the Straits of Juan de Fuca about a hundred miles into the heart of one of the

noblest coniferous forests on the face of the globe. All its
scenery is wonderful – broad river-like reaches sweeping
in beautiful curves around bays and capes and jutting
promontories, opening here and there into smooth, blue,
lake-like expanses dotted with islands and feathered with
tall, spiry evergreens, their beauty doubled on the bright
mirror-water.

Sailing from Victoria, the Olympic Mountains are seen
right ahead, rising in bold relief against the sky, with jagged
crests and peaks from six to eight thousand feet high – small
residual glaciers and ragged snow-fields beneath them in
wide amphitheatres opening down through the forest-filled
valleys. These valleys mark the courses of the Olympic
glaciers at the period of their greatest extension, when
they poured their tribute into that portion of the great
northern ice-sheet that overswept Vancouver Island and
filled the strait between it and the mainland.

On the way up to Olympia, then a hopeful little town
situated at the end of one of the longest fingers of the
Sound, one is often reminded of Lake Tahoe, the scenery
of the widest expanses is so lake-like in the clearness and
stillness of the water and the luxuriance of the surrounding forests. Doubling cape after cape, passing uncounted
islands, new combinations break on the view in endless
variety, sufficient to satisfy the lover of wild beauty through
a whole life. When the clouds come down, blotting out
everything, one feels as if at sea; again lifting a little, some
islet may be seen standing alone with the tops of its trees
dipping out of sight in grey misty fringes; then the ranks of
spruce and cedar bounding the water's edge come to view;
and when at length the whole sky is clear the colossal cone
of Mount Rainier may be seen in spotless white, looking
down over the dark woods from a distance of fifty or sixty
miles, but so high and massive and so sharply outlined,
it seems to be just back of a strip of woods only a few
miles wide.

Mount Rainier, or Tahoma (the Indian name), is the
noblest of the volcanic cones extending from Lassen Butte
and Mount Shasta along the Cascade Range to Mount
Baker. One of the most telling views of it hereabouts is

obtained near Tacoma. From a bluff back of the town it was revealed in all its glory, laden with glaciers and snow down to the forested foothills around its finely curved base. Up to this time (1879) it had been ascended but once. From observations made on the summit with a single aneroid barometer, it was estimated to be about 14,500ft. high. Mount Baker, to the northward, is about 10,700ft. high, a noble mountain. So also are Mount Adams, Mount St Helens, and Mount Hood. The latter, overlooking the town of Portland, is perhaps the best known. Rainier, about the same height as Shasta, surpasses them all in massive icy grandeur – the most majestic solitary mountain I had ever yet beheld. How eagerly I gazed and longed to climb it and study its history only the mountaineer may know, but I was compelled to turn away and bide my time.

The species forming the bulk of the woods here is the Douglas spruce (*Pseudotsuga douglasii*), one of the greatest of the western giants. A specimen that I measured near Olympia was about three hundred feet in height and twelve feet in diameter four feet above the ground. It is a widely distributed tree, extending northward through British Columbia, southward through Oregon and California, and eastward to the Rocky Mountains. The timber is used for ship-building, spars, piles, and the framework of houses, bridges, etc. In the California lumber markets it is known as 'Oregon pine'. In Utah, where it is common on the Wahsatch Mountains, it is called 'red pine'. In California, on the western slope of the Sierra Nevada, it forms, in company with the yellow pine, sugar pine, and incense cedar, a pretty well-defined belt at a height of from three to six thousand feet above the sea; but it is only in Oregon and Washington, especially in this Puget Sound region, that it reaches its very grandest development – tall, straight, and strong, growing down close to tide-water.

All the towns of the Sound had a hopeful, thrifty aspect. Port Townsend, picturesquely located on a grassy bluff, was the port of clearance for vessels sailing to foreign parts. Seattle was famed for its coalmines, and claimed to be the coming town of the North Pacific Coast. So also did its rival, Tacoma, which had been selected as the terminus of the much-talked-of Northern Pacific Railway. Several coal-veins of astonishing thickness were discovered the winter before on the Carbon River, to the east of Tacoma, one of them said to be no less than twenty-one feet, another twenty feet, another fourteen, with many smaller ones, the aggregate thickness of all the veins being upwards of a hundred feet. Large deposits of magnetic iron ore and brown hematite, together with limestone, had been discovered in advantageous proximity to the coal, making a bright outlook for the Sound region in general in connection with its railroad hopes, its unrivalled timber resources, and its far-reaching geographical relations.

After spending a few weeks in the Puget Sound region with a friend from San Francisco, we engaged passage on the little mail steamer California, at Portland, Oregon, for Alaska. The sail down the broad lower reaches of the Columbia and across its foamy bar, around Cape Flattery, and up the Juan de Fuca Strait, was delightful; and after calling again at Victoria and Port Townsend we got fairly off for icy Alaska.

TWO

Alexander Archipelago and the Home
I Found in Alaska

To the lover of pure wildness Alaska is one of the most wonderful countries in the world. No excursions that I know of may be made into any other American wilderness where so marvellous an abundance of noble, newborn scenery is so charmingly brought to view as on the trip through the Alexander Archipelago to Fort Wrangell and Sitka. Gazing from the deck of the steamer, one is borne smoothly over calm blue waters, through the midst of countless forest-clad islands. The ordinary discomforts of a sea voyage are not felt, for nearly all the whole long way is on inland waters that are about as waveless as rivers and lakes. So numerous are the islands that they seem to have been sown broadcast; long tapering vistas between the largest of them open in every direction.

Day after day in the fine weather we enjoyed, we seemed to float in true fairyland, each succeeding view seeming more and more beautiful, the one we chanced to have before us the most surprisingly beautiful of all. Never before this had I been embosomed in scenery so hopelessly beyond description. To sketch picturesque bits, definitely bounded, is comparatively easy – a lake in the woods, a glacier meadow, or a cascade in its dell; or even a grand master view of mountains beheld from some commanding outlook after climbing from height to height above the forests. These may be attempted, and more or less telling pictures made of them; but in these coast landscapes there is such indefinite, on-leading expansiveness, such a multitude of features without apparent redundance, their lines graduating delicately into one another in endless succession, while the whole is so fine, so tender, so ethereal, that all penwork seems hopelessly unavailing.

Tracing shining ways through fiord and sound, past forests and waterfalls, islands and mountains and far azure
headlands, it seems as if surely we must at length reach
the very paradise of the poets, the abode of the blessed.

Some idea of the wealth of this scenery may be gained
from the fact that the coast-line of Alaska is about twenty-
six thousand miles long, more than twice as long as all the
rest of the United States. The islands of the Alexander
Archipelago, with the straits, channels, canals, sounds,
passages, and fiords, form an intricate web of land and
water embroidery sixty or seventy miles wide, fringing the
lofty ice chain of coast mountains from Puget Sound to
Cook Inlet; and, with infinite variety, the general pattern
is harmonious throughout its whole extent of nearly a
thousand miles. Here you glide into a narrow channel
hemmed in by mountain walls, forested down to the
water's edge, where there is no distant view, and your
attention is concentrated on the objects close about you
– the crowded spires of the spruces and hemlocks rising
higher and higher on the steep green slopes; stripes of
paler green where winter avalanches have cleared away
the trees, allowing grasses and willows to spring up; zigzags
of cascades appearing and disappearing among the bushes
and trees; short, steep glens with brawling streams hidden
beneath alder and dogwood, seen only where they emerge
on the brown algae of the shore; and retreating hollows,
with lingering snow-banks marking the fountains of ancient
glaciers. The steamer is often so near the shore that you
may distinctly see the cones clustered on the tops of the
trees, and the ferns and bushes at their feet.

But new scenes are brought to view with magical rapidity.
Rounding some bossy cape, the eye is called away into
far-reaching vistas, bounded on either hand by headlands
in charming array, one dipping gracefully beyond another
and growing fainter and more ethereal in the distance.
The tranquil channel stretching river-like between, may be
stirred here and there by the silvery plashing of upspringing
salmon, or by flocks of white gulls floating like waterlilies
among the sun spangles; while mellow, tempered sunshine
is streaming over all, blending sky, land, and water in pale,

misty blue. Then, while you are dreamily gazing into the depths of this leafy ocean lane, the little steamer, seeming hardly larger than a duck, turning into some passage not visible until the moment of entering it, glides into a wide expanse – a sound filled with islands, sprinkled and clustered in forms and compositions such as nature alone can invent; some of them so small the trees growing on them seem like single handfuls culled from the neighbouring woods and set in the water to keep them fresh, while here and there at wide intervals you may notice bare rocks just above the water, mere dots punctuating grand, outswelling sentences of islands.

The variety we find, both as to the contours and the collocation of the islands, is due chiefly to differences in the structure and composition of their rocks, and the unequal glacial denudation different portions of the coast were subjected to. This influence must have been especially heavy toward the end of the glacial period, when the main ice-sheet began to break up into separate glaciers. Moreover, the mountains of the larger islands nourished local glaciers, some of them of considerable size, which sculptured their summits and sides, forming in some cases wide cirques with canyons or valleys leading down from them into the channels and sounds. These causes have produced much of the bewildering variety of which nature is so fond, but none the less will the studious observer see the underlying harmony – the general trend of the islands in the direction of the flow of the main ice-mantle from the mountains of the Coast Range, more or less varied by subordinate foothill ridges and mountains. Furthermore, all the islands, great and small, as well as the headlands and promontories of the mainland, are seen to have a rounded, over-rubbed appearance produced by the over-sweeping ice-flood during the period of greatest glacial abundance.

The canals, channels, straits, passages, sounds, etc., are subordinate to the same glacial conditions in their forms, trends, and extent as those which determined the forms, trends, and distribution of the land-masses, their basins being the parts of the pre-glacial margin of the continent, eroded to varying depths below sea-level, and into which, of course, the ocean waters flowed as the ice was melted out of them. Had the general glacial denudation been much less, these ocean ways over which we are sailing would have been valleys and canyons and lakes; and the islands rounded hills and ridges, landscapes with undulating features like those found above sea-level wherever the rocks and glacial conditions are similar. In general, the island-bound channels are like rivers, not only in separate reaches as seen from the deck of a vessel, but continuously so for hundreds of miles in the case of the longest of them. The tide-currents, the fresh driftwood, the inflowing streams, and the luxuriant foliage of the out-leaning trees on the shores make this resemblance all the more complete. The largest islands look like part of the mainland in any view to be had of them from the ship, but far the greater number are small, and appreciable as islands, scores of them being less than a mile long. These the eye easily takes in and revels in their beauty with ever fresh delight. In their relations to each other the individual members of a group have evidently been derived from the same general rock-mass, yet they never seem broken or abridged in any way as to their contour lines, however abruptly they may dip their sides. Viewed one by one, they seem detached beauties, like extracts from a poem, while, from the completeness of their lines and the way that their trees are arranged, each seems a finished stanza in itself. Contemplating the arrangement of the trees on these small islands, a distinct impression is produced of their having been sorted and harmonized as to size like a well-balanced bouquet. On some of the smaller tufted islets a group of tapering spruces is planted in the middle, and two smaller groups that evidently correspond with each other are planted on the ends at about equal distances from the central group; or the whole appears as one group with marked fringing trees that match each other spreading around the sides, like flowers leaning outward against the rim of a vase. These harmonious tree relations are so constant that they evidently are the result of design, as much so as the arrangement of the feathers of birds or the scales of fishes.

Thus perfectly beautiful are these blessed evergreen islands, and their beauty is the beauty of youth, for though the freshness of their verdure must be ascribed to the bland moisture with which they are bathed from warm ocean-currents, the very existence of the islands, their features, finish, and peculiar distribution, are all immediately referable to ice-action during the great glacial winter just now drawing to a close.

We arrived at Wrangell 14 July, and after a short stop of a few hours went on to Sitka and returned on the 20th to Wrangell, the most inhospitable place at first sight I had ever seen. The little steamer that had been my home in the wonderful trip through the archipelago, after taking the mail, departed on her return to Portland, and as I watched her gliding out of sight in the dismal blurring rain, I felt strangely lonesome. The friend that had accompanied me thus far now left for his home in San Francisco, with two other interesting travellers who had made the trip for health and scenery, while my fellow passengers, the missionaries, went direct to the Presbyterian home in the old fort. There was nothing like a tavern or lodging-house in the village, nor could I find any place in the stumpy, rocky, boggy ground about it that looked dry enough to camp on until I could find a way into the wilderness to begin my studies. Every place within a mile or two of the town seemed strangely shelterless and inhospitable, for all the trees had long ago been felled for building-timber and firewood. At the worst, I thought, I could build a bark hut on a hill back of the village, where something like a forest loomed dimly through the draggled clouds.

I had already seen some of the high glacier-bearing mountains in distant views from the steamer, and was anxious to reach them. A few whites of the village, with whom I entered into conversation, warned me that the Indians were a bad lot, not to be trusted, that the woods were well-nigh impenetrable, and that I could go nowhere without a canoe. On the other hand, these natural difficulties made the grand wild country all the more attractive, and I determined to get into the heart of it somehow or other with a bag of hardtack, trusting to my usual good luck. My present difficulty was in finding a first base camp. My only hope was on the hill. When I was strolling past the old fort I happened to meet one of the missionaries, who kindly asked me where I was going to take up my quarters.

'I don't know', I replied. 'I have not been able to find quarters of any sort. The top of that little hill over there seems the only possible place.'

He then explained that every room in the mission house was full, but he thought I might obtain leave to spread my blanket in a carpenter-shop belonging to the mission. Thanking him, I ran down to the sloppy wharf for my bundle of baggage, laid it on the shop floor, and felt glad and snug among the dry sweet-smelling shavings.

The carpenter was at work on a new Presbyterian mission building, and when he came in I explained that Dr Jackson had suggested that I might be allowed to sleep on the floor, and after I assured him that I would not touch his tools or be in his way, he goodnaturedly gave me the freedom of the shop and also of his small private side room where I would find a wash-basin.

I was here only one night, however, for Mr Vanderbilt, a merchant, who with his family occupied the best house in the fort, hearing that one of the late arrivals, whose business none seemed to know, was compelled to sleep in the carpenter-shop, paid me a good-Samaritan visit and after a few explanatory words on my glacier and forest studies, with fine hospitality offered me a room and a place at his table. Here I found a real home, with freedom to go on all sorts of excursions as opportunity offered. Annie Vanderbilt, a little doctor of divinity two years old, ruled the household with love sermons and kept it warm.

Mr Vanderbilt introduced me to prospectors and traders and some of the most influential of the Indians. I visited the mission school and the home for Indian girls kept by Mrs MacFarland, and made short excursions to the nearby forests and streams, and studied the rate of growth of the different species of trees and their age, counting the annual rings on stumps in the large clearings made by the military when the fort was occupied, causing wondering speculation among the Wrangell folk, as was reported by Mr Vanderbilt.

'What can the fellow be up to?' they inquired. 'He seems to spend most of his time among stumps and weeds. I saw him the other day on his knees, looking at a stump as if he expected to find gold in it. He seems to have no serious object whatever.'

One night when a heavy rainstorm was blowing I unwittingly caused a lot of wondering excitement among the whites as well as the superstitious Indians. Being anxious to see how the Alaska trees behave in storms and hear the songs they sing, I stole quietly away through the grey drenching blast to the hill back of the town, without being observed. Night was falling when I set out and it was pitch dark when I reached the top. The glad, rejoicing storm in glorious voice was singing through the woods, noble compensation for mere body discomfort. But I wanted a fire, a big one, to see as well as hear how the storm and trees were behaving. After long, patient groping I found a little dry punk in a hollow trunk and carefully stored it beside my matchbox and an inch or two of candle in an inside pocket that the rain had not yet reached; then, wiping some dead twigs and whittling them into thin shavings, stored them with the punk. I then made a little conical bark hut about a foot high, and, carefully leaning over it and sheltering it as much as possible from the driving rain, I wiped and stored a lot of dead twigs, lighted the candle, and set it in the hut, carefully added pinches of punk and shavings, and at length got a little blaze, by the light of which I gradually added larger shavings, then twigs all set on end astride the inner flame, making the little hut higher and wider. Soon I had light enough to enable me to select the best dead branches and large sections of bark, which were set on end, gradually increasing the height and corresponding light of the hut fire. A considerable area was thus well lighted, from which I gathered abundance of wood, and kept adding to the fire until it had a strong, hot heart and sent up a pillar of flame thirty or forty feet high, illuminating a wide circle in spite of the rain, and casting a red glare into the flying clouds. Of all the thousands of camp-fires I have elsewhere built none was just like this one, rejoicing in triumphant strength and beauty in the heart of the rain-laden gale. It was wonderful – the illumined rain and clouds mingled together and the trees glowing against the jet background, the colours of the mossy, lichened trunks with sparkling streams pouring down the furrows of the bark, and the grey-bearded old patriarchs bowing low and chanting in passionate worship!

My fire was in all its glory about midnight, and, having made a bark shed to shelter me from the rain and partially dry my clothing, I had nothing to do but look and listen and join the trees in their hymns and prayers.

Neither the great white heart of the fire nor the quivering enthusiastic flames shooting aloft like auroral lances could be seen from the village on account of the trees in front of it and its being back a little way over the brow of the hill; but the light in the clouds made a great show, a portentous sign in the stormy heavens unlike anything ever before seen or heard of in Wrangell. Some wakeful Indians, happening to see it about midnight, in great alarm aroused the Collector of Customs and begged him to go to the missionaries and get them to pray away the frightful omen, and inquired anxiously whether white men had ever seen anything like that sky-fire, which instead of being quenched by the rain was burning brighter and brighter. The Collector said he had heard of such strange fires, and this one he thought might perhaps be what the white man called a 'volcano, or an *ignis fatuus*'. When Mr Young was called from his bed to pray, he, too, confoundedly astonished and at a loss for any sort of explanation, confessed that he had never seen anything like it in the sky or anywhere else in such cold wet weather, but that it was probably some sort of spontaneous combustion, 'that the white man called St Elmo's fire, or Will-of-the-wisp'. These explanations, though not convincingly clear, perhaps served to veil their own astonishment and in some measure to diminish the superstitious fears of the natives; but from what I heard, the few whites who happened to see the strange light wondered about as wildly as the Indians.

I have enjoyed thousands of camp-fires in all sorts of weather and places, warm-hearted, short-flamed, friendly little beauties glowing in the dark on open spots in High Sierra gardens, daisies and lilies circled about them, gazing like enchanted children; and large fires in silver fir forests, with spires of flame towering like the trees about them, and sending up multitudes of starry sparks to enrich the sky; and still greater fires on the mountains in winter, changing camp climate to summer, and making the frosty snow look like beds of white flowers, and oftentimes mingling their swarms of swift-flying sparks with falling snow-crystals when the clouds were in bloom. But this Wrangell camp-fire, my first in Alaska, I shall always remember for its triumphant storm-defying grandeur, and the wondrous beauty of the psalm-singing, lichen-painted trees which it brought to light.

THREE

Wrangell Island and Alaska Summers

Wrangell Island is about fourteen miles long, separated from the mainland by a narrow channel or fiord, and trending in the direction of the flow of the ancient ice-sheet. Like all its neighbours, it is densely forested down to the water's edge with trees that never seem to have suffered from thirst or fire or the axe of the lumberman in all their long century lives. Beneath soft, shady clouds, with abundance of rain, they flourish in wonderful strength and beauty to a good old age, while the many warm days, half cloudy, half clear, and the little groups of pure sun-days enable them to ripen their cones and send myriads of seeds flying every autumn to insure the permanence of the forests and feed the multitude of animals.

The Wrangell village was a rough place. No mining hamlet in the placer gulches of California, nor any backwoods village I ever saw, approached it in picturesque, devil-may-care *abandon*. It was a lawless bedraggle of wooden huts and houses, built in crooked lines wrangling around the boggy shore of the island for a mile or so in the general form of the letter S, without the slightest subordination to the points of the compass or to building laws of any kind. Stumps and logs, like precious monuments, adorned its two streets, each stump and log, on account of the moist climate, moss-grown and tufted with grass and bushes, but muddy on the sides below the limit of the bogline. The ground in general was an oozy, mossy bog on a foundation of jagged rocks, full of concealed pitholes. This picturesque rock, bog and stump obstructions, however, were not so very much in the way, for there were no wagons or carriages there. There was not a horse on the island. The domestic animals were represented by chickens, a lonely cow, a few sheep, and hogs of a breed well calculated to deepen and complicate the mud of the streets.

Most of the permanent residents of Wrangell were engaged in trade. Some little trade was carried on in fish and furs, but most of the quickening business of the place was derived from the Cassiar gold-mines, some two hundred and fifty or three hundred miles inland, by way of the Stickeen River and Dease Lake. Two stern-wheel steamers plied on the river between Wrangell and Telegraph Creek at the head of navigation, a hundred and fifty miles from Wrangell, carrying freight and passengers and connecting with pack-trains for the mines. These placer mines, on tributaries of the Mackenzie River, were discovered in the year 1874. About eighteen hundred miners and prospectors were said to have passed through Wrangell that season of 1879, about half of them being Chinamen. Nearly a third of this whole number set out from here in the month of February, travelling on the Stickeen River, which usually remains safely frozen until toward the end of April. The main body of the miners, however, went up on the steamers in May and June. On account of the severe winters they were all compelled to leave the mines the end of September. Perhaps about two thirds of them passed the winter in Portland and Victoria and the towns of Puget Sound. The rest remained here in Wrangell, dozing away the long winter as best they could.

Indians, mostly of the Stickeen tribe, occupied the two ends of the town, the whites, of whom there were about forty or fifty, the middle portion; but there was no determinate line of demarcation, the dwellings of the Indians being mostly as large and solidly built of logs and planks as those of the whites. Some of them were adorned with tall totem poles.

The fort was a quadrangular stockade with a dozen block and frame buildings located upon rising ground just back of the business part of the town. It was built by our Government shortly after the purchase of Alaska, and was abandoned in 1872, reoccupied by the military in 1875, and finally abandoned and sold to private parties in 1877. In the fort and about it there were a few good, clean homes, which shone all the more brightly in their sombre surroundings. The ground occupied by the fort, by being carefully levelled and drained was dry, though formerly a portion of the general swamp, showing how easily the whole town could have been improved. But in spite of disorder and squalor, shaded with clouds, washed and wiped by rain and sea winds, it was triumphantly salubrious through all the seasons. And though the houses seemed to rest uneasily among the miry rocks and stumps, squirming at all angles as if they had been tossed and twisted by earthquake shocks, and showing but little more relation to one another than may be observed among moraine boulders, Wrangell was a tranquil place. I never heard a noisy brawl in the streets, or a clap of thunder, and the waves seldom spoke much above a whisper along the beach. In summer the rain comes straight down, steamy and tepid. The clouds are usually united, filling the sky, not racing along in threatening ranks suggesting energy of an overbearing destructive kind, but forming a bland, mild, laving bath. The cloudless days are calm, pearl-grey, and brooding in tone, inclining to rest and peace; the islands seem to drowse and float on the glassy water, and in the woods scarce a leaf stirs.

The very brightest of Wrangell days are not what Californians would call bright. The tempered sunshine sifting through the moist atmosphere makes no dazzling glare, and the town, like the landscape, rests beneath a hazy, hushing, Indian-summerish spell. On the longest days the sun rises about three o'clock, but it is daybreak at midnight. The cocks crowed when they woke, without reference to the dawn, for it is never quite dark; there were only a few full-grown roosters in Wrangell, half a dozen or so, to awaken the town and give it a civilized character. After sunrise a few languid smoke-columns might be seen, telling the first stir of the people. Soon an Indian or two might be noticed here and there at the doors of their barnlike cabins, and a merchant getting ready for trade; but scarcely a sound was heard, only a dull, muffled stir gradually deepening. There were only two white babies in the town, so far as I saw, and as for Indian babies, they woke and ate and made no crying sound. Later you might hear the croaking of ravens, and the strokes of an axe on firewood. About eight or nine o'clock the town was awake, Indians, mostly women and children, began to gather on the front platforms of the half-dozen stores, sitting carelessly on their blankets, every other face hideously blackened, a naked circle around the eyes, and perhaps a spot on the cheek-bone and the nose where the smut had been rubbed off. Some of the little children were also blackened, and none were over-clad, their light and airy costume consisting of a calico shirt reaching only to the waist. Boys eight or ten years old sometimes had an additional garment – a pair of castaway miner's overalls wide enough and ragged enough for extravagant ventilation. The larger girls and young women were arrayed in showy calico, and wore jaunty straw hats, gorgeously ribboned, and glowed among the blackened and blanketed old crones like scarlet tanagers in a flock of blackbirds. The women, seated on the steps and platform of the traders' shops, could hardly be called loafers, for they had berries to sell, basketfuls of huckleberries, large yellow salmon-berries, and bog raspberries that looked wondrous fresh and clean amid the surrounding squalor. After patiently waiting for purchasers until hungry, they ate what they could not sell, and went away to gather more.

Yonder you see a canoe gliding out from the shore, containing perhaps a man, a woman, and a child or two, all paddling together in natural, easy rhythm. They are going to catch a fish, no difficult matter, and when this is done their day's work is done. Another party puts out to capture bits of driftwood, for it is easier to procure fuel in this way than to drag it down from the outskirts of the woods through rocks and bushes. As the day advances, a fleet of canoes may be seen along the shore, all fashioned alike, high and long beak-like prows and sterns, with lines as fine as those of the breast of a duck. What the mustang is to the Mexican *vaquero*, the canoe is to these coast Indians. They skim along the shores to fish and hunt and trade, or merely to visit their neighbours, for they are sociable, and have family pride remarkably well developed, meeting often to inquire after each other's health, attend potlatches and dances, and gossip concerning coming marriages, births, deaths, etc. Others seem to sail for the pure pleasure of the thing, their canoes decorated with handfuls of the tall purple epilobium.

Yonder goes a whole family, grandparents and all, making a direct course for some favourite stream and camp-ground. They are going to gather berries, as the baskets tell. Never before in all my travels, north or south, had I found so lavish an abundance of berries as here. The woods and meadows are full of them, both on the lowlands and mountains – huckleberries of many species, salmon-berries, blackberries, raspberries, with service-berries on dry open places, and cranberries in the bogs, sufficient for every bird, beast, and human being in the territory and thousands of tons to spare. The huckleberries are especially abundant. A species that grows well up on the mountains is the best and largest, a half-inch and more in diameter and delicious in flavour. These grow on bushes three or four inches to a foot high. The berries of the commonest species are smaller and grow almost everywhere on the low grounds on bushes from three to six or seven feet high. This is the species on which the Indians depend most for food, gathering them in large quantities, beating them into a paste, pressing the paste into cakes about an inch thick, and drying them over a slow fire to enrich their winter stores. Salmon-berries and service-berries are preserved in the same way.

A little excursion to one of the best huckleberry-fields adjacent to Wrangell, under the direction of the Collector of Customs, to which I was invited, I greatly enjoyed. There were nine Indians in the party, mostly women and children going to gather huckleberries. As soon as we had arrived at the chosen camp-ground on the bank of a trout stream, all ran into the bushes and began eating berries before anything in the way of camp-making was done, laughing and chattering in natural animal enjoyment. The Collector went up the stream to examine a meadow at its head with reference to the quantity of hay it might yield for his cow, fishing by the way. All the Indians except the two eldest boys who joined the Collector, remained among the berries.

The fishermen had rather poor luck, owing, they said, to the sunny brightness of the day, a complaint seldom heard in this climate. They got good exercise however, jumping from boulder to boulder in the brawling stream, running along slippery logs and through the bushes that fringe the bank, casting here and there into swirling pools at the foot of cascades, imitating the tempting little skips and whirls of flies so well known to fishing persons, but perhaps still better known to Indian boys. At the lake-basin the Collector, after he had surveyed his hay-meadow, went around it to the inlet of the lake with his brown pair of attendants to try their luck, while I botanised in the delightful flora which called to mind the cool sphagnum and carex bogs of Wisconsin and Canada. Here I found many of my old favourites the heathworts – kalmia, pyrola, chiogenes, huckleberry, cranberry, etc. On the margin of the meadow darling linnaea was in its glory; purple panicled grasses in full flower reached over my head, and some of the carices and ferns were almost as tall. Here, too, on the edge of the woods I found the wild apple tree, the first I had seen in Alaska. The Indians gather the fruit, small and sour as it is, to flavour their fat salmon. I never saw a richer bog and meadow growth anywhere. The principal forest-trees are hemlock, spruce, and Nootka cypress, with a few pines (*P. contorta*) on the margin of the meadow, some of them nearly a hundred feet high, draped with grey usnea, the bark also grey with scale lichens.

We met all the berry-pickers at the lake, excepting only a small girl and the camp-keeper. In their bright colours they made a lively picture among the quivering bushes, keeping up a low pleasant chanting as if the day and the place and the berries were according to their own hearts. The children carried small baskets, holding two or three quarts; the women two large ones swung over their shoulders. In the afternoon, when the baskets were full, all started back to the camp-ground, where the canoe was left. We parted at the lake, I choosing to follow quietly the stream through the woods. I was the first to arrive at camp. The rest of the party came in shortly afterwards, singing and humming like heavy-laden bees. It was interesting to note how kindly they held out handfuls of the best berries to the little girl, who welcomed them all in succession with smiles and merry words that I did not understand. But there was no mistaking the kindliness and serene good nature.

While I was at Wrangell the chiefs and head men of the Stickeen tribe got up a grand dinner and entertainment in honour of their distinguished visitors, three doctors of divinity and their wives, fellow passengers on the steamer with me, whose object was to organise the Presbyterian church. To both the dinner and dances I was invited, was adopted by the Stickeen tribe, and given an Indian name (Ancoutahan) said to mean adopted chief. I was inclined to regard this honour as being unlikely to have any practical value, but I was assured by Mr Vanderbilt, Mr Young and others that it would be a great safeguard while I was on my travels among the different tribes of the archipelago. For travellers without an Indian name might be killed and robbed without the offender being called to account as long as the crime was kept secret from the whites; but, being adopted by the Stickeens, no one belonging to the other tribes would dare attack me, knowing that the Stickeens would hold them responsible.

The dinner-tables were tastefully decorated with flowers, and the food and general arrangements were in good taste, but there was no trace of Indian dishes. It was mostly imported canned stuff served Boston fashion. After the dinner we assembled in Chief Shakes' large block-house and were entertained with lively examples of their dances and amusements, carried on with great spirit, making a very novel barbarous durbar. The dances seemed to me wonderfully like those of the American Indians in general, a monotonous stamping accompanied by hand-clapping, head-jerking, and explosive grunts kept in time to grim drum-beats. The chief dancer and leader scattered great quantities of downy feathers like a snowstorm as blessings on everybody, while all chanted, 'Hee-ee-ah-ah, hee-ee-ah-ah', jumping up and down until all were bathed in perspiration.

After the dancing excellent imitations were given of the gait, gestures, and behaviour of several animals under different circumstances – walking, hunting, capturing, and devouring their prey, etc. While all were quietly seated, waiting to see what next was going to happen, the door of the big house was suddenly thrown open and in bounced a bear, so true to life in form and gestures we were all startled, though it was only a bear-skin nicely fitted on a man who was intimately acquainted with the animals and knew how to imitate them. The bear shuffled down into the middle of the floor and made the motion of jumping into a stream and catching a wooden salmon that was ready for him, carrying it out on to the bank, throwing his head around to listen and see if anyone was coming, then tearing it to pieces, jerking his head from side to side, looking and listening in fear of hunters' rifles. Besides the bear dance, there were porpoise and deer dances with one of the party imitating the animals by stuffed specimens with an Indian inside, and the movements were so accurately imitated that they seemed the real thing.

These animal plays were followed by serious speeches, interpreted by an Indian woman: 'Dear Brothers and Sisters, this is the way we used to dance. We liked it long ago when we were blind, we always danced this way, but now we are not blind. The Good Lord has taken pity upon us and sent his son, Jesus Christ, to tell us what to do. We have danced to-day only to show you how blind we were to like to dance in this foolish way. We will not dance any more.'

Another speech was interpreted as follows: 'Dear Brothers and Sisters, the chief says, "this is the way we used to dance and play. We do not wish to do so any more. We will give away all the dance dresses you have seen us wearing, though we value them very highly." He says he feels much honoured to have so many white brothers and sisters at our dinner and plays.'

Several short explanatory remarks were made all through

the exercises by Chief Shakes, presiding with grave dignity. The last of his speeches concluded thus: 'Dear Brothers and Sisters, we have been long, long in the dark. You have led us into strong guiding light and taught us the right way to live and the right way to die. I thank you for myself and all my people, and I give you my heart.'

At the close of the amusements there was a potlatch when robes made of the skins of deer, wild sheep, marmots, and sables were distributed, and many of the fantastic head-dresses that had been worn by Shamans. One of these fell to my share.

The floor of the house was strewn with fresh hemlock boughs, bunches of showy wild flowers adorned the walls, and the hearth was filled with huckleberry branches and epilobium. Altogether it was a wonderful show.

I have found southeastern Alaska a good, healthy country to live in. The climate of the islands and shores of the mainland is remarkably bland and temperate and free from extremes of either heat or cold throughout the year. It is rainy, however – so much so that hay-making will hardly ever be extensively engaged in here, whatever the future may show in the way of the development of mines, forests, and fisheries. This rainy weather, however, is of good quality, the best of the kind I ever experienced, mild in temperature, mostly gentle in its fall, filling the fountains of the rivers and keeping the whole land fresh and fruitful, while anything more delightful than the shining weather in the midst of the rain, the great round sun-days of July and August, may hardly be found anywhere, north or south. An Alaska summer day is a day without night. In the Far North, at Point Barrow, the sun does not set for weeks, and even here in southeastern Alaska it is only a few degrees below the horizon at its lowest point, and the topmost colours of the sunset blend with those of the sunrise, leaving no gap of darkness between. Midnight is only a low noon, the middle point of the gloaming. The thin clouds that are almost always present and then coloured yellow and red, making a striking advertisement of the sun's progress beneath the horizon. The day opens slowly. 'The low arc of light steals around to the northeastward with gradual increase of height and span and intensity of tone; and when at length the sun appears, it is without much of that stirring, impressive pomp, of flashing, awakening, triumphant energy, suggestive of the Bible imagery, a bridegroom coming out of his chamber and rejoicing like a strong man to run a race. The red clouds with yellow edges dissolve in hazy dimness; the islands, with greyish-white ruffs of mist about them, cast ill-defined shadows on the glistening waters, and the whole down-bending firmament becomes pearlgrey. For three or four hours after sunrise there is nothing especially impressive in the landscape. The sun, though seemingly unclouded, may almost be looked in the face, and the islands and mountains, with their wealth of woods and snow and varied beauty of architecture, seem comparatively sleepy and uncommunicative.

As the day advances toward high noon, the sunflood streaming through the damp atmosphere lights the water levels and the sky to glowing silver. Brightly play the ripples about the bushy edges of the islands and on the plume-shaped streaks between them, ruffled by gentle passing wind-currents. The warm air throbs and makes itself felt as a life-giving, energising ocean, embracing all the landscape, quickening the imagination, and bringing to mind the life and motion about us – the tides, the rivers, the flood of light streaming through the satiny sky; the marvellous abundance of fishes feeding in the lower ocean; the misty flocks of insects in the air; wild sheep and goats on a thousand grassy ridges; beaver and mink far back on many a running stream; Indians floating and basking along the shores; leaves and crystals drinking the sunbeams; and glaciers on the mountains, making valleys and basins for new rivers and lakes and fertile beds of soil.

Through the afternoon, all the way down to the sunset, the day grows in beauty. The light seems to thicken and become yet more generously fruitful without losing its soft mellow brightness. Everything seems to settle into conscious repose. The winds breathe gently or are wholly at rest. The few clouds visible are downy and luminous and combed out fine on the edges. Gulls here and there, winnowing the air on easy wing, are brought into striking relief; and every stroke of the paddles of Indian hunters in their canoes is told by a quick, glancing flash. Bird choirs in the grove are scarce heard as they sweeten the brooding stillness; and the sky, land, and water meet and blend in one inseparable scene of enchantment. Then comes the sunset with its purple and gold, not a narrow arch on the horizon, but oftentimes filling all the sky. The level cloud-bars usually present are fired on the edges, and the spaces of clear sky between them are greenish-yellow or pale amber, while the orderly flocks of small overlapping clouds, often seen higher up, are mostly touched with crimson like the out-leaning sprays of maple-groves in the beginning of an Eastern Indian Summer. Soft, mellow purple flushes the sky to the zenith and fills the air, fairly steeping and transfiguring the islands and making all the water look like wine. After the sun goes down, the glowing gold vanishes, but because it descends on a curve nearly in the same plane with the horizon, the glowing portion of the display lasts much longer than in more southern latitudes, while the upper colours with gradually lessening intensity of tone sweep around to the north, gradually increase to the eastward, and unite with those of the morning.

The most extravagantly coloured of all the sunsets I have yet seen in Alaska was one I enjoyed on the voyage from Portland to Wrangell, when we were in the midst of one of the most thickly islanded parts of the Alexander Archipelago. The day had been showery, but late in the afternoon the clouds melted away from the west, all save a few that settled down in narrow level bars near the horizon. The evening was calm and the sunset colours came on gradually, increasing in extent and richness of tone by slow degrees as if requiring more time than usual to ripen. At a height of about thirty degrees there was a heavy cloud-bank, deeply reddened on its lower edge and the projecting parts of its face. Below this were three horizontal belts of purple edged with gold, while a vividly defined, spreading fan of flame streamed upward across the purple bars and faded in a feather edge of dull red. But beautiful and impressive as was this painting on the sky, the most novel and exciting effect was in the body of the atmosphere itself, which, laden with moisture, became one mass of colour – a fine translucent purple haze in which the islands with softened outlines seemed to float, while a dense red ring lay around the base of each of them as a fitting border. The peaks, too, in the distance, and the snow-fields and glaciers and fleecy rolls of mist that lay in the hollows, were flushed with a deep, rosy alpenglow of ineffable loveliness. Everything near and far, even the ship, was comprehended in the glorious picture and the general colour effect. The mission divines we had aboard seemed then to be truly divine as they gazed transfigured in the celestial glory. So also seemed our bluff, storm-fighting old captain, and his tarry sailors and all.

About one third of the summer days I spent in the Wrangell region were cloudy with very little or no rain, one third decidedly rainy, and one third clear. According to a record kept here of a hundred and forty-seven days beginning 17 May of that year, there were sixty-five on which rain fell, forty-three cloudy with no rain, and thirty-nine clear. In June rain fell on eighteen days, in July eight days, in August fifteen days, in September twenty days. But on some of these days there was only a few minutes' rain, light showers scarce enough to count, while as a general thing the rain fell so gently and the temperature was so mild, very few of them could be called stormy or dismal; even the bleakest, most bedraggled of them all usually had a flush of late or early colour to cheer them, or some white illumination about the noon hours. I never before saw so much rain fall with so little noise. None of the summer winds make roaring storms, and thunder is seldom heard. I heard none at all. This wet, misty weather seems perfectly healthful. There is no mildew in the houses, as far as I have seen, or any tendency toward mouldiness in nooks hidden from the sun; and neither among the people nor the plants do we find anything flabby or dropsical.

In September clear days were rare, more than three fourths of them were either decidedly cloudy or rainy, and the rains of this month were, with one wild exception, only moderately heavy, and the clouds between showers drooped and crawled in a ragged, unsettled way without betraying hints of violence such as one often sees in the gestures of mountain storm-clouds.

July was the brightest month of the summer, with fourteen days of sunshine, six of them in uninterrupted succession, with a temperature at 7 am of about 60°, at 12 am, 70°. The average 7 am temperature for June was 54.3°; the average 7 am temperature for July was 55.3°; at 12 m the average temperature was 61.45°; the average 7 am temperature for August was 54.12°; 12 m, 61.48°; the average 7 am temperature for September was 52.14°; and 12 m, 56.12°.

The highest temperature observed here during the summer was seventy-six degrees. The most remarkable characteristic of this summer weather, even the brightest of it, is the velvet softness of the atmosphere. On the mountains of California, throughout the greater part of the year, the presence of an atmosphere is hardly recognized, and the thin, white, bodiless light of the morning comes to the peaks and glaciers as a pure spiritual essence, the most impressive of all the terrestrial manifestations of God. The clearest of Alaskan air is always appreciably substantial, so much so that it would seem as if one might test its quality by rubbing it between the thumb and finger. I never saw summer days so white and so full of subdued lustre.

The winter storms, up to the end of December when I left Wrangell, were mostly rain at a temperature of thirty-five or forty degrees, with strong winds which sometimes roughly lash the shores and carry scud far into the woods. The long nights are then gloomy enough and the value of snug homes with crackling yellow cedar fires may be finely appreciated. Snow falls frequently, but never to any great depth or to lie long. It is said that only once since the settlement of Fort Wrangell has the ground been covered to a depth of four feet. The mercury seldom falls more than five or six degrees below the freezing-point, unless the wind blows steadily from the mainland. Back from the coast, however, beyond the mountains, the winter months are very cold. On the Stickeen River at Glenora, less than a thousand feet above the level of the sea, a temperature of from thirty to forty degrees below zero is not uncommon.

FOUR

The Stickeen River

The most interesting of the short excursions we made from Fort Wrangell was the one up the Stickeen River to the head of steam navigation. From Mount St Elias the coast range extends in a broad, lofty chain beyond the southern boundary of the territory, gashed by stupendous canyons, each of which carries a lively river, though most of them are comparatively short, as their highest sources lie in the icy solitudes of the range within forty or fifty miles of the coast. A few, however, of these foaming, roaring streams – the Alsek, Chilcat, Chilcoot, Taku, Stickeen, and perhaps others – head beyond the range with some of the southwest branches of the Mackenzie and Yukon.

The largest side branches of the main-trunk canyons of all these mountain streams are still occupied by glaciers which descend in showy ranks, their massy, bulging snouts lying back a little distance in the shadows of the walls, or pushing forward among the cotton-woods that line the banks of the rivers, or even stretching all the way across the main canyons, compelling the rivers to find a channel beneath them.

The Stickeen was, perhaps, the best known of the rivers that cross the Coast Range, because it was the best way to the Mackenzie River Cassiar gold-mines. It is about three hundred and fifty miles long, and is navigable for small steamers a hundred and fifty miles to Glenora, and sometimes to Telegraph Creek, fifteen miles farther. It first pursues a westerly course through grassy plains darkened here and there with groves of spruce and pine; then, curving southward and receiving numerous tributaries from the north, it enters the Coast Range, and sweeps across it through a magnificent canyon three thousand to five thousand feet deep, and more than a hundred miles long. The majestic cliffs and mountains forming the canyon-walls display endless variety of form and sculpture, and are wonderfully adorned and enlivened with glaciers and waterfalls, while throughout almost its whole extent the floor is a flowery landscape garden, like Yosemite. The most striking features are the glaciers hanging over the cliffs, descending the side canyons and pushing forward to the river, greatly enhancing the wild beauty of all the others.

Gliding along the swift-flowing river, the views change with bewildering rapidity. Wonderful, too, are the changes dependent on the seasons and the weather. In spring, when the snow is melting fast, you enjoy the countless rejoicing waterfalls; the gentle breathing of warm winds; the colours of the young leaves and flowers when the bees are busy and wafts of fragrance are drifting hither and thither from miles of wild roses, clover, and honeysuckle; the swaths of birch and willow on the lower slopes following the melting of the winter avalanche snow-banks; the bossy cumuli swelling in white and purple piles above the highest peaks; grey rain-clouds wreathing the outstanding brows and battlements of the walls; and the breaking-forth of the sun after the rain; the shining of the leaves and streams and crystal architecture of the glaciers; the rising of fresh fragrance; the song of the happy birds; and the serene colour-grandeur of the morning and evening sky. In summer you find the groves and gardens in full dress; glaciers melting rapidly under sunshine and rain; waterfalls in all their glory; the river rejoicing in its strength; young birds trying their wings; bears enjoying salmon and berries; all the life of the canyon brimming full like the streams. In autumn comes rest, as if the year's work were done. The rich hazy sunshine streaming over the cliffs calls forth the last of the gentians and goldenrods; the groves and thickets and meadows bloom again as their leaves change to red and yellow petals; the rock also, and the glaciers, seem to bloom like the plants in the mellow golden light. And so goes the song, change succeeding change in sublime harmony through all the wonderful seasons and weather.

*   *   *

My first trip up the river was made in the spring with the missionary party soon after our arrival at Wrangell. We left Wrangell in the afternoon and anchored for the night above the river delta, and started up the river early next morning when the heights above the 'Big Stickeen' Glacier and the smooth domes and copings and arches of solid snow along the tops of the canyon walls were glowing in the early beams. We arrived before noon at the old trading-post called 'Buck's' in front of the Stickeen Glacier, and remained long enough to allow the few passengers who wished a nearer view to cross the river to the terminal moraine. The sunbeams streaming through the ice pinnacles along its terminal wall produced a wonderful glory of colour, and the broad, sparkling crystal prairie and the distant snowy fountains were wonderfully attractive and made me pray for opportunity to explore them.

Of the many glaciers, a hundred or more, that adorn the walls of the great Stickeen River Canyon, this is the largest. It draws its sources from snowy mountains within fifteen or twenty miles of the coast, pours through a comparatively narrow canyon about two miles in width in a magnificent cascade, and expands in a broad fan five or six miles in width, separated from the Stickeen River by its broad terminal moraine, fringed with spruces and willows. Around the beautifully drawn curve of the moraine the Stickeen River flows, having evidently been shoved by the glacier out of its direct course. On the opposite side of the canyon another somewhat smaller glacier, which now terminates four or five miles from the river, was once united front to front with the greater glacier, though at first both were tributaries of the main Stickeen Glacier which once filled the whole grand canyon. After the main trunk canyon was melted out, its side branches, drawing their sources from a height of three or four to five or six thousand feet, were cut off, and of course became separate glaciers, occupying cirques and branch canyons along the tops and sides of the walls. The Indians have a tradition that the river used to run through a tunnel under the united fronts of the two large tributary glaciers mentioned above, which entered the main canyon from either side; and that on one occasion an Indian, anxious to get rid of his wife, had her sent adrift in a canoe down through the ice tunnel, expecting that she would trouble him no more. But to his surprise she floated through under the ice in safety. All the evidence connected with the present appearance of these two glaciers indicates that they were united and formed a dam across the river after the smaller tributaries had been melted off and had receded to a greater or lesser height above the valley floor.

The big Stickeen Glacier is hardly out of sight ere you come upon another that pours a majestic crystal flood through the evergreens, while almost every hollow and tributary canyon contains a smaller one, the size, of course, varying with the extent of the area drained. Some are like mere snow-banks; others, with the blue ice apparent, depend in massive bulging curves and swells, and graduate into the river-like forms that maze through the lower forested regions and are so striking and beautiful that they are admired even by the passing miners with gold-dust in their eyes.

Thirty-five miles above the Big Stickeen Glacier is the 'Dirt Glacier', the second in size. Its outlet is a fine stream, abounding in trout. On the opposite side of the river there is a group of five glaciers, one of them descending to within a hundred feet of the river.

Near Glenora, on the northeastern flank of the main Coast Range, just below a narrow gorge called 'The Canyon', terraces first make their appearance, where great quantities of moraine material have been swept through the flood-choked gorge and of course outspread and deposited on the first open levels below. Here, too, occurs a marked change in climate and consequently in forests and general appearance of the face of the country. On account of destructive fires the woods are younger and are composed of smaller trees about a foot to eighteen inches in diameter and seventy-five feet high, mostly two-leaved pines which hold their seeds for several years after they are ripe. The woods here are without a trace of those deep accumulations of mosses, leaves, and decaying trunks which make so damp and unclearable a mass in the coast forests. Whole mountain-sides are covered with grey moss and lichens where the forest has been utterly destroyed. The river-bank cotton-woods are also smaller, and the birch and contorta pines mingle freely with the coast hemlock and spruce. The birch is common on the lower slopes and is very effective, its round, leafy, pale-green head contrasting with the dark, narrow spires of the conifers and giving a striking character to the forest. The 'tamarac pine' or black pine, as the variety of *P. contorta* is called here, is yellowish-green, in marked contrast with the dark lichen-draped spruce which grows above the pine at a height of about two thousand feet, in groves and belts where it has escaped fire and snow avalanches. There is another handsome spruce hereabouts, *Picea alba*, very slender and graceful in habit, drooping at the top like a mountain hemlock. I saw fine specimens a hundred and twenty-five feet high on deep bottom land a few miles below Glenora. The tops of some of them were almost covered with dense clusters of yellow and brown cones.

We reached the old Hudson's Bay trading-post at Glenora about one o'clock, and the captain informed me that he would stop here until the next morning, when he would make an early start for Wrangell.

At a distance of about seven or eight miles to the northeastward of the landing, there is an outstanding group of mountains crowning a spur from the main chain of the Coast Range, whose highest point rises about eight thousand feet above the level of the sea; and as Glenora is only a thousand feet above the sea, the height to be overcome in climbing this peak is about seven thousand feet. Though the time was short I determined to climb it, because of the advantageous position it occupied for general views of the peaks and glaciers of the east side of the great range.

Although it was now twenty minutes past three and the days were getting short, I thought that by rapid climbing I could reach the summit before sunset in time to get a general view and a few pencil sketches, and make my way back to the steamer in the night. Mr Young, one of the missionaries, asked permission to accompany me, saying that he was a good walker and climber and would not delay me or cause any trouble. I strongly advised him not to go, explaining that it involved a walk, coming and going of fourteen or sixteen miles, and a climb through brush and boulders of seven thousand feet, a fair day's work for a seasoned mountaineer to be done in less than half a day and part of a night. But he insisted that he was a strong walker, could do a mountaineer's day's work in half a day, and would not hinder me in any way.

'Well, I have warned you', I said, 'and will not assume responsibility for any trouble that may arise'.

He proved to be a stout walker, and we made rapid progress across a brushy timbered flat and up the mountain slopes, open in some places, and in others thatched with dwarf firs, resting a minute here and there to refresh ourselves with huckleberries, which grew in abundance in open spots. About half an hour before sunset, when we were near a cluster of crumbling pinnacles that formed the summit, I had ceased to feel anxiety about the mountaineering strength and skill of my companion, and pushed rapidly on. In passing around the shoulder of the highest pinnacle, where the rock was rapidly disintegrating and the danger of slipping was great, I shouted in a warning voice, 'Be very careful here, this is dangerous'.

Mr Young was perhaps a dozen or two yards behind me, but out of sight. I afterwards reproached myself for not stopping and lending him a steadying hand, and showing him the slight footsteps I had made by kicking out little blocks of the crumbling surface, instead of simply warning him to be careful. Only a few seconds after giving this warning, I was startled by a scream for help, and hurrying back, found the missionary face downward, his arms outstretched, clutching little crumbling knobs on the brink of a gully that plunges down a thousand feet or more to a small residual glacier. I managed to get below him, touched one of his feet, and tried to encourage him by saying, 'I am below you. You are in no danger. You can't slip past me and I will soon get you out of this.'

He then told me that both of his arms were dislocated. It was almost impossible to find available footholds on the treacherous rock, and I was at my wits' end to know how to get him rolled or dragged to a place where I could get about him, find out how much he was hurt, and a way back down the mountain. After narrowly scanning the cliff and making footholds, I managed to roll and lift him a few yards to a place where the slope was less steep, and there I attempted to set his arms. I found, however, that this was impossible in such a place. I therefore tied his arms to his sides with my suspenders and necktie, to prevent as much as possible inflammation from movement. I then left him, telling him to lie still, that I would be back in a few minutes, and that he was now safe from slipping. I hastily examined the ground and saw no way of getting him down except by the steep glacier gully. After scrambling to an outstanding point that commands a view of it from top to bottom, to make sure that it was not interrupted by sheer precipices, I concluded that with great care and the digging of slight footholds he could be slid down to the glacier, where I could lay him on his back and perhaps be able to set his arms. Accordingly, I cheered him up, telling him I had found a way, but that it would require lots of time and patience. Digging a footstep in the sand or crumbling rock five or six feet beneath him, I reached up, took hold of him by one of his feet, and gently slid him down on his back, placed his heels in the step, then descended another five or six feet, dug heel notches, and slid him down to them. Thus the whole distance was made by a succession of narrow steps at very short intervals, and the glacier was reached perhaps about midnight. Here I took off one of my boots, tied a handkerchief around his wrist for a good hold, placed my heel in his arm pit, and succeeded in getting one of his arms in place, but my utmost strength was insufficient to reduce the dislocation of the other. I therefore bound it closely to his side, and asked him if in his exhausted and trembling condition he was still able to walk.

'Yes', he bravely replied.

So, with a steadying arm around him and many stops for rest, I marched him slowly down in the starlight on the comparatively smooth, unfissured surface of the little glacier to the terminal moraine, a distance of perhaps a mile, crossed the moraine, bathed his head at one of the outlet streams, and after many rests reached a dry place and made a brush fire. I then went ahead looking for an open way through the bushes to where larger wood could be had, made a good lasting fire of resiny silver-fir roots, and a leafy bed beside it. I now told him I would run down the mountain, hasten back with help from the boat, and carry him down in comfort. But he would not hear of my leaving him.

'No, no', he said, 'I can walk down. Don't leave me.'

I reminded him of the roughness of the way, his nerve-shaken condition, and assured him I would not be gone long. But he insisted on trying, saying on no account whatever must I leave him. I therefore concluded to try to get him to the ship by short walks from one fire and resting-place to another. While he was resting I went ahead, looking for the best way through the brush and rocks, then returning, got him on his feet and made him lean on my shoulder while I steadied him to prevent his falling. This slow, staggering struggle from fire to fire lasted until long after sunrise. When at last we reached the ship and stood at the foot of the narrow single plank without side rails that reached from the bank to the deck at a considerable angle, I briefly explained to Mr Young's companions, who stood looking down at us, that he had been hurt in an accident, and requested one to assist me in getting him aboard. But strange to say, instead of coming down to help, they made haste to reproach him for having gone on a 'wild-goose chase' with Muir.

'These foolish adventures are well enough for Mr Muir', they said, 'but you, Mr Young, have a work to do; you have a family; you have a church, and you have no right to risk your life on treacherous peaks and precipices'.

The captain, Nat Lane, son of Senator Joseph Lane, had been swearing in angry impatience for being compelled to make so late a start and thus encounter a dangerous wind in a narrow gorge, and was threatening to put the missionaries ashore to seek their lost companion, while he went on down the river about his business. But when he heard my call for help, he hastened forward, and elbowed the divines away from the end of the gangplank, shouting in angry irreverence, 'Oh, blank! This is no time for preaching! Don't you see the man is hurt?'

He ran down to our help, and while I steadied my trembling companion from behind, the captain kindly led him up the plank into the saloon, and made him drink a large glass of brandy. Then, with a man holding down his shoulders, we succeeded in getting the bone into its socket, notwithstanding the inflammation and contraction of the muscles and ligaments. Mr Young was then put to bed, and he slept all the way back to Wrangell.

In his mission lectures in the East, Mr Young oftentimes told his story. I made no record of it in my notebook and never intended to write a word about it; but after a miserable, sensational caricature of the story had appeared in a respectable magazine, I though it but fair to my brave companion that it should be told just as it happened.

FIVE

A Cruise in the Cassiar

Shortly after our return to Wrangell the missionaries planned a grand mission excursion up the coast of the mainland to the Chilcat country, which I gladly joined, together with Mr Vanderbilt, his wife, and a friend from Oregon. The river steamer Cassiar was chartered, and we had her all to ourselves, ship and officers at our command to sail and stop where and when we would, and of course everybody felt important and hopeful. The main object of the missionaries was to ascertain the spiritual wants of the warlike Chilcat tribe, with a view to the establishment of a church and school in their principal village; the merchant and his party were bent on business and scenery; while my mind was on the mountains, glaciers, and forests.

This was toward the end of July, in the very brightest and best of Alaska summer weather, when the icy mountains towering in the pearly sky were displayed in all their glory, and the islands at their feet seemed to float and drowse on the shining mirror waters.

After we had passed through the Wrangell Narrows, the mountains of the mainland came in full view, gloriously arrayed in snow and ice, some of the largest and most river-like of the glaciers flowing through wide, high-walled valleys like Yosemite, their sources far back and concealed, others in plain sight, from their highest fountains to the level of the sea.

Cares of every kind were quickly forgotten, and though the Cassiar engines soon began to wheeze and sigh with doleful solemnity, suggesting coming trouble, we were too happy to mind them. Every face glowed with natural love of wild beauty. The islands were seen in long perspective, their forests dark green in the foreground, with varying tones of blue growing more and more tender in the distance; bays full of hazy shadows, graduating into open, silvery fields of light, and lofty headlands with fine arching insteps dipping their feet in the shining water. But every eye was turned to the mountains. Forgotten now were the Chilcats and missions while the word of God was being read in these majestic hieroglyphics blazoned along the sky. The earnest, childish wonderment with which this glorious page of Nature's Bible was contemplated was delightful to see. All evinced eager desire to learn.

'Is that a glacier', they asked, 'down in that canyon? And is it all solid ice?'

'Yes.'

'How deep is it?'

'Perhaps five hundred or a thousand feet.'

'You say it flows. How can hard ice flow?'

'It flows like water, though invisibly slow.'

'And where does it come from?'

'From snow that is heaped up every winter on the mountains.'

'And how, then, is the snow changed into ice?'

'It is welded by the pressure of its own weight.'

'Are these white masses we see in the hollows glaciers also?'

'Yes.'

'Are those bluish draggled masses hanging down from beneath the snow-fields what you call the snouts of the glaciers?'

'Yes.'

'What made the hollows they are in?'

'The glaciers themselves, just as travelling animals make their own tracks.'

'How long have they been there?'

'Numberless centuries', etc. I answered as best I could, keeping up a running commentary on the subject in general, while busily engaged in sketching and noting my own observations, preaching glacial gospel in a rambling way, while the Cassiar, slowly wheezing and creeping along the shore, shifted our position so that the icy canyons were opened to view and closed again in regular succession, like the leaves of a book.

About the middle of the afternoon we were directly opposite a noble group of glaciers some ten in number, flowing from a chain of crater-like snow fountains, guarded around their summits and well down their sides by jagged peaks and cols and curving mural ridges. From each of the larger clusters of fountains, a wide, sheer-walled canyon opens down to the sea. Three of the trunk glaciers descend to within a few feet of the sea-level. The largest of the three, probably about fifteen miles long, terminates in a magnificent valley like Yosemite, in an imposing wall of ice about two miles long, and from three to five hundred feet high, forming a barrier across the valley from wall to wall. It was to this glacier that the ships of the Alaska Ice Company resorted for the ice they carried to San Francisco and the Sandwich Islands, and, I believe, also to China and Japan. To load, they had only to sail up the fiord within a short distance of the front and drop anchor in the terminal moraine.

Another glacier, a few miles to the south of this one, receives two large tributaries about equal in size, and then flows down a forested valley to within a hundred feet or so of sea-level. The third of this low-descending group is four or five miles farther south, and, though less imposing than either of the two sketched above, is still a truly noble object, even as imperfectly seen from the channel, and would of itself be well worth a visit to Alaska to any lowlander so unfortunate as never to have seen a glacier.

The boilers of our little steamer were not made for sea water, but it was hoped that fresh water would be found at available points along our course where streams leap down the cliffs. In this particular we failed, however, and were compelled to use salt water an hour or two before reaching Cape Fanshawe, the supply of fifty tons of fresh water brought from Wrangell having then given out. To make matters worse, the captain and engineer were not in accord concerning the working of the engines. The captain repeatedly called for more steam, which the engineer refused to furnish, cautiously keeping the pressure low because the salt water foamed in the boilers and some of it passed over into the cylinders, causing heavy thumping at the end of each piston stroke, and threatening to knock out the cylinder-heads. At seven o'clock in the evening we had made only about seventy miles, which caused dissatisfaction, especially among the divines, who thereupon called a meeting in the cabin to consider what had better be done. In the discussions that followed much indignation and economy were brought to light. We had chartered the boat for sixty dollars per day, and the round trip was to have been made in four or five days. But at the present rate of speed it was found that the cost of the trip for each passenger would be five or ten dollars above the first estimate. Therefore, the majority ruled that we must return next day to Wrangell, the extra dollars outweighing the mountains and missions as if they had suddenly become dust in the balance.

Soon after the close of this economical meeting, we came to anchor in a beautiful bay, and as the long northern day had still hours of good light to offer, I gladly embraced the opportunity to go ashore to see the rocks and plants. One of the Indians, employed as a deck hand on the steamer, landed me at the mouth of a stream. The tide was low, exposing a luxuriant growth of algae, which sent up a fine, fresh sea smell. The shingle was composed of slate, quartz, and granite, named in the order of abundance. The first land plant met was a tall grass, nine feet high, forming a meadow-like margin in front of the forest. Pushing my way well back into the forest, I found it composed almost entirely of spruce and two hemlocks (*Picea sitchensis, Tsuga heterophylla* and *T. mertensiana*) with a few specimens of yellow cypress. The ferns were developed in remarkable beauty and size – aspidiums, one of which is about six feet high, a woodsia, lomaria, and several species of polypodium. The underbrush is chiefly alder, rubus, ledum, three species of vaccinium, and *Echinopanax horrida*, the whole about from six to eight feet high, and in some places closely intertangled and hard to penetrate. On the opener spots beneath the trees the ground is covered to a depth of two or three feet with mosses of indescribable freshness and beauty, a few dwarf cornels often planted on their rich furred bosses, together with pyrola, coptis, and Solomon's-seal. The tallest of the trees are about a hundred and fifty feet high, with a diameter of about four or five feet, their branches mingling together and making a perfect shade. As the twilight began to fall, I sat down on the mossy instep of a spruce. Not a bush or tree was moving; every leaf seemed hushed in brooding repose. One bird, a thrush, embroidered the silence with cheery notes, making the solitude familiar and sweet, while the solemn monotone of the stream sifting through the woods seemed like the very voice of God, humanized, terrestrialized, and entering one's heart as to a home prepared for it. Go where we will, all the world over, we seem to have been there before.

The stream was bridged at short intervals with picturesque, moss-embossed logs, and the trees on its banks, leaning over from side to side, made high embowering arches. The log bridge I crossed was, I think, the most beautiful of the kind I ever saw. The massive log is plushed to a depth of six inches or more with mosses of three or four species, their different tones of yellow shading finely into each other, while their delicate fronded branches and foliage lie in exquisite order, inclining outward and down the sides in rich, furred, clasping sheets overlapping and felted together until the required thickness is attained. The pedicels and spore-cases give a purplish tinge, and the whole bridge is enriched with ferns and a row of small seedling trees and currant bushes with coloured leaves, every one of which seems to have been culled from the woods for this special use, so perfectly do they harmonise in size, shape, and colour with the mossy cover, the width of the span, and the luxuriant, brushy abutments.

Sauntering back to the beach, I found four or five Indian deck hands getting water, with whom I returned aboard the steamer, thanking the Lord for so noble an addition to my life as was this one big mountain, forest, and glacial day.

Next morning most of the company seemed uncomfortably conscience-stricken, and ready to do anything in the way of compensation for our broken excursion that would not cost too much. It was not found difficult, therefore, to convince the captain and disappointed passengers that instead of creeping back to Wrangell direct we should make an expiatory branch-excursion to the largest of the three low-descending glaciers we had passed. The Indian pilot, well acquainted with this part of the coast, declared himself willing to guide us. The water in these fiord channels is generally deep and safe, and though at wide intervals rocks rise abruptly here and there, lacking only a few feet in height to enable them to take rank as islands, the flat-bottomed Cassiar drew but little more water than a duck, so that even the most timid raised no objection on this score. The cylinder-heads of our engines were the main source of anxiety; provided they could be kept on all might yet be well. But in this matter there was evidently some distrust, the engineer having imprudently informed some of the passengers that in consequence of using salt water in his frothing boilers the cylinder-heads might fly off at any moment. To the glacier, however, it was at length decided we should venture.

Arriving opposite the mouth of its fiord, we steered straight inland between beautiful wooded shores, and the grand glacier came in sight in its granite valley, glowing in the early sunshine and extending a noble invitation to come and see. After we passed between the two mountain rocks that guard the gate of the fiord, the view that was unfolded fixed every eye in wondering admiration. No words can convey anything like an adequate conception of its sublime grandeur – the noble simplicity and fineness of the sculpture of the walls; their magnificent proportions; their cascades, gardens, and forest adornments; the placid fiord between them; the great white and blue ice wall, and the snow-laden mountains beyond. Still more important are words in telling the peculiar awe one experiences in entering these mansions of the icy North, notwithstanding it is only the natural effect of appreciable manifestations of the presence of God.

Standing in the gateway of this glorious temple, and regarding it only as a picture, its outlines may be easily traced, the water foreground of a pale-green colour, a smooth mirror sheet sweeping back five or six miles like one of the lower reaches of a great river, bounded at the head by a bevelled barrier wall of blueish-white ice four or five hundred feet high. A few snowy mountain-tops appear beyond it, and on either hand rise a series of majestic, pale-grey granite rocks from three to four thousand feet high, some of them thinly forested and striped with bushes and flowery grass on narrow shelves, especially about half-way up, others severely sheer and bare and built together into walls like those of Yosemite, extending far beyond the ice barrier, one immense brow appearing beyond another with their bases buried in the glacier. This is a Yosemite Valley in process of formation, the modelling and sculpture of the walls nearly completed and well planted, but no groves as yet or gardens or meadows on the raw and unfinished bottom. It is as if the explorer, in entering the Merced Yosemite, should find the walls nearly in their present condition, trees and flowers in the warm nooks and along the sunny portions of the moraine-covered brows, but the bottom of the valley still covered with water and beds of gravel and mud, and the grand glacier that formed it slowly receding but still filling the upper half of the valley.

Sailing directly up the edge of the low, outspread, water-washed terminal moraine, scarce noticeable in a general view, we seemed to be separated from the glacier only by a bed of gravel a hundred yards or so in width; but on so grand a scale are all the main features of the valley, we afterwards found the distance to be a mile or more.

The captain ordered the Indian deck hands to get out the canoe, take as many of us ashore as wished to go, and accompany us to the glacier in case we should need their help. Only three of the company, in the first place, availed themselves of this rare opportunity of meeting a glacier in the flesh – Mr Young, one of the doctors, and myself. Paddling to the nearest and driest-looking part of the moraine flat, we stepped ashore, but gladly wallowed back into the canoe; for the grey mineral mud, a paste made of fine-ground mountain meal kept unstable by the tides, at once began to take us in, swallowing us feet foremost with becoming glacial deliberation. Our next attempt, made nearer the middle of the valley, was successful, and we soon found ourselves on firm gravelly ground, and made haste to the huge ice wall, which seemed to recede as we advanced. The only difficulty we met was a network of icy streams, at the largest of which we halted, not willing to get wet in fording. The Indian attendant promptly carried us over on his back. When my turn came I told him I would ford, but he bowed his shoulders in so ludicrously persuasive a manner I thought I would try the queer mount, the only one of the kind I had enjoyed since boyhood days in playing leapfrog. Away staggered my perpendicular mule over the boulders into the brawling torrent, and in spite of top-heavy predictions to the contrary, crossed without a fall. After being ferried in this way over several more of these glacial streams, we at length reached the foot of the glacier wall. The doctor simply played tag on it, touched it gently as if it were a dangerous wild beast, and hurried back to the boat, taking the portage Indian with him for safety, little knowing what he was missing. Mr Young and I traced the glorious crystal wall, admiring its wonderful architecture, the play of light in the rifts and caverns, and the structure of the ice as displayed in the less fractured sections, finding fresh beauty everywhere and facts for study. We then tried to climb it, and by dint of patient zigzagging and doubling among the crevasses, and cutting steps here and there, we made our way up over the brow and back a mile or two to a height of about seven hundred feet. The whole front of the glacier is gashed and sculptured into a maze of shallow caves and crevasses, and a bewildering variety of novel architectural forms, clusters of glittering lance-tipped spires, gables, and obelisks, bold outstanding bastions and plain mural cliffs, adorned along the top with fretted cornice and battlement, while every gorge and crevasse, groove and hollow, was filled with light, shimmering and throbbing in pale-blue tones of ineffable tenderness and beauty. The day was warm, and back on the broad melting bosom of the glacier beyond the crevassed front, many streams were rejoicing, gurgling, ringing, singing, in frictionless channels worn down through the white disintegrated ice of the surface into the quick and living blue, in which they flowed with a grace of motion and flashing of light to be found only on the crystal hillocks and ravines of a glacier.

Along the sides of the glacier we saw the mighty flood grinding against the granite walls with tremendous pressure, rounding outswelling bosses, and deepening the retreating hollows into the forms they are destined to have when, in the fullness of appointed time, the huge ice tool shall be withdrawn by the sun. Every feature glowed with intention, reflecting the plans of God. Back a few miles from the front, the glacier is now probably but little more than a thousand feet deep; but when we examine the records on the walls, the rounded, grooved, striated, and polished features so surely glacial, we learn that in the earlier days of the ice age they were all over-swept, and that this glacier has flowed at a height of from three to four thousand feet above its present level, when it was at least a mile deep.

Standing here, with facts so fresh and telling and held up so vividly before us, every seeing observer, not to say geologist, must readily apprehend the earth-sculpturing, landscape-making action of flowing ice. And here, too, one learns that the world, though made, is yet being made; that this is still the morning of creation; that mountains long conceived are now being born, channels traced for coming rivers, basins hollowed for lakes; that moraine soil is being ground and outspread for coming plants, – coarse boulders and gravel for forests, finer soil for grasses and flowers – while the finest part of the grist, seen hastening out to sea in the draining streams, is being stored away in darkness and builded particle on particle, cementing and crystallizing, to make the mountains and valleys and plains of other predestined landscapes, to be followed by still others in endless rhythm and beauty.

Gladly would we have camped out on this grand old landscape mill to study its ways and works; but we had no bread and the captain was keeping the Cassiar whistle screaming for our return. Therefore, in mean haste, we threaded our way back through the crevasses and down the blue cliffs, snatched a few flowers from a warm spot on the edge of the ice, plashed across the moraine streams, and were paddled aboard, rejoicing in the possession of so blessed a day, and feeling that in very foundational truth we had been in one of God's own temples and had seen Him and heard Him working and preaching like a man.

Steaming solemnly out of the fiord and down the coast, the islands and mountains were again passed in review; the clouds that so often hide the mountaintops even in good weather were now floating high above them, and the transparent shadows they cast were scarce perceptible on the white glacier fountains. So abundant and novel are the objects of interest in a pure wilderness that unless you are pursuing special studies it matters little where you go, or how often to the same place. Wherever you chance to be always seems at the moment of all places the best; and you feel that there can be no happiness in this world or in any other for those who may not be happy here. The bright hours were spent in making notes and sketches and getting more of the wonderful region into memory. In particular a second view of the mountains made me raise my first estimate of their height. Some of them must be seven or eight thousand feet at the least. Also the glaciers seemed larger and more numerous. I counted nearly a hundred, large and small, between a point ten or fifteen miles to the north of Cape Fanshawe and the mouth of the Stickeen River. We made no more landings, however, until we had passed through the Wrangell Narrows and dropped anchor for the night in a small sequestered bay. This was about sunset, and I eagerly seized the opportunity to go ashore in the canoe and see what I could learn. It is here only a step from the marine algae to terrestrial vegetation of almost tropical luxuriance. Parting the alders and huckleberry bushes and the crooked stems of the prickly panax, I made my way into the woods, and lingered in the twilight doing nothing in particular, only measuring a few of the trees, listening to learn what birds and animals might be about, and gazing along the dusky aisles.

In the meantime another excursion was being invented, one of small size and price. We might have reached Fort Wrangell this evening instead of anchoring here; but the owners of the Cassiar would then receive only ten dollars fare from each person, while they had incurred considerable expense in fitting up the boat for this special trip, and had treated us well. No, under the circumstances, it would never do to return to Wrangell so meanly soon.

It was decided, therefore, that the Cassiar Company should have the benefit of another day's hire, in visiting the old deserted Stickeen village fourteen miles to the south of Wrangell.

'We shall have a good time', one of the most influential of the party said to me in a semi-apologetic tone, as if dimly recognizing my disappointment in not going on to Chilcat. 'We shall probably find stone axes and other curiosities. Chief Kadachan is going to guide us, and there are interesting old buildings and totem poles to be seen.'

It seemed strange, however, that so important a mission to the most influential of the Alaskan tribes should end in a deserted village. But divinity abounded nevertheless; the day was divine and there was plenty of natural religion in the newborn landscapes that were being baptized in sunshine, and sermons in the glacial boulders on the beach where we landed.

The site of the old village is on an outswelling strip of ground about two hundred yards long and fifty wide, sloping gently to the water with a strip of gravel and tall grass in front, dark woods back of it, and charming views over the water among the islands – a delightful place. The tide was low when we arrived, and I noticed that the exposed boulders on the beach – granite erratics that had been dropped by the melting ice toward the close of the glacial period – were piled in parallel rows at right angles to the shore-line, out of the way of the canoes that had belonged to the village.

Most of the party sauntered along the shore; for the ruins were overgrown with tall nettles, elder bushes, and prickly rubus vines through which it was difficult to force a way. In company with the most eager of the relic-seekers and two Indians, I pushed back among the dilapidated dwellings. They were deserted some sixty or seventy years before, and some of them were at least a hundred years old. So said our guide, Kadachan, and his word was corroborated by the venerable aspect of the ruins. Though the damp climate is destructive, many of the house timbers were still in a good state of preservation, particularly those hewn from the yellow cypress, or cedar as it is called here. The magnitude of the ruins and the excellence of the workmanship manifest in them was astonishing as belonging to Indians. For example, the first dwelling we visited was about forty feet square, with walls built of planks two feet wide and six inches thick. The ridgepole of yellow cypress was two feet in diameter, forty feet long, and as round and true as if it had been turned in a lathe; and, though lying in the damp weeds, it was still perfectly sound. The nibble marks of the stone adze were still visible, though crusted over with scale lichens in most places. The pillars that had supported the ridgepole were still standing in some of the ruins. They were all, as far as I observed, carved into life-size figures of men, women, and children, fishes, birds, and various other animals, such as the beaver, wolf, or bear. Each of the wall planks had evidently been hewn out of a whole log, and must have required sturdy deliberation as well as skill. Their geometrical truthfulness was admirable. With the same tools not one in a thousand of our skilled mechanics could do as good work. Compared with it the bravest work of civilized backwoodsmen is feeble and bungling. The completeness of form, finish, and proportion of these timbers suggested skill of a wild and positive kind, like that which guides the woodpecker in drilling round holes, and the bee in making its cells.

The carved totem-pole monuments are the most striking of the objects displayed here. The simplest of them consisted of a smooth, round post fifteen or twenty feet high and about eighteen inches in diameter, with the figure of some animal on top – a bear, porpoise, eagle, or raven, about life-size or larger. These were the totems of the families that occupied the houses in front of which they stood. Others supported the figure of a man or woman, life-size or larger, usually in a sitting posture, said to resemble the dead whose ashes were contained in a closed cavity in the pole. The largest were thirty or forty feet high, carved from top to bottom into human and animal totem figures, one above another, with their limbs grotesquely doubled and folded. Some of the most imposing were said to commemorate some event of an historical character. But a telling display of family pride seemed to have been the prevailing motive. All the figures were more or less rude, and some were broadly grotesque, but there was never any feebleness or obscurity in the expression. On the contrary, every feature showed grave force and decision; while the childish audacity displayed in the designs, combined with manly strength in their execution, was truly wonderful.

The coloured lichens and mosses gave them a venerable air, while the larger vegetation often found on such as were most decayed produced a picturesque effect. Here, for example, is a bear five or six feet long, reposing on top of his lichen-clad pillar, with paws comfortably folded, a tuft of grass growing in each ear and rubus bushes along his back. And yonder is an old chief poised on a taller pillar, apparently gazing out over the landscape in contemplative mood, a tuft of bushes leaning back with a jaunty air from the top of his weatherbeaten hat, and downy mosses about his massive lips. But no rudeness or grotesqueness that may appear, however combined with the decorations that nature has added, may possibly provoke mirth. The whole work is serious in aspect and brave and true in execution.

Similar monuments are made by other Thlinkit tribes. The erection of a totem pole is made a grand affair, and is often talked of for a year or two beforehand. A feast, to which many are invited, is held, and the joyous occasion is spent in eating, dancing, and the distribution of gifts. Some of the larger specimens cost a thousand dollars or more. From one to two hundred blankets, worth three dollars apiece, are paid to the genius who carves them, while the presents and feast usually cost twice as much, so that only the wealthy families can afford them. I talked with an old Indian who pointed out one of the carvings he had made in the Wrangell village, for which he told me had received forty blankets, a gun, a canoe, and other articles, all together worth about $170. Mr Swan, who has contributed much information concerning the British Columbian and Alaskan tribes, describes a totem pole that cost $2500. They are always planted firmly in the ground and stand fast, showing the sturdy erectness of their builders.

While I was busy with my pencil, I heard chopping going on at the north end of the village, followed by a heavy thud, as if a tree had fallen. It appeared that after digging about the old hearth in the first dwelling visited without finding anything of consequence, the archaeological doctor called the steamer deck hands to one of the most interesting of the totems and directed them to cut it down, saw off the principal figure – a woman measuring three feet three inches across the shoulders – and convey it aboard the steamer, with a view to taking it on East to enrich some museum or other. This sacrilege came near causing trouble and would have cost us dear had the totem not chanced to belong to the Kadachan family, the representative of which is a member of the newly organized Presbyterian Church. Kadachan looked very seriously into the face of the reverend doctor and pushed home the pertinent question: 'How would you like to have an Indian go to a graveyard and break down and carry away a monument belonging to your family?'

However, the religious relations of the parties and a few trifling presents embedded in apologies served to hush and mend the matter.

Some time in the afternoon the steamer whistle called us together to finish our memorable trip. There was no trace of decay in the sky; a glorious sunset gilded the water and cleared away the shadows of our meditations among the ruins. We landed at the Wrangell wharf at dusk, pushed our way through a group of inquisitive Indians, across the two crooked streets, and up to our homes in the fort. We had been away only three days, but they were so full of novel scenes and impressions the time seemed indefinitely long, and our broken Chilcat excursion, far from being a failure as it seemed to some, was one of the most memorable of my life.

SIX

The Cassiar Trail

I made a second trip up the Stickeen in August and from the head of navigation pushed inland for general views over dry grassy hills and plains on the Cassiar trail.

Soon after leaving Telegraph Creek I met a merry trader who encouragingly assured me that I was going into the most wonderful region in the world, that 'the scenery up the river was full of the very wildest freaks of nature, surpassing all other sceneries either natural or artificial, on paper or in nature. And give yourself no bothering care about provisions, for wild food grows in prodigious abundance everywhere. A man was lost four days up there, but he feasted on vegetables and berries and got back to camp in good condition. A mess of wild parsnips and pepper, for example, will actually do you good. And here's my advice – go slow and take the pleasures and sceneries as you go.'

At the confluence of the first North Fork of the Stickeen I found a band of Toltan or Stick Indians catching their winter supply of salmon in willow traps, set where the fish are struggling in swift rapids on their way to the spawning-grounds. A large supply had already been secured, and of course the Indians were well fed and merry. They were camping in large booths made of poles set on end in the ground, with many binding cross-pieces on which tons of salmon were being dried. The heads were strung on separate poles and the roes packed in willow baskets, all being well smoked from fires in the middle of the floor. The largest of the booths near the bank of the river was about forty feet square. Beds made of spruce and pine boughs were spread all around the walls, on which some of the Indians lay asleep; some were braiding ropes, others sitting and lounging, gossiping and courting, while a little baby was swinging in a hammock. All seemed to be light-hearted and jolly, with work enough and wit enough to maintain health and comfort. In the winter they are said to dwell in substantial huts in the woods, where game, especially caribou, is abundant. They are pale copper-coloured, have small feet and hands, are not at all negroish in lips or cheeks like some of the coast tribes, nor so thickset, short-necked, or heavy-featured in general. One of the most striking of the geological features of this region are immense gravel deposits displayed in sections on the walls of the river gorges. About two miles above the North Fork confluence there is a bluff of basalt three hundred and fifty feet high, and above this a bed of gravel four hundred feet thick, while beneath the basalt there is another bed at least fifty feet thick.

From 'Ward's', seventeen miles beyond Telegraph, and about fourteen hundred feet above sea-level, the trail ascends a gravel ridge to a pine-and-fir-covered plateau twenty-one hundred feet above the sea. Thence for three miles the trail leads through a forest of short, closely planted trees to the second North Fork of the Stickeen, where a still greater deposit of stratified gravel is displayed, a section at least six hundred feet thick resting on a red jaspery formation.

Nine hundred feet above the river there is a slightly dimpled plateau diversified with aspen and willow groves and mossy meadows. At 'Wilson's', one and a half miles from the river, the ground is carpeted with dwarf manzanita and the blessed *Linnoea borealis*, and forested with small pines, spruces, and aspens, the tallest fifty to sixty feet high.

From Wilson's to 'Caribou', fourteen miles, no water was visible, though the nearly level, mossy ground is swampy-looking. At 'Caribou Camp', two miles from the river, I saw two fine dogs, a Newfoundland and a spaniel. Their owner told me that he paid only twenty dollars for the team and was offered one hundred dollars for one of them a short time afterwards. The Newfoundland, he said, caught salmon on the ripples, and could be sent back for miles to fetch horses. The fine jet-black curly spaniel helped to carry the dishes from the table to the kitchen, went for water when ordered, took the pail and set it down at the stream-side, but could not be taught to dip it full. But their principal work was hauling camp-supplies on sleds up the river in winter. These two were said to be able to haul a load of a thousand pounds when the ice was in fairly good condition. They were fed on dried fish and oatmeal boiled together.

The timber hereabouts is mostly willow or poplar on the low ground, with here and there pine, birch, and spruce about fifty feet high. None seen much exceeded a foot in diameter. Thousand-acre patches have been destroyed by fire. Some of the green trees had been burned off at the root, the raised roots, packed in dry moss, being readily attacked from beneath. A range of mountains about five thousand to six thousand feet high trending nearly north and south for sixty miles is forested to the summit. Only a few cliff-faces and one of the highest points patched with snow are treeless. No part of this range as far as I could see is deeply sculptured, though the general denudation of the country must have been enormous as the gravel-beds show.

At the top of a smooth, flowery pass about four thousand feet above the sea, beautiful Dease Lake comes suddenly in sight, shining like a broad tranquil river between densely forested hills and mountains. It is about twenty-seven miles long, one to two miles wide, and its waters, tributary to the Mackenzie, flow into the Arctic Ocean by a very long, round-about, romantic way, the exploration of which in 1789 from Great Slave Lake to the Arctic Ocean must have been a glorious task for the heroic Scotchman, Alexander Mackenzie, whose name it bears.

Dease Creek, a fine rushing stream about forty miles long and forty or fifty feet wide, enters the lake from the west, drawing its sources from grassy mountain-ridges. Thibert Creek, about the same size, and McDames and Defot Creeks, with their many branches, head together in the same general range of mountains or on moor-like tablelands on the divide between the Mackenzie and Yukon and Stickeen. All these Mackenzie streams have proved rich in gold. The wing-dams, flumes, and sluice-boxes on the lower five or ten miles of their courses showed wonderful industry, and the quantity of glacial and perhaps preglacial gravel displayed was enormous. Some of the beds were not unlike those of the so-called Dead Rivers of California. Several ancient drift-filled channels on Thibert Creek, blue at bed rock, were exposed and had been worked. A considerable portion of the gold, though mostly coarse, had no doubt come from considerable distances, as boulders included in some of the deposits show. The deepest beds, though known to be rich, had not yet been worked to any great depth on account of expense. Diggings that yield less than five dollars a day to the man were considered worthless. Only three of the claims on Defot Creek, eighteen miles from the mouth of Thibert Creek, were then said to pay. One of the nuggets from this creek weighed forty pounds.

While wandering about the banks of these gold-besprinkled streams, looking at the plants and mines and miners, I was so fortunate as to meet an interesting French Canadian, an old *coureur de bois*, who after a few minutes' conversation invited me to accompany him to his gold-mine on the head of Defot Creek, near the summit of a smooth, grassy mountain-ridge which he assured me commanded extensive views of the region at the heads of Stickeen, Taku, Yukon, and Mackenzie tributaries. Although heavy-laden with flour and bacon, he strode lightly along the rough trails as if his load was only a natural balanced part of his body. Our way at first lay along Thibert Creek, now on gravel benches, now on bed rock, now close down on the bouldery edge of the stream. Above the mines the stream is clear and flows with a rapid current. Its banks are embossed with moss and grass and sedge well mixed with flowers – daisies, larkspurs, solidagos, parnassia, potentilla, strawberry, etc. Small strips of meadow occur here and there, and belts of slender arrowy fir and spruce with moss-clad roots grow close to the water's edge. The creek is about forty-five miles long, and the richest of its goldbearing beds so far discovered were on the lower four miles of the creek; the higher four-or-five-dollars-a-day diggings were considered very poor on account of the high price of provisions and shortness of the season. After crossing many smaller streams with their strips of trees and meadows, bogs and bright wild gardens, we arrived at the Le Claire cabin about the middle of the afternoon. Before entering it he threw down his burden and made haste to show me his favourite flower, a blue forget-me-not, a specimen of which he found within a few rods of the cabin, and proudly handed it to me with the finest respect, and telling its many charms and lifelong associations, showed in every endearing look and touch and gesture that the tender little plant of the mountain wilderness was truly his best-loved darling.

After luncheon we set out for the highest point on the dividing ridge about a mile above the cabin, and sauntered and gazed until sundown, admiring the vast expanse of open rolling prairie-like highlands dotted with grooves and lakes, the fountain-heads of countless cool, glad streams.

Le Claire's simple, childlike love of nature, preserved undimmed through a hard wilderness life, was delightful to see. The grand landscapes with their lakes and streams, plants and animals, all were dear to him. In particular he was fond of the birds that nested near his cabin, watched the young, and in stormy weather helped their parents to feed and shelter them. Some species were so confiding they learned to perch on his shoulders and take crumbs from his hand.

A little before sunset snow began to fly, driven by a cold wind, and by the time we reached the cabin, though we had not far to go, everything looked wintry. At half-past nine we ate supper, while a good fire crackled cheerily in the ingle and a wintry wind blew hard. The little log cabin was only ten feet long, eight wide, and just high enough under the roof peak to allow one to stand upright. The bedstead was not wide enough for two, so Le Claire spread the blankets on the floor, and we gladly lay down after our long, happy walk, our heads under the bedstead, our feet against the opposite wall, and though comfortably tired, it was long ere we fell asleep, for Le Claire, finding me a good listener, told many stories of his adventurous life with Indians, bears and wolves, snow and hunger, and of his many camps in the Canadian woods, hidden like the nests and dens of wild animals; stories that have a singular interest to everybody, for they awaken inherited memories of the lang, lang syne when we were all wild. He had nine children, he told me, the youngest eight years of age, and several of his daughters were married. His home was in Victoria.

Next morning was cloudy and windy, snowy and cold, dreary December weather in August, and I gladly ran out to see what I might learn. A grey ragged-edged cloud capped the top of the divide, its snowy fringes drawn out by the wind. The flowers, though most of them were buried or partly so, were to some extent recognizable, the bluebells bent over, shining like eyes through the snow, and the gentians, too, with their corollas twisted shut; cassiope I could recognize under any disguise; and two species of dwarf willow with their seeds already ripe, one with comparatively small leaves, were growing in mere cracks and crevices of rock-ledges where the dry snow could not lie. Snowbirds and ptarmigan were flying briskly in the cold wind, and on the edge of a grove I saw a spruce from which a bear had stripped large sections of bark for food.

About nine o'clock the clouds lifted and I enjoyed another wide view from the summit of the ridge of the vast grassy fountain region with smooth rolling features. A few patches of forest broke the monotony of colour, and the many lakes, one of them about five miles long, were glowing like windows. Only the highest ridges were whitened with snow, while rifts in the clouds showed beautiful bits of yellow-green sky. The limit of tree growth is about five thousand feet.

Throughout all this region from Glenora to Cassiar the grasses grow luxuriantly in openings in the woods and on dry hillsides where the trees seem to have been destroyed by fire, and over all the broad prairies above the timber-line. A kind of bunch-grass in particular is often four or five feet high, and close enough to be mowed for hay. I never anywhere saw finer or more bountiful wild pasture. Here the caribou feed and grow fat, braving the intense winter cold, often forty to sixty degrees below zero. Winter and summer seem to be the only seasons here. What may fairly be called summer lasts only two or three months, winter nine or ten, for of pure well-defined spring or autumn there is scarcely a trace. Were it not for the long severe winters, this would be a capital stock country, equalling Texas and the prairies of the old West. From my outlook on the Defot ridge I saw thousands of square miles of this prairie-like region drained by tributaries of the Stickeen, Taku, Yukon, and Mackenzie Rivers.

Le Claire told me that the caribou, or reindeer, were very abundant on this ground. A flock of fifty or more was seen a short time before at the head of Defot Creek – fine, hardy, able animals like their near relatives the reindeer of the Arctic tundras. The Indians hereabouts, he said, hunted them with dogs, mostly in the autumn and winter. On my return trip I met several bands of these Indians on the march, going north to hunt. Some of the men and women were carrying puppies on top of their heavy loads of dried salmon, while the grown dogs had saddle-bags filled with odds and ends strapped on their backs. Small puppies, unable to carry more than five or six pounds, were thus made useful. I overtook another band going south, heavy laden with furs and skins to trade. An old woman, with short dress and leggings, was carrying a big load of furs and skins, on top of which was perched a little girl about three years old.

A brown, speckled marmot, one of Le Claire's friends, was getting ready for winter. The entrance of his burrow was a little to one side of the cabin door. A well-worn trail led to it through the grass and another to that of his companion, fifty feet away. He was a most amusing pet, always on hand at meal times for bread-crumbs and bits of bacon-rind, came when called, answering in a shrill whistle, moving like a squirrel with quick, nervous impulses, jerking his short flat tail. His fur clothing was neat and clean, fairly shining in the wintry light. The snowy weather that morning must have called winter to mind; for as soon as he got his breakfast, he ran to a tuft of dry grass, chewed it into fuzzy mouthfuls, and carried it to his nest, coming and going with admirable industry, forecast and confidence. None watching him as we did could fail to sympathize with him; and I fancy that in practical weather wisdom no government forecaster with all his advantages surpasses this little Alaska rodent, every hair and nerve a weather instrument.

I greatly enjoyed this little inland side trip – the wide views; the miners along the branches of the great river, busy as moles and beavers; young men dreaming and hoping to strike it rich and rush home to marry their girls faithfully waiting; others hoping to clear off weary farm mortgages, and brighten the lives of the anxious home folk; but most, I suppose, just struggling blindly for gold enough to make them indefinitely rich to spend their lives in aimless affluence, honour, and ease. I enjoyed getting acquainted with the trees, especially the beautiful spruce and silver fir; the flower gardens and great grassy caribou pastures; the cheery, able marmot mountaineer; and above all the friendship and kindness of Mr Le Claire, whom I shall never forget. Bidding goodbye, I sauntered back to the head of navigation on the Stickeen, happy and rich without a particle of obscuring gold-dust care.

SEVEN

Glenora Peak

On the trail to the steamboat-landing at the foot of Dease Lake, I met a Douglas squirrel, nearly as red and rusty in colour as his Eastern relative the chickaree. Except in colour he differs but little from the California Douglas squirrel. In voice, language, gestures, temperament, he is the same fiery, indomitable little king of the woods. Another darker and probably younger specimen met near the Caribou House, barked, chirruped, and showed off in fine style on a tree within a few feet of us.

'What does the little rascal mean?' said my companion, a man I had fallen in with on the trail. 'What is he making such a fuss about? I cannot frighten him.'

'Never mind,' I replied; 'just wait until I whistle "Old Hundred" and you will see him fly in disgust'. And so he did, just as his California brethren do. Strange that no squirrel or spermophile I yet have found ever seemed to have anything like enough of Scotch religion to enjoy this grand old tune.

The taverns along the Cassiar gold trail were the worst I had ever seen, rough shacks with dirt floors, dirt roofs, and rough meals. The meals are all alike – a potato, a slice of something like bacon, some grey stuff called bread, and a cup of muddy, semi-liquid coffee like that which the California miners call 'slickens' or 'slumgullion'. The bread was terrible and sinful. How the Lord's good wheat could be made into stuff so mysteriously bad is past finding out. The very de'il, it would seem, in wicked anger and ingenuity, has been the baker.

On our walk from Dease Lake to Telegraph Creek we had one of these rough luncheons at three o'clock in the afternoon of the first day, then walked on five miles to Ward's, where we were solemnly assured that we could not have a single bite of either supper or breakfast, but as a great favour we might sleep on his best grey bunk. We replied that, as we had lunched at the lake, supper would not be greatly missed, and as for breakfast we would start early and walk eight miles to the next road-house. We set out at half-past four, glad to escape into the fresh air, and reached the breakfast place at eight o'clock. The landlord was still abed, and when at length he came to the door, he scowled savagely at us as if our request for breakfast was preposterous and criminal beyond anything ever heard of in all goldful Alaska. A good many in those days were returning from the mines dead broke, and he probably regarded us as belonging to that disreputable class. Anyhow, we got nothing and had to tramp on.

As we approached the next house, three miles ahead, we saw the tavern-keeper keenly surveying us, and, as we afterwards learned, taking me for a certain judge whom for some cause he wished to avoid, he hurriedly locked his door and fled. Half a mile farther on we discovered him in a thicket a little way off the trail, explained our wants, marched him back to his house, and at length obtained a little sour bread, sour milk, and old salmon, our only lonely meal between the Lake and Telegraph Creek.

We arrived at Telegraph Creek, the end of my two-hundred-mile walk, about noon. After luncheon I went on down the river to Glenora in a fine canoe owned and manned by Kitty, a stout, intelligent-looking Indian woman, who charged her passengers a dollar for the fifteen-mile trip. Her crew was four Indian paddlers. In the rapids she also plied the paddle, with stout, telling strokes, and a keen-eyed old man, probably her husband, sat high in the stern and steered. All seemed exhilarated as we shot down through the narrow gorge on the rushing, roaring, throttled river, paddling all the more vigorously the faster the speed of the stream, to hold good steering way. The canoe danced lightly amid grey surges and spray as if alive and enthusiastically enjoying the adventure. Some of the passengers were pretty thoroughly drenched. In unskilful hands the frail dugout would surely have been wrecked or upset. Most of the season goods for the Cassiar gold camps were carried from Glenora to Telegraph Creek in canoes, the steamers not being able to overcome the rapids except during high water. Even then they had usually to line two of the rapids – that is, take a line ashore, make it fast to a tree on the bank, and pull up on the capstan. The freight canoes carried about three or four tons, for which fifteen dollars per ton was charged. Slow progress was made by poling along the bank out of the swiftest part of the current. In the rapids a tow line was taken ashore, only one of the crew remaining aboard to steer. The trip took a day unless a favouring wind was blowing, which often happened.

Next morning I set out from Glenora to climb Glenora Peak for the general view of the great Coast Range that I failed to obtain on my first ascent on account of the accident that befell Mr Young when we were within a minute or two of the top. It is hard to fail in reaching a mountain-top that one starts for, let the cause be what it may. This time I had no companion to care for, but the sky was threatening. I was assured by the local weather-prophets that the day would be rainy or snowy because the peaks in sight were muffled in clouds that seemed to be getting ready for work. I determined to go ahead, however, for storms of any kind are well worth while, and if driven back I could wait and try again.

With crackers in my pocket and a light rubber coat that a kind Hebrew passenger on the steamer Gertrude loaned me, I was ready for anything that might offer, my hopes for the grand view rising and falling as the clouds rose and fell. Anxiously I watched them as they trailed their draggled skirts across the glaciers and fountain peaks as if thoughtfully looking for the places where they could do the most good. From Glenora there is first a terrace of two hundred feet above the river covered mostly with bushes, yellow apocynum in the open spaces, together with carpets of dwarf manzanita, bunch-grass, and a few of the compositae, galiums, etc. Then comes a flat stretch a mile wide, extending to the foothills, covered with birch, spruce, fir and poplar, now mostly killed by fire and the ground strewn with charred trunks. From this black forest the mountain rises in rather steep slopes covered with a luxuriant growth of bushes, grass, flowers and a few trees, chiefly spruce and fir, the firs gradually dwarfing into a beautiful chaparral, the most beautiful, I think, I have ever seen, the flat fan-shaped plumes thickly foliaged and imbricated by snow pressure, forming a smooth, handsome thatch which bears cones and thrives as if this repressed condition were its very best. It extends up an elevation of about fifty-five hundred feet. Only a few trees more than a foot in diameter and more than fifty feet high are found higher than four thousand feet above the sea. A few poplars and willows occur on moist places, gradually dwarfing like the conifers. Alder is the most generally distributed of the chaparral bushes, growing nearly everywhere; its crinkled stems an inch or two thick form a troublesome tangle to the mountaineer. The blue geranium, with leaves red and showy at this time of the year, is perhaps the most telling of the flowering plants. It grows up to five thousand feet or more. Larkspurs are common, with epilobium, senecio, erigeron, and a few solidagos. The harebell appears at about four thousand feet and extends to the summit, dwarfing in stature but maintaining the size of its handsome bells until they seem to be lying loose and detached on the ground as if like snow flowers they had fallen from the sky; and, though frail and delicate-looking, none of its companions is more enduring or rings out the praises of beauty-loving Nature in tones more appreciable to mortals, not forgetting even cassiope, who also is here and her companion, bryanthus, the loveliest and most widely distributed of the alpine shrubs. Then come crowberry, and two species of huckle-berry, one of them from about six inches to a foot high with delicious berries, the other a most lavishly prolific and contented-looking dwarf, few of the bushes being more than two inches high, counting to the topmost leaf, yet each bearing from ten to twenty or more large berries. Perhaps more than half the bulk of the whole plant is fruit, the largest and finest-flavoured of all the huckleberries or blueberries I ever tasted, spreading fine feasts for the grouse and ptarmigan and many others of Nature's mountain people. I noticed three species of dwarf willows, one with narrow leaves, growing at the very summit of the mountain in cracks of the rocks, as well as on patches of soil, another with large, smooth leaves now turning yellow. The third species grows between the others as to elevation; its leaves, then orange-coloured, are strikingly pitted and reticulated. Another alpine shrub, a species of sericocarpus, covered with handsome heads of feathery achenia, beautiful dwarf echiverias with flocks of purple flowers pricked into their bright grass-green, cushion-like bosses of moss-like foliage, and a fine forget-me-not reach to the summit. I may also mention a large mertensia, a fine anemone, a veratrum, six feet high, a large blue daisy, growing up to three to four thousand feet, and at the summit a dwarf species, with dusky, hairy involucres, and a few ferns, aspidium, gymnogramma, and small rock cheilanthes, leaving scarce a foot of ground bare, though the mountain looks bald and brown in the distance like those of the desert ranges of the Great Basin in Utah and Nevada.

Charmed with these plant people, I had almost forgotten to watch the sky until I reached the top of the highest peak, when one of the greatest and most impressively sublime of all the mountain views I have ever enjoyed came full in sight – more than three hundred miles of closely packed peaks of the great Coast Range, sculptured in the boldest manner imaginable, their naked tops and dividing ridges dark in colour, their sides and the canyons, gorges and valleys between them loaded with glaciers and snow. From this standpoint I counted upwards of two hundred glaciers, while dark-centred luminous clouds with fringed edges hovered and crawled over them, now slowly descending, casting transparent shadows on the ice and snow, now rising high above them, lingering like loving angels guarding the crystal gifts they had bestowed. Although the range as seen from this Glenora mountain-top seems regular in its trend, as if the main axis were simple and continuous, it is, on the contrary, far from simple. In front of the highest ranks of peaks are others of the same form with their own glaciers, and lower peaks before these, and yet lower ones with their ridges and canyons, valleys and foothills. Alps rise beyond alps as far as the eye can reach, and clusters of higher peaks here and there closely crowded together; clusters, too, of needles and pinnacles innumerable like trees in groves. Everywhere the peaks seem comparatively slender and closely packed, as if Nature had here been trying to see how many noble well-dressed mountains could be crowded into one grand range.

The black rocks, too steep for snow to lie upon, were brought into sharp relief by white clouds and snow and glaciers, and these again were outlined and made tellingly plain by the rocks. The glaciers so grandly displayed are of every form, some crawling through gorge and valley like monster glittering serpents; others like broad cataracts pouring over cliffs into shadowy gulfs; others, with their main trunks winding through narrow canyons, display long, white finger-like tributaries descending from the summits of pinnacled ridges. Others lie back in fountain cirques walled in all around save at the lower edge, over which they pour in blue cascades. Snow, too, lay in folds and patches of every form on blunt, rounded ridges in curves, arrowy lines, dashes, and narrow ornamental flutings among the summit peaks and in broad radiating wings on smooth slopes. And on many a bulging headland and lower ridge there lay heavy, over-curling copings and smooth, white domes where wind-driven snow was pressed and wreathed and packed into every form and in every possible place and condition. I never before had seen so richly sculptured a range or so many awe-inspiring inaccessible mountains crowded together. If a line were drawn east and west from the peak on which I stood, and extended both ways to the horizon, cutting the whole round landscape in two equal parts, then all of the south half would be bounded by these icy peaks, which would seem to curve around half the horizon and about twenty degrees more, though extending in a general straight, or but moderately curved, line. The deepest and thickest and highest of all this wilderness of peaks lie to the southwest. They are probably from about nine to twelve thousand feet high, springing to this elevation from near the sea-level. The peak on which these observations were made is somewhere about seven thousand feet high, and from here I estimated the height of the range. The highest peak of all, or that seemed so to me, lies to the westward at an estimated distance of about one hundred and fifty to two hundred miles. Only its solid white summit was visible. Possibly it may be the topmost peak of St Elias. Now look northward around the other half of the horizon, and instead of countless peaks crowding into the sky, you see a low brown region, heaving and swelling in gentle curves, apparently scarcely more waved than a rolling prairie. The so-called canyons of several forks of the upper Stickeen are visible, but even where best seen in the foreground and middle ground of the picture, they are like mere sunken gorges, making scarce perceptible marks on the landscape, while the tops of the highest mountain-swells show only small patches of snow and no glaciers.

Glenora Peak, on which I stood, is the highest point of a spur that puts out from the main range in a northerly direction. It seems to have been a rounded, broad-backed ridge which has been sculptured into its present irregular form by short residual glaciers, some of which, a mile or two long, are still at work.

As I lingered, gazing on the vast show, luminous shadowy clouds seemed to increase in glory of colour and motion, now fondling the highest peaks with infinite tenderness of touch, now hovering above them like eagles over their nests.

When night was drawing near, I ran down the flowery slopes exhilarated, thanking God for the gift of this great day. The setting sun fired the clouds. All the world seemed new-born. Every thing, even the commonest, was seen in new light and was looked at with new interest as if never seen before. The plant people seemed glad, as if rejoicing with me, the little ones as well as the trees, while every feature of the peak and its travelled boulders seemed to know what I had been about and the depth of my joy, as if they could read faces.

EIGHT

Exploration of the Stickeen Glaciers

Next Day I planned an excursion to the so-called Dirt Glacier, the most interesting to Indians and steamer men of all the Stickeen glaciers from its mysterious floods. I left the steamer Gertrude for the glacier delta an hour or two before sunset. The captain kindly loaned me his canoe and two of his Indian deck hands, who seemed much puzzled to know what the rare service required of them might mean, and on leaving bade a merry adieu to their companions. We camped on the west side of the river opposite the front of the glacier, in a spacious valley surrounded by snowy mountains. Thirteen small glaciers were in sight and four waterfalls. It was a fine, serene evening, and the highest peaks were wearing turbans of flossy, gossamer cloud-stuff. I had my supper before leaving the steamer, so I had only to make a camp-fire, spread my blanket, and lie down. The Indians had their own bedding and lay beside their own fire.

The Dirt Glacier is noted among the river men as being subject to violent flood outbursts once or twice a year, usually in the late summer. The delta of this glacier stream is three or four miles wide where it fronts the river, and the many rough channels with which it is guttered and the uprooted trees and huge boulders that roughen its surface manifest the power of the floods that swept them to their places; but under ordinary conditions the glacier discharges its drainage water into the river through only four or five of the delta-channels.

Our camp was made on the south or lower side of the delta, below all the draining streams, so that I would not have to ford any of them on my way to the glacier. The Indians chose a sand-pit to sleep in; I chose a level spot back of a drift log. I had but little to say to my companions as they could speak no English, nor I much Thlinkit or Chinook. In a few minutes after landing they retired to their pit and were soon asleep and asnore. I lingered by the fire until after ten o'clock, for the night sky was clear, and the great white mountains in the starlight seemed nearer than by day and to be looking down like guardians of the valley, while the waterfalls, and the torrents escaping from beneath the big glacier, roared in a broad, low monotone, sounding as if close at hand, though, as it proved next day, the nearest was three miles away. After wrapping myself in my blankets, I still gazed into the marvellous sky and made out to sleep only about two hours. Then, without waking the noisy sleepers, I arose, ate a piece of bread, and set out in my shirt-sleeves, determined to make the most of the time at my disposal. The captain was to pick us up about noon at a woodpile about a mile from here; but if in the mean time the steamer should run aground and he should need his canoe, a three-whistle signal would be given.

Following a dry channel for about a mile, I came suddenly upon the main outlet of the glacier, which in the imperfect light seemed as large as the river, about one hundred and fifty feet wide, and perhaps three or four feet deep. A little farther up it was only about fifty feet wide and rushing on with impetuous roaring force in its rocky channel, sweeping forward sand, gravel, cobblestones and boulders, the bump and rumble sounds of the largest of these rolling stones being readily heard in the midst of the roaring. It was too swift and rough to ford, and no bridge tree could be found, for the great floods had cleared everything out of their way. I was therefore compelled to keep on up the right bank, however difficult the way. Where a strip of bare boulders lined the margin, the walking was easy, but where the current swept close along the ragged edge of the forest, progress was difficult and slow on account of snow-crinkled and interlaced thickets of alder and willow, reinforced with fallen trees and thorny devil's-club (*Echinopanax horridum*), making a jungle all but impenetrable. The mile of this extravagantly difficult growth through which I struggled, inch by inch, will not soon be forgotten. At length arriving within a few hundred yards of the glacier, full of panax barbs, I found that both the glacier and its unfordable stream were pressing hard against a shelving cliff, dangerously steep, leaving no margin, and compelling me to scramble along its face before I could get on to the glacier. But by sunrise all these cliff, jungle and torrent troubles were overcome and I gladly found myself free on the magnificent ice-river.

The curving, out-bulging front of the glacier is about two miles wide, two hundred feet high, and its surface for a mile or so above the front is strewn with moraine detritus, giving it a strangely dirty, dusky look, hence its name, the 'Dirt Glacier', this detritus-laden portion being all that is seen in passing up the river. A mile or two beyond the moraine-covered part I was surprised to find alpine plants growing on the ice, fresh and green, some of them in full flower. These curious glacier gardens, the first I had seen, were evidently planted by snow avalanches from the high walls. They were well watered, of course, by the melting surface of the ice and fairly well nourished by humus still attached to the roots, and in some places formed beds of considerable thickness. Seedling trees and bushes also were growing among the flowers. Admiring these novel floating gardens, I struck out for the middle of the pure white glacier, where the ice seemed smoother, and then held straight on for about eight miles, where I reluctantly turned back to meet the steamer, greatly regretting that I had not brought a week's supply of hardtack to allow me to explore the glacier to its head, and then trust to some passing canoe to take me down to Buck Station, from which I could explore the Big Stickeen Glacier.

Altogether, I saw about fifteen or sixteen miles of the main trunk. The grade is almost regular, and the walls on either hand are about from two to three thousand feet high, sculptured like those of Yosemite Valley. I found no difficulty of an extraordinary kind. Many a crevasse had to be crossed, but most of them were narrow and easily jumped, while the few wide ones that lay in my way were crossed on sliver bridges or avoided by passing around them. The structure of the glacier was strikingly revealed on its melting surface. It is made up of thin vertical or inclined sheets or slabs set on edge and welded together. They represent, I think, the successive snowfalls from heavy storms on the tributaries. One of the tributaries on the right side, about three miles above the front, has been entirely melted off from the trunk and has receded two or three miles, forming an independent glacier. Across the mouth of this abandoned part of its channel the main glacier flows, forming a dam which gives rise to a lake. On the head of the detached tributary there are some five or six small residual glaciers, the drainage of which, with that of the snowy mountain slopes above them, discharges into the lake, whose outlet is through a channel or channels beneath the damming glacier. Now these sub-channels are occasionally blocked and the water rises until it flows alongside of the glacier, but as the dam is a moving one, a grand outburst is sometimes made, which, draining the large lake, produces a flood of amazing power, sweeping down immense quantities of moraine material and raising the river all the way down to its mouth, so that several trips may occasionally be made by the steamers after the season of low water has laid them up for the year. The occurrence of these floods are, of course, well known to the Indians and steamboat men, though they know nothing of their cause. They simply remark, 'The Dirt Glacier has broken out again'.

I greatly enjoyed my walk up this majestic ice-river, charmed by the pale-blue, ineffably fine light in the crevasses, moulins, and wells, and the innumerable azure pools in basins of azure ice, and the network of surface streams, large and small, gliding, swirling with wonderful grace of motion in their frictionless channels, calling forth devout admiration at almost every step and filling the mind with a sense of Nature's endless beauty and power. Looking ahead from the middle of the glacier, you see the broad white flood, though apparently rigid as iron, sweeping in graceful curves between its high mountain-like walls, small glaciers hanging in the hollows on either side, and snow in every form above them, and the great down-plunging granite buttresses and headlands of the walls marvellous in bold massive sculpture; forests in side canyons to within fifty feet of the glacier; avalanche pathways overgrown with alder and willow; innumerable cascades keeping up a solemn harmony of water sounds blending with those of the glacier moulins and rills; and as far as the eye can reach, tributary glaciers at short intervals silently descending from their high, white fountains to swell the grand central ice-river.

In the angle formed by the main glacier and the lake that gives rise to the river floods, there is a massive granite dome sparsely feathered with trees, and just beyond this yosemitic rock is a mountain, perhaps ten thousand feet high, laden with ice and snow which seemed pure pearly white in the morning light. Last evening as seen from camp it was adorned with a cloud streamer, and both the streamer and the peak were flushed in the alpenglow. A mile or two above this mountain, on the opposite side of the glacier, there is a rock like the Yosemite Sentinel; and in general all the wall rocks as far as I saw them are more or less yosemitic in form and colour and streaked with cascades.

But wonderful as this noble ice-river is in size and depth and in power displayed, far more wonderful was the vastly greater glacier three or four thousand feet, or perhaps a mile, in depth, whose size and general history is inscribed on the sides of the walls and over the tops of the rocks in characters which have not yet been greatly dimmed by the weather. Comparing its present size with that when it was in its prime, is like comparing a small rivulet to the same stream when it is a roaring torrent.

The return trip to the camp past the shelving cliff and through the weary devil's-club jungle was made in a few hours. The Indians had gone off picking berries, but were on the watch for me and hailed me as I approached. The captain had called for me, and, after waiting three hours, departed for Wrangell without leaving any food, to make sure, I suppose, of a quick return of his Indians and canoe. This was no serious matter, however, for the swift current swept us down to Buck Station, some thirty-five miles distant, by eight o'clock. Here I remained to study the 'Big

Stickeen Glacier', but the Indians set out for Wrangell soon after supper, though I invited them to stay till morning.

The weather that morning, 27 August, was dark and rainy, and I tried to persuade myself that I ought to rest a day before setting out on new ice work. But just across the river the 'Big Glacier' was staring me in the face, pouring its majestic flood through a broad mountain gateway and expanding in the spacious river valley to a width of four or five miles, while dim in the grey distance loomed its high mountain fountains. So grand an invitation displayed in characters so telling was of course irresistible, and body-care and weather-care vanished.

Mr Choquette, the keeper of the station, ferried me across the river, and I spent the day in getting general views and planning the work that had been long in mind. I first traced the broad, complicated terminal moraine to its southern extremity, climbed up the west side along the lateral moraine three or four miles, making my way now on the glacier, now on the moraine-covered bank, and now compelled to climb up through the timber and brush in order to pass some rocky headland, until I reached a point commanding a good general view of the lower end of the glacier. Heavy, blotting rain then began to fall, and I retraced my steps, oftentimes stopping to admire the blue ice-caves into which glad, rejoicing streams from the mountain-side were hurrying as if going home, while the glacier seemed to open wide its crystal gateways to welcome them.

The following morning blotting rain was still falling, but time and work was too precious to mind it. Kind Mr Choquette put me across the river in a canoe, with a lot of biscuits his Indian wife had baked for me and some dried salmon, a little sugar and tea, a blanket, and a piece of light sheeting for shelter from rain during the night, all rolled into one bundle.

'When shall I expect you back?' inquired Choquette, when I bade him good-bye.

'Oh, any time,' I replied. 'I shall see as much as possible of the glacier, and I know not how long it will hold me.'

'Well, but when will I come to look for you, if anything

happens? Where are you going to try to go? Years ago
Russian officers from Sitka went up the glacier from here
and none ever returned. It's a mighty dangerous glacier,
all full of damn deep holes and cracks. You've no idea
what ticklish deceiving traps are scattered over it.'

'Yes, I have,' I said. 'I have seen glaciers before, though
none so big as this one. Do not look for me until I make
my appearance on the river-bank. Never mind me. I am
used to caring for myself.' And so, shouldering my bundle,
I trudged off through the moraine boulders and thickets.

My general plan was to trace the terminal moraine to its
extreme north end, pitch my little tent, leave the blanket
and most of the hardtack, and from this main camp go
and come as hunger required or allowed.

After examining a cross-section of the broad moraine,
roughened by concentric masses, marking interruptions in
the recession of the glacier of perhaps several centuries, in
which the successive moraines were formed and shoved
together in closer or wider order, I traced the moraine
to its northeastern extremity and ascended the glacier for
several miles along the left margin, then crossed it at the
grand cataract and down the right side to the river, and
along the moraine to the point of beginning.

On the older portions of this moraine I discovered several
kettles in process of formation and was pleased to find that
they conformed in the most striking way with the theory I
had already been led to make from observations on the old
kettles which form so curious a feature of the drift covering
Wisconsin and Minnesota and some of the larger moraines
of the residual glaciers in the California Sierra. I found a pit
eight or ten feet deep with raw shifting sides countersunk
abruptly in the rough moraine material, and at the bottom,
on sliding down by the aid of a lithe spruce tree that was
being undermined, I discovered, after digging down a foot
or two, that the bottom was resting on a block of solid
blue ice which had been buried in the moraine perhaps a
century or more, judging by the age of the tree that had
grown above it. Probably more than another century will
be required to complete the formation of this kettle by the
slow melting of the buried ice-block. The moraine material

of course was falling in as the ice melted, and the sides maintained an angle as steep as the material would lie. All sorts of theories have been advanced for the formation of these kettles, so abundant in the drift over a great part of the United States, and I was glad to be able to set the question at rest, at least as far as I was concerned.

The glacier and the mountains about it are on so grand a scale and so generally inaccessible in the ordinary sense, it seemed to matter but little what course I pursued. Everything was full of interest, even the weather, though about as unfavourable as possible for wide views, and scrambling through the moraine jungle brush kept one as wet as if all the way was beneath a cascade.

I pushed on, with many a rest and halt to admire the bold and marvellously sculptured ice-front, looking all the grander and more striking in the grey mist with all the rest of the glacier shut out, until I came to a lake about two hundred yards wide and two miles long with scores of small bergs floating in it, some aground, close inshore against the moraine, the light playing on their angles and shimmering in their blue caves in ravishing tones. This proved to be the largest of the series of narrow lakelets that lie in shallow troughs between the moraine and the glacier, a miniature Arctic Ocean, its ice-cliffs played upon by whispering, rippling wavelets and its small berg floes drifting in its currents or with the wind, or stranded here and there along its rocky moraine shore.

Hundreds of small rills and good-sized streams were falling into the lake from the glacier, singing in low tones, some of them pouring in sheer falls over blue cliffs from narrow ice-valleys, some spouting from pipelike channels in the solid front of the glacier, others gurgling out of arched openings at the base. All these water-streams were riding on the parent ice-stream, their voices joined in one grand anthem telling the wonders of their near and far-off mountains. The lake itself is resting in a basin of ice, and the forested moraine, though seemingly cut off from the glacier and probably more than a century old, is in great part resting on buried ice left behind as the glacier receded, and melting slowly on account of the protection afforded by the moraine detritus, which keeps shifting and falling on the inner face long after it is overgrown with lichens, mosses, grasses, bushes, and even good-sized trees; these changes going on with marvellous deliberation until in fullness of time the whole moraine settles down upon its bed-rock foundation.

The outlet of the lake is a large stream, almost a river in size, one of the main draining streams of the glacier. I attempted to ford it where it begins to break in rapids in passing over the moraine, but found it too deep and rough on the bottom. I then tried to ford at its head, where it is wider and glides smoothly out of the lake, bracing myself against the current with a pole, but found it too deep, and when the icy water reached my shoulders I cautiously struggled back to the moraine. I next followed down through the rocky jungle to a place where in breaking across the moraine dam it was only about thirty-five feet wide. Here I found a spruce tree, which I felled for a bridge; it reached across, about ten feet of the top holding in the bank brush. But the force of the torrent, acting on the submerged branches and the slender end of the trunk, bent it like a bow and made it very unsteady, and after testing it by going out about a third of the way over, it seemed likely to be carried away when bent deeper into the current by my weight. Fortunately, I discovered another larger tree well situated a little farther down, which I felled, and though a few feet in the middle was submerged, it seemed perfectly safe.

As it was now getting late, I started back to the lakeside where I had left my bundle, and in trying to hold a direct course found the interlaced jungle still more difficult than it was along the bank of the torrent. For over an hour I had to creep and struggle close to the rocky ground like a fly in a spider-web without being able to obtain a single glimpse of any guiding feature of the landscape. Finding a little willow taller than the surrounding alders, I climbed it, caught sight of the glacier-front, took a compass bearing, and sunk again into the dripping, blinding maze of brush, and at length emerged on the lake-shore seven hours after leaving it, all this time as wet as though I had been swimming, thus completing a trying day's work. But everything was deliciously fresh, and I found new and old plant friends, and lessons on Nature's Alaska moraine landscape-gardening that made everything bright and light.

It was now near dark, and I made haste to make up my flimsy little tent. The ground was desperately rocky. I made out, however, to level down a strip large enough to lie on, and by means of slim alder stems bent over it and tied together soon had a home. While thus busily engaged I was startled by a thundering roar across the lake. Running to the top of the moraine, I discovered that the tremendous noise was only the outcry of a newborn berg about fifty or sixty feet in diameter, rocking and wallowing in the waves it had raised as if enjoying its freedom after its long grinding work as a part of the glacier. After this fine last lesson I managed to make a small fire out of wet twigs, got a cup of tea, stripped off my dripping clothing, wrapped myself in a blanket and lay brooding on the gains of the day and plans for the morrow, glad, rich, and almost comfortable.

It was raining hard when I awoke, but I made up my mind to disregard the weather, put on my dripping clothing, glad to know it was fresh and clean; ate biscuits and a piece of dried salmon without attempting to make a tea fire; filled a bag with hardtack, slung it over my shoulder, and with my indispensable ice-axe plunged once more into the dripping jungle. I found my bridge holding bravely in place against the swollen torrent, crossed it and beat my way around pools and logs and through two hours of tangle back to the moraine on the north side of the outlet – a wet weary battle but not without enjoyment. The smell of the washed ground and vegetation made every breath a pleasure, and I found *Calypso borealis*, the first I had seen on this side of the continent, one of my darlings, worth any amount of hardship; and I saw one of my Douglas squirrels on the margin of a grassy pool. The drip of the rain on the various leaves was pleasant to hear. More especially marked were the flat low-toned bumps and splashes of large drops from the trees on the broad horizontal leaves of *Echinopanax horridum*, like the drumming of thunder-shower drops on veratrum and palm leaves, while the mosses were indescribably beautiful, so fresh, so bright, so cheerily green, and all so low and calm and silent, however heavy and wild the wind and the rain blowing and pouring above them. Surely never a particle of dust has touched leaf or crown of all these blessed mosses; and how bright were the red rims of the cladonia cups beside them, and the fruit of the dwarf cornel! And the wet berries, Nature's precious jewellry, how beautiful they were! – huckleberries with pale bloom and a crystal drop on each; red and yellow salmon-berries, with clusters of smaller drops; and the glittering, berry-like raindrops, adorning the interlacing arches of bent grasses and sedges around the edges of the pools, every drop a mirror with all the landscape in it. A' that and a' that and twice as muckle's a' that in this glorious Alaska day, recalling, however different, George Herbert's 'Sweet day, so cool, so calm, so bright'.

In the gardens and forests of this wonderful moraine one might spend a whole joyful life.

When I at last reached the end of the great moraine and the front of the mountain that forms the north side of the glacier basin, I tried to make my way along its side, but, finding the climbing tedious and difficult, took to the glacier and fared well, though a good deal of step-cutting was required on its ragged, crevassed margin. When night was drawing nigh, I scanned the steep mountainside in search of an accessible bench, however narrow, where a bed and a fire might be gathered for a camp. About dark great was my delight to find a shelf with a few small mountain hemlocks growing in cleavage joints. Projecting knobs below it enabled me to build a platform for a fireplace and a bed and by industrious creeping from one fissure to another, cutting bushes and small trees and sliding them down to within reach of my rock-shelf, I made out to collect wood enough to last through the night. In an hour or two I had a cheery fire, and spent the night in turning from side to side, steaming and drying after being wet two days and a night. Fortunately this night it did not rain, but it was very cold.

Pushing on next day, I climbed to the top of the glacier by ice-steps and along its side to the grand cataract two miles wide where the whole majestic flood of the glacier pours like a mighty surging river down a steep declivity in its channel. After gazing a long time on the glorious show, I discovered a place beneath the edge of the cataract where it flows over a hard, resisting granite rib, into which I crawled and enjoyed the novel and instructive view of a glacier pouring over my head, showing not only its grinding, polishing action, but how it breaks off large angular boulder-masses – a most telling lesson in earth sculpture, confirming many I had already learned in the glacier basins of the High Sierra of California. I then crossed to the south side, noting the forms of the huge blocks into which the glacier was broken in passing over the brow of the cataract, and how they were welded.

The weather was now clear, opening views according to my own heart far into the high snowy fountains. I saw what seemed the farthest mountains, perhaps thirty miles from the front, everywhere winter-bound, but thick forested, however steep, for a distance of at least fifteen miles from the front, the trees, hemlock and spruce, clinging to the rock by root-holds among cleavage joints. The greatest discovery was in methods of denudation displayed beneath the glacier.

After a few more days of exhilarating study I returned to the river-bank opposite Choquette's landing. Promptly at sight of the signal I made, the kind Frenchman came across for me in his canoe. At his house I enjoyed a rest while writing out notes; then examined the smaller glacier fronting the one I had been exploring, until a passing canoe bound for Fort Wrangell took me aboard.

NINE

A Canoe Voyage to Northward

I arrived at Wrangell in a canoe with a party of Cassiar miners in October while the icy regions to the northward still burned in my mind. I had met several prospectors who had been as far as Chilcat at the head of Lynn Canal, who told wonderful stories about the great glaciers they had seen there. All the high mountains up there, they said, seemed to be made of ice, and if glaciers 'are what you are after, that's the place for you,' and to get there 'all you have to do is to hire a good canoe and Indians who know the way'.

But it now seemed too late to set out on so long a voyage. The days were growing short and winter was drawing nigh when all the land would be buried in snow. On the other hand, though this wilderness was new to me, I was familiar with storms and enjoyed them. The main channels extending along the coast remain open all winter, and, their shores being well forested, I knew that it would be easy to keep warm in camp, while abundance of food could be carried. I determined, therefore, to go ahead as far north as possible, to see and learn what I could, especially with reference to future work. When I made known my plans to Mr Young, he offered to go with me, and, being acquainted with the Indians, procured a good canoe and crew, and with a large stock of provisions and blankets, we left Wrangell 14 October, eager to welcome weather of every sort, as long as food lasted.

I was anxious to make an early start, but it was half-past two in the afternoon before I could get my Indians together – Toyatte, a grand old Stickeen nobleman, who was made captain, not only because he owned the canoe, but for his skill in woodcraft and seamanship; Kadachan, the son of a Chilcat chief; John, a Stickeen, who acted as interpreter; and Sitka Charley. Mr Young, my companion, was an adventurous evangelist, and it was the opportunities the trip might afford to meet the Indians of the different tribes on our route with reference to future missionary work, that induced him to join us.

When at last all were aboard and we were about to cast loose from the wharf, Kadachan's mother, a woman of great natural dignity and force of character, came down the steps alongside the canoe oppressed with anxious fears for the safety of her son. Standing silent for a few moments, she held the missionary with her dark, bodeful eyes, and with great solemnity of speech and gesture accused him of using undue influence in gaining her son's consent to go on a dangerous voyage among unfriendly tribes; and like and ancient sibyl foretold a long train of bad luck from storms and enemies, and finished by saying, 'If my son comes not back, on you will be his blood, and you shall pay. I say it.'

Mr Young tried in vain to calm her fears, promising Heaven's care as well as his own for her precious son, assuring her that he would faithfully share every danger that he encountered, and if need be die in his defence.

'We shall see whether or not you die', she said, and turned away.

Toyatte also encountered domestic difficulties. When he stepped into the canoe I noticed a cloud of anxiety on his grand old face, as if his doom now drawing near was already beginning to overshadow him. When he took leave of his wife, she refused to shake hands with him, wept bitterly, and said that his enemies, the Chilcat chiefs, would be sure to kill him in case he reached their village. But it was not on this trip that the old hero was to meet his fate, and when we were fairly free in the wilderness and a gentle breeze pressed us joyfully over the shining waters these gloomy forebodings vanished.

We first pursued a westerly course, through Sumner Strait, between Kupreanof and Prince of Wales Islands, then, turning northward, sailed up the Kiku Strait through the midst of innumerable picturesque islets, across Prince Frederick's Sound, up Chatham Strait, thence north-westward through Icy Strait and around the then uncharted

Glacier Bay. Thence returning through Icy Strait, we sailed up the beautiful Lynn Canal to the Davidson Glacier and the lower village of the Chilcat tribe and returned to Wrangell along the coast of the mainland, visiting the icy Sum Dum Bay and the Wrangell Glacier on our route. Thus we made a journey more than eight hundred miles long, and though hardships and perhaps dangers were encountered, the great wonderland made compensation beyond our most extravagant hopes. Neither rain nor snow stopped us, but when the wind was too wild, Kadachan and the old captain stayed on guard in the camp and John and Charley went into the woods deer-hunting, while I examined the adjacent rocks and woods. Most of our camp-grounds were in sheltered nooks where good firewood was abundant, and where the precious canoe could be safely drawn up beyond reach of the waves. After supper we sat long around the fire, listening to the Indian's stories about the wild animals, their hunting-adventures, wars, traditions, religion, and customs. Every Indian party we met we interviewed, and visited every village we came to.

Our first camp was made at a place called the Island of the Standing Stone, on the shore of a shallow bay. The weather was fine. The mountains of the mainland were unclouded, excepting one, which had a horizontal ruff of dull slate colour, but its icy summit covered with fresh snow towered above the cloud, flushed like its neighbours in the alpenglow. All the large islands in sight were densely forested, while many small rock islets in front of our camp were treeless or nearly so. Some of them were distinctly glaciated even below the tide-line, the effects of wave washing and general weathering being scarce appreciable as yet. Some of the larger islets had a few trees, others only grass. One looked in the distance like a two-masted ship flying before the wind under press of sail.

Next morning the mountains were arrayed in fresh snow that had fallen during the night down to within a hundred feet of the sea-level. We made a grand fire, and after an early breakfast pushed merrily on all day along beautiful forested shores embroidered with autumn-coloured bushes. I noticed some pitchy trees that had been deeply hacked for kindling-wood and torches, precious conveniences to belated voyagers on stormy nights. Before sundown we camped in a beautiful nook of Deer Bay, shut in from every wind by grey-bearded trees and fringed with rose bushes, rubus, potentilla, asters, etc. Some of the lichen tresses depending from the branches were six feet in length.

A dozen rods or so from our camp we discovered a family of Kake Indians snugly sheltered in a portable bark hut, a stout middle-aged man with his wife, son, and daughter, and his son's wife. After our tent was set and fire made, the head of the family paid us a visit and presented us with a fine salmon, a pair of mallard ducks, and a mess of potatoes. We paid a return visit with gifts of rice and tobacco, etc. Mr Young spoke briefly on mission affairs and inquired whether their tribe would be likely to welcome a teacher or missionary. But they seemed unwilling to offer an opinion on so important a subject. The following words from the head of the family was the only reply:

'We have not much to say to you fellows. We always do to Boston men as we have done to you, give a little of whatever we have, treat everybody well and never quarrel. This is all we have to say.'

Our Kake neighbours set out for Fort Wrangell next morning, and we pushed gladly on toward Chilcat. We passed an island that had lost all its trees in a storm, but a hopeful crop of young ones was springing up to take their places. I found no trace of fire in these woods. The ground was covered with leaves, branches, and fallen trunks perhaps a dozen generations deep, slowly decaying, forming a grand mossy mass of ruins, kept fresh and beautiful. All that is repulsive about death was here hidden beneath abounding life. Some rocks along the shore were completely covered with crimson-leafed huckle-berry bushes; one species still in fruit might well be called the winter huckle-berry. In a short walk I found vetches eight feet high leaning on raspberry bushes, and tall ferns and *Smilacina unifolia* with leaves six inches wide growing on yellow-green moss, producing a beautiful effect.

Our Indians seemed to be enjoying a quick and merry reaction from the doleful domestic dumps in which the voyage was begun. Old and young behaved this afternoon like a lot of truant boys on a lark. When we came to a pond fenced off from the main channel by a moraine dam, John went ashore to seek a shot at ducks. Creeping up behind the dam, he killed a mallard fifty or sixty feet from the shore and attempted to wave it within reach by throwing stones back of it. Charley and Kadachan went to his help, enjoying the sport, especially enjoying their own blunders in throwing in front of it and thus driving the duck farther out. To expedite the business John then tried to throw a rope across it, but failed after repeated trials, and so did each in turn, all laughing merrily at their awkward bungling. Next they tied a stone to the end of the rope to carry it further and with better aim, but the result was no better. Then majestic old Toyatte tried his hand at the game. He tied the rope to one of the canoe-poles, and taking aim threw it, harpoon fashion, beyond the duck, and the general merriment was redoubled when the pole got loose and floated out to the middle of the pond. At length John stripped, swam to the duck, threw it ashore, and brought in the pole in his teeth, his companions meanwhile making merry at his expense by splashing the water in front of him and making the dead duck go through the motions of fighting and biting him in the face as he landed.

The morning after this delightful day was dark and threatening. A high wind was rushing down the strait dead against us, and just as we were about ready to start, determined to fight our way by creeping close inshore, pelting rain began to fly. We concluded therefore to wait for better weather. The hunters went out for deer and I to see the forests. The rain brought out the fragrance of the drenched trees, and the wind made wild melody in their tops, while every brown bole was embroidered by a network of rain rills. Perhaps the most delightful part of my ramble was along a stream that flowed through a leafy arch beneath overleaning trees which met at the top. The water was almost black in the deep pools and fine clear amber in the shallows. It was the pure, rich wine of the woods with a pleasant taste, bringing spicy spruce groves and widespread bog and beaver meadows to mind. On this amber stream I discovered an interesting fall. It is only a few feet high, but remarkably fine in the curve of its brow and blending shades of colour, while the mossy, bushy pool into which it plunges is inky black, but wonderfully brightened by foam bells larger than common that drift in clusters on the smooth water around the rim, each of them carrying a picture of the overlooking trees leaning together at the tips like the teeth of moss capsules before they rise.

I found most of the trees here fairly loaded with mosses. Some broadly palmated branches had beds of yellow moss so wide and deep that when wet they must weigh a hundred pounds or even more. Upon these moss-beds ferns and grasses and even good-sized seedling trees grow, making beautiful hanging gardens in which the curious spectacle is presented of old trees holding hundreds of their own children in their arms, nourishing by rain and dew and the decaying leaves showered down to them by their parents. The branches upon which these beds of mossy soil rest become flat and irregular like weathered roots or the antlers of deer, and at length die; and when the whole tree has thus been killed it seems to be standing on its head with roots in the air. A striking example of this sort stood near the camp and I called the missionary's attention to it.

'Come, Mr Young,' I shouted. 'Here's something wonderful, the most wonderful tree you ever saw; it is standing on its head.'

'How in the world', said he in astonishment, 'could that tree have been plucked up by the roots, carried high in the air, and dropped down head foremost into the ground. It must have been the work of a tornado.'

Toward evening the hunters brought in a deer. They had seen four others, and at the camp-fire talk said that deer abounded on all the islands of considerable size and along the shores of the mainland. But few were to be found in the interior on account of wolves that ran them down where they could not readily take refuge in the water. The Indians, they said, hunted them on the islands with trained dogs which went into the woods and drove them out, while the hunters lay in wait in canoes at the points where they were likely to take to the water. Beaver and black bear also abounded on this large island. I saw but few birds there, only ravens, jays, and wrens. Ducks, gulls, bald eagles, and jays are the commonest birds hereabouts. A flock of swans flew past, sounding their startling human-like cry which seemed yet more striking in this lonely wilderness. The Indians said that geese, swans, cranes, etc., making their long journeys in regular order thus called aloud to encourage each other and enable them to keep stroke and time like men in rowing or marching (a sort of 'Row, brothers, row', or 'Hip, hip' of marching soldiers).

18 October was about half sunshine, half rain and wet snow, but we paddled on through the midst of the innumerable islands in more than half comfort, enjoying the changing effects of the weather on the dripping wilderness. Strolling a little way back into the woods when we went ashore for luncheon, I found fine specimens of cedar, and here and there a birch, and small thickets of wild apple. A hemlock, felled by Indians for bread-bark, was only twenty inches thick at the butt, a hundred and twenty feet long, and about five hundred and forty years old at the time it was felled. The first hundred of its rings measured only four inches, showing that for a century it had grown in the shade of taller trees and at the age of one hundred years was yet only a sapling in size. On the mossy trunk of an old prostrate spruce about a hundred feet in length thousands of seedlings were growing. I counted seven hundred on a length of eight feet, so favourable is this climate for the development of tree seeds and so fully do these trees obey the command to multiply and replenish the earth. No wonder these islands are densely clothed with trees. They grow on solid rocks and logs as well as on fertile soil. The surface is first covered with a plush of mosses in which the seeds germinate; then the interlacing roots form a sod, fallen leaves soon cover their feet, and the young trees, closely crowded together, support each

other, and the soil becomes deeper and richer from year to year.

I greatly enjoyed the Indian's camp-fire talk this evening on their ancient customs, how they were taught by their parents ere the whites came among them, their religion, ideas connected with the next world, the stars, plants, the behaviour and language of animals under different circumstances, manner of getting a living, etc. When our talk was interrupted by the howling of a wolf on the opposite side of the strait, Kadachan puzzled the minister with the question, 'Have wolves souls?' The Indians believe that they have, giving as foundation for their belief that they are wise creatures who know how to catch seals and salmon by swimming slyly upon them with their heads hidden in a mouthful of grass, hunt deer in company, and always bring forth their young at the same and most favourable time of the year. I inquired how it was that with enemies so wise and powerful the deer were not all killed. Kadachan replied that wolves knew better than to kill them all and thus cut off their most important food-supply. He said they were numerous on all the large islands, more so than on the mainland, that Indian hunters were afraid of them and never ventured far into the woods alone, for these large grey and black wolves attacked man whether they were hungry or not. When attacked, the Indian hunter, he said, climbed a tree or stood with his back against a tree or rock as a wolf never attacks face to face. Wolves, and not bears, Indians regard as masters of the woods, for they sometimes attack and kill bears, but the wolverine they never attack, 'for', said John, 'wolves and wolverines are companions in sin and equally wicked and cunning'.

On one of the small islands we found a stockade, sixty by thirty-five feet, built, our Indians said, by the Kake tribe during one of their many warlike quarrels. Toyatte and Kadachan said these forts were common throughout the canoe waters, showing that in this foodful, kindly wilderness, as in all the world beside, man may be man's worst enemy.

We discovered small bits of cultivation here and there, patches of potatoes and turnips, planted mostly on the

cleared sites of deserted villages. In spring the most industrious families sailed to their little farms of perhaps a
quarter of an acre or less, and ten or fifteen miles from
their villages. After preparing the ground, and planting
it, they visited it again in summer to pull the weeds and
speculate on the size of the crop they were likely to have
to eat with their fat salmon. The Kakes were then busy
digging their potatoes, which they complained were this
year injured by early frosts.

We arrived at Klugh-Quan, one of the Kupreanof Kake
villages, just as a funeral party was breaking up. The body
had been burned and gifts were being distributed – bits
of calico, handkerchiefs, blankets, etc., according to the
rank and wealth of the deceased. The death ceremonies
of chiefs and head men, Mr Young told me, are very weird
and imposing, with wild feasting, dancing and singing. At
this little place there are some eight totem poles of bold
and intricate design, well executed, but smaller than those
of Stickeens. As elsewhere throughout the archipelago, the
bear, raven, eagle, salmon, and porpoise are the chief
figures. Some of the poles have square cavities, mortised
into the back, which are said to contain the ashes of
members of the family. These recesses are closed by a
plug. I noticed one that was caulked with a rag where the
joint was imperfect.

Strolling about the village, looking at the tangled vegetation, sketching the totems, etc., I found a lot of human
bones scattered on the surface of the ground or partly
covered. In answer to my inquiries, one of our crew
said they probably belonged to Sitka Indians slain in
war. These Kakes are shrewd, industrious, and rather
good-looking people. It was at their largest village that
an American schooner was seized and all the crew except
one man murdered. A gunboat sent to punish them burned
the village. I saw the anchor of the ill-fated vessel lying near
the shore.

Though all the Thlinkit tribes believe in witch-craft,
they are less superstitious in some respects than many
of the lower classes of whites. Chief Yana Taowk seemed
to take pleasure in kicking the Sitka bones that lay in his

way, and neither old nor young showed the slightest trace of superstitious fear of the dead at any time.

It was at the northmost of the Kupreanof Kake villages that Mr Young held his first missionary meeting, singing hymns, praying, and preaching, and trying to learn the number of the inhabitants and their readiness to receive instruction. Neither here nor in any of the other villages of the different tribes that we visited was there anything like a distinct refusal to receive school-teachers or ministers. On the contrary, with but one or two exceptions, all with apparent good faith declared their willingness to receive them, and many seemed heartily delighted at the prospect of gaining light on subjects so important and so dark to them. All had heard ere this of the wonderful work of the Reverend Mr Duncan at Metlakatla, and even those chiefs who were not at all inclined to anything like piety were yet anxious to procure schools and churches that their people should not miss the temporal advantages of knowledge, which with their natural shrewdness they were not slow to recognize. 'We are all children', they said, 'groping in the dark. Give us this light and we will do as you bid us.'

The chief of the first Kupreanof Kake village we came to was a venerable-looking man, perhaps seventy years old, with massive head and strongly marked features, a bold Roman nose, deep, tranquil eyes, shaggy eyebrows, a strong face set in a halo of long grey hair. He seemed delighted at the prospect of receiving a teacher for his people. 'This is just what I want', he said. 'I am ready to bid him welcome'.

'This', said Yana Taowk, chief of the larger north village, 'is a good work you bring us. We will be glad to come out of our darkness into your light. You Boston men must be favourites of the Great Father. You know all about God, and ships and guns and the growing of things to eat. We will sit quiet and listen to the words of any teacher you send us.'

While Mr Young was preaching, some of the congregation smoked, talked to each other, and answered the shouts of their companions outside, greatly to the disgust of Toyatte and Kadachan, who regarded the Kakes as mannerless barbarians. A little girl, frightened at the strange exercises, began to cry and was turned out of doors. She cried in a strange, low, wild tone, quite unlike the screech crying of the children of civilization.

The following morning we crossed Prince Frederick Sound to the west coast of Admiralty Island. Our frail shell of a canoe was tossed like a bubble on the swells coming in from the ocean. Still, I suppose, the danger was not so great as it seemed. In a good canoe, skilfully handled, you may safely sail from Victoria to Chilcat, a thousand-mile voyage frequently made by Indians in their trading operations before the coming of the whites. Our Indians, however, dreaded this crossing so late in the season. They spoke of it repeatedly before we reached it as the one great danger of our voyage.

John said to me just as we left the shore, 'You and Mr Young will be scared to death on this broad water'.

'Never mind us, John', we merrily replied, 'perhaps some of you brave Indian sailors may be the first to show fear'.

Toyatte said he had not slept well a single night thinking of it, and after we rounded Cape Gardner and entered the comparatively smooth Chatham Strait, they all rejoiced, laughing and chatting like frolicsome children.

We arrived at the first of the Hootsenoo villages on Admiralty Island shortly after noon and were welcomed by everybody. Men, women, and children made haste to the beach to meet us, the children staring as if they had never before seen a Boston man. The chief, a remarkably good-looking and intelligent fellow, stepped forward, shook hands with us Boston fashion, and invited us to his house. Some of the curious children crowded in after us and stood around the fire staring like half-frightened wild animals. Two old women drove them out of the house, making hideous gestures, but taking good care not to hurt them. The merry throng poured through the round door, laughing and enjoying the harsh gestures and threats of the women as all a joke, indicating mild parental government in general. Indeed, in all my travels I never saw a child, old or young, receive a blow or even a harsh word. When our cook began to prepare luncheon our host said through his interpreter that he was sorry we could not eat Indian food, as he was anxious to entertain us. We thanked him, of course, and expressed our sense of his kindness. His brother, in the mean time, brought a dozen turnips, which he peeled and sliced and served in a clean dish. These we ate raw as dessert, reminding me of turnip-field feasts when I was a boy in Scotland. Then a box was brought from some corner and opened. It seemed to be full of tallow or butter. A sharp stick was thrust into it, and a lump of something five or six inches long, three or four wide, and an inch thick was dug up, which proved to be a section of the back fat of a deer, preserved in fish oil and seasoned with boiled spruce and other spicy roots. After stripping off the lard-like oil, it was cut into small pieces and passed round. It seemed white and wholesome, but I was unable to taste it even for manner's sake. This disgust, however, was not noticed, as the rest of the company did full justice to the precious tallow and smacked their lips over it as a great delicacy. A lot of potatoes about the size of walnuts, boiled and peeled and added to a potful of salmon, made a savoury stew that all seemed to relish. An old, cross-looking, wrinkled crone presided at the steaming chowder-pot, and as she peeled the potatoes with her fingers she, at short intervals, quickly thrust one of the best into the mouth of a little wild-eyed girl that crouched beside her, a spark of natural love which charmed her withered face and made all the big gloomy house shine. In honour of our visit, our host put on a genuine white shirt. His wife also dressed in her best and put a pair of dainty trousers on her two-year-old boy, who seemed to be the pet and favourite of the large family and indeed of the whole village. Toward evening messengers were sent through the village to call everybody to a meeting. Mr Young delivered the usual missionary sermon and I also was called on to say something. Then the chief arose and made an eloquent reply, thanking us for our good words and for the hopes we had inspired of obtaining a teacher for their children. In particular, he said, he wanted to hear all we could tell him about God.

This village was an offshoot of a larger one, ten miles to

the north, called Killisnoo. Under the prevailing patriarchal form of government each tribe is divided into comparatively few families; and because of quarrels, the chief of this branch moved his people to this little bay, where the beach offered a good landing for canoes. A stream which enters it yields abundance of salmon, while in the adjacent woods and mountains berries, deer, and wild goats abound.

'Here', he said, 'we enjoy peace and plenty; all we lack is a church and a school, particularly a school for the children'. His dwelling so much with benevolent aspect on the children of the tribe showed, I think, that he truly loved them and had a right intelligent insight concerning their welfare. We spent the night under his roof, the first we had ever spent with Indians, and I never felt more at home. The loving kindness bestowed on the little ones made the house glow.

Next morning, with the hearty good wishes of our Hootsenoo friends, and encouraged by the gentle weather, we sailed gladly up the coast, hoping soon to see the Chilcat glaciers in their glory. The rock hereabouts is mostly a beautiful blue marble, waveworn into a multitude of small coves and ledges. Fine sections were thus revealed along the shore, which with their colours, brightened with showers and late-blooming leaves and flowers, beguiled the weariness of the way. The shingle in front of these marble cliffs is also mostly marble, well polished and rounded and mixed with a small percentage of glacier-borne slate and granite erratics.

We arrived at the upper village about half-past one o'clock. Here we saw Hootsenoo Indians in a very different light from that which illumined the lower village. While we were yet half a mile or more away, we heard sounds I had never before heard – a storm of strange howls, yells, and screams rising from a base of gasping, bellowing grunts and groans. Had I been alone, I should have fled as from a pack of fiends, but our Indians quietly recognized this awful sound, if such stuff could be called sound, simply as the 'whiskey howl' and pushed quietly on. As we approached the landing, the demoniac howling so greatly increased I tried to dissuade Mr Young from attempting to say a single word in the village, and as for preaching one might as well try to preach in Tophet. The whole village was afire with bad whiskey. This was the first time in my life that I learned the meaning of the phrase 'a howling drunk'. Even our Indians hesitated to venture ashore, notwithstanding whiskey storms were far from novel to them. Mr Young, however, hoped that in this Indian Sodom at least one man might be found so righteous as to be in his right mind and able to give trustworthy information. Therefore I was at length prevailed on to yield consent to land. Our canoe was drawn up on the beach and one of the crew left to guard it. Cautiously we strolled up the hill to the main row of houses, now a chain of alcoholic volcanoes. The largest house, just opposite the landing, was about forty feet square, built of immense planks, each hewn from a whole log, and, as usual, the only opening was a mere hole about two and a half feet in diameter, closed by a massive hinged plug like the breach of a cannon. At the dark door-hole a few black faces appeared and were suddenly withdrawn. Not a single person was to be seen on the street. At length a couple of old, crouching men, hideously blackened, ventured out and stared at us, then, calling to their companions, other black and burning heads appeared, and we began to fear that like the Alloway Kirk witches the whole legion was about to sally forth. But, instead, those outside suddenly crawled and tumbled in again. We were thus allowed to take a general view of the place and return to our canoe unmolested. But ere we could get away, three old women came swaggering and grinning down to the beach, and Toyatte was discovered by a man with whom he had once had a business misunderstanding, who, burning for revenge, was now jumping and howling and threatening as only a drunken Indian may, while our heroic old captain, in severe icy majesty, stood erect and motionless, uttering never a word. Kadachan, on the contrary, was well nigh smothered with the drunken caresses of one of his father's *tillicums* (friends), who insisted on his going back with him into the house. But reversing the words of St Paul in his account of his shipwreck, it came to pass that we at length got safe to sea and by hard rowing managed to reach a fine harbour before dark, fifteen sweet, serene miles from the howlers.

Our camp this evening was made at the head of a narrow bay bordered by spruce and hemlock woods. We made our beds beneath a grand old Sitka spruce five feet in diameter, whose broad, winglike branches were outspread immediately above our heads. The night picture as I stood back to see it in the firelight was this one great tree, relieved against the gloom of the woods back of it, the light on the low branches revealing the shining needles, the brown, sturdy trunk grasping an outswelling mossy bank, and a fringe of illuminated bushes within a few feet of the tree with the firelight on the tips of the sprays.

Next morning, soon after we left our harbour, we were caught in a violent gust of wind and dragged over the seething water in a passionate hurry, though our sail was close-reefed, flying past the grey headlands in most exhilarating style, until fear of being capsized made us drop our sail and run into the first little nook we came to for shelter. Captain Toyatte remarked that in this kind of wind no Indian would dream of travelling, but since Mr Young and I were with him he was willing to go on, because he was sure that the Lord loved us and would not allow us to perish.

We were now within a day or two of Chilcat. We had only to hold a direct course up the beautiful Lynn Canal to reach the large Davidson and other glaciers at its head in the canyons of the Chilcat and Chilcoot Rivers. But rumours of trouble among the Indians there now reached us. We found a party taking shelter from the stormy wind in a little cove, who confirmed the bad news that the Chilcats were drinking and fighting, that Kadachan's father had been shot, and that it would be far from safe to venture among them until blood-money had been paid and the quarrels settled. I decided, therefore, in the mean time to turn westward and go in search of the wonderful 'ice-mountains' that Sitka Charley had been telling us about. Charley, the youngest of my crew, noticing my interest in glaciers, said that when he was a boy he had gone with his father to hunt seals in a large bay full of ice, and that though it was long since he had been there, he thought he could find his way to it. Accordingly, we pushed eagerly on across Chatham Strait to the north end of Icy Strait, toward the new and promising ice-field.

On the south side of Icy Strait we ran into a picturesque bay to visit the main village of the Hoona tribe. Rounding a point on the north shore of the bay, the charmingly located village came in sight, with a group of the inhabitants gazing at us as we approached. They evidently recognized us as strangers or visitors from the shape and style of our canoe, and perhaps even determining that white men were aboard, for these Indians have wonderful eyes. While we were yet half a mile off, we saw a flag unfurled on a tall mast in front of the chief's house. Toyatte hoisted his United States flag in reply, and thus arrayed we made for the landing. Here we were met and received by the chief, Kashoto, who stood close to the water's edge, barefooted and bareheaded, but wearing so fine a robe and standing so grave, erect, and serene, his dignity was complete. No white man could have maintained sound dignity under circumstances so disadvantageous. After the usual formal salutations, the chief, still standing as erect and motionless as a tree, said that he was not much acquainted with our people and feared that his house was too mean for visitors so distinguished as we were. We hastened of course to assure him that we were not proud of heart, and would be glad to have the honour of his hospitality and friendship. With a smile of relief he then led us into his large fort house to the seat of honour prepared for us. After we had been allowed to rest unnoticed and unquestioned for fifteen minutes or so, in accordance with good Indian manners in case we should be weary or embarrassed, our cook began to prepare luncheon; and the chief expressed great concern at his not being able to entertain us in Boston fashion.

Luncheon over, Mr Young as usual requested him to call his people to a meeting. Most of them were away at outlying camps gathering winter stores. Some ten or twelve men, however, about the same number of women, and a crowd of wondering boys and girls were gathered in, to whom Mr Young preached the usual gospel sermon. Toyatte prayed in Thlinkit, and the other members of the crew joined in the hymn-singing. At the close of the mission exercises the chief arose and said that he would now like to hear what the other white chief had to say. I directed John to reply that I was not a missionary, that I came only to pay a friendly visit and see the forests and mountains of their beautiful country. To this he replied, as others had done in the same circumstances, that he would like to hear me on the subject of their country and themselves; so I had to get on my feet and make some sort of a speech, dwelling principally on the brotherhood of all races of people, assuring them that God loved them and that some of their white brethren were beginning to know them and become interested in their welfare; that I seemed this evening to be among old friends with whom I had long been acquainted, though I had never been here before; that I would always remember them and the kind reception they had given us; advised them to heed the instructions of sincere self-denying mission men who wished only to do them good and desired nothing but their friendship and welfare in return. I told them that in some far-off countries, instead of receiving the missionaries with glad and thankful hearts, the Indians killed and ate them; but I hoped, and indeed felt sure, that his people would find a better use for missionaries than putting them, like salmon, in pots for food. They seemed greatly interested, looking into each other's faces with emphatic nods and a-ahs and smiles.

The chief then slowly arose and, after standing silent a minute or two, told us how glad he was to see us; that he felt as if his heart had enjoyed a good meal; that we were the first to come humbly to his little out-of-the-way village to tell his people about God; that they were all like children groping in darkness, but eager for light; that they would gladly welcome a missionary and teacher and use them well; that he could easily believe that whites and Indians were the children of one Father just as I had told them in my speech; that they differed little and resembled each other a great deal, calling attention to the similarity of hands, eyes, legs, etc., making telling gestures in the most natural style of eloquence and dignified composure.

'Oftentimes', he said, 'when I was on the high mountains in the fall, hunting wild sheep for meat, and for wool to make blankets, I have been caught in snowstorms and held in camp until there was nothing to eat, but when I reached my home and got warm, and had a good meal, then my body felt good. For a long time my heart has been hungry and cold, but to-night your words have warmed my heart, and given it a good meal, and now my heart feels good.'

The most striking characteristic of these people is their serene dignity in circumstances that to us would be novel and embarrassing. Even the little children behave with natural dignity, come to the white men when called, and restrain their wonder at the strange prayers, hymn-singing, etc. This evening an old woman fell asleep in the meeting and began to snore; and though both old and young were shaken with suppressed mirth, they evidently took great pains to conceal it. It seems wonderful to me that these so-called savages can make one feel at home in their families. In good breeding, intelligence, and skill in accomplishing whatever they try to do with tools they seem to me to rank above most of our uneducated white labourers. I have never yet seen a child ill-used, even to the extent of an angry word. Scolding, so common a curse in civilization, is not known here at all. On the contrary the young are fondly indulged without being spoiled. Crying is very rarely heard.

In the house of this Hoona chief a pet marmot (Parry's) was a great favourite with old and young. It was therefore delightfully confiding and playful and human. Cats were petted, and the confidence with which these cautious, thoughtful animals met strangers showed that they were kindly treated.

There were some ten or a dozen houses, all told, in the village. The count made by the chief for Mr Young showed some seven hundred and twenty-five persons in the tribe.

TEN

The Discovery of Glacier Bay

From here, on 24 October, we set sail for Guide Charley's ice-mountains. The handle of our heaviest axe was cracked, and as Charley declared that there was no firewood to be had in the big ice-mountain bay, we would have to load the canoe with a store for cooking at an island out in the Strait a few miles from the village. We were therefore anxious to buy or trade for a good sound axe in exchange for our broken one. Good axes are rare in rocky Alaska. Soon or late an unlucky stroke on a stone concealed in moss spoils the edge. Finally one in almost perfect condition was offered by a young Hoona for our broken-handled one and a half-dollar to boot; but when the broken axe and money were given he promptly demanded an additional twenty-five cents' worth of tobacco. The tobacco was given him, then he required a half-dollar's worth more of tobacco, which was also given; but when he still demanded something more, Charley's patience gave way and we sailed in the same condition as to axes as when we arrived. This was the only contemptible commercial affair we encountered among these Alaskan Indians.

We reached the wooded island about one o'clock, made coffee, took on a store of wood, and set sail direct for the icy country, finding it very hard indeed to believe the woodless part of Charley's description of the Icy Bay, so heavily and uniformly are all the shores forested wherever we had been. In this view we were joined by John, Kadachan and Toyatte, none of them on all their lifelong canoe travels having ever seen a woodless country.

We held a northwesterly course until long after dark, when we reached a small inlet that sets in near the mouth of Glacier Bay, on the west side. Here we made a cold camp on a desolate snow-covered beach in stormy sleet and darkness. At daybreak I looked eagerly in every direction to learn what kind of place we were in; but gloomy rain-clouds covered the mountains, and I could see nothing that would give me a clue, while Vancouver's chart, hither-to a faithful guide, here failed us altogether. Nevertheless, we made haste to be off; and fortunately, for just as we were leaving the shore, a faint smoke was seen across the inlet, toward which Charley, who now seemed lost, gladly steered. Our sudden appearance so early that grey morning had evidently alarmed our neighbours, for as soon as we were within hailing distance an Indian with his face blackened fired a shot over our heads, and in a blunt, bellowing voice roared, 'Who are you?'

Our interpreter shouted, 'Friends and the Fort Wrangell missionary'.

Then men, women, and children swarmed out of the hut, and awaited our approach on the beach. One of the hunters having brought his gun with him, Kadachan sternly rebuked him, asking with superb indignation whether he was not ashamed to meet a missionary with a gun in his hands. Friendly relations, however, were speedily established, and as a cold rain was falling, they invited us to enter their hut. It seemed very small and was jammed full of oily boxes and bundles; nevertheless, twenty-one persons managed to find shelter in it about a smoky fire. Our hosts proved to be Hoona seal-hunters laying in their winter stores of meat and skins. The packed hut was passably well ventilated, but its heavy, meaty smells were not the same to our noses as those we were accustomed to in the sprucy nooks of the evergreen woods. The circle of black eyes peering at us through a fog of reek and smoke made a novel picture. We were glad, however, to get within reach of information, and of course asked many questions concerning the ice-mountains and the strange bay, to most of which our inquisitive Hoona friends replied with counter-questions as to our object in coming to such a place, especially so late in the year. They had heard of Mr Young and his work at Fort Wrangell, but could not understand what a missionary could be doing in such a place as this. Was he going to preach to the seals and gulls, they asked, or to the ice-mountains? And could they take his word? Then John explained that only the friend of the missionary was seeking ice-mountains, that Mr Young had already preached many good words in the villages we had visited, their own among the others, that our hearts were good and every Indian was our friend. Then we gave them a little rice, sugar, tea, and tobacco, after which they began to gain confidence and to speak freely. They told us that the big bay was called by them Sit-a-da-kay, or Ice Bay; that there were many large ice-mountains in it, but no gold-mines; and that the ice-mountain they knew best was at the head of the bay, where most of the seals were found.

Notwithstanding the rain, I was anxious to push on and grope our way beneath the clouds as best we could, in case worse weather should come; but Charley was ill at ease, and wanted one of the seal-hunters to go with us, for the place was much changed. I promised to pay well for a guide, and in order to lighten the canoe proposed to leave most of our heavy stores in the hut until our return. After a long consultation one of them consented to go. His wife got ready his blanket and a piece of cedar matting for his bed, and some provisions – mostly dried salmon, and seal sausage made of strips of lean meat plaited around a core of fat. She followed us to the beach, and just as we were pushing off said with a pretty smile, 'It is my husband that you are taking away. See that you bring him back.'

We got under way about 10 am. The wind was in our favour, but a cold rain pelted us, and we could see but little of the dreary, treeless wilderness which we had now fairly entered. The bitter blast, however, gave us good speed; our bedraggled canoe rose and fell on the waves as solemnly as a big ship. Our course was northwestward, up the southwest side of the bay, near the shore of what seemed to be the mainland, smooth marble islands being on our right. About noon we discovered the first of the great glaciers, the one I afterward named for James Geikie, the noted Scotch geologist. Its lofty blue cliffs, looming through the draggled skirts of the clouds, gave a tremendous impression of savage power, while the roar of the new-born icebergs thickened and emphasized the general roar of the storm. An hour and a half beyond the Geikie Glacier we ran into a slight harbour where the shore is low, dragged the canoe beyond the reach of drifting icebergs, and, much against my desire to push ahead, encamped, the guide insisting that the big ice-mountain at the head of the bay could not be reached before dark, that the landing there was dangerous even in daylight, and that this was the only safe harbour on the way to it. While camp was being made, I strolled along the shore to examine the rocks and the fossil timber that abounds here. All the rocks are freshly glaciated, even below the sea-level, nor have the waves as yet worn off the surface polish, much less the heavy scratches and grooves and lines of glacial contour.

The next day being Sunday, the minister wished to stay in camp; and so, on account of the weather, did the Indians. I therefore set out on an excursion, and spent the day alone on the mountain-slopes above the camp, and northward, to see what I might learn. Pushing on through rain and mud and sludgy snow, crossing many brown, boulder-choked torrents, wading, jumping, and wallowing in snow up to my shoulders was mountaineering of the most trying kind. After crouching cramped and benumbed in the canoe, poulticed in wet or damp clothing night and day, my limbs had been asleep. This day they were awakened and in the hour of trial proved that they had not lost the cunning learned on many a mountain peak of the High Sierra. I reached a height of fifteen hundred feet, on the ridge that bounds the second of the great glaciers. All the landscape was smothered in clouds and I began to fear that as far as wide views were concerned I had climbed in vain. But at length the clouds lifted a little, and beneath their grey fringes I saw the berg-filled expanse of the bay, and the feet of the mountains that stand about it, and the imposing fronts of five huge glaciers, the nearest being immediately beneath me. This was my first general view of Glacier Bay, a solitude of ice and snow and newborn rocks, dim, dreary, mysterious. I held the ground I had so dearly won for an hour or two, sheltering myself from the blast as best I could, while with benumbed fingers I sketched what I could see of the landscape, and wrote a few lines in my notebook. Then, breasting the snow again, crossing the shifting avalanche slopes and torrents, I reached camp about dark, wet and weary and glad.

While I was getting some coffee and hardtack, Mr Young told me that the Indians were discouraged, and had been talking about turning back, fearing that I would be lost, the canoe broken, or in some other mysterious way the expedition would come to grief if I persisted in going farther. They had been asking him what possible motive I could have in climbing mountains when storms were blowing; and when he replied that I was only seeking knowledge, Toyatte said, 'Muir must be a witch to seek knowledge in such a place as this and in such miserable weather'.

After supper, crouching about a dull fire of fossil wood, they became still more doleful, and talked in tones that accorded well with the wind and waters and growling torrents about us, telling sad old stories of crushed canoes, drowned Indians, and hunters frozen in snowstorms. Even brave old Toyatte, dreading the treeless, forlorn appearance of the region, said that his heart was not strong, and that he feared his canoe, on the safety of which our lives depended, might be entering a skookum-house (jail) of ice, from which there might be no escape; while the Hoona guide said bluntly that if I was so fond of danger, and meant to go close up to the noses of the ice-mountains, he would not consent to go any farther; for we should all be lost, as many of his tribe had been, by the sudden rising of bergs from the bottom. They seemed to be losing heart with every howl of the wind, and fearing that they might fail me now that I was in the midst of so grand a congregation of glaciers, I made haste to reassure them, telling them that for ten years I had wandered alone among mountains and storms, and good luck always followed me; that with me, therefore, they need fear nothing. The storm would soon cease and the sun would shine to show us the way we should go, for God cares for us and guides us as long as we are trustful and brave, therefore all childish fear must be put away. This little speech did good. Kadachan, with some show of enthusiasm, said he liked to travel with good-luck people; and dignified old Toyatte declared that now his heart was strong again, and he would venture on with me as far as I liked for my 'wawa' was 'delait' (my talk was very good). The old warrior even became a little sentimental, and said that even if the canoe was broken he would not greatly care, because on the way to the other world he would have good companions.

Next morning it was still raining and snowing, but the south wind swept us bravely forward and swept the bergs from our course. In about an hour we reached the second of the big glaciers, which I afterwards named for Hugh Miller. We rowed up its fiord and landed to make a slight examination of its grand frontal wall. The berg-producing portion we found to be about a mile and a half wide, and broken into an imposing array of jagged spires and pyramids, and flat-topped towers and battlements, of many shades of blue, from pale, shimmering, limpid tones in the crevasses and hollows, to the most startling, chilling, almost shrieking vitriol blue on the plain mural spaces from which bergs had just been discharged. Back from the front for a few miles the glacier rises in a series of wide steps, as if this portion of the glacier had sunk in successive sections as it reached deep water, and the sea had found its way beneath it. Beyond this it extends indefinitely in a gently rising prairie-like expanse, and branches along the slopes and canyons of the Fairweather Range.

From here a run of two hours brought us to the head of the bay, and to the mouth of the northwest fiord, at the head of which lie the Hoona sealing-grounds, and the great glacier now called the Pacific, and another called the Hoona. The fiord is about five miles long, and two miles wide at the mouth. Here our Hoona guide had a store of dry wood, which we took aboard. Then, setting sail, we were driven wildly up the fiord, as if the storm-wind were saying, 'Go, then, if you will, into my icy chamber; but you shall stay in until I am ready to let you out.' All this time sleety rain was falling on the bay, and snow on the mountains; but soon after we landed the sky began to open. The camp was made on a rocky bench near the front

of the Pacific Glacier, and the canoe was carried beyond
the reach of the bergs and berg-waves. The bergs were now
crowded in a dense pack against the discharging front, as if
the storm-wind had determined to make the glacier take
back her crystal off-spring and keep them at home.

While camp affairs were being attended to, I set out to
climb a mountain for comprehensive views; and before I
had reached a height of a thousand feet the rain ceased,
and the clouds began to rise from the lower altitudes,
slowly lifting their white skirts, and lingering in majestic,
wing-shaped masses about the mountains that rise out of
the broad, icy sea, the highest of all the white mountains,
and the greatest of all the glaciers I had yet seen. Climbing
higher for a still broader outlook, I made notes and
sketched, improving the precious time while sunshine
streamed through the luminous fringes of the clouds and
fell on the green waters of the fiord, the glittering bergs,
the crystal bluffs of the vast glacier, the intensely white,
far-spreading fields of ice, and the ineffably chaste and
spiritual heights of the Fairweather Range, which were now
hidden, now partly revealed, the whole making a picture
of icy wildness unspeakably pure and sublime.

Looking southward, a broad ice-sheet was seen extending in a gently undulating plain from the Pacific Fiord in
the foreground to the horizon, dotted and ridged here
and there with mountains which were as white as the
snow-covered ice in which they were half, or more than
half, submerged. Several of the great glaciers of the bay
flow from this one grand fountain. It is an instructive
example of a general glacier covering the hills and dales
of a country that is not yet ready to be brought to the light
of day – not only covering but creating a landscape with the
features it is destined to have when, in the fullness of time,
the fashioning ice-sheet shall be lifted by the sun, and the
land become warm and fruitful. The view to the westward
is bounded and almost filled by the glorious Fairweather
Mountains, the highest among them springing aloft in
sublime beauty to a height of nearly sixteen thousand
feet, while from base to summit every peak and spire and
dividing ridge of all the mighty host was spotless white, as

if painted. It would seem that snow could never be made to lie on the steepest slopes and precipices unless plastered on when wet, and then frozen. But this snow could not have been wet. It must have been fixed by being driven and set in small particles like the storm-dust of drifts, which, when in this condition, is fixed not only on sheer cliffs, but in massive, overcurling cornices. Along the base of this majestic range sweeps the Pacific Glacier, fed by innumerable cascading tributaries, and discharging into the head of its fiord by two mouths only partly separated by the brow of an island rock about one thousand feet high, each nearly a mile wide.

Dancing down the mountain to camp, my mind glowing like the sunbeaten glaciers, I found the Indians seated around a good fire, entirely happy now that the farthest point of the journey was safely reached and the long, dark storm was cleared away. How hopefully, peacefully bright that night were the stars in the frosty sky, and how impressive was the thunder of the icebergs, rolling, swelling, reverberating through the solemn stillness! I was too happy to sleep.

About daylight next morning we crossed the fiord and landed on the south side of the rock that divides the wall of the great glacier. The whiskered faces of seals dotted the open spaces between the bergs, and I could not prevent John and Charley and Kadachan from shooting at them. Fortunately, few, if any, were hurt. Leaving the Indians in charge of the canoe, I managed to climb to the top of the wall by a good deal of step-cutting between the ice and dividing rock, and gained a good general view of the glacier. At one favourable place I descended about fifty feet below the side of the glacier, where its denuding, fashioning action was clearly shown. Pushing back from here, I found the surface crevassed and sunken in steps, like the Hugh Miller Glacier, as if it were being undermined by the action of tide waters. For a distance of fifteen or twenty miles the river-like ice-flood is nearly level, and when it recedes, the ocean water will follow it, and thus form a long extension of the fiord, with features essentially the same as those now extending into the continent farther south, where many great glaciers once poured into the sea, though scarce a vestige of them now exists. Thus the domain of the sea has been, and is being, extended in these ice-sculptured lands, and the scenery of their shores enriched. The brow of the dividing rock is about a thousand feet high, and is hard beset by the glacier. A short time ago it was at least two thousand feet below the surface of the over-sweeping ice; and under present climatic conditions it will soon take its place as a glacier-polished island in the middle of the fiord, like a thousand others in the magnificent archipelago. Emerging from its icy sepulchre, it gives a most telling illustration of the birth of a marked feature of a landscape. In this instance it is not the mountain, but the glacier, that is in labour, and the mountain itself is being brought forth.

The Hoona Glacier enters the fiord on the south side, a short distance below the Pacific, displaying a broad and far-reaching expanse, over which many lofty peaks are seen; but the front wall, thrust into the fiord, is not nearly so interesting as that of the Pacific, and I did not observe any bergs discharged from it.

In the evening, after witnessing the unveiling of the majestic peaks and glaciers and their baptism in the down-pouring sunbeams, it seemed inconceivable that nature could have anything finer to show us. Nevertheless, compared with what was to come the next morning, all that was as nothing. The calm dawn gave no promise of anything uncommon. Its most impressive features were the frosty clearness of the sky and a deep, brooding stillness made all the more striking by the thunder of the newborn bergs. The sunrise we did not see at all, for we were beneath the shadows of the fiord cliffs; but in the midst of our studies, while the Indians were getting ready to sail, we were startled by the sudden appearance of a red light burning with a strange unearthly splendour on the topmost peak of the Fairweather Mountains. Instead of vanishing as suddenly as it had appeared, it spread and spread until the whole range down to the level of the glaciers was filled with the celestial fire. In colour it was at first a vivid crimson, with a thick, furred appearance, as fine as the alpenglow, yet indescribably rich and deep – not in the least like a garment or mere external flush or bloom through which one might expect to see the rocks or snow, but every mountain apparently was glowing from the heart like molten metal fresh from a furnace. Beneath the frosty shadows of the fiord we stood hushed and awe-stricken, gazing at the holy vision; and had we seen the heavens opened and God made manifest, our attention could not have been more tremendously strained. When the highest peak began to burn, it did not seem to be steeped in sunshine, however glorious, but rather as if it had been thrust into the body of the sun itself. Then the supernal fire slowly descended, with a sharp line of demarcation separating it from the cold, shaded region beneath; peak after peak, with their spires and ridges and cascading glaciers, caught the heavenly glow, until all the mighty host stood transfigured, hushed, and thoughtful, as if awaiting the coming of the Lord. The white, rayless light of morning, seen when I was alone amid the peaks of the California Sierra, had always seemed to me the most telling of all the terrestrial manifestations of God. But here the mountains themselves were made divine, and declared His glory in terms still more impressive. How long we gazed I never knew. The glorious vision passed away in a gradual, fading change through a thousand tones of colour to pale yellow and white, and then the work of the ice-world went on again in everyday beauty. The green waters of the fiord were filled with sun-spangles; the fleet of icebergs set forth on their voyages with the upspringing breeze; and on the innumerable mirrors and prisms of these bergs, and on those of the shattered crystal walls of the glaciers, common white light and rainbow light began to burn, while the mountains shone in their frosty jewellry, and loomed again in the thin azure in serene terrestrial majesty. We turned and sailed away, joining the outgoing bergs, while 'Gloria in excelsis' still seemed to be sounding over all the white landscape, and our burning hearts were ready for any fate, feeling that, whatever the future might have in store, the treasures we had gained this glorious morning would enrich our lives forever.

When we arrived at the mouth of the fiord, and rounded

the massive granite headland that stands guard at the entrance on the north side, another large glacier, now named the Reid, was discovered at the head of one of the northern branches of the bay. Pushing ahead into this new fiord, we found that it was not only packed with bergs, but that the spaces between the bergs were crusted with new ice, compelling us to turn back while we were yet several miles from the discharging frontal wall. But though we were not then allowed to set foot on this magnificent glacier, we obtained a fine view of it, and I made the Indians cease rowing while I sketched its principal features. Thence, after steering northeastward a few miles, we discovered still another large glacier, now named the Carroll. But the fiord into which this glacier flows was, like the last, utterly inaccessible on account of ice, and we had to be content with a general view and sketch of it, gained as we rowed slowly past at a distance of three or four miles. The mountains back of it and on each side of its inlet are sculptured in a singularly rich and striking style of architecture, in which subordinate peaks and gables appear in wonderful profusion, and an imposing conical mountain with a wide, smooth base stands out in the main current of the glacier, a mile or two back from the discharging ice-wall.

We now turned southward down the eastern shore of the bay, and in an hour or two discovered a glacier of the second class, at the head of a comparatively short fiord that winter had not yet closed. Here we landed, and climbed across a mile or so of rough boulder-beds, and back upon the wildly broken, receding front of the glacier, which, though it descends to the level of the sea, no longer sends off bergs. Many large masses, detached from the wasting front by irregular melting, were partly buried beneath mud, sand, gravel, and boulders of the terminal moraine. Thus protected, these fossil icebergs remain unmelted for many years, some of them for a century or more, as shown by the age of trees growing above them, though there are no trees here as yet. At length melting, a pit with sloping sides is formed by the falling in of the overlying moraine material into the space at first occupied by the buried ice. In this way are formed the curious depressions in drift-covered regions called kettles or sinks. On these decaying glaciers we may also find many interesting lessons on the formation of boulders and boulder-beds, which in all glaciated countries exert a marked influence on scenery, health and fruitfulness.

Three or four miles farther down the bay, we came to another fiord, up which we sailed in quest of more glaciers, discovering one in each of the two branches into which the fiord divides. Neither of these glaciers quite reaches tide-water. Notwithstanding the apparent fruitfulness of their fountains, they are in the first stage of decadence, the waste from melting and evaporation being greater now than the supply of new ice from their snowy fountains. We reached the one in the north branch, climbed over its wrinkled brow, and gained a good view of the trunk and some of the tributaries, and also of the sublime grey cliffs of its channel.

Then we sailed up the south branch of the inlet, but failed to reach the glacier there, on account of a thin sheet of new ice. With the tent-poles we broke a lane for the canoe for a little distance; but it was slow work, and we soon saw that we could not reach the glacier before dark. Nevertheless, we gained a fair view of it as it came sweeping down through its gigantic gateway of massive Yosemite rocks three or four thousand feet high. Here we lingered until sundown, gazing and sketching; then turned back, and encamped on a bed of cobblestones between the forks of the fiord.

We gathered a lot of fossil wood and after supper made a big fire, and as we sat around it the brightness of the sky brought on a long talk with the Indians about the stars; and their eager, childlike attention was refreshing to see as compared with the deathlike apathy of weary town-dwellers, in whom natural curiosity has been quenched in toil and care and poor shallow comfort.

After sleeping a few hours, I stole quietly out of the camp, and climbed the mountain that stands between the two glaciers. The ground was frozen, making the climbing difficult in the steepest places; but the views over the icy bay, sparkling beneath the stars, were enchanting. It seemed then a sad thing that any part of so precious a night had been lost in sleep. The starlight was so full that I distinctly saw not only the berg-filled bay, but most of the lower portions of the glaciers, lying pale and spirit-like amid the mountains. The nearest glacier in particular was so distinct that it seemed to be glowing with light that came from within itself. Not even in dark nights have I ever found any difficulty in seeing large glaciers; but on this mountain-top, amid so much ice, in the heart of so clear and frosty a night, everything was more or less luminous, and I seemed to be poised in a vast hollow between two skies of almost equal brightness. This exhilarating scramble made me glad and strong and I rejoiced that my studies called me before the glorious night succeeding so glorious a morning had been spent!

I got back to camp in time for an early breakfast, and by daylight we had everything packed and were again under way. The fiord was frozen nearly to its mouth, and though the ice was so thin it gave us but little trouble in breaking a way for the canoe, yet it showed us that the season for exploration in these waters was well-nigh over. We were in danger of being imprisoned in a jam of icebergs, for the water-spaces between them freeze rapidly, binding the floes into one mass. Across such floes it would be almost impossible to drag a canoe, however industriously we might ply the axe, as our Hoona guide took great pains to warn us. I would have kept straight down the bay from here, but the guide had to be taken home, and the provisions we left at the bark hut had to be got on board. We therefore crossed over to our Sunday storm-camp, cautiously boring a way through the bergs. We found the shore lavishly adorned with a fresh arrival of assorted bergs that had been left stranded at high tide. They were arranged in a curving row, looking intensely clear and pure on the grey sand, and, with the sunbeams pouring through them, suggested the jewel-paved streets of the New Jerusalem.

On our way down the coast, after examining the front of the beautiful Geikie Glacier, we obtained our first broad view of the great glacier afterwards named the Muir, the last of all the grand company to be seen, the stormy weather having hidden it when we first entered the bay. It was now perfectly clear, and the spacious prairie-like glacier, with its many tributaries extending far back into the snowy recesses of its fountains, made a magnificent display of its wealth, and I was strongly tempted to go and explore it at all hazards. But winter had come, and the freezing of its fiords was an insurmountable obstacle. I had, therefore, to be content for the present with sketching and studying its main features at a distance.

When we arrived at the Hoona hunting-camp, men, women, and children came swarming out to welcome us. In the neighbourhood of this camp I carefully noted the lines of demarcation between the forested and deforested regions. Several mountains here are only in part deforested, and the lines separating the bare and the forested portions are well defined. The soil, as well as the trees, had slid off the steep slopes, leaving the edge of the woods raw-looking and rugged.

At the mouth of the bay a series of moraine islands show that the trunk glacier that occupied the bay halted here for some time and deposited this island material as a terminal moraine; that more of the bay was not filled in shows that, after lingering here, it receded comparatively fast. All the level portions of trunks of glaciers occupying ocean fiords, instead of melting back gradually in times of general shrinking and recession, as inland glaciers with sloping channels do, melt almost uniformly over all the surface until they become thin enough to float. Then, of course, with each rise and fall of the tide, the sea water, with a temperature usually considerably above the freezing-point, rushes in and out beneath them, causing rapid waste of the nether surface, while the upper is being wasted by the weather, until at length the fiord portions of these great glaciers become comparatively thin and weak and are broken up and vanish almost simultaneously.

Glacier Bay is undoubtedly young as yet. Vancouver's chart, made only a century ago, shows no trace of it, though found admirably faithful in general. It seems probable, therefore, that even then the entire bay was occupied by a glacier of which all those described above, great though they are, were only tributaries. Nearly as great a change has taken place in Sum Dum Bay since Vancouver's visit, the main trunk glacier there having receded from eighteen to twenty-five miles from the line marked on his chart. Charley, who was here when a boy, said that the place had so changed that he hardly recognized it, so many new islands had been born in the meantime and so much ice had vanished. As we have seen, this Icy Bay is being still farther extended by the recession of the glaciers. That this whole system of fiords and channels was added to the domain of the sea by glacial action is to my mind certain.

We reached the island from which we had obtained our store of fuel about half-past six and camped here for the night, having spent only five days in Sitadaka, sailing round it, visiting and sketching all the six glaciers excepting the largest, though I landed only on three of them, – the Geikie, Hugh Miller, and Grand Pacific – the freezing of the fiords in front of the others rendering them inaccessible at this late season.

ELEVEN

The Country of the Chilcats

On 30 October we visited a camp of Hoonas at the mouth of a salmon-chuck. We had seen some of them before, and they received us kindly. Here we learned that peace reigned in Chilcat. The reports that we had previously heard were, as usual in such cases, wildly exaggerated. The little camp hut of these Indians was crowded with the food-supplies they had gathered – chiefly salmon, dried and tied in bunches of convenient size for handling and transporting to their villages, bags of salmon-roe, boxes of fish-oil, a lot of mountain-goat mutton, and a few porcupines. They presented us with some dried salmon and potatoes, for which we gave them tobacco and rice. About 3 pm we reached their village, and in the best house, that of a chief, we found the family making whiskey. The still and mash were speedily removed and hidden away with apparent shame as soon as we came in sight. When we entered and passed the regular greetings, the usual apologies as to being unable to furnish Boston food for us and inquiries whether we could eat Indian food were gravely made. Toward six or seven o'clock Mr Young explained the object of his visit and held a short service. The chief replied with grave deliberation, saying that he would be heartily glad to have a teacher sent to his poor ignorant people, upon whom he now hoped the light of a better day was beginning to break. Hereafter he would gladly do whatever the white teachers told him to do and would have no will of his own. This under the whiskey circumstances seemed too good to be true. He thanked us over and over again for coming so far to see him, and complained that Port Simpson Indians, sent out on a missionary tour by Mr Crosby, after making a good-luck board for him and nailing it over his door, now wanted to take it away. Mr Young promised to make him a

new one, should this threat be executed, and remarked that
since he had offered to do his bidding he hoped he would
make no more whiskey. To this the chief replied with fresh
complaints concerning the threatened loss of his precious
board, saying that he thought the Port Simpson Indians
were very mean in seeking to take it away, but that now
he would tell them to take it as soon as they liked for he
was going to get a better one at Wrangell. But no effort
of the missionary could bring him to notice or discuss the
whiskey business. The luck board nailed over the door was
about two feet long and had the following inscription: 'The
Lord will bless those who do his will. When you rise in the
morning, and when you retire at night give him thanks.
Heccla Hockla Popla.'

This chief promised to pray like a white man every
morning, and to bury the dead as the whites do. 'I often
wondered', he said, 'where the dead went to. Now I am
glad to know'; and at last acknowledged the whiskey, saying
he was sorry to have been caught making the bad stuff.
The behaviour of all, even the little ones circled around
the fire, was very good. There was no laughter when the
strange singing commenced. They only gazed like curious,
intelligent animals. A little daughter of the chief with the
glow of the firelight on her eyes made an interesting picture,
head held aslant. Another in the group, with upturned eyes,
seeming to half understand the strange words about God,
might have passed for one of Raphael's angels.

The chief's house was about forty feet square, of the
ordinary fort kind, but better built and cleaner than usual.
The side-room doors were neatly panelled, though all the
lumber had been nibbled into shape with a small narrow
Indian adze. We had our tent pitched on a grassy spot
near the beach, being afraid of wee beasties; which greatly
offended Kadachan and old Toyatte, who said, 'If this is
the way you are to do up at Chilcat, we will be ashamed
of you.' We promised them to eat Indian food and in every
way behave like good Chilcats.

We set out direct for Chilcat in the morning against a
brisk head wind. By keeping close inshore and working
hard, we made about ten miles by two or three o'clock,

when, the tide having turned against us, we could make scarce any headway, and therefore landed in a sheltered cove a few miles up the west side of Lynn Canal. Here I discovered a fine growth of yellow cedar, but none of the trees were very large, the tallest only seventy-five to one hundred feet high. The flat, drooping, plume-like branchlets hang edgewise, giving the trees a thin, open, airy look. Nearly every tree that I saw in a long walk was more or less marked by the knives and axes of the Indians, who use the bark for matting, for covering house-roofs, and making temporary portable huts. For this last purpose sections five or six feet long and two or three wide are pressed flat and secured from warping or splitting by binding them with thin strips of wood at the end. These they carry about with them in their canoes, and in a few minutes they can be put together against slim poles and made into a rainproof hut. Every paddle that I have seen along the coast is made of the light, tough, handsome yellow wood of this tree. It is a tree of moderately rapid growth and usually chooses ground that is rather boggy and mossy. Whether its network of roots makes the bog or not, I am unable as yet to say.

Three glaciers on the opposite side of the canal were in sight, descending nearly to sea-level, and many smaller ones that melt a little below timber-line. While I was sketching these, a canoe hove in sight, coming on at a flying rate of speed before the wind. The owners, eager for news, paid us a visit. They proved to be Hoonas, a man, his wife, and four children, on their way home from Chilcat. The man was sitting in the stern steering and holding a sleeping child in his arms. Another lay asleep at his feet. He told us that Sitka Jack had gone up to the main Chilcat village the day before he left, intending to hold a grand feast and potlatch, and that whiskey up there was flowing like water. The news was rather depressing to Mr Young and myself, for we feared the effect of the poison on Toyatte's old enemies. At 8.30 pm we set out again on the turn of the tide, though the crew did not relish this night work. Naturally enough, they liked to stay in camp when wind and tide were against us, but didn't care to make up lost time after dark however wooingly wind and tide might flow and blow. Kadachan, John and Charley rowed, and Toyatte steered and paddled, assisted now and then by me. The wind moderated and almost died away, so that we made about fifteen miles in six hours, when the tide turned and snow began to fall. We ran into a bay nearly opposite Berner's Bay, where three or four families of Chilcats were camped, who shouted when they heard us landing and demanded our names. Our men ran to the huts for news before making camp. The Indians proved to be hunters, who said there were plenty of wild sheep on the mountains back a few miles from the head of the bay. This interview was held at three o'clock in the morning, a rather early hour. But Indians never resent any such disturbance provided there is anything worthwhile to be said or done. By four o'clock we had our tents set, a fire made and some coffee, while the snow was falling fast. Toyatte was out of humour with this night business. He wanted to land an hour or two before we did, and then, when the snow began to fall and we all wanted to find a camping-ground as soon as possible, he steered out into the middle of the canal, saying grimly that the tide was good. He turned, however, at our orders, but read us a lecture at the first opportunity, telling us to start early if we were in a hurry, but not to travel in the night like thieves.

After a few hours' sleep, we set off again, with the wind still against us and the sea rough. We were all tired after making only about twelve miles, and camped in a rocky nook where we found a family of Hoonas in their bark hut beside their canoe. They presented us with potatoes and salmon and a big bucketful of berries, salmon-roe, and grease of some sort, probably fish-oil, which the crew consumed with wonderful relish.

A fine breeze was blowing next morning from the south, which would take us to Chilcat in a few hours, but unluckily the day was Sunday and the good wind was refused. Sunday, it seemed to me, could be kept as well by sitting in the canoe and letting the Lord's wind waft us quietly on our way. The day was rainy and the clouds hung low. The trees here are remarkably well developed, tall and straight. I observed three or four hemlocks which had been struck by lightning – the first I noticed in Alaska. Some of the species on windy outjutting rocks become very picturesque, almost as much so as old oaks, the foliage becoming dense and the branchlets tufted in heavy plume-shaped horizontal masses.

Monday was a fine clear day, but the wind was dead ahead, making hard, dull work with paddles and oars. We passed a long stretch of beautiful marble cliffs enlivened with small merry waterfalls, and toward noon came in sight of the front of the famous Chilcat or Davidson Glacier, a broad white flood reaching out two or three miles into the canal with wonderful effect. I wanted to camp beside it but the head wind tired us out before we got within six or eight miles of it. We camped on the west side of a small rocky island in a narrow cove. When I was looking among the rocks and bushes for a smooth spot for a bed, I found a human skeleton. My Indians seemed not in the least shocked or surprised, explaining that it was only the remains of a Chilcat slave. Indians never bury or burn the bodies of slaves, but just cast them away anywhere. Kind Nature was covering the poor bones with moss and leaves, and I helped in the pitiful work.

The wind was fair and joyful in the morning, and away we glided to the famous glacier. In an hour or so we were directly in front of it and beheld it in all its crystal glory descending from its white mountain fountains and spreading out in an immense fan three or four miles wide against its tree-fringed terminal moraine. But, large as it is, it long ago ceased to discharge bergs.

The Chilcats are the most influential of all the Thlinkit tribes. Whenever on our journey I spoke of the interesting characteristics of other tribes we had visited, my crew would invariably say, 'Oh, yes, these are pretty good Indians, but wait till you have seen the Chilcats'. We were now only five or six miles distant from their lower village, and my crew requested time to prepare themselves to meet their great rivals. Going ashore on the moraine with their boxes that had not been opened since we left

Fort Wrangell, they sat on boulders and cut each other's hair, carefully washed and perfumed themselves and made a complete change in their clothing, even to white shirts, new boots, new hats, and bright neckties. Meanwhile, I scrambled across the broad, brushy, forested moraine, and on my return scarcely recognized my crew in their dress suits. Mr Young also made some changes in his clothing, while I, having nothing dressy in my bag, adorned my cap with an eagle's feather I found on the moraine, and thus arrayed we set forth to meet the noble Thlinkits.

We were discovered while we were several miles from the village, and as we entered the mouth of the river we were hailed by a messenger from the chief, sent to find out who we were and the objects of our extraordinary visit.

'Who are you?' he shouted in a heavy, far-reaching voice. 'What are your names? What do you want? What have you come for?'

On receiving replies, he shouted the information to another messenger, who was posted on the river-bank at a distance of a quarter of a mile or so, and he to another and another in succession, and by this living telephone the news was delivered to the chief as he sat by his fireside. A salute was then fired to welcome us, and a swarm of musket-bullets, flying scarce high enough for comfort, pinged over our heads. As soon as we reached the landing at the village, a dignified young man stepped forward and thus addressed us:

'My chief sent me to meet you, and to ask if you would do him the honour to lodge in his house during your stay in our village?'

We replied, of course, that we would consider it a great honour to be entertained by so distinguished a chief.

The messenger then ordered a number of slaves, who stood behind him, to draw our canoe out of the water, carry our provisions and bedding into the chief's house, and then carry the canoe back from the river where it would be beyond the reach of floating ice. While we waited, a lot of boys and girls were playing on a meadow near the landing – running races, shooting arrows, and wading in the icy river without showing any knowledge of our presence beyond quick stolen glances. After all was made secure, he conducted us to the house, where we found seats of honour prepared for us.

The old chief sat barefooted by the fireside, clad in a calico shirt and blanket, looking down, and though we shook hands as we passed him he did not look up. After we were seated, he still gazed into the fire without taking the slightest notice of us for about ten or fifteen minutes. The various members of the chief's family, also – men, women, and children – went about their usual employment and play as if entirely unconscious that strangers were in the house, it being considered impolite to look at visitors or speak to them before time had been allowed them to collect their thoughts and prepare any message they might have to deliver.

At length, after the politeness period had passed, the chief slowly raised his head and glanced at his visitors, looked down again, and at last said, through our interpreter:

'I am troubled. It is customary when strangers visit us to offer them food in case they might be hungry, and I was about to do so, when I remembered that the food of you honourable white chiefs is so much better than mine that I am ashamed to offer it.'

We, of course, replied that we would consider it a great honour to enjoy the hospitality of so distinguished a chief as he was.

Hearing this, he looked up, saying, 'I feel relieved'; or, in John the interpreter's words, 'He feels good now, he says he feels good'.

He then ordered one of his family to see that the visitors were fed. The young man who was to act as steward took up his position in a corner of the house commanding a view of all that was going on, and ordered the slaves to make haste to prepare a good meal; one to bring a lot of the best potatoes from the cellar and wash them well; another to go out and pick a basketful of fresh berries; another to broil a salmon; while others made a suitable fire, pouring oil on the wet wood to make it blaze. Speedily the feast was prepared and passed around. The first course was potatoes, the second fish-oil and salmon, next berries and rose-hips; then the steward shouted the important news, in a loud voice like a herald addressing an army, 'That's all!' and left his post.

Then followed all sorts of questions from the old chief. He wanted to know what Professor Davidson had been trying to do a year or two ago on a mountain-top back of the village, with many strange things looking at the sun when it grew dark in the daytime; and we had to try to explain eclipses. He asked us if we could tell him what made the water rise and fall twice a day, and we tried to explain that the sun and moon attracted the sea by showing how a magnet attracted iron.

Mr Young, as usual, explained the object of his visit and requested that the people might be called together in the evening to hear his message. Accordingly all were told to wash, put on their best clothing, and come at a certain hour. There was an audience of about two hundred and fifty, to whom Mr Young preached. Toyatte led in prayer, while Kadachan and John joined in the singing of several hymns. At the conclusion of the religious exercises the chief made a short address of thanks, and finished with a request for the message of the other chief. I again tried in vain to avoid a speech by telling the interpreter to explain that I was only travelling to see the country, the glaciers, and mountains and forests, etc., but these subjects, strange to say, seemed to be about as interesting as the gospel, and I had to deliver a sort of lecture on the fine foodful country God had given them and the brotherhood of man, along the same general lines I had followed at other villages. Some five similar meetings were held here, two of them in the daytime, and we began to feel quite at home in the big block-house with our hospitable and warlike friends.

At the last meeting an old white-haired shaman of grave and venerable aspect, with a high wrinkled forehead, big, strong Roman nose and light-coloured skin, slowly and with great dignity arose and spoke for the first time.

'I am an old man', he said, 'but I am glad to listen to those strange things you tell, and they may well be true, for what is more wonderful than the flight of birds in the air? I remember the first white man I ever saw. Since that long, long-ago time I have seen many, but never until now have I ever truly known and felt a white man's heart. All the white men I have heretofore met wanted to get something from us. They wanted furs and they wished to pay for them as small a price as possible. They all seemed to be seeking their own good – not our good. I might say that through all my long life I have never until now heard a white man speak. It has always seemed to me while trying to speak to traders and those seeking gold-mines that it was like speaking to a person across a broad stream that was running fast over stones and making so loud a noise that scarce a single word could be heard. But now, for the first time, the Indian and the white man are on the same side of the river, eye to eye, heart to heart. I have always loved my people. I have taught them and ministered to them as well as I could. Hereafter, I will keep silent and listen to the good words of the missionaries, who know God and the places we go to when we die so much better than I do.'

At the close of the exercises, after the last sermon had been preached and the last speech of the Indian chief and headsmen had been made, a number of the sub-chiefs were talking informally together. Mr Young, anxious to know what impression he had made on the tribe with reference to mission work, requested John to listen and tell him what was being said.

'They are talking about Mr Muir's speech', he reported. 'They say he knows how to talk and beats the preacher far.' Toyatte also, with a teasing smile, said: 'Mr Young, mika tillicum hi yu tola wawa' (Your friend leads you far in speaking).

Later, when the sending of a missionary and teacher was being considered, the chief said they wanted me, and, as an inducement, promised that if I would come to them they would always do as I directed, follow my councils, give me as many wives as I liked, build a church and school, and pick all the stones out of the paths and make them smooth for my feet.

They were about to set out on an expedition to the

Hootsenoos to collect blankets as indemnity or blood-money for the death of a Chilcat woman from drinking whiskey furnished by one of the Hootsenoo tribe. In case of their refusal to pay, there would be fighting, and one of the chiefs begged that we would pray them good luck, so that no one would be killed. This he asked as a favour, after begging that we would grant permission to go on this expedition, promising that they would avoid bloodshed if possible. He spoke in a very natural and easy tone and manner, always serene and so much of a polished diplomat that all polish was hidden. The younger chief stood while speaking, the elder sat on the floor. None of the congregation had a word to say, though they gave approving nods and shrugs.

The house was packed at every meeting, two a day. Some climbed on the roof to listen around the smoke opening. I tried in vain to avoid speech-making, but, as usual, I had to say something at every meeting. I made five speeches here, all of which seemed to be gladly heard, particularly what I said on the different kinds of white men and their motives, and their own kindness and good manners in making strangers feel at home in their houses.

The chief had a slave, a young and good-looking girl, who waited on him, cooked his food, lighted his pipe for him, etc. Her servitude seemed by no means galling. In the morning, just before we left on the return trip, interpreter John overhead him telling her that after the teacher came from Wrangell, he was going to dress her well and send her to school and use her in every way as if she were his own daughter. Slaves are still owned by the richest of the Thlinkits. Formerly, many of them were sacrificed on great occasions, such as the opening of a new house or the erection of a totem pole. Kadachan ordered John to take a pair of white blankets out of his trunk and wrap them about the chief's shoulders, as he sat by the fire. This gift was presented without ceremony or saying a single word. The chief scarcely noticed the blankets, only taking a corner in his hand, as if testing the quality of the wool. Toyatte had been an inveterate enemy and fighter of the Chilcats, but now, having joined the church, he wished to forget the past and bury all the hard feuds and be universally friendly and peaceful. It was evident, however, that he mistrusted the proud and warlike Chilcats and doubted the acceptance of his friendly advances, and as we approached their village became more and more thoughtful.

'My wife said that my old enemies would be sure to kill me. Well, never mind. I am an old man and may as well die as not.' He was troubled with palpitations, and oftentimes, while he suffered, he put his hand over his heart and said, 'I hope the Chilcats will shoot me here'.

Before venturing up the river to the principal village, located some ten miles up the river, we sent Sitka Charley and one of the young Chilcats as messengers to announce our arrival and inquire whether we would be welcome to visit them, informing the chief that both Kadachan and Toyatte were Mr Young's friends and mine, that we were 'all one meat' and any harm done them would also be done to us.

While our messengers were away, I climbed a pure-white, dome-crowned mountain about fifty-five hundred feet high and gained noble telling views to the northward of the main Chilcat glaciers and the multitude of mighty peaks from which they draw their sources. At a height of three thousand feet I found a mountain hemlock, considerably dwarfed, in company with Sitka spruce and the common hemlock, the tallest about twenty feet high, sixteen inches in diameter. A few stragglers grew considerably higher, say at about four thousand feet. Birch and two-leaf pine were common.

The messengers returned next day, bringing back word that we would all be heartily welcomed excepting Toyatte; that the guns were loaded and ready to be fired to welcome us, but that Toyatte, having insulted a Chilcat chief not long ago in Wrangell, must not come. They also informed us in their message that they were very busy merrymaking with other visitors, Sitka Jack and his friends, but that if we could get up to the village through the running ice on the river, they would all be glad to see us; they had been drinking and Kadachan's father, one of the principal chiefs, said plainly that he had just waked up out of a ten days' sleep. We were anxious to make this visit, but, taking the difficulties and untoward circumstances into account, the danger of being frozen in at so late a time, while Kadachan would not be able to walk back on account of a shot in his foot, the danger also from whiskey, the awakening of old feuds on account of Toyatte's presence, etc., we reluctantly concluded to start back on the home journey at once. This was on Friday and a fair wind was blowing, but our crew, who loved dearly to rest and eat in these big hospitable houses, all said that Monday would be *hyas klosh* for the starting-day. I insisted, however, on starting Saturday morning, and succeeded in getting away from our friends at ten o'clock. Just as we were leaving, the chief who had entertained us so handsomely requested a written document to show that he had not killed us, so in case we were lost on the way home he could not be held accountable in any way for our death.

TWELVE

The Return to Fort Wrangell

The day of our start for Wrangell was bright and the Hoon, the north wind strong. We passed around the east side of the larger island which lies near the south extremity of the point of land between the Chilcat and the Chilcoot channels and thence held a direct course down the east shore of the canal. At sunset we encamped in a small bay at the head of a beautiful harbour three or four miles south of Berner's Bay, and the next day, being Sunday, we remained in camp as usual, though the wind was fair and it is not a sin to go home. The Indians spent most of the day in washing, mending, eating, and singing hymns with Mr Young, who also gave them a Bible lesson, while I wrote notes and sketched. Charley made a sweathouse and all the crew got good baths. This is one of the most delightful little bays we have thus far enjoyed, girdled with tall trees whose branches almost meet, and with views of pure-white mountains across the broad, river-like canal.

Seeing smoke back in the dense woods, we went ashore to seek it and discovered a Hootsenoo whiskey-factory in full blast. The Indians said that an old man, a friend of theirs, was about to die and they were making whiskey for his funeral.

Our Indians were already out of oily flesh, which they regard as a necessity and consume in enormous quantities. The bacon was nearly gone and they eagerly inquired for flesh at every camp we passed. Here we found skinned carcasses of porcupines and a heap of wild mutton lying on the confused hut floor. Our cook boiled the porcupines in a big pot with a lot of potatoes we obtained at the same hut, and although the potatoes were protected by their skins, the awfully wild penetrating porcupine flavour found a way through the skins and flavoured them to the very heart. Bread and beans and dried fruit we had in abundance, and none of these rank aboriginal dainties ever came nigh any meal of mine. The Indians eat the hips of wild roses entire like berries, and I was laughed at for eating only the outside of this fruit and rejecting the seeds.

When we were approaching the village of the Auk tribe, venerable Toyatte seemed to be unusually pensive, as if weighed down by some melancholy thought. This was so unusual that I waited attentively to find out the cause of his trouble.

When at last he broke silence it was to say, 'Mr Young, Mr Young' – he usually repeated the name – 'I hope you will not stop at the Auk village'.

'Why, Toyatte?' asked Mr Young.

'Because they are a bad lot, and preaching to them can do no good.'

'Toyatte', said Mr Young, 'have you forgotten what Christ said to his disciples when he charged them to go forth and preach the gospel to everybody; and that we should love our enemies and do good to those who use us badly?'

'Well', replied Toyatte, 'if you preach to them, you must not call on me to pray, because I cannot pray for Auks.'

'But the Bible says we should pray for all men, however bad they may be.'

'Oh, yes, I know that, Mr Young; I know it very well. But Auks are not men, good or bad – they are dogs.'

It was now nearly dark and quite so ere we found a harbour, not far from the fine Auk Glacier which descends into the narrow channel that separates Douglas Island from the mainland. Two of the Auks followed us to our camp after eight o'clock and inquired into our object in visiting them, that they might carry the news to their chief. One of the chief's houses is opposite our camp a mile or two distant, and we concluded to call on him next morning.

I wanted to examine the Auk Glacier in the morning, but tried to be satisfied with a general view and sketch as we sailed around its wide fanshaped front. It is one of the most beautiful of all the coast glaciers that are in the first stage of decadence. We called on the Auk chief at daylight, when he was yet in bed, but he arose goodnaturedly, put on a calico shirt, drew a blanket around his legs, and comfortably seated himself beside a small fire that gave light enough to show his features and those of his children and the three women that one by one came out of the shadows. All listened attentively to Mr Young's message of goodwill. The chief was a serious, sharp-featured, dark-complexioned man, sensible-looking and with good manners. He was very sorry, he said, that his people had been drinking in his absence and had used us so ill; he would like to hear us talk and would call his people together if we would return to the village. This offer we had to decline. We gave him good words and tobacco and bade him good-bye.

The scenery all through the channel is magnificent, something like Yosemite Valley in its lofty avalanche-swept wall cliffs, especially on the mainland side, which are so steep few trees can find footing. The lower island side walls are mostly forested. The trees are heavily draped with lichens, giving the woods a remarkably grey, ancient look. I noticed a good many two-leafed pines in boggy spots. The water was smooth, and the reflections of the lofty walls striped with cascades were charmingly distinct.

It was not easy to keep my crew full of wild flesh. We called at an Indian summer camp on the mainland about noon, where there were three very squalid huts crowded and jammed full of flesh of many colours and smells, among which we discovered a lot of bright fresh trout, lovely creatures about fifteen inches long, their sides adorned with vivid red spots. We purchased five of them and a couple of salmon for a box of gun-caps and a little tobacco. About the middle of the afternoon we passed through a fleet of icebergs, their number increasing as we neared the mouth of the Taku Fiord, where we camped, hoping to explore the flord and see the glaciers where the bergs, the first we had seen since leaving Icy Bay, are derived.

We left camp at six o'clock, nearly an hour before daybreak. My Indians were glad to find the fiord barred by a violent wind, against which we failed to make any headway; and as it was too late in the season to wait for better weather, I reluctantly gave up this promising work for another year, and directed the crew to go straight ahead down the coast. We sailed across the mouth of the happy inlet at fine speed, keeping a man at the bow to look out for the smallest of the bergs, not easily seen in the dim light, and another bailing the canoe as the tops of some of the white caps broke over us. About two o'clock we passed a large bay or fiord, out of which a violent wind was blowing, though the main Stephens Passage was calm. About dusk, when we were all tired and anxious to get into camp, we reached the mouth of Sum Dum Bay, but nothing like a safe landing could we find. Our experienced captain was indignant, as well he might be, because we did not see fit to stop early in the afternoon at a good camp-ground he had chosen. He seemed determined to give us enough of night sailing as a punishment to last us for the rest of the voyage. Accordingly, though the night was dark and rainy and the bay full of icebergs, he pushed grimly on, saying that we must try to reach an Indian village on the other side of the bay or an old Indian fort on an island in the middle of it. We made slow, weary, anxious progress while Toyatte, who was well acquainted with every feature of this part of the coast and could find his way in the dark, only laughed at our misery. After a mile or two of this dismal night work we struck across toward the island, now invisible, and came near being wrecked on a rock which showed a smooth round back over which the waves were breaking. In the hurried Indian shouts that followed and while we were close against the rock, Mr Young shouted, as he leaned over against me, 'It's a whale, a whale!' evidently fearing its tail, several specimens of these animals, which were probably still on his mind, having been seen in the forenoon. While we were passing along the east shore of the island we saw a light on the opposite shore, a joyful sight, which Toyatte took for a fire in the Indian village, and steered for it. John stood in the bow, as guide through the bergs. Suddenly, we ran aground on a sand bar. Clearing this, and running back half a mile or so, we again stood for the light, which

now shone brightly. I thought it strange that Indians should
have so large a fire. A broad white mass dimly visible back
of the fire Mr Young took for the glow of the fire on the
clouds. This proved to be the front of a glacier. After we
had effected a landing and stumbled up toward the fire
over a ledge of slippery, algae-covered rocks, and through
the ordinary tangle of shore grass, we were astonished to
find white men instead of Indians, the first we had seen for
a month. They proved to be a party of seven gold-seekers
from Fort Wrangell. It was now about eight o'clock and
they were in bed, but a jolly Irishman got up to make
coffee for us and find out who we were, where we had
come from, where going, and the objects of our travels.
We unrolled our chart and asked for information as to the
extent and features of the bay. But our benevolent friend
took great pains to pull wool over our eyes, and made
haste to say that if 'ice and sceneries' were what we were
looking for, this was a very poor, dull place. There were
'big rocks, gulches and sceneries' of a far better quality
down the coast on the way to Wrangell. He and his party
were prospecting, he said, but thus far they had found only
a few colours and they proposed going over to Admiralty
Island in the morning to try their luck.

In the morning, however, when the prospectors were to
have gone over to the island, we noticed a smoke half a
mile back on a large stream, the outlet of the glacier we
had seen the night before, and an Indian told us that the
white men were building a big log house up there. It
appeared that they had found a promising placer mine in
the moraine and feared we might find it and spread the
news. Daylight revealed a magnificent fiord that brought
Glacier Bay to mind. Miles of bergs lay stranded on
the shores, and the waters of the branch fiords, not
on Vancouver's chart, were crowded with them as far
as the eye could reach. After breakfast we set out to
explore an arm of the bay that trends southeastward,
and managed to force a way through the bergs about
ten miles. Farther we could not go. The pack was so
close no open water was in sight, and, convinced at last
that this part of my work would have to be left for another

year, we struggled across to the west side of the fiord and camped.

I climbed a mountain next morning, hoping to gain a view of the great fruitful glaciers at the head of the fiord or, at least, of their snowy fountains. But in this also I failed; for at a distance of about sixteen miles from the mouth of the fiord a change to the northward in its general trend cut off all its upper course from sight.

Returning to camp baffled and weary, I ordered all hands to pack up and get out of the ice as soon as possible. And how gladly was that order obeyed! Toyatte's grand countenance glowed like a sun-filled glacier, as he joyfully and teasingly remarked that 'the big Sum Dum ice-mountain had hidden his face from me and refused to let me pay him a visit'. All the crew worked hard boring a way down the west side of the fiord, and early in the afternoon we reached comparatively open water near the mouth of the bay. Resting a few minutes among the drifting bergs, taking last lingering looks at the wonderful place I might never see again, and feeling sad over my weary failure to explore it, I was cheered by a friend I little expected to meet here. Suddenly, I heard the familiar whirr of an ouzel's wings, and, looking up, saw my little comforter coming straight from the shore. In a second or two he was with me, and flew three times around my head with a happy salute, as if saying, 'Cheer up, old friend, you see I am here and all's well'. He then flew back to the shore, alighted on the topmost jag of a stranded iceberg, and began to nod and bow as though he were on one of his favourite rocks in the middle of a sunny California mountain cataract.

Mr Young regretted not meeting the Indians here, but mission work also had to be left until next season. Our happy crew hoisted sail to a fair wind, shouted 'Good-bye, Sum Dum!' and soon after dark reached a harbour a few miles north of Hobart Point.

We made an early start the next day, a fine, calm morning, glided smoothly down the coast, admiring the magnificent mountains arrayed in their winter robes, and early in the afternoon reached a lovely harbour on an island five or six miles north of Cape Fanshawe. Toyatte predicted a heavy winter storm, though only a mild rain was falling as yet. Everybody was tired and hungry, and as the voyage was nearing the end, I consented to stop here. While the shelter tents were being set up and our blankets stowed under cover, John went out to hunt and killed a deer within two hundred yards of the camp. When we were at the camp-fire in Sum Dum Bay, one of the prospectors, replying to Mr Young's complaint that they were oftentimes out of meat, asked Toyatte why he and his men did not shoot plenty of ducks for the minister. 'Because the duck's friend would not let us', said Toyatte; 'when we want to shoot, Mr Muir always shakes the canoe'.

Just as we were passing the south headland of Port Houghton Bay, we heard a shout, and a few minutes later saw four Indians in a canoe paddling rapidly after us. In about an hour they overtook us. They were an Indian, his son, and two women with a load of fish-oil and dried salmon to sell and trade at Fort Wrangell. They camped within a dozen yards of us; with their sheets of cedar bark and poles they speedily made a hut, spread spruce boughs in it for a carpet, unloaded the canoe, and stored their goods under cover. Toward evening the old man came smiling with a gift for Toyatte – a large fresh salmon, which was promptly boiled and eaten by our captain and crew as if it were only a light refreshment like a biscuit between meals. A few minutes after the big salmon had vanished, our generous neighbour came to Toyatte with a second gift of dried salmon, which after being toasted a few minutes tranquilly followed the fresh one as though it were a mere mouthful. Then, from the same generous hands, came a third gift – a large milk-panful of huckleberries and grease boiled together – and, strange to say, this wonderful mess went smoothly down to rest on the broad and deep salmon foundation. Thus refreshed, and appetite sharpened, my sturdy crew made haste to begin on the buck, beans, bread, etc., and boiling and roasting, managed to get comfortably full on but little more than half of it by sundown, making a good deal of sport of my pity for the deer and refusing to eat any of it and nicknaming me the ice *ancou* and the deer and duck's *tillicum*.

Sunday was a wild, driving, windy day with but little rain but big promise of more. I took a walk back in the woods. The timber here is very fine, about as large as any I have seen in Alaska, much better than farther north. The Sitka spruce and the common hemlock, one hundred and fifty and two hundred feet high, are slender and handsome. The Sitka spruce makes good firewood even when green, the hemlock very poor. Back a little way from the sea, there was a good deal of yellow cedar, the best I had yet seen. The largest specimen that I saw and measured on the trip was five feet three inches in diameter and about one hundred and forty feet high. In the evening Mr Young gave the Indians a lesson, calling in our Indian neighbours. He told them the story of Christ coming to save the world. The Indians wanted to know why the Jews had killed him. The lesson was listened to with very marked attention. Toyatte's generous friend caught a devil-fish about three feet in diameter to add to his stores of food. It would be very good, he said, when boiled in berry and coliconoil soup. Each arm of this savage animal with its double row of button-like suction discs closed upon any object brought within reach with a grip nothing could escape. The Indians tell me that devil-fish live mostly on crabs, mussels and clams, the shells of which they easily crunch with their strong, parrot-like beaks. That was a wild, stormy, rainy night. How the rain soaked us in our tents!

'Just feel that', said the minister in the night, as he took my hand and plunged it into a pool about three inches deep in which he was lying.

'Never mind', I said, 'it is only water. Everything is wet now. It will soon be morning and we will dry at the fire.'

Our Indian neighbours were, if possible, still wetter. Their hut had been blown down several times during the night. Our tent leaked badly, and we were lying in a mossy bog, but around the big camp-fire we were soon warm and half dry. We had expected to reach Wrangell by this time. Toyatte said the storm might last several days longer. We were out of tea and coffee, much to Mr Young's distress. On my return from a walk I brought in a good big bunch of glandular ledum and boiled it in the teapot. The result of this experiment was a bright, clear amber-coloured, rank-smelling liquor which I did not taste, but my suffering companion drank the whole potful and praised it. The rain was so heavy we decided not to attempt to leave camp until the storm somewhat abated, as we were assured by Toyatte that we would not be able to round Cape Fanshawe, a sheer, outjutting headland, the nose as he called it, past which the wind sweeps with great violence in these southeastern storms. With what grateful enthusiasm the trees welcomed the life-giving rain! Strong, towering spruces, hemlocks, and cedars tossed their arms, bowing, waving, in every leap, quivering and rejoicing together in the grey, roaring storm. John and Charley put on their gun-coats and went hunting for another deer, but returned later in the afternoon with clean hands, having fortunately failed to shed any more blood. The wind still held in the south, and Toyatte, grimly trying to comfort us, told us that we might be held here a week or more, which we should not have minded much, for we had abundance of provisions. Mr Young and I shifted our tent and tried to dry blankets. The wind moderated considerably, and at 7 am we started but met a rough sea and so stiff a wind we barely succeeded in rounding the cape by all hands pulling their best. Thence we struggled down the coast, creeping close to the shore and taking advantage of the shelter of protecting rocks, making slow, hard-won progress until about the middle of the afternoon, when the sky opened and the blessed sun shone out over the beautiful waters and forests with rich amber light; and the high, glacier-laden mountains, adorned with fresh snow, slowly came to view in all their grandeur, the bluish-grey clouds crawling and lingering and dissolving until every vestige of them vanished. The sunlight made the upper snow-fields pale creamy yellow, like that seen on the Chilcat mountains the first day of our return trip. Shortly after the sky cleared, the wind abated and changed around to the north, so that we ventured to hoist our sail, and then the weary Indians had rest. It was interesting to note how speedily the heavy swell that had been rolling for the last two or three days was subdued by the comparatively light breeze from the opposite direction. In a few minutes the sound was smooth and no trace of the storm was left, save the fresh snow and the discoloration of the water. All the water of the sound as far as I noticed was pale coffee-colour like that of the streams in boggy woods. How much of this colour was due to the inflow of the flooded streams many times increased in size and number by the rain, and how much to the beating of the waves along the shore stirring up vegetable matter in shallow bays, I cannot determine. The effect, however, was very marked.

About four o'clock we saw smoke on the shore and ran in for news. We found a company of Taku Indians, who were on their way to Fort Wrangell, some six men and about the same number of women. The men were sitting in a bark hut, handsomely reinforced and embowered with fresh spruce boughs. The women were out at the side of a stream, washing their many bits of calico. A little girl, six or seven years old, was sitting on the gravelly beach, building a playhouse of white quartz pebbles, scarcely caring to stop her work to gaze at us. Toyatte found a friend among the men, and wished to encamp beside them for the night, assuring us that this was the only safe harbour to be found within a good many miles. But we resolved to push on a little farther and make use of the smooth weather after being stormbound so long, much to Toyatte and his companion's disgust. We rowed about a couple of miles and ran into a cozy cove where wood and water were close at hand. How beautiful and homelike it was! plushy moss for mattresses decked with red cornel berries, noble spruce standing guard about us and spreading kindly protecting arms. A few ferns, aspidiums, polypodiums, with dewberry vines, coptis, pyrola, leafless huckleberry bushes, and ledum grow beneath the trees. We retired at eight o'clock, and just then Toyatte, who had been attentively studying the sky, presaged rain and another southeaster for the morrow.

The sky was a little cloudy next morning, but the air was still and the water smooth. We all hoped that Toyatte, the old weather prophet, had misread the sky signs. But before reaching Point Vanderpeut the rain began to fall and the dreaded southeast wind to blow, which soon increased to a stiff breeze, next thing to a gale, that lashed the sound into ragged white caps. Cape Vanderpeut is part of the terminal of an ancient glacier that once extended six or eight miles out from the base of the mountains. Three large glaciers that once were tributaries still descend nearly to the sea-level, though their fronts are back in narrow fiords, eight or ten miles from the sound. A similar point juts out into the sound five or six miles to the south, while the missing portion is submerged and forms a shoal.

All the cape is forested save a narrow strip about a mile long, composed of large boulders against which the waves beat with loud roaring. A bar of foam a mile or so farther out showed where the waves were breaking on a submerged part of the moraine, and I supposed that we would be compelled to pass around it in deep water, but Toyatte, usually so cautious, determined to cross it, and after giving particular directions, with an encouraging shout every oar and paddle was strained to shoot through a narrow gap. Just at the most critical point a big wave heaved us aloft and dropped us between two huge rounded boulders, where, had the canoe been a foot or two closer to either of them, it must have been smashed. Though I had offered no objection to our experienced pilot's plan, it looked dangerous, and I took the precaution to untie my shoes so they could be quickly shaken off for swimming. But after crossing the bar we were not yet out of danger, for we had to struggle hard to keep from being driven ashore while the waves were beating us broadside on. At length we discovered a little inlet, into which we gladly escaped. A pure-white iceberg, weathered to the form of a cross, stood amid drifts of kelp and the black rocks of the wave-beaten shore in sign of safety and welcome. A good fire soon warmed and dried us into common comfort. Our narrow escape was the burden of conversation as we sat around the fire. Captain Toyatte told us of two similar adventures while he was a strong young man. In both of them his canoe was smashed and he swam ashore out of the

surge with a gun in his teeth. He says that if we had struck
the rocks he and Mr Young would have been drowned,
all the rest of us probably would have been saved. Then,
turning to me, he asked me if I could have made a fire in
such a case without matches, and found a way to Wrangell
without canoe or food.

We started about daybreak from our blessed white cross
harbour, and, after rounding a bluff cape opposite the
mouth of Wrangell Narrows, a fleet of icebergs came
in sight, and of course I was eager to trace them to
their source. Toyatte naturally enough was greatly excited
about the safety of his canoe and begged that we should
not venture to force a way through the bergs, risking the
loss of the canoe and our lives now that we were so near
the end of our long voyage.

'Oh, never fear, Toyatte', I replied. 'You know we are
always lucky – the weather is good. I only want to see the
Thunder Glacier for a few minutes, and should the bergs
be packed dangerously close, I promise to turn back and
wait until next summer.'

Thus assured, he pushed rapidly on until we entered
the fiord, where we had to go cautiously slow. The bergs
were close packed almost throughout the whole extent
of the fiord, but we managed to reach a point about
two miles from the head – commanding a good view
of the down-plunging lower end of the glacier and blue,
jagged ice-wall. This was one of the most imposing of the
first-class glaciers I had as yet seen, and with its magnificent
fiord formed a fine triumphant close for our season's ice
work. I made a few notes and sketches and turned back
in time to escape from the thickest packs of bergs before
dark. Then Kadachan was stationed in the bow to guide
through the open portion of the mouth of the fiord and
across Soutchoi Strait. It was not until several hours after
dark that we were finally free from ice. We occasionally
encountered stranded packs on the delta, which in the
starlight seemed to extend indefinitely in every direction.
Our danger lay in breaking the canoe on small bergs hard
to see and in getting too near the larger ones that might
split or roll over.

'Oh, when will we escape from this ice?' moaned much-enduring old Toyatte.

We ran aground in several places in crossing the Stickeen delta, but finally succeeded in groping our way over muddy shallows before the tide fell, and encamped on the boggy shore of a small island, where we discovered a spot dry enough to sleep on, after tumbling about in a tangle of bushes and mossy logs.

We left our last camp 21 November at daybreak. The weather was calm and bright. Wrangell Island came into view beneath a lovely rosy sky, all the forest down to the water's edge silvery grey with a dusting of snow. John and Charley seemed to be seriously distressed to find themselves at the end of their journey while a portion of the stock of provisions remained uneaten. 'What is to be done about it?' they asked, more than half in earnest. The fine, strong, and specious deliberation of Indians was well illustrated on this eventful trip. It was fresh every morning. They all behaved well, however, exerted themselves under tedious hardships without flinching for days or weeks at a time; never seemed in the least nonplussed; were prompt to act in every exigency; good as servants, fellow travellers, and even friends.

We landed on an island in sight of Wrangell and built a big smoky signal fire for friends in town, then set sail, unfurled our flag, and about noon completed our long journey of seven or eight hundred miles. As we approached the town, a large canoeful of friendly Indians came flying out to meet us, cheering and handshaking in lusty Boston fashion. The friends of Mr Young had intended to come out in a body to welcome him back, but had not had time to complete their arrangements before we landed. Mr Young was eager for news. I told him there could be no news of importance about a town. We only had real news, drawn from the wilderness. The mail steamer had left Wrangell eight days before, and Mr Vanderbilt and family had sailed on her to Portland. I had to wait a month for the next steamer, and though I would have liked to go again to Nature, the mountains were locked for the winter and canoe excursions no longer safe.

So I shut myself up in a good garret alone to wait and work. I was invited to live with Mr Young but concluded to prepare my own food and enjoy quiet work. How grandly long the nights were and short the days! At noon the sun seemed to be about an hour high, the clouds coloured like sunset. The weather was rather stormy. North winds prevailed for a week at a time, sending down the temperature to near zero and chilling the vapour of the bay into white reek, presenting a curious appearance as it streamed forward on the wind, like combed wool. At Sitka the minimum was eight degrees plus; at Wrangell, near the storm-throat of the Stickeen, zero. This is said to be the coldest weather ever experienced in southeastern Alaska.

THIRTEEN

Alaska Indians

Looking back on my Alaska travels, I have always been glad that good luck gave me Mr Young as a companion, for he brought me into confiding contact with the Thlinkit tribes, so that I learned their customs, what manner of men they were, how they lived and loved, fought and played, their morals, religion, hopes and fears, and superstitions, how they resembled and differed in their characteristics from our own and other races. It was easy to see that they differed greatly from the typical American Indian of the interior of this continent. They were doubtless derived from the Mongol stock. Their down-slanting oval eyes, wide cheek-bones, and rather thick, outstanding upper lips at once suggest their connection with the Chinese or Japanese. I have not seen a single specimen that looks in the least like the best of the Sioux, or indeed of any of the tribes to the east of the Rocky Mountains. They also differ from other North American Indians in being willing to work, when free from contamination of bad whites. They manage to feed themselves well, build good substantial houses, bravely fight their enemies, love their wives and children and friends, and cherish a quick sense of honour. The best of them prefer death to dishonour, and sympathize with their neighbours in their misfortunes and sorrows. Thus when a family loses a child by death, neighbours visit them to cheer and console. They gather around the fire and smoke, talk kindly and naturally, telling the sorrowing parents not to grieve too much, reminding them of the better lot of their child in another world and of the troubles and trials the little ones escape by dying young, all this in a perfectly natural, straightforward way, wholly unlike the vacant, silent, hesitating behaviour of most civilized friends, who oftentimes in such cases seem nonplussed, awkward, and afraid to speak, however sympathetic.

The Thlinkits are fond and indulgent parents. In all my travels I never heard a cross, fault-finding word, or anything like scolding inflicted on an Indian child, or ever witnessed a single case of spanking, so common in civilized communities. They consider the want of a son to bear their name and keep it alive the saddest and most deplorable ill-fortune imaginable.

The Thlinkit tribes give a hearty welcome to Christian missionaries. In particular they are quick to accept the doctrine of the atonement, because they themselves practice it, although to many of the civilized whites it is a stumbling-block and rock of offence. As an example of their own doctrine of atonement they told Mr Young and me one evening that twenty or thirty years ago there was a bitter war between their own and the Sitka tribe, great fighters, and pretty evenly matched. After fighting all summer in a desultory, squabbling way, fighting now under cover, now in the open, watching for every chance for a shot, none of the women dared venture to the salmon-streams or berry-fields to procure their winter stock of food. At this crisis one of the Stickeen chiefs came out of his block-house fort into an open space midway between their fortified camps, and shouted that he wished to speak to the leader of the Sitkas.

When the Sitka chief appeared he said:

'My people are hungry. They dare not go to the salmon-streams or berry-fields for winter supplies, and if this war goes on much longer most of my people will die of hunger. We have fought long enough; let us make peace. You brave Sitka warriors go home, and we will go home, and we will all set out to dry salmon and berries before it is too late.'

The Sitka chief replied:

'You may well say let us stop fighting, when you have had the best of it. You have killed ten more of my tribe than we have killed of yours. Give us ten Stickeen men to balance our blood-account; then, and not till then, will we make peace and go home.'

'Very well', replied the Stickeen chief, 'you know my rank. You know that I am worth ten common men and more. Take me and make peace.'

This noble offer was promptly accepted; the Stickeen chief stepped forward and was shot down in sight of the fighting bands. Peace was thus established, and all made haste to their homes and ordinary work. That chief literally gave himself a sacrifice for his people. He died that they might live. Therefore, when missionaries preached the doctrine of atonement, explaining that when all mankind had gone astray, had broken God's laws and deserved to die, God's son came forward, and, like the Stickeen chief, offered himself as a sacrifice to heal the cause of God's wrath and set all the people of the world free, the doctrine was readily accepted.

'Yes, your words are good', they said. 'The Son of God, the Chief of chiefs, the Maker of all the world, must be worth more than all mankind put together; therefore, when His blood was shed, the salvation of the world was made sure.'

A telling illustration of the ready acceptance of this doctrine was displayed by Shakes, head chief of the Stickeens at Fort Wrangell. A few years before my first visit to the Territory, when the first missionary arrived, he requested Shakes to call his people together to hear the good word he had brought them. Shakes accordingly sent out messengers throughout the village, telling his people to wash their faces, put on their best clothing, and come to the block-house to hear what their visitor had to say. When all were assembled, the missionary preached a Christian sermon on the fall of man and the atonement whereby Christ, the Son of God, the Chief of chiefs, had redeemed all mankind, provided that this redemption was voluntarily accepted with repentance of their sins and the keeping of his commandments.

When the missionary had finished his sermon, Chief Shakes slowly arose, and, after thanking the missionary for coming so far to bring them good tidings and taking so much unselfish interest in the welfare of his tribe, he advised his people to accept the new religion, for he felt satisfied that because the white man knew so much more than the Indian, the white man's religion was likely to be better than theirs.

'The white man', said he, 'makes great ships. We, like children, can only make canoes. He makes his big ships go with the wind, and he also makes them go with fire. We chop down trees with stone axes; the Boston man with iron axes, which are far better. In everything the ways of the white man seem to be better than ours. Compared with the white man we are only blind children, knowing not how best to live either here or in the country we go to after we die. So I wish you to learn this new religion and teach it to your children, that you may all go when you die into that good heaven country of the white man and be happy. But I am too old to learn a new religion, and besides, many of my people who have died were bad and foolish people, and if this word the missionary has brought us is true, and I think it is, many of my people must be in that bad country the missionary calls 'Hell', and I must go there also, for a Stickeen chief never deserts his people in time of trouble. To that bad country, therefore, I will go, and try to cheer my people and help them as best I can to endure their misery.'

Toyatte was a famous orator. I was present at the meeting at Fort Wrangell at which he was examined and admitted as a member of the Presbyterian Church. When called upon to answer the questions as to his ideas of God, and the principal doctrines of Christianity, he slowly arose in the crowded audience, while the missionary said, 'Toyatte, you do not need to rise. You can answer the questions seated.'

To this he paid no attention, but stood several minutes without speaking a word, never for a moment thinking of sitting down like a tired woman while making the most important of all the speeches of his life. He then explained in detail what his mother had taught him as to the character of God, the great Maker of the world; also what the shamans had taught him; the thoughts that often came to his mind when he was alone on hunting expeditions, and what he first thought of the religion which the missionaries had brought them. In all his gestures, and in the language in which he expressed himself, there was a noble simplicity and earnestness and majestic bearing which made the sermons and behaviour of the three distinguished divinity doctors present seem commonplace in comparison.

Soon after our return to Fort Wrangell this grand old man was killed in a quarrel in which he had taken no other part than that of peacemaker. A number of the Taku tribe came to Fort Wrangell, camped near the Stickeen village, and made merry, manufacturing and drinking *hootchenoo*, a vile liquor distilled from a mash made of flour, dried apples, sugar and molasses and drunk hot from the still. The manufacture of *hootchenoo* being illegal, and several of Toyatte's tribe having been appointed deputy constables to prevent it, they went to the Taku camp and destroyed as much of the liquor as they could find. The Takus resisted, and during the quarrel one of the Stickeens struck a Taku in the face – an unpardonable offence. The next day messengers from the Taku camp gave notice to the Stickeens that they must make atonement for that blow, or fight with guns. Mr Young, of course, was eager to stop the quarrel and so was Toyatte. They advised the Stickeen who had struck the Taku to return to their camp and submit to an equal blow in the face from the Taku. He did so; went to the camp, said he was ready to make atonement, and invited the person whom he had struck to strike him. This the Taku did with so much force that the balance of justice was again disturbed. The attention of the Takus was called to the fact that this atoning blow was far harder than the one to be atoned for, and immediately a sort of general free fist-fight began, and the quarrel was thus increased in bitterness rather than diminished.

Next day the Takus sent word to the Stickeens to get their guns ready, for tomorrow they would come up and fight them, thus boldy declaring war. The Stickeens in great excitement assembled and loaded their guns for the coming strife. Mr Young ran hither and thither amongst the men of his congregation, forbidding them to fight, reminding them that Christ told them when they were struck to offer the other cheek instead of giving a blow in return, doing everything in his power to still the storm, but all in vain. Toyatte stood outside one of the big block-houses with his men about him, awaiting the onset of the Takus. Mr Young tried hard to get him away to a place of safety, reminding him that he belonged to his church and no longer had any right to fight. Toyatte calmly replied:

'Mr Young, Mr Young, I am not going to fight. You see I have no gun in my hand; but I cannot go inside of the fort to a place of safety like women and children while my young men are exposed to the bullets of their enemies. I must stay with them and share their dangers, but I will not fight. But you, Mr Young, *you* must go away; you are a minister and you are an important man. It would not do for you to be exposed to bullets. Go to your home in the fort; pretty soon "hi yu poogh"' (much shooting).

At the first fire Toyatte fell, shot through the breast. Thus died for his people the noblest old Roman of them all.

On this first Alaska excursion I saw Toyatte under all circumstances – in rain and snow, landing at night in dark storms, making fires, building shelters, exposed to all kinds of discomfort, but never under any circumstances did I ever see him do anything, or make a single gesture, that was not dignified, or hear him say a word that might not be uttered anywhere. He often deplored the fact that he had no son to take his name at his death, and expressed himself as very grateful when I told him that his name would not be forgotten – that I had named one of the Stickeen glaciers for him.

Sum Dum Bay

I arrived early on the morning of the eighth of August on the steamer California to continue my explorations of the fiords to the northward which were closed by winter the previous November. The noise of our cannon and whistle was barely sufficient to awaken the sleepy town. The morning shout of one good rooster was the only evidence of life and health in all the place. Everything seemed kindly and familiar – the glassy water; evergreen islands; the Indians with their canoes and baskets and blankets and berries; the jet ravens, prying and flying about the streets and spruce trees; and the bland, hushed atmosphere brooding tenderly over all.

How delightful it is, and how it makes one's pulses bound to get back into this reviving northland wilderness! How truly wild it is, and how joyously one's heart responds to the welcome it gives, its waters and mountains shining and glowing like enthusiastic human faces! Gliding along the shores of its network of channels, we may travel thousands of miles without seeing any mark of man, save at long intervals some little Indian village or the faint smoke of a camp-fire. Even these are confined to the shore. Back a few yards from the beach the forests are as trackless as the sky, while the mountains, wrapped in their snow and ice and clouds, seem never before to have been looked at.

For those who really care to get into hearty contact with the coast region, travel by canoe is by far the better way. The larger canoes carry from one to three tons, rise lightly over any waves likely to be met on the inland channels, go well under sail, and are easily paddled alongshore in calm weather or against moderate winds, while snug harbours where they may ride at anchor or be pulled up on a smooth beach are to be found almost everywhere. With plenty of provisions packed in boxes, and blankets and warm clothing in rubber or canvas bags, you may be truly independent, and enter into partnership with Nature; to be carried with the winds and currents, accept the noble invitations offered all along your way to enter the mountain fiords, the homes of the waterfalls and glaciers, and encamp almost every night beneath hospitable trees.

I left Fort Wrangell the 16th of August, accompanied by Mr Young, in a canoe about twenty-five feet long and five wide, carrying two small square sails and manned by two Stickeen Indians – Captain Tyeen and Hunter Joe – and a half-breed named Smart Billy. The day was calm, and bright, fleecy, clouds hung about the lowest of the mountain-brows, while far above the clouds the peaks were seen stretching grandly away to the northward with their ice and snow shining in as calm a light as that which was falling on the glassy waters. Our Indians welcomed the work that lay before them, dipping their oars in exact time with hearty good will as we glided past island after island across the delta of the Stickeen into Soutchoi Channel.

By noon we came in sight of a fleet of icebergs from Hutli Bay. The Indian name of this icy fiord is Hutli, or Thunder Bay, from the sound made by the bergs in falling and rising from the front of the inflowing glacier.

As we floated happily on over the shining waters, the beautiful islands, in ever-changing pictures, were an unfailing source of enjoyment; but chiefly our attention was turned upon the mountains. Bold granite headlands with their feet in the channel, or some broad-shouldered peak of surpassing grandeur, would fix the eye, or some one of the larger glaciers, with far-reaching tributaries clasping entire groups of peaks and its great crystal river pouring down through the forest between grey ridges and domes. In these grand picture lessons the day was spent, and we spread our blankets beneath a Menzies spruce on moss two feet deep.

Next morning we sailed around an outcurving bank of boulders and sand ten miles long, the terminal moraine of a grand old glacier on which last November we met a perilous adventure. It is located just opposite three large converging glaciers which formerly united to form the vanished trunk of the glacier to which the submerged moraine belonged. A few centuries ago it must have been the grandest feature of this part of the coast, and, so well preserved are the monuments of its greatness, the noble old ice-river may be seen again in imagination about as vividly as if present in the flesh, with snow-clouds crawling about its fountains, sunshine sparkling on its broad flood, and its ten-mile ice-wall planted in the deep waters of the channel and sending off its bergs with loud resounding thunder.

About noon we rounded Cape Fanshawe, scudding swiftly before a fine breeze, to the delight of our Indians, who had now only to steer and chat. Here we overtook two Hoona Indians and their families on their way home from Fort Wrangell. They had exchanged five sea-otter furs, worth about a hundred dollars apiece, and a considerable number of fur-seal, land-otter, marten, beaver and other furs and skins, some $800 worth, for a new canoe valued at eighty dollars, some flour, tobacco, blankets and a few barrels of molasses for the manufacture of whiskey. The blankets were not to wear, but to keep as money, for the almighty dollar of these tribes is a Hudson's Bay blanket. The wind died away soon after we met, and as the two canoes glided slowly side by side, the Hoonas made minute inquiries as to who we were and what we were doing so far north. Mr Young's object in meeting the Indians as a missionary they could in part understand, but mine in searching for rocks and glaciers seemed past comprehension, and they asked our Indians whether gold-mines might not be the main object. They remembered, however, that I had visited their Glacier Bay ice-mountains a year ago, and seemed to think there might be, after all, some mysterious interest about them of which they were ignorant. Toward the middle of the afternoon they engaged our crew in a race. We pushed a little way ahead for a time, but, though possessing a considerable advantage, as it would seem, in our long oars, they at length overtook us and kept up until after dark, when we camped together in the rain on the bank of a salmon-stream among dripping grass and bushes some twenty-five miles beyond Cape Fanshawe.

These cold northern waters are at times about as brilliantly phosphorescent as those of the warm South, and so they were this evening in the rain and darkness, with the temperature of the water at forty-nine degrees, the air fifty-one. Every stroke of the oar made a vivid surge of white light, and the canoes left shining tracks.

As we neared the mouth of the well-known salmon-stream where we intended making our camp, we noticed jets and flashes of silvery light caused by the startled movement of the salmon that were on their way to the spawning-grounds. These became more and more numerous and exciting, and our Indians shouted joyfully, 'Hi yu salmon! Hi yu muck-a-muck!' while the water about the canoe and beneath the canoe was churned by thousands of fins in silver fire. After landing two of our men to commence camp-work, Mr Young and I went up the stream with Tyeen to the foot of a rapid, to see him catch a few salmon for supper. The stream was so filled with them there seemed to be more fish than water in it, and we appeared to be sailing in boiling, seething silver light marvellously relieved in the jet darkness. In the midst of the general auroral glow and the specially vivid flashes made by the frightened fish darting ahead and to right and left of the canoe, our attention was suddenly fixed by a long, steady, comet-like blaze that seemed to be made by some frightful monster that was pursuing us. But when the portentous object reached the canoe, it proved to be only our little dog, Stickeen.

After getting the canoe into a side eddy at the foot of the rapids, Tyeen caught half a dozen salmon in a few minutes by means of a large hook fastened to the end of a pole. They were so abundant that he simply groped for them in a random way, or aimed at them by the light they themselves furnished. That food to last a month or two may thus be procured in less than an hour is a striking illustration of the fruitfulness of these Alaskan waters.

Our Hoona neighbours were asleep in the morning at sunrise, lying in a row, wet and limp like dead salmon. A little boy about six years old, with no other covering than a remnant of a shirt, was lying peacefully on his back like

Tam o'Shanter, despising wind and rain and fire. He is up now, looking happy and fresh, with no clothes to dry and no need of washing while this weather lasts. The two babies are firmly strapped on boards, leaving only their heads and hands free. Their mothers are nursing them, holding the boards on end, while they sit on the ground with their breasts level with the little prisoners' mouths.

This morning we found out how beautiful a nook we had got into. Besides the charming picturesqueness of its lines, the colours about it, brightened by the rain, made a fine study. Viewed from the shore, there was first a margin of dark-brown algae, then a bar of yellowish-brown, next a dark bar on the rugged rocks marking the highest tides, then a bar of granite boulders with grasses in the seams, and above this a thick, bossy, overleaning fringe of bushes coloured red and yellow and green. A wall of spruces and hemlocks draped and tufted with grey and yellow lichens and mosses embowered the camp-ground and overarched the little river, while the camp-fire smoke, like a stranded cloud, lay motionless in their branches. Down on the beach ducks and sandpipers in flocks of hundreds were getting their breakfasts, bald eagles were seen perched on dead spars along the edge of the woods, heavy-looking and overfed, gazing stupidly like gorged vultures, and porpoises were blowing and lunging outside.

As for the salmon, as seen this morning urging their way up the swift current – tens of thousands of them, side by side, with their backs out of the water in shallow places now that the tide was low – nothing that I could write might possibly give anything like a fair conception of the extravagance of their numbers. There was more salmon apparently, bulk for bulk, than water in the stream. The struggling multitudes, crowding one against another, could not get out of our way when we waded into the midst of them. One of our men amused himself by seizing them above the tail and swinging them over his head. Thousands could thus be taken by hand at low tide, while they were making their way over the shallows among the stones.

Whatever may be said of other resources of the Territory, it is hardly possible to exaggerate the importance of the fisheries. Not to mention cod, herring, halibut, etc., there are probably not less than a thousand salmon-streams in southeastern Alaska as large or larger than this one (about forty feet wide) crowded with salmon several times a year. The first run commenced that year in July, while the king salmon, one of the five species recognized by the Indians, was in the Chilcat River about the middle of the November before.

From this wonderful salmon-camp we sailed joyfully up the coast to explore icy Sum Dum Bay, beginning my studies where I left off the previous November. We started about six o'clock, and pulled merrily on through fog and rain, the beautiful wooded shore on our right, passing bergs here and there, the largest of which, though not over two hundred feet long, seemed many times larger as they loomed grey and indistinct through the fog. For the first five hours the sailing was open and easy, nor was there anything very exciting to be seen or heard, save now and then the thunder of a falling berg rolling and echoing from cliff to cliff, and the sustained roar of cataracts.

About eleven o'clock we reached a point where the fiord was packed with ice all the way across, and we ran ashore to fit a block of wood on the cutwater of our canoe to prevent its being battered or broken. While Captain Tyeen, who had had considerable experience among berg ice, was at work on the canoe, Hunter Joe and Smart Billy prepared a warm lunch.

The sheltered hollow where we landed seems to be a favourite camping-ground for the Sum Dum seal-hunters. The pole-frames of tents, tied with cedar bark, stood on level spots strewn with seal bones, bits of salmon, and spruce bark.

We found the work of pushing through the ice rather tiresome. An opening of twenty or thirty yards would be found here and there, then a close pack that had to be opened by pushing the smaller bergs aside with poles. I enjoyed the labour, however, for the fine lessons I got, and in an hour or two we found zigzag lanes of water, through which we paddled with but little interruption, and had leisure to study the wonderful variety of forms

the bergs presented as we glided past them. The largest
we saw did not greatly exceed two hundred feet in length,
or twenty-five or thirty-feet in height above the water.
Such bergs would draw from one hundred and fifty to
two hundred feet of water. All those that have floated
long undisturbed have a projecting base at the water-line,
caused by the more rapid melting of the immersed portion.
When a portion of the berg breaks off, another base line is
formed, and the old one, sharply cut, may be seen rising at
all angles, giving it a marked character. Many of the oldest
bergs are beautifully ridged by the melting out of narrow
furrows strictly parallel throughout the mass, revealing the
bedded structure of the ice, acquired perhaps centuries ago,
on the mountain snow fountains. A berg suddenly going to
pieces is a grand sight, especially when the water is calm
and no motion is visible save perchance the slow drift of
the tide-current. The prolonged roar of its fall comes with
startling effect, and heavy swells are raised that haste away
in every direction to tell what has taken place, and tens of
thousands of its neighbours rock and swash in sympathy,
repeating the news over and over again. We were too near
several larger ones that fell apart as we passed them, and
our canoe had narrow escapes. The seal-hunters, Tyeen
says, are frequently lost in these sudden berg accidents.

In the afternoon, while we were admiring the scenery,
which, as we approached the head of the fiord, became
more and more sublime, one of our Indians called attention
to a flock of wild goats on a mountain overhead, and soon
afterwards we saw two other flocks, at a height of about
fifteen hundred feet, relieved against the mountains as
white spots. They are abundant here and throughout the
Alaskan Alps in general, feeding on the grassy slopes
above the timber-line. Their long, yellowish hair is shed
at this time of year and they were snowy white. None of
nature's cattle are better fed or better protected from the
cold. Tyeen told us that before the introduction of guns
they used to hunt them with spears, chasing them with
their wolf-dogs, and thus bringing them to bay among the
rocks, where they were easily approached and killed.

The upper half of the fiord is about from a mile to a

mile and a half wide, and shut in by sublime Yosemite cliffs, nobly sculptured, and adorned with waterfalls and fringes of trees, bushes, and patches of flowers; but amid so crowded a display of novel beauty it was not easy to concentrate the attention long enough on any portion of it without giving more days and years than our lives could afford. I was determined to see at least the grand fountain of all this ice. As we passed headland after headland, hoping as each was rounded we should obtain a view of it, it still remained hidden.

'Ice-mountain hi yu kumtux hide' – glaciers know how to hide extremely well – said Tyeen, as he rested for a moment after rounding a huge granite shoulder of the wall whence we expected to gain a view of the extreme head of the fiord. The bergs, however, were less closely packed and we made good progress, and at half-past eight o'clock, fourteen and a half hours after setting out, the great glacier came in sight at the head of a branch of the fiord that comes in from the northeast.

The discharging front of this fertile, fast-flowing glacier is about three quarters of a mile wide, and probably eight or nine hundred feet deep, about one hundred and fifty feet of its depth rising above the water as a grand blue barrier wall. It is much wider a few miles farther back, the front being jammed between sheer granite walls from thirty-five hundred to four thousand feet high. It shows grandly from where it broke on our sight, sweeping boldly forward and downward in its majestic channel, swaying from side to side in graceful fluent lines around stern unflinching rocks. While I stood in the canoe making a sketch of it, several bergs came off with tremendous dashing and thunder, raising a cloud of ice-dust and spray to a height of a hundred feet or more.

'The ice-mountain is well disposed toward you', said Tyeen. 'He is firing his big guns to welcome you'.

After completing my sketch and entering a few notes, I directed the crew to pull around a lofty burnished rock on the west side of the channel, where, as I knew from the trend of the canyon, a large glacier once came in; and what was my delight to discover that the glacier was still there and still pouring its ice into a branch of the fiord. Even the Indians shared my joy and shouted with me. I expected only one first-class glacier here, and found two. They are only about two miles apart. How glorious a mansion that precious pair dwell in! After sunset we made haste to seek a camp-ground. I would fain have shared these upper chambers with the two glaciers, but there was no landing-place in sight, and we had to make our way back a few miles in the twilight to the mouth of the side canyon where we had seen timber on the way up. There seemed to be a good landing as we approached the shore, but, coming nearer, we found that the granite fell directly into deep water without leading any level margin, though the slope a short distance back was not very steep.

After narrowly scanning the various seams and steps that roughened the granite, we concluded to attempt a landing rather than grope our way further down the fiord through the ice. And what a time we had climbing on hands and knees up the slippery glacier-polished rocks to a shelf some two hundred feet above the water and dragging provisions and blankets after us! But it proved to be a glorious place, the very best camp-ground of all the trip – a perfect garden, ripe berries nodding from a fringe of bushes around its edges charmingly displayed in the light of our big fire. Close alongside there was a lofty mountain capped with ice, and from the blue edge of the ice-cap there were sixteen silvery cascades in a row, falling about four thousand feet, each one of the sixteen large enough to be heard at least two miles.

How beautiful was the firelight on the nearest larkspurs and geraniums and daisies of our garden! How hearty the wave greeting on the rocks below brought to us from the two glaciers! And how glorious a song the sixteen cascades sang!

The cascade songs made us sleep all the sounder, and we were so happy as to find in the morning that the berg waves had spared our canoe. We set off in high spirits down the fiord and across to the right side to explore a remarkably deep and narrow branch of the main fiord that I had noted on the way up, and that, from the magnitude of the glacial characters on the two colossal rocks that guard the entrance, promised a rich reward for our pains.

After we had sailed about three miles up this side fiord, we came to what seemed to be its head, for trees and rocks swept in a curve around from one side to the other without showing any opening, although the walls of the canyon were seen extending back indefinitely, one majestic brow beyond the other.

When we were tracing this curve, however, in a leisurely way, in search of a good landing, we were startled by Captain Tyeen shouting, 'Skookum chuck! Skookum chuck!' (strong water, strong water), and found our canoe was being swept sideways by a powerful current, the roar of which we had mistaken for a waterfall. We barely escaped being carried over a rocky bar on the boiling flood, which, as we afterwards learned, would have been only a happy shove on our way. After we had made a landing a little distance back from the brow of the bar, we climbed the highest rock near the shore to seek a view of the channel beyond the inflowing tide rapids, to find out whether or no we could safely venture in. Up over rolling, mossy, bushy burnished rock waves we scrambled for an hour or two, which resulted in a fair view of the deep-blue waters of the fiord stretching on and on along the feet of the most majestic Yosemite rocks we had yet seen. This determined our plan of shooting the rapids and exploring it to its furthest recesses. This novel interruption of the channel is a bar of exceedingly hard resisting granite, over which the great glacier that once occupied it swept, without degrading it to the general level, and over which tide-waters now rush in and out with the violence of a mountain torrent.

Returning to the canoe, we pushed off, and in a few moments were racing over the bar with lightning speed through hurrahing waves and eddies and sheets of foam, our little shell of a boat tossing lightly as a bubble. Then, rowing across a belt of back-flowing water, we found ourselves on a smooth mirror reach between granite walls of the very wildest and most exciting description, surpassing in some ways those of the far-famed Yosemite Valley.

As we drifted silent and awe-stricken beneath the shadows of the mighty cliffs, which, in their tremendous height and abruptness, seemed to overhang at the top, the Indians gazing intently, as if they, too, were impressed with the strange, awe-inspiring grandeur that shut them in, one of them at length broke the silence by saying. 'This must be a good place for woodchucks; I hear them calling'.

When I asked them, further on, how they thought this gorge was made, they gave up the question, but offered an opinion as to the formation of rain and soil. The rain, they said, was produced by the rapid whirling of the earth by a stout mythical being called Yek. The water of the ocean was thus thrown up, to descend again in showers, just as it is thrown off a wet grindstone. They did not, however, understand why the ocean water should be salt, while the rain from it is fresh. The soil, they said, for the plants to grow on is formed by the washing of the rain on the rocks and gradually accumulating. The grinding action of ice in this connection they had not recognized.

Gliding on and on, the scenery seemed at every turn to become more lavishly fruitful in forms as well as more sublime in dimensions – snowy falls booming in splendid dress; colossal domes and battlements and sculptured arches of a fine neutral-grey tint, their bases laved by the blue fiord water; green ferny dells; bits of flower-bloom on ledges; fringes of willow and birch; and glaciers above all. But when we approached the base of a majestic rock like the Yosemite Half Dome at the head of the fiord, where two short branches put out, and came in sight of another glacier of the first order sending off bergs, our joy was complete. I had a most glorious view of it, sweeping in grand majesty from high mountain fountains, swaying around one mighty bastion after another, until it fell into the fiord in shattered overleaning fragments. When we had feasted awhile on this unhoped-for treasure, I directed the Indians to pull to the head of the left fork of the fiord, where we found a large cascade with a volume of water great enough to be called a river, doubtless the outlet of a receding glacier not in sight from the fiord.

This is in form and origin a typical Yosemite valley,

though as yet its floor is covered with ice and water – ice above and beneath, a noble mansion in which to spend a winter and a summer! It is about ten miles long, and from three quarters of a mile to a mile wide. It contains ten large falls and cascades, the finest one on the left side near the head. After coming in an admirable rush over a granite brow where it is first seen at a height of nine hundred or a thousand feet, it leaps a sheer precipice of about two hundred and fifty feet, then divides and reaches the tide-water in broken rapids over boulders. Another about a thousand feet high drops at once on to the margin of the glacier two miles back from the front. Several of the others are upwards of three thousand feet high, descending through narrow gorges as richly feathered with ferns as any channel that water ever flowed in, though tremendously abrupt and deep. A grander array of rocks and waterfalls I have never yet beheld in Alaska.

The amount of timber on the walls is about the same as that on the Yosemite walls, but owing to greater moisture, there is more small vegetation – bushes, ferns, mosses, grasses, etc.; though by far the greater portion of the area of the wall-surface is bare and shining with the polish it received when occupied by the glacier that formed the fiord. The deep-green patches seen on the mountains back of the walls at the limits of vegetation are grass, where the wild goats, or chamois rather, roam and feed. The still greener and more luxuriant patches farther down in gullies and on slopes where the declivity is not excessive, are made up mostly of willows, birch, and huckleberry bushes, with a varying amount of prickly ribes and rubus and echinopanax. This growth, when approached, especially on the lower slopes near the level of the sea at the jaws of the great side canyons, is found to be the most impenetrable and tedious and toilsome combination of fighting bushes that the weary explorer ever fell into, incomparably more punishing than the buckthorn and manzanita tangles of the Sierra.

The cliff gardens of this hidden Yosemite are exceedingly rich in colour. On almost every rift and bench, however small, as well as on the wider table-rocks where a little soil has lodged, we found gay multitudes of flowers, far more brilliantly coloured than would be looked for in so cool and beclouded a region – larkspurs, geraniums, painted-cups, blue-bells, gentians, saxifrages, epilobiums, violets, parnassia, veratrum, spiranthes and other orchids, fritillaria, smilax, asters, daisies, bryanthus, cassiope, linnaea, and a great variety of flowering ribes and rubus and heathworts. Many of the above, though with soft stems and leaves, are yet as brightly painted as those of the warm sunlands of the south. The heathworts in particular are very abundant and beautiful, both in flower and fruit, making delicate green carpets for the rocks, flushed with pink bells, or dotted with red and blue berries. The tallest of the grasses have ribbon leaves well tempered and arched, and with no lack of bristly spikes and nodding purple panicles. The alpine grasses of the Sierra, making close carpets on the glacier meadows, I have not yet seen in Alaska.

The ferns are less numerous in species than in California, but about equal in the number of fronds. I have seen three aspidiums, two woodsias, a lomaria, polypodium, cheilanthes and several species of pteris.

In this eastern arm of Sum Dum Bay and its Yosemite branch, I counted from my canoe, on my way up and down, thirty small glaciers back of the walls, and we saw three of the first order; also thirty-seven cascades and falls, counting only those large enough to make themselves heard several miles. The whole bay, with its rocks and woods and ice, reverberates with their roar. How many glaciers may be disclosed in the other great arm that I have not seen as yet, I cannot say, but, judging from the bergs it sends down, I guess not less than a hundred pour their turbid streams into the fiord, making about as many joyful, bouncing cataracts.

About noon we began to retrace our way back into the main fiord, and arrived at the gold-mine camp after dark, rich and weary.

On the morning of 21 August I set out with my three Indians to explore the right arm of this noble bay, Mr Young having decided, on account of mission work, to remain at the gold-mine. So here is another fine lot of Sum Dum ice – thirty-five or forty square miles of bergs, one great glacier of the first class descending into the fiord at the head, the fountain whence all these bergs were derived, and thirty-one smaller glaciers that do not reach tide-water; also nine cascades and falls, large size, and two rows of Yosemite rocks from three to four thousand feet high, each row about eighteen or twenty miles long, burnished and sculptured in the most telling glacier style, and well trimmed with spruce groves and flower gardens; a' that and more of a kind that cannot here be catalogued.

For the first five or six miles there is nothing excepting the icebergs that is very striking in the scenery as compared with that of the smooth unencumbered outside channels, where all is so evenly beautiful. The mountain-wall on the right as you go up is more preciptious than usual, and a series of small glaciers is seen along the top of it, extending their blue-crevassed fronts over the rims of pure-white snow fountains, and from the end of each front a hearty stream coming in a succession of falls and rapids over the terminal moraines, through patches of dwarf willows, and then through the spruce woods into the bay, singing and dancing all the way down. On the opposite side of the bay from here there is a small side bay about three miles deep, with a showy group of glacier-bearing mountains back of it. Everywhere else the view is bounded by comparatively low mountains densely forested to the very top.

After sailing about six miles from the mine, the experienced mountaineer could see some evidence of an opening from this wide lower portion, and on reaching it, it proved to be the continuation of the main west arm, contracted between stupendous walls of grey granite, and crowded with bergs from shore to shore, which seem to bar the way against everything but wings. Headland after headland, in most imposing array, was seen plunging sheer and bare from dizzy heights, and planting its feet in the ice-encumbered water without leaving a spot on which one could land from a boat, while no part of the great glacier that pours all these miles of ice into the fiord was visible. Pushing our way slowly through the packed bergs, and passing headland after headland, looking eagerly forward, the glacier and its fountain mountains were still beyond sight, cut off by other projecting headland capes, toward which I urged my way, enjoying the extraordinary grandeur of the wild unfinished Yosemite. Domes swell against the sky in fine lines as lofty and perfect in form as those of the California valley, and rock-fronts stand forward, as sheer and nobly sculptured. No ice-work that I have ever seen surpasses this, either in the magnitude of the features or effectiveness of composition.

On some of the narrow benches and tables of the walls rows of spruce trees and two-leaved pines were growing, and patches of considerable size were found on the spreading bases of those mountains that stand back inside the canyons, where the continuity of the walls is broken. Some of these side canyons are cut down to the level of the water and reach far back, opening views into groups of glacier fountains that give rise to many a noble stream; while all along the tops of the walls on both sides small glaciers are seen, still busily engaged in the work of completing their sculpture. I counted twenty-five from the canoe. Probably the drainage of fifty or more pours into this fiord. The average elevation at which they melt is about eighteen hundred feet above sea-level, and all of them are residual branches of the grand trunk that filled the fiord and overflowed its walls when there was only one Sum Dum glacier.

The afternoon was wearing away as we pushed on and on through the drifting bergs without our having obtained a single glimpse of the great glacier. A Sum Dum seal-hunter, whom we met groping his way deftly through the ice in a very small, unsplitable cottonwood canoe, told us that the ice-mountain was yet fifteen miles away. This was toward the middle of the afternoon, and I gave up sketching and making notes and worked hard with the Indians to reach it before dark. About seven o'clock we approached what seemed to be the extreme head of the fiord, and still no great glacier in sight – only a small one, three or four miles long, melting a thousand feet above the sea. Presently, a narrow side opening appeared between tremendous cliffs sheer to a height of four thousand feet or more, trending nearly at right angles to the general trend of the fiord, and apparently terminated by a cliff, scarcely less abrupt or high, at a distance of a mile or two. Up this bend we toiled against wind and tide, creeping closely along the wall on the right side, which, as we looked upward, seemed to be leaning over, while the waves beating against the bergs and rocks made a discouraging kind of music. At length, toward nine o'clock, just before the grey darkness of evening fell, a long, triumphant shout told that the glacier, so deeply and desperately hidden, was at last hunted back to its benmost bore. A short distance around a second bend in the canyon, I reached a point where I obtained a good view of it as it pours its deep, broad flood into the fiord in a majestic course from between the noble mountains, its tributaries, each of which would be regarded elsewhere as a grand glacier, converging from right and left from a fountain set far in the silent fastnesses of the mountains.

'There is your lost friend', said the Indians laughing; 'he says, "Sagh-a-ya"' (how do you do)? And while berg after berg was being born with thundering uproar, Tyeen said, 'Your friend has klosh tumtum (good heart). Hear! Like the other big-hearted one he is firing his guns in your honour.'

I stayed only long enough to make an outline sketch, and then urged the Indians to hasten back some six miles to the mouth of a side canyon I had noted on the way up as a place where we might camp in case we should not find a better. After dark we had to move with great caution through the ice. One of the Indians was stationed in the bow with a pole to push aside the smaller fragments and look out for the most promising openings, through which he guided us, shouting, 'Friday! Tucktay!' (shoreward, seaward) about ten times a minute. We reached this landing-place after ten o'clock, guided in the darkness by the roar of a glacier torrent. The ground was all boulders and it was hard to find a place among them, however small, to lie on. The Indians anchored the canoe well out from the shore and passed the night in it to guard against berg-waves and drifting waves, after assisting me to set my tent in some sort of way among the stones well back beyond the reach of the tide. I asked them as they were returning to the canoe if they were not going to eat something. They answered promptly:

'We will sleep now, if your ice friend will let us. We will eat to-morrow, but we can find some bread for you if you want it.'

'No', I said, 'go to rest. I, too, will sleep now and eat tomorrow.' Nothing was attempted in the way of light or fire. Camping that night was simply lying down. The boulders seemed to make a fair bed after finding the best place to take their pressure.

During the night I was awakened by the beating of the spent ends of berg-waves against the side of my tent, though I had fancied myself well beyond their reach. These special waves are not raised by wind or tide, but by the fall of large bergs from the snout of the glacier, or sometimes by the overturning or breaking of large bergs that may have long floated in perfect poise. The highest berg-waves oftentimes travel half a dozen miles or farther before they are much spent, producing a singularly impressive uproar in the far recesses of the mountains on calm dark nights when all beside is still. Far and near they tell the news that a berg is born, repeating their story again and again, compelling attention and reminding us of earthquake-waves that roll on for thousands of miles, taking their story from continent to continent.

When the Indians came ashore in the morning and saw the condition of my tent they laughed heartily and said, 'Your friend [meaning the big glacier] sent you a good word last night, and his servant knocked at your tent and said, "Sagh-a-ya, are you sleeping well?"'

I had fasted too long to be in very good order for hard work, but while the Indians were cooking, I made out to push my way up the canyon before breakfast to seek the glacier that once came into this fiord, knowing from the size and muddiness of the stream that drains it that it must be quite large and not far off. I came in sight of it after a hard scramble of two hours through thorny chaparral and across steep avalanche taluses of rocks and snow. The front reaches across the canyon from wall to wall, covered with rocky detritus, and looked dark and forbidding in the shadow cast by the cliffs, while from a low, cavelike hollow its draining stream breaks forth, a river in size, with a reverberating roar that stirs all the canyon. Beyond, in a cloudless blaze of sunshine, I saw many tributaries, pure and white as new-fallen snow, drawing their sources from clusters of peaks and sweeping down waving slopes to unite their crystal currents with the trunk glacier in the central canyon. This fine glacier reaches to within two hundred and fifty feet of the level of the sea, and would even yet reach the fiord and send off bergs but for the waste it suffers in flowing slowly through the trunk canyon, the declivity of which is very slight.

Returning, I reached camp and breakfast at ten o'clock; then had everything packed into the canoe, and set off leisurely across the fiord to the mouth of another wide and low canyon, whose lofty outer cliffs, facing the fiord, are telling glacial advertisements. Gladly I should have explored it all, traced its streams of water and streams of ice, and entered its highest chambers, the homes and fountains of the snow. But I had to wait. I only stopped an hour or two, and climbed on to the top of a rock through the common underbrush whence I had a good general view. The front of the main glacier is not far distant from the fiord, and sends off small bergs into a lake. The walls of its tributary canyons are remarkably jagged and high, cut in red variegated rock, probably slate. On the way back to the canoe I gathered ripe salmon-berries an inch and a half in diameter, ripe huckleberries, too, in great abundance, and several interesting plants I had not before met in the territory.

About noon, when the tide was in our favour, we set out on the return trip to the gold-mine camp. The sun shone free and warm. No wind stirred. The water spaces between the bergs were smooth as glass, reflecting the unclouded sky, and doubling the ravishing beauty of the bergs as the sunlight streamed through their innumerable angles in rainbow colours.

Soon a light breeze sprang up, and dancing lily spangles on the water mingled their glory of light with that burning on the angles of the ice.

On days like this, true sun-days, some of the bergs show a purplish tinge, though most are white from the disintegrating of their weathered surfaces. Now and then a new-born one is met that is pure blue crystal throughout, freshly broken from the fountain or recently exposed to the air by turning over. But in all of them, old and new, there are azure caves and rifts of ineffable beauty, in which the purest tones of light pulse and shimmer, lovely and untainted as anything on earth or in the sky.

As we were passing the Indian village I presented a little tobacco to the headmen as an expression of regard, while they gave us a few smoked salmon, after putting many questions concerning my exploration of their bay and bluntly declaring their disbelief in the ice business.

About nine o'clock we arrived at the gold camp, where we found Mr Young ready to go on with us the next morning, and thus ended two of the brightest and best of all my Alaska days.

FIFTEEN

From Taku River to Taylor Bay

I never saw Alaska looking better than it did when we bade farewell to Sum Dum on 22 August and pushed on northward up the coast toward Taku. The morning was clear, calm, bright – not a cloud in all the purple sky, nor wind, however gentle, to shake the slender spires of the spruces or dew-laden grass around the shores. Over the mountains and over the broad white bosoms of the glaciers the sunbeams poured, and rosy as ever, fell on fields of ripening wheat, drenching the forests and kindling the glassy waters and icebergs into a perfect blaze of coloured light. Every living thing seemed joyful, and nature's work was going on in glowing enthusiasm, not less appreciable in the deep repose that brooded over every feature of the landscape, suggesting the coming fruitfulness of the icy land and showing the advance that has already been made from glacial winter to summer. The care-laden commercial lives we lead close our eyes to the operations of God as a workman, though openly carried on that all who will look may see. The scarred rocks here and the moraines make a vivid showing of the old winter-time of the glacial period, and mark the bounds of the *mer-de-glace* that once filled the bay and covered the surrounding mountains. Already that sea of ice is replaced by water, in which multitudes of fishes are fed, while the hundred glaciers lingering about the bay and the streams that pour from them are busy night and day bringing in sand and mud and stones, at the rate of tons every minute, to fill it up. Then, as the seasons grow warmer, there will be fields here for the plough.

Our Indians, exhilarated by the sunshine, were garrulous as the gulls and plovers, and pulled heartily at the oars, evidently glad to get out of the ice with a whole boat.

'Now for Taku', they said, as we glided over the shining

water. 'Good-bye, Ice-Mountains; good-bye, Sum Dum.' Soon a light breeze came, and they unfurled the sail and laid away their oars and began, us usual in such free times, to put their goods in order, unpacking and sunning provisions, guns, ropes, clothing, etc. Joe has an old flintlock musket suggestive of Hudson's Bay times, which he wished to discharge and reload. So, stepping in front of the sail, he fired at a gull that was flying past before I could prevent him, and it fell slowly with outspread wings alongside the canoe, with blood dripping from its bill. I asked him why he had killed the bird, and followed the question by a severe reprimand for his stupid cruelty, to which he could offer no other excuse than that he had learned from the whites to be careless about taking life. Captain Tyeen denounced the deed as likely to bring bad luck.

Before the whites came most of the Thlinkits held with Agassiz, that animals have souls, and that it was wrong and unlucky to even speak disrespectfully of the fishes or any of the animals that supplied them with food. A case illustrating their superstitious beliefs in this connection occurred at Fort Wrangell while I was there the year before. One of the sub-chiefs of the Stickeens had a little son five or six years old, to whom he was very much attached, always taking him with him in his short canoe-trips, and leading him by the hand while going about town. Last summer the boy was taken sick, and gradually grew weak and thin, whereupon his father became alarmed, and feared, as is usual in such obscure cases, that the boy had been bewitched. He first applied in his trouble to Dr Carliss, one of the missionaries, who gave medicine, without effecting the immediate cure that the fond father demanded. He was, to some extent, a believer in the powers of missionaries, both as to material and spiritual affairs, but in so serious an exigency it was natural that he should go back to the faith of his fathers. Accordingly, he sent for one of the shamans, or medicine-men, of his tribe, and submitted the case to him, who, after going through the customary incantations, declared that he had discovered the cause of the difficulty.

'Your boy', he said, 'has lost his soul, and this is the way it happened. He was playing among the stones down on the beach when he saw a crawfish in the water, and made fun of it, pointing his finger at it and saying, "Oh, you crooked legs! Oh, you crooked legs! You can't walk straight; you go sidewise", which made the crab so angry that he reached out his long nippers, seized the lad's soul, pulled it out of him and made off with it into deep water. And', continued the medicine-man, 'unless his stolen soul is restored to him and put back in its place he will die. Your boy is really dead already; it is only his lonely empty body that is living now, and though it may continue to live in this way for a year or two, the boy will never be of any account, not strong, nor wise, nor brave.'

The father then inquired whether anything could be done about it; was the soul still in possession of the crab, and if so, could it be recovered and re-installed in his forlorn son? Yes, the doctor rather thought it might be charmed back and re-united, but the job would be a difficult one, and would probably cost about fifteen blankets.

After we were fairly out of the bay into Stephens Passage, the wind died away, and the Indians had to take to their oars again, which ended our talk. On we sped over the silvery level, close alongshore. The dark forests extending far and near, planted like a field of wheat, might seem monotonous in general views, but the appreciative observer, looking closely, will find no lack of interesting variety, however far he may go. The steep slopes on which they grow allow almost every individual tree, with its peculiarities of form and colour, to be seen like an audience on seats rising above one another – the blue-green, sharply-tapering spires of the Menzies spruce, the warm yellow-green Mertens spruce with their finger-like tops all pointing in the same direction, or drooping gracefully like leaves of grass, and the airy, feathery, brownish-green Alaska cedar. The outer fringe of bushes along the shore and hanging over the brows of the cliffs, the white mountains above, the shining water beneath, the changing sky over all, form pictures of divine beauty in which no healthy eye may ever grow weary.

Toward evening at the head of a picturesque bay we

came to a village belonging to the Taku tribe. We found
it silent and deserted. Not a single shaman or policeman
had been left to keep it. These people are so happily rich
as to have but little of a perishable kind to keep, nothing
worth fretting about. They were away catching salmon,
our Indians said. All the Indian villages hereabouts are thus
abandoned at regular periods every year, just as a tent is left
for a day, while they repair to fishing, berrying and hunting
stations, occupying each in succession for a week or two
at a time, coming and going from the main, substantially
built villages. Then, after their summer's work is done,
the winter supply of salmon dried and packed, fish-oil and
seal-oil stored in boxes, berries and spruce bark pressed
into cakes, their trading-trips completed, and the year's
stock of quarrels with the neighbouring tribe patched up
in some way, they devote themselves to feasting, dancing
and hootchenoo drinking. The Takus, once a powerful and
warlike tribe, were at this time, like most of the neighbouring tribes, whiskied nearly out of existence. They had a
larger village on the Taku River, but, according to the
census taken that year by the missionaries, they numbered
only 269 in all – 109 men, 79 women, and 81 children,
figures that show the vanishing condition of the tribe at a
glance.

Our Indians wanted to camp for the night in one of
the deserted houses, but I urged them on into the clean
wilderness until dark, when we landed on a rocky beach
fringed with devil's-clubs, greatly to the disgust of our
crew. We had to make the best of it, however, as it was
too dark to seek farther. After supper was accomplished
among the boulders, they retired to the canoe, which they
anchored a little way out, beyond low tide, while Mr Young
and I at the expense of a good deal of scrambling and
panax stinging, discovered a spot on which we managed
to sleep.

The next morning, about two hours after leaving our
thorny camp, we rounded a great mountain rock nearly
a mile in height and entered the Taku fiord. It is about
eighteen miles long and from three to five miles wide,
and extends directly back into the heart of the mountains,

draining hundreds of glaciers and streams. The ancient glacier that formed it was far too deep and broad and too little concentrated to erode one of those narrow canyons, usually so impressive in sculpture and architecture, but it is all the more interesting on this account when the grandeur of the ice work accomplished is recognized. This fiord, more than any other I have examined, explains the formation of the wonderful system of channels extending along the coast from Puget Sound to about latitude 59 degrees, for it is a marked portion of the system – a branch of Stephens Passage. Its trends and general sculpture are as distinctly glacial as those of the narrowest fiord, while the largest tributaries of the great glacier that occupied it are still in existence. I counted some forty-five altogether, big and little, in sight from the canoe in sailing up the middle of the fiord. Three of them, drawing their sources from magnificent groups of snowy mountains, came down to the level of the sea and formed a glorious spectacle. The middle one of the three belongs to the first class, pouring its majestic flood, shattered and crevassed, directly into the fiord, and crowding about twenty-five square miles of it with bergs. The next below it also sends off bergs occasionally, though a narrow strip of glacial detritus separates it from the tide-water. That forenoon a large mass fell from it, damming its draining stream, which at length broke the dam, and the resulting flood swept forward thousands of small bergs across the mud-flat into the fiord. In a short time all was quiet again; the flood-waters receded, leaving only a large blue scar on the front of the glacier and stranded bergs on the moraine flat to tell the tale.

These two glaciers are about equal in size – two miles wide – and their fronts are only about a mile and a half apart. While I sat sketching them from a point among the drifting icebergs where I could see far back into the heart of their distant fountains, two Taku seal-hunters, father and son, came gliding toward us in an extremely small canoe. Coming along side with a goodnatured 'Sagh-a-ya', they inquired who we were, our objects, etc., and gave us information about the river, their village, and two other large glaciers that descend nearly to the sea-level a few miles up the river canyon. Crouching in their little shell of a boat among the great bergs, with paddle and barbed spear, they formed a picture as arctic and remote from anything to be found in civilization as ever was sketched for us by the explorers of the Far North.

Making our way through the crowded bergs to the extreme head of the fiord, we entered the mouth of the river, but were soon compelled to turn back on account of the strength of the current. The Taku River is a large stream, nearly a mile wide at the mouth, and, like the Stickeen, Chilcat and Chilcoot, draws its sources from far inland, crossing the mountain-chain from the interior through a majestic canyon, and draining a multitude of glaciers on its way.

The Taku Indians, like the Chilcats, with a keen appreciation of the advantages of their position for trade, hold possession of the river and compel the Indians of the interior to accept their services as middle-men, instead of allowing them to trade directly with the whites.

When we were baffled in our attempt to ascend the river, the day was nearly done, and we began to seek a camp-ground. After sailing two or three miles along the left side of the fiord, we were so fortunate as to find a small nook described by the two Indians, where firewood was abundant, and where we could drag our canoe up the bank beyond reach of the berg-waves. Here we were safe, with a fine outlook across the fiord to the great glaciers and near enough to see the birth of the icebergs and the wonderful commotion they make, and hear their wild, roaring rejoicing. The sunset sky seemed to have been painted for this one mountain mansion, fitting it like a ceiling. After the fiord was in shadow the level sunbeams continued to pour through the miles of bergs with ravishing beauty, reflecting and refracting the purple light like cut crystal. Then all save the tips of the highest became dead white. These, too, were speedily quenched, the glowing points vanishing like stars sinking beneath the horizon. And after the shadows had crept higher, submerging the glaciers and the ridges between them, the divine alpenglow still lingered on their highest fountain peaks as they stood transfigured in glorious array. Now the last of the twilight purple has vanished, the stars begin to shine, and all trace of the day is gone. Looking across the fiord the water seems perfectly black, and the two great glaciers are seen stretching dim and ghostly into the shadowy mountains now darkly massed against the starry sky.

Next morning it was raining hard, everything looked dismal, and on the way down the fiord a growling head wind battered the rain in our faces, but we held doggedly on and by 10 am got out of the fiord into Stephens Passage. A breeze sprung up in our favour that swept us bravely on across the passage and around the end of Admiralty Island by dark. We camped in a boggy hollow on a bluff among scraggy, usnea-bearded spruces. The rain, bitterly cold and driven by a stormy wind, thrashed us well while we floundered in the stumpy bog trying to make a fire and supper.

When daylight came we found our camp-ground a very savage place. How we reached it and established ourselves in the thick darkness it would be difficult to tell. We crept along the shore a few miles against strong head winds, then hoisted sail and steered straight across Lynn Canal to the mainland, which we followed without great difficulty, the wind having moderated toward evening. Near the entrance to Icy Strait we met a Hoona who had seen us last year and who seemed glad to see us. He gave us two salmon, and we made him happy with tobacco and then pushed on and camped near Sitka Jack's deserted village.

Though the wind was still ahead next morning, we made about twenty miles before sundown and camped on the west end of Farewell Island. We bumped against a hidden rock and sprung a small leak that was easily stopped with resin. The salmon-berries were ripe. While climbing a bluff for a view of our course, I discovered moneses, one of my favourites and saw many well-travelled deer-trails, though the island is cut off from the mainland and other islands by at least five or six miles of icy, berg-encumbered water.

We got under way early next day – a grey, cloudy morning with rain and wind. Fair and head winds were about evenly balanced throughout the day. Tides run fast here,

like great rivers. We rowed and paddled around Point
Wimbleton against both wind and tide, creeping close to
the feet of the huge, bold rocks of the north wall of Cross
Sound, which here were very steep and awe-inspiring as
the heavy swells from the open sea coming in past Cape
Spencer dashed white against them, tossing our frail canoe
up and down lightly as a feather. The point reached by
vegetation shows that the surf dashes up to a height of
about seventy-five or a hundred feet. We were awestricken
and began to fear that we might be upset should the
ocean waves rise still higher. But little Stickeen seemed
to enjoy the storm, and gazed at the foam-wreathed cliffs
like a dreamy, comfortable tourist admiring the sunset.
We reached the mouth of Taylor Bay about two or three
o'clock in the afternoon, when we had a view of the open
ocean before we entered the bay. Many large bergs from
Glacier Bay were seen drifting out to sea past Cape Spencer. We reached the head of the fiord now called Taylor
Bay at five o'clock and camped near an immense glacier with a front about three miles wide stretching across
from wall to wall. No icebergs are discharged from it, as
it is separated from the water of the fiord at high tide
by a low, smooth mass of outspread, overswept moraine
material, netted with torrents and small shallow rills from
the glacier-front, with here and there a lakelet, and patches
of yellow mosses and garden spots bright with epilobium,
saxifrage, grass-tufts, sedges and creeping willows on the
higher ground. But only the mosses were sufficiently abundant to make conspicuous masses of colour to relieve the
dull slaty grey of the glacial mud and gravel. The front of
the glacier, like all those which do not discharge icebergs,
is rounded like a brow, smooth-looking in general views,
but cleft and furrowed, nevertheless, with chasms and
grooves in which the light glows and shimmers in glorious
beauty. The granite walls of the fiord, though very high,
are not deeply sculptured. Only a few deep side canyons
with trees, bushes, grassy and flowery spots interrupt their
massive simplicity, leaving but few of the cliffs absolutely
sheer and bare like those of Yosemite, Sum Dum or Taku.
One of the side canyons is on the left side of the fiord, the

other on the right, the tributaries of the former leading over
by a narrow tide-channel to the bay next to the eastward,
and by a short portage over into a lake into which pours a
branch glacier from the great glacier. Still another branch
from the main glacier turns to the right. Counting all three
of these separate fronts, the width of this great Taylor Bay
Glacier must be about seven or eight miles.

While camp was being made, Hunter Joe climbed the
eastern wall in search of wild mutton, but found none.
He fell in with a brown bear, however, and got a shot
at it, but nothing more. Mr Young and I crossed the
moraine slope, splashing through pools and streams up to
the ice-wall, and made the interesting discovery that the
glacier had been advancing of late years, ploughing up and
shoving forward moraine soil that had been deposited long
ago, and overwhelming and grinding and carrying away
the forests on the sides and front of the glacier. Though
not now sending off icebergs, the front is probably far
below sea-level at the bottom, thrust forward beneath its
wave-washed moraine.

Along the base of the mountain-wall we found abundance of salmon-berries, the largest measuring an inch and
a half in diameter. Strawberries, too, are found hereabouts.
Some which visiting Indians brought us were as fine in size
and colour and flavour as any I ever saw anywhere. After
wandering and wondering an hour or two, admiring the
magnificent rock and crystal scenery about us, we returned
to camp at sundown, planning a grand excursion for the
morrow.

I set off early in the morning of 30 August before anyone
else in camp had stirred, not waiting for breakfast, but only
eating a piece of bread. I had intended getting a cup of
coffee, but a wild storm was blowing and calling, and I
could not wait. Running out against the rain-laden gale
and turning to catch my breath I saw that the minister's
little dog had left his bed in the tent and was coming boring
through the storm, evidently determined to follow me. I
told him to go back, that such a day as this had nothing
for him.

'Go back', I shouted, 'and get your breakfast'. But he

simply stood with his head down, and when I began to urge my way again, looking around, I saw he was still following me. So I at last told him to come on if he must and gave him a piece of the bread I had in my pocket.

Instead of falling, the rain, mixed with misty shreds of clouds, was flying in level sheets, and the wind was roaring as I had never heard wind roar before. Over the icy levels and over the woods, on the mountains, over the jagged rocks and spires and chasms of the glacier it boomed and moaned and roared, filling the fiord in even, grey, structureless gloom, inspiring and awful. I first struggled up in the face of the blast to the east end of the ice-wall, where a patch of forest had been carried away by the glacier when it was advancing. I noticed a few stumps well out on the moraine flat, showing that its present bare, raw condition was not the condition of fifty or a hundred years ago. In front of this part of the glacier there is a small moraine lake about half a mile in length, around the margin of which are a considerable number of trees standing knee-deep, and of course dead. This also is a result of the recent advance of the ice.

Pushing up through the ragged edge of the woods on the left margin of the glacier, the storm seemed to increase in violence, so that it was difficult to draw breath in facing it; therefore I took shelter back of a tree to enjoy it and wait, hoping that it would at last somewhat abate. Here the glacier, descending over an abrupt rock, falls forward in grand cascades, while a stream swollen by the rain was now a torrent – wind, rain, ice-torrent and water-torrent in one grand symphony.

At length the storm seemed to abate somewhat, and I took off my heavy rubber boots, with which I had waded the glacial streams on the flat, and laid them with my overcoat on a log, where I might find them on my way back, knowing I would be drenched anyhow, and firmly tied my mountain shoes, tightened my belt, shouldered my ice-axe, and, thus free and ready for rough work, pushed on, regardless as possible of mere rain. Making my way up a steep granite slope, its projecting polished bosses encumbered here and there by boulders and the ground and bruised ruins of the ragged edge of the forest that had been uprooted by the glacier during its recent advance, I traced the side of the glacier for two or three miles, finding everywhere evidence of its having encroached on the woods, which here run back along its edge for fifteen or twenty miles. Under the projecting edge of this vast ice-river I could see down beneath it to a depth of fifty feet or so in some places, where logs and branches were being crushed to pulp, some of it almost fine enough for paper, though most of it stringy and coarse.

After thus tracing the margin of the glacier for three or four miles, I chopped steps and climbed to the top, and as far as the eye could reach, the nearly level glacier stretched indefinitely away in the grey cloudy sky, a prairie of ice. The wind was now almost moderate, though rain continued to fall, which I did not mind, but a tendency to mist in the drooping draggled clouds made me hesitate about attempting to cross to the opposite shore. Although the distance was only six or seven miles, no traces at this time could be seen of the mountains on the other side, and in case the sky should grow darker, as it seemed inclined to do, I feared that when I got out of sight of land and perhaps into a maze of crevasses I might find difficulty in winning a way back.

Lingering awhile and sauntering about in sight of the shore, I found this eastern side of the glacier remarkably free from large crevasses. Nearly all I met were so narrow I could step across them almost anywhere, while the few wide ones were easily avoided by going up or down along their sides to where they narrowed. The dismal cloud ceiling showed rifts here and there, and, thus encouraged, I struck out for the west shore, aiming to strike it five or six miles above the front wall, cautiously taking compass bearings at short intervals to enable me to find my way back should the weather darken again with mist or rain or snow. The structure lines of the glacier itself were, however, my main guide. All went well. I came to a deeply furrowed section about two miles in width where I had to zigzag in long, tedious tacks and make narrow doublings, tracing the edges of wide longitudinal furrows and chasms until

I could find a bridge connecting their sides, oftentimes making the direct distance ten times over. The walking was good of its kind, however, and by dint of patient doubling and axe-work on dangerous places, I gained the opposite shore in about three hours, the width of the glacier at this point being about seven miles. Occasionally, while making my way, the clouds lifted a little, revealing a few bald, rough mountains sunk to the throat in the broad, icy sea which encompassed them on all sides, sweeping on forever and forever as we count them, wearing them away, giving them the shape they are destined to take when in the fullness of time they shall be parts of new landscapes.

Ere I lost sight of the east-side mountains, those on the west came in sight, so that holding my course was easy, and, though making haste, I halted for a moment to gaze down into the beautiful pure blue crevasses and to drink at the lovely blue wells, the most beautiful of all Nature's water-basins, or at the rills and streams outspread over the ice-land prairie, never ceasing to admire their lovely colour and music as they glided and swirled in their blue crystal channels and potholes, and the rumbling of the moulins, or mills, where streams poured into blue-walled pits of unknown depth, some of them as regularly circular as if bored with augers. Interesting, too, were the cascades over blue cliffs, where streams fell into crevasses or slid almost noiselessly down slopes so smooth and frictionless their motion was concealed. The round or oval wells, however, from one to ten feet wide, and from one to twenty or thirty feet deep, were perhaps the most beautiful of all, the water so pure as to be almost invisible. My widest view did not probably exceed fifteen miles, the rain and mist making distances seem greater.

On reaching the farther shore and tracing it a few miles to northward, I found a large portion of the glacier-current sweeping out westward in a bold and beautiful curve around the shoulder of a mountain as if going direct to the open sea. Leaving the main trunk, it breaks into a magnificent uproar of pinnacles and spires and up-heaving, splashing wave-shaped masses, a crystal cataract incomparably greater and wilder than a score of Niagaras.

Tracing its channel three or four miles, I found that it fell into a lake, which it fills with bergs. The front of this branch of the glacier is about three miles wide. I first took the lake to be the head of an arm of the sea, but, going down to its shore and tasting it, I found it fresh, and by my aneroid perhaps less than a hundred feet above sea-level. It is probably separated from the sea only by a moraine dam. I had not time to go around its shores, as it was now near five o'clock and I was about fifteen miles from camp, and I had to make haste to recross the glacier before dark, which would come on about eight o'clock. I therefore made haste up to the main glacier, and, shaping my course by compass and the structure lines of the ice, set off from the land out on to the grand crystal prairie again. All was so silent and so concentrated, owing to the low dragging mist, the beauty close about me was all the more keenly felt, though tinged with a dim sense of danger, as if coming events were casting shadows. I was soon out of sight of land, and the evening dusk that on cloudy days precedes the real night gloom came stealing on and only ice was in sight, and the only sounds, save the low rumbling of the mills and the rattle of falling stones at long intervals, were the low, terribly earnest moanings of the wind or distant waterfalls coming through the thickening gloom. After two hours of hard work I came to a maze of crevasses of appalling depth and width which could not be passed apparently either up or down. I traced them with firm nerve developed by the danger, making wide jumps, poising cautiously on dizzy edges after cutting footholds, taking wide crevasses at a grand leap at once frightful and inspiring. Many a mile was thus travelled, mostly up and down the glacier, making but little real headway, running much of the time as the danger of having to pass the night on the ice became more and more imminent. This I could do, though with the weather and my rain-soaked condition it would be trying at best. In treading the mazes of this crevassed section I had frequently to cross bridges that were only knife-edges for twenty or thirty feet, cutting off the sharp tops and leaving them flat so that little Stickeen could follow me. These I had to straddle, cutting off the top as I progressed and hitching gradually ahead like a boy riding a rail fence. All this time the little dog followed me bravely, never hesitating on the brink of any crevasse that I had jumped, but now that it was becoming dark and the crevasses became more troublesome, he followed close at my heels instead of scampering far and wide, where the ice was at all smooth, as he had in the forenoon. No land was now in sight. The mist fell lower and darker and snow began to fly. I could not see far enough up and down the glacier to judge how best to work out of the bewildering labyrinth, and how hard I tried while there was yet hope of reaching camp that night! A hope which was fast growing dim like the sky. After dark, on such ground, to keep from freezing, I could only jump up and down until morning on a piece of flat ice between the crevasses, dance to the boding music of the winds and waters, and as I was already tired and hungry I would be in bad condition for such ice work. Many times I was put to my mettle, but with a firm-braced nerve, all the more unflinching as the dangers thickened, I worked out of that terrible ice-web, and with blood fairly up Stickeen and I ran over common danger without fatigue. Our very hardest trial was in getting across the very last of the sliver bridges. After examining the first of the two widest crevasses, I followed its edge half a mile or so up and down and discovered that its narrowest spot was about eight feet wide, which was the limit of what I was able to jump. Moreover, the side I was on – that is, the west side – was about a foot higher than the other, and I feared that in case I should be stopped by a still wider impassable crevasse ahead that I would hardly be able to take back that jump from its lower side. The ice beyond, however, as far as I could see it, looked temptingly smooth. Therefore, after carefully making a socket for my foot on the rounded brink, I jumped, but found that I had nothing to spare and more than ever dreaded having to retrace my way. Little Stickeen jumped this, however, without apparently taking a second look at it, and we ran ahead joyfully over smooth, level ice, hoping we were now leaving all danger behind us. But hardly had we gone a hundred or two yards when to our dismay we found ourselves on the very widest of all the longitudinal crevasses we had yet encountered. It was about forty feet wide. I ran anxiously up the side of it to northward eagerly hoping that I could get around its head, but my worst fears were realized when at a distance of about a mile or less it ran into the crevasse that I had just jumped. I then ran down the edge for a mile or more below the point where I had first met it, and found that its lower end also united with the crevasse I had jumped, showing dismally that we were on an island two or three hundred yards wide and about two miles long and the only way of escape from this island was by turning back and jumping again that crevasse which I dreaded, or venturing ahead across the giant crevasse by the very worst of the sliver bridges I had ever seen. It was so badly weathered and melted down that it formed a knife-edge, and extended across from side to side in a low, drooping curve like that made by a loose rope attached at each end at the same height. But the worst difficulty was that the ends of the down-curving sliver were attached to the sides at a depth of about eight or ten feet below the surface of the glacier. Getting down to the end of the bridge, and then after crossing it getting up the other side, seemed hardly possible. However, I decided to dare the dangers of the fearful sliver rather than to attempt to retrace my steps. Accordingly I dug a low groove in the rounded edge for my knees to rest in and, leaning over, began to cut a narrow foothold on the steep, smooth side. When I was doing this, Stickeen came up behind me, pushed his head over my shoulder, looked into the crevasses and along the narrow knife-edge, then turned and looked in my face, muttering and whining as if trying to say, 'Surely you are not going down there'. I said, 'Yes, Stickeen, this is the only way'. He then began to cry and ran wildly along the rim of the crevasse, searching for a better way, then, returning baffled, of course, he came behind me and lay down and cried louder and louder.

After getting down one step I cautiously stooped and cut another and another in succession until I reached the point where the sliver was attached to the wall. There, cautiously balancing, I chipped down the upcurved end of the bridge until I had formed a small level platform about a foot wide, then, bending forward, got astride of the end of the sliver, steadied myself with my knees, then cut off the top of the sliver, hitching myself forward an inch or two at a time, leaving it about four inches wide for Stickeen. Arrived at the farther end of the sliver, which was about seventy-five feet long, I chipped another little platform on its upcurved end, cautiously rose to my feet, and with infinite pains cut narrow notch steps and finger-holds in the wall and finally got safely across. All this dreadful time poor little Stickeen was crying as if his heart was broken, and when I called to him in as reassuring a voice as I could muster, he only cried the louder, as if trying to say that he never, never could get down there – the only time that the brave little fellow appeared to know what danger was. After going away as if I was leaving him, he still howled and cried without venturing to try to follow me. Returning to the edge of the crevasse, I told him that I must go, that he could come if he only tried, and finally in despair he hushed his cries, slid his little feet slowly down into my footsteps out on the big sliver, walked slowly and cautiously along the sliver as if holding his breath, while the snow was falling and the wind was moaning and threatening to blow him off. When he arrived at the foot of the slope below me, I was kneeling on the brink ready to assist him in case he should be unable to reach the top. He looked up along the row of notched steps I had made, as if fixing them in his mind, then with a nervous spring he whizzed up and passed me out on to the level ice, and ran and cried and barked and rolled about fairly hysterical in the sudden revulsion from the depth of despair to triumphant joy. I tried to catch him and pet him and tell him how good and brave he was, but he would not be caught. He ran round and round, swirling like autumn leaves in an eddy, lay down and rolled head over heels. I told him we still had far to go and that we must now stop all nonsense and get off the ice before dark. I knew by the ice-lines that every step was now taking me nearer the shore and soon it came in sight. The headland four or five miles back from the front, covered with spruce trees, loomed faintly but surely through the mist and light fall of snow not more than two miles away. The ice now proved good all the way across, and we reached the lateral moraine just at dusk, then with trembling limbs, now that the danger was over, we staggered and tumbled down the bouldery edge of the glacier and got over the dangerous rocks by the cascades while yet a faint light lingered. We were safe, and then, too, came limp weariness such as no ordinary work ever produces, however hard it may be. Wearily we stumbled down through the woods, over logs and brush and roots, devil's-clubs pricking us at every faint blundering tumble. At last we got out on the smooth mud slope with only a mile of slow but sure dragging of weary limbs to camp. The Indians had been firing guns to guide me and had a fine supper and fire ready, though fearing they would be compelled to seek us in the morning, a care not often applied to me. Stickeen and I were too tired to eat much, and, strange to say, too tired to sleep. Both of us, springing up in the night again and again, fancied we were still on that dreadful ice bridge in the shadow of death.

Nevertheless, we arose next morning in newness of life. Never before had rocks and ice and trees seemed to beautiful and wonderful, even the cold, biting rain-storm that was blowing seemed full of loving kindness, wonderful compensation for all that we had endured, and we sailed down the bay through the grey, driving rain rejoicing.

SIXTEEN

Glacier Bay

While Stickeen and I were away, a Hoona, one of the head men of the tribe, paid Mr Young a visit, and presented him with porpoise meat and berries and much interesting information. He naturally expected a return visit, and when we called at his house, a mile or two down the fiord, he said his wives were out in the rain gathering fresh berries to complete a feast prepared for us. We remained, however, only a few minutes, for I was not aware of this arrangement or of Mr Young's promise until after leaving the house. Anxiety to get around Cape Wimbelton was the cause of my haste, fearing the storm might increase. On account of this ignorance, no apologies were offered him, and the upshot was that the good Hoona became very angry. We succeeded, however, in the evening of the same day, in explaining our haste, and by sincere apologies and presents made peace.

After a hard struggle we got around stormy Wimbelton and into the next fiord to the northward (Klunastucksana – Dundas Bay). A cold, drenching rain was falling, darkening but not altogether hiding its extraordinary beauty, made up of lovely reaches and side fiords, feathery headlands and islands, beautiful every one and charmingly collocated. But how it rained, and how cold it was, and how weary we were pulling most of the time against the wind! The branches of this bay are so deep and so numerous that, with the rain and low clouds concealing the mountain landmarks, we could hardly make out the main trends. While groping and gazing among the islands through the misty rain and clouds, we discovered wisps of smoke at the foot of a sheltering rock in front of a mountain, where a choir of cascades were chanting their rain songs. Gladly we made for this camp, which proved to belong to a rare old Hoona sub-chief, so tall and wide and dignified in demeanour he looked grand even in the sloppy weather, and every inch a chief in spite of his bare legs and the old shirt and draggled, ragged blanket in which he was dressed. He was given to much handshaking, gripping hard, holding on and looking you gravely in the face while most emphatically speaking in Thlinkit, not a word of which we understood until interpreter John came to our help. He turned from one to the other of us, declaring, as John interpreted, that our presence did him good like food and fire, that he would welcome white men, especially teachers, and that he and all his people compared to ourselves were only children. When Mr Young informed him that a missionary was about to be sent to his people, he said he would call them all together four times and explain that a teacher and preacher were coming and that they therefore must put away all foolishness and prepare their hearts to receive them and their words. He then introduced his three children, one a naked lad five or six years old who, as he fondly assured us, would soon be a chief, and later to his wife, an intelligent-looking woman of whom he seemed proud. When we arrived she was out at the foot of the cascade mountain gathering salmon-berries. She came in dripping and loaded. A few of the fine berries saved for the children she presented, proudly and fondly beginning with the youngest, whose only clothing was a nose-ring and a string of beads. She was lightly apparelled in a cotton gown and bit of blanket, thoroughly bedraggled, but after unloading her berries she retired with a dry calico gown around the corner of a rock and soon returned fresh as a daisy and with becoming dignity took her place by the fireside. Soon two other berry-laden women came in, seemingly enjoying the rain like the bushes and trees. They put on little clothing so that they may be the more easily dried, and as for the children, a thin shirt of sheeting is the most they encumber themselves with, and get wet and half dry without seeming to notice it while we shiver with two or three dry coats. They seem to prefer being naked. The men also wear but little in wet weather. When they go out for all day they put on a single blanket, but in choring around camp, getting firewood, cooking, or looking after their precious canvas, they seldom wear anything, braving wind and rain in utter nakedness to avoid the bother of drying clothes. It is a rare sight to see the children bringing in big chunks of firewood on their shoulders, balancing in crossing boulders with firmly set bow-legs and bulging back muscles.

We gave Ka-hood-oo-shough, the old chief, some tobacco and rice and coffee, and pitched our tent near his hut among tall grass. Soon after our arrival the Taylor Bay sub-chief came in from the opposite direction from ours, telling us that he came through a cut-off passage not on our chart. As stated above, we took pains to conciliate him and soothe his hurt feelings. Our words and gifts, he said, had warmed his sore heart and made him glad and comfortable.

The view down the bay among the islands was, I thought, the finest of this kind of scenery that I had yet observed.

The weather continued cold and rainy. Nevertheless Mr Young and I and our crew, together with one of the Hoonas, an old man who acted as guide, left camp to explore one of the upper arms of the bay, where we were told there was a large glacier. We managed to push the canoe several miles up the stream that drains the glacier to a point where the swift current was divided among rocks and the banks were overhung with alders and willows. I left the canoe and pushed up the right bank past a magnificent waterfall some twelve hundred feet high, and over the shoulder of a mountain, until I secured a good view of the lower part of the glacier. It is probably a lobe of the Taylor Bay or Brady Glacier.

On our return to camp, thoroughly drenched and cold, the old chief came to visit us, apparently as wet and cold as ourselves.

'I have been thinking of you all day', he said, 'and pitying you, knowing how miserable you were, and as soon as I saw your canoe coming back I was ashamed to think that I had been sitting warm and dry at my fire while you were out in the storm; therefore I made haste to strip off my dry clothing and put on these wet rags to share your misery and show how much I love you.'

I had another long talk with Ka-hood-oo-shough the next day.

'I am not able', he said, 'to tell you how much good your words have done me. Your words are good, and they are strong words. Some of my people are foolish, and when they make their salmon-traps they do not take care to tie the poles firmly together, and when the big rain-floods come the traps break and are washed away because the people who made them are foolish people. But your words are strong words and when storms come to try them they will stand the storms.'

There was much hand shaking as we took our leave and assurances of eternal friendship. The grand old man stood on the shore watching us and waving farewell until we were out of sight.

We now steered for the Muir Glacier and arrived at the front on the east side the evening of the third, and camped on the end of the moraine, where there was a small stream. Captain Tyeen was inclined to keep at a safe distance from the tremendous threatening cliffs of the disharging wall. After a good deal of urging he ventured within half a mile of them, on the east side of the fiord, where with Mr Young I went ashore to seek a camp-ground on the moraine, leaving the Indians in the canoe. In a few minutes after we landed a huge berg sprung aloft with awful commotion, and the frightened Indians incontinently fled down the fiord, plying their paddles with admirable energy in the tossing waves until a safe harbour was reached around the south end of the moraine. I found a good place for a camp in a slight hollow where a few spruce stumps afforded firewood. But all efforts to get Tyeen out of his harbour failed. 'Nobody knew', he said, 'how far the angry ice mountain could throw waves to break his canoe'. Therefore I had my bedding and some provisions carried to my stump camp, where I could watch the bergs as they were discharged and get night views of the brow of the glacier and its sheer jagged face all the way across from side to side of the channel. One night the water was luminous and the surge from discharging icebergs churned the water into silver fire, a glorious sight in the darkness. I also went back up the east side of the glacier five or six miles and ascended a mountain between its first two eastern tributaries, which, though covered with grass near the top, was exceedingly steep and difficult. A bulging ridge near the top I discovered was formed of ice, a remnant of the glacier when it stood at this elevation which had been preserved by moraine material and later by a thatch of dwarf bushes and grass.

Next morning at daybreak I pushed eagerly back over the comparatively smooth eastern margin of the glacier to see as much as possible of the upper fountain region. About five miles back from the front I climbed a mountain twenty-five hundred feet high, from the flowery summit of which, the day being clear, the vast glacier and its principal branches were displayed in one magnificent view. Instead of a stream of ice winding down a mountain-walled valley like the largest of the Swiss glaciers, the Muir looks like a broad undulating prairie streaked with medial moraines and gashed with crevasses, surrounded by numberless mountains from which flow its many tributary glaciers. There are seven main tributaries from ten to twenty miles long and from two to six miles wide where they enter the trunk, each of them fed by many secondary tributaries; so that the whole number of branches, great and small, pouring from the mountain fountains perhaps number upward of two hundred, not counting the smallest. The area drained by this one grand glacier can hardly be less than seven or eight hundred miles, and probably contains as much ice as all the eleven hundred Swiss glaciers combined. Its length from the frontal wall back to the head of its farthest fountain seemed to be about forty or fifty miles, and the width just below the confluence of the main tributaries about twenty-five miles. Though apparently motionless as the mountains, it flows on forever, the speed varying in every part with the seasons, but mostly with the depth of the current, and the declivity, smoothness and directness of the different portions of the basin. The flow of the central cascading portion near the front, as determined by Professor Reid, is at the rate of from two and a half to five inches an hour, or from five to ten feet a day. A strip of the main trunk about a mile in width, extending along the eastern margin about fourteen miles to a lake filled with bergs, has so little motion and is so little interrupted by crevasses, a hundred horsemen might ride abreast over it without encountering very much difficulty.

But far the greater portion of the vast expanse looking smooth in the distance is torn and crumpled into a bewildering network of hummocky ridges and blades, separated by yawning gulfs and crevasses, so that the explorer, crossing it from shore to shore, must always have a hard time. In hollow spots here and there in the heart of the icy wilderness are small lakelets fed by swift-glancing streams that flow without friction in blue shining channels, making delightful melody, singing and ringing in silvery tones of peculiar sweetness, radiant crystals like flowers ineffably fine growing in dazzling beauty along their banks. Few, however, will be likely to enjoy them. Fortunately to most travellers the thundering ice-wall, while comfortably accessible, is also the most strikingly interesting portion of the glacier.

The mountains about the great glacier were also seen from this standpoint in exceedingly grand and telling views, ranged and grouped in glorious array. Along the valleys of the main tributaries to the north-westward I saw far into their shadowy depths, one noble peak in its snowy robes appearing beyond another in fine perspective. One of the most remarkable of them, fashioned like a superb crown with delicately fluted sides, stands in the middle of the second main tributary, counting from left to right. To the westward the magnificent Fairweather Range is displayed in all its glory, lifting its peaks and glaciers into the blue sky. Mount Fairweather, though not the highest, is the noblest and most majestic in port and architecture of all the sky-dwelling company. La Perouse, at the south end of the range, is also a magnificent mountain, symmetrically peaked and sculptured, and wears its robes of snow and glaciers in noble style. Lituya, as seen from here, is an immense tower, severely plain and massive. It makes a fine and terrible and lonely impression. Crillon, though the loftiest of all (being nearly sixteen thousand feet high), presents no well-marked features. Its ponderous glaciers have ground it away into long, curling ridges until, from this point of view, it resembles a huge twisted shell. The lower summits about the Muir Glacier, like this one, the first that I climbed, are richly adorned and enlivened with flowers, though they make but a faint show in general views. Lines and dashes of bright green appear on the lower slopes as one approaches them from the glacier, and a fainter green tinge may be noticed on the subordinate summits at a height of two thousand or three thousand feet. The lower are mostly alder bushes and the topmost a lavish profusion of flowering plants, chiefly cassiope, vaccinium, pyrola, erigeron, gentiana, campanula, anemone, larkspur and columbine, with a few grasses and ferns. Of these cassiope is at once the commonest and the most beautiful and influential. In some places its delicate stems make mattresses more than a foot thick over several acres, while the bloom is so abundant that a single handful plucked at random contains hundreds of its pale pink bells. The very thought of this Alaska garden is a joyful exhilaration. Though the storm-beaten ground it is growing on is nearly half a mile high, the glacier centuries ago flowed over it as a river flows over a boulder; but out of all the cold darkness and glacial crushing and grinding comes this warm, abounding beauty and life to teach us that what we in our faithless ignorance and fear call destruction is creation finer and finer.

When night was approaching I scrambled down out of my blessed garden to the glacier, and returned to my lonely camp, and, getting some coffee and bread, again went up the moraine to the east end of the great ice-wall. It is about three miles long, but the length of the jagged, berg-producing portion that stretches across the fiord from side to side like a huge green-and-blue barrier is only about two miles and rises above the water to a height of from two hundred and fifty to three hundred feet. Soundings made by Captain Carroll show that seven hundred and twenty feet of the wall is below the surface, and a third unmeasured portion is buried beneath the moraine detritus deposited at the foot of it. Therefore, were the water and rocky detritus cleared away, a sheer precipice of ice would be presented nearly two miles long and more than a thousand feet high. Seen from a distance, as you come up the fiord, it seems comparatively regular in form, but it is far otherwise; bold, jagged capes jut forward into the fiord, alternating with deep re-entering angles and craggy hollows with plain bastions, while the top is roughened with innumerable spires and pyramids and sharp hacked blades leaning and toppling or cutting straight into the sky.

The number of bergs given off varies somewhat with the weather and the tides, the average being about one every five or six minutes, counting only those that roar loud enough to make themselves heard at a distance of two or three miles. The very largest, however, may under favourable conditions be heard ten miles or even farther. When a large mass sinks from the upper fissured portion of the wall, there is first a keen, prolonged, thundering roar, which slowly subsides into a low muttering growl, followed by numerous smaller grating clashing sounds from the agitated bergs that dance in the waves about the newcomer as if in welcome; and these again are followed by the swash and roar of the waves that are raised and hurled up the beach against the moraines. But the largest and most beautiful of the bergs, instead of thus falling from the upper weathered portion of the wall, rise from the submerged portion with a still grander commotion, springing with tremendous voice and gestures nearly to the top of the wall, tons of water streaming like hair down their sides, plunging and rising again and again before they finally settle in perfect poise, free at last, after having formed part of the slow-crawling glacier for centuries. And as we contemplate their history, as they sail calmly away down the fiord to the sea, how wonderful it seems that ice formed from pressed snow on the far-off mountains two or three hundred years ago should still be pure and lovely in colour after all its travel and toil in the rough mountain quarries, grinding and fashioning the features of predestined landscapes.

When sunshine is sifting through the midst of the multitude of icebergs that fill the fiord and through the jets of radiant spray ever rising from the tremendous dashing and splashing of the falling and upspringing bergs, the effect is indescribably glorious. Glorious, too, are the shows they make in the night when the moon and stars are shining. The berg-thunder seems far louder than by day, and the projecting buttresses seem higher as they stand forward in the pale light, relieved by gloomy hollows, while the new-born bergs are dimly seen, crowned with faint lunar rainbows in the up-dashing spray. But it is in the darkest nights when storms are blowing and the waves are phosphorescent that the most impressive displays are made. Then the long range of ice-bluffs is plainly seen stretching through the gloom in wierd, unearthly splendour, luminous wave foam dashing against every bluff and drifting berg; and ever and anon amid all this wild auroral splendour some huge new-born berg dashes the living water into yet brighter foam, and the streaming torrents pouring from its sides are worn as robes of light, while they roar in awful accord with the winds and waves, deep calling unto deep, glacier to glacier, fròm fiord to fiord over all the wonderful bay.

After spending a few days here, we struck across to the main Hoona village on the south side of Icy Strait, thence by a long cut-off with one short portage to Chatham Strait, and thence down through Peril Strait, sailing all night, hoping to catch the mail steamer at Sitka. We arrived at the head of the strait about daybreak. The tide was falling, and rushing down with the swift current as if descending a majestic cataract was a memorable experience. We reached Sitka the same night, and there I paid and discharged my crew, making allowance for a couple of days or so for the journey back home to Fort Wrangell, while I boarded the steamer for Portland and thus ended my exploration for this season.

In Camp at Glacier Bay

I left San Francisco for Glacier Bay on the steamer City of Pueblo, 14 June 1890, at 10 am, this being my third trip to southeastern Alaska and fourth to Alaska, including northern and western Alaska as far as Unalaska and Pt Barrow and the northeastern coast of Siberia. The bar at the Golden Gate was smooth, the weather cool and pleasant. The redwoods in sheltered coves approach the shore closely, their dwarfed and shorn tops appearing here and there in ravines along the coast up to Oregon. The wind-swept hills, beaten with scud, are of course bare of trees. Along the Oregon and Washington coast the trees get nearer the sea, for spruce and contorted pine endure the briny winds better than the redwoods. We took the inside passage between the shore and Race Rocks, a long range of islets on which many a good ship has been wrecked. The breakers from the deep Pacific, driven by the gale, made a glorious display of foam on the bald islet rocks, sending spray over the tops of some of them a hundred feet high or more in sublime, curving jagged-edged and flame-shaped sheets. The gestures of these upspringing, purple-tinged waves as they dashed and broke were sublime and serene, combining displays of graceful beauty of motion and form with tremendous power – a truly glorious show. I noticed several small villages on the green slopes between the timbered mountains and the shore. Long Branch made quite a display of new houses along the beach, north of the mouth of the Columbia.

I had pleasant company on the Pueblo and sat at the chief engineer's table, who was a good and merry talker. An old San Francisco lawyer, rather stiff and dignified, knew my father-in-law, Dr Strentzel. Three ladies, opposed to the pitching of the ship, were absent from table the greater part of the way. My best talker was an old Scandinavian sea-captain, who was having a new bark built at Port Blakely – an interesting old salt, every sentence of his conversation flavoured with sea-brine, bluff and hearty as a sea-wave, keen-eyed, courageous, self-reliant, and so stubbornly sceptical he refused to believe even in glaciers.

'After you see your bark', I said, 'and find everything being done to your mind, you had better go on to Alaska and see the glaciers'.

'Oh, I haf seen many glaciers already'.

'But are you sure that you know what a glacier is?' I asked.

'Vell, a glacier is a big mountain all covered up with ice'.

'Then a river', said I, 'must be a big mountain all covered with water'.

I explained what a glacier was and succeeded in exciting his interest. I told him he must reform, for a man who neither believed in God nor glaciers must be very bad, indeed the worst of all unbelievers.

At Port Townsend I met Mr Loomis, who had agreed to go with me as far as the Muir Glacier. We sailed from here on the steamer Queen. We touched again at Victoria, and I took a short walk into the adjacent woods and gardens and found the flowery vegetation in its glory, especially the large wild rose for which the region is famous, and the spiraea and English honeysuckle of the gardens.

18 June. We sailed from Victoria on the Queen at 10.30 am. The weather all the way to Fort Wrangell was cloudy and rainy, but the scenery is delightful even in the dullest weather. The marvellous wealth of forests, islands, and waterfalls, the cloud-wreathed heights, the many avalanche slopes and slips, the pearl-grey tones of the sky, the browns of the woods, their purple flower edges and mist fringes, the endless combinations of water and land and ever-shifting clouds – none of these greatly interest the tourists. I noticed one of the small whales that frequent these channels and mentioned the fact, then called attention to a charming group of islands, but they turned their eyes from the islands, saying 'Yes, yes, they are very fine, but where did you see the whale?'

The timber is larger and apparently better every way as you go north from Victoria, that is on the islands, perhaps on account of fires from less rain to the southward. All the islands have been overswept by the ice-sheet and are but little changed as yet, save a few of the highest summits which have been sculptured by local residual glaciers. All have approximately the form of greatest strength with reference to the overflow of an ice-sheet, excepting those mentioned above, which have been more or less eroded by local residual glaciers. Every channel also has the form of greatest strength with reference to ice-action. Islands, as we have seen, are still being born in Glacier Bay and elsewhere to the northward.

I found many pleasant people aboard, but strangely ignorant on the subject of earth-sculpture and landscape-making. Professor Niles, of the Boston Institute of Technology, is aboard; also Mr Russell and Mr Kerr of the Geological Survey, who are now on their way to Mount St Elias, hoping to reach the summit; and a granddaughter of Peter Burnett, the first governor of California.

We arrived at Wrangell in the rain at 10.30 pm. There was a grand rush on shore to buy curiosities and see totem poles. The shops were jammed and mobbed, high prices paid for shabby stuff manufactured expressly for tourist trade. Silver bracelets hammered out of dollars and half dollars by Indian smiths are the most popular articles, then baskets, yellow cedar toy canoes, paddles, etc. Most people who travel look only at what they are directed to look at. Great is the power of the guidebook-maker, however ignorant. I inquired for my old friends Tyeen and Shakes, who were both absent.

20 June. We left Wrangell early this morning and passed through the Wrangell Narrows at high tide. I noticed a few bergs near Cape Fanshawe from Wrangell Glacier. The water ten miles from Wrangell is coloured with particles derived mostly from the Stickeen River glaciers and Le Conte Glacier. All the waters of the channels north of

Wrangell are green or yellowish from glacier erosion. We had a good view of the glaciers all the way to Juneau, but not of their high, cloud-veiled fountains. The stranded bergs on the moraine bar at the mouth of Sum Dum Bay looked just as they did when I first saw them ten years ago.

Before reaching Juneau, the Queen proceeded up the Taku Inlet that the passengers might see the fine glacier at its head, and ventured to within half a mile of the berg-discharging front, which is about three quarters of a mile wide. Bergs fell but seldom, perhaps one in half an hour. The glacier makes a rapid descent near the front. The inlet, therefore, will not be much extended beyond its present limit by the recession of the glacier. The grand rocks on either side of its channel show ice-action in telling style. The Norris Glacier, about two miles below the Taku, is a good example of a glacier in the first stage of decadence. The Taku River enters the head of the inlet a little to the east of the glaciers, coming from beyond the main coast range. All the tourists are delighted at seeing a grand glacier in the flesh. The scenery is very fine here and in the channel at Juneau. On Douglas Island there is a large mill of 240 stamps, all run by one small water-wheel, which, however, is acted on by water at enormous pressure. The forests around the mill are being rapidly nibbled away. Wind is here said to be very violent at times, blowing away people and houses and sweeping scud far up the mountain-side. Winter snow is seldom more than a foot or two deep.

21 June. We arived at Douglas Island at five in the after-noon and went sight-seeing through the mill. Six hundred tons of low-grade quartz are crushed per day. Juneau, on the mainland opposite the Douglas Island mills, is quite a village, well supplied with stores, churches, etc. A dance-house in which Indians are supposed to show native dances of all sorts is perhaps the best-patronized of all the places of amusement. A Mr Brooks, who prints a paper here, gave us some information on Mount St Elias, Mount Wrangell and the Cook Inlet and Prince William Sound region. He told Russell that he would never reach the summit of St Elias, that it was inaccessible. He saw no glaciers that discharged bergs into the sea at Cook Inlet, but many in Prince William Sound.

22 June. Leaving Juneau at noon, we had a good view of the Auk Glacier at the mouth of the channel between Douglas Island and the mainland, and of Eagle Glacier a few miles north of the Auk on the east side of Lynn Canal. Then the Davidson Glacier came in sight, finely curved, striped with medial moraines, and girdled in front by its magnificent tree-fringed terminal moraine; and besides these many others of every size and pattern on the mountains bounding Lynn Canal, most of them comparatively small, completing their sculpture. The mountains on either hand and at the head of the canal are strikingly beautiful at any time of the year. The sky today is mostly clear, with just clouds enough hovering about the mountains to show them to best advantage as they stretch onward in sustained grandeur like two separate and distinct ranges, each mountain with its glaciers and clouds and fine sculpture glowing bright in smooth, graded light. Only a few of them exceed five thousand feet in height; but as one naturally associates great height with ice-and-snow-laden mountains and with glacial sculpture so pronounced, they seem much higher. There are now two canneries at the head of Lynn Canal. The Indians furnish some of the salmon at ten cents each. Everybody sits up to see the midnight sky. At this time of the year there is no night here, though the sun drops a degree or two below the horizon. One may read at twelve o'clock San Francisco time.

23 June. Early this morning we arrived in Glacier Bay. We passed through crowds of bergs at the mouth of the bay, though, owing to wind and tide, there were but few at the front of Muir Glacier. A fine, bright day, the last of a group of a week or two, as shown by the dryness of the sand along the shore and on the moraine – rare weather hereabouts. Most of the passengers went ashore and climbed the moraine on the east side to get a view of the glacier from a point a little higher than the top of

the front wall. A few ventured on a mile or two farther.
The day was delightful, and our one hundred and eighty
passengers were happy, gazing at the beautiful blue of the
bergs and the shattered pinnacled crystal wall, awed by the
thunder and commotion of the falling and rising icebergs,
which ever and anon sent spray flying several hundred
feet into the air and raised swells that set all the fleet of
bergs in motion and roared up the beach, telling the story
of the birth of every iceberg far and near. The number
discharged varies much, influenced in part no doubt by
the tides and weather and seasons, sometimes one every
five minutes for half a day at a time on the average,
though intervals of twenty or thirty minutes may occur
without any considerable fall, then three or four immense
discharges will take place in as many minutes. The sound
they make is like heavy thunder, with a prolonged roar after
deep thudding sounds – a perpetual thunderstorm easily
heard three or four miles away. The roar in our tent and
the shaking of the ground one or two miles distant from
points of discharge seems startlingly near.

I had to look after camp-supplies and left the ship late
this morning, going with a crowd to the glacier; then,
taking advantage of the fine weather, I pushed off alone
into the silent icy prairie to the east, to Nunatak Island,
about five hundred feet above the ice. I discovered a small
lake on the larger of the two islands, and many battered
and ground fragments of fossil wood, large and small.
They seem to have come from trees that grew on the
island perhaps centuries ago. I mean to use this island as
a station in setting out stakes to measure the glacial flow.
The top of Mount Fairweather is in sight at a distance
of perhaps thirty miles, the ice all smooth on the eastern
border, wildly broken in the central portion. I reached the
ship at 2.30 pm. I had intended getting back at noon and
sending letters and bidding friends goodbye, but could not
resist this glacier saunter. The ship moved off as soon as I
was seen on the moraine bluff, and Loomis and I waved
our hats in farewell to the many wavings of handkerchiefs
of acquaintances we had made on the trip.

Our goods – blankets, provisions, tent, etc. – lay in a

rocky moraine hollow within a mile of the great terminal wall of the glacier, and the discharge of the rising and falling icebergs kept up an almost continuous thundering and echoing, while a few gulls flew about on easy wing or stood like specks of foam on the shore. These were our neighbours.

After my twelve-mile walk, I ate a cracker and planned the camp. I found that one of my boxes had been left on the steamer, but still we have more than enough of everything. We obtained two cords of dry wood at Juneau which Captain Carroll kindly had his men carry up the moraine to our camp-ground. We piled the wood as a wind-break, then laid a floor of lumber brought from Seattle for a square tent, nine feet by nine. We set the tent, stored our provisions in it, and made our beds. This work was done by 11.30 pm, good daylight lasting to this time. We slept well in our roomy cotton house, dreaming of California home nests in the wilderness of ice.

25 June. A rainy day. For a few hours I kept count of the number of bergs discharged, then sauntered along the beach to the end of the crystal wall. A portion of the way is dangerous, the moraine bluff being capped by an overlying lobe of the glacier, which as it melts sends down boulders and fragments of ice, while the strip of sandy shore at high tide is only a few rods wide, leaving but little room to escape from the falling moraine material and the berg-waves. The view of the ice-cliffs, pinnacles, spires and ridges was very telling, a magnificent picture of nature's power and industry and love of beauty. About a hundred or a hundred and fifty feet from the shore a large stream issues from an arched, tunnel-like channel in the wall of the glacier, the blue of the ice hall being of an exquisite tone, contrasting with the strange, sooty, smoky, brown-coloured stream. The front wall of the Muir Glacier is about two and a half or three miles wide. Only the central portion about two miles wide discharges icebergs. The two wings advanced over the washed and stratified moraine deposits have little or no motion melting and receding as fast, or perhaps faster, than it advances. they have been advanced at least a mile over the old re-formed moraines, as is shown by the overlying, angular, recent moraine deposits, now being laid down, which are continuous with the medial moraines of the glacier.

In the old stratified moraine banks, trunks and branches of trees showing but little sign of decay occur at a height of about a hundred feet above tide-water. I have not yet compared this fossil wood with that of the opposite shore deposits. That the glacier was once withdrawn considerably back of its present limit seems plain. Immense torrents of water had filled in the inlet with stratified moraine-material, and for centuries favourable climatic conditions allowed forests to grow upon it. At length the glacier advanced, probably three or four miles, uprooting and burying the trees which had grown undisturbed for centuries. Then came a great thaw, which produced the flood that deposited the uprooted trees. Also the trees which grew around the shores above reach of floods were shed off, perhaps by the thawing of the soil that was resting on the buried margin of the glacier, left on its retreat and protected by a covering of moraine-material from melting as fast as the exposed surface of the glacier. What appear to be remnants of the margin of the glacier when it stood at a much higher level still exist on the left side and probably all along its banks on both sides just below its present terminus.

26 June. We fixed a mark on the left wing to measure the motion if any. It rained all day, but I had a grand tramp over mud, ice and rock to the east wall of the inlet. Brown metamorphic slate, close-grained in places, dips away from the inlet, presenting edges to ice-action, which has given rise to a singularly beautiful and striking surface, polished and grooved and fluted.

All the next day it rained. The mountains were smothered in dull-coloured mist and fog, the great glacier looming through the gloomy grey fog fringes with wonderful effect. The thunder of bergs booms and rumbles through the foggy atmosphere. It is bad weather for exploring but delightful nevertheless, making all the strange, mysterious region yet stranger and more mysterious.

28 June. A light rain. We were visited by two parties of Indians. A man from each canoe came ashore, leaving the women in the canoe to guard against the berg-waves. I tried my Chinook and made out to say that I wanted to hire two of them in a few days to go a little way back on the glacier and round the bay. They are seal-hunters and promised to come again with 'Charley', who 'hi yu kumtux wawa Boston' – knew well how to speak English.

I saw three huge bergs born. Spray rose about two hundred feet. Lovely reflections showed of the pale-blue tones of the ice-wall and mountains in the calm water. Mirages are common, making the stranded bergs along the shore look like the sheer frontal wall of the glacier from which they were discharged.

I am watching the ice-wall, berg life and behaviour, etc. Yesterday and today a solitary small flycatcher was feeding about camp. A sandpiper on the shore, loons, ducks, gulls and crows, a few of each and a bald eagle are all the birds I have noticed thus far. The glacier is thundering gloriously.

30 June. Clearing clouds and sunshine. In less than a minute I saw three large bergs born. First there is usually a preliminary thundering of comparatively small masses as the large mass begins to fall, then the grand crash and boom and reverberating roaring. Oftentimes three of four heavy main throbbing thuds and booming explosions are heard as the main mass falls in several pieces, and also secondary thuds and thunderings as the mass or masses plunge and rise again and again ere they come to rest. Seldom, if ever, do the towers, battlements and pinnacles into which the front of the glacier is broken fall forward headlong from their bases like falling trees at the water-level or above or below it. They mostly sink vertically or nearly so, as if undermined by the melting action of the water of the inlet, occasionally maintaining their upright position after sinking far below the level of

the water and rising again a hundred feet or more into the
air with water streaming like hair down their sides from
their crowns, then launch forward and fall flat with yet
another thundering report, raising spray in magnificent,
flame-like, radiating jets and sheets, occasionally to the
very top of the front wall. Illumined by the sun, the spray
and angular crystal masses are indescribably beautiful.
Some of the discharges pour in fragments from clefts in the
wall like waterfalls, white and mealy-looking, even dusty
with minute swirling ice-particles, followed by a rushing
succession of thunder-tones combining into a huge, blunt,
solemn roar. Most of these crumbling discharges are from
the excessively shattered central part of the ice-wall; the
solid deep-blue masses from the ends of the wall forming
the large bergs rise from the bottom of the glacier.

Many lesser reports are heard at a distance of a mile or
more from the fall of pinnacles into crevasses or from the
opening of new crevasses. The berg discharges are very
irregular, from three to twenty-two an hour. On one rising
tide, six hours, there were sixty bergs discharged, large
enough to thunder and be heard at distances of from three
quarters to one and a half miles; and on one succeeding
falling tide, six hours, sixty-nine were discharged.

1 July. We were awakened at four o'clock this morning by the whistle of the steamer George W. Elder. I
went out on the moraine and waved my hand in salute
and was answered by a toot from the whistle. Soon a
party came ashore and asked if I was Professor Muir.
The leader, Professor Harry Fielding Reid of Cleveland,
Ohio, introduced himself and his companion, Mr Cushing,
also of Cleveland and six or eight young students who had
come well provided with instruments to study the glacier.
They landed seven or eight tons of freight and pitched
camp beside ours. I am delighted to have companions so
congenial – we have now a village.

As I set out to climb the second mountain, three thousand feet high, on the east side of the glacier, I met many
tourists returning from a walk on the smooth east margin
of the glacier, and had to answer many questions. I had

a hard climb, but wonderful views were developed and I sketched the glacier from this high point and most of its upper fountains.

Many fine alpine plants grew here, an anemone on the summit, two species of cassiope in shaggy mats, three or four dwarf willows, large blue hairy lupines eighteen inches high, parnassia, phlox, solidago, dandelion, white-flowered bryanthus, daisy, pedicularis, epilobium, etc., with grasses, sedges, mosses and lichens, forming a delightful deep spongy sod. Woodchucks stood erect and piped dolefully for an hour 'Chee-chee!' with jaws absurdly stretched to emit so thin a note – rusty-looking, seedy fellows, also a smaller striped species which stood erect and cheeped and whistled like a Douglas squirrel. I saw three or four species of birds. A finch flew from her nest at my feet; and I almost stepped on a family of young ptarmigan ere they scattered, little bunches of downy brown silk, small but able to run well. They scattered along a snow-bank, over boulders, through willows, grass and flowers, while the mother, very lame, tumbled and sprawled at my feet. I stood still until the little ones began to peep; the mother answered 'Too-too-too' and showed admirable judgment and devotion. She was in brown plumage with white on the wing primaries. She had fine grounds on which to lead and feed her young.

Not a cloud in the sky today; a faint film to the north vanished by noon, leaving all the sky full of soft, hazy light. The magnificent mountains around the widespread tributaries of the glacier; the great, gently undulating, prairie-like expanse of the main trunk, bluish on the east, pure white on the west and north; its trains of moraines in magnificent curving lines and many colours – black, grey, red and brown; the stormy, cataract-like, crevassed sections; the hundred fountains; the lofty, pure white Fairweather Range; the thunder of the plunging bergs; the fleet of bergs sailing tranquilly in the inlet – formed a glowing picture of nature's beauty and power.

2 July. I crossed the inlet with Mr Reid and Mr Adams today. The stratified drift on the west side all the way from top to base contains fossil wood. On the east side, as far as I have seen it, the wood occurs only in one stratum at a height of about a hundred and twenty feet in sand and clay. Some in a bank of the west side are rooted in clay soil. I noticed a large grove of stumps in a washed-out channel near the glacier-front but had no time to examine closely. Evidently a flood carrying great quantities of sand and gravel had overwhelmed and broken off these trees, leaving high stumps. The deposit, about a hundred feet or more above them, had been recently washed out by one of the draining streams of the glacier, exposing a part of the old forest floor certainly two or three centuries old.

I climbed along the right bank of the lowest of the tributaries and set a signal flag on a ridge fourteen hundred feet high. This tributary is about one and a fourth or one and a half miles wide and has four secondary tributaries. It reaches tide-water but gives off no bergs. Later I climbed the large Nunatak Island, seven thousand feet high, near the west margin of the glacier. It is composed of crumbling granite draggled with washed boulders, but has some enduring bosses which on sides and top are polished and scored rigidly, showing that it had been heavily overswept by the glacier when it was thousands of feet deeper than now, like a submerged boulder in a river-channel. This island is very irregular in form, owing to the variations in the structure joints of the granite. It has several small lakelets and has been loaded with glacial drift, but by the melting of the ice about its flanks is shedding it off, together with some of its own crumbling surface. I descended a deep rock gully on the north side, the rawest, dirtiest, dustiest, most dangerous that I have seen hereabouts. There is also a large quantity of fossil wood scattered on this island, especially on the north side, that on the south side having been cleared off and carried away by the first tributary glacier, which, being lower and melting earlier, has allowed the soil of the moraine material to fall, together with its forest and be carried off. That on the north side is now being carried off or buried. The last of the main ice foundation is melting and the moraine material re-formed over and over again, and the fallen tree-trunks, decayed or half decayed or in a fair state of preservation, are also unburied and buried again or carried off to the terminal or lateral moraine.

I found three small seedling Sitka spruces, feeble beginnings of a new forest. The circumference of the island is about seven miles. I arrived at camp about midnight, tired and cold. Sailing across the inlet in a cranky rotten boat through the midst of icebergs was dangerous, and I was glad to get ashore.

4 July. I climbed the east wall to the summit, about thirty-one hundred feet or so, by the northern-most ravine next to the yellow ridge, finding about a mile of snow in the upper portion of the ravine and patches on the summit. A few of the patches probably lie all the year, the ground beneath them is so plantless. On the edge of some of the snow-banks I noticed cassiope. The thin, green, mosslike patches seen from camp are composed of a rich, shaggy growth of cassiope, white-flowered bryanthus, dwarf vaccinium with bright pink flowers, saxifrages, anemones, blue-bells, gentians, small erigeron, pedicularis, dwarf willow and a few species of grasses. Of these, *Cassiope tetragona* is far the most influential and beautiful. Here it forms mats a foot thick and an acre or more in area, the sections being measured by the size and drainage of the soil-patches. I saw a few plants anchored in the less crumbling parts of the steep-faced bosses and steps – parnassia, potentilla, hedysarum, lutkea, etc. The lower, rough-looking patches half-way up the mountain are mostly alder bushes ten or fifteen feet high. I had a fine view of the top of the mountain-mass which forms the boundary wall of the upper portion of the inlet on the west side, and of several glaciers, tributary to the first of the eastern tributaries of the main Muir Glacier. Five or six of these tributaries were seen, most of them now melted off from the trunk and independent. The highest peak to the eastward has an elevation of about five thousand feet or a little less. I also had glorious views of the Fairweather Range, La Pérouse, Crillon, Lituya, and Fairweather. Mount Fairweather is the most beautiful of all the giants that stand guard about Glacier Bay. When the sun is shining on it from the east or south its magnificent glaciers and colours are brought out in most telling display. In the late afternoon its features become less distinct. The atmosphere seems pale and hazy, though around to the north and northeastward of Fairweather innumerable white peaks are displayed, the highest fountain-heads of the Muir Glacier crowded together in bewildering array, most exciting and inviting to the mountaineer. Altogether I have had a delightful day, a truly glorious celebration of the fourth.

6 July. I sailed three or four miles down the east coast of the inlet with the Reid party's cook, who is supposed to be an experienced camper and prospector, and landed at a stratified moraine-bank. It was here that I camped in 1880, a point at that time less than half a mile from the front of the glacier, now one and a half miles. I found my Indian's old camp made just ten years ago and Professor Wright's of five years ago. Their alder-bough beds and fireplace were still marked and but little decayed. I found thirty-three species of plants in flower, not counting willows – a showy garden on the shore only a few feet above high tide, watered by a fine stream. Lutkea, hedysarum, parnassia, epilobium, bluebell, solidago, habenaria, strawberry with fruit half grown, arctostaphylos, mertensia, erigeron, willows, tall grasses and alder are the principal species. There are many butterflies in this garden. Gulls are breeding near here. I saw young in the water today.

On my way back to camp I discovered a group of monumental stumps in a washed-out valley of the moraine and went ashore to observe them. They are in the dry course of a flood-channel about eighty feet above mean tide and four or five hundred yards back from the shore, where they have been pounded and battered by boulders rolling against them and over them, making them look like gigantic shaving-brushes. The largest is about three feet in diameter and probably three hundred years old. I mean to return and examine them at leisure. A smaller stump, still firmly rooted, is standing astride of an old crumbling trunk, showing that at least two generations of trees flourished here undisturbed by the advance or retreat of the glacier or by its draining stream-floods. They are Sitka spruces and the wood is mostly in a good state of preservation. How these trees were broken off without being uprooted is dark to me at present. Perhaps most of their companions were uprooted and carried away.

7 July. Another fine day; scarce a cloud in the sky. The icebergs in the bay are miraged in the distance to look like the frontal wall of a great glacier. I am writing letters in anticipation of the next steamer, the Queen.

She arrived about 2.30 pm with two hundred and thirty tourists. What a show they made with their ribbons and kodaks! All seemed happy and enthusiastic, though it was curious to see how promptly all of them ceased gazing when the dinner-bell rang, and how many turned from the great thundering crystal world of ice to look curiously at the Indians that came alongside to sell trinkets, and how our little camp and kitchen arrangements excited so many to loiter and waste their precious time prying into our poor hut.

8 July. A fine clear day. I went up the glacier to observe stakes and found that a marked point near the middle of the current had flowed about a hundred feet in eight days. On the medial moraine one mile from the front there was no measureable displacement. I found a raven devouring a tom-cod that was alive on a shallow at the mouth of the creek. It had probably been wounded by a seal or eagle.

10 July. I have been getting acquainted with the main features of the glacier and its fountain mountains with reference to an exploration of its main tributaries and the upper part of its prairie-like trunk, a trip I have long had in mind. I have been building a sled and must now get fully ready to start without reference to the weather. Yesterday evening I saw a large blue berg just as it was detached sliding down from the front. Two of Professor Reid's party rowed out to it as it sailed past the camp, estimating it to be two hundred and forty feet in length and one hundred feet high.

EIGHTEEN

My Sled-trip on the Muir Glacier

I started off the morning of 11 July on my memorable sled-trip to obtain general views of the main upper part of the Muir Glacier and its seven principal tributaries, feeling sure that I would learn something and at the same time get rid of a severe bronchial cough that followed an attack of the grippe and had troubled me for three months. I intended to camp on the glacier every night, and did so, and my throat grew better every day until it was well, for no lowland microbe could stand such a trip. My sled was about three feet long and made as light as possible. A sack of hardtack, a little tea and sugar and a sleeping-bag were firmly lashed on it so that nothing could drop off however much it might be jarred and dangled in crossing crevasses.

Two Indians carried the baggage over the rocky moraine to the clear glacier at the side of one of the eastern Nunatak Islands. Mr Loomis accompanied me to this first camp and assisted in dragging the empty sled over the moraine. We arrived at the middle Nunatak Island about nine o'clock. Here I sent back my Indian carriers, and Mr Loomis assisted me the first day in hauling the loaded sled to my second camp at the foot of Hemlock Mountain, returning the next morning.

13 July. I skirted the mountain to eastward a few miles and was delighted to discover a group of trees high up on its ragged rocky side, the first trees I had seen on the shores of Glacier Bay or on those of any of its glaciers. I left my sled on the ice and climbed the mountain to see what I might learn. I found that all the trees were mountain hemlock (*Tsuga mertensiana*), and were evidently the remnant of an old well-established forest, standing on the only ground that was stable, all the rest of the forest below it having been sloughed off with the soil from the disintegrating slate bed rock. The lowest of the trees stood at an elevation of about two thousand feet above the sea, the highest at about three thousand feet or a little higher. Nothing could be more striking than the contrast between the raw, crumbling, deforested portions of the mountain, looking like a quarry that was being worked, and the forested part with its rich, shaggy beds of cassiope and bryanthus in full bloom and its sumptuous cushions of flower-enamelled mosses. These garden-patches are full of gay colours of gentian, erigeron, anemone, larkspur and columbine and are enlivened with happy birds and bees and marmots. Climbing to an elevation of twenty-five hundred feet, which is about fifteen hundred feet above the level of the glacier at this point, I saw and heard a few marmots and three ptarmigans that were as tame as barnyard fowls. The sod is sloughing off on the edges, keeping it ragged. The trees are storm-bent from the southeast. A few are standing at an elevation of nearly three thousand feet; at twenty-five hundred feet, pyrola, veratrum, vaccinium, fine grasses, sedges, willows, mountain-ash, buttercups and acres of the most luxuriant cassiope are in bloom.

A lake encumbered with icebergs lies at the end of Divide Glacier. A spacious, level-floored valley beyond it, eight or ten miles long, with forested mountains on its west side, perhaps discharges to the southeastward into Lynn Canal. The divide of the glacier is about opposite the third of the eastern tributaries. Another berg-dotted lake into which the drainage of the Braided Glacier flows, lies a few miles to the westward and is one and a half miles long. Berg Lake is next the remarkable Girdled Glacier to the southeastward.

When the ice-period was in its prime, much of the Muir Glacier that now flows northward into Howling Valley flowed southward into Glacier Bay as a tributary of the Muir. All the rock contours show this, and so do the medial moraines. Berg Lake is crowded with bergs because they have no outlet and melt slowly. I heard none discharged. I had a hard time crossing the Divide Glacier, on which I camped. Half a mile back from the lake I gleaned a little fossil wood and made a fire on moraine boulders for tea. I slept fairly well on the sled. I heard the roar of four cascades on a shaggy green mountain on the west side of Howling Valley and saw three wild goats fifteen hundred feet up in the steep grassy pastures.

14 July. I rose at four o'clock this cloudy and dismal morning and looked for my goats, but saw only one. I thought there must be wolves where there were goats, and in a few minutes heard their low, dismal, far-reaching howling. One of them sounded very near and came nearer until it seemed to be less than a quarter of a mile away on the edge of the glacier. They had evidently seen me, but I was unable to catch sight of any of them. About half an hour later, while I was eating breakfast, they began howling again, so near I began to fear they had a mind to attack me, and I made haste to the shelter of a big square boulder, where, though I had no gun, I might be able to defend myself from a front attack with my alpenstock. After waiting half an hour or so to see what these wild dogs meant to do, I ventured to proceed on my journey to the foot of Snow Dome, where I camped for the night.

There are six tributaries on the northwest side of Divide arm, counting to the Grey Glacier, next after Granite Canyon Glacier going northwest. Next is Dirt Glacier, which is dead. I saw bergs on the edge of the main glacier a mile back from here which seem to have been left by the draining of a pool in a sunken hollow. A circling rim of driftwood, back twenty rods on the glacier, marks the edge of the lakelet shore where the bergs lie scattered and stranded. It is now half past ten o'clock and getting dusk as I sit by my little fossil-wood fire writing these notes. A strange bird is calling and complaining. A stream is rushing into a glacier well on the edge of which I am camped, back a few yards from the base of the mountain for fear of falling stones. A few small ones are rattling down the steep slope. I must go to bed.

15 July. I climbed the dome to plan a way, scan the glacier, and take bearings, etc., in case of storms. The main divide is about fifteen hundred feet; the second divide, about fifteen hundred also, is about one and one half miles southeastward. The flow of water on the glacier noticeably diminished last night though there was no frost. It is now already increasing. Stones begin to roll into the crevasses and into new positions, sliding against each other, half turning over or falling on moraine ridges. Mud pellets with small pebbles slip and roll slowly from ice-hummocks again and again. How often and by how many ways are boulders finished and finally brought to anything like permanent form and place in beds for farms and fields, forests and gardens. Into crevasses and out again, into moraines, shifted and reinforced and reformed by avalanches, melting from pedestals, etc. Rain, frost and dew help in the work; they are swept in rills, caught and ground in pot-hole mills. Moraines of washed pebbles, like those on glacier margins, are formed by snow avalanches deposited in crevasses, then weathered out and projected on the ice as shallow raised moraines. There is one such at this camp.

A ptarmigan is on a rock twenty yards distant, as if on show. It has red over the eye, a white line, not conspicuous, over the red, belly white, white markings over the upper parts on ground of brown and black wings, mostly white as seen when flying, but the coverts the same as the rest of the body. Only about three inches of the folded primaries show white. The breast seems to have golden iridescent colours, white under the wings. It allowed me to approach within twenty feet. It walked down a sixty degree slope of the rock, took flight with a few whirring wingbeats, then sailed with wings perfectly motionless four hundred yards down a gentle grade and vanished over the brow of a cliff. Ten days ago Loomis told me that he found a nest with nine eggs. On the way down to my sled I saw four more ptarmigans. They utter harsh notes when alarmed. 'Crack, chuck, crack', with the *r* rolled and prolonged. I also saw fresh and old goat-tracks and some bones that suggest wolves.

There is a pass through the mountains at the head of the third glacier. Fine mountains stand at the head on each side. The one on the northeast side is the higher and finer every way. It has three glaciers, tributary to the third. The third glacier has altogether ten tributaries, five on each side. The mountain on the left side of White Glacier is about six thousand feet high. The moraines of Girdled Glacier seem scarce to run anywhere. Only a little material is carried to Berg Lake. Most of it seems to be at rest as a terminal on the main glacier-field, which here has little motion. The curves of these last as seen from this mountain-top are very beautiful.

It has been a glorious day, all pure sunshine. An hour or more before sunset the distant mountains, a vast host, seemed more softly ethereal than ever, pale blue, ineffably fine, all angles and harshness melted off in the soft evening light. Even the snow and the grinding, cascading glaciers became divinely tender and fine in this celestial amethystine light. I got back to camp at 7.15, not tired. After my hardtack supper I could have climbed the mountain again and got back before sunrise, but dragging the sled tires me. I have been out on the glacier examining a moraine-like mass about a third of a mile from camp. It is perhaps a mile long, a hundred yards wide, and is thickly strewn with wood. I think that it has been brought down the mountain by a heavy snow avalanche, loaded on the ice, then carried away from the shore in the direction of the flow of the glacier. This explains detached moraine-masses. This one seems to have been derived from a big roomy cirque or amphitheatre on the northwest side of this Snow Dome Mountain.

To shorten the return journey I was tempted to glissade down what appeared to be a snow-filled ravine, which was very steep. All went well until I reached a bluish spot which proved to be ice, on which I lost control of myself and rolled into a gravel talus at the foot without a scratch. Just as I got up and was getting myself orientated, I heard a loud fierce scream, uttered in an exulting, diabolical tone of voice which startled me, as if an enemy, having seen me fall, was glorying in my death. Then suddenly two ravens came swooping from the sky and alighted on the jag of rock within a few feet of me, evidently hoping that I had been maimed and that they were going to have a feast. But as they stared at me, studying my condition, impatiently waiting for bone-picking time, I saw what they were up to and shouted, 'Not yet, not yet!'

16 July. At 7 am I left camp to cross the main glacier. Six ravens came to the camp as soon as I left. What wonderful eyes they must have! Nothing that moves in all this icy wilderness escapes the eyes of these brave birds. This is one of the loveliest mornings I ever saw in Alaska; not a cloud or faintest hint of one in all the wide sky. There is a yellowish haze in the east, white in the west, mild and mellow as a Wisconsin Indian Summer, but finer, more ethereal, God's holy light making all divine.

In an hour or so I came to the confluence of the first of the seven grand tributaries of the main Muir Glacier and had a glorious view of it as it comes sweeping down in wild cascades from its magnificent, pure white, mountain-girt basin to join the main crystal sea, its many fountain peaks, clustered and crowded, all pouring forth their tribute to swell its grand current. I crossed its front a little below its confluence, where its shattered current, about two or three miles wide, is reunited, and many rills and good-sized brooks glide gurgling and ringing in pure blue channels, giving delightful animation to the icy solitude.

Most of the ice-surface crossed today has been very uneven, and hauling the sled and finding a way over hummocks has been fatiguing. At times I had to lift the sled bodily and to cross many narrow, nerve-trying, ice-sliver bridges, balancing astride of them and cautiously shoving the sled ahead of me with temendous chasms on either side. I had made perhaps not more than six or eight miles in a straight line by six o'clock this evening when I reached ice so hummocky and tedious I concluded to camp and not try to take the sled any farther. I intend to leave it here in the middle of the basin and carry my sleeping-bag and provisions the rest of the way across to the west side. I am cozy and comfortable here resting in the midst of glorious icy scenery, though very tired. I made out to get a cup of tea by means of a few shavings and splinters whittled from the bottom board of my sled, and made a fire in a little can, a small campfire, the smallest I ever made or saw, yet it answered well enough as far as tea was concerned. I crept into my sack before eight o'clock as the wind was cold and my feet wet. One of my shoes is about worn out. I may have to put on a wooden sole. This day has been cloudless throughout, with lovely sunshine, a purple evening and morning. The circumference of mountains beheld from the midst of this world of ice is marvellous, the vast plain reposing in such soft tender light, the fountain mountains so clearly cut, holding themselves aloft with their loads of ice in supreme strength and beauty of architecture. I found a skull and most of the other bones of a goat on the glacier about two miles from the nearest land. It had probably been chased out of its mountain home by wolves and devoured here. I carried its horns with me. I saw many considerable depressions in the glacial surface, also a pitlike hole, irregular, not like the ordinary wells along the slope of the many small dirt-clad hillocks, faced to the south. Now the sun is down and the sky is saffron yellow, blending and fading into purple around to the south and north. It is a curious experience to be lying in bed writing these notes, hummock waves rising in every direction, their edges marking a multitude of crevasses and pits, while all around the horizon rise peaks innumerable of most intricate style of architecture. Solemnly growling and grinding moulins contrast with the sweet low-voiced whispering and warbling of a network of rills, singing like water-ouzels, glinting, gliding with indescribable softness and sweetness of voice. They are all around, one within a few feet of my hard sled bed.

17 July. Another glorious cloudless day is dawning in yellow and purple and soon the sun over the eastern peak will blot out the blue peak shadows and make all the vast white ice prairie sparkle. I slept well last night in the middle of the icy sea. The wind was cold but my sleeping-bag enabled me to lie neither warm nor intolerably cold. My three-months cough is gone. Strange that with such work and exposure one should know nothing of sore throats and of what are called colds. My heavy, thick-soled shoes, resoled just before starting on the trip six days ago, are about worn out and my feet have been wet every night. But no harm comes of it, nothing but good. I succeeded in getting a warm breakfast in bed. I reached over the edge of my sled, got hold of a small cedar stick that I had been carrying, whittled a lot of thin shavings from it, stored them on my breast, then set fire to a piece of paper in a shallow tin can, added a pinch of shavings, held the cup of water that always stood at my bedside over the tiny blaze with one hand, and fed the fire by adding little pinches of shavings until the water boiled, then pulling my bread sack within reach, made a good warm breakfast, cooked and eaten in bed. Thus refreshed, I surveyed the wilderness of crevassed, hummocky ice and concluded to try to drag my little sled a mile or two farther, then, finding encouragement, persevered, getting it across innumerable crevasses and streams and around several lakes and over and through the midst of hummocks, and at length reached the western shore between five and six o'clock this evening, extremely fatigued. This I consider a hard job well done, crossing so wildly broken a glacier, fifteen miles of it from Snow Dome Mountain, in two days with a sled weighing altogether not less than a hundred pounds. I found innumerable crevasses, some of them brimful of water. I crossed in most places just where the ice was close pressed and welded after descending cascades and was being shoved over an upward slope, thus closing the crevasses at the bottom, leaving only the upper sun-melted bevelled portion open for water to collect in.

Vast must be the drainage from this great basin. The waste in sunshine must be enormous, while in dark weather rains and winds also melt the ice and add to the volume produced by the rain itself. The winds also, though in temperature they may be only a degree or two above freezing-point, dissolve the ice as fast, or perhaps faster, than clear sunshine. Much of the water caught in tight crevasses doubtless freezes during the winter and gives rise to many of the irregular veins seen in the structure of the glacier. Saturated snow also freezes at times and is incorporated with the ice, as only from the lower part of the glacier is the snow melted during the summer. I have noticed many traces of this action. One of the most beautiful things to be seen on the glacier is the myriads of minute and intensely brilliant radiant lights burning in rows on the banks of streams and pools and lakelets from the tips of crystals melting in the sun, making them look as if bordered with diamonds. These gems are rayed like stars and twinkle; no diamond radiates keener or more brilliant light. It was perfectly glorious to think of this divine light burning over all this vast crystal sea in such ineffably fine effulgence, and over how many other of icy Alaska's glaciers where nobody sees it. To produce these effects I fancy the ice must be melting rapidly, as it was being melted today. The ice in these pools does not melt with anything like an even surface, but in long branches and leaves, making fairy forests of points, while minute bubbles of air are constantly being set free. I am camped tonight on what I call Quarry Mountain from its raw, loose, plantless condition, seven or eight miles above the front of the glacier. I found enough fossil wood for tea. Glorious is the view to the eastward from this camp. The sun has set, a few clouds appear, and a torrent rushing down a gully and under the edge of the glacier is making a solemn roaring. No tinkling, whistling rills this night. Ever and anon I hear a falling boulder. I have had a glorious and instructive day, but am excessively weary and to bed I go.

18 July. I felt tired this morning and meant to rest today. But after breakfast at 8 am I felt I must be up and doing, climbing, sketching new views up the great tributaries from the top of Quarry Mountain. Weariness vanished and I could have climbed, I think, five thousand feet. Anything seems easy after sled-dragging over hummocks and crevasses, and the constant nerve-strain in jumping crevasses so as not to slip in making the spring. Quarry Mountain is the barest I have ever seen, a raw quarry with infinite abundance of loose decaying granite all on the go. Its slopes are excessively steep. A few patches of epilobium make gay purple spots of colour. Its seeds fly everywhere seeking homes. Quarry Mountain is cut across into a series of parallel ridges by oversweeping ice. It is still overswept in three places by glacial flows a half to three quarters of a mile wide, finely arched at the top of the divides. I have been sketching, though my eyes are much inflamed and I can scarce see. All the lines I make appear double. I fear I shall not be able to make the few more sketches I want tomorrow, but must try. The day has been gloriously sunful, the glacier pale yellow toward five o'clock. The hazy air, white with a yellow tinge, gives an Indian-summerish effect. Now the blue evening shadows are creeping out over the icy plain, some ten miles long, with sunny yellow belts between them. Boulders fall now and again with dull, blunt booming, and the gravel pebbles rattle.

19 July. Nearly blind. The light is intolerable and I fear I may be long unfitted for work. I have been lying on my back all day with a snow poultice bound over my eyes. Every object I try to look at seems double; even the distant mountain-ranges are doubled, the upper an exact copy of the lower, though somewhat faint. This is the first time in Alaska that I have had too much sunshine. About four o'clock this afternoon, when I was waiting for the evening shadows to enable me to get nearer the main camp, where I could be more easily found in case my eyes should become still more inflamed and I should be unable to travel, thin clouds cast a grateful shade over all the glowing landscape. I gladly took advantage of these kindly clouds to make an effort to cross the few miles of the glacier that lay between me and the shore of the inlet. I made a pair of goggles but am afraid to wear them. Fortunately the ice here is but little broken, therefore I pulled my cap well down and set off about five o'clock. I got on pretty well and camped on the glacier in sight of the main camp, which from here in a straight line is only five or six miles away. I went ashore on Granite Island and gleaned a little fossil wood with which I made tea on the ice.

20 July. I kept wet bandages on my eyes last night as long as

I could, and feel better this morning, but all the mountains still seem to have double summits, giving a curiously unreal aspect to the landscape. I packed everything on the sled and moved three miles farther down the glacier, where I want to make measurements. Twice today I was visited on the ice by a hummingbird, attracted by the red lining of the bear-skin sleeping-bag.

I have gained some light on the formation of gravel-beds along the inlet. The material is mostly sifted and sorted by successive rollings and washings along the margins of the glacier-tributaries, where the supply is abundant beyond anything I ever saw elsewhere. The lowering of the surface of a glacier when its walls are not too steep leaves a part of the margin buried and protected from the wasting sunshine beneath the lateral moraines. Thus a marginal valley is formed, clear ice on one side, or nearly so, buried ice on the other. As melting goes on, the marginal trough, or valley, grows deeper and wider, since both sides are being melted, the land side slower. The dead, protected ice in melting first sheds off the large boulders, as they are not able to lie on slopes where smaller ones can. Then the next larger ones are rolled off and pebbles and sand in succession. Meanwhile this material is subjected to torrent-action, as if it were cast into a trough. When floods come it is carried forward and stratified, according to the force of the current, sand, mud, or larger material. This exposes fresh surfaces of ice and melting goes on again, until enough material has been undermined to form a veil in front; then follows another washing and carrying-away and depositing where the current is allowed to spread. In melting, protected margin terraces are often-times formed. Perhaps these terraces mark successive heights of the glacial surface. From terrace to terrace the grist of stone is rolled and sifted. Some, meeting only feeble streams, have only the fine particles carried away and deposited in smooth beds; others, coarser, from swifter streams, overspread the fine beds, while many of the large boulders no doubt roll back upon the glacier to go on their travels again.

It has been cloudy mostly today, though sunny in the afternoon, and my eyes are getting better. The steamer

Queen is expected in a day or two, so I must try to get down to the inlet tomorrow and make signal to have some of the Reid party ferry me over. I must hear from home, write letters, get rest and more to eat.

Near the front of the glacier the ice was perfectly free, apparently, of anything like a crevasse, and in walking almost carelessly down it I stopped opposite the large granite Nunatak Island, thinking that I would there be partly sheltered from the wind. I had not gone a dozen steps toward the island when I suddenly dropped into a concealed water-filled crevasse, which on the surface showed not the slightest sign of its existence. This crevasse like many others was being used as the channel of a stream, and at some narrow point the small cubical masses of ice into which the glacier surface disintegrates were jammed and extended back farther and farther till they completely covered and concealed the water. Into this I suddenly plunged, after crossing thousands of really dangerous crevasses, but never before had I encountered a danger so completely concealed. Down I plunged over head and ears, but of course bobbed up again, and after a hard struggle succeeded in dragging myself out over the farther side. Then I pulled my sled over close to Nunatak cliff, made haste to strip off my clothing, threw it in a sloppy heap and crept into my sleeping-bag to shiver away the night as best I could.

21 July. Dressing this rainy morning was a miserable job, but might have been worse. After wringing my sloppy underclothing, getting it on was far from pleasant. My eyes are better and I feel no bad effect from my icy bath. The last trace of my three months' cough is gone. No lowland grippe microbe could survive such experiences.

I have had a fine telling day examining the ruins of the old forest of Sitka spruce that no great time ago grew in a shallow mud-filled basin near the southwest corner of the glacier. The trees were protected by a spur of the mountain that puts out here, and when the glacier advanced they were simply flooded with fine sand and overborne. Stumps by the hundred, three to fifteen feet high, rooted in a stream of fine blue mud on cobbles, still have their bark on. A stratum of decomposed bark, leaves, cones and old trunks is still in place. Some of the stumps are on rocky ridges of gravelly soil about one hundred and twenty-five feet above sea. The valley has been washed out by the stream now occupying it, one of the glacier's draining streams a mile long or more and an eighth of a mile wide.

I got supper early and was just going to bed, when I was startled by seeing a man coming across the moraine, Professor Reid, who had seen me from the main camp and who came with Mr Loomis and the cook in their boat to ferry me over. I had not intended making signals for them until tomorrow but was glad to go. I had been seen also by Mr Case and one of his companions, who were on the western mountain-side above the fossil forest, shooting ptarmigans. I had a good rest and sleep and leisure to find out how rich I was in new facts and pictures and how tired and hungry I was.

NINETEEN

Auroras

A few days later I set out with Professor Reid's party to visit some of the other large glaciers that flow into the bay, to observe what changes have taken place in them since October, 1879, when I first visited and sketched them. We found the upper half of the bay closely choked with bergs, through which it was exceedingly difficult to force a way. After slowly struggling a few miles up the east side, we dragged the whale-boat and canoe over rough rocks into a fine garden and comfortably camped for the night.

The next day was spent in cautiously picking a way across to the west side of the bay; and as the strangely scanty stock of provisions was already about done, and the ice-jam to the northward seemed impenetrable, the party decided to return to the main camp by a comparatively open, roundabout way to the southward, while with the canoe and a handful of food-scraps I pushed on northward. After a hard, anxious struggle, I reached the mouth of the Hugh Miller fiord about sundown, and tried to find a camp-spot on its steep, boulder-bound shore. But no landing-place where it seemed possible to drag the canoe above high-tide mark was discovered after examining a mile or more of this dreary forbidding barrier, and as night was closing down, I decided to try to grope my way across the mouth of the fiord in the starlight to an open sandy spot on which I had camped in October, 1879, a distance of about three or four miles.

With the utmost caution I picked my way through the sparkling bergs, and after an hour or two of this nerve-trying work, when I was perhaps less than half-way across and dreading the loss of the frail canoe which would include the loss of myself, I came to a pack of very large bergs which loomed threateningly, offering no visible thoroughfare.

Paddling and pushing to right and left, I at last discovered a sheer-walled opening about four feet wide and perhaps two hundred feet long, formed apparently by the splitting of a huge iceberg. I hesitated to enter this passage, fearing that the slightest change in the tide-current might close it, but ventured nevertheless, judging that the dangers ahead might not be greater than those I had already passed. When I had got about a third of the way in, I suddenly discovered that the smooth-walled ice-lane was growing narrower, and with desperate haste backed out. Just as the bow of the canoe cleared the sheer walls they came together with a growling crunch. Terror-stricken, I turned back, and in an anxious hour or two gladly reached the rock-bound shore that had at first repelled me, determined to stay on guard all night in the canoe or find some place where with the strength that comes in a fight for life I could drag it up the boulder wall beyond ice danger. This at last was happily done about midnight, and with no thought of sleep I went to bed rejoicing.

My bed was two boulders, and as I lay wedged and bent on their up-bulging sides, beguiling the hard, cold time in gazing into the starry sky and across the sparkling bay, magnificent upright bars of light in bright prismatic colours suddenly appeared, marching swiftly in close succession along the northern horizon from west to east as if in diligent haste, an auroral display very different from any I had ever before beheld. Once long ago in Wisconsin I saw the heavens draped in rich purple auroral clouds fringed and folded in most magnificent forms; but in this glory of light, so pure, so bright, so enthusiastic in motion, there was nothing in the least cloud-like. The short colour-bars, apparently about two degrees in height, though blending, seemed to be as well defined as those of the solar spectrum.

How long these glad, eager soldiers of light held on their way I cannot tell; for sense of time was charmed out of mind and the blessed night circled away in measureless rejoicing enthusiasm.

In the early morning after so inspiring a night I launched my canoe feeling able for anything, crossed the mouth of

the Hugh Miller fiord, and forced a way three or four miles
along the shore of the bay, hoping to reach the Grand
Pacific Glacier in front of Mount Fairweather. But the
farther I went, the ice-pack, instead of showing inviting
little open streaks here and there, became so much harder
jammed that on some parts of the shore the bergs, drifting
south with the tide, were shoving one another out of the
water beyond high-tide line. Farther progress to northward
was thus rigidly stopped, and now I had to fight for a
way back to my cabin, hoping that by good tide luck I
might reach it before dark. But at sundown I was less
than half-way home, and though very hungry was glad
to land on a little rock island with a smooth beach for
the canoe and a thicket of alder bushes for fire and bed
and a little sleep. But shortly after sundown, while these
arrangements were being made, lo and behold another
aurora enriching the heavens! and though it proved to be
one of the ordinary almost colourless kind, thrusting long,
quivering lances toward the zenith from a dark cloudlike
base, after last night's wonderful display one's expectations
might well be extravagant and I lay wide awake watching.

On the third night I reached my cabin and food. Professor Reid and his party came in to talk over the results
of our excursions, and just as the last one of the visitors
opened the door after bidding good-night, he shouted,
'Muir, come look here. Here's something fine.'

I ran out in auroral excitement, and sure enough here
was another aurora, as novel and wonderful as the marching rainbow-coloured columns – a glowing silver bow span-
ning the Muir Inlet in a magnificent arch right under the
zenith, or a little to the south of it, the ends resting on
the top of the mountain-walls. And though colourless and
steadfast, its intense, solid, white splendour, noble proportions and fineness of finish excited boundless admiration.
In form and proportion it was like a rainbow, a bridge of
one span five miles wide; and so brilliant, so fine and solid
and homogeneous in every part, I fancy that if all the stars
were raked together into one windrow, fused and welded
and run through some celestial rolling-mill, all would be
required to make this one glowing white colossal bridge.

After my last visitor went to bed, I lay down on the moraine in front of the cabin and gazed and watched. Hour after hour the wonderful arch stood perfectly motionless, sharply defined and substantial-looking as if it were a permanent addition to the furniture of the sky. At length while it yet spanned the inlet in serene unchanging splendour, a band of fluffy, pale grey, quivering ringlets came suddenly all in a row over the eastern mountain-top, glided in nervous haste up and down the under side of the bow and over the western mountain-wall. They were about one and a half times the apparent diameter of the bow in length, maintained a vertical posture all the way across, and slipped swiftly along as if they were suspended like a curtain on rings. Had these lively auroral fairies marched across the fiord on the top of the bow instead of shuffling along the under side of it, one might have fancied they were a happy band of spirit people on a journey making use of the splendid bow for a bridge. There must have been hundreds of miles of them; for the time required for each to cross from one end of the bridge to the other seemed only a minute or less, while nearly an hour elapsed from their first appearance until the last of the rushing throng vanished behind the western mountain, leaving the bridge as bright and solid and steadfast as before they arrived. But later, half an hour or so, it began to fade. Fissures or cracks crossed it diagonally through which a few stars were seen, and gradually it became thin and nebulous until it looked like the Milky Way, and at last vanished, leaving no visible monument of any sort to mark its place.

I now returned to my cabin, replenished the fire, warmed myself, and prepared to go to bed, though too aurorally rich and happy to go to sleep. But just as I was about to retire, I thought I had better take another look at the sky, to make sure that the glorious show was over; and, contrary to all reasonable expectations, I found that the pale foundation for another bow was being laid right overhead like the first. Then losing all thought of sleep, I ran back to my cabin, carried out blankets and lay down on the moraine to keep watch until daybreak, that none of the sky wonders of the glorious night within reach of my eyes might be lost.

I had seen the first bow when it stood complete in full splendour, and its gradual fading decay. Now I was to see the building of a new one from the beginning. Perhaps in less than half an hour the silvery material was gathered, condensed, and welded into a glowing, evenly proportioned arc like the first and in the same part of the sky. Then in due time over the eastern mountain-wall came another throng of restless electric auroral fairies, the infinitely fine pale-grey garments of each lightly touching those of their neighbours as they swept swiftly along the under side of the bridge and down over the western mountain like the merry band that had gone the same way before them, all keeping quivery step and time to music too fine for mortal ears.

While the gay throng was gliding swiftly along, I watched the bridge for any change they might make upon it, but not the slightest could I detect. They left no visible track, and after all had passed the glowing arc stood firm and apparently immutable, but at last faded slowly away like its glorious predecessor.

Excepting only the vast purple aurora mentioned above, said to have been visible over nearly all the continent, these two silver bows in supreme, serene, supernal beauty surpassed everything auroral I ever beheld.

TO MY DOG BLANCO

My dear dumb friend, low lying there,
  A willing vassal at my feet;
Glad partner of my home and fare,
  My shadow in the street;

I look into your great brown eyes,
  Where love and loyal homage shine,
And wonder where the difference lies
  Between your soul and mine!

I scan the whole broad earth around
  For that one heart which, leal and true,
Bears friendship without end or bound,
  And find the prize in you.

Ah, Blanco! did I worship God
  As truly as you worship me,
Or follow where my Master trod
  With your humility:

Did I sit fondly at His feet
  As you, dear Blanco, sit at mine,
And watch Him with a love as sweet,
  My life would grow divine!

J.G. HOLLAND

Stickeen

In the summer of 1880 I set out from Fort Wrangell in a canoe to continue the exploration of the icy region of southeastern Alaska, begun in the fall of 1879. After the necessary provisions, blankets, etc., had been collected and stowed away, and my Indian crew were in their places ready to start, while a crowd of their relatives and friends on the wharf were bidding them good-by and good-luck, my companion, the Rev. S. H. Young, for whom we were waiting, at last came aboard, followed by a little black dog, that immediately made himself at home by curling up in a hollow among the baggage. I like dogs, but this one seemed so small and worthless that I objected to his going, and asked the missionary why he was taking him.

'Such a little helpless creature will only be in the way,' I said; 'you had better pass him up to the Indian boys on the wharf, to be taken home to play with the children. This trip is not likely to be good for toy-dogs. The poor silly thing will be in rain and snow for weeks or months, and will require care like a baby.'

But his master assured me that he would be no trouble at all; that he was a perfect wonder of a dog, could endure cold and hunger like a bear, swim like a seal, and was wondrous wise and cunning, etc., making out a list of virtues to show he might be the most interesting member of the party.

Nobody could hope to unravel the lines of his ancestry. In all the wonderfully mixed and varied dog-tribe I never saw any creature very much like him, though in some of his sly, soft, gliding motions and gestures he brought the fox to mind. He was short-legged and bunchy-bodied, and his hair, though smooth, was long and silky and slightly waved, so that when the wind was at his back it ruffled, making him look shaggy. At first sight his only noticeable feature was his fine tail, which was about as airy and shady as a squirrel's, and was carried curling forward almost to his nose. On closer inspection you might notice his thin sensitive ears, and sharp eyes with cunning tan-spots above them. Mr Young told me that when the little fellow was a pup about the size of a woodrat he was presented to his wife by an Irish prospector at Sitka, and that on his arrival at Fort Wrangell he was adopted with enthusiasm by the Stickeen Indians as a sort of new good-luck totem, was named 'Stickeen' for the tribe, and became a universal favorite; petted, protected, and admired wherever he went, and regarded as a mysterious fountain of wisdom.

On our trip he soon proved himself a queer character – odd, concealed, independent, keeping invincibly quiet, and doing many little puzzling things that piqued my curiosity. As we sailed week after week through the long intricate channels and inlets among the innumerable islands and mountains of the coast, he spent most of the dull days in sluggish ease, motionless, and apparently as unobserving as if in deep sleep. But I discovered that somehow he always knew what was going on. When the Indians were about to shoot at ducks or seals, or when anything along the shore was exciting our attention, he would rest his chin on the edge of the canoe and calmly look out like a dreamy-eyed tourist. And when he heard us talking about making a landing, he immediately roused himself to see what sort of a place we were coming to, and made ready to jump overboard and swim ashore as soon as the canoe neared the beach. Then, with a vigorous shake to get rid of the brine in his hair, he ran into the woods to hunt small game. But though always the first out of the canoe, he was always the last to get into it. When we were ready to start he could never be found, and refused to come to our call. We soon found out, however, that though we could not see him at such times, he saw us, and from the cover of the briers and huckleberry bushes in the fringe of the woods was watching the canoe with wary eye. For as soon as we were fairly off he came trotting down the beach, plunged into the surf, and swam after us, knowing well that we would cease rowing and take him in. When the contrary little vagabond came alongside, he was lifted by the neck, held at arm's length a moment to drip, and dropped aboard. We tried to cure him of this trick by compelling him to swim a long way, as if we had a mind to abandon him; but this did no good: the longer the swim the better he seemed to like it.

Though capable of great idleness, he never failed to be ready for all sorts of adventures and excursions. One pitch – dark rainy night we landed about ten o'clock at the mouth of a salmon stream when the water was phosphorescent. The salmon were running, and the myriad fins of the onrushing multitude were churning all the stream into a silvery glow, wonderfully beautiful and impressive in the ebon darkness. To get a good view of the show I set out with one of the Indians and sailed up through the midst of it to the foot of a rapid about half a mile from camp, where the swift current dashing over rocks made the luminous glow most glorious. Happening to look back down the stream, while the Indian was catching a few of the struggling fish, I saw a long spreading fan of light like the tail of a comet, which we thought must be made by some big strange animal that was pursuing us. On it came with its magnificent train, until we imagined we could see the monster's head and eyes; but it was only Stickeen, who, finding I had left the camp, came swimming after me to see what was up.

When we camped early, the best hunter of the crew usually went to the woods for a deer, and Stickeen was sure to be at his heels, provided I had not gone out. For, strange to say, though I never carried a gun, he always followed me, forsaking the hunter and even his master to share my wanderings. The days that were too stormy for sailing I spent in the woods, or on the adjacent mountains, wherever my studies called me; and Stickeen always insisted on going with me, however wild the weather, gliding like a fox through dripping huckleberry bushes and thorny tangles of panax and rubus, scarce stirring their rain-laden leaves; wading and wallowing through snow, swimming icy streams, skipping over logs and rocks and the crevasses of glaciers with the patience and endurance of a determined mountaineer, never tiring or getting discouraged. Once he followed me over a glacier the surface of which was so crusty and rough that it cut his feet until every step was marked with blood; but he trotted on with Indian fortitude until I noticed his red track, and, taking pity on him, made him a set of moccasins out of a handkerchief. However great his troubles he never asked help or made any complaint, as if, like a philosopher, he had learned that without hard work and suffering there could be no pleasure worth having.

Yet none of us was able to make out what Stickeen was really good for. He seemed to meet danger and hardships without anything like reason, insisted on having his own way, never obeyed an order, and the hunter could never set him on anything, or make him fetch the birds he shot. His equanimity was so steady it seemed due to want of feeling; ordinary storms were pleasures to him, and as for mere rain, he flourished in it like a vegetable. No matter what advances you might make, scarce a glance or a tail-wag would you get for your pains. But though he was apparently as cold as a glacier and about as impervious to fun, I tried hard to make his acquaintance, guessing there must be something worth while hidden beneath so much courage, endurance, and love of wild-weathery adventure. No super-annuated mastiff or bulldog grown old in office surpassed this fluffy midget in stoic dignity. He sometimes reminded me of a small, squat, unshakable desert cactus. For he never displayed a single trace of the merry, tricksy, elfish fun of the terriers and collies that we all know, nor of their touching affection and devotion. Like children, most small dogs beg to be loved and allowed to love; but Stickeen seemed a very Diogenes, asking only to be let alone: a true child of the wilderness, holding the even tenor of his hidden life with the silence and serenity of nature. His strength of character lay in his eyes. They looked as old as the hills, and as young, and as wild. I never tired of looking into them: it was like looking into a landscape; but they were small and rather deep-set, and had no explaining lines around them to give out particulars. I was accustomed to look into the faces of plants and animals, and I watched the little sphinx more and more keenly as an interesting study. But there is no estimating the wit and wisdom concealed and latent in our lower fellow mortals until made manifest by profound experiences; for it is through suffering that dogs as well as saints are developed and made perfect.

After we had explored the Sundum and Tahkoo fiords and their glaciers, we sailed through Stephen's Passage into Lynn Canal and thence through Icy Strait into Cross Sound, searching for unexplored inlets leading toward the great fountain ice-fields of the Fairweather Range. Here, while the tide was in our favour, we were accompanied by a fleet of icebergs drifting out to the ocean from Glacier Bay. Slowly we paddled around Vancouver's Point, Wimbleton, our frail canoe tossed like a feather on the massive heaving swells coming in past Cape Spenser. For miles the sound is bounded by precipitous mural cliffs, which, lashed with wave-spray and their heads hidden in clouds, looked terribly threatening and stern. Had our canoe been crushed or upset we could have made no landing here, for the cliffs, as high as those of Yosemite, sink sheer into deep water. Eagerly we scanned the wall on the north side for the first sign of an opening fiord or harbor, all of us anxious except Stickeen, who dozed in peace or gazed dreamily at the tremendous precipices when he heard us talking about them. At length we made the joyful discovery of the mouth of the inlet now called 'Taylor Bay,' and about five o'clock reached the head of it and encamped in a spruce grove near the front of a large glacier.

While camp was being made, Joe the hunter climbed the mountain wall on the east side of the fiord in pursuit of wild goats, while Mr Young and I went to the glacier. We found that it is separated from the waters of the inlet by a tide-washed moraine, and extends, an abrupt barrier, all the way across from wall to wall of the inlet, a distance of about three miles. But our most interesting discovery was that it had recently advanced, though again slightly receding. A portion of the terminal moraine had been plowed up and shoved forward, uprooting and overwhelming the woods on the east side. Many of the trees were down and buried, or nearly so, others were leaning a way from the ice-cliffs, ready to fall, and some stood erect, with the bottom of the ice-plow still beneath their roots and its lofty crystal spires towering high above their tops. The spectacle presented by these century-old trees standing close beside a spiry wall of ice, with their branches almost touching it, was most novel and striking. And when I climbed around the front, and a little way up the west side of the glacier, I found that it had swelled and increased in height and width in accordance with its advance, and carried away the outer ranks of trees on its bank.

On our way back to camp after these first observations I planned a far-and-wide excursion for the morrow. I awoke early, called not only by the glacier, which had been on my mind all night, but by a grand floodstorm. The wind was blowing a gale from the north and the rain was flying with the clouds in a wide passionate horizontal flood, as if it were all passing over the country instead of falling on it. The main perennial streams were booming high above their banks, and hundreds of new ones, roaring like the sea, almost covered the lofty gray walls of the inlet with white cascades and falls. I had intended making a cup of coffee and getting something like a breakfast before starting, but when I heard the storm and looked out I made haste to join it; for many of Nature's finest lessons are to be found in her storms, and if careful to keep in right relations with them, we may go safely abroad with them, rejoicing in the grandeur and beauty of their works and ways, and chanting with the old Norsemen, 'The blast of the tempest aids our oars, the hurricane is our servant and drives us whither we wish to go.' So, omitting breakfast, I put a piece of bread in my pocket and hurried away.

Mr Young and the Indians were asleep, and so, I hoped, was Stickeen; but I had not gone a dozen rods before he left his bed in the tent and came boring through the blast after me. That a man should welcome storms for their exhilarating music and motion, and go forth to see God making landscapes, is reasonable enough; but what fascination could there be in such tremendous weather for a dog? Surely nothing akin to human enthusiasm for scenery or geology. Anyhow, on he came, breakfastless, through the choking blast. I stopped and did my best to turn him back. 'Now don't,' I said, shouting to make myself heard in the storm, 'now don't, Stickeen. What has got into your queer noddle now? You must be daft. This wild day has nothing for you. There is no game abroad, nothing but weather. Go back to camp and keep warm, get a good breakfast with your master, and be sensible for once. I can't carry you all day or feed you, and this storm will kill you.'

But Nature, it seems, was at the bottom of the affair, and she gains her ends with dogs as well as with men, making us do as she likes, shoving and pulling us along her ways, however rough, all but killing us at times in getting her lessons driven hard home. After I had stopped again and again, shouting good warning advice, I saw that he was not to be shaken off; as well might the earth try to shake off the moon. I had once led his master into trouble, when he fell on one of the topmost jags of a mountain and dislocated his arm; now the turn of his humble companion was coming. The pitiful little wanderer just stood there in the wind, drenched and blinking, saying doggedly, 'Where thou goest I will go.' So at last I told him to come on if he must, and gave him a piece of the bread I had in my pocket; then we struggled on together, and thus began the most memorable of all my wild days.

The level flood, driving hard in our faces, thrashed and washed us wildly until we got into the shelter of a grove on the east side of the glacier near the front, where we stopped awhile for breath and to listen and look out. The exploration of the glacier was my main object, but the wind was too high to allow excursions over its open surface, where one might be dangerously shoved while balancing for a jump on the brink of a crevasse. In the mean time the storm was a fine study. Here the end of the glacier, descending an abrupt swell of resisting rock about five hundred feet high, leans forward and falls in ice cascades. And as the storm came down the glacier from the North, Stickeen and I were beneath the main current of the blast, while favorably located to see and hear it. What a psalm the storm was singing, and how fresh the smell of the washed earth and leaves, and how sweet the still small voices of the storm! Detached wafts and swirls were coming through the woods, with music from the leaves and branches and furrowed boles, and even from the splintered rocks and ice-crags overhead, many of the tones soft and low and flute-like, as if each leaf and tree, crag and spire were a tuned reed. A broad torrent, draining the side of the glacier, now swollen by scores of new streams from the mountains, was rolling boulders along its rocky channel, with thudding, bumping, muffled sounds, rushing towards the bay with tremendous energy, as if in haste to get out of the mountains; the waters above and beneath calling to each other, and all to the ocean, their home.

Looking southward from our shelter, we had this great torrent and the forested mountain wall above it on our left, the spiry ice-crags on our right, and smooth gray gloom ahead. I tried to draw the marvellous scene in my note-book, but the rain blurred the page in spite of all my pains to shelter it, and the sketch was almost worthless. When the wind began to abate, I traced the east side of the glacier. All the trees standing on the edge of the woods were barked and bruised, showing high-ice mark in a very telling way, while tens of thousands of those that had stood for centuries on the bank of the glacier farther out lay crushed and being crushed. In many places I could see down fifty feet or so beneath the margin of the glacier-mill, where trunks from one to two feet in diameter were being ground to pulp against outstanding rock-ribs and bosses of the bank.

About three miles above the front of the glacier I climbed to the surface of it by means of axe-steps made easy for Stickeen. As far as the eye could reach, the level, or nearly level, glacier stretched away indefinitely beneath the gray sky, a seemingly boundless prairie of ice. The rain continued, and grew colder, which I did not mind, but a dim snowy look in the drooping clouds made me hesitate about venturing far from land. No trace of the west shore was visible, and in case the clouds should settle and give snow, or the wind again become violent, I feared getting caught in a tangle of crevasses. Snow-crystals, the flowers of the mountain clouds, are frail, beautiful things, but terrible when flying on storm-winds in darkening, benumbing swarms, or, when welded together into glaciers full of deadly crevasses. Watching the weather, I sauntered about on the crystal sea. For a mile or two out I found the ice remarkably safe. The marginal crevasses were mostly narrow, while the few wider ones were easily avoided by passing around them, and the clouds began to open here and there.

Thus encouraged, I at last pushed out for the other side; for Nature can make us do anything she likes. At first we made rapid progress, and the sky was not very threatening, while I took bearings occasionally with a pocket compass to enable me to find my way back more surely in case the storm should become blinding; but the structure lines of the glacier were my main guide. Toward the west side we came to a closely crevassed section in which we had to make long, narrow tacks and doublings, tracing the edges of tremendous transverse and longitudinal crevasses, many of which were from twenty to thirty feet wide, and perhaps a thousand feet deep – beautiful and awful. In working a way through them I was severely cautious, but Stickeen came on as unhesitating as the flying clouds. The widest crevasse that I could jump he would leap without so much as halting to take a look at it. The weather was now making quick changes, scattering bits of dazzling brightness through the wintry gloom; at rare intervals, when the sun broke forth wholly free, the glacier was seen from shore to shore with a bright array of encompassing mountains partly revealed, wearing the clouds as garments, while the prairie bloomed and sparkled with irised light from myriads of washed crystals. Then suddenly all the glorious show would be darkened and blotted out.

Stickeen seemed to care for none of these things, bright or dark, nor for the crevasses, wells, moulins, or swift flashing streams into which he might fall. The little adventurer was only about two years old, yet nothing seemed novel to him, nothing daunted him. He showed neither caution nor curiosity, wonder nor fear, but bravely trotted on as if glaciers were playgrounds. His stout, muffled body seemed all one skipping muscle, and it was truly wonderful to see how swiftly and to all appearance heedlessly he flashed across nerve-trying chasms six or eight feet wide. His courage was so unwavering that it seemed to be due to dullness of perception, as if he were only blindly bold; and I kept warning him to be careful. For we had been close companions on so many wilderness trips that I had formed the habit of talking to him as if he were a boy and understood every word.

We gained the west shore in about three hours; the width of the glacier here being about seven miles. Then I pushed northward in order to see as far back as possible into the fountains of the Fairweather Mountains, in case the clouds should rise. The walking was easy along the margin of the forest, which, of course, like that on the other side, had been invaded and crushed by the swollen, overflowing glacier. In an hour or so, after passing a massive headland, we came suddenly on a branch of the glacier, which, in the form of a magnificent ice-cascade two miles wide, was pouring over the rim of the main basin in a westerly direction, its surface broken into wave-shaped blades and shattered blocks, suggesting the wildest updashing, heaving, plunging motion of a great river cataract. Tracing it down three or four miles, I found that it discharged into a lake, filling it with icebergs.

I would gladly have followed the lake outlet to tide-water, but the day was already far spent, and the threatening sky called for haste on the return trip to get off the ice before dark. I decided therefore to go no farther, and, after taking a general view of the wonderful region, turned back, hoping to see it again under more favorable auspices. We made good speed up the cañon of the great ice-torrent, and out on the main glacier until we had left the west shore about two miles behind us. Here we got into a difficult network of crevasses, the gathering clouds began to drop misty fringes, and soon the dreaded snow came flying thick and fast. I now began to feel anxious about finding a way in the blurring storm. Stickeen showed no trace of fear. He was still the same silent, able little hero. I noticed, however, that after the storm-darkness came on he kept close up behind me. The snow urged us to make still greater haste, but at the same time hid our way. I pushed on as best I could, jumping innumerable crevasses, and for every hundred rods or so of direct advance travelling a mile in doubling up and down in the turmoil of chasms and dislocated iceblocks. After an hour or two of this work we came to a series of longitudinal crevasses of appalling width, and almost straight and regular in trend, like immense furrows. These I traced with firm nerve, excited and strengthened by the danger, making wide jumps, poising cautiously on their dizzy edges after cutting hollows for my feet before making the spring, to avoid possible slipping or any uncertainty on the farther sides, where only one trial is granted – exercise at once frightful and inspiring. Stickeen followed seemingly without effort.

Many a mile we thus travelled, mostly up and down, making but little real headway in crossing, running instead of walking most of the time as the danger of being compelled to spend the night on the glacier became threatening. Stickeen seemed able for anything. Doubtless we could have weathered the storm for one night, dancing on a flat spot to keep from freezing, and I faced the threat without feeling anything like despair; but we were hungry and wet, and the wind from the mountains was still thick with snow and bitterly cold, so of course that night would have seemed a very long one. I could not see far enough through the blurring snow to judge in which general direction the least dangerous route lay, while the few dim, momentary glimpses I caught of mountains through rifts in the flying clouds were far from encouraging either as weather signs or as guides. I had simply to grope my way from crevasse to crevasse, holding a general direction by the ice-structure, which was not to be seen everywhere, and partly by the wind. Again and again I was put to my mettle, but Stickeen followed easily, his nerve apparently growing more unflinching as the danger increased. So it always is with mountaineers when hard beset. Running hard and jumping, holding every minute of the remaining daylight, poor as it was, precious, we doggedly persevered and tried to hope that every difficult crevasse we overcame would prove to be the last of its kind. But on the contrary, as we advanced they became more deadly trying.

At length our way was barred by a very wide and

straight crevasse, which I traced rapidly northward a mile
or so without finding a crossing or hope of one; then down
the glacier about as far, to where it united with another
uncrossable crevasse. In all this distance of perhaps two
miles there was only one place where I could possibly
jump it, but the width of this jump was the utmost I
dared attempt, while the danger of slipping on the farther
side was so great that I was loath to try it. Furthermore, the
side I was on was about a foot higher than the other, and
even with this advantage the crevasse seemed dangerously
wide. One is liable to underestimate the width of crevasses
where the magnitudes in general are great. I therefore
stared at this one mighty keenly, estimating its width
and the shape of the edge on the farther side, until I
thought that I could jump it if necessary, but that in case
I should be compelled to jump back from the lower side
I might fail. Now, a cautious mountaineer seldom takes
a step on unknown ground which seems at all dangerous
that he cannot retrace in case he should be stopped by
unseen obstacles ahead. This is the rule of mountaineers
who live long, and, though in haste, I compelled myself to
sit down and calmly deliberate before I broke it.

Retracing my devious path in imagination as if it were
drawn on a chart, I saw that I was recrossing the glacier
a mile or two farther up stream than the course pursued
in the morning, and that I was now entangled in a section
I had not before seen. Should I risk this dangerous jump,
or try to regain the woods on the west shore, make a fire,
and have only hunger to endure while waiting for a new
day? I had already crossed so broad a stretch of dangerous
ice that I saw it would be difficult to get back to the woods
through the storm, before dark, and the attempt would
most likely result in a dismal night-dance on the glacier;
while just beyond the present barrier the surface seemed
more promising, and the east shore was now perhaps about
as near as the west. I was therefore eager to go on. But this
wide jump was a dreadful obstacle.

At length, because of the dangers already behind me, I
determined to venture against those that might be ahead,
jumped and landed well, but with so little to spare that

I more than ever dreaded being compelled to take that jump back from the lower side. Stickeen followed, making nothing of it, and we ran eagerly forward, hoping we were leaving all our troubles behind. But within the distance of a few hundred yards we were stopped by the widest crevasse yet encountered. Of course I made haste to explore it, hoping all might yet be remedied by finding a bridge or a way around either end. About three-fourths of a mile upstream I found that it united with the one we had just crossed, as I feared it would. Then, tracing it down, I found it joined the same crevasse at the lower end also, maintaining throughout its whole course a width of forty to fifty feet. Thus to my dismay I discovered that we were on a narrow island about two miles long, with two barely possible ways of escape: one back by the way we came, the other ahead by an almost inaccessible sliver-bridge that crossed the great crevasse from near the middle of it!

After this nerve-trying discovery I ran back to the sliver-bridge and cautiously examined it. Crevasses, caused by strains from variations in the rate of motion of different parts of the glacier and convexities in the channel, are mere cracks when they first open, so narrow as hardly to admit the blade of a pocket-knife, and gradually widen according to the extent of the strain and the depth of the glacier. Now some of these cracks are interrupted, like the cracks in wood, and in opening, the strip of ice between overlapping ends is dragged out, and may maintain a continuous connection between the sides, just as the two sides of a slivered crack in wood that is being split are connected. Some crevasses remain open for months or even years, and by the melting of their sides continue to increase in width long after the opening strain has ceased; while the sliver-bridges, level on top at first and perfectly safe, are at length melted to thin, vertical, knife-edged blades, the upper portion being most exposed to the weather; and since the exposure is greatest in the middle, they at length curve downward like the cables of suspension bridges. This one was evidently very old, for it had been weathered and wasted until it was the most dangerous and inaccessible that ever lay in my way. The width of the crevasse was here about fifty feet, and the sliver crossing diagonally was about seventy feet long; its thin knife-edge near the middle was depressed twenty-five or thirty feet below the level of the glacier, and the upcurving ends were attached to the sides eight or ten feet below the brink. Getting down the nearly vertical wall to the end of the sliver and up the other side were the main difficulties, and they seemed all but insurmountable. Of the many perils encountered in my years of wandering on mountains and glaciers none seemed so plain and stern and merciless as this. And it was presented when we were wet to the skin and hungry, the sky dark with quick driving snow, and the night near. But we were forced to face it. It was a tremendous necessity.

Beginning, not immediately above the sunken end of the bridge, but a little to one side, I cut a deep hollow on the brink for my knees to rest in. Then, leaning over, with my shorthandled axe I cut a step sixteen or eighteen inches below, which on account of the sheerness of the wall was necessarily shallow. That step, however, was well made; its floor sloped slightly inward and formed a good hold for my heels. Then, slipping cautiously upon it, and crouching as low as possible, with my left side toward the wall, I steadied myself against the wind with my left hand in a slight notch, while with the right I cut other similar steps and notches in succession, guarding against losing balance by glinting of the axe, or by wind-gusts, for life and death were in every stroke and in the niceness of finish of every foothold.

After the end of the bridge was reached I chipped it down until I had made a level platform six or eight inches wide, and it was a trying thing to poise on this little slippery platform while bending over to get safely astride of the sliver. Crossing was then comparatively easy by chipping off the sharp edge with short, careful strokes, and hitching forward an inch or two at a time, keeping my balance with my knees pressed against the sides. The tremendous abyss on either hand I studiously ignored. To me the edge of that blue sliver was then all the world. But the most trying part of the adventure, after working my way across inch by inch and chipping another small platform, was to rise from the

safe position astride and to cut a step-ladder in the nearly
vertical face of the wall, – chipping, climbing, holding on
with feet and fingers in mere notches. At such times one's
whole body is eye, and common skill and fortitude are
replaced by power beyond our call or knowledge. Never
before had I been so long under deadly strain. How I got
up that cliff I never could tell. The thing seemed to have
been done by somebody else. I never have held death in
contempt, though in the course of my explorations I have
oftentimes felt that to meet one's fate on a noble mountain,
or in the heart of a glacier, would be blessed as compared
with death from disease, or from some shabby lowland
accident. But the best death, quick and crystal-pure, set
so glaringly open before us, is hard enough to face, even
though we feel gratefully sure that we have already had
happiness enough for a dozen lives.

But poor Stickeen, the wee, hairy, sleekit beastie, think
of him! When I had decided to dare the bridge, and while
I was on my knees chipping a hollow on the rounded brow
above it, he came behind me, pushed his head past my
shoulder, looked down and across, scanned the sliver and
its approaches with his mysterious eyes, then looked me
in the face with a startled air of surprise and concern,
and began to mutter and whine; saying as plainly as if
speaking with words, 'Surely, you are not going into that
awful place.' This was the first time I had seen him gaze
deliberately into a crevasse, or into my face with an eager,
speaking, troubled look. That he should have recognized
and appreciated the danger at the first glance showed
wonderful sagacity. Never before had the daring midget
seemed to know that ice was slippery or that there was
any such thing as danger anywhere. His looks and tones of
voice when he began to complain and speak his fears were
so human that I unconsciously talked to him in sympathy
as I would to a frightened boy, and in trying to calm his
fears perhaps in some measure moderated my own. 'Hush
your fears, my boy,' I said, 'we will get across safe, though
it is not going to be easy. No right way is easy in this rough
world. We must risk our lives to save them. At the worst
we can only slip, and then how grand a grave we will have,

and by and by our nice bones will do good in the terminal moraine.'

But my sermon was far from reassuring him: he began to cry, and after taking another piercing look at the tremendous gulf, ran away in desperate excitement, seeking some other crossing. By the time he got back, baffled of course, I had made a step or two. I dared not look back, but he made himself heard; and when he saw that I was certainly bent on crossing he cried aloud in despair. The danger was enough to daunt anybody, but it seems wonderful that he should have been able to weigh and appreciate it so justly. No mountaineer could have seen it more quickly or judged it more wisely, discriminating between real and apparent peril.

When I gained the other side, he screamed louder than ever, and after running back and forth in vain search for a way of escape, he would return to the brink of the crevasse above the bridge, moaning and wailing as if in the bitterness of death. Could this be the silent, philosophic Stickeen? I shouted encouragement, telling him the bridge was not so bad as it looked, that I had left it flat and safe for his feet, and he could walk it easily. But he was afraid to try. Strange so small an animal should be capable of such big, wise fears. I called again and again in a reassuring tone to come on and fear nothing; that he could come if he would only try. He would hush for a moment, look down again at the bridge, and shout his unshakable conviction that he could never, never come that way; then lie back in despair, as if howling, 'O-o-oh! What a place! No-o-o, I can never go-o-o down there!' His natural composure and courage had vanished utterly in a tumultuous storm of fear. Had the danger been less, his distress would have seemed ridiculous. But in this dismal, merciless abyss lay the shadow of death, and his heartrending cries might well have called Heaven to his help. Perhaps they did. So hidden before, he was now transparent, and one could see the workings of his heart and mind like the movements of a clock out of its case. His voice and gestures, hopes and fears, were so perfectly human that none could mistake them; while he seemed to understand every word of mine.

I was troubled at the thought of having to leave him out all night, and of the danger of not finding him in the morning. It seemed impossible to get him to venture. To compel him to try through fear of being abandoned, I started off as if leaving him to his fate, and disappeared back of a hummock; but this did no good; he only lay down and moaned in utter hopeless misery. So, after hiding a few minutes, I went back to the brink of the crevasse and in a severe tone of voice shouted across to him that now I must certainly leave him, I could wait no longer, and that, if he would not come, all I could promise was that I would return to seek him next day. I warned him that if he went back to the woods the wolves would kill him, and finished by urging him once more by words and gestures to come on, come on.

He knew very well what I meant, and at last, with the courage of despair, hushed and breathless, he crouched down on the brink in the hollow I had made for my knees, pressed his body against the ice as if trying to get the advantage of the friction of every hair, gazed into the first step, put his little feet together and slid them slowly, slowly over the edge and down into it, bunching all four in it and almost standing on his head. Then, without lifting his feet, as well as I could see through the snow, he slowly worked them over the edge of the step and down into the next and the next in succession in the same way, and gained the end of the bridge. Then, lifting his feet with the regularity and slowness of the vibrations of a seconds pendulum, as if counting and measuring *one-two-three*, holding himself steady against the gusty wind, and giving separate attention to each little step, he gained the foot of the cliff, while I was on my knees leaning over to give him a lift should he succeed in getting within reach of my arm. Here he halted in dead silence, and it was here I feared he might fail, for dogs are poor climbers. I had no cord. If I had had one, I would have dropped a noose over his head and hauled him up. But while I was thinking whether an available cord might be made out of clothing, he was looking keenly into the series of notched steps and finger-holds I had made, as if counting them, and fixing the position of each one of them in his mind. Then suddenly up he came in a springy rush, hooking his paws into the steps and notches so quickly that I could not see how it was done, and whizzed past my head, safe at last!

And now came a scene! 'Well done, well done, little boy! Brave boy!' I cried, trying to catch and caress him; but he would not be caught. Never before or since have I seen anything like so passionate a revulsion from the depths of despair to exultant, triumphant, uncontrollable joy. He flashed and darted hither and thither as if fairly demented, screaming and shouting, swirling round and round in giddy loops and circles like a leaf in a whirlwind, lying down, and rolling over and over, sidewise and heels over head, and pouring forth a tumultuous flood of hysterical cries and sobs and gasping mutterings. When I ran up to him to shake him, fearing he might die of joy, he flashed off two or three hundred yards, his feet in a mist of motion; then, turning suddenly, came back in a wild rush and launched himself at my face, almost knocking me down, all the time screeching and screaming and shouting as if saying, 'Saved! saved! saved!' Then away again, dropping suddenly at times with his feet in the air, trembling and fairly sobbing. Such passionate emotion was enough to kill him. Moses' stately song of triumph after escaping the Egyptians and the Red Sea was nothing to it. Who could have guessed the capacity of the dull, enduring little fellow for all that most stirs this mortal frame? Nobody could have helped crying with him!

But there is nothing like work for toning down excessive fear or joy. So I ran ahead, calling him in as gruff a voice as I could command to come on and stop his nonsense, for we had far to go and it would soon be dark. Neither of us feared another trial like this. Heaven would surely count one enough for a lifetime. The ice ahead was gashed by thousands of crevasses, but they were common ones. The joy of deliverance burned in us like fire, and we ran without fatigue, every muscle with immense rebound glorying in its strength. Stickeen flew across everything in his way, and not till dark did he settle into his normal fox-like trot. At last the cloudy mountains came in sight, and we soon felt the solid rock beneath our feet, and were safe. Then came weakness. Danger had vanished, and so had our strength. We tottered down the lateral moraine in the dark, over boulders and tree trunks, through the bushes and devil-club thickets of the grove where we had sheltered ourselves in the morning, and across the level mud-slope of the terminal moraine. We reached camp about ten o'clock, and found a big fire and a big supper. A party of Hoona Indians had visited Mr Young, bringing a gift of porpoise meat and wild strawberries, and Hunter Joe had brought in a wild goat. But we lay down, too tired to eat much, and soon fell into a troubled sleep. The man who said, 'The harder the toil, the sweeter the rest,' never was profoundly tired. Stickeen kept springing up and muttering in his sleep, no doubt dreaming that he was still on the brink of the crevasse; and so did I, that night and many others long afterward, when I was overtired.

Thereafter Stickeen was a changed dog. During the rest of the trip, instead of holding aloof, he always lay by my side, tried to keep me constantly in sight, and would hardly accept a morsel of food, however tempting, from any hand but mine. At night, when all was quiet about the camp-fire, he would come to me and rest his head on my knee with a look of devotion as if I were his god. And often as he caught my eye he seemed to be trying to say, 'Wasn't that an awful time we had together on the glacier?'

Nothing in after years has dimmed that Alaska storm-day. As I write it all comes rushing and roaring to mind as if I were again in the heart of it. Again I see the gray flying clouds with their rain-floods and snow, the ice-cliffs towering above the shrinking forest, the majestic ice-cascade, the vast glacier outspread before its white mountain fountains, and in the heart of it the tremendous crevasse, – emblem of the valley of the shadow of death, – low clouds trailing over it, the snow falling into it; and on its brink I see little Stickeen, and I hear his cries for help and his shouts of joy. I have known many dogs, and many a story I could tell of their wisdom and devotion; but to none do I owe so much as to Stickeen. At first the least promising and least known of my dog-friends, he suddenly became the best known of them all. Our storm-battle for life brought him to light, and through him as through a window I have ever since been looking with deeper sympathy into all my fellow mortals.

None of Stickeen's friends knows what finally became of him. After my work for the season was done I departed for California, and I never saw the dear little fellow again. In reply to anxious inquiries his master wrote me that in the summer of 1883 he was stolen by a tourist at Fort Wrangell and taken away on a steamer. His fate is wrapped in mystery. Doubtless he has left this world – crossed the last crevasse – and gone to another. But he will not be forgotten. To me Stickeen is immortal.

Select Bibliography

The Mountains of California (Century, New York, 1894)
Our National Parks (Houghton Mifflin & Co., Boston, 1901)
Stickeen (1909; Houghton Mifflin, Boston, 1923)
My First Summer in the Sierra (Houghton Mifflin, Boston, 1911)
The Yosemite (Century, New York, 1912)
The Story of My Boyhood and Youth (Houghton Mifflin, Boston, 1913)
Travels in Alaska (Houghton Mifflin, Boston, 1915)
A Thousand Mile Walk to the Gulf (Houghton Mifflin, Boston, 1916)
The Cruise of the Corwin (Houghton Mifflin, Boston, 1917)
Steep Trails (Houghton Mifflin, Boston, 1918)
The Eight Wilderness Discovery Books ed. Terry Gifford (Diadem/Mountain, London, 1992)

COLLECTED LETTERS AND JOURNALS

The Life and Letters of John Muir, ed. William Frederic Badé (1924)
John of the Mountains: The Unpublished Journals of John Muir, ed. Linnie Marsh Wolfe (1938, University of Wisconsin Press, 1979)
John Muir, The Life and Letters and Other Writings, ed. Terry Gifford (Baton-Wicks/Mountain Publishing, 1996)
The John Muir Papers Microfilm Edition, available at The National Library of Scotland.

BOOKS ABOUT JOHN MUIR

Rediscovering America: John Muir in his Time and Ours, Frederick Turner (Sierra Club Books, San Francisco 1985)
The Pathless Way: John Muir and the American Wilderness, Michael P. Cohen (University of Wisconsin Press, 1984)

CONTACTS

The John Muir Trust
FREEPOST, Musselburgh, Midlothian EH21 7BR
Phone: 0131 554 0114; Fax 0131 555 2112

Dunbar's John Muir Association
c/o John Muir House, 128 High Street, Dunbar EH42 1EL

CANONGATE CLASSICS

Books listed in alphabetical order by author.

The Land of the Leal James Barke
  ISBN 0 86241 142 4   £4.95
The House with the Green Shutters
  George Douglas Brown
  ISBN 0 86241 549 7   £4.99
Witchwood John Buchan
  ISBN 0 86241 202 1   £4.99
The Life of Robert Burns Catherine Carswell
  ISBN 0 86241 292 7   £5.99
The Complete Brigadier Gerard Arthur Conan Doyle
  ISBN 0 86241 534 9   £4.99
Dance of the Apprentices Edward Gaitens
  ISBN 0 86241 297 8
Ringan Gilhaize John Galt
  ISBN 0 86241 552 7   £6.99
A Scots Quair: (Sunset Song, Cloud Howe, Grey
  Granite) Lewis Grassic Gibbon
  ISBN 0 86241 532 2   £5.99
Sunset Song Lewis Grassic Gibbon
  ISBN 0 86241 179 3   £3.99
Memoirs of a Highland Lady vols. I&II
  Elizabeth Grant of Rothiemurchus
  ISBN 0 86241 396 6   £7.99
The Highland Lady in Ireland
  Elizabeth Grant of Rothiemurchus
  ISBN 0 86241 361 3   £7.95
Highland River Neil M. Gunn
  ISBN 0 86241 358 3   £5.99
Sun Circle Neil M. Gunn
  ISBN 0 86241 587 X   £5.99
Gillespie J. MacDougall Hay
  ISBN 0 86241 427 X   £6.99
The Private Memoirs and Confessions of a Justified Sinner
  James Hogg
  ISBN 0 86241 340 0   £3.99
Fergus Lamont Robin Jenkins
  ISBN 0 86241 310 9   £4.95
Just Duffy Robin Jenkins
  ISBN 0 86241 551 9   £4.99
The Changeling Robin Jenkins
  ISBN 0 86241 228 5   £4.99

Most Canongate Classics are available at good bookshops. If you experience difficulty in obtaining the title you want, please contact us at 14 High Street, Edinburgh EH1 1TE.